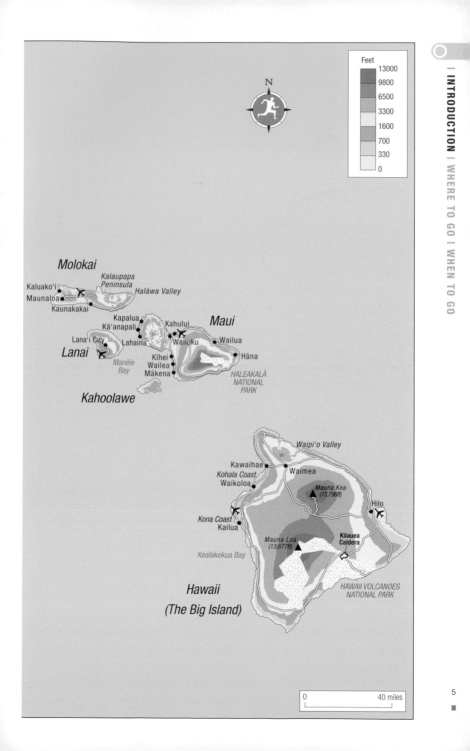

Feet
13000
9800
6500
3300
1600
700
330
0

N

Molokai
Kaluako'i
Maunaloa
Kaunakakai
Kalaupapa
Peninsula
Halāwa Valley

Kapalua
Kā'anapali
Lana'i City
Lanai
Lahaina
Manēle
Bay
Kahului
Wailuku
Kīhei
Wailea
Mākena
Maui
Wailua
Hāna
HALEAKALĀ
NATIONAL
PARK

Kahoolawe

Waipi'o Valley
Kawaihae
Kohala Coast
Waikoloa
Waimea
Mauna Kea
(13,796ft)
Hilo

Kona Coast
Kailua
Mauna Loa
(13,677ft)
Kīlauea
Caldera

Kealakekua Bay

Hawaii
(The Big Island)
HAWAII VOLCANOES
NATIONAL PARK

0   40 miles

Introduction to

Hawaii

Renowned the world over for their palm-fringed beaches and spectacular scenery, the ravishing islands of Hawaii poke up from the Pacific more than two thousand miles off the west coast of America. Of the seven that are inhabited, only six welcome visitors: Oahu, the site of state capital Honolulu and its resort annex of Waikīkī; Hawaii itself, known as the Big Island in a vain attempt to avoid confusion; Maui; Lanai; Molokai; and Kauai.

The islands are the eroded summits of submarine volcanoes; the entire chain now stretches almost to Japan, though most have dwindled to tiny atolls. Each of the main islands is much wetter on its north and east – **windward** – coasts, characterized by stupendous sea cliffs, verdant stream-cut valleys, and dense tropical vegetation. The south and west – **leeward** or "Kona" – coasts are much drier, often virtually barren, and make ideal locations for big resorts.

Hawaii combines top-quality hotels and restaurants with almost unlimited opportunities not only for sheer self-indulgence, but also for activities such as surfing, diving, and hiking. Visiting Hawaii does not, however, have to be expensive; budget facilities are listed throughout this book, together with advice on making the most of your money.

Despite the crowds, the islands have not been ruined by tourism. Resort development is concentrated in surprisingly small regions – Waikīkī is the classic example, holding half the state's hotel rooms in just two square miles – and it's always possible to venture off into pristine wilderness or to camp on the seashore or mountainside.

▲ Nā Pali coast, Kauai

▲ Nā Pali coast, Kauai

Where to go

T he key decision in any Hawaiian itinerary is whether to go to **Oahu**, and specifically **Waikīkī**, which holds virtually all its accommodation. If you prefer cities and nightlife to deserted beaches – or if you don't want to drive – then it's worth spending three or four days in Waikīkī. Otherwise, unless you're a **surfer** heading for the legendary North Shore, you may end up wishing you'd allowed for more time elsewhere.

Each of the so-called **neighbor islands** has its own strengths and weaknesses. Maui, Kauai, and the Big Island all offer accommodation for every budget, and cost the same to reach from Oahu, as well as being accessible by direct flights from the US West Coast.

Fact file

• Hawaii's **first human settlers**, Polynesian voyagers, arrived less than two thousand years ago. The first European sailor known to have reached the islands was England's **Captain Cook**, in 1778. Hawaii remained an independent kingdom until 1898, when it became a territory of the United States. It was admitted as the **fiftieth US state** in 1959.

• The state's **population** is 1.29 million people, of whom 910,000 live on Oahu. The Big Island holds 176,000, Maui almost 150,000, and Kauai almost 63,000. Molokai has around 8000, and Lanai just 2200, while Niihau is home to a mere 130 citizens.

• Fewer than ten percent of Hawaii's citizens consider themselves to be "**Native Hawaiians**," while over forty percent are of **Asian descent** (mostly Japanese or Filipino), 26.5 percent say they are "**White**," and 2.2 percent that they are "**Black**." Over half of all marriages are classified as interracial, so such statistics grow ever more meaningless.

• 6.5 million tourists visit Hawaii each year, of whom 4.3 million come from the US, and around 1.1 million from Japan. By far the **most popular island** remains Oahu, with 4 million visitors a year. Maui comes second, welcoming 2.9 million, while 1.2 million spend time on the Big Island, and 930,000 on Kauai. Around 60,000 visit Lanai and 50,000 visit Molokai, while Niihau is barred to outsiders altogether.

• Mauna Kea on the Big Island is the **highest mountain** in the Pacific, at 13,796 feet. Locals ski and snowboard at the summit. Mount Wai'ale'ale on Kauai is the **wettest place** on earth, receiving an average of 451 inches per year.

Hawaiian food and ritual

Eating was a serious business in ancient Hawaii, attended by many rituals and taboos. Only men were allowed to cook or prepare food. Women were forbidden to eat pork, bananas, or coconuts, as well as several kinds of fish, or to use the same utensils or even eat at the same table as the men.

These days, although Hawaii boasts many fabulous restaurants, there's no such thing as an authentic "Hawaiian" restaurant.

At a *lū'au*, a "feast" staged for tourists, you can sample such traditional foods as *poi*, a purple-gray paste made from the root of the taro plant (which is still being cultivated in the traditional painstaking way in such time-hallowed spots as Molokai's Hālawa Valley and Kauai's Hanalei Valley); *kālua* pork, an entire pig wrapped in leaves and baked in an underground oven; *poke*, marinated raw fish, shellfish, or octopus; and *lomi-lomi*, made with raw salmon. You're unlikely, however, to be given another historically authentic specialty: boiled hairless dogs. For more on eating and drinking, see p.28.

The best for **beaches** is probably Maui, followed by Kauai and then the Big Island; for **scenery**, and also **hiking**, Kauai beats the Big Island, with Maui well behind. The Big Island boasts the awesome spectacle of the world's most active **volcano** – Kīlauea, which has been erupting ever since 1983 – although slumbering Haleakalā on Maui is also impressive.

Among more specialized interests, Maui offers the best conditions for **windsurfing** and **whale-watching**; Maui and the Big Island are equally well equipped for **diving**, **snorkeling**, and **golf**; and the Big Island is the best suited for a **touring** vacation. The appeal of the lesser islands rests largely on their seclusion; **Molokai** is a down-home, inexpensive, and very traditional Hawaiian island, while **Lanai** has become a haven for the mega-rich.

Visitors in search of **ancient Hawaii** may be disappointed by how few vestiges remain. The Hawaiians themselves destroyed many of their *heiaus* (temples), and traces of the pre contact way of life tend to survive only in out-of-the-way places. Otherwise, what is presented as "historic" usually post-dates the missionary impact. The former plantation villages often have an appealing air of the nineteenth-century West, with their false-front stores and wooden boardwalks, but of the larger towns only Honolulu on Oahu, Lahaina on Maui, and Kailua on the Big Island offer much sense of history.

If you have **one week** or less, it's best sense to concentrate on a single island. Five days on either Kauai or the Big Island, combined with two days in Waikīkī, makes a good introduction to the state, while if you fly direct to Maui you can explore that island and still have time to cross over to Molokai or Lanai. With **two weeks**, you could spend four or five days each on three of the major islands – though it would be easy to fill a week or more on the Big Island – and perhaps a couple of days on Molokai as well. Any more than two weeks, and you can consider seeing all the major islands.

Hawaiian language

Almost everyone in Hawaii speaks English, and as a rule the **Hawaiian language** is only encountered in the few words – such as *aloha* or "love," the all-purpose island greeting, and *mahalo*, meaning "thank you" – that have passed into general local usage. A glossary of Hawaiian words appears on p.456.

The **Hawaiian alphabet** consists of just twelve letters, together with two punctuation marks, the macron and the glottal stop. Strictly speaking, the word Hawaii should be written **Hawai'i**, with the glottal stop to show that the two "i"s are pronounced separately; the correct forms for the other islands are O'ahu, Lāna'i, Moloka'i, Kaua'i, Ni'ihau, and Maui. Convention has it, however, that words in common English usage are written without their Hawaiian punctuation. Thus, although this book uses Hawaiian place names wherever possible, all the island names appear in their familiar English form.

When to go

▶ Hula dancer

Although Hawaii's **high season** for tourism is mid-December to March, when typical room rates for mid-range hotels rise by perhaps $30 per night, its climate remains constant year-round.

Specific information for each island appears throughout this book. In general, Hawaii is not prone to extremes. **Temperatures** in the major coastal resorts vary between a daily maximum of around 80°F (27°C) from January to March up to perhaps 87°F (30°C) from July to October. Average minimum temperatures remain in the region of 68°F (20°C) at sea level year-round, though warm clothing is necessary at the summits of the volcanoes on Maui or the Big Island. **Rainfall** is heaviest from December to March. Even so, while the mountaintops are among the wettest places on earth, you'd be unlucky to get enough rain in any of the resort areas to spoil your vacation.

The main seasonal variation is in the state of the **ocean**. Along protected stretches of shoreline, you can swim all year round in beautiful seas where the water temperature stays between 75°F and 82°F (24–28°C). From October to April, however, high surf renders unsheltered beaches dangerous in the extreme, and some beaches lose their sand altogether. Conditions on specific beaches are indicated throughout this book; see also p.34.

For most of the year, the trade winds blow in from the northeast, though they're occasionally replaced by humid "Kona winds" from the south. Hurricanes are very rare, though tsunamis do hit from time to time, generally as a result of earthquakes or landslides caused by volcanic eruptions.

◀ Windsurfing at Ho'okipa Beach, Maui

19

things not to miss

It's not possible to see everything that Hawaii has to offer in one trip – and we don't suggest you try. What follows is a selective taste of the highlights on the islands: unique tropical wonders, fabulous beaches, exhilarating outdoor activities, and fashionable resorts. They're arranged in five color-coded categories, which you can browse through to find the very best things to see, do, and experience. All highlights have a page reference to take you straight into the Guide, where you can find out more.

01 **Haleakalā Crater** Page **272** ● Every day, legions of visitors drive through the darkness to catch the unforgettable moment when the sun's first rays strike the multi-colored crater of Haleakalā, at the core of eastern Maui.

02 Kona coffee Page **145** • Be sure not to leave the Big Island without sampling some strong, flavorful Kona coffee, a gourmet specialty grown on the slopes above Kealakekua Bay.

03 Hanauma Bay Page **101** • Just a short bus ride out from Waikīkī, lagoon-like Hanauma Bay formed when a crater wall collapsed, to create Oahu's best-loved snorkeling destination.

04 Garden of the Gods Page **306** • These eerie rock formations, located down a dirt road in central Lanai, make a superb spot to catch a radiant sunset.

05 Kōke'e State Park Page **403** • Perched above the dazzling rainbow-hued gorge of Waimea Canyon, this lushly vegetated state park offers breathtaking views of the remote valleys along Kauai's North Shore.

06 **'Akaka Falls** Page **180** • Mighty 'Akaka Falls is simply the largest of countless waterfalls that cascade down the richly vegetated flanks of the Big Island's Hāmākua coast.

07 **Unique wildlife** Pages **276** & **407** • From silversword plants to the rarest '*ō'ō 'a'ā* honey-creeper, you'll never cease to be awed by the islands' tropical flora and fauna.

08 **Mauna Kea** Page **187** • Even Hawaii sees a little snow sometimes – at least if you drive to the summit of the Pacific's highest mountain, on the Big Island. It's a surreal landscape, where powerful astronomical telescopes stand juxtaposed with traditional Hawaiian shrines.

09 **Oahu's Circle-Island Drive** Page **104** • To get away from the bustle on Oahu, drive the full length of the gorgeous windward shore, pausing at the many remote beaches along the way.

10 Big Beach

Page **262** • Beyond its resorts and high-rise hotels, Maui still holds enticing unspoiled beaches, where you may well find the sands undisturbed by a single footprint. One of the most gorgeous is Oneloa Beach, popularly known as "Big Beach".

11 Surfing Page **33** & *Blue Hawaii* **color section** • This traditional Polynesian sport may have spread all over the globe, but for locals and tourists alike, Hawaii's thunderous waves still represent the ultimate challenge.

12 Kalaupapa Peninsula Page **323** • Pilgrims flock to take the legendary Molokai Mule Ride down to Father Damien's celebrated leper colony, located on an all-but-inaccessible promontory at the foot of the world's tallest sea cliffs.

13 **Merrie Monarch festival** Page **176** • Hula shows and festivals take place on all the islands throughout the year, but this Big Island event is the highlight of the annual calendar.

14 **Whale migrations** Page **34** • Cavorting humpback whales, who spend each winter calving in the warm Hawaiian waters, are frequently visible off the beaches of West Maui.

15 **Helicopter trips** Page **340** • Taking a helicopter tour of Kauai is the perfect, albeit expensive, way to get a bird's-eye view of the island's spectacular scenery – its hidden waterfalls, tall sea cliffs, and lush valleys.

16 **The Kīlauea eruption** Page **203** • Kīlauea volcano on the Big Island, whose name means "much spewing," has been in a constant state of eruption since 1983; see it from a helicopter or, when conditions are right, on foot.

17 **The Feast at Lele** Page **233** • Set on the beach in lovely Lahaina, Maui, the Feast at Lele offers a sublime combination of wonderful food, beautiful scenery, and a great Polynesian show.

18 **Kalalau Trail**
Page **382** • Perhaps the most exhilarating and demanding trail in all the islands, this coastal hike traces Kauai's North Shore for eleven stupendous miles.

19 **Waiʻānapanapa State Park** Page **285** • Not far from the time-forgotten village of Hāna, this ravishing black-sand beach offers the best camping along the Maui coast.

Basics

Basics

Getting there

You'll almost certainly have to fly to get to the Hawaiian islands. Although Honolulu receives by far the most flights, there are direct services to Maui, the Big Island and Kauai as well, so there's no need to pass through Honolulu if you don't plan to spend any time in Oahu. Though the winter is peak season in Hawaii, fares are typically highest between June and August, and again around Christmas and New Year. As a rule, flying on weekdays costs less than weekends.

The simplest way to save money on a trip to Hawaii is to buy a **package** deal, for example through the operators listed on p.21, which includes both flight and accommodation (and possibly car rental as well). Even if you normally prefer to travel independently, you'll probably get a better deal on room rates if you book as part of a package.

Flights from the US and Canada

Most **flights** to Hawaii from the US mainland and Canada land at the state capital, **Honolulu**, on the island of Oahu. Virtually every large US airline flies to Honolulu, with United being the major carrier; Hawaiian Airlines also runs its own services to and from the western states. The only other airports that receive nonstop flights from the continental US are Kahului on **Maui**, Kona/Keahole on the **Big Island**, and Līhu'e on **Kauai**.

So long as you arrive in Honolulu by about 7pm, you should be able to connect with an onward flight to any of the other islands. In most cases it will be with the main inter-island carrier, Hawaiian Airlines; for more details, see p.22.

As for the **journey time**, crossing the Pacific from the West Coast to Honolulu

Arrival

You'll find information on **arrival** and getting to your destination from the airport in the relevant Guide chapters. For Oahu details, see p.53; for the Big Island, see p.135; for Maui, see p.245; and for Kauai, see p.347.

takes roughly five hours. For details on time differences, see p.41.

Flights from the US

Not surprisingly, most nonstop flights **to Hawaii** leave from the **West Coast** – and most go to **Honolulu**. Both **Los Angeles** and **San Francisco** are served by five carriers: Hawaiian, United, American, Continental, and Delta. The only other places connected to Honolulu by nonstop flights are **San Diego** and **Portland** by Delta and Hawaiian; **Oakland** by Hawaiian; **Orange County** by Continental; **Seattle** by Delta, Hawaiian, and Alaska; **Phoenix** by United and Hawaiian; **Salt Lake City**, **Atlanta**, and **Detroit** by Delta; **Denver** by United; **Dallas** by American; and **Chicago** by United and American.

An increasing number of nonstop flights connect the continental US with the Neighbor Islands. Nonstop flights to Kahului airport on **Maui** are operated from **Los Angeles** by Alaska, American, Continental, Delta, and United; from **San Francisco** by Continental and United; from **Seattle** by Hawaiian and Alaska; from **Oakland** and **Portland** by Hawaiian; from **Orange County** by Continental; from **Dallas** by American; and from **Phoenix** and **Chicago** by United.

Both Kona on the **Big Island** and Līhu'e on **Kauai** are connected with the same four cities by nonstop flights: **Los Angeles** on Hawaiian, United, American, and Delta; **San Francisco** and **Phoenix** on United; and **Seattle** on Alaska.

Typical round-trip **fares** to Hawaii from West-Coast cities range from around $350 up to perhaps $600; expect to pay more like $650 up to $850 anywhere east of

the Rockies. As there are so few nonstop flights from the Midwest and East Coast, and those that do exist tend to charge premium rates, most travelers from those areas fly via California.

Flights from Canada

Vancouver is the main Canadian hub for nonstop flights to Hawaii. **WestJet** flies to Honolulu and Maui from Vancouver year-round, as well as, in winter only, to Honolulu from Victoria and Calgary; to Maui from Victoria and Edmonton; and to the Big Island and Kauai from Vancouver. Round-trip **fares** start at around Can$450, going up to Can$750. In addition, **Air Canada** flies nonstop daily to Honolulu from Vancouver, with fares generally starting at more like Can$600 and ranging up to Can$1000.

Getting to Hawaii from anywhere else in Canada will require you to change planes either in Vancouver, or on the US mainland, which gives you more flexibility.

Flights from the UK and Ireland

Unless you're visiting Hawaii as part of a round-the-world trip, the only cost-effective way to reach the islands from the **UK** or **Ireland** is to fly via the mainland United States or Canada. Your options, therefore, are more or less the same as they are for North Americans; fly to one of the US cities mentioned on p.19 and change there for your onward trip.

With a ten-hour flight across the Atlantic to the West Coast, and a five-hour flight over the Pacific, that makes for a very long journey. However, it is possible to get to any of the four major islands – Oahu, Maui, Kauai and the Big Island – on the same day that you set off from London, thanks to the ten- or eleven-hour time difference (see p.41) and the great number of flights that leave the West Coast each afternoon. In any case, it's the journey home that's really exhausting – if you fly direct, you're likely to arrive home on the second morning after you leave, having "lost" two nights' sleep.

Connections **from Ireland** are more problematic. If you fly direct to the US mainland, you'll have to spend a night before

catching an onward flight to Hawaii, though it is possible to catch an early-morning plane to London and pick up a flight from there.

A typical return ticket from London to Hawaii **costs** around £650 from January to March, and more like £850 in July and August.

Flights from Australia and New Zealand

There's no shortage of flights from Australia and New Zealand to **Honolulu**, and very little price difference between airlines. Several airlines operate daily services, with journey times of around nine hours.

From Australia, most flights to Honolulu are out of **Sydney**. Both Air Canada, code sharing with United, and Qantas, code sharing with American Airlines, offer daily nonstop service, from around Aus$850 in low season up to more like Aus$1500 in high season. For around the same price, United flies via Auckland.

From New Zealand, the best deals to Honolulu are the direct flights out of Auckland offered by Air New Zealand, which can cost as little as NZ$1500 return in low season (going up to around NZ$2000 in high season), and by Air Canada, which tend to be a little more expensive. For similarly low fares, Qantas can also take you from Auckland to Honolulu via either Sydney or Western Samoa.

Airlines, agents and operators

Airlines

Aer Lingus ⓦ www.aerlingus.com
Air Canada ⓦ www.aircanada.com
Air New Zealand ⓦ www.airnz.co.nz
Alaska Airlines ⓦ www.alaskaair.com
American Airlines ⓦ www.aa.com
British Airways ⓦ www.ba.com
Continental Airlines ⓦ www.continental.com
Delta ⓦ www.delta.com
Hawaiian Airlines ⓦ www.hawaiianair.com
Qantas Airways ⓦ www.qantas.com
United Airlines ⓦ www.united.com
US Airways ⓦ www.usair.com
Virgin Atlantic ⓦ www.virgin-atlantic.com
WestJet ⓦ www.westjet.com

Six steps to a better kind of travel

At Rough Guides we are passionately committed to travel. We feel strongly that only through traveling do we truly come to understand the world we live in and the people we share it with – plus tourism has brought a great deal of **benefit** to developing economies around the world over the last few decades. But the extraordinary growth in tourism has also damaged some places irreparably, and of course **climate change** is exacerbated by most forms of transport, especially flying. This means that now more than ever it's important to **travel thoughtfully** and **responsibly**, with respect for the cultures you're visiting – not only to derive the most benefit from your trip but also to preserve the best bits of the planet for everyone to enjoy. At Rough Guides we feel there are six main areas in which you can make a difference:

- Consider what you're contributing to the **local economy**, and how much the services you use do the same, whether it's through employing local workers and guides or sourcing locally grown produce and local services.
- Consider the **environment** on holiday as well as at home. Water is scarce in many developing destinations, and the biodiversity of local flora and fauna can be adversely affected by tourism. Try to patronize businesses that take account of this.
- Travel with a purpose, not just to tick off experiences. Consider **spending longer** in a place, and getting to know it and its people.
- Give thought to how often you **fly**. Try to avoid short hops by air and more harmful night flights.
- Consider **alternatives to flying**, travelling instead by bus, train, boat and even by bike or on foot where possible.
- Make your trips **"climate neutral"** via a reputable carbon offset scheme. All Rough Guide flights are offset, and every year we donate money to a variety of charities devoted to combating the effects of climate change.

Agents and operators

In the US

American Airlines Vacations ⓦ www.aavacations .com. Package tours to Hawaii, including flight, accommodation, and car rental.

Backroads ⓦ www.backroads.com. Biking or multi-sport tours of the Big Island, with stays in top-quality accommodation, priced from $3000 for five nights, not including airfares.

Continental Airlines Vacations ⓦ www .covacations.com. Individually tailored Hawaiian vacations, including flights, hotel, and car rental.

Delta Vacations ⓦ www.deltavacations.com. Good-value Hawaiian package vacations with all combinations of flights, hotel, and car rental. A five-night stay in Waikīkī from New York starts at under $1000.

Globus and Cosmos ⓦ www.globusandcosmos .com. Independent and escorted tours in multi-island combinations: eight days on Oahu and Maui, or thirteen days on Oahu, Maui, Kauai, and the Big Island. Land-only rates start around $2300.

New England Hiking Holidays ⓦ www .nehikingholidays.com. Guided seven-day springtime hiking tours of the Big Island, for $2095, excluding airfare.

Pleasant Hawaiian Holidays ⓦ www .pleasantholidays.com. The leading supplier of independent packages, combining flights, car rental, accommodation, and so forth, on any island. Eight days on Maui, Oahu or both from LA start under $1000.

Sierra Club ⓦ www.sierraclub.org. Guided wilderness tours, geared towards families, on all the islands; a week-long trip to Hawaii Volcanoes National Park on the Big Island costs around $1900.

Tauck Tours ⓦ www.tauck.com. Fully escorted tours, staying at the very top hotels. Eleven nights on Oahu, Kauai, Maui and the Big Island costs $3740, excluding airfare.

United Vacations ⓦ www.unitedvacations.com. Custom-made individual vacations, combining islands and hotels to your specifications. Four-night trips from the West Coast start at around $800.

Windsurfari ⓦ www.windsurfari.com. Wind-surfing and custom vacation packages on Maui,

including condo, car, and equipment rental – but not flights – from $600 per week.

In the UK

Bon Voyage www.bon-voyage.co.uk. A range of packages, customized holidays, and special offers from around £1200 for twelve nights (flight plus accommodation).

Funway Holidays www.funwayholidays.co.uk. Well-priced flight-and-hotel packages from the UK to Big Island, Kauai, Maui, and Oahu, from around £1100 for two weeks. Car rental and other add-ons available too.

Hawaiian Dream www.hawaiian-dream.co.uk. Packages and bespoke holidays from a long-standing Hawaii specialist. Their "twin centre" deal costs from £1830 per person for seven nights on Big Island and Maui (including flights).

North America Travel Service www.north americatravelservice.co.uk. Puts together tailor-made packages to suit your requirements.

United Vacations www.unitedvacations .co.uk. Good-value flight-and-hotel packages from around £1100 for two weeks, with all the usual add-ons available.

Virgin Holidays www.virginholidays.co.uk. All-inclusive flight-and-hotel deals on all the main islands, usually booked in combination with either California or Las Vegas.

In Australia

Creative Tours www.creativeholidays.com.au. A range of hotel-only bookings or full packages to Big Island, Kauai, Maui, and Oahu, from $1229 for a four-night break.

Inter-island travel

Apart from a couple of small-scale ferry services from Maui, all travel between the Hawaiian islands is done by air. The route between Honolulu and Kahului on Maui ranks as the busiest domestic route in the entire US, with more than three million passengers each year. Honolulu is the main hub; apart from very short hops, it's unusual to be able to fly between two of the outer islands without a stop on Oahu.

Flights and fares

The major airline for inter-island travel, **Hawaiian** (☎1-800/367-5320, www .hawaiianair.com), connects Honolulu up to twenty times daily with the airports at Kona and Hilo on the Big Island, Kahului on Maui, and Līhu'e on Kauai. They also fly nonstop from Kahului to both Big Island airports, and to Kauai.

Island Air (☎1-800/652-6541, www .islandair.com) flies from Honolulu to Molokai, Lanai, and both Kahului and Kapalua on Maui; from Kahului to Kona, Kauai, and Molokai; from Kapalua to Molokai; and from Molokai to Lanai.

Budget airline **Go!** (☎1-888/435-9462, www.iflygo.com) connects Honolulu with all the other islands, including Lanai and Molokai,

as well as around one daily nonstop service between Maui and both Kona and Molokai.

Finally, a small commuter airline, **Pacific Wings** (☎1-888/575-4546, www.pacific wings.com), offers connections between Maui and Molokai, and also between Waimea on the Big Island and both Maui and Honolulu.

Price competition being strong, all the airlines charge similar **fares**, with typical one-way rates from Honolulu to Kahului starting at around $60, and flights between the other islands generally costing more like $100.

Don't expect to be able to fly late in the evening; the last scheduled flights on all the airlines usually depart at around 7pm from Honolulu, and 8pm from the Neighbor Islands.

Ferries and cruises

Hawaii's much-vaunted **Super Ferry**, which was expected to provide regular services between Oahu and the other major islands, made its first sailing between Honolulu and Maui in 2007, but controversy centering on its environmental impact caused it to abandon operations forever in 2009.

That leaves only two scheduled ferry services in Hawaii, both of which depart from Lahaina on Maui. **Expeditions** (☏808/661-3756 or 1-800/695-2624, ⊛www.go-lanai .com) runs five boats each day to Manele Bay on Lanai, while the **Molokai Princess** (☏808/662-3535 or 1-877/500-6284, ⊛www .mauiprincess.com) makes two daily round-trips between Lahaina and Kaunakakai on Molokai. For details of both, see p.229.

The main operator of **cruises** between the islands is Norwegian Cruise Lines (☏1-866/234-7350, ⊛www.ncl.com). They offer weekly, week-long cruises out of Honolulu that visit Kauai, Maui, and the Big Island, for typical per-person fares of $1300 and up.

Getting around

The only way to explore the Hawaiian islands at all thoroughly is to drive. Those planning a completely Waikīkī-centered vacation will find that Oahu has a reasonable public-transport system; everywhere else, if you're not on a package tour, you'll be floundering from the moment you touch down at the airport. "Getting around" sections for each island, with details of public transport and island tours, appear in the introductions to each chapter.

By car

Demand for **rental cars** in Hawaii is high – in addition to the millions of tourists, there are all the locals who can't take their cars when they travel from island to island. That said, there's such a plentiful supply that competition is fierce, and Honolulu has the lowest average rental rates of any major US city.

The **national rental chains** are represented on all the major islands, and every airport has at least one outlet. Make reservations online; most individual offices cannot even advise on rates or availability. With so much competition, and so many short-lived special offers, it's hard to quote specific prices, but a target rate for the cheapest economy car with unlimited mileage should be something around $35 per day or $150 per week. Avis and Hertz allow drivers to pay the weekly rate even when driving different cars on different islands; all the rest charge separately for each vehicle. To rent a car, drivers must be over 21, and those between ages 21 and 24 often have to supply additional guarantees or simply pay extra.

Before you commit yourself to a rate, check whether your airline – or your hotel, B&B, or hostel – can offer a discount on car rental. Some hotels even supply free cars for guests who stay for a week or longer.

When you rent, you'll probably be pressured to pay perhaps $20 extra per day for **Collision Damage Waiver** (CDW), a form of insurance that absolves you of liability for any damage to your vehicle. Controversially, Hawaii is a "no-fault state," meaning that drivers are held responsible for whatever befalls their own vehicle, so CDW cover is more important here than elsewhere. American car-owners should call their insurance companies to check if they're covered by policies they already hold; some credit-card companies also provide card holders with car-rental insurance coverage. Whether or not you choose to buy CDW is

a purely personal decision. Some people regard it as little short of extortion; others feel it gives them peace of mind.

Car rental companies

Alamo ⓦ www.alamo.com
Avis ⓦ www.avis.com
Budget ⓦ www.budget.com
Dollar ⓦ www.dollar.com
Enterprise ⓦ www.enterprise.com
Hertz ⓦ www.hertz.com
National ⓦ www.nationalcar.com
Thrifty ⓦ www.thrifty.com

Driving in Hawaii

On the whole, **driving** in Hawaii is both easy and enjoyable. Most of the islands effectively have just one main road, so there's little risk of getting lost, and with such small distances to cover no one seems to be in too much of a hurry.

However, there are a few provisos. **Honolulu** is a large and confusing city, with major rush-hour traffic congestion and a shortage of parking spaces. Since the city has a good bus system, there's no real need to drive while you're there, and renting a car at the airport after a tiring flight can be a recipe for disaster. Elsewhere, the **coastal highways** can be slow and tortuous, and often narrow to a single lane to cross tiny bridges. Bear in mind, too, that it's dark by 7pm, and stretches of road between towns are not lit, so driving at night can be difficult.

Apart from the fact that in Hawaii, as in the rest of the US, you drive on the right, the one rule of the road that can trouble foreign visitors is that, unless specifically prohibited, drivers are allowed, after a careful pause, to **turn right on a red light**.

Typical **gas prices** are around thirty percent above the US average, so you can easily pay $3.25 per gallon. Keep a closer eye on your fuel gauge than usual; sightseeing expeditions can carry you 25 miles into the wilderness on dead-end roads, which makes for a fifty-mile round-trip before you see another gas station.

Cycling

As detailed throughout the Guide, **bikes** are available for rent on all the Hawaiian islands, usually for in town use rather than long-distance explorations. Safety considerations have, however, led to recent restrictions on "**downhill cycling adventures,**" in which groups of tourists are taken by van to some appropriately lofty spot and then allowed to freewheel back to base. Thus the daily dawn descent from the top of Haleakalā on Maui now starts several miles below the summit, as detailed on p.270. Cycles are not allowed on hiking trails in national or state parks.

Some of the companies listed on p.21 organize guided **cycle-touring** vacations, but few visitors bring their own bikes and tour the islands themselves. There's no great reason why not; the Big Island in particular would make an excellent destination for a camping trip by bike, while all the main highways on Maui have cycle lanes.

Public transport

While Oahu boasts an excellent bus network – detailed on p.55 – **public transport** on the other islands is minimal in the extreme. Maui, Kauai, and the Big Island have limited bus systems, Lanai has a very localized shuttle service, and Molokai has nothing at all. To get to or from the airport, you can always call a taxi or minivan service, but that's no way to go sightseeing. The only **railroads** still operating in Hawaii are the "Sugar Cane Train," which offers daily musical excursions between Lahaina and Kā'anapali on Maui (see p.230), and a short stretch in southwest Oahu, where the Hawaii Railway Society runs Sunday-afternoon jaunts (see p.122).

Accommodation

Although the average cost of a single night's accommodation in Hawaii may sound alarming at $170, that figure has dropped slightly since the recession kicked in, and is in any case boosted by the $300–400 rates for the lavish resorts at the top end of the spectrum. On all the islands, you can expect to find a reasonable standard of hotel, condo, or B&B for around $100 per night: Molokai is the cheapest, followed in ascending order by Oahu, the Big Island, Kauai, Maui, and Lanai. Overall occupancy rates seem to hover around seventy percent or lower, so it's usually possible to book a room at short notice.

All these prices are based on the hotel's own **rack rates** – the rate you'll be offered if you simply walk through the door and ask for a room. While there's little room for bargaining in the smaller inns or B&Bs, in the larger hotels it's very possible to find significantly cheaper rates online, or to cut costs by buying a **package deal** through one of the operators or airlines listed on p.21.

Detailed advice on where to stay on each individual island, with specific recommendations, appears at the start of the relevant chapter. With the exception of the Big Island, it's relatively easy to explore each island from a single base. Few people tour from place to place on any one island, staying in a different town each night, and hotels much prefer guests to make reservations well in advance.

Resorts

If you haven't visited a major tropical vacation destination before, you may not be familiar with the concept of a **resort**, in the sense of an individual property, run most often by a major chain such as *Hyatt Regency* or *Hilton*. These gigantic, sprawling enclaves, each holding hundreds or even thousands of rooms, are more than just hotels. Often located far from any town, they are equipped with their own restaurants, stores, swimming pools, beaches, golf courses, tennis courts, walking trails, and anything else you can think of, all designed to ensure that guests never feel the need to leave the property. Such luxury doesn't come cheap – typical ocean-view rooms are likely to cost over $350 a night, and suites can go for $2500 or more – and since the resorts are located purely for sun rather than culture or even scenery, they often hold little to remind you that you're in Hawaii at all.

This kind of development was pioneered on Maui and the Big Island during the 1960s, when entrepreneurs realized that the islands' leeward coasts were dry and hot enough to make it worth constructing brand-new

Accommodation price codes

Throughout this book, **accommodation prices** have been graded with the symbols below, according to the least expensive double room for most of the year, not including state taxes of 13.42 percent.

Both hostels and budget hotels usually keep the same rates throughout the year, but in more expensive properties, rooms that are normally priced above $100 tend to rise by an average of $20–40 in the peak seasons – from Christmas to Easter and June to August. However, it's possible to obtain much better rates for top-range accommodation by booking your room as part of an all-inclusive package.

❶ $40 and under	❹ $101–150	❼ $251–300
❷ $41–70	❺ $151–200	❽ $301–400
❸ $71–100	❻ $201–250	❾ $401 and over

oases from scratch. Where beaches didn't exist they were sculpted into the coastline; coconut palms were flown in and replanted; and turf was laid on top of the lava to build championship-quality golf courses.

Hawaii's prime resort concentrations can be found in Waikoloa, Mauna Lani, and Mauna Kea on the Big Island; Po'ipū on Kauai; and Kā'anapali, Kapalua, and Wailea on Maui. Additional individual resorts scattered around the islands include the *Ihilani Resort* and *Turtle Bay Resort* on Oahu, the *Lodge at Kō'ele* and *Manele Bay Hotel* on Lanai, and the *Princeville Hotel* on Kauai.

Hotels, motels, and condos

In addition to the paramount example of Waikīkī on Oahu, large clusters of conventional **hotels** have grown up in areas such as Kīhei on Maui, Kailua on the Big Island, and Wailua on Kauai. While these may look far less opulent than the resorts described above – and barely distinguishable from each other – the standard of the rooms is dependably high. You can expect an en-suite bathroom, as well as a balcony (universally known as a *lānai*) of some kind. Room rates vary from perhaps $300 per night at the top of the spectrum down to around $100, and virtually every hotel has at least one **restaurant**.

The distinction between a hotel room and a **condominium** apartment is not always clear; the same building may hold some private condo apartments and others rented by the night to short-term guests. The difference lies in the types of facilities each offers. An individual condo unit is likely to be more comfortable and better equipped than a typical hotel room, usually with a kitchenette, but on the other hand, a condominium building may not have a lobby area, daily housekeeping service, restaurants, or other hotel amenities.

Incidentally, many of Hawaii's oldest hotels rank among its very best. That's because regulations dictating how close to the ocean it's possible to build have become much stricter in recent years, so delightful beachfront accommodations like the *Hanalei Colony Resort* on Kauai, and the *Mauian* and its neighbors on Maui's Napili Bay, could never be constructed these days.

Motels on the usual American model are rare, and representatives of the national motel chains all but nonexistent. Certain older towns do, however, retain basic hotels that were originally built to accommodate migrant agricultural laborers. In most cases these are minimally equipped flophouses, which may charge as little as $30 per night, though those that haven't shut down altogether have tended to upgrade over time.

Bed and breakfasts

The definition of **bed and breakfast** accommodation stretches from a simple room or two in a private home, through self-contained, self-catering cottages, to luxurious fifteen-room inns; surprisingly, not all include breakfast. In principle, however, the standards are very high. The cheapest rooms, perhaps sharing a bathroom with one other guest room, start around $75 per night, while for $150 per night you can expect your own well-furnished apartment, with all facilities. The owners are often friendly and full of advice on making the most of your vacation.

Most small-scale B&Bs are located away from the busier tourist areas, in the more scenic, but slightly wetter or cooler parts of the islands where people actually choose to live. Thus there are particular concentrations in the upcountry meadowlands of Maui and the Big Island, across the mountains from Honolulu on Oahu's windward coast, and a couple of miles back from the ocean on the east coast of Kauai. If you plan to spend a night or two at Hawaii Volcanoes National Park on the Big Island, there's little alternative to the wide assortment of B&Bs in the nearby village of Volcano.

For a reliable selection of top-quality B&Bs on all the islands, contact local agencies like **Hawaii's Best Bed & Breakfasts** (☏808/263-3100 or 1-800/262-9912, ⓦwww .bestbnb.com) or **Bed & Breakfast Hawaii** (☏808/822-7771 or 1-800/733-1632, ⓦwww .bandb-hawaii.com).

Vacation rentals

For families in particular, renting a home makes a convenient alternative to staying in a hotel. **Vacation rentals** are widely available on all the islands, concentrated in very much the same areas as the hotels and B&Bs, and

Hostels

Each of the largest islands has at least one budget **hostel**, where you can get a bed in a dormitory for around $22 per night or a very basic, private double room for $35–50. Few of these are affiliated to international hosteling organizations, and some only admit non-US citizens. As a rule, they're strongly geared towards young surfers and backpackers.

Big Island
Arnott's Lodge, Hilo (p.172)
Hilo Bay Hostel, Hilo (p.172)
Holo Holo In, Volcano (p.207)
JoMamas Pāhoa, Pāhoa (p.101)
Koa Wood Hale Inn, Kailua (p.137)
Pineapple Park, Hilo (p.172)
Pineapple Park, Kealakekua (p.147)

Maui
Banana Bungalow, Wailuku (p.248)
Lahaina's Last Resort, Lahaina (p.229)
Northshore Hostel, Wailuku (p.248)

Oahu
Backpacker's Vacation Inn,
  Pūpūkea (p.119)
Hosteling International Honolulu,
  Honolulu (p.62)
Hosteling International Waikīkī,
  Waikīkī (p.57)
Polynesian Hostel Beach Club,
  Waikīkī (p.57)
Waikīkī Beachside, Waikīkī (p.57)

especially, of course, close to the beaches. Rates are broadly similar to those for hotel accommodation, with a similar range from the basic to the luxurious. Indeed, many vacation rentals are privately owned condos in the self-same blocks that also hold hotel rooms.

Vacation rental websites

Ⓦ www.hawaiianbeachrentals.com
Ⓦ www.homeaway.com
Ⓦ www.vacationhomerentals.com
Ⓦ www.vrbo.com

Food and drink

Hawaii-bound visitors hoping for memorable culinary experiences can sample from an array of cuisines, brought to the islands by immigrants from all over the world. In addition, the presence of thousands of tourists, many prepared to pay top rates for good food, means that the islands have some truly superb fine-dining restaurants, run by internationally renowned chefs.

Local restaurants

While the national fast-food chains are well represented in Hawaii, and pretty much anything eaten in the mainland US is available in Hawaii, locally owned budget restaurants, diners, and takeout stands throughout the state serve a hybrid cuisine that draws on the traditions of Japan, China, Korea, and the Philippines as well as the US mainland. The resultant mixture has a slight but definite

Hawaiian twist. In fact, the term **"local"** food has a distinct meaning in Hawaii, and specifically applies to this multicultural mélange.

Breakfast tends to be the standard combination of eggs, meat, pancakes, muffins, or toast. At midday, the most popular option is the **plate lunch**, a tray holding meat and rice as well as potato or macaroni salad and costing between $6 and $9. **Bento** is the Japanese version, with mixed meats and rice; in Filipino diners, you'll be offered

adobo, which is pork or chicken stewed with garlic and vinegar and served in a similar way. Korean barbecue, **kal bi** – prepared with sesame – is especially tasty, with the word "barbecue" indicating that the meat or fish has been marinated rather than necessarily cooked on an open grill. One simple but filling recipe – thought to be of Chinese origin – is **saimin** (pronounced *sy-min* not *say-min*), a bowl of clear soup filled with noodles and other mixed ingredients that has become something of a Hawaiian state dish. **Spam musubi** is an individual-sized block of rice topped by grilled Spam – to all intents it's a piece of Spam sushi (more than half of all the Spam eaten in the US is consumed in Hawaii). The carbohydrate-packed **loco moco** is a fried egg served on a hamburger with gravy and rice, while the favorite local dessert is **shave ice**, slushy scrapings of ice flavored with rainbow-colored syrups. Finally, a **malasada** is a sweet Portuguese donut, best eaten hot and fresh.

Food in general is often referred to as *kaukau*, and the general term for snacks is **pūpūs** (pronounced *poo-poos*) – the kind of finger food that is given away at early evening Happy Hours.

Fine dining

Some of the world's most lavish and inventive **restaurants** can be found in the more exclusive resort regions of Hawaii. The distinctively Hawaiian cuisine being created in such places, known variously as **Pacific Rim**, **Euro-Asian**, or **Hawaii Regional**, combines foods and techniques from all the countries and ethnic groups that have figured in Hawaiian history, and uses the freshest ingredients possible. The top chefs – such as Roy Yamaguchi, who runs **Roy's** restaurants on all four major islands, and Peter Merriman, who owns restaurants on Maui, Kauai and the Big Island – seek to preserve natural flavors by such methods as flash-frying meat and fish like the Chinese, baking it whole like the Hawaiians, or serving it raw like the Japanese. The effect is enhanced by the delicate addition of Thai herbs and spices,

Hawaiian fish

Although the ancient Hawaiians were expert offshore fishermen, as well as being highly sophisticated fish farmers, most of the **fish** eaten in Hawaii nowadays is imported. Local fishing is not done on a large enough scale to meet the demand, and in any case many of the species that tourists enjoy thrive in much cooler waters. Thus salmon and crab come from Alaska, mussels from New Zealand, and so on, although Maine lobsters are farmed in the cold waters of the deep ocean off Honokōhau on the Big Island, and **aquafarms** on several islands are raising freshwater species.

Some of the **Pacific** species caught nearby are listed below by their common Hawaiian names. Of these it's worth trying *opah*, which is chewy and salty like swordfish; the chunky *'ōpakapaka*, which because of its red color (associated with happiness) is often served on special occasions; the succulent white *ono* (Hawaiian for "delicious"); the beautifully tender *moi*, often steamed or fried whole in Chinese restaurants; and the dark *ahi*, the most popular choice for sashimi.

ahi	yellow-fin tuna	*mano*	shark
aku	skipjack tuna	*moi*	thread fish
a'u	swordfish or marlin	*onaga*	red snapper
'ehu	red snapper	*ono*	mackerel/tuna-like fish
hāpu'upu'u	sea bass	*'ōpae*	shrimp
hebi	spear fish	*opah*	moonfish
kākū	barracuda	*'ōpakapaka*	pink snapper
kalekale	pink snapper	*pāpio*	pompano
kāmano	salmon	*uhu*	parrot fish
kūmū	red goat fish	*uku*	gray snapper
lehi	yellow snapper	*ulua*	jack fish
mahimahi	dorado or dolphin fish	*weke*	goat fish

and by the sheer inventiveness that it shares with modern Californian cooking.

Throughout the islands, you'll also find plenty of conventional **American** shrimp and steak specialists, as well as high-class **Italian**, **Thai**, and **Chinese** places. Many of the larger hotels hold authentic and very good **Japanese** restaurants, which tend to specialize in discreet sushi and sashimi dining rather than the flamboyant teppanyaki style, where knife-juggling chefs cook at your table.

Local ingredients

As well as the many kinds of fish listed in the box on p.29, widely used local ingredients include **ginger** and **macadamia nuts** (large, creamy, and somewhat bland white nuts said to contain a hundred calories per nut, even when they aren't coated with chocolate). Bright red **'ohelo berries**, which taste like cranberries, are served up in gourmet restaurants, but they were once sacred to the volcano goddess Pele, and to eat one was punishable by death. **Avocados** are widely grown and are even richer than you may be used to, as are fruits such as **guava** (an imported pest that's a staple for hikers, as it grows wild along most wilderness trails), **papaya**, and **mango**. Watch out also for the small yellow **apple bananas**, with their distinct savory tang and, of course, the ever-present **coconut**.

Drink

The usual range of **wines** (mostly Californian, though both Maui and the Big Island have their own tiny wineries) and **beers** (mainly imported either from the mainland or Mexico) are sold at Hawaiian restaurants and bars, but at some point every visitor seems to insist on getting wiped out by a tropical **cocktail** or two. Among the most popular are the **Mai Tai**, which should contain at least two kinds of rum, together with orange Curaçao and lemon juice; the **Blue Hawaii**, in which vodka is colored with blue Curaçao; and the **Planter's Punch**, made with light rum, grenadine, bitters, and lemon juice.

Tap **water** is safe to drink, though it's a scarce enough resource in places that some restaurants will only bring it to your table on request.

Deliciously rich local coffees are available in small cafés and espresso bars throughout the state. Hawaii's most famous gourmet product, **Kona coffee**, refers only to coffees grown on the southwestern slopes of the Big Island – see p.145 – but coffee is also grown on Kauai, Molokai, Oahu and Maui.

Entertainment and festivals

If you consider wild nightlife essential to the success of your Hawaiian vacation, head straight for the bright lights and glitter of Waikīkī. Everywhere else on the islands, with the possible exception of Lahaina on Maui, is likely to prove disappointing. That's not to say there's nothing going on at all, but Hawaii is a rural state, and away from Honolulu there's nothing larger than a small country town. On Maui they call 10pm "Maui midnight" because everyone has gone to bed; Kauai and the Big Island are even sleepier.

Entertainment listings for Honolulu and Waikīkī appear on pp.96–98. Otherwise most of the nightlife in Hawaii is arranged by the major **hotels** – almost all put on some form of entertainment for their guests, and many feature live musicians every night, with a strong but not exclusive emphasis on Hawaiian music. **Restaurants** and **cafés** also use live music to attract diners, whether in the form of full-fledged bands or simple acoustic strummers.

Unless you coincide with one of the major annual festivals, you're unlikely to see an authentic **hula** performance, though all the main islands have several commercial *lū'aus*, a sort of mocked-up version of the open-air, ocean-front Hawaiian feasts that are traditionally held to celebrate a baby's first birthday. These can be great fun if you're in the right mood, but they seldom bring you into contact with locals. Big-name touring musicians tend to perform in Honolulu, and with luck on Maui as well, while the other islands have to settle for regular concert appearances by the stars of the Hawaiian music scene. For more about hula and Hawaiian music, see p.438.

A festival calendar

January–February

Ka Molokai Makahiki Kaunakakai (Molokai), late Jan ⓦ www.molokaievents.com. Festival of ancient Hawaiian sports.

Chinese New Year Chinatown, Honolulu (Oahu), Jan/Feb ⓦ www.chinatownhi.com. Street celebrations in Honolulu.

Maui Whale Festival Maui, Feb ⓦ www.maui whalefestival.org. A month of whale-related events.

March–April

Honolulu Festival Downtown Honolulu and Waikīkī (Oahu), early March ⓦ www.honolulufestival.com. Hawaii's place in the Pacific is celebrated through dance, arts, and crafts.

Kona Brewers Festival Kailua (Big Island), mid-March ⓦ www.konabrewersfestival.com. Beery times on the Big Island.

Merrie Monarch Festival Hilo (Big Island), week after Easter ⓦ www.merriemonarch.com. The biggest international hula festival (see p.176).

May–June

Lei Day Throughout Hawaii, May 1. Public holiday with statewide celebrations.

Kanaka Ikaika Molokai–Oahu kayak race Molokai, mid-May ⓦ www.y2kanu.com. Prestigious men's kayak event.

Molokai Ka Hula Piko Pāpōhaku Beach Park (Molokai), third Sat in May ⓦ www.molokaievents .com. Hula festival (see p.331).

International Festival of Canoes Lahaina (Maui), late May ⓦ www.mauifestivalofcanoes .com. A tribute to Polynesian seafaring.

Nā Hōkū Hanohano O Hawai'I Waikīkī (Oahu), late May ⓦ www.nahokufestival.com. Four-day music festival.

Kauai Polynesian Festival Līhu'e (Kauai), late May ⓦ www.kauaipolynesianfestival.org. Four-day dance and music festival.

Kamehameha Day Throughout Hawaii, June 11. Statewide celebrations.

Maui Film Festival Wailea (Maui), mid-June ⓦ www.mauifilmfestival.com. Small-scale film festival with a Pacific emphasis.

King Kamehameha Hula Festival Blaisdell Center, Honolulu (Oahu), late June ⓦ www.hula comp.com. A traditional and contemporary hula, performed by both men and women.

Hawaiian Slack Key Guitar Festival Maui Arts & Cultural Center (Maui), late June ⓦ www.slackkey festival.com. A glorious cavalcade of Hawaiian music.

Pu'uhonua O Hōnaunau Cultural Festival Big Island, late June ⓦ www.nps.gov/puho. The "Place of Refuge" celebrates its heritage.

Flavors of Honolulu food festival Civic Center Grounds, Honolulu (Oahu), late June. A chance to sample Hawaii's various ethnic traditions.

July–August

Parker Ranch Rodeo Waimea (Big Island), July 4 ⓦ www.parkerranch.com. Hawaii's largest and oldest ranch honors its cowboy past.

Makawao Rodeo Makawao (Maui), July 4. Maui's principal rodeo event.

Big Island Hawaiian Music Festival Hilo (Big Island), mid-July ⓦ www.ehcc.org. The Big Island's largest music festival.

Prince Lot Hula Festival Moanalua Gardens, Honolulu (Oahu), third Sat in July ⓦ www.mgf -hawaii.org. A chance to sample Hawaii's various ethnic traditions.

Hawaiian International Billfish Tournament Kailua (Big Island), early Aug ⓦ www.hibtfishing .com. Competitive sport-fishing event.

Hawaiian Slack Key Guitar Festival Kapiolani Park, Waikīkī (Oahu), mid-Aug ⓦ www.slackkey festival.com. See June, above.

September–October

Hawaiian Slack Key Guitar Festival Sheraton Keauhou (Big Island), early Sept ⓦ www.slackkey festival.com. See June, above.

Aloha Festival Consecutive festivals on each island, Sept–Oct ⓦ www.alohafestivals.com. Parades, performances, and assorted cultural events.

Kauai Mokihana Festival Kauai, late Sept ⓦ www.maliefoundation.org. Week-long hula, music, and crafts festival.

Na Wahine O Ke Kai Molokai to Oahu, late Sept ⓦ www.ohcra.com. Women's outrigger canoe race.
Molokai Hoe Molokai to Oahu, early Oct. Men's outrigger canoe race.
Ironman Triathlon World Championship Kailua (Big Island), early Oct ⓦ www.ironman.com. The ultimate test of athletic endurance (see p.138).
Halloween parade Lahaina (Maui) and Waikīkī (Oahu), Oct 31. Notoriously boisterous parades.

November–December

Hawaii International Film Festival Honolulu (Oahu), first two weeks Nov ⓦ www.hiff.org. Prestigious celebration of global and especially Pacific film.
Hawaiian Slack-key Guitar Festival Līhu'e (Kauai), early Nov ⓦ www.slackkeyfestival.com. See June, above.

Kona Coffee Cultural Festival South Kona (Big Island), early Nov ⓦ www.konacoffeefest.com. All sorts of coffee-themed events.
Hāmākua Music Festival Honoka'a (Big Island), Nov ⓦ www.hamakuamusicfestival.com. Charming, small-scale local music festival.
Triple Crown of Surfing Oahu, Nov–Dec ⓦ www.triplecrownofsurfing.com. World-famous surfing event centered on three main contests on Oahu's North Shore: the Hawaiian Pro (Ali'i Beach Park, Hale'iwa) in mid-Nov; the World Cup (Sunset Beach), late Nov/early Dec; and the Pipe Masters (Banzai Pipeline), early Dec.
Honolulu Marathon Oahu, second Sun in Dec ⓦ www.honolulumarathon.org. Starting on Ala Moana Blvd and finishing at Kapiolani Park, Honolulu's annual marathon attracts around 25,000 participants.

Ocean sports and beach safety

Hawaii's vast tourism industry is rooted in the picture-book appeal of its palm-fringed sandy beaches and crystal-clear turquoise ocean. Opportunities for sea sports are almost infinite, ranging from snorkeling and scuba diving to fishing and whale-watching, as well as Hawaii's greatest gift to the world, the art of surfing. Hawaiian beaches can be deadly as well as beautiful, however, and you need to know exactly what you're doing before you enter the water.

No one owns any stretch of beach in Hawaii. Every beach in the state – defined as the area below the vegetation line – is regarded as **public property**. That doesn't mean that you're entitled to stroll across any intervening land between the ocean and the nearest highway; always use the clearly signposted "public right of way" footpaths. Whatever impression the large oceanfront hotels may attempt to convey, they can't stop you from using the beaches out front; they can only restrict, but not refuse to supply, parking places for non-guests.

What constitutes the **best beach** in Hawaii is a matter of personal taste, and each of the major islands holds candidates. For sheer looks, head for **Mākena Beach** on Maui, **Kailua Beach** on Oahu, **Kē'ē Beach** on Kauai, **Kehena Beach** on the Big Island, or

Pāpōhaku Beach on Molokai. If you want to swim in safety as well, then try **Hāpuna Beach** on the Big Island, **'Anini** on Kauai, **Kailua** on Oahu, or the **Kama'ole** beaches on Maui. And for glamour, of course, there's no beating **Waikīkī**.

Ocean sports

With average water temperatures of between 75°F and 82°F (24–28°C), the sea in Hawaii is ideal for a wide range of ocean sports.

Snorkeling

Probably the easiest activity for beginners is **snorkeling**. Equipped with mask, snorkel, and fins, you can while away hours and days having face-to-face encounters with the rainbow-colored populations of Hawaii's

reefs and lava pools. Well-known sites include **Hānauma Bay** in southeast Oahu, **Kealakekua Bay** on the Big Island, and the islet of **Molokini** off Maui.

You can **rent** snorkel equipment on all the islands, at rates ranging upwards from $7 per day/$15 per week. One reliable source on every island is Snorkel Bob's (Ⓦwww.snorkelbob.com).

Scuba diving

With endless networks of submarine lava tubes to explore, and the chance to get close to some amazing marine life forms, Hawaii makes a great **scuba diving** destination. The Big Island and Maui are the most popular of the islands, but experts rate Lanai even higher, and Kauai is also acquiring a reputation; you'll find a detailed overview, plus lists of diving-boat operators, in the introduction to each chapter. The typical cost for a two-tank boat diving trip for a certified diver is around $110; beginners pay around $25 more than that, and every operator offers short courses leading to certification. Note that for medical reasons you shouldn't dive within 24 hours of flying or even ascending significantly above sea level, for example by driving towards the summits of Haleakalā on Maui or Mauna Kea on the Big Island.

Surfing

The place that invented **surfing** – long before the foreigners came – remains its greatest arena. A recurring theme in ancient legends has young men frittering away endless days in the waves rather than facing up to their duties (see p.426); now young people from all over the world flock to Hawaii to do just that. The sport was popularized a century ago by champion Olympic swimmer **Duke Kahanamoku**, the original Waikīkī Beach Boy. He toured the world with his 16ft board, demonstrating his skills to admiring crowds, and was responsible for introducing surfing to Australia.

Waikīkī lost its best surf breaks when it was re-landscaped at the start of the tourist boom, but with advances in techniques and technology, surfing has never been more popular. Oahu's fabled **North Shore** is a haven for surf bums, who ride the waves around Waimea Bay and hang out in the coffee bars of Hale'iwa. Favored spots elsewhere include **Hanalei Bay** on Kauai and **Honolua Bay** on Maui, but surfing at such legendary sites is for experts only. However much you've surfed at home, you need to be very sure you're up to it before you have a go in Hawaii; start by sampling the conditions at the lesser surf-spots to be found on all the islands. Be warned that surfing is forbidden at some of Hawaii's most popular beaches, to prevent collisions with ordinary bathers.

Surfing lessons for beginners are on offer in most tourist areas, costing anything from $25 per hour and coming with a guarantee that you'll ride a wave on your own before it's over. They're great fun, and they really work. An equally exhilarating way to get a taste for the surf is to use a smaller **boogie-board**, which you lie on. Variations such as stand-up **paddle boarding** and **kitesurfing** have also become extremely popular in recent years; tuition is widely available.

Windsurfing

Hawaii is also the spiritual home of **windsurfing**. Maui is the prime goal for enthusiasts from around the world, and many of them find that Hawaiian waters present challenges on a vastly different scale to what they're used to at home. If you find an oceanfront parking lot on Maui filled with shiny rental cars and bursting with tanned tourists sporting Lycra clothing and expensive equipment, the chances are you're at a beginners' beach. Salt-caked local rustbuckets and cut-off denims are the markers of demanding beaches like **Ho'okipa Beach Park**, the venue for windsurfing's World Cup.

Fishing

Big-game **fishing**, for marlin especially, is a major attraction for many visitors to Hawaii. On the Kona coast of the **Big Island**, Kailua plays host each August to the prestigious Hawaiian International Billfish Tournament, while fishing charter vessels are available year-round at Honokōhau Harbor, a few miles north. A smaller selection of boats leave from Lahaina and Mā'alaea harbors on **Maui**.

Details on fishing regulations, and licenses for freshwater fishing ($5–25), can be obtained online from the Division of Aquatic Resources (Ⓦwww.hawaii.gov/dlnr).

Whale-watching

Around a quarter of the North Pacific's twenty thousand **humpback whales** winter in Hawaiian waters, between late November and early April. They're especially fond of the shallow channels between Maui, Molokai, and Lanai, and are often clearly visible from the coastal highways. In season, **whale-watching** boats set off from all the major islands, and most operators are confident enough to guarantee sightings.

Ocean safety

Hawaii is the remotest archipelago on earth, which means that **waves** have two thousand miles of the Pacific Ocean to build up their strength before they come crashing into the islands. Anyone born in Hawaii is brought up with a healthy respect for the sea, and learns to watch out for all sorts of signs before they swim. You'll be told to throw sticks into the waves to see how they move, or to look for disturbances in the surf that indicate powerful currents. Unless you have local expertise, however, you're better off sticking to the official beach parks and most popular spots, especially those that are shielded by offshore reefs. Not all beaches have lifeguards and warning flags, and unattended beaches are not necessarily safe. Look for other bathers, but whatever your experience elsewhere, don't assume you'll be able to cope with the same conditions as the local kids. Always ask for advice and above all follow the cardinal rule – **never turn your back on the water**.

The beaches that have the most accidents and **drownings** are those where waves of four feet or more break directly onto the shore. This varies according to the season, so beaches that are idyllic in summer can be storm-tossed death traps between October and April. If you get caught in a rip current

or undertow and find yourself being dragged out to sea, stay calm and remember that the vast majority of such currents disappear within a hundred yards of the shore. Never exhaust yourself by trying to swim against them, but simply allow yourself to be carried out until the force weakens, and then swim first to one side and then back to the shore.

Sea creatures to avoid include *wana* (black spiky **sea urchins**), Portuguese man-of-war **jellyfish**, and **coral** in general, which can give painful, infected cuts. **Shark attacks** are much rarer than popular imagination suggests, though there were four fatalities in Hawaii during the 1990s, and there have been two more in the 2000s. Those that do happen are usually due to "misunder-standings," such as surfers idling on their boards who look a bit too much like turtles from below. That probably occurred in the notorious case of 13-year-old Kauai surfer Bethany Hamilton, who lost her left arm while surfing at Tunnels Beach in 2003.

Sun safety

Only expose yourself to the harsh **tropical sun** in moderation; a mere fifteen to thirty minutes is the safe recommendation for the first day. The sun is strongest between 10am and 3pm, and even on overcast days human skin still absorbs harmful UV rays. Use plenty of **sunscreen** – doctors recommend Sun Protection Factor (SPF) 30 for Hawaii – and reapply after swimming. Note, however, that some marine life sanctuaries forbid the use of sunscreen by bathers, which should be enough to discourage you from swimming altogether. Drink lots of (nonalcoholic) liquids as well, to stave off dehydration.

Hiking and camping

Hawaii is one of the most exciting hiking destinations imaginable. Well-maintained trails guide walkers through scenery that ranges from dense tropical rainforest to remote deserts and active volcanoes. At times, you can find yourself in some pretty uncompromising wilderness.

However, **camping** in Hawaii need not be a battle with the elements. All the islands hold lovely oceanfront campgrounds where you don't have to do anything more than drive in and pitch your tent; some offer cabins for rent so you needn't even do that.

Camping

Advice on the best **campgrounds** on each island, and how to obtain permits to stay at them, is given in the introduction to each chapter of the Guide. The majority of campgrounds are in the public **parks** scattered across each island. There's a complicated hierarchy of county, state, and national parks, each with different authorities, so it's not always obvious whom to contact about a particular spot. However, one thing you cannot do is just set up your tent on some unoccupied piece of land; only camp at designated sites.

On a camping (as opposed to backpacking) vacation, your best bet is to spend most of your time at the **county beach parks** ranged along the shoreline of each island. The most appealing are on the **Big Island**, where Spencer Beach Park and Punalu'u are especially attractive, and along the north shore of **Kauai**, but Maui and Oahu also have their moments.

County authorities are engaged in a constant struggle to discourage semi-permanent encampments of homeless local people from developing at certain sites, so precise regulations on maximum lengths of stay, and even whether a particular park is open at all, tend to change at a moment's notice. On Oahu, for example, all public campgrounds are closed on Wednesday and Thursday nights.

Many of the campgrounds in Hawaii's **state** and **national** parks are in remote spots that can only be reached on foot, but they tend to be set amid utterly sublime scenery. Among the best are the backcountry sites along the **Kalalau Trail** on Kauai's Nā Pali coast, and the national park campgrounds in **Hawaii Volcanoes** park on the Big Island and atop **Haleakalā** on Maui, both of which also offer rudimentary cabins for rent.

For a full list of state parks and their facilities, see ⓦ www.hawaiistateparks.org.

Hiking

All the best **hiking trails** in Hawaii are described in detail in the relevant chapters (see also the *Hiking in Hawaii* color section). Every island has at least one inspiring trail, but the two best destinations for hikers have to be Kauai and the Big Island.

Kauai has the dual attractions of the spectacular Nā Pali coast, where the **Kalalau Trail** clings to the cliffs through eleven miles of magnificent unspoiled valleys, and Kōke'e State Park, high above, where the **Alaka'i Swamp Trail** and the **Awa'awapuhi Trail** trek through the rainforest for amazing overviews of similar rugged scenery.

On the Big Island, it would be easy to spend a week day-hiking trails such as the **Kīlauea Iki** trail in Volcanoes National Park, without the thrill wearing off, and there's potential for countless longer backpacking expeditions.

Maui offers the **Sliding Sands Trail** through the heart of Haleakalā, and mountain hikes like the **Waihe'e Ridge Trail**, while on Molokai, with local guides, you can clamber through the verdant **Halawa Valley** to reach a pair of superb waterfalls. Even Honolulu itself has the lovely rainforest trails through **Makiki** and **Mānoa** valleys.

As a rule, all trails remain passable all year, but you can expect conditions to be much muddier between November and April.

National parks admissions

Hawaii has two full-fledged national parks, **Healeakalā** on Maui (p.269) and **Hawaii Volcanoes** on the Big Island (p.193), while the Big Island also holds a national monument, the **Puʻuhonua O Hōnaunau** (p.150).

All charge for admission, but also sell the park system's national passes. The $80 **National Parks** pass, which provides admission to all national parks and monuments for the bearer and any accompanying passengers, can also be bought online at ⓦwww.store.usgs.gov/pass. Both the **Access Pass**, free to US citizens or residents with disabilities, and the **Senior Pass**, available to US citizens or residents aged over 62 for a $10 one-time fee, offer unlimited admission for life to all national parks in the US.

Equipment and safety

Hiking **trails** in Hawaii tend to fall into two basic types. There are the beautiful scenic ones, to waterfalls or through lush valleys, which tend to be very wet and muddy; and then there are the harsh exposed ones across rugged volcanic terrain, where the bare lava rock is capable of slashing any footwear to ribbons. Either way, a sturdy pair of **hiking boots** is essential. Other **equipment** should include rain gear, a flashlight, insect repellent, sunscreen and sunglasses, some attention-seeking device such as a whistle or a piece of brightly colored clothing, and a basic first aid kit. If you're backpacking, of course, you'll need a waterproof tent and sleeping bag as well. Take things slowly if you're heading up the volcanoes on Maui or the Big Island, as there's a real risk of altitude sickness; if you feel symptoms such as a heavy pulse, shortness of breath, headache, and nausea, come back down again. Warm clothing is also essential, especially with night temperatures low enough to cause hypothermia.

While hiking, be wary of following even dry streambeds and never wade across streams that are more than waist-high. Allow plenty of time to finish any trail by sunset, which is never later than 7pm and usually much earlier. On typical Hawaiian trails you shouldn't reckon on walking more than 1.5 miles per hour. Most hiking deaths occur when hikers are stranded on cliffs or ledges and then panic; certain trails, as indicated throughout this book, but especially on Kauai, have some really hair-raising spots that you should avoid if you're prone to vertigo.

Carry plenty of **water** when you hike, and drink it as you need it – don't try to conserve water supplies, as it takes more water to recover from dehydration than it does to prevent it. Never drink untreated water; **leptospirosis**, a bacterial disease carried by rats and mice in particular, can be contracted through drinking stream water (filtering alone will not purify it) or even from wading through fresh water if you have any cuts or abrasions. Symptoms range from diarrhea, fever and chills through to kidney or heart failure, and appear in anything from two to twenty days. In the case of infection, seek treatment immediately; for more information, see ⓦwww.hawaii.gov/health.

Shopping

Honolulu is very much the shopping capital of Hawaii, and any stories you may have heard about Japanese tourists coming to Hawaii specifically to shop apply almost exclusively to Honolulu, where malls like the Ala Moana Center hold outlets of all the big names in world fashion. Residents of the other islands, too, tend to think nothing of flying over to Oahu for a day's shopping, though Maui, especially, now also holds its fair share of tourist-oriented malls. The prints, posters, and T-shirts piled high along the sidewalks of Waikīkī and other tourist areas are all well and good if you think that a gecko on a surfboard is real neat, but stores and galleries selling high-quality indigenous arts and crafts are few and far between. For more on shops and malls in Honolulu and Waikīkī, see p.99.

Hawaiian crafts and produce

Some of the most attractive products of Hawaii are just too ephemeral to take home. That goes for virtually all the orchids and tropical flowers on sale everywhere, and unfortunately it's also true of *leis*.

Leis (pronounced *lays*) are flamboyant decorative garlands, usually composed of flowers such as the fragrant *melia* (the plumeria or frangipani) or the bright-red *lehua* blossom (from the *'ō'hia* tree), but sometimes also made from feathers, shells, seeds, or nuts. They're worn by both men and women, above all on celebrations or gala occasions – election-winning politicians are absolutely deluged in them, as are the statues of Kamehameha the Great and Queen Lili'uokalani in Honolulu on state holidays. Sadly, not every arriving tourist is

festooned with a *lei* these days, but you'll probably be way-*lei*ed at a *lū'au* or some such occasion, while if you're around for Lei Day (May 1), everyone's at it. If you want to buy one, most towns have a store or two with a supply of flower *leis* kept in refrigerated cabinets, but Chinatown in Honolulu is the acknowledged center of the art.

Colorful Hawaiian **clothing**, such as aloha shirts and the cover-all "Mother Hubbard"-style *mu'umu'u* dress, is sold everywhere, though classic designs are surprisingly rare and you tend to see the same stylized prints over and over again. Otherwise, the main local crafts to look out for are *lau hala* **weaving**, in which mats, hats, baskets, and the like are created by plaiting the large leaves (*lau*) of the spindly legged pandanus (*hala*) tree, and **wood turning**, with fine bowls made from native dark woods such as *koa*.

Travel essentials

Costs

Although it's possible to have an inexpensive vacation in Hawaii, there's no getting away from the fact that **prices** on the islands are consistently higher – on the scale of around forty percent – than in the rest of the United

States. Locals call it the "Paradise Tax" – the price you pay for living in paradise.

How much you spend each day is, of course, up to you, but it's hard to get any sort of breakfast for under $10, a cheap lunch can easily come to $17, and an evening

meal in a restaurant, with drinks, is likely to cost $30 or more per person, even if you're trying to economize. In the main tourist areas it's usually possible to find a dorm bed in a hostel for around $25, but otherwise even the cheapest hotels tend to charge over $80 a night for a double room, and a rental car with gas won't cost less than $30 a day. It's easy to spend $100 per person per day before you've done anything: pay for a snorkel cruise or a lū'au, and you've cleared $150.

Throughout the Guide, you'll find detailed price information for lodging and eating on all the islands. Unless otherwise indicated, hotel price symbols (explained on p.26) refer to the price of a double room (excluding tax) for most of the year, while restaurant prices are for food only and don't include drinks or service.

A state **sales tax** (technically a general excise tax, though the difference is highly abstruse) of 4.17 percent is imposed on all transactions, and is almost never included in the prices displayed in stores or on menus. As hotels collect an additional 9.25 percent **room tax**, a total surcharge of 13.42 percent is added to accommodation bills.

Crime and personal safety

For travelers, Hawaii poses no serious issues regarding **crime** or **personal safety**. You should, however, try to avoid leaving valuables in any unattended vehicle – **break-ins** are a problem at isolated hiking trailheads in particular – or leaving your belongings on the beach while you're in the sea. Certain beaches, detailed where necessary throughout this book, also serve as evening partying places for locals, who can be intimidating to outsiders.

Electricity

Hawaii's **electricity** supply, like that on the US mainland, uses 100 volts AC. Plugs are standard American two-pins.

Entry requirements for foreign travelers

Under the **visa waiver scheme**, passport-holders from Britain, Ireland, Australia, New Zealand, and most European countries do not require visas for trips to the US, so long as they stay less than ninety days, and have an onward or return ticket. However, anyone planning to use the visa waiver scheme is required to apply for **travel authorization** in advance, online. It's a very quick and straight-forward process, via the website ⓦwww.cbp.gov/xp/cgov/travel/. Fail to do so, however, and you may well be denied entry. Once you have authorization, you can simply fill in the visa waiver form that's handed out on incoming planes. Immigration control takes place at your point of arrival on US soil.

In addition, your passport must be **machine-readable**, with a barcode-style number. All children need to have their own individual passports. Holders of older, non-readable passports should either obtain new ones or apply for visas prior to travel.

Prospective visitors from parts of the world not mentioned above need a valid passport and a non-immigrant visitor's visa. How you'll obtain a visa depends on what country you're in and your status when you apply, so call the nearest US embassy or consulate. For full details visit ⓦhttp://travel.state.gov.

Gay and lesbian travelers

The greatest concentration of **gay and lesbian activism** in Hawaii is in Honolulu, though the state as a whole is liberal on social issues. During the 1990s, Hawaii was at the forefront of the national movement towards the legalization of same-sex marriages, and a 1997 state law granted equal rights to same-gender couples and their families in most areas of the law. "Gay marriage" as such, however, is still not on the statute book; Hawaii's Senate approved a civil unions bill early in 2010, but the governor seems unlikely to sign it into law.

Listings for Honolulu's gay and lesbian scene appear on p.98. Gay-friendly **accommodation** can be found on all the islands, including the *Waikīkī Beachside Hotel & Hostel* (see p.57) and *Cabana at Waikīkī* (see p.60) in Waikīkī; the *Sunseeker Resort* (see p.256) on Maui; *Mahina Kai* (see p.363) on Kauai; and *Hale Ohia* (see p.207) on the Big Island.

Pacific Ocean Holidays (☎808/545-5252 or 1-800/735-6600, ⓦwww.gayhawaii vacations.com) organizes all-inclusive **package vacations** in Hawaii for gay and

lesbian travelers, and maintains the useful ⓦ www.gayhawaii.com **website**.

The best-known gay **beaches** are Queen's Surf and Diamond Head on Oahu, Donkey Beach on Kauai, Honokōhau Beach on the Big Island, and the Little Beach at Mākena on Maui.

Health

No **inoculations** or **vaccinations** are required by law in order to enter Hawaii, though some authorities suggest a polio vaccination.

Medical resources for travelers

CDC ☏1-800/232-4636, ⓦ www.cdc.gov/travel. Official US government travel health site. **International Society for Travel Medicine** ☏1-404/373-8282, ⓦ www.istm.org. Has a full list of travel health clinics.

Hospitals

For all **emergencies** call ☏911. **Hospitals** providing 24-hour assistance in **Honolulu** include Kuakini Medical Center, 347 Kuakini St (☏808/536-2236); Moanalua Medical Center, 3288 Moanalua Rd (☏808/432-0000); the Queens Medical Center, 1301 Punchbowl St (☏808/538-9011); and the Straub Clinic and Hospital, 888 S King St (☏808/522-4000).

The **Big Island** holds the following hospitals: Hilo Medical Center, 1190 Waiānuenue Ave, Hilo (☏808/974-4700); Ka'ū Hospital, 1 Kamani St, Pahala (☏808/928-2050); Kohala Hospital, 54-383 Hospital Rd, Kapa'au (☏808/889-6211); Kona Community Hospital, 79-1019 Haukapila St, Kealakekua (☏808/322-9311); and North Hawaii Community Hospital, 67-1125 Māmalahoa Hwy, Waimea (☏808/885-4444).

Maui hospitals include: Maui Memorial Medical Center, 221 Mahalani St, Wailuku (☏808/244-9056), and Kīhei-Wailea Medical Center, 221 Pi'ikea Ave, Kīhei (☏808/874-8100); there is no hospital in Lahaina.

On **Kauai**, contact the Wilcox Memorial Hospital and Kauai Medical Clinic, 3-3420 Kūhīō Hwy, Līhu'e (☏808/245-1100). **Lanai**'s only hospital is Lanai Community Hospital, 628 Seventh St, Lāna'i City (☏808/565-8450); while **Molokai** holds the Molokai General Hospital, 280 Home Olu Place, Kaunakakai (☏808/553-5331).

Insurance

In view of the high cost of medical care in the US, all travelers visiting the US from overseas should be sure to buy some form of **travel insurance**. American and Canadian citizens may already be covered – some homeowners' or renters' policies are valid on vacation, and credit cards such as American Express often include some medical or other insurance, while most Canadians are covered for medical mishaps overseas by their provincial health plans. If you only need trip cancellation/interruption coverage (to supplement your existing plan), this is generally available at about $6 per $100.

Internet

Internet access is widely available in Hawaii. Most public and university libraries offer free access; hostels tend to have a computer or two where guests can check email; and both copier outlets and internet cafés allow customers to go online, typically for around $4 per hour. Almost all hotels offer some form of **wi-fi**, usually in every room (though

Rough Guides travel insurance

Rough Guides has teamed up with WorldNomads.com to offer great **travel insurance** deals. Policies are available to residents of over 150 countries, with cover for a wide range of **adventure sports**, 24hr emergency assistance, high levels of medical and evacuation cover and a stream of **travel safety information**. Roughguides.com users can take advantage of their policies online 24/7, from anywhere in the world – even if you're already traveling. And since plans often change when you're on the road, you can extend your policy and even claim online. Roughguides.com users who buy travel insurance with WorldNomads.com can also leave a positive footprint and donate to a community development project. For more information go to ⓦ **www .roughguides.com/shop**.

in the larger resorts especially a fee is often charged), and also in the lobby (which is more likely to be free).

Mail

There are **post offices** in all the main towns, generally open between 8.30am and 4pm on weekdays and for an hour or two on Saturday mornings. Mail service is extremely slow, as all mail between Hawaii and the rest of the world, and even between Hawaiian islands other than Oahu, is routed via Honolulu. From anywhere except Honolulu, allow a week for your letter to reach destinations in the US and two weeks or more for the rest of the world. From Honolulu itself, reckon on four days to the mainland US and eight days to anywhere else.

Maps

The best general-purpose **maps** of the individual islands – there's one each for Oahu, the Big Island, Maui, and Kauai, while Molokai and Lanai are combined on a single sheet – are published by the University of Hawaii, and are widely available at island bookstores.

Plenty of free maps are also distributed on the islands themselves – you'll almost certainly get a booklet of maps from your rental car agency. These can be useful for pinpointing specific hotels and restaurants, but only the University of Hawaii maps are at all reliable for minor roads.

If you need detailed **hiking maps**, call the state parks office in Honolulu or on each specific island, as detailed in the relevant chapters; their free map of Kauai, for example, is excellent. You could also buy the **topographic maps** produced by the United States Geological Survey (@www.usgs.gov), which are widely sold at specialist bookstores in Hawaii.

Money

For most services, it's taken for granted that you'll be paying with a **credit card**. Hotels and car rental companies routinely require an imprint of your card whether or not you intend to use it to pay. Most visitors find that there's no reason to carry large amounts of cash or travelers' checks to Hawaii. **ATMs** that accept most cards issued by domestic and foreign banks can be found almost everywhere; call your own bank if you're in any doubt.

If you do want to take **travelers' checks** – which offer the great security of knowing that lost or stolen checks will be replaced – be sure to get them issued in US dollars. Foreign currency, whether cash or travelers' checks, can be hard to exchange, so foreign travelers should change some of their money into dollars at home.

Opening hours and public holidays

Opening hours for specific attractions are detailed throughout this book. In general, most businesses geared towards tourists are open every day, with shops typically opening from 10am until 8pm or later, while government offices, banks, and the like tend to be open between 9am and 5pm on weekdays, and closed at weekends and public holidays.

Phones

The **telephone area code** for the entire state of Hawaii is ☏808. Calls within any one island count as local, so you don't need to dial the area code. To call another island, put ☏1-808 before the phone number; charges vary according to the time of day and distance involved.

Public holidays

As well as observing the national public holidays, Hawaii also has a number of its own:

Jan 1	New Year's Day
Third Mon in Jan	Dr Martin Luther King Jr's Birthday
Third Mon in Feb	Presidents' Day
March 26	Prince Kūhiō Day
Easter Monday	
May 1	Lei Day
Last Mon in May	Memorial Day
June 11	Kamehameha Day
July 4	Independence Day
Third Fri in Aug	Admission Day
First Mon in Sept	Labor Day
Second Mon in Oct	Columbus Day
Nov 11	Veterans' Day
Fourth Thurs in Nov	Thanksgiving
Dec 25	Christmas Day

Calling home from abroad

Hotels impose huge surcharges, so it's best to use a **phone card** for long-distance calls. In preference to the ones issued by the major phone companies, you'll find it simpler and cheaper to choose from the various pre-paid cards sold in almost all supermarkets and general stores, which can be used from your hotel room or any public phone (though note that pay phones are becoming increasingly rare).

To place a call **from Hawaii** to the rest of the world, dial ☎011 then the relevant country code as follows:

Australia	☎61
Britain	☎44
Canada	☎1
Ireland	☎353
New Zealand	☎64

To make an international call **to Hawaii**, dial your country's international access code, then 1 for the US, then 808 for Hawaii.

Cell phones

If you want to use your **cell** (**mobile**) **phone** in Hawaii, you'll need to check with your phone provider whether it will work there, and what the call charges are. For overseas visitors, the rates are likely to be very high indeed.

Restrooms

Doors in some **restrooms** are labeled in Hawaiian: *Kāne* for Men, *Wahine* for Women.

Senior travelers

Hawaii is a popular destination for **senior travelers**; most attractions offer reduced rates for seniors and many hotels have special deals on rooms in quiet periods. For discounts on accommodation and vehicle rental, US residents aged 50 or over should consider joining the American Association of Retired Persons (☎1-888/687-2277, ⓦwww .aarp.org). The Senior Pass, which entitles holders to free admission to US National Parks, is detailed on p.36.

Exploritas (previously known as Elderhostel) runs programs each summer on the Hawaiian islands, in conjunction with the University of Hawaii at Hilo on the Big Island (☎1-800/454-5768, ⓦwww.exploritas.org). Participating senior citizens take courses in various aspects of Hawaiian culture and history, with fees covering boarding, lodging, and tuition.

Smoking

Smoking is **banned** in all restaurants and bars in Hawaii.

Time

Unlike most of the US, Hawaii does not observe Daylight Saving Time. Therefore, from 2am on the second Sunday in March until 2am on the first Sunday in November, the **time difference** between Hawaii and the US West Coast is three hours, not the usual two; the time difference between Hawaii and the mountain region is four hours, not three; and the islands are six hours earlier than the East Coast, not five. Hawaiian time is from ten to eleven hours behind the UK. In fact it's behind just about everywhere else; although New Zealand and Australia might seem to be two and four hours respectively behind Honolulu time, they're on the other side of the International Date Line, so are actually almost a full day ahead.

Tipping

Wait staff in restaurants expect **tips** of at least fifteen percent, in bars a little less. Hotel porters and bellhops should receive at least $2 per piece of luggage, and housekeeping staff at least $2 per night.

Tourist information

The **Hawaii Visitors and Convention Bureau (HVCB)** has offices (known as chapters) on every island. Its official website, ⓦwww.go hawaii.com, also holds links to businesses and operators on all the islands, though bear in mind that they pay to have their activities publicized.

Racks of leaflets, brochures, and magazines – a good source of free offers and discount coupons – are prominently displayed in all major hotels, malls, and airports. In heavily touristed areas such as Waikīkī, Kīhei and Lahaina on Maui, Kapa'a on Kauai, and Kailua

on the Big Island, you'll also find plenty of **activities centers**. Masquerading as information kiosks, these are primarily concerned with persuading you to buy tickets for some specific activity such as a cruise, horse ride, island tour, or whatever; the worst are fronts for time-share companies as well.

Hawaii Visitors Bureau offices

Main Office 1-800/464-2924, @www.gohawaii .com.
Big Island Visitors Bureau 250 Keawe St, Hilo ☎808/961-5797 or 1-800/648-2441; and 65-1158 Mamalahoa Hwy, Waimea ☎808/885-1655, @www.bigisland.org.
Kauai Visitors Bureau 4334 Rice St, Līhuʻe ☎808/245-3971 or 1-800/262-1400, @www .kauaidiscovery.com.
Lanai Visitors Bureau 431 Seventh St, Lānaʻi City, HI 96763 ☎808/565-7600 or 1-800/947-4774, @www.visitlanai.net.
Maui Visitors Bureau 1727 Wili Pā Loop, Wailuku ☎1-800/525-6284, @www.visitmaui.com.
Molokai Visitors Association 2 Kamoi St, Kaunakakai ☎808/553-5221 or 1-800/800-6367, @www.molokai-hawaii.com.
Oahu Visitors Bureau 733 Bishop St, Suite 1250, Honolulu ☎808/524-0722 or 1-887/525-6248, @www.visit-oahu.com.

Useful websites

Web addresses for hotels, activity operators, and other businesses are listed throughout the Guide. You can also find copious links and listings on sites such as @www.aloha -hawaii.com, www.maui.net, and www.kauai .com. The most useful sites for news and listings are run by the two daily Honolulu newspapers, the *Star Bulletin* (@www.star bulletin.com) and the *Advertiser* (@www .honoluluadvertiser.com), and also the weekly papers on each island such as *Honolulu Weekly* (@www.honoluluweekly.com), *Maui Weekly* (@www.mauiweekly.com), the *Molokai Dispatch* (@www.themolokaidispatch.com), and the *Hawaii Island Journal* (@www.hawaii islandjournal.com).

Travelers with disabilities

When it comes to meeting the needs of **travelers with disabilities**, Hawaii is among the best-equipped vacation destinations in the world – indeed Oahu has been ranked as the most accessible place in the United States by the Society for the Advancement of Travel for the Handicapped (@www.sath.org).

The **State of Hawaii Disability and Communication Access Board** produces reports on facilities for disabled travelers on each of the islands, which you can download from @www.state.hi.us/health /dcab/. In addition, Access–Able (@www .access–able.com) carries information on the accessibility of hotels and other facilities throughout Hawaii.

Rental cars with hand controls are available from Avis and Hertz outlets; arrangements should be made at least a month in advance. On Oahu, CR Newton (☎808/949-8389 or 1-800/545-2078, @www.crnewton .com) rents wheelchairs, scooters, and crutches. Most TheBus vehicles are adapted to suit passengers with physical disabilities.

Guide dogs for the blind are exempt from Hawaii's otherwise strict **quarantine** regulations; full details can be obtained from the Animal Quarantine Facility (☎808/483-7151, @www.hawaii.gov).

Traveling with children

Hawaii is a hugely popular destination for travelers with young **children**. The biggest attraction of course is the ocean; be sure to follow local advice (as well as the information in this book) as to the safety of specific beaches, and ideally use those that have lifeguards. Activity operators of all kinds offer special facilities and reduced rates for kids. Hotels cater especially well for kids; extra beds are always available, perhaps for a small additional charge. Children are invariably welcome in restaurants.

Weddings

To get **married** in Hawaii, you must have a valid state license, available from the Department of Health, Marriage License Office, 1250 Punchbowl St, Honolulu (☎808/586-4545, @www.hawaii.gov/health), or agents on the other islands (hotels have details). Licenses cost $60 and are valid for thirty days; there's no waiting period. Weddings are very big business; most major resorts offer their own marriage planners, and the Hawaii Visitors Bureau keeps full lists of organizers.

Guide

Guide

Oahu

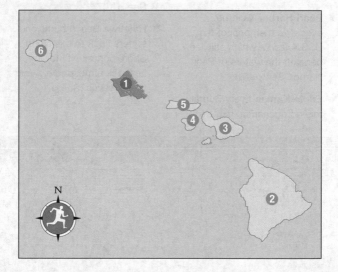

CHAPTER 1 # Highlights

* **Waikīkī Beach** Learn to surf, or just sip a cocktail, on Hawaii's most famous beach. See p.63

* **Nu'uanu Pali State Wayside** Site of an ancient battle and now a breathtaking viewpoint overlooking windward Oahu. See p.85

* **Bishop Museum** The world's finest collection of Polynesian artifacts brings Pacific history to life. See p.86

* **Pearl Harbor** Visit the evocative memorial of the USS *Arizona*, which still lies beneath the waters of Pearl Harbor. See p.87

* **Eddie Kamae** Every Sunday, this octogenarian 'ukulele virtuoso offers Oahu's finest weekly musical treat. See p.97

* **Ala Moana Center** Every visitor to Honolulu spends at least half a day in this vast, cosmopolitan shopping mall. See p.99

* **Kailua Beach** Lapped by gentle turquoise waters, this gorgeous golden strand is Oahu's loveliest beach – and President Obama's favorite. See p.107

* **Hale'iwa** Beach bums and surfers flock to this North Shore community for its laidback atmosphere... and those waves. See p.117

▲ Waikīkī Beach

1

Oahu

Around three quarters of the population of Hawaii – just over 900,000 people – live on the island of **Oahu**. Around half of them are packed into the city of **Honolulu**, which remains the financial and political powerhouse of the whole archipelago. While it's a genuinely vibrant city in its own right, the fact that ninety percent of visitors to Hawaii spend at least one night on Oahu inevitably means that tourism dominates the local economy.

The vast majority of Oahu's hotel rooms are squeezed into the tower-block enclave of **Waikīkī**, just east of downtown Honolulu. Although that's a blessing for local residents, it makes it hard for visitors to create their own personal, individual travel experiences. Surfers flock to the fabled **North Shore**, just over an hour's drive away, but almost everyone else ends up in Waikīkī, where even the most determined hedonist can find the hectic resort lifestyle palls after a few days.

That said, Honolulu itself is a remarkably attractive city, ringed by eroded volcanoes and reaching back into gorgeous valleys, and as a major world crossroads it has a broad ethnic mix, plus strong cultural traditions and lively nightlife. Great **beaches** are scattered all over the island – not just in Waikīkī – while plantation towns, ancient ruins, and luscious scenery await more adventurous explorers.

Tourist organizations like to claim that Oahu means "the gathering place." Both the translation, and the suggestion that to see Hawaii, you should first see Oahu, are spurious. Don't feel that Oahu is a place to avoid, but if you spend more than a few days in Waikīkī at the start of your Hawaiian vacation, you may end up wishing you'd moved on to the other islands a little sooner.

A brief history of Oahu

Before the coming of the foreigners, Oahu was probably the least significant of the four major Hawaiian islands. Nonetheless, it was among the very first places in Hawaii to attract Polynesian settlers. Traces of occupation dating back to 200 AD have been found at Kahana Valley and Bellows Field. The windward valleys held sizeable agricultural populations, while the sheltered coastline of Pearl Harbor supported an intricate network of fishponds. Not until the eighteenth century, however, did any individual chief manage to subdue the whole island, and by that time the rulers of both Maui and the Big Island were capable of launching successful invasions.

Captain Cook never set foot on Oahu. However, shortly after he died at Kealakekua Bay in 1779, his two ships put in at Waimea Bay on Oahu's North Shore. By the time Captain Vancouver returned in 1792, the island had been conquered by Chief Kahekili of Maui. In 1793, Captain William Brown, a British fur trader, spotted a safe anchorage near the mouth of the Nuʻuanu Stream. The Hawaiians knew this as *He Awa Kou*, "the harbor of Kou," but Brown renamed it **Honolulu**, or "fair haven," and the name soon attached itself to the fishing village nearby.

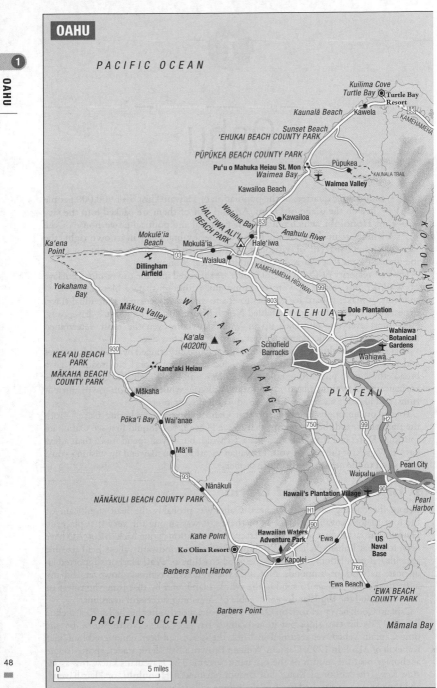

OAHU

PACIFIC OCEAN

Kuilima Cove
Turtle Bay
Turtle Bay Resort
Kawela
83
KAMEHAMEHA
Kaunalā Beach
Sunset Beach
'EHUKAI BEACH COUNTY PARK
PŪPŪKEA BEACH COUNTY PARK
Pūpukea
Pu'u o Mahuka Heiau St. Mon
Waimea Bay
KAUNALA TRAIL
Waimea Valley
Kawailoa Beach
Waialua Bay
Kawailoa
Ka'ena Point
83
Anahulu River
Mokulē'ia Beach
HALE'IWA ALI'I
BEACH PARK
Hale'iwa
Mokulā'ia
Waialua
KAMEHAMEHA HIGHWAY
Dillingham Airfield
03
K
O
'
O
L
A
U
99
Yokahama Bay
Mākua Valley
803
LEILEHUA
Dole Plantation
WAI'ANAE
Wahiawa Botanical Gardens
Ka'ala (4020ft)
Schofield Barracks
Wahiawā
KEA'AU BEACH PARK
Kane'aki Heiau
RANGE
PLATEAU
MĀKAHA BEACH COUNTY PARK
Mākaha
750
99
H2
Pōka'i Bay
Wai'anae
Pearl City
Waipahu
Mā'ili
Nānākuli
93
Hawaii's Plantation Village
90
Pearl Harbor
NĀNĀKULI BEACH COUNTY PARK
H1
US Naval Base
Kahe Point
90
Ko Olina Resort
Hawaiian Waters Adventure Park
Kapolei
'Ewa
Barbers Point Harbor
760
'Ewa Beach
'EWA BEACH COUNTY PARK
PACIFIC OCEAN
Barbers Point
Māmala Bay

0   5 miles

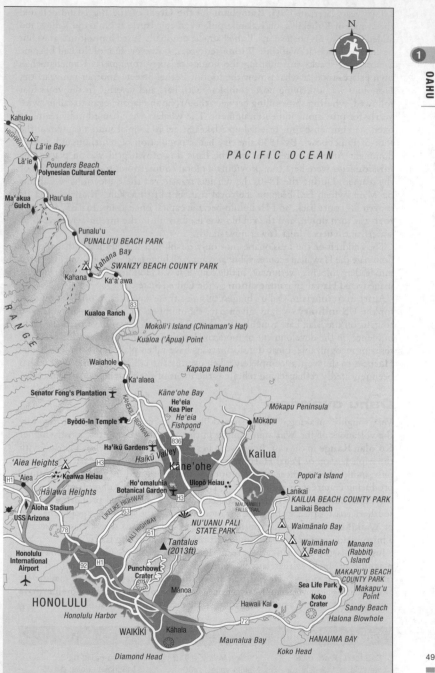

N

PACIFIC OCEAN

Kahuku

Lāʻie Bay

Lāʻie

Pounders Beach
Polynesian Cultural Center

Maʻakua Gulch

Hauʻula

Punaluʻu

PUNALUʻU BEACH PARK

Kahana *Bay*

SWANZY BEACH COUNTY PARK

Kahana

Kaʻaʻawa

83

Kualoa Ranch

Mokoliʻi Island (Chinaman's Hat)

Kualoa (ʻĀpua) Point

Waiahole

Kaʻalaea

Kapapa Island

Senator Fong's Plantation

Kāneʻohe Bay

**Heʻeia
Kea Pier**
*Heʻeia
Fishpond*

Mōkapu Peninsula

Byōdō-In Temple

Mōkapu

Haʻikū Gardens

836

Haikū Valley

Kāneʻohe

Kailua

RANGE

KOʻOLAU RANGE

KAHEKILI HIGHWAY

'Aiea Heights

H3

Hālawa Heights

Keaiwa Heiau

H1

'Aiea

Popoiʻa Island

**Hoʻomaluhia
Botanical Garden**

Ulopō Heiau

Lanikai

KAILUA BEACH COUNTY PARK
Lanikai Beach

H3

MAUNAWILI FALLS TRAIL

Aloha Stadium

USS Arizona

78

LIKELIKE HIGHWAY

63

Waimānalo Bay

*NUʻUANU PALI
STATE PARK*

72

PALI HIGHWAY

61

**Waimānalo
Beach**

*Manana
(Rabbit)
Island*

**Honolulu
International
Airport**

92

H1

**Punchbowl
Crater**

▲ *Tantalus
(2013ft)*

*MAKAPUʻU BEACH
COUNTY PARK*

Sea Life Park

*Makapuʻu
Point*

Mānoa

**Koko
Crater**

Sandy Beach

HONOLULU

Hawaii Kai

72

Honolulu Harbor

Kāhala

Halona Blowhole

WAIKĪKĪ

Maunalua Bay

HANAUMA BAY

Diamond Head

Koko Head

Two years later, in 1795, **Kamehameha the Great** of the Big Island defeated the armies of Kahekili's son Kalanikūpule in an epic battle at Nuʻuanu Valley, and added Oahu to his possessions. Kamehameha originally based himself in a grass hut beside the beach at **Waikīkī**. Within ten years, however, Honolulu had become a cluster of shacks surrounding the homes of sixty foreigners; Kamehameha's own palace stood at what is now the foot of Bethel Street. Another ten years on, Honolulu was a thriving port, complete with bars and taverns. In the years that followed, **whaling** ships sailing between the Arctic and Japan began to call in twice yearly for provisions and entertainment. The whalers were hauled in by teams of oxen – an immense rope reached up Alakea Street to loop around a capstan at the foot of Punchbowl. By 1830 the city had a population of ten thousand, with a dominant American presence, and the basic downtown grid was in place. The **missionaries** were here too, providing a moral counterpoint to the lawlessness of the seamen. During the 1840s the whalers transferred their affections to Lahaina on Maui, which had become the royal seat, but in time King Kamehameha III moved his court back, and Honolulu became capital once again. In 1857, the city **fort** was torn down, and the rubble was used to fill in the fifteen-acre stretch of waterfront where Aloha Tower now stands.

The children of the missionaries not only established the businesses that were to dominate the Hawaiian economy, but also amassed huge landholdings, and gravitated into leading roles in government. In due course, it was Honolulu's American elite that maneuvered Hawaii into **annexation** by the United States.

Apart from **tourism**, Oahu's biggest business these days is as an offshore outpost for the **US military**; on any given day, the numbers of military personnel and tourists on the island are roughly the same. These two forces have been the main influences in the development of modern Honolulu. While the city's historic core remains recognizable, great transformations have taken place on its fringes. **Pearl Harbor**, to the west, is completely taken over by the US Navy, while Waikīkī has been repeatedly reshaped and rebuilt as the focus of the thriving tourist industry.

Oahu overview

Very roughly speaking, Oahu is shaped like a butterfly, with its wings formed by the volcanoes of the **Waiʻanae Range** in the west and the wetter, mostly higher **Koʻolau Range** in the east. In between lies the narrow, flat Leilehua Plateau, with the triple lagoon of **Pearl Harbor** at its southern end. The symmetrical outline is only spoiled by the more recent eruptions that elongated its southeast coastline, producing craters such as Punchbowl, Diamond Head, and Koko Head.

With all its suburbs, **Honolulu** stretches along a substantial proportion of the southern coast, squeezed between the mountains and the sea. It's the golden beaches of **Waikīkī** that draw in the tourists, but the city also boasts world-class museums, a historic downtown area, and some surprisingly rural hiking trails.

Just across the Koʻolaus, the green cliffs of the **east** or **windward coast** are magnificent, lined with relatively safe and secluded beaches and indented with time-forgotten valleys. Towns such as **Kailua**, **Kāneʻohe**, and **Lāʻie** may be far from exciting, but you're unlikely to tire of the sheer beauty of the shoreline drive – so long as you time your forays to miss the peak-hour traffic jams.

Oahu favorites: hikes		
Diamond Head, p.69	Kahana Valley, p.110	Mānoa Falls, p.83
Hauʻula, p.112	Makiki Valley, p.80	Maunawili Falls, p.105

Oahu favorites: beaches

Swimming beaches

Kailua Beach Park, p.107   Waikīkī Beach, p.63
Mālaekahana Bay, p.112   Waimānolo Beach, p.104
Sandy Beach, p.103

Snorkel spots

Hanauma Bay, p.101   Shark's Cove, p.119
Sans Souci Beach, p.67

Surf sites

'Ehukai Beach Park, p.120   Sunset Beach, p.120
Mākaha Beach, p.123   Waimea Bay Beach Park, p.118
Pūpūkea Beach Park, p.119

Mere mortals can only marvel at the winter waves that make the **North Shore** the world's premier surfing destination; for anyone other than experts, entering the water at that time is almost suicidal. However, **Waimea**, **Sunset**, and **'Ehukai** beaches are compelling spectacles, little **Hale'iwa** makes a refreshing contrast to Waikīkī, and in summer you may manage to find a safe spot somewhere along the North Shore for a swim.

Although the **west** or **leeward coast** of Oahu also holds some fine beaches – including the prime surf spot of Mākaha – it remains very much off the beaten track. There's just one route in and out of this side of the island, and the locals are happy to keep it that way.

Getting around Oahu

Oahu is blessed with an exemplary network of public **buses**, officially named **TheBus** (☎ 808/848-5555, ⓦ www.thebus.org), which radiates out from downtown Honolulu and the Ala Moana Center to cover the whole island. All journeys cost $2.25 (ages 6–17 $1), with free transfers to any connecting route. One of the best sightseeing routes is TheBus #52 or #55, which circles the whole of the Ko'olau Range, including the North Shore and the windward coast, still for just $2.25. The complete circuit takes four hours, not that there's any point doing it without getting off a few times along the way. The one disadvantage with TheBus is that you can't carry large bags or bulky items (including surfboards), which rules out using it to get to or from the airport.

For details of transportation between Waikīkī and the airport, see p.63. Services in Honolulu and Waikīkī are summarized on p.55, together with companies offering **island tours**. If you want to explore Oahu at your own pace, you'd do best to rent a **car**. However, a car is a liability in Waikīkī itself – traffic is heavy, and parking is so expensive it can even work out cheaper to rent a car anew each morning.

Where to stay

The overwhelming majority of Oahu visitors stay in **Waikīkī**, a couple of miles east of central Honolulu – see p.56 for detailed accommodation listings. The city itself holds a handful of hotels, but there are very few alternatives in the rest of the island; the only hotels are the *Turtle Bay Resort* and *Ihilani* resorts, at the far northeast and southwest corners respectively, while the bargain *Backpackers Vacation Inn*, on the North Shore, caters to the surf crowd. Other than a few tiny B&Bs at Kailua and Kāne'ohe on the windward coast, that's about it.

According to official figures, the average room in Waikīkī costs around $150. There's a heavy premium for oceanfront accommodation, however, and away from the beach – bearing in mind that nowhere in Waikīkī is more than a few minutes' walk from the sea – you can normally find something for half that. You're unlikely to find yourself stranded if you arrive without a reservation, and several hostels cater for budget travelers.

You can **camp** in county parks on Oahu for free, and in state parks for $18 per campsite per night, with a permit from the relevant office. However, few sites are worth recommending, and none that's especially convenient to Honolulu. Furthermore, all county and state campgrounds are closed on both Wednesday and Thursday nights, and you can't stay at any one site for more than five days in one month. The best **state parks** are Keaīwa Heiau (see p.115), and Mālaekahana Bay (p.112); appealing **county parks** include Bellows Field Beach (p.104), Kaiaka Bay Beach Park, a mile out of Haleʻiwa (p.117), and Keaʻau Beach Park on the Leeward Shore (p.123). State parks can be **booked** no more than thirty days in advance, either via Ⓦwww.hawaiistateparks.org, or by visiting Room 310, 1151 Punchbowl St, Honolulu (Mon–Fri 8.30am–3.30pm; Ⓣ808/587-0300). County permits can be obtained, in person only, from 650 S King St (Mon–Fri 7.45am–4pm; Ⓣ808/523-4525, Ⓦwww.honolulu.gov/parks) or from subsidiary "City Halls" in the Ala Moana Center (Mon–Fri 9am–4pm, Sat 8am–4pm; Ⓣ808/973-2600) and elsewhere.

When to go

Of all major US cities, Honolulu is said to have both the *lowest* average annual maximum temperature and the *highest* minimum, at 85°F and 60°F respectively. Neither fluctuates more than a few degrees between summer and winter. Waikīkī remains a balmy tropical year-round resort, and the only seasonal variation likely to make much difference to travelers is the state of the **surf** on the North Shore. For surfers, the time to come is from October to April, when mighty winter waves scour the sand off many beaches and curl in at heights of twenty feet or more. In summer, the surf bums head home, and some North Shore beaches are even safe for family swimming.

As for **room rates**, peak season in Waikīkī runs from December to March, and many mid-range hotels lower their prices by twenty or thirty dollars during the rest of the year. Waikīkī is pretty crowded all year, though, and coming in summer will not yield significant savings.

Honolulu and Waikīkī

Stretching for around a dozen miles along the southern coast of Oahu, and home to 400,000 people, **HONOLULU** is by far Hawaii's largest city. As the site of the islands' major **airport** and of the legendary beaches and skyscrapers of **WAIKĪKĪ**, it also provides most visitors with their first taste of Hawaii. Many, unfortunately, leave without ever realizing quite how out of keeping it is with the rest of the state.

Honolulu only came into being after the arrival of the foreigners; from the early days of sandalwood and whaling, through the rise of King Sugar and the development of Pearl Harbor, to its modern incarnation as a tourist playground, the fortunes of the city have depended on the ever-increasing integration of Hawaii into the global economy. Benefits of this process include an exhilarating energy and dynamism, and the cosmopolitan air that comes from being such an international meeting place. The major drawback has been the rampant over development of Waikīkī.

The **setting** is beautiful, right on the Pacific Ocean and backed by the dramatic *pali* (cliffs) of the Ko'olau mountains. **Downtown Honolulu**, centered around administrative buildings that date from the final days of the Hawaiian monarchy, nestles at the foot of the extinct **Punchbowl** volcano, now a military cemetery. It's a manageable size, and a lot quieter than its glamorous image might suggest. Immediately west is livelier **Chinatown**, while the **airport** lies four or five miles further west again, just before the sheltered inlet of **Pearl Harbor**.

The distinct district of **Waikīkī**, three miles east of downtown, is conspicuous not only for its towering hotels but also for the furrowed brow of another extinct volcano, **Diamond Head**, just to the east. Although Waikīkī is a small suburb, and one that many Honolulu residents avoid, for package tourists it's the tail that wags the dog. They spend their days on Waikīkī's beaches, and their nights in its hotels, restaurants, and bars; apart from the odd expedition to the nearby **Ala Moana** shopping mall, the rest of Honolulu might just as well not exist.

The sun-and-fun appeal of Waikīkī may wear off after a few days, but it still makes an excellent base for a longer stay on Oahu. Downtown Honolulu is easily accessible, and has top-quality museums like the **Bishop Museum** and the **Academy of Arts**, as well as some superb rainforest hikes, especially in the **Makiki** and **Mānoa** valleys. You can also get a bus to just about anywhere on the island, while the North Shore beaches are less than two hours' drive away.

Arrival and information

For details of **flights** to and from Honolulu's **International Airport**, see pp.19–20 (long-distance), and p.22 (inter-island). Roughly five miles west of downtown, its runways extend out to sea on a coral reef. The main **Overseas Terminal** is flanked by smaller **Inter-Island** and **Commuter** terminals, connected by free Wikiwiki shuttles. All are located on a loop road, constantly circled by hotel and rental-car pick-up vans, taxis, and minibuses.

Virtually every arriving tourist heads straight to Waikīkī; if you don't have a **hotel or hostel reservation** use the courtesy phones in the baggage claim area. Competing **shuttle buses**, such as Airport Waikīkī Express (☎808/954-8652 or 1-866/898-2519, ⓦwww.robertshawaii.com; $9 one-way, $15 round-trip), and Island Express (☎808/944-1879, ⓦwww.islandexpresstransport.com; $11 one-way), pick up outside the terminals and will carry passengers to any Waikīkī hotel. A **taxi** from the airport to Waikīkī costs $25–30, depending on traffic.

In addition, **TheBus** #19 and #20 run to Waikīkī from the airport, leaving from outside the Departures lounge of the Overseas Terminal. The ride costs $2.25 one-way, but you have to be traveling light: TheBus won't carry large bags, cases, or backpacks.

Car rental outlets abound. The nine-mile – not at all scenic – **drive** from the airport to Waikīkī takes anything from 25 to 75 minutes. The quickest route is to follow H-1 as far as possible, running inland of downtown Honolulu, and then watch out for the Waikīkī exit.

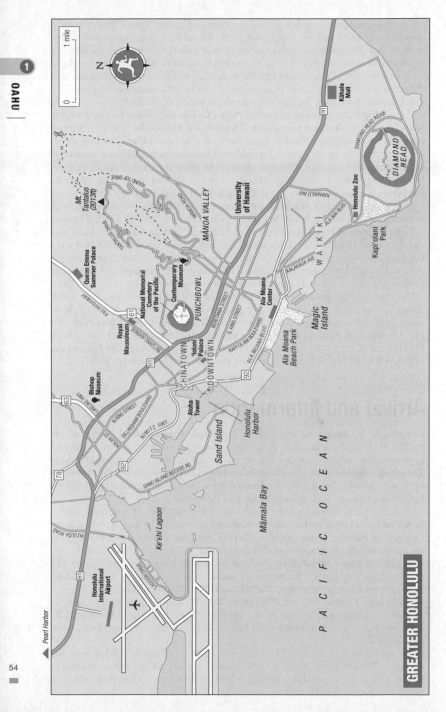

GREATER HONOLULU

Information

There are no visitor **information** centers worth visiting in Waikīkī or Honolulu. The best place to pick up printed material is the Arrivals hall at the airport, but almost every hotel runs its own information desk with further racks of brochures, and kiosks around Kalākaua Avenue offer greatly discounted rates for island tours, helicopter rides, dinner cruises, surfing lessons, and so on. Useful **websites** for advance information are run by the Hawaii Visitors Bureau (☎808/923-1811 or 1-800/464-2924, ⓦwww.gohawaii.com) and the island of Oahu (ⓦwww.visit-oahu.com).

The main **post offices** are at 330 Saratoga Rd in Waikīkī (Mon, Tues, Thurs & Fri 8am–4.30pm, Wed 8am–6pm, Sat 9am–noon); at the Ala Moana Center (Mon–Fri 8.30am–5pm, Sat 8.30am–4.15pm); 335 Merchant St downtown (Mon, Tues, Thurs & Fri 8am–4.30pm, Wed 8am–6pm); and at the airport.

City transport

While renting a car enables you to explore Oahu in much greater depth, **driving** in Honolulu is seldom pleasant. The **traffic** on major roads, such as H-1 along the city's northern flanks, and the Pali and Likelike highways across the mountains, can be horrendous, and **parking** is always a problem. You may find it easier to travel by **bus**, thanks to the exemplary TheBus network.

Buses

A network of over sixty **bus** routes, officially named TheBus and centered on downtown Honolulu and the Ala Moana Center, covers the whole of Oahu (☎808/848-5555, ⓦwww.thebus.org). All journeys cost $2.25 (ages 6–17 $1), with free transfers on to any connecting route if you ask as you board. The **4-Day Pass**, available from ABC stores in Waikīkī, offers four days' unlimited travel on TheBus for $25; $50 **monthly passes** are also available. The most **popular routes** with Waikīkī-based tourists are #2 to downtown, #8 to Ala Moana, #19 and #20 to the airport, #20 and #42 to Pearl Harbor, #22 to Hanauma Bay, #57 to Kailua and Kāne'ohe,

---

Bus and walking tours

Countless operators in Waikīkī offer **bus tours** of Honolulu and Oahu, such as Polynesian Adventure Tours (☎808/833-3000 or 1-800/622-3011, ⓦwww.polyad.com), E Noa Tours (☎808/591-2561 or 1-800/824-8804, ⓦwww.enoa.com), and Roberts (☎808/954-8652 or 1-866/898-2519, ⓦwww.robertshawaii.com). Typical choices range from $24 for an excursion to Pearl Harbor, or $30 for a half-day tour of Pearl Harbor and downtown Honolulu, to $60–100 for a full-day island tour.

Organized **walking tours**, on the other hand, are less widely available – perhaps because both Waikīkī and downtown Honolulu are so easy to explore on your own. However, the Clean Air Team organizes various walks, including tours of Honolulu and Waikīkī, and a weekly jaunt up Diamond Head (prices vary, some walks free; ☎808/948-3299). In addition, Ohana Tours offer a fascinating two-hour weekend jaunt around downtown Honolulu, starting at the King Kamehameha statue (Sat & Sun 9am, $15; ☎808/204-7331, ⓦwww.ohanatours.org), while Chinatown tours are detailed on p.75.

For more energetic **hiking** in different areas all over the island, the Hawaii chapter of the Sierra Club sponsors treks and similar activities on weekends (☎808/538-6616, ⓦwww.sierraclubhawaii.com/outings), as does the Hawaii Nature Center, less frequently (☎808/955-0100, ⓦwww.hawaiinaturecenter.org).

and the bargain "**Circle Island**" buses that take four hours to loop all the way around Oahu, still for just $2.25: #52 (clockwise) and #55 (counterclockwise).

For tourists, the main alternative to TheBus is the ridiculously expensive **Waikīkī Trolley** (Ⓦ www.waikikitrolley.com; one-day pass $25, ages 4–11 $13; four-day pass $43/$17), which runs open-sided trolleys on three separate lines. The **Red Line** tours from Waikīkī via downtown Honolulu to Chinatown, and back along the waterfront via Ala Moana (8.30am–5.20pm, every 35min); the **Green Line** connects Waikīkī with Diamond Head, by way of the zoo and aquarium (8.30am–4.30pm, every 35–70min); and the **Pink Line** simply shuttles between Waikīkī and the Ala Moana Center (9.30am–9pm, every 10min; $2 one-way fare this route only).

Car and bike rental

All the major **car rental** chains have outlets at the airport, and many have offices in Waikīkī as well; you may find better room-and-car deals through your hotel. Bear in mind that Waikīkī hotels charge anything from $10 to $25 per night for **parking**, although there are meters on the backstreets of Waikīkī, near the Ala Wai Canal. Downtown, the largest metered parking lot is on the edge of Chinatown at Smith and Beretania streets. Several companies in and near Waikīkī rent out **bicycles**, **mopeds** and **motorbikes**, including Big Kahuna Rentals, 407 Seaside Ave (Ⓣ 808/924-2736 or 1-888/451-5544, Ⓦ www.bigkahunarentals.com), and the good-value Mopeds Direct, 750 Kapahulu Ave (Ⓣ 808/732-3366, Ⓦ www.mopedsdirect.net). Typical rates for bikes are $15 per day (8am–6pm) or $20 for 24 hours; mopeds cost around $40 per day, or from $175 per week; and a Harley-Davidson motorbike will set you back perhaps $155 for a day, $750 for a week.

Given the steep mountains and busy highways that separate Honolulu from the rest of the island, a bicycle is only really practicable for getting between downtown Honolulu and Waikīkī.

Taxis

Honolulu **taxi** firms include Charley's (Ⓣ 808/531-1333, Ⓦ www.charleystaxi .com), and TheCab (Ⓣ 808/422-2222, Ⓦ www.thecabhawaii.com). Riding from Waikīkī to downtown Honolulu typically costs $12–16.

Accommodation

Almost all the **accommodation** in the city of Honolulu is confined to **Waikīkī**, which holds an extraordinary concentration of hotels in all price ranges. Room rates at the upper end in particular have dropped significantly since the economic downturn, but unless you're happy to spend at least $200 per night for world-class luxury, most Waikīkī rooms are far from exciting. The many anonymous tower blocks charge at least $120 for a standard en-suite double room, with perhaps another $50 for an ocean view, and $50 more again if they're right on the seafront. Few have any personal touch, and there are no B&Bs. Assuming that you're committed to staying in Waikīkī in the first place, decide what you plan to do, and how much you want to spend. The very cheapest option is a dorm bed in a hostel, but as long as you don't mind missing out on a sea view, or having to walk a few minutes to the beach, you can find adequate rooms for around $75 a night. To get your first-choice hotel in peak season, always **reserve** well in advance. However, it's usually possible to find something at short notice.

Outrigger and Ohana hotels

The family-oriented **Outrigger** chain currently runs nine hotels in Waikīkī, divided into two categories: five of the most luxurious carry the Outrigger name, while the rest are **Ohana** ("family" in Hawaiian) hotels.

Although Outrigger has moved upmarket in recent years, most obviously by spearheading the redevelopment of the Beach Walk area, all their properties remain competitively priced. They're particularly price-sensitive in times of recession, so it's often possible to find bargain rates online, at www.outrigger.com and www.ohana hotels.com. At all the Ohana properties, you can expect to pay well under $150 per night for a clean, well-maintained room with standard but smart hotel furnishings.

For phone **reservations**, contact Outrigger at ☏1-866/956-4262 and Ohana at ☏1-866/968-8744; if you're calling from outside the US and Canada, both are on ☏303/369-7777.

Outrigger hotels

Luana Waikīkī, 2045 Kalākaua Ave (see p.61) ➍–➐
Reef On The Beach, 2169 Kālia Rd ➎–➑
Regency on Beach Walk, 255 Beach Walk ➐–➒
Waikīkī On The Beach, 2335 Kalākaua Ave (see p.61) ➎–➒
Waikīkī Shore, 2161 Kālia Rd ➐–➒

Ohana hotels

Waikīkī Beachcomber, 2300 Kalākaua Ave ➍
Waikīkī East, 150 Ka'iulani Ave (see p.61) ➍
Waikīkī Malia, 2211 Kūhiō Ave ➌
Waikīkī West, 2330 Kūhiō Ave ➌

Except for the top-of-the-line properties, there's little point choosing a hotel with a **swimming pool** – most are squeezed onto rooftop terraces, and overlooked by thousands of rooms in the surrounding high-rises. There are no **campgrounds** in Waikīkī, and camping at Honolulu's only site, Sand Island State Park, is not recommended.

Although Waikīkī is part of Honolulu, hotels listed below as being in "Honolulu" are outside Waikīkī.

Waikīkī hostels

Hosteling International Waikīkī 2417 Prince Edward St ☏808/926-8313, ⓦwww.hostelsaloha .com. Informal, AYH-affiliated hostel, in a turquoise four-story building a couple of minutes from the heart of Waikīkī Beach. Beds in four-person, single-sex dorms are $25 ($28 for non-members), while the five double studio rooms cost $58 or $64; shared kitchen and patio. Office open 7am–3am; no curfew; seven-day max stay. Reservations recommended. ➊–➋

Polynesian Hostel Beach Club 2584 Lemon Rd ☏808/922-1340, ⓦwww.polynesian beachclub.com. Clean, safe, and efficient private hostel, a block from the sea at the Diamond Head end of Waikīkī. All the air-conditioned dorms have en-suite bathrooms; some hold four bunk beds

($25 per person), some six ($23 per person). "Semi-private" rooms, sharing a bathroom, cost $40 single, $50 double, and a studio is $70. Van tours offered. Free wi-fi and use of snorkel gear and boogie-boards, plus cheap surfboard, bike and moped rentals. ➊–➌

Waikīkī Beachside Hotel & Hostel 2556 Lemon Rd ☏808/923-9566, ⓦwww.waikikibeachside hostel.com. By far the liveliest of the Lemon Rd hostels, near the park in eastern Waikīkī, although not literally "beachside." Beds in eight-person dorms cost $20, in four-person dorms $35; they also have "semi-private" double rooms, sharing bathroom and kitchen, for $75. It looks smarter from the outside than it does once you go in, but amenities include free continental breakfast and wi-fi, plus snorkel and surf equipment rental, and they have their own café, too. ➊–➌

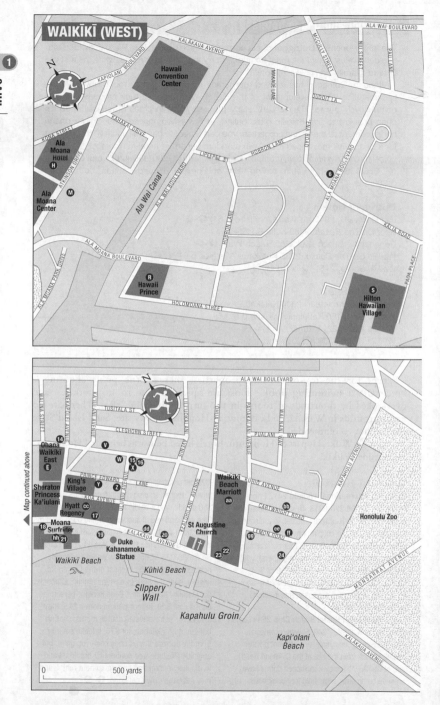

WAIKĪKĪ (WEST)

N

ALA WAI BOULEVARD

KALĀKAUA AVENUE

KAPIOLANI BOULEVARD

Hawaii
Convention
Center

McCULLY STREET

HILL STREET

PAU LANE

MĀKALEI LANE

KAHAKAI DRIVE

ELM ROAD

DUDOIT LA.

KONA STREET

Ala
Moana
Hotel
H

ATKINSON DRIVE

LIPEEPEE ST

HOBRON LANE

ALA MOANA BOULEVARD

6

KĀLIA ROAD

Ala
Moana
Center
M

Ala Wai Canal

ALA WAI BOULEVARD

HOBRON LANE

ALA MOANA BOULEVARD

R
Hawaii
Prince

HOLOMOANA STREET

ALA MOANA PARK DRIVE

PAOA PLACE

S
Hilton
Hawaiian
Village

Map continued above ◀

N

ALA WAI BOULEVARD

TUSITALA ST.

WALINA STREET

KANEKAPOLEI AVENUE

KAIULANI AVENUE

CLEGHORN STREET

LILIUOKALANI AVENUE

ŌHUA AVENUE

PAOKALANI AVENUE

WAI NANI WAY

PUALANI WAY

KAPAHULU AVENUE

14
Ohana
Waikīkī
East
E

V

W **15 16**
X

PRINCE EDWARD

KŪHIŌ AVENUE

Waikīkī
Beach
Marriott
aa

King's
Village
Y **Z**

LANE

KOA AVENUE

KAIULANI AVENUE

KEALOHILANI AVENUE

CARTWRIGHT ROAD

bb

Honolulu Zoo

Sheraton
Princess
Ka'iulani

Hyatt
Regency **cc**
17

dd

St Augustine
Church
✝

ee **ff**

Moana
Surfrider
18
hh 21

19

KALĀKAUA AVENUE

20

LEMON ROAD

gg

Duke
Kahanamoku
Statue

23 **22**

24

Waikīkī Beach

Kūhiō Beach

MONSARRAT AVENUE

Slippery
Wall

Kapahulu Groin

Kapi'olani
Beach

KALĀKAUA AVENUE

0   500 yards

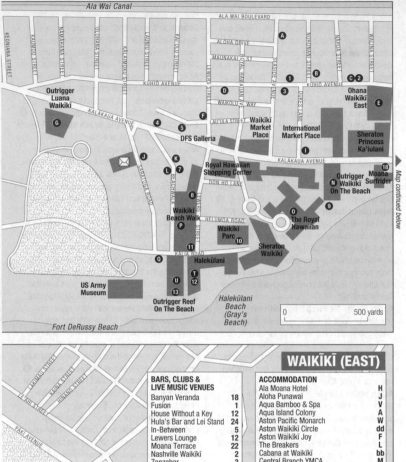

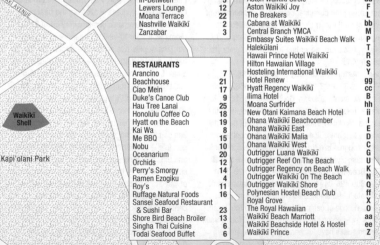

WAIKĪKĪ (EAST)

BARS, CLUBS & LIVE MUSIC VENUES

Banyan Veranda	18
Fusion	1
House Without a Key	12
Hula's Bar and Lei Stand	24
In-Between	5
Lewers Lounge	12
Moana Terrace	22
Nashville Waikīkī	2
Zanzabar	3

RESTAURANTS

Arancino	7
Beachhouse	21
Ciao Mein	17
Duke's Canoe Club	9
Hau Tree Lanai	25
Honolulu Coffee Co	18
Hyatt on the Beach	19
Kai Wa	8
Me BBQ	15
Nobu	10
Oceanarium	20
Orchids	12
Perry's Smorgy	14
Ramen Ezogiku	4
Roy's	11
Ruffage Natural Foods	16
Sansei Seafood Restaurant & Sushi Bar	23
Shore Bird Beach Broiler	13
Singha Thai Cuisine	6
Todai Seafood Buffet	6

ACCOMMODATION

Ala Moana Hotel	H
Aloha Punawai	J
Aqua Bamboo & Spa	V
Aqua Island Colony	A
Aston Pacific Monarch	W
Aston Waikīkī Circle	dd
Aston Waikīkī Joy	F
The Breakers	L
Cabana at Waikīkī	bb
Central Branch YMCA	M
Embassy Suites Waikīkī Beach Walk	P
Halekūlani	T
Hawaii Prince Hotel Waikīkī	R
Hilton Hawaiian Village	S
Hosteling International Waikīkī	Y
Hotel Renew	gg
Hyatt Regency Waikīkī	cc
Ilima Hotel	B
Moana Surfrider	hh
New Otani Kaimana Beach Hotel	ii
Ohana Waikīkī Beachcomber	I
Ohana Waikīkī East	E
Ohana Waikīkī Malia	D
Ohana Waikīkī West	C
Outrigger Luana Waikīkī	G
Outrigger Reef On The Beach	U
Outrigger Regency on Beach Walk	K
Outrigger Waikīkī On The Beach	N
Outrigger Waikīkī Shore	Q
Polynesian Hostel Beach Club	ff
Royal Grove	X
The Royal Hawaiian	O
Waikīkī Beach Marriott	aa
Waikīkī Beachside Hotel & Hostel	ee
Waikīkī Prince	Z

59

Waikīkī hotels

Aloha Punawai 305 Saratoga Rd ☎808/923-5211 or 1-866/713-9694, ⓦwww.alternative-hawaii.com /alohapunawai. Miniature hotel, opposite the post office, whose nineteen well-priced studios and apartments – all air-conditioned – are furnished in a bare-bones Japanese style. All units have kitchens, bathrooms, and balconies, but no phones, only the slightly pricier "deluxe" options sleep three guests. ❹

Aqua Bamboo & Spa 2425 Kūhiō Ave ☎808/922-7777 or 1-866/971-2782, ⓦwww.aquaresorts.com. Very central and stylish "boutique hotel," two blocks from the beach, with fewer than a hundred nicely upgraded rooms spread across its twelve stories. All have appealing furnishings and live plants, with at least one *lānai*, plus wide-screen TV and free wi-fi and internet. ❹

Aqua Island Colony 445 Seaside Ave ☎808/923-2345 or 1-866/971-2782, ⓦwww.aquaresorts.com. Anonymous-looking 44-story high-rise at the quieter inland side of Waikīkī, still just five minutes' walk from the beach. All its conventional hotel rooms and more luxurious suites are furnished to a reasonable standard and have balconies, though the bathrooms can be small. ❸

Aston Pacific Monarch 2427 Kūhiō Ave ☎808/923-9805 or 1-877/997-6667, ⓦwww .pacific-monarch.com. Tall condo building in the heart of Waikīkī holding small, plain but good-value studios with kitchenettes, plus larger four-person suites with full kitchens and *lānais*, and a rooftop swimming pool. ❹

Aston Waikīkī Circle 2464 Kalākaua Ave ☎808/923-1571 or 1-877/997-6667, ⓦwww .astonhotels.com. Bright and cheery turquoise-and-white octagonal tower, dwarfed by its surroundings but among the cheapest options on the oceanfront. Each of its thirteen circular floors is divided into eight identical rooms with two double beds and *lānai*; prices vary according to how much sea you can see. ❹

Aston Waikīkī Joy 320 Lewers St ☎808/923-2300 or 1-877/997-6667, ⓦwww.astonhotels.com. Good-value little hotel, with quirky though dated pastel-trimmed decor, from the airy garden lobby through to the faded but perfectly adequate rooms, all of which have whirlpool baths and incongruous retro hi-fi systems. Free continental breakfast, plus an on-site café and karaoke bar. ❹

The Breakers 250 Beach Walk ☎808/923-3181 or 1-800/426-0494, ⓦwww.breakers-hawaii.com. Intimate, old-fashioned Polynesian hotel on the western edge of central Waikīkī, close to the beach. All its two-person studio apartments and four-person garden suites have kitchenettes, phones, and a/c, there's a bar and grill beside the flower-surrounded pool, and there's even a Japanese teahouse. Limited free parking. ❹

Cabana at Waikīkī 2551 Cartwright Rd ☎808/926-5555 or 1-877/902-2121, ⓦwww .cabana-waikiki.com. Boutique hotel, gay-friendly but no longer marketed especially towards gay men. All its nineteen nice but not exquisite mini-suites hold kitchenettes and extra daybeds, and guests get free breakfasts, plus free cocktails some nights. There's a small, clothes-optional outdoor hot tub. ❹

Embassy Suites Waikīkī Beach Walk 201 Beach Walk ☎808/921-2345 or 1-800/362-2779, ⓦwww.embassysuiteswaikiki.com. Showpiece all-suite hotel in the modern Beach Walk development, offering huge suites, albeit not quite with ocean views, and a very good pool area, with lots of sunbathing space. Welcoming staff and some nice Polynesian touches. ❻

Halekūlani 2199 Kālia Rd ☎808/923-2311 or 1-800/367-2343, ⓦwww.halekulani.com. Stunning oceanfront hotel, arranged around an exquisite courtyard and pool, in a prime location for views along the beach to Diamond Head, but aloof from the resort bustle. Probably the most luxurious option in Waikīkī – even if you're not staying in the opulent Vera Wang honeymoon suite, you'll have a huge room with *lānai*, a deep bath and walk-in shower, and DVD player. It's also home to a lavish spa and the highly rated *Orchids* (see p.92) and *La Mer* restaurants, while the open-air *House Without a Key* bar (see p.97) is perfect for sunset cocktails. ❾

Hawaii Prince Hotel Waikīkī 100 Holomoana St ☎808/956-1111 or 1-888/977-4623, ⓦwww .princeresortshawaii.com. Extremely classy Japanese-styled hotel, overlooking the yacht harbor and just a short walk from the Ala Moana Center, so ten minutes' walk from the beach. Its twin towers have spacious and very comfortable rooms with floor-to-ceiling ocean views (though not *lānais*), plus two good restaurants, and it even has its own golf course, albeit half an hour's drive away. Look for great deals online, such as third night free or two rooms for the price of one. ❺–❾

Hilton Hawaiian Village 2005 Kālia Rd ☎808/949-4321 or 1-800/445-8667, ⓦwww .hawaiianvillage.hilton.com. With 3400 rooms and counting – choose those in the Ali'i Tower if possible – the *Hilton* is the largest hotel in Hawaii and the largest non-casino hotel in the US (the second-largest in the world). A scaled-down version of Waikīkī, it holds a hundred of the same stores and restaurants you'd find out on the streets. As the center of Waikīkī is a 15min walk away, and there's a good pool, a great stretch of beach (see p.64), and even a lagoon populated by penguins and flamingos, there's little incentive to leave the hotel

precincts. Everything from parking and internet to in-room coffee incurs extra charges. ❼

Hotel Renew 129 Paoakalani Ave ☎ 808/687-7700 or 1-888/485-7639, ⓦ www.hotelrenew.com. Very tasteful "designer boutique" hotel, with plenty of Japanese furnishings and general trimmings, where rates include free internet and, often, breakfast. ❺

Hyatt Regency Waikīkī Resort and Spa 2424 Kalākaua Ave ☎ 808/923-1234 or 1-800/492-8804, ⓦ www.waikiki.hyatt.com. Very lavish, very central property, across the road from the heart of Waikīkī Beach, and consisting of two enormous towers engulfing a central atrium equipped with cascading waterfalls and tropical vegetation. The 1229 "over-sized" rooms are cunningly arrayed to maximize ocean views, and there's an upmarket shopping mall, an open-air pool with hot tubs and rocking chairs to watch the sunset, and spa. The *Ciao Mein* restaurant is reviewed on p.92. ❽

Ilima Hotel 445 Nohonani St ☎ 808/923-1877 or 1-800/801-9366, ⓦ www.ilima.com. Good-value, small and very pink hotel, near the canal on the *mauka* side of central Waikīkī and catering to a mainly local clientele. The spacious condo units each offer two double beds, a kitchen, additional sofa beds, and free local calls and internet, and there's limited free parking. ❺

Moana Surfrider 2365 Kalākaua Ave ☎ 808/922-3111 or 1-866/716-8109, ⓦ www.moana-surfrider .com. Waikīkī's oldest hotel, built at the end of the nineteenth century (see p.68). Despite extensive restoration, the "Colonial" architectural style of the original building – now the focus of the Banyan wing – remains intact, though these days it's flanked by two huge towers. The main lobby, with its tongue-and-groove walls, memorabilia cabinets, soothing sea breezes and old-time atmosphere, is a delight – that said, prepare yourself to pick through countless Japanese wedding parties – and the beachfront setting, with its broad veranda and colossal banyan tree, is unsurpassed. New managers Westin Resorts have greatly upgraded the actual guest rooms, and added an oceanfront spa. ❼

🏃 **New Otani Kaimana Beach Hotel** 2863 Kalākaua Ave ☎ 808/923-1555 or 1-800/356-8264, ⓦ www.kaimana.com. Intimate Japanese-toned hotel, stylish and airy, on quiet and secluded Sans Souci Beach (see p.67). Half a mile east of the bustle of central Waikīkī, it boasts the lovely backdrop of Diamond Head. Its *Hau Tree Lanai* restaurant is reviewed on p.92. Valet parking only. ❺

Ohana Waikīkī East 150 Ka'iulani Ave ☎ 808/922-5353 or 1-866/968-8744, ⓦ www .ohanahotels.com. While the rooms – and the bathrooms – are on the small side, the staff and services are as good as you'd expect of the Ohana

chain, and the convenient location, a block back from the beach, close to several good restaurants, makes it a very dependable option, especially for budget-conscious families. ❹

🏃 **Outrigger Luana Waikīkī** 2045 Kalākaua Ave ☎ 808/955-6000 or 1-866/956-4262, ⓦ www.outrigger.com. Smart condo block, back from the beach at the western end of Waikīkī, that's one of the jewels in the Outrigger chain. Characterful, individually styled kitchenette studios and hotel rooms, with an upscale Hawaiian flavor. ❹–❼

Outrigger Waikīkī On The Beach 2335 Kalākaua Ave ☎ 808/923-0711 or 1-866/956-4262, ⓦ www .outrigger.com. Flagship Outrigger hotel, in prime position close to the center of Waikīkī Beach, with good restaurants and entertainment. The rooms closest to the ocean offer great views and facilities, including huge whirlpool baths; those further back are less special, but rates can be very reasonable for such a choice location. ❺–❾

Royal Grove 151 Uluniu Ave ☎ 808/923-7691, ⓦ www.royalgrovehotel.com. Small-scale, family-run hotel, with a homey feel, in central Waikīkī. While it's undeniably run down, the prices are unbeatable. Facilities improve the more you're prepared to pay; avoid the most basic rooms in the Mauka wing, which lack a/c, and hold two single beds. There's also a courtyard pool, a piano for guest use, and retro bric-a-brac scattered around the shared spaces. Weekly rates apply April–Nov only. ❷

🏃 **The Royal Hawaiian** 2259 Kalākaua Ave ☎ 808/923-7311 or 1-866/716-8110, ⓦ www.royal-hawaiian.com. The 1920s "Pink Palace" (see p.68) remains Waikīkī's best-loved landmark. The atmospheric original building, which seeps vintage glamour, still commands a great expanse of beach and looks over a lawn to the sea; pink through and through, it remains a lovely place to hang out, with elegant rooms and peaceful gardens at the back. Sadly, though, it's now flanked by a less atmospheric tower-block holding additional suites. As well as a pool shared with the *Sheraton*, there's a full-service spa; the 'Aha 'Aina *lū'au*, held on the ocean-facing lawn on Monday evenings, is reviewed on p.97. ❽

Waikīkī Beach Marriott Resort & Spa 2552 Kalākaua Ave ☎ 808/922-6611 or 1-888/236-2427, ⓦ www.marriottwaikiki.com. This huge property consists of two giant towers facing the eastern end of Waikīkī Beach; while not historic, it has a stylish, contemporary Hawaiian feel, and offers Waikīkī's best value at the top end of the spectrum. As well as a state-of-the-art spa, it holds several good restaurants, including the wonderful *Sansei* (see p.93), while the *Moana Terrace* hosts superb Hawaiian musicians (see p.97). ❻

Waikīkī Prince 2431 Prince Edward St ☏ 808/922-1544, ⓦ www.waikikiprince.com. Slightly drab but perfectly adequate and very central budget hotel (not to be confused with the upscale *Hawaii Prince*; see p.60). Rooms have a/c, en-suite baths, and basic cooking facilities, but no phones, and maid service is not daily; the "very small" and "small" categories are even cheaper than "economy" units, while "standard" is top of the range. Office 9am–6pm only; seventh night free April–Nov. ❷

Honolulu hostels

Central Branch YMCA 401 Atkinson Drive ☏ 808/941-3344, ⓦ www.ymcahonolulu.org. Set in attractive grounds opposite the Ala Moana Center, just outside Waikīkī, with an on-site swimming pool and a beach nearby. Accommodations include plain rooms with shared bath for men only ($42 single/$62 double), plus small but slightly nicer en-suite doubles available to women too ($52 single/$72 double). All guests must reserve in advance; no walk-ins accepted. ❷

Hosteling International Honolulu 2323-A Seaview Ave ☏ 808/946-0591, ⓦ www.hostels aloha.com. Youth hostel in college residence in Mānoa, a couple of miles north of Waikīkī on TheBus #6 or #18 from the Ala Moana Center. Office 8am–noon and 4pm–midnight; no curfew. Beds in single-sex dorms (two are male, three female) cost $20 for AYH/IYHA members, $23 for non-members, while private doubles cost $50 and $56 respectively, with a three-night max stay for non-members. ❶–❷

Honolulu hotels and B&Bs

Ala Moana Hotel 410 Atkinson Drive ☏ 808/955-4811, 1-800/446-8990 (HI) or 1-800/367-6025 (US & Canada), ⓦ www.alamoanahotel.com.

Thousand-room tower block alongside the Ala Moana Center, five minutes' walk from Waikīkī. Managed by Outrigger, it consists of individually-owned condo units, of varying but generally high standard. Though targeted primarily at business visitors and shopaholics, it offers the lively *Rumours* nightclub and some good restaurants, and there's an excellent beach not far away (ooo p.79). Rooms ❹, suites ❼

Aston at the Executive Center 1088 Bishop St ☏ 808/539-3000 or 1-877/997-6667, ⓦ www .astonhotels.com. All-suite, forty-story downtown skyscraper, enjoying great harbor views. Geared to business travelers, but the prices compare well with similar-standard Waikīkī hotels. ❺

Mānoa Valley Inn 2001 Vancouver Drive ☏ 808/947-6019, ⓦ www.manoavalleyinn .com. One of Honolulu's most relaxing options: a plush, antique-filled B&B inn, near the University of Hawaii in lush Mānoa Valley, with five en-suite rooms, a two-bedroom suite, and a self-contained cottage. Waikīkī feels a lot farther away than the mile it really is. Linger over breakfast on a wicker chair on the back porch. ❸–❺

Ohana Honolulu Airport Hotel 3401 N Nimitz Hwy ☏ 808/836-0661 or 1-866/968-8744, ⓦ www.honoluluairporthotel.com. Three-hundred-room chain hotel, close to the airport by a noisy freeway, and served by free 24-hour shuttles; the rooms are acceptable, but it's not a place you'd spend more than one night. ❹

Pagoda Hotel 1525 Rycroft St ☏ 808/941-6611 or 1-800/367-6060, ⓦ www.pagodahotel.com. Tower block, within easy walking distance of the Ala Moana Center halfway between downtown Honolulu and Waikīkī, that's very much a budget option used largely by visitors from the other islands. Ageing hotel rooms and one- and two-bedroom suites, plus two pools and a "floating restaurant." ❸

Waikīkī

On any one day, half of all the tourists in Hawaii are crammed into the tiny, surreal enclave of **WAIKĪKĪ**, three miles east of downtown Honolulu. Effectively, it's an island in its own right, a two-mile-long, quarter-mile-wide strip sealed off from the rest of the city by the Ala Wai Canal and almost completely surrounded by water. Jostling for position along the shoreline, its skyscrapers hold enough hotel rooms to accommodate more than a hundred thousand guests, restaurants by the hundred, and stores providing anything the visitor could possibly want.

Long before Kamehameha the Great built a thatched hut here at the start of the nineteenth century, Waikīkī – "spouting water" – was a favored residence of Oahu chiefs. They coveted not only its waterfront coconut groves and well-stocked fishponds, but also the then mosquito-free swamps and wetlands that lay immediately behind them. By the end of that century, however, with Hawaii annexed by

the United States, it was considered all but useless. Waikīkī's value lay instead in its being the best beach within easy reach of Honolulu. When the *Moana* hotel went up in 1901, a handful of inns were already dotted among the luxurious homes of missionary and merchant families.

Since the 1920s, when the Ala Wai Canal was dug to divert the mountain streams to flow around the edge of Waikīkī, and the central area was filled in with chunks of coral, Waikīkī has mushroomed beyond belief. Looking beyond the tower blocks, to Diamond Head or the mysterious valleys that recede into the mountains, will remind you that you're on a Pacific island, but there's precious little of the real Hawaii left in Waikīkī.

As long as you're prepared to enter into the spirit of rampant commercialism, you can have a great time in Waikīkī. You could even, just about, survive with little money, buying snacks from the omnipresent ABC convenience stores, but there's little point – there's almost nothing to see, and the only alternative to surfing and sunbathing is to shop until you drop.

Waikīkī Beach

Viewed objectively, **Waikīkī Beach** ranks pretty low on any list of Hawaii's best beaches. Even on Oahu, it's not hard to find a stretch of deserted, palm-fringed, tropical shoreline, whereas at Waikīkī you can hardly see the sand for the sunbathers, and the traffic on Kalākaua Avenue outroars the surf.

Somehow, however, that barely matters. Waikīkī Beach may be crowded, but it's crowded with enthusiastic holiday-makers, wringing every moment of pleasure from being on one of the world's most famous beaches. Simply glance towards the ocean, and you'll be caught up in the ever-changing action. At the edge of the water, family groups splash and thrash while oblivious honeymooners gaze hand-in-hand at the horizon; beyond them, circling surfers await the next wave, now and then parting abruptly to allow outrigger canoes to glide through; further still, pleasure yachts and parasailers race back and forth; and, out in the deep-water channel, cruise liners, merchant ships, aircraft carriers, and oil tankers make their stately way towards the docks of Honolulu and Pearl Harbor.

Meanwhile, the beach itself plays host to a constant parade of characters: undiscovered starlets in impenetrable sunshades sashay around in the latest swimsuits; local beach boys busy themselves making new friends and renting out the occasional surfboard; over-excited children dart between the sedate seniors with their fancy deckchairs and bulging coolers; and determined European backpackers pick their way through the throng on their dogged search for the perfect plot of sand. On the sidewalk behind, jet-lagged new arrivals wonder how they'll ever get through the crush to dabble their toes in the Pacific for the first time.

Waikīkī's natural setting is as beguiling as its melee of activity. To the east, the sharp profile of **Diamond Head** rises up from the ocean, while straight inland the lush green Ko'olau mountains soar between the skyscrapers. In the early evening, especially, as the orange sun sinks far out to sea and the silhouettes of the palm trees grow ever starker, the overall effect is magical.

Few visitors, however, realize that Waikīkī Beach is almost entirely artificial. Ever since the landscaping that created Waikīkī swept its natural beaches away, so much sand has been shipped in – much of it from Pāpōhaku Beach, on Molokai (see p.331) – that the contours of the sea bottom have been permanently altered. As a result, the **surfing** conditions at the birthplace of the modern sport are no longer all that spectacular – which explains why the experts head straight up to Oahu's North Shore.

Although the name Waikīkī Beach applies to the full length of the Waikīkī shoreline, from the Ala Wai Harbor in the west to within a couple of hundred yards of Diamond Head, many distinct sections within this stretch also have their own names.

Central Waikīkī Beach

The **center** of the beach – the segment that everyone tends to call Waikīkī Beach – is the point near Duke Kahanamoku's statue (see p.67) where the buildings on the ocean side of Kalākaua Avenue come to a halt, and the sidewalk turns into a beachfront promenade. Swimmers here enjoy the best conditions of the entire seafront, with softly shelving sands, and waters that are generally calm.

With so many visitors eager to sample Hawaii's signature **watersports**, this is also the prime spot for commercial activity operators. Several concession stands rent out **surfboards**, typically for $10 per hour, and offer **surfing lessons** for beginners at around $40 per hour, with prices ranging upwards if you want a solo lesson. You can also take a $10 ride in a colorful, traditional **outrigger canoe**, paddled by experts – it's a similarly exhilarating experience to surfing, but requires far less effort. Thanks to all that sand, however, **snorkeling** conditions throughout Waikīkī are poor; keen snorkelers should head instead for Hanauma Bay, eight miles east (see p.101).

Royal-Moana Beach

To the **west**, central Waikīkī Beach merges into **Royal–Moana Beach**, fronting the *Royal Hawaiian* and *Moana Surfrider* hotels. The crowds along this narrow, busy strip can make walking here a struggle, but the swimming is, again, excellent. It's also ideal for **novice surfers**: head slightly to the right as you enter the water to reach the easy break known as Canoes' Surf. The waves are slightly stronger further left, at the Queen's Surf break. Conditions for almost everything are generally at their best early in the day, when the water is clearest and the sun not so hot.

Halekūlani Beach

West of the *Royal Hawaiian*, a raised walkway curves in front of the *Sheraton Waikīkī*, where the sea comes right over the sand. After a tiny little "pocket beach," where the swimming is fine but to find any shade you have to crouch beneath some very low branches, a long arrow-straight walkway squeezes between the waves and the opulent *Halekūlani Hotel*. At the far end comes a slightly larger stretch of beach, extending for a hundred yards or so from the *Halekūlani* as far as the *Outrigger Reef* resort. Generally known as either **Halekūlani Beach** or **Gray's Beach**, this was renowned to the ancient Hawaiians as Kawehewehe, where the waters were said to have special healing properties. It, too, is a popular swimming spot, though erosion has scoured away much of the sand on the seabed, so reef shoes are advisable.

Fort DeRussy and Kahanamoku beaches

Beyond Gray's Beach, the sands grow broader as you pass in front of the military base and the *Hale Koa* hotel which, although reserved for military personnel, has a beachfront bar open to all customers. The walking can be a bit slow on the thick sand of **Fort DeRussy Beach** itself, but it's backed by some pleasant lawns and an open pavilion sheltered by interlaced trees. Concessions stands here rent out surf-and boogie-boards, along with huge, garish pedaloes. Few people swim at this point, however, as the ocean floor is sharp and rocky.

The westernmost section of the Waikīkī shorefront, **Kahanamoku Beach**, flanks the *Hilton Hawaiian Village*. Duke Kahanamoku's grandfather was granted most of the twenty-acre plot on which the hotel now stands in 1848. Thanks to its carefully sculpted shelf of sand, the beach where Duke was raised is ideal for family bathing, but it lacks the concentrated glamour or excitement of central Waikīkī.

Watersports and cruises

All Oahu's **water-based activities** listed below are readily accessible to visitors based in Waikīkī. Shop around at hotel **activities desks**, or **"activity centers"** such as Hawaii Tour & Travels (135 Uluniu Ave; ☎808/931-6003, ⓦwww.hawaiitourandtravels.com) or Tom Barefoot (☎1-800/779-6305, ⓦwww.tombarefoot.com) to find cheaper rates than those quoted by the operators.

Dinner and sightseeing cruises

Ali'i Kai Catamaran ☎808/954-8652 or 1-866/898-2519, ⓦwww.robertshawaii.com. This giant catamaran offers kitsch sunset dinner cruises along Waikīkī Beach, leaving from Pier 5, near Honolulu's Aloha Tower, at 5.30pm daily. $63, ages 3–11 $37.

Navatek I ☎808/973-9811 or 1-800/548-6262, ⓦwww.atlantisadventures.com. Huge catamaran, based at Pier 6 in Honolulu, which provides evening dinner cruises (from $80 for adults and $48 for children), complete with bland entertainment, and also a lunch buffet cruise, which includes whale-watching in winter ($62, ages 2–12 $32).

Outrigger Catamaran ☎808/922-2210, ⓦwww.outriggercatamaranhawaii.com. Regular departures from Halekūlani Beach, immediately in front of Waikīkī's *Outrigger Reef* hotel, including 90min sunset and sail-powered trips for $41, and longer snorkel cruises for $49, plus whale-watching in winter.

Star of Honolulu ☎808/983-7827 or 1-800/334-6191, ⓦwww.starofhonolulu.com. Dinner cruises from Pier 8 beside Aloha Tower. The enormous ship has four decks; seven-course French dinners with jazz on the top deck cost $172, with no child reductions. All other passengers get to see the same Polynesian revue, with a steak-and-lobster dinner on decks 2 and 3 costing $128 for adults, $77 for kids, and the bottom deck costing $88 (kids $53) for crab and steak, or $77 ($46) for a buffet. Daytime cruises are cheaper, with 2hr 30min whale-watching trips from $40 in winter.

Diving

Two-tank scuba-diving boat trips on Oahu typically cost $100–120. The best sites near Waikīkī are the wrecks visited by Atlantis Submarines, as described below; otherwise Wai'anae in the west offers good conditions, Hanauma Bay has a good shore dive – contact **Hanauma Bay Dive Tours** (☎808/256-8956 or 1-800/505-8956, ⓦwww.hanaumabay-hawaii.com) – and there are some fine sites on the North Shore that can only be dived in summer. Other operators include **Surf 'n' Sea** in Hale'iwa (☎808/637-9887 or 1-800/899-7873, ⓦwww.surfnsea.com), and **Ocean Concepts** in Wai'anae (☎808/677-7975 or 1-800/808-3483, ⓦwww.oceanconcepts.com).

Submarines

Atlantis Submarines ☎808/973-9811 or 1-800/548-6262, ⓦwww.atlantisadventures.com. In this claustrophobic but thrilling adventure, passengers are ferried from the *Hilton Hawaiian Village* to rendezvous with two separate submarines about a mile off Waikīkī. The 64-seater (adults $104, under-12s, who must be at least 3ft tall, $48) is a bit more comfortable than the 48-seater ($89/$41), but the 45min cruise on either is substantially the same, descending a hundred feet beneath the waves to pass a sunken airplane and an artificial reef before circling a full-size shipwreck, with a certainty of seeing colorful fish and a likelihood of spotting sharks and turtles.

Other watersports

Surfboard rental, **surfing lessons**, and **outrigger canoe** rides in Waikīkī are detailed on p.64; for details of Surf 'n' Sea, the North Shore's major operator, see p.117. The best place on Oahu to rent a **kayak** is Kailua Bay on the windward coast; for details of operators, see p.107. You can **parasail** off Waikīkī, although the boats set off from Kewalo Basin to the west, with X-treme Parasail (☎808/737-3599, ⓦwww.xtremeparasail.com) or Hawaiian Parasail (☎808/737-1280).

Kūhiō Beach

Large segments of the long beach that runs **east** of central Waikīkī did not exist
until well after World War II. Now, however, Kūhiō Beach is among Waikīkī's
busiest areas. The protective walls and breakwaters that jut into the ocean here
shelter two separate lagoons in which swimming is both safe and comfortable.

The easternmost wall, the **Kapahulu Groin**, projects from the end of Kapahulu
Avenue, following the line of the vanished Kuʻekaunahi Stream. Standing well
above the waterline, it makes a good vantage point for photos of the Waikīkī
panorama. On the other hand, the long, seaweed-covered **Slippery Wall**, parallel
to the beach roughly fifty yards out, is washed over by every wave. Daredevil
locals boogie-board just outside the wall, but don't join them; the currents are
fearsomely strong. Neither should you swim east of the Groin; it's easy to blunder
into deep spots created by underwater drifts.

At 6pm each night, a conch horn signals the start of a free **hula show** on the lawns
beside Kūhiō Beach. With island musicians and dancers performing by the light of
flaming torches, it's a perfect way to relax at sunset, at the end of another hard day.

Kapiʻolani Park Beach

East of the Kapahulu Groin, at the end of the built-up section of Waikīkī, comes
a gap in the beach where the sand all but disappears and the waters are not suitable
for bathing. Not far beyond, however, **Kapiʻolani Park Beach** (either side of the
Waikīkī Aquarium; see p.69), is a favorite with local families and fitness freaks, and
also has a strong gay presence. Banyans and coconut palms offer plenty of free shade
and its lawns make a perfect picnic spot. Waikīkī's only substantial unspoiled coral
reef runs a short distance offshore, shielding a pleasant, gentle swimming area. The
most used segment of the beach, nearest Waikīkī, is **Queen's Surf Beach Park**.

When this book went to press, the dilapidated concrete facade of the decaying
War Memorial Natatorium was still standing a short way past the Aquarium,
though the city authorities have pledged to destroy it and replace it with newly
restored beach. A curious combination of World War I memorial and swimming
pool, the Natatorium opened with a hundred-meter swim by Duke Kahanamoku
(see opposite) in 1927, but never really recovered from being used for training by
the US Navy during World War II.

▲ Queen's Surf Beach Park

Sans Souci and Kaluahole beaches

East of the Natatorium, palm-fringed **Sans Souci Beach** commemorates one of Waikīkī's earliest guesthouses, built in 1884 and twice stayed in by Robert Louis Stevenson. In addition to being sheltered enough for young children, the beach also offers decent snorkeling. The *New Otani Kaimana Beach* hotel (see p.61), now occupying the site of the *Sans Souci*, marks the return of buildings to the shoreline and is as far as most visitors would think to stroll along Waikīkī Beach. However, beyond it lies the **Outrigger Canoe Club Beach**, the preserve of surfers and snorkelers.

As Kalākaua Avenue heads out of Waikīkī, curving away from the shoreline to join Diamond Head Road and skirt the base of the volcano, it passes a little scrap of sandy beach known as **Kaluahole Beach** or **Diamond Head Beach**. Though too small for anyone to want to spend much time on the beach itself, it does offer some decent swimming, and makes a good launching-point for windsurfers.

Diamond Head Beach Park and beyond

Officially **Diamond Head Beach Park**, the coast immediately east of Kaluahole Beach is much too rocky and exposed for ordinary swimmers. It is, however, noteworthy as the site of the 55ft-high **Diamond Head Lighthouse**, built in 1899 and still in use.

A short distance further on, the highway, by now raised well above sea level, rounds the point of Diamond Head; the island of Molokai is visible across the water on clear days. Little scraps of sand cling here and there to the shoreline, but those who pick their way down to the ocean from the three roadside lookouts that constitute **Kuilei Cliffs Beach Park** tend to be keen surfers.

Opposite the intersection where Diamond Head Road loops back inland and Kāhala Avenue continues beside the ocean, **Ka'alāwai Beach**, at the end of short Kulumanu Place, is a narrow patch of white sand favored by snorkelers and surfers.

Inland Waikīkī

Away from the beaches, any walking you do in Waikīkī is more likely to be from necessity than from choice; there's little in the way of conventional sightseeing. The inland roads may once have been picturesque lanes that meandered between the coconut groves and taro fields, but they're now lined by dull concrete malls and hotels. In addition, the daytime **heat** can make walking more than a few blocks uncomfortable.

However, vestiges of the old Waikīkī are still scattered here and there, as pointed out by the helpful surfboard-shaped placards of the waterfront **Waikīkī Historical Trail**. A couple of museums illustrate aspects of Hawaiian history, and the lawns of Kapi'olani Park to the east offer a welcome break. It may come as a surprise that for some people Waikīkī still counts as home; you'll probably see groups of seniors strumming their 'ukuleles or playing chess in the oceanfront pavilions.

West from the Duke Kahanamoku statue

The logical place to start a walking tour is in the middle of Waikīkī Beach, on seafront **Kalākaua Avenue**, where a statue of **Duke Kahanamoku** (1890–1968) is always wreathed in bright flower *leis*. The archetypal "Beach Boy," Duke represented the US in three Olympics, winning swimming golds in 1912 and 1920. His exhibition tours popularized surfing all over the world, and as Sheriff of Honolulu he welcomed celebrity visitors to Hawaii until his death in 1968. Sadly, the statue stands with its back to the ocean, a pose Duke seldom adopted in life; otherwise he'd be gazing at the spot where in 1917 he rode a single 35ft wave a record total of one and a quarter miles.

Slightly west of the statue, alongside a small police station in a railed enclosure, are four large boulders known as the **sacred stones** of either Uluꞌkou (the name of this spot) or Kapaemāhū. These are said to embody the healing and spiritual powers of a Tahitian magician-priest and three of his brother wizards, who set them in place before returning to their home island of Raiatea in the fourteenth century.

A little further west, the wedge of the **Moana Surfrider** forces Kalākaua Avenue away from the ocean. Though not Waikīkī's first hotel, the *Moana* is the oldest left standing, and has been transformed back to a close approximation of its original 1901 appearance. Like all Waikīkī hotels, the *Moana* is happy to allow non-guests in for a peek. At any time, the luxurious settees of its long Beaux Arts lobby make an ideal spot to catch up with the newspapers.

Follow Kalākaua Avenue west from here, and you'll come to the upmarket **Royal Hawaiian Shopping Center**, and across from that the funkier open-air **International Marketplace**, which has a bargain food court (see p.99). Once the site of an ancient *heiau*, and later of the ten-thousand-strong royal Helumoa coconut grove, the beachfront here is today dominated by the **Royal Hawaiian Hotel**, also known as the "Pink Palace." Its Spanish-Moorish architecture was all the rage when it opened in 1927, with a room rate of $14 per night, but its grandeur is now somewhat swamped by a towering new wing. The area west of the *Royal Hawaiian* has been redeveloped in recent years to create a glitzy modern shopping mall known as **Waikīkī Beach Walk**. Also featuring a couple of high-end hotels, and fancy restaurants including a branch of *Roy's* (see p.93), it segues into the upscale end of Kalākaua Avenue to form a futuristic cityscape that's very different to the rest of **Waikīkī**.

Fort DeRussy

On maps, the military base of **Fort DeRussy** looks like a welcome expanse of green at the western edge of the main built-up area of Waikīkī. In fact, it's largely taken up by parking lots and tennis courts, and is not a place to stroll for pleasure. At its oceanfront side, however, the **US Army Museum** (Tues–Sat 9am–5pm; free; Ⓦ www.hiarmymuseumsoc.org) is located in a low concrete structure which, as Battery Randolph, housed massive artillery pieces that were directed by observers stationed atop Diamond Head during World War II. Displays here trace the history of warfare in Hawaii back to Kamehameha the Great, though the bulk of the collection consists of the guns and cannons that have defended Honolulu since the US Army first arrived, four days after annexation in 1898. One photo shows a young, giggling Shirley Temple perched astride a gun barrel during the 1930s, but the mood swiftly changes with a detailed chronicle of the state's pivotal role during the Pacific campaign against Japan.

East from the Duke Kahanamoku statue

The first thing you come to as you head **east** from the Duke Kahanamoku statue is a magnificent, well-groomed Indian banyan tree, supported by two "trunks" that on close inspection turn out to be tangled masses of aerial roots. This area has been attractively landscaped in the last few years, and kitted out with appealing little lagoons and waterfalls as well as shaded pavilions and open-air benches.

Beyond the eastern limit of central Waikīkī, as defined by Kapuhulu Avenue, lies Hawaii's first-ever public park, **Kapiꞌolani Park**. This much-needed breathing space was established in 1877 by King David Kalākaua, and named for his queen. It originally held a number of ponds, until the completion of the Ala Wai Canal in 1928 cut off its supply of fresh water. Now locals flock to its open green lawns, with joggers pounding the footpaths, and t'ai chi practitioners exercising in slow motion beneath the banyans. The adjoining **Waikīkī Shell** hosts large concerts, especially in summer, while the Royal Hawaiian Band performs on the park's **bandstand** on Sundays at 2pm.

Honolulu Zoo

Honolulu Zoo occupies a verdant wedge on the fringes of Kapiʻolani Park (daily 9am–4.30pm; $12, ages 4–12 $3; Ⓦ www.honoluluzoo.org), with its main entrance barely a minute's walk from Waikīkī. Sadly, it's all a bit too run-down and unkempt to merit a thorough recommendation, and it's surprisingly hard to spot many of its animals in their ageing enclosures. On the positive side, the tropical undergrowth and blossoming trees can look pretty against the backdrop of Diamond Head, and kids may enjoy the chance to see species that range from wallowing hippos and gray kangaroos to unfortunate monkeys trapped on tiny islands in a crocodile-infested lagoon. The zoo's pride and joy, the African Savanna exhibit, is a world of reddish mud where the "black" rhinos end up pretty much the color of their surroundings.

Waikīkī Aquarium

A few minutes' walk further east along the Kapiʻolani Park waterfront stands the disappointingly small **Waikīkī Aquarium** (daily 9am–5pm; $9, ages 13–17 $4, ages 5–12 $2; Ⓦ www.waquarium.org). Windows in its indoor galleries offer views into the turquoise world of Hawaiian reef fish, among them the lurid red frogfish and a teeming mass of small sharks. The highlight has to be the "leafy sea dragon," a bizarre Australian relative of the relatively normal seahorse; there's also a tank devoted to sea life from Hanauma Bay (see p.101). Outside, the mocked-up "edge of the reef," complete with artificial tide pools, feels a bit pointless with the real thing just a few feet away. A nearby tank holds two Hawaiian monk seals, dog-like not only in appearance but also in their willingness to perform tawdry tricks for snacks.

Diamond Head

The craggy 762ft pinnacle of **Diamond Head**, immediately southeast along the coast from Waikīkī, is Honolulu's most famous landmark. It's among the youngest of the chain of volcanic cones – others include Punchbowl (p.79) and Koko Head (p.102) – that stretch across southeast Oahu. All were created by brief blasts of the Koʻolau vent, which reawakened a few hundred thousand years ago after slumbering for more than two million years. The most recent date back less than ten thousand years, so further eruptions are possible. Diamond Head itself was formed in a few days or even hours: its southwestern side is so much higher than the others because the trade winds were blowing from the northeast at the time.

Ancient Hawaiians knew Diamond Head as either Leiʻahi ("wreath of fire," a reference to beacons lit on the summit to guide canoes) or Laeʻahi ("brow of the yellow-fin tuna"). They built *heiaus* in and around it, slid down its walls to Waikīkī on *hōlua* land-sleds as sport, and threw convicted criminals from the rim. Its modern name derives from the mistake of some nineteenth-century English sailors, who stumbled across what they thought were diamonds on its slopes and rushed back to town with their pockets bulging with glittering but worthless calcite crystals. For most of the twentieth century the interior was sealed off by the US armed forces, who based long-range artillery here during World War I, and after Pearl Harbor used the bunkers to triangulate the guns of Waikīkī's Fort DeRussy. Only in the 1960s was it reopened as the **Diamond Head State Monument** public park (Ⓦ www.hawaiistateparks.org).

Access to the crater is via a short road tunnel that drills through the walls, around two miles by road from Waikīkī; it's not a particularly pleasant walk, so most people either drive or catch bus #22 or #58 from Kūhiō Avenue in Waikīkī.

Because the floor of the crater stands well above sea level – it's gradually filling in as the walls erode – Diamond Head is not quite so dramatic from the inside. In fact, the lawns of the crater interior are oddly bland, almost suburban. Often parched, but a vivid green after rain, they're dotted with now-defunct military installations.

The climb to the rim

The only reason anyone comes to Diamond Head is to hike the hot half-hour trail up to the rim for a grand **panorama** of Oahu's entire southern coast. So many walkers hit the trail each day, plenty of whom treat the undertaking as a joyless endurance test, that this is very far from a wilderness experience, and serious hikers looking for natural splendors are advised to head elsewhere. Not that this is an easy climb; it's surprisingly steep, with several long concrete staircases, and it's exposed to the morning sun, so unprepared tourists often end up in distress. Bring water, and wear suitable footwear and a hat.

Rangers at the parking lot collect $5 per vehicle, or $1 from each walk-in hiker; the paved trail is open daily from 6am until 6pm. Having first climbed slowly away from the crater floor, it meanders up the inside walls. Many of the holes visible but out of reach on the hillside are ancient burial caves. Before long, you enter the vast network of ugly military bunkers and passageways that riddle the crater. After passing through the first long, dark and cramped tunnel, take time to catch your breath before tackling the very tall, narrow flight of yellow-painted concrete steps that leads up between two high walls to the right.

At the top of the steps, you come to another tunnel, then climb a dark spiral staircase through cramped tiers of fortifications, equipped with eye-slit windows and camouflaged from above. Beyond that, a final outdoor staircase leads to the summit, where you get your first sweeping views of Waikīkī and Honolulu. In theory a geodetic plate marks the highest point, but no matter how often it's replaced it soon gets stolen again. On days when a *kona* (southwest) wind is blowing, planes landing at Honolulu Airport approach from the east, passing low enough over Diamond Head for you to see the passengers inside.

Weary hikers who can't face the walk back to Waikīkī can catch the waiting taxis in the parking lot back on the crater floor.

Downtown Honolulu

Downtown Honolulu, the administrative heart of first the kingdom, and now the state, of Hawaii, stands a few blocks west of the original city center. Most of the compact grid of streets where the port grew up is now taken up by Chinatown, while downtown is generally considered to focus on the cluster of buildings that surround ʻIolani Palace, home to Hawaii's last monarchs. This is certainly an attractive district, with several well-preserved historic buildings, but it's not a very lively one. At lunchtime on weekdays office workers scurry through the streets, but the rest of the time the contrast with the frenzy of Waikīkī is striking. With few shops, bars, or restaurants to lure outsiders, the whole place is usually empty by 8pm.

ʻIolani Palace

Stately, four-square **ʻIolani Palace**, dominating downtown from the center of its spacious gardens, was the official home of the last two monarchs of Hawaii. It was built for **King David Kalākaua** in 1882, and he lived here until his death in 1891. For his sister and successor, **Queen Liliʻuokalani**, it was first a palace, and

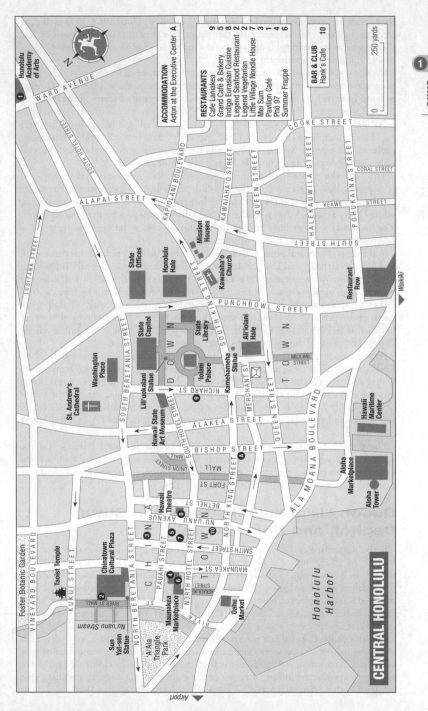

CENTRAL HONOLULU

ACCOMMODATION
Aston at the Executive Center **A**

RESTAURANTS
Cafe Laniakea	9
Grand Café & Bakery	5
Indigo Eurasian Cuisine	8
Legend Seafood Restaurant	2
Legend Vegetarian	7
Little Village Noodle House	3
Mei Sum	1
Pavilion Café	4
Phở 97	6

BAR & CLUB
Hank's Cafe	10
Summer Frappé	

0   250 yards

then, after her overthrow in 1893 (see p.422), a prison. Until 1968, by which time termites had pretty much eaten up this palace like they did its predecessor, it was the Hawaiian state capitol building. Following the completion of the new Capitol in 1969, it became a museum.

Daily except Sunday, the palace can be visited in three different ways. The first-floor **state apartments**, reached via grand exterior staircases, and the royal family's **private quarters** on the second floor can be seen on **guided tours** in the morning (9–11.15am, every 15min; $20, ages 5–12 $5, under-5s not admitted; reservations on ☎808/522-0832, ⓦ www.iolanipalace.org), or on self-guided **audio tours** later on (11.45am–3pm; $13, ages 5–12 $5, no under-5s). The self-guided **basement galleries** are open to visitors on either kind of tour, or you can also pay to access only those galleries (9am–5pm; $6, ages 5–12 $3, under-5s free).

Although the palace has become a symbol for the sovereignty movement, and is occasionally the scene of large pro-independence demonstrations, the tours are firmly apolitical. Guides revel in the lost romance of the Hawaiian monarchy while barely acknowledging that it was illegally overthrown by the United States. The fact that visitors have to shuffle around in cotton bootees to protect the *koa*-wood floors adds to the air of unreality.

In the large **Throne Room**, Kalākaua held formal balls to celebrate his coronation and fiftieth birthday, and Lili'uokalani was tried for treason for allegedly supporting moves for her own restoration. The *kapu* stick separating the thrones of Kalākaua and his wife Kapi'olani was made from a narwhal tusk given to Kalākaua by a sea captain. Other reception rooms lead off from the grand central hall, with all wall space taken up by portraits of Hawaiian and other monarchs. Though the plush upstairs **bedrooms** feel similarly impersonal, there's one touching exhibit – a quilt made by Queen Lili'uokalani during her eight months under house arrest.

Prize items in the basement include two wooden calabashes presented to King Kalākaua on his fiftieth birthday in 1886. One, the tall, slender *ipu* of Lono'ikimakahiki I, was then claimed to be five hundred years old. Retrieved from the royal burial ground at Ka'awaloa on the Big Island, it was said to have once held all the winds of the world. Among other extraordinary treasures are a feather cloak seized by Kamehameha I from his defeated rival Kīwala'o in 1782 (see p.417), and Kalākaua's own crown.

The palace's **ticket office** is housed in the castellated 'Iolani Barracks on the west side of the grounds, an odd structure that predates the palace by about fifteen years, and also holds a gift store. Anyone **driving** to the palace will find plenty of metered visitor parking within the palace grounds.

Queen Lili'uokalani statue, the State Capitol, and Honolulu Hale

On the northern side of 'Iolani Palace, beyond the impressive banyan tree at the foot of the palace steps, a walkway separates the grounds from the State Capitol to the north. At its center, a statue of **Queen Lili'uokalani** looks haughtily towards the state's present-day legislators. Festooned with *leis* and plumeria blossoms, she's depicted holding copies of her mournful song *Aloha 'Oe*, the Hawaiian creation chant known as the *Kumulipo*, and her draft Constitution of 1893, which precipitated the coup d'état against her.

Hawaii's **State Capitol** is a bizarre edifice, propped up on pillars, and with each of its two legislative chambers shaped like a volcano. It took little more than twenty years from its opening in 1969 for flaws in its design to force its closure for extensive and very expensive rebuilding. In front of the main entrance, there's a peculiar cubic statue of Father Damien (see p.326), created by Marisol Escobar in 1968.

The seat of Honolulu's city government – **Honolulu Hale**, opposite the eastern end of the walkway – is a more successful architectural experiment. An airy 1920s melding of Italianate and Spanish-Mission styles, with whitewashed walls, ornate patterned ceilings, and red-tiled roofs, it boasts a grand central atrium that's packed with colorful murals and sculptural flourishes.

The Kamehameha statue and Ali'iolani Hale

The flower-bedecked, gilt figure of **Kamehameha the Great** (1758–1819), the first man to rule all the islands of Hawaii, stares northwards across King Street towards 'Iolani Palace from outside Ali'iolani Hale. Kamehameha is depicted wearing the *'ahu'ula* (royal cloak), *malo* (loincloth), *ka'ei* (sash), and *mahiole* (feather helmet), and clutching a spear. The work of Thomas R. Gould, an American sculptor based in Florence, the statue was commissioned in 1878 to celebrate the centenary of the arrival of Captain Cook. On its way to Hawaii, however, it was lost in a shipwreck, so a second copy was cast and dispatched. That arrived in 1880 and was unveiled by King Kalākaua at his coronation in 1883; surplus insurance money from the lost statue paid for the sequence of four panels depicting scenes from Kamehameha's life around its base. Meanwhile, the original statue was found floating off the Falkland Islands. Purchased by a whaling captain in Port Stanley, it too turned up in Hawaii, and was packed off to Kamehameha's birthplace on the Big Island. Ceremonies at the Honolulu statue on June 11 each year mark Kamehameha Day, a state holiday.

Erected in 1874, **Ali'iolani Hale** – "House of the Heavenly King" in Hawaiian – was Hawaii's first library and national museum; it was also the first building taken over by the conspirators who overthrew the monarchy in 1893. Throughout its history, however, its main function has been as the home of the state's Supreme Court. On the first floor, the fascinating **Judiciary History Center** (Mon–Fri 8am–4pm; free; ⓦwww.jhchawaii.net) outlines the story of Hawaiian law from the days of the ancient *kapu* onwards. There's also a scale model of Honolulu in 1850, watched over by the now-vanished fort and with thatched huts still dotted among its Victorian mansions.

Hawaii State Art Museum

Immediately west of 'Iolani Palace, across Richards Street from the palace ticket office, the excellent **Hawaii State Art Museum** (Tues–Sat 10am–4pm; free; ⓦwww.hawaii.gov/sfca) fills the second floor of an impressive 1920s Spanish-Mission building with displays of the state's collection of contemporary art. Broadly speaking, the 'Ewa galleries to the west hold small-scale works in different media which explore Hawaii's natural and urban environment. Look out for the most popular painting, taken from Masami Teraoka's hilarious Hanauma Bay Series, in which local snorkelers are deliberately styled after Japan's *ukiyo-e* tradition of brightly colored woodblock prints. The Diamond Head galleries to the east feature displays on Pacific voyaging, including a model of the *Hōkūle'a* canoe, some fine *koa*-wood carved bowls, and large, lyrical paintings of Hawaiian landscapes.

Kawaiaha'o Church

Although **Kawaiaha'o Church** (Mon–Fri 8am–4pm, Sunday service 9am; free), just east of 'Iolani Palace, was erected in 1842, less than twenty years after the first Christian missionaries came to Hawaii (see p.418), it was the fifth church to stand on this site. According to its Protestant minister, Rev Hiram Bingham, each of its four predecessors was a thatched "cage in a haymow." This one, by contrast, was built with thousand-pound chunks of living coral, hacked from the reef. It's not especially huge, but the columned portico is grand enough, topped by a square clock-tower.

Inside, broad balconies run down both sides of the nave, lined with royal portraits. Below, plaques on the walls honor early figures of Hawaiian Christianity, such as Henry 'Opukaha'ia (see p.418). The plushest pews – at the back of the church, upholstered in velvet and marked off by *kahili* standards – were reserved for royalty.

In the church **gardens**, a fountain commemorates the site of a spring known as *Ka wai a Ha'o*, "the water of Ha'o." A rare treasure in this barren region, it was reserved for *ali'i nui*, or high chiefs, such as chiefess Ha'o. The small mausoleum in the grounds fronting the church holds the remains of **King Lunalilo**, who ruled for less than two years after his election in 1872. The rest of the graves in the **cemetery** around the back serve as a brief introduction to Hawaii's nineteenth-century missionary elite, with an abundance of Castles and Cookes, Alexanders and Baldwins, and the only president of the Republic, Sanford B. Dole.

The Mission Houses

The lives of Hawaii's first Christian missionaries are recalled in the restored **Mission Houses** behind Kawaiaha'o Church. Cheek by jowl at 553 S King St, these three nineteenth-century buildings commemorate the pioneers of the Sandwich Islands Mission, who arrived from Boston in 1820.

To see inside them all, you have to join a guided tour (Tues–Sat 11am, 1pm & 2.45pm; $10, under-19s $6; ⓦwww.missionhouses.org), though you can also visit the largest, the **Chamberlain House**, on your own (Tues–Sat 10am–4pm; $6, or included in tour). That started life in 1831 as the mission storehouse, a role that when the missionary families became increasingly embroiled in the economy of the islands turned it into the commercial headquarters of Castle and Cooke, one of the original "Big Five" (see p.420).

The oldest edifice, the two-story **Frame House**, was shipped from New England in 1821. Reluctant to let outsiders build permanent structures, the king only allowed it to go up with the words "When you go away, take everything with you." The house, whose tiny windows were entirely unsuited to the heat of Honolulu, was home to four missionary families. A kitchen had to be added because cooking outdoors attracted too much attention from the islanders, as it was *kapu* (taboo) for women to prepare food.

One of the missionaries' first acts, in 1823, was to set up the **Print House**, which produced the first Hawaiian-language Bible – *Ka Palapala Hemolele*. The current building – not the original, but its 1841 replacement – holds a replica of its imported Ramage printing press, whose limitations were among the reasons why to this day the Hawaiian alphabet only has twelve letters.

Honolulu Academy of Arts

Honolulu residents take great pride in the stunning fine art on display at the **Academy of Arts**, 900 S Beretania St (Tues–Sat 10am–4.30pm, Sun 1–5pm, second Thurs of month 10am–9pm; tours Tues–Sat 10.15am, 11.30am & 1.30pm, Sun 1.15pm; open 11am–5pm, with free admission, on third Sun of month; otherwise $10, seniors and students $5, under-13s free; ⓣ808/532-8700, ⓦwww.honoluluacademy.org). Two or three hours wandering the galleries of this elegant former private home, with its Eastern-influenced architecture, open courtyards and fountains, is time well spent.

Precisely which of the Academy's superb collection of **paintings** is on show at any one time varies, but a fine selection always adorns the galleries surrounding the **Mediterranean Court**. Highlights include Van Gogh's *Wheat Field*, Gauguin's *Two Nudes on a Tahitian Beach*, and one of Monet's *Water Lilies*. Other pieces date from the Italian Renaissance, with two separate *Apostles* by Carlo Crivelli, as well as engravings by Rembrandt and Dürer; more recent canvases include lesser works

by Picasso, Léger, Braque, Matisse, and Tanguy. Under the theme of "East meets West," the final parts of this section explore cross-cultural contacts between Europe, India, and China. An entire room on Captain Cook and the Pacific is papered with gloriously romantic French wallpaper from around 1804, depicting an idyllic South Seas landscape in which Cook's death is a minor unfortunate detail.

An even larger area on the first floor is devoted to **Asian** art and artifacts, with Korean, Japanese, "pan-Asian Buddhist," and, especially, **Chinese** works. Among the latter are beautiful Neolithic-era ceramics, four-thousand-year-old jade blades, and columns from a two-thousand-year-old Han tomb that resemble Easter Island statues. There then follows a cornucopia of masterpieces: Buddhist and Shinto deities, plus *netsuke* (toggles) and samurai armor from Japan; Tibetan *thangkas* (religious images); Indian carvings ranging from Rajasthani sandstone screens to a stone Chola statue of Krishna; Mayan effigies and Indonesian stick figures; Melanesian masks incorporating boars' tusks and cobwebs; and pottery from the pueblos of Arizona and New Mexico. One last street-level gallery holds the Academy's **Modern and Contemporary** collection, which ranges from a Francis Bacon triptych to a Nam June Paik video installation.

Upstairs on the second floor of the newer Luce Pavilion, most of the works in **The Arts of Hawaii** are of mainly historic interest. Although you can find finer collections of ancient Hawaiian artifacts at the Bishop Museum (see p.86) or 'Iolani Palace (see p.70), the early depictions of Hawaii here by Western artists are well worth seeing.

The Academy's appealing and inexpensive **courtyard café** makes a highly recommended lunchtime stop (Tues–Sat 11.30am–1.30pm; reservations ⓣ808/532-8734).

Chinatown

Barely five minutes' walk west of 'Iolani Palace, a pair of matching stone dragons flank either side of Hotel Street, marking the transition between downtown Honolulu and the oldest part of the city, **Chinatown**. For well over a century, this was renowned as the city's red-light district. Though almost all the pool halls, massage parlors, and tawdry bars that formerly lined the narrow streets are gone, its fading green clapboard storefronts and bustling market ambience still make Chinatown seem like another world. Cosmopolitan, atmospheric, and historic in equal proportions, it's the one local neighborhood that's genuinely fun to explore on your own, though you can join an organized **walking tour** of Chinatown with the Hawaii Heritage Center, 1040 Smith St, which also runs a little museum displaying musical instruments (tours Wed & Fri 9.30am, $10; museum Mon–Sat 9am–2pm, $1; ⓣ808/521-2749).

While Chinatown retains its traditional Asian flavor, it's also attracted a considerable influx in recent years of hip, creative types, who are most evident in its lively **art scene**. The regular **First Friday** event, in which galleries stay open 5 to 8pm on the first Friday of each month, enables visitors to take early-evening strolls from gallery to gallery before adjourning to local bars and restaurants.

For general information on Chinatown, see Ⓦwww.chinatownhi.com.

Exploring Chinatown

Of the district's two main axes, North Hotel and Maunakea streets, **Hotel Street** best lives up to the old lowlife reputation, with neon signs advertising long-gone fleshpots and drunken sailors lurching to and from assorted sawdust-floored bars. At the intersection with Maunakea Street stands the ornate hundred-year-old facade of **Wo**

Fat's Chop Sui restaurant, now occupied by a Chinese supermarket. Its main rival as the leading local landmark is the painstakingly restored Art Deco **Hawaii Theatre**, further east at 1130 Bethel St. Guided tours of the theater ($5) take place every Tuesday at 11am, but a better way to appreciate its gorgeous interior is by attending a performance; contact ⓣ808/528-0506 or ⓦwww.hawaiitheatre.com for schedules.

Many of Chinatown's old walled courtyards have been converted into open malls, but the businesses within remain much the same. Apothecaries and herbalists weigh out dried leaves in front of endless arrays of bottles, shelves, and wooden cabinets, while deft-fingered women gather around tables to thread *leis*. Every hole-in-the-wall store holds a fridge bursting with colorful blooms, and appetizing food smells waft from backstreet bakeries. If you get hungry, browse through the Oriental food specialties at **Oahu Market**, on North King and Kekaulike. One of the fastest-selling items is *ahi* (yellow-fin tuna), used for making sashimi or *poke*, but this is also the place to go if you're looking for pig snouts or salmon heads. However, for the best fast-food in Chinatown, visit the **Maunakea Marketplace**, a couple of blocks north and entered from either Hotel or Maunakea streets. Another tempting food market, piled high with shiny eggplants, great mountains of gnarled ginger roots, and twitchy live crabs, it also houses a good little food court. The temperature is likely to be sweltering, but the choice of cuisines – Filipino, Vietnamese, Korean, Thai, Malaysian, Hong Kong – is good, and at the lowest prices in Honolulu.

Chinatown is bordered to the west by Nu'uanu Stream, which flows down to Honolulu Harbor. **River Street**, running alongside, becomes a restaurant-filled pedestrian mall between Beretania and Kukui streets. At the port end stands a *lei*-swaddled statue of the revolutionary hero **Sun Yat-sen**, who was raised in Hawaii and became the first President of the Republic of China in 1912, while over Kukui Street at the opposite end is the tiny, ornate-roofed Lum Hai So Tong **Taoist temple**, erected by a "friendly society" in 1899 and now perched above a couple of little stores. Most of the interior of the block next to the mall is occupied by the **Chinatown Cultural Plaza**, filled with slightly tacky souvenir stores and conventional businesses that cater to the Chinese community.

Foster Botanical Garden

At the top end of River Street, and entered via a short driveway that leads off North Vineyard Boulevard beside the Kuan Yin Buddhist temple, is the fourteen-acre **Foster Botanical Garden** (daily 9am–4.30pm, last admission 4pm; adults $5, under-13s $1; guided tour, no extra charge, Mon–Sat 1pm). Established in the nineteenth century as a sanctuary for Hawaiian plants and testing ground for foreign species, it's one of Honolulu's best-loved city parks. Although, thanks to the H-1 freeway racing along its northern flank, it's not exactly quiet, it's usually filled with birds. Different sections cover spices and herbs, flowering orchids, and tropical trees. As well as sausage trees from Mozambique, the latter collection includes a spectacular "cannonball tree," a giant *quipo*, and a *bo* (or *peepal*) tree supposedly descended from the *bo* tree at Bodh Gaya in north India where the Buddha achieved enlightenment.

Waterfront Honolulu

It's all too easy to lose sight of the fact that central Honolulu stands just a few yards up from the turquoise waters of the Pacific, clean enough here to support conspicuous populations of bright tropical fish. Unfortunately, pedestrians exploring Chinatown or downtown have to brave the fearsome traffic of the **Nimitz Highway** to reach the ocean. That effort is rewarded by a short but enjoyable stroll

along the segment of the waterfront that stretches for a couple of hundred yards east of the venerable **Aloha Tower**. Until 1857, this area was covered by the waves; then the city fort, at Fort and Queen streets, was torn down, and the rubble used to fill in a fifteen-acre expanse of the sea floor. Now, in addition to watching the comings and goings of **Honolulu Harbor**, you can join a sunset dinner cruise or similar expedition from the piers nearby or learn something of the port's history in the **Hawaii Maritime Center**.

Long and surprisingly quiet **beaches** fringe the shoreline a little further to the east, especially in the vicinity of the **Ala Moana** district, home to the city's largest beach park as well as a huge shopping mall.

Aloha Tower

The **Aloha Tower**, on Pier 9 of Honolulu Harbor, was built in 1926 to serve as a control center for the port's traffic and a landmark for arriving cruise passengers. At 184ft high, it was then the tallest building in Honolulu; with its four giant clock-faces, each surmounted by the word "ALOHA," it was also the most photographed.

These days, feeling somewhat cut off from the city, it's the center-piece of the not particularly thriving **Aloha Tower Marketplace** shopping mall. After-work downtowners keep the mall's restaurants and music venues busy in the evenings, especially at weekends, but during the day it's heavily dependent on day-trippers from Waikīkī, who don't necessarily materialize, and often seems forlorn. However, with the mall walkways ending right at the dockside, and several of the restaurants and bars offering large open-air terraces, this still makes an appealing place to get a sense of the ongoing life of the port. Cargo vessels from all over the world tie up alongside, and there's always something going on out in the water.

Taking a free trip up to the tenth-floor **Observation Deck** of the now rather shabby Aloha Tower itself is also worthwhile (daily 9am–5pm). Balconies on each of its four sides offer views that are just short of ugly – freeways, airport runways, and grimy harbor installations – but provide an excellent orientation to the city. As you look towards Diamond Head, which may well be obscured by haze, the twin pink-trimmed "stereo speakers" of the Waterfront Towers condominiums loom above the black glass of Waterfront Plaza; meanwhile, Pearl Harbor sprawls to the west, and the green mountains soar inland.

Hawaii Maritime Center

A short walk east of the Aloha Marketplace, at Pier 7, exhibits at the **Hawaii Maritime Center**, in theory, illustrate Hawaii's seafaring past in riveting detail. However, when this book went to press, it had been "temporarily" closed since April 2009, due to budget cuts at the Bishop Museum, which manages it. Check Ⓦ www.bishopmuseum .org to see whether it has reopened, and thus whether you'll be able to enjoy displays on such themes as Captain Cook, the whaling industry, the growth of tourism, and the renaissance of Polynesian voyaging.

East to Waikīkī: Ala Moana

East of Aloha Tower and the Maritime Center, **Ala Moana Boulevard** runs along the shoreline towards Waikīkī, passing a few more of Honolulu's main **shopping malls** – the Ward Warehouse, the Ward Centre, and the pick of the bunch, the **Ala Moana Center**. For details, see p.99.

The first spot where you can enter the ocean in this stretch is Point Panic in **Kakaʻako Waterfront State Park**. Serious board- and body-surfers swear by its

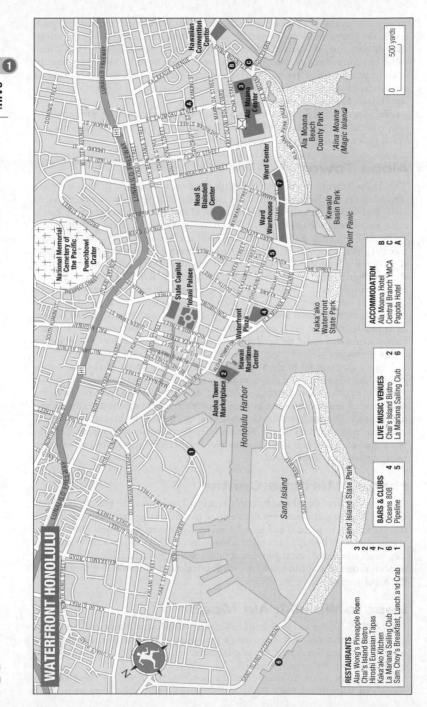

WATERFRONT HONOLULU

RESTAURANTS
Alan Wong's Pineapple Room	3
Chai's Island Bistro	2
Hiroshi Eurasian Tapas	4
Kaka'ako Kitchen	7
La Mariana Sailing Club	6
Sam Choy's Breakfast, Lunch and Crab	1

BARS & CLUBS
Oceans 808	4
Pipeline	5

LIVE MUSIC VENUES
Chai's Island Bistro	2
La Mariana Sailing Club	6

ACCOMMODATION
Ala Moana Hotel	B
Central Branch YMCA	C
Pagoda Hotel	A

0   500 yards

powerful waves, but a lack of sand, an abundance of sharks, and the fact that the surf hammers straight into a stone wall ensure that few visitors are tempted to join them. Even though there's no beach, the park itself is nice enough, with its grassy hills, paved pathways, and pavilions. Next up, across from the Ward Warehouse, **Kewalo Basin Park** occupies the thin oceanfront groin that shelters the Kewalo Basin harbor, used by several small-boat operators.

Though tourists tend not to realize it, the long green lawns across Ala Moana Boulevard from the malls flank a superb **beach** – the long white-sand strand preserved as the **Ala Moana Beach County Park**. Honolulu city-dwellers come here to enjoy excellent facilities and, especially during working hours, a relative absence of crowds. Like most of the beaches in Waikīkī, it's artificial, having been constructed on a garbage dump during the 1930s. Inshore swimming is generally safe and good, and there's potential for snorkeling around the reef; just watch out for the steep drop-off, only a few yards out at low tide.

At its eastern end, Ala Moana Beach curves out and around a long promontory. Known as **Magic Island** or **'Aina Moana**, this too is artificial. It was one of the most ambitious elements of the state's plans to expand tourism in the early 1960s, the idea being to reclaim an "island" of shallow coral reef, connect it to the mainland, and build luxury hotels on it. The hotels never materialized, so the vast sums of money involved have instead resulted in the creation of a tranquil park with roomy lawns, a gently sloping beach, and a lovely little crescent lagoon at its tip. It's worth wearing reef shoes if you go in the water, however; the sea floor remains rocky. Honolulu's mayor proposed renaming Magic Island after President Obama in 2009, but so far it doesn't look likely to happen.

Tantalus and Makiki Heights

If constant glimpses of the mountains that soar inland of downtown Honolulu entice you into exploring, there's no better choice of route than **Tantalus** and **Round Top** drives. They're actually a single eight-mile road that climbs up one flanking ridge of **Makiki Valley** and then wriggles back down the other, changing its name from Tantalus Drive in the west to Round Top Drive in the east. Along the way you'll get plenty of views of Honolulu and Waikīkī, but the real attraction is the dense rainforest that cloaks the hillside, its greenery often meeting overhead to form a tunnel. It's a slow drive, which in places narrows to just a single lane of traffic, but a spellbinding one.

To join Tantalus Drive from downtown, follow signs for the Punchbowl cemetery until you reach the right turn onto Pūowaina Drive, and head straight on instead. Coming from Waikīkī, take Makiki Street up from Wilder Avenue, which runs parallel to and just north of H-1 west of the University. It's also possible to skip the bulk of the circuit by taking **Makiki Heights Drive**, which holds the stimulating **Contemporary Museum** as well as trailheads for some superb mountain **hikes**.

Punchbowl: National Memorial Cemetery

The extinct volcanic caldera known as Punchbowl, perched above downtown Honolulu, makes an evocative setting for the **National Memorial Cemetery of the Pacific** (March–Sept daily 8am–6.30pm; Oct–Feb daily 8am–5.30pm). To ancient Hawaiians, this was Pūowaina, the hill of human sacrifices; somewhere within its high encircling walls stood a sacrificial temple. It's now possible to drive right into the crater – having first spiralled around the base of the cone to meet up with Pūowaina Drive from the back – and park along its perimeter road.

Beneath the lawns that carpet the bowl-shaped interior, over twenty-five thousand dead of US Pacific wars, and also Vietnam, lie buried. Famous names here include the Hawaiian astronaut Ellison Onizuka, killed when the *Challenger* shuttle exploded, but no graves are singled out for special attention. Instead, each gravestone, marked perhaps with a bouquet of ginger and heliconia, is recessed into the grass, with space left for their families or still-living veterans to join those laid to rest. At the opposite end to the entrance rises the imposing marble staircase of the **Honolulu Memorial**, where ten "Courts of the Missing" commemorate a further 28,778 service personnel listed as missing in action.

Only when you climb the footpath to the top of the crater rim and find yourself looking straight down Punchbowl Street to the Capitol do you appreciate how close this all is to downtown Honolulu. During World War II, before the creation of the cemetery, this ridge held heavy artillery trained out to sea.

Contemporary Museum

At 2411 Makiki Heights Drive, a short distance east of that road's intersection with Mott-Smith Drive, a grand 1920s country estate houses the lovely **Contemporary Museum** (Tues–Sat 10am–4pm, Sun noon–4pm; $8, free third Thurs of month, under-13s free; ⓣ808/526-1322, ⓦwww.tcmhi.org). The grounds are tastefully landscaped with ornamental Oriental gardens that offer a superb overview of Honolulu and are packed with playful sculptures, while the venue itself is really more of an art gallery than a museum, and hosts exhibitions of up-to-the-minute fine art. Few last more than eight weeks, but each is installed with lavish attention to detail. A separate pavilion houses a permanent display of the sets created by David Hockney for the Metropolitan Opera's production of Ravel's *L'Enfant et les Sortilèges*; a recording of the work plays constantly. Excellent lunches, with daily specials priced at $10–12, are available at the on-site *Contemporary Café* (Tues–Sat 11.30am–2.30pm, Sun noon–2.30pm; ⓣ808/523-3362), and there's also a very good gift store.

Makiki Forest Recreation Area

Honolulu's finest **hiking trails** wind their way across and around the slopes of **Makiki Valley**. The network is most easily accessed via a short, clearly signed spur road that leads inland from a hairpin bend in Makiki Heights Drive, roughly half a mile east of the Contemporary Museum, or half a mile west of the intersection with Makiki Street. Follow the dead-end road to park in a large lot, just beyond a sign that announces you've entered the **Makiki Forest Recreation Area**.

Walking a little further on brings you to the green trailers of the **Hawaii Nature Center**, a volunteer educational group that works mainly with schoolchildren and organizes guided hikes, open to all, on weekends (ⓣ808/955-0100 or ⓦwww .hawaiinaturecenter.org). If you haven't already picked up trail maps from the state office downtown (see p.52), you might find some at the center.

Makiki Valley trails

To take the best loop hike in Makiki Valley, you don't need to go as far as the Nature Center. Set off instead across the Kanealole Stream, which flows parallel to the road on its right-hand side, on the clearly signed **Maunalaha Trail**. At a T-junction a short way up, the Kanealole Trail is arrowed left, and the Maunalaha to the right. Follow the Maunalaha, and you swiftly switchback onto the ridge for a long straight climb, often stepping from one exposed tree root to the next. Despite being in the shade most of the way, it's a grueling haul. Looking back through the deep green woods, you'll glimpse the towers of downtown Honolulu and then of Waikīkī. At first you can see the valleys to either side of the ridge, but

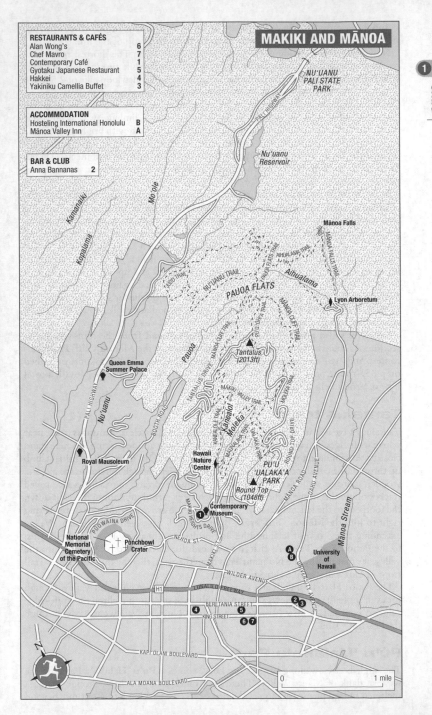

MAKIKI AND MĀNOA

RESTAURANTS & CAFÉS
Alan Wong's   6
Chef Mavro   7
Contemporary Café   1
Gyotaku Japanese Restaurant   5
Hakkei   4
Yakiniku Camellia Buffet   3

ACCOMMODATION
Hosteling International Honolulu   B
Mānoa Valley Inn   A

BAR & CLUB
Anna Bannanas   2

NU'UANU PALI STATE PARK

Nu'uanu Reservoir

Mānoa Falls

AIHUALAMA TRAIL

PAUOA FLATS TRAIL

NU'UANU TRAIL

'AIHUALAMA

PAUOA FLATS

Aihualama

MĀNOA FALLS TRAIL

Lyon Arboretum

MĀNOA CLIFF TRAIL

PU'U 'OHIA TRAIL

▲ Tantalus (2013ft)

Pauoa

MĀNOA CLIFF TRAIL

Queen Emma Summer Palace

TANTALUS DRIVE

MAKIKI VALLEY TRAIL

Kanealoi

Moleka

MOLEKA TRAIL

ROUND TOP DRIVE

KANEALOLE TRAIL

MAUNALAHA TRAIL

DALEKA TRAIL

Nu'uanu

PALI HIGHWAY

BOOTH ROAD

Royal Mausoleum ▲

Hawaii Nature Center

PU'U 'UALAKA'A PARK

▲ Round Top (1048ft)

OAHU AVENUE

MĀNOA ROAD

Mānoa Stream

① Contemporary Museum

MAKIKI HEIGHTS DRIVE

PUOWAINA DRIVE

National Memorial Cemetery of the Pacific

Punchbowl Crater

NEHOA ST

MAKIKI ST

Ⓐ Ⓑ

University of Hawaii

UNIVERSITY AVENUE

WILDER AVENUE

H1 LUNALILO FREEWAY

BERETANIA STREET

④   ⑤   ② ③

KING STREET

⑥ ⑦

KAPI'OLANI BOULEVARD

ALA MOANA BOULEVARD

N

0   1 mile

before long only Mānoa Valley to the east is visible. After roughly three-quarters of a mile, you come to a **four-way intersection** at the top of the hill.

Now you have to decide just how far you want to walk. The shortest route back to the trailhead is simply to return the way you came, while turning **left** onto the **Makiki Valley Trail** lets you complete a highly recommended loop hike of 2.5 miles. The first stretch of the Makiki Valley Trail is the most gorgeous of the lot. A gentle descent angled along the steep valley wall, it heads inland to cross Moleka Stream at Herring Springs, amid a profusion of tiny bright flowers. Climbing away again you're treated to further ravishing views of the high valley, bursting with bright gingers and fruit trees. Birds are audible all around, and dangling lianas festoon the path. Take **Kanealole Trail**, which cuts away to the left shortly before this trail meets Tantalus Drive, and you'll drop back down through endless guava trees to your starting point near the Nature Center.

Alternatively, you can head **right** at the four-way intersection to take the **'Ualaka'a Trail**, adding an enjoyable if muddy half-mile to the loop trip. Plunging into the forest, the level path soon passes some extraordinary banyans, perched on the steep slopes with their many trunks, which have engulfed older trees. Having rounded the ridge, where magnificent Cook pines march along the crest in parallel rows, an arm-span apart, you curve back to cross Round Top Drive twice. In between the two crossings, a short spur trail leads left and up to the hike's highest point. A clearing here perfectly frames Diamond Head against the ocean, with Waikīkī to the right. Once you rejoin the main trail on the far side of Round Top Drive – it starts fifty yards to the right – a brief woodland walk, down to the left, returns you to the four-way junction.

Finally, it's also possible to continue **straight ahead** from the four-way intersection. As first the **Moleka Trail**, and subsequently the **Mānoa Cliff Trail**, this route brings you in roughly three miles to the Nu'uanu Pali Lookout, described on p.85. You're now almost four miles from your car, so you're faced with a total hike of around eight miles.

Tantalus trails

Tantalus Drive is at its highest just below the 2013ft pinnacle of **Tantalus** itself, near where it changes its name to Round Top Drive. Two roadside parking lots here stand close to the trailhead for the three-quarter-mile **Pu'u 'Ōhi'a Trail**. The initial climb up through the eucalyptus trees to the summit is steep enough to require the aid of a wooden staircase, which comes out after a few hundred yards onto a little-used paved track. Follow this to the right until you reach an electrical substation, then cut down the footpath to the left, which leads through a dense grove of bamboo before veering right to join the **Mānoa Cliff Trail**. By now you'll have seen vast Nu'uanu Valley extending away to your left; heading left brings you, in a couple of hundred yards, to the **Pauoa Flats Trail**. As that in turn heads for three quarters of a mile into the valley, it's met first by the Nu'uanu Trail from the west, then by the Aihualama Trail from Mānoa Falls (see p.84) from the east.

The Pauoa Flats Trail ends at a vantage point high above Nu'uanu Valley, though for even more dramatic views you can double back slightly and climb the knife-edge ridge to your left, from where it's obvious how Nu'uanu Valley cuts right through the heart of Oahu.

Pu'u 'Ualaka'a Park

The single best view along Round Top Drive comes at **Pu'u 'Ualaka'a Park**, on the western flank of Mānoa Valley. There's not much of a park here, though there's a sheltered hilltop picnic pavilion at the first of its two parking lots. Continue beyond

that to the second lot, where a paved walkway leads to a railed-off viewing area right at the end of the ridge, and you'll be rewarded with a panorama of Oahu's entire southern coast. The twin craters of Diamond Head to the left and Punchbowl to the right readily draw the eye, but looking away west you can see beyond the airport and Pearl Harbor and all the way to Barber's Point. Pools of glass in the parking lot attest to many break-ins, so don't spend too long away from your vehicle.

The small summit that separates the two lots is Round Top itself. The Hawaiians called it 'Ualaka'a ("rolling sweet potato"), because Kamehameha the Great decreed the planting of sweet potatoes here, which when dug up rolled down the hillside.

Mānoa Valley

Although just a couple of miles north of Waikīkī, **Mānoa Valley** is light-years away from the commercial hustle of the city. Behind the **University of Hawaii** – a magnet for students from around the Pacific, but of no great appeal for casual visitors – lies a quiet residential suburb that peters out as it narrows into the mountains, culminating in a spectacular **waterfall**.

Mānoa Falls

To drive to the uppermost reaches of Mānoa Valley, continue along University Avenue beyond the university campus, cross East Mānoa Road onto Oahu Avenue, then turn right onto Mānoa Road itself. Immediately you'll see the silver stream of Mānoa Falls amid the trees at the head of the valley. Mānoa Road comes to a halt just beyond the **Lyon Arboretum**, which preserves Hawaiian and imported trees in a reasonable approximation of their native environment (Mon–Fri 9am–4pm, Sat 9am–3pm; $5 suggested donation; ⓦ www.hawaii.edu/lyonarboretum). Several short trails crisscross beneath the canopy.

Barack Obama's Oahu

Although **Barack Obama**'s political career has played out far from the islands, Hawaiians take understandable pride in the first Hawaii-born president. Obama's roots on Oahu run deep. His parents met as students at the **University of Hawaii**, and he was born at Honolulu's Kapiolani Hospital for Women and Children on August 4, 1961.

The young Obama lived on Oahu until the age of 6, initially in exclusive **Hawaii Kai**, and subsequently in **Mānoa Valley**, near the university, at 2277 Kamehameha Ave and 2234 University Ave. After four years in Indonesia, he returned to spend the rest of his education at Hawaii's leading private school, **Punahou School**, where he played on the state championship basketball team. His youthful haunts included Sandy Beach and Honolulu's various beach parks, while his first job was at the *Baskin Robbins* ice-cream parlor at 1618 S King St. During this period he lived with his grandparents at 1617 S Beretania St, still near the university but within easy reach of both Waikīkī and downtown Honolulu. His grandfather is buried in Punchbowl cemetery, while the ashes of both his mother – Stanley Ann Dunham, who died aged 52 in 1995 – and his grandmother were scattered near the **Halona Blowhole**.

As President, Obama has spent winter vacations in rented houses near the gorgeous beach in the windward town of **Kailua**. As well as body-surfing at **Sandy Beach**, hiking to **Mānoa Falls**, and snorkeling at **Hanauma Bay** – specially opened for the presidential party on a Tuesday – he continues to enjoy local treats like shave ice and takeout lunches from Kapahulu neighborhood restaurants such as *Zippy's* and the *Rainbow Drive-In*.

At three quarters of a mile each way, the hike to **Mānoa Falls**, towering 160ft high at the head of Mānoa Valley, is the most rewarding short trail on Oahu. Considering how close it is to the heart of Honolulu, it offers an amazing sense of delving deep into a gorgeous tropical rainforest. Expect to spend around an hour and a half away from your vehicle, and don't wait to get bitten before you cover yourself with mosquito repellent. The only legal place to park is in the large lot of the defunct Paradise Park, where there's usually an attendant to collect the $5 fee; this area is notorious for **break-ins**, so don't leave valuables in your car.

The **trail** to the falls follows straight on ahead from the end of the road. Having passed over a footbridge and through a soggy meadow, it's soon climbing beside one of the two main tributaries of Mānoa Stream. After scrambling from root to protruding root, over intertwined banyans and bamboos, you come out at the soaring high falls, where the flat, mossy cliff-face is at enough of an angle that the water flows rather than falls into the small pool at its base. Sadly, thanks to recent landslides, access to the foot of the falls is strictly forbidden.

Many hikers combine the falls trek with tackling the much more demanding **Aihualama Trail**, which switchbacks steeply up to the west from an inconspicuous intersection just short of the falls. After something over a mile, it comes out atop the ridge, amid a thick cluster of bamboo, to connect with the Makiki network of trails half a mile short of the Nu'uanu Lookout (see p.82).

Pali Highway

Of the three roads that negotiate the Ko'olau Mountains to connect Honolulu with windward Oahu, only the **Pali Highway** and **Likelike Highway** hold much potential for sightseeing. Both can get hideously congested at peak times, but the Pali Highway in particular is an exhilarating drive, whether you head straight for the clifftop **Nu'uanu Pali Lookout**, or call in at the various **royal sites** on the way up.

The third route, the **H-3** freeway, opened in 1997. Originally intended for military use as a direct link between Pearl Harbor and the Marine Corps base at Kāne'ohe, it serves primarily as a commuter route between the windward communities and Honolulu.

Royal Mausoleum

The Gothic-influenced **Royal Mausoleum** is located very near the top of Nu'uanu Avenue, shortly before it joins the Pali Highway. It's very easy to miss and frankly it's not worth losing any sleep over if you do. The drab, gray mausoleum (Mon–Fri 8am–4pm; free), built in 1865 to replace the overcrowded Kamehameha family tomb at 'Iolani Palace, is now simply a chapel, as the bodies it held for its first forty years or so were later moved to various sarcophagi dotted around the lawns. Kamehameha the Great was buried in secret on the Big Island (see p.138), but most of his closest family, as Christians, now lie here. His widow, Ka'ahumanu, along with Kamehamehas II to V, are in the pink granite tomb to the left, while members of the separate Kalākaua dynasty were reinterred in the gilded vault beneath the central black column.

Queen Emma Summer Palace

A couple of miles up the Pali Highway, just over half a mile after its intersection with Nu'uanu Avenue, a former royal retreat stands on the brow of a small hill to the right of the road. The **Queen Emma Summer Palace** made a welcome escape from the heat of Honolulu for the former Emma Rooke, who married King Kamehameha IV

The Battle of Nu'uanu Valley

For early foreign visitors, the ride to the top of Nu'uanu Pali was an essential part of a Hawaiian itinerary. As their horses struggled up, native guides would recount tales of the epic **Battle of Nu'uanu Valley** in 1795, in which Kamehameha the Great (from the Big Island) defeated Kalanikūpule and conquered Oahu. Kamehameha's army landed at Honolulu to find Kalanikūpule waiting for them in Nu'uanu Valley. Kamehameha sent men along the tops of the ridges to either side, and advanced towards Kalanikūpule in the center himself. By this time, Kamehameha's entourage included Europeans and, crucially, a few European guns. Isaac Davis, who five years previously had been the sole survivor of a Hawaiian raid on a small boat on the Big Island (see p.234), positioned himself at the front of the attack.

Before the usual ritual of challenges and counter-challenges could even begin, Davis killed Kalanikūpule's leading general with a single lucky shot. The soldiers of Oahu turned and ran, pursued all the way to the head of the valley. When they reached the top, where the thousand-foot Nu'uanu Pali **precipice** drops away on the far side, they had no choice. Almost to a man, they hurtled to their deaths. Kalanikūpule managed to hide out in Oahu's mountains for several months, before he was captured and sacrificed to Kamehameha's personal war god.

in 1856, was queen consort until 1863, and lived here until her death in 1885. It's now run as a somewhat cloying shrine to Emma by the Daughters of Hawaii, a group composed of descendants of missionary families (daily 9am–4pm; $6, under-12s $1; ⓦ www.daughtersofhawaii.org).

Behind its entrance stairway and six Doric pillars, the single-story white frame house is surprisingly small. Guided tours proceed at a snail's pace through rooms lined with royal souvenirs; only the splendidly grumpy Princess Ruth relieves the monotony of the official portraits. Among touching memorabilia of the young Prince Albert Edward – Queen Emma's only child, who died aged 4 – are his beautiful *koa*-wood crib, and a fireman's outfit he wore in a parade. Gifts from Queen Victoria, after whose husband the boy was named, make up a large proportion of the items on display. Both Victoria and Emma were widowed – Emma was only 27 when her husband died, a year after their son – and the two women exchanged presents for the rest of their lives.

Nu'uanu Pali State Wayside

Half a mile up the Pali Highway beyond Queen Emma's Palace, an inconspicuous right turn leads onto **Nu'uanu Pali Drive**. Other than having to drive slower, you lose nothing by taking this detour, which curves back to meet the highway two miles up. There are no specific stops en route, but the dense tropical canopy, lit with flashes of color, makes for an appealing drive.

Back on the highway, it's now just a mile until the next right turn – confusingly, it too is Nu'uanu Pali Drive – which leads in a few hundred yards to **Nu'uanu Pali State Wayside** (daily sunrise–sunset; parking $3). Miss this, and you'll bypass a staggering overview of the cliffs of windward Oahu; the highway goes into a tunnel at this point, and emerges much lower down the hillside. At the edge of a small parking lot – another notorious spot for **vehicle break-ins** – the railed viewing area of the **Nu'uanu Pali Lookout** turns out to be perched near the top of a magnificent curtain of green velvet, plunging more than a thousand feet. Straight ahead lie the sprawling coastal communities of **Kailua** and **Kāne'ohe**, separated by the Mōkapu Peninsula, but your eye is likely to be drawn to the north, where the mighty *pali* seems to stretch away forever, with a waterfall in every fold.

It was over this fearsome drop that the defeated warriors of Oahu were driven in 1795 (see p.85). Notches higher up the ridge are said to have been cut to provide fortified positions for the defenders, an estimated four hundred of whose skulls were found down below when the Pali Highway was built a century later. The stairs that head down to the right lead to the highway's original route as it edges its way above the precipice. It's blocked off about a mile along, but walking to the end makes a good, if windy, mountain hike.

To continue across the island, drive back down to rejoin the highway where you left it. To the right, Nu'uanu Pali Drive crosses over the tunnel and meets the highway's other carriageway on the far side, to drop back into Honolulu.

Likelike Highway

You're most likely to use the Pali Highway (see p.84) to get to windward Oahu from Honolulu, but the **Likelike Highway** is a less spectacular alternative. Pronounced *leek-e-leek-e*, the road is named after the younger sister of Queen Lili'uokalani. Starting roughly two miles west of the Pali Highway, it runs through residential Kalihi Valley and then passes through its own tunnel to emerge just above Kāne'ohe. There's no great reason to cross the island this way, but you'll have to drive a short stretch of Likelike Highway to visit the superb Bishop Museum.

Bishop Museum

The best museum of Hawaiian history, anthropology, and natural history – and the world's finest collection of the arts of the Pacific – is located in the largely residential Kahili neighborhood, two miles northwest of downtown Honolulu. To reach the **Bishop Museum**, at 1525 Bernice St, catch TheBus #2 from Waikīkī or drive to the foot of Likelike Highway and follow the signs from the first exit on the right (daily except Tues 9am–5pm; adults $18, ages 4–12 and seniors $15; prices include planetarium; ☎808/847-3511, ⓦ www.bishopmuseum.org).

The Bishop Museum was founded in 1889 by Charles Reed Bishop to preserve the heirlooms left by his wife, Princess Bernice Pauahi, the last direct descendant of Kamehameha the Great. Spread across four large buildings on a twelve-acre hillside estate, it sets out to present authentic Polynesian culture. Extensive recent rebuilding has left it better than ever; air conditioning has made it possible to display artifacts previously considered too delicate, while the exhibits have been reoriented into the first person, referring to Hawaiian culture in terms of "we" instead of the previous "they".

The first section you come to, beyond the ticket hall, is the **planetarium** where navigator Nainoa Thompson of the *Hōkūle'a* studied the virtual sky during the 1970s, to reinvent traditional Polynesian navigational techniques, as described on pp.429–431. Shows take place daily at 11.30am, 1.30pm, and 3.30pm.

The museum's huge main building, and in particular the beautifully remodeled **Hawaiian Hall**, its original core, focuses largely on Hawaiian history. Prize artifacts include Kamehameha the Great's personal wooden effigy of the war god Kūkā'ilimoku, found in a cave in Kona on the Big Island; a crested feather helmet that probably belonged to Kalaniopu'u of the Big Island; and the only known Akua Loa ("long god"), an image of Lono bedecked in albatross carcases. A scale model depicts the Big Island's Waha'ula *heiau*, overrun by lava from Kīlauea during the 1990s; while there's also a sharkskin drum that once announced human sacrifices in a similar *luakini* temple on the seaward slopes of Diamond Head. The thorough overview of Hawaii's post-contact history on

the top floor doesn't mince words when it comes to the illegality of the islands' annexation by the US.

In the other half of the main building, not affected by the renovations, the **Polynesian Hall** emphasizes the full diversity of Polynesia. After the breaking of the *kapu* (see p.417), the Hawaiians themselves set about destroying the relics of their ancient religion; most other Polynesian cultures have preserved far more of their heritage. Among stunning exhibits are woven-grass masks and dance costumes from Vanikoro, modeled skulls and figures from Vanuato, stark white and red sorcery charms from Papua New Guinea, and stick charts used by Micronesian navigators. The Maoris of New Zealand are represented by the facade of a storehouse, carved in high relief with human figures and inlaid with abalone-shell eyes.

Next door, the **Castle Building** hosts top-quality temporary exhibitions, while across the lawn the **Science Adventure Center** holds high-tech displays on earth and life sciences, aimed largely at local schoolchildren. Its centerpiece is an enormous artificial volcano, which constantly "erupts" fountains of glowing orange liquid; kids can twiddle knobs to mimic the natural forces responsible for different kinds of eruption. Down in the basement, another less spectacular volcano pumps out black wax that piles up in much the same way as the Hawaiian islands themselves.

The Bishop Museum holds an excellent bookstore as well as a snack bar.

Pearl Harbor

Ancient Hawaiians knew the vast inlet of **Pearl Harbor**, reaching deep into the heart of Oahu, as *Wai Momi*, "water of pearl," on account of its pearl-bearing oysters. Their canoes had no need of deep-water anchorages, but Westerners came to realize that by dredging its entrance they could create the finest harbor in the Pacific. Such was its strategic potential that the desire to control Pearl Harbor played a large role in the eventual annexation of Hawaii by the United States. The US first received permission to develop installations here in 1887, in return for granting Hawaiian sugar duty-free access to US markets, and construction of the naval base commenced in 1908.

To this day, the 12,600-acre Pearl Harbor Naval Complex is the headquarters from which the US Pacific Fleet patrols just over a hundred million square miles of ocean. The entire fleet consists of approximately 180 ships, fifteen hundred aircraft and 125,000 personnel, while Pearl Harbor itself is the home port for around eleven surface vessels and eighteen nuclear submarines. Even though there's a small city's worth of operations, only the **Arizona Memorial**, commemorating the surprise Japanese attack with which Pearl Harbor remains synonymous, is open to civilians, so half a day is plenty of time to visit.

Arizona Memorial

Almost half the victims of the December 1941 Japanese attack on Pearl Harbor were aboard the battleship **USS Arizona**. Hit by an armor-piercing shell that detonated its magazine and lifted its bow 20ft out of the water, it sank within nine minutes. Of its crew of 1514 – who had earned the right to sleep in late that Sunday morning by coming second in a military band competition – 1177 were killed. The *Arizona* still lies submerged where it came to rest, out in the waters of the harbor along "Battleship Row," next to Ford Island. Its wreck is spanned (though not touched) by the curving white **Arizona Memorial**, maintained by the National Park Service in honor of all the victims of the attack; small boats ferry a stream of visitors out from the mainland.

The **visitor center** for the memorial is located six miles west of Honolulu, just over a mile after Kamehameha Highway cuts off to the left of H-1 (center open daily 7am–5pm, tours 8am–3pm; closed New Year, Thanksgiving & Christmas Day; free; ⓉTAX 808/422-0561, ⓌWEB www.nps.gov/usar). It takes up to an hour to drive across town from Waikīkī; the large warning signs restricting admission to the naval base don't apply to memorial visitors. TheBus #20 runs direct from Waikīkī, as do overpriced commercial tours (typically around $25 per person; see p.55). No reservations are accepted, so each individual has to pick up a numbered ticket for the free memorial tour on arrival. The average wait before you're called to board the ferry, of around ninety minutes, can easily extend to two or three hours in peak season. Many people try to beat the crowds by arriving early, but if anything your chances of a short wait may be better in the afternoon. No bags of any kind are permitted on the ferry.

The attack on Pearl Harbor

As the winter of **1941** approached, with German soldiers occupying most of Europe and moving into Soviet Russia, and Japanese forces advancing through Southeast Asia, the United States remained outside the global conflict. However, negotiations to halt Japanese progress had stalled, and on November 27 the US government sent secret "war warnings" to its military units. The version received in Hawaii read: "Japanese future action unpredictable but **hostile action** possible at any moment. If hostilities cannot, repeat cannot, be avoided the United States desires that Japan commit the first overt act."

A few days earlier, a 33-vessel attack fleet, including six aircraft carriers, had sailed from northern Japan. Conventional wisdom was that it must be heading towards the Philippines, site of the furthest-flung US Pacific base, and B-17 "Flying Fortress" aircraft were sent from Hawaii to bolster the islands' defenses. In fact, Hawaii itself, where **Pearl Harbor** was the headquarters of the US Pacific Fleet, was the target. The Japanese fleet sailed an icy, rarely used northerly course, keeping well clear of usual shipping lanes and maintaining strict radio silence. The Japanese did not expect to achieve complete surprise and were prepared to engage the US fleet in battle if they met on the open sea; but reconnaissance flights from Pearl Harbor only covered the likeliest angle of attack, from the southwest, and the Japanese approach was not detected. By the early morning of December 7, the fleet was in position 230 miles northwest of Oahu.

The first wave of the attack was launched at 6am. As the 183 aircraft passed over the western Wai'anae mountains, they were picked up by radar screens at a tracking station. When the operators called Honolulu with news of the sighting, they were told "Well, don't worry about it," in the belief that these were replacement B-17s arriving from the mainland. Meanwhile, the cloud cover had lifted to give the attackers a perfect view of Pearl Harbor, where seven of the US fleet's nine battleships lay at anchor along "Battleship Row." At 7.53am, Commander Mitsuo Fuchida sent the codeword "Tora! Tora! Tora!" (Tiger! Tiger! Tiger!) to his flagship, the *Akagai*, signalling that a surprise attack was under way.

Within two hours the US Navy lost eighteen warships: eight battleships, three light cruisers, three destroyers and four auxiliary craft. In addition to 87 Navy planes, simultaneous attacks on other bases on Oahu destroyed 77 Air Force planes and damaged 128 more. The planes were parked wingtip-to-wingtip on the airfields, to make them easier to protect against sabotage by possible Japanese agents; instead it left them utterly exposed to aerial attack. During the onslaught, the expected squadron of B-17s arrived from California; unarmed, several were shot down.

In total, 2403 US military personnel were killed, and 1178 wounded. The Japanese lost 29 aircraft, plus five midget submarines that had sneaked into Pearl Harbor during the previous night. Ten hours later, Japanese aircraft did indeed attack Clark Airfield

Perhaps because so many of the 1.5 million annual visitors are Japanese, the displays in the visitor center are surprisingly even-handed, calling the attack "a daring gamble" by Admiral Yamamoto to knock out the US fleet and give the Japanese time to conquer Southeast Asia. The center has long been scheduled to hold a new **museum** covering all aspects of the attack and its aftermath, but until that's completed, the best place to get a sense of what happened is in the waterfront **garden** outside. From here, you see the low and undramatic mountain ridges that ring Pearl Harbor, together with the gap down the center of the island through which the first planes arrived. Captioned photographs illustrate the disposition of the ships on the fateful morning, as well as their eventual fate.

When your number finally comes up, you're shown a twenty-minute film that pays tribute to "one of the most brilliantly planned and executed attacks in naval history."

in the Philippines, destroying large numbers of aircraft. The next day, declaring the United States to be at war with Japan, **President Franklin D. Roosevelt** condemned the "dastardly" Pearl Harbor attack as "a date which will live in infamy."

The official postwar **inquiry** into "the greatest military and naval disaster in our nation's history" was told that the fleet was based in Hawaii in the first place, despite its weakness, because to leave it in the relative safety of the US West Coast would have signaled a lack of US will to resist Japanese expansion. As to whether the fleet's vulnerability had invited the attack, Japanese plans were drawn up expecting a much larger fleet at Pearl Harbor, and they were disappointed to find that both US aircraft carriers were out of port. The fact that the Japanese withdrew from Hawaii almost immediately, instead of following up their initial success by destroying port installations or even invading the islands, suggests that if anything they overestimated US defenses.

No proof supports revisionist assertions that Roosevelt knew the attack was coming, but allowed it to happen to create an excuse to join the war. It makes no sense, if Roosevelt did know, that he didn't at least alert US defenses a few hours in advance, when an unprovoked Japanese attack was demonstrably imminent.

Mistakes were certainly made. Navy authorities were never told, for example, of intercepted messages from Tokyo in which the Japanese consulate in Honolulu was asked to divide the moorings in Pearl Harbor into five separate areas and specify which ships were anchored in each section. The best explanation can probably be found in a pair of statements by the two leading protagonists. The overall Japanese commander, reporting to his superiors a fortnight later, wrote that "Good luck, together with negligence on the part of the arrogant enemy, enabled us to launch a successful surprise attack." Admiral Husband E. Kimmel, in charge of the US Pacific Fleet, was asked informally why he had left the ships exposed in Pearl Harbor, and replied, "I never thought those little yellow sons-of-bitches could pull off such an attack, so far from Japan."

In the long run, the Japanese decision to provoke the US into all-out **war in the Pacific** was to prove suicidal. What's more, most of the vessels damaged and even sunk at Pearl Harbor eventually returned to active service. Only the *Arizona* and the *Utah* could not be salvaged, while the *Oklahoma* sank once again, five hundred miles off the Big Island. By contrast, just two of the Japanese ships involved survived the war; four of the anti-aircraft carriers were sunk during the Battle of Midway. In 1945, the *West Virginia*, risen from the waters of Pearl Harbor, was in Tokyo Bay to witness the Japanese surrender.

In a little-known footnote, the *Phoenix*, which was unscathed by the 1941 onslaught, was sold to Argentina ten years later. Renamed the *General Belgrano*, the last surviving warship from the attack on Pearl Harbor was sunk by the British during the Falklands War in 1982.

▲ The Arizona Memorial, Pearl Harbor

Crisp-uniformed Navy personnel then usher you onto open-sided boats, which they steer for ten minutes across a tiny fraction of the naval base. You disembark at the memorial, whose white marble walls are inscribed with the names of the dead. The outline of the *Arizona* is still discernible in the clear blue waters, and still seeping oil, while here and there rusty metal spurs poke above the surface. All those who died when the *Arizona* went down remain entombed in the wreckage, occasionally joined by veteran survivors who choose to be buried here. You're free to stay for as long as you choose, although almost everyone simply returns on the next boat, which usually arrives in around fifteen minutes.

USS Bowfin Submarine Museum and Park

Located alongside the *Arizona* visitor center, but entirely separate, the privately owned **USS Bowfin Submarine Museum and Park** serves as an alternative distraction if you have a couple of hours to wait before your ferry (daily 7am–5pm; sub and museum $10, under-13s $4; museum only $5, under-13s $3; ☏808/423-1341, ⓦwww.bowfin.org). Its main focus, the claustrophobic *Bowfin* itself, is a still-floating, 83-man submarine that survived World War II unscathed, having sunk 44 enemy vessels. Once you've explored it on a self-guided audio tour – complete with the captain's account of one of the *Bowfin*'s most hair-raising missions – you can learn more about twentieth-century submarines in the adjoining museum.

The park outside, to which access is free, holds various missiles and torpedoes, including a Polaris A-1 ballistic missile, and the Japanese naval equivalent of a *kamikaze* airplane, a *kaiten*. Such manned, single-seater torpedoes were designed for suicide attacks on larger ships; only one, piloted by its inventor, ever succeeded in sinking a US Navy ship. A memorial garden alongside commemorates 52 US submarines lost during the war in the Pacific, listing over 3500 crew "On Eternal Patrol."

USS Missouri

The decommissioned battleship **USS Missouri**, also known as the "Mighty Mo," is permanently moored close to the Arizona Memorial. The last battleship constructed by the United States, she was christened in January 1944. After service in the Pacific

and Korean wars, she was decommissioned in 1955 and remained mothballed until being refitted in 1986. Operation Desert Storm saw the *Missouri* firing Tomahawk missiles into Iraq, but she was finally retired once more in 1992, as the last operational battleship in the world.

The *Missouri* now lives at Pearl Harbor on the basis that the place where World War II began for the United States should also hold the spot where it ended; the Japanese surrender of September 2, 1945, was signed on the deck of the *Missouri*, then moored in Tokyo Bay.

Since the battleship is located alongside Ford Island, on the naval base, visitors can only reach it by shuttle bus. These depart from the USS *Bowfin* visitor center, which is also where you purchase tickets (daily 9am–5pm, tickets sold 8am–4pm; $20, ages 4–12 $10; Battle Stations Tour additional $25, ages 10–12 $12; ☎808/973-2494 or 1-877/644-4489, ⓦwww.ussmissouri.org).

Having crossed the harbor on a retracting bridge, you're deposited at the entrance gate. Depending on whether you want to join a 35-minute guided tour, follow an audio or iPod tour, or simply wander at your own pace – all options are included in the admission price – you're then shepherded either towards your personal guide or simply left to climb up to the deck. The overwhelming first impression is the *Missouri*'s sheer size; at 887ft long, she's the length of three football fields and armed with colossal twin gun turrets. By contrast, once you go below decks, the crew's quarters are cramped in the extreme, bringing home the full claustrophobic reality of her long and dangerous missions. The principal highlights are the dimly lit Combat Engagement Center, set up as it was during the Gulf War but now looking very antiquated; the surrender site, on the deck nearby; and the spot where a *kamikaze* fighter careered into the side of the ship, as captured in a dramatic photo. Visitors on the $25 Battle Stations Tour get to see additional areas including an engine room and gun turret.

Eating

With most of its hundred thousand daily visitors eating out at least once a day, **Waikīkī** supports an incredible range of **restaurants**. In the rest of **Honolulu**, you'll find somewhere to eat pretty much anywhere you go – the shopping malls are packed with numerous, albeit bland, options – but only the restaurants of **Chinatown** merit a special trip from Waikīkī.

Waikīkī

Almost all of Waikīkī's hotels have an on-site American restaurant, and usually one or two other more specialized alternatives as well. As you'd expect, the standards in the major hotels are high, but out on the streets the emphasis is on keeping prices down, rather than quality up. Many of the better restaurants don't bother to open for lunch, but takeouts, fast-food chains and snack bars are everywhere you turn; the largest concentrations are along **Kūhiō Avenue** and, with more Japanese offerings, on **Kalākaua Avenue** west of Lewers Street. The easiest **fast-food** option is the food court in the International Marketplace on Kalākaua.

Arancino 255 Beach Walk ☎808/923-5557, ⓦwww.arancino.com. Authentic Italian trattoria in central Waikīkī. Appetizers to share cost $12–20, while pasta and pizza entrees range from $11 up to the tasty spaghetti alla pescatore ($29), with all kinds of fish swimming in olive oil and garlic. There's another branch at the *Waikīkī Beach*

Marriott (☎808/931-6273), open for breakfast as well. Daily 11.30am–2.30pm & 5–10.30pm.
Beachhouse *Moana Surfrider*, 2365 Kalākaua Ave ☎808/921-4600, ⓦwww.beachhousewaikiki.com. Fancy restaurant in one of Waikīkī's most atmospheric old hotels. Full "complete" ($28) or continental ($20) breakfasts start the day off, while as well as

$20–25 lunchtime salads and sandwiches, they serve an elaborate afternoon tea that's a Waikīkī tradition: $32.50 buys a plate of finger sandwiches and pastries and a pot of tea to enjoy as you listen to a Hawaiian guitarist, while $48 gets you a glass of fizz, some berries, and a sandalwood fan too. For dinner there's a lavish $90 tasting menu, also available with wine pairings, or you can also go à la carte, with entrees like lamb chops at $38; your meal is accompanied by live Hawaiian music. Mon–Sat 7–11am, 1–4pm & 5.30–9pm, Sun 9am–1pm, 3–4pm & 5.30–9pm.

Ciao Mein *Hyatt Regency Waikīkī*, 2424 Kalākaua Ave ☎808/923-2426. Huge, opulent restaurant serving an odd but successful mixture of Chinese and Italian cuisine. Few dishes actually combine the two, though "Collision Cuisine" specials at around $26 include "Hot Bean Salmon alla Siciliana" and seafood *funn* lasagne. Chinese entrees include sizzling Mongolian beef and honey walnut shrimp (both $28), and there are vegetarian options, too; a four-course set menu costs $49. They seem to give up on Chinese altogether when it comes to desserts, which include a rich tiramisu. Daily 6–10pm.

Duke's Canoe Club *Outrigger Waikīkī*, 2335 Kalākaua Ave ☎808/922-2268, ⓦwww.dukeswaikiki.com. Right on the beach, with an open-air *lānai*, this crowded chain restaurant offers great views along with a feast of retro tiki and surf styling, vintage photos and memorabilia. The buffet breakfasts (until 10.30am) are not bad value at $15, but for lunch it's best to ignore the buffet ($14) in favor of the *pūpū* menu, which ranges from nachos to sashimi. At night, the large, unimaginative dinner menu is lined with chicken, steak, and fish entrees at $20–30. Big-name Hawaiian musicians play Fri–Sun 4–6pm. Daily 6.30am–midnight.

Hau Tree Lanai *New Otani Kaimana Beach Hotel*, 2863 Kalākaua Ave ☎808/921-7066. Open-air restaurant, set beneath two magnificent spreading *hau* trees beside Sans Souci Beach. Well away from the fray of Waikīkī Beach, it's a peaceful spot, perfect for romantic sunsets. Cuisine is mostly Continental/American, with Pacific Rim touches: choose from top-quality breakfasts (go for the sweetbread French toast with coco-macadamia nut), lunches ranging from sandwiches to crab-cake burgers or seared garlic *ahi* (around $17), or dinner entrees like duck confit or seafood mixed grill ($25–40). Daily 7–10.45am, 11.45am–2pm & 5.30–9pm.

Honolulu Coffee Co *Moana Surfrider*, 2365 Kalākaua Ave ☎808/533-1500. This airy streetside coffee house adjoining the *Moana Surfrider* has huge open windows, paneling, and simple darkwood furniture. Espresso drinks, Kona coffee,

juices, and smoothies, along with fresh pastries. Daily 6am–10pm.

Hyatt on the Beach 2146 Kalākaua Ave ☎808/926-8616. This rather unlikely budget-café offshoot of the *Hyatt Regency* is right on the edge of the actual beach, across the street from the hotel, and as such quite irresistible for its low-priced takeout snacks which you eat at oceanfront tables. "Local," very un-*Hyatt* offerings include spam'n'eggs for $5.50, *loco moco* for $8, and shave ice. Daily 7am–6pm.

Kai Wa Beach Walk level 2, 226 Lewers St ☎808/924-1555, ⓦwww.kai-wa.com. Stylish Japanese restaurant, upstairs in the Beach Walk development, serving full sushi, sashimi, and teppan-yaki dinners with entrees up to $40, and well-priced lunch specials like the $15 salmon plate, along with *donburi* (rice) and hot and cold noodles. Mon–Fri 11.30am–2pm & 5–10.30pm, Sat & Sun 5–10.30pm.

Me BBQ 151 Uluniu Ave ☎808/926-9717. The barbecue in question at this tiny takeout is Korean rather than American, so most diners at the adjoining outdoor tables are enjoying plates of tangy beef ribs for under $10, though you can also get eggs and Portuguese sausages. Mon–Sat 7am–9pm.

Nobu *Waikīkī Parc*, 2233 Helumoa Rd ☎808/237-6999, ⓦwww.nobumatsuhisa.com. The first Hawaiian outpost of Japanese-Peruvian chef Nobu Matsuhisa's empire, set alongside the *Parc* hotel's ultra-smart lobby. Exquisite, and expensive, sushi, sashimi, and "special dishes," both cold like the $18 sashimi tacos, and hot, as with the $20 *Nobu* fish'n'chips. The full chef's tasting menu starts at $90. Daily 5.30–11pm.

Oceanarium *Pacific Beach Hotel*, 2490 Kalākaua Ave ☎808/921-6111. Functionally furnished restaurant with one big gimmick – one wall of the dining room is a three-story aquarium, so as you eat your meal you can watch four hundred live fish, plus the occasional scuba diver. The food itself is much less enthralling than the view, and all comes in buffet form, priced at $17.50 for breakfast, $15.50 for lunch, and $35 for dinner, when along with prime rib and seafood they prepare several kinds of *nigiri* sushi. Brunch costs $24 Sat, $29 Sun. Mon–Fri 6–10am, 11am–2pm & 4.30–10pm, Sat & Sun 11am–2.30pm & 4.30–10pm.

Orchids *Halekūlani*, 2199 Kālia Rd ☎808/923-2311. Afroth with orchids in the classiest hotel on Waikīkī Beach, this elegant yet relaxed seafood restaurant, open to the ocean and affording divine views of Diamond Head, is pricey but outstanding. Fusing Asian and island cooking, it offers a Madras seafood curry at lunch for $23, but it's most romantic at night, when entrees like *moi* with hearts of palm and steamed *onaga* start at $30

and the "Hawaii Centric" set menu costs $59. The elaborate Sunday brunch is a local favorite for special occasions. Mon–Sat 7.30–11am, 11.30am–2pm & 6–10pm, Sun 9.30am–2.30pm & 6–10pm.

Perry's Smorgy 2380 Kūhiō Ave ☎808/926-0184, ⓦwww.perryssmorgy.com. All-you-can-eat buffet, served indoors or in a Japanese-style garden. Though the food neither looks edible nor tastes of anything much, *Perry's* is always crowded with bargain-hunters. Choose from the $8 breakfast (ham, beef hash, sausages, pancakes, pastries, juices), the $9 lunch (mahimahi, Southern fried chicken, garlic bread, rice, baked macaroni, desserts), the $12 dinner (beef, shrimp, ribs, turkey, teriyaki chicken), or the $12 Sunday brunch. Mon–Sat 7–11am, 11.30am–2.30pm & 5–9pm, Sun 11.30am–2.30pm & 5–9pm.

Ramen Ezogiku 2146 Kalākaua Ave ☎808/926-8616. Bright, efficient noodle place (with two Waikīkī outlets), usually busy with Japanese tourists, which serves up large bowls of meat or seafood ramen or rice for well under $10, plus plump *gyoza* pork dumplings for $4.50. Daily 11am–11pm.

Roy's 226 Lewers St ☎808/923-7697, ⓦwww .roysrestaurant.com. Waikīkī finally has its first outlet of *Roy's* wildly popular chain of fusion-cuisine restaurants, in this glitzy, buzzy location in the Beach Walk development. Much bigger than it looks from the outside, it serves all *Roy's* beautifully presented, colorful signature dishes, like the succulent *misoyaki* butterfish, for lunch and dinner. Expect to pay around $40 for a full meal. Daily 11am–11pm.

Ruffage Natural Foods 2443 Kūhiō Ave ☎808/922-2042. Tiny wholefood grocery with a takeout counter and limited patio seating. The selection is great, with granola breakfasts and delicious $5 real-fruit and honey smoothies; avocado and bean-sprout sandwiches and vegan burritos; and salads, pasta, and tofu dishes. Most items cost around $7. From 6.30pm onwards, the front section transforms into an inexpensive sushi bar. Daily 9am–10.30pm.

Sansei Seafood Restaurant & Sushi Bar *Waikīkī Beach Marriott Resort*, 2552 Kalākaua Ave ☎808/931-6286, ⓦwww.sanseihawaii.com. Outstanding, well-priced food, whether you go for the Pacific Rim menu or stick to the sushi bar.

Sushi starts at $5 (try the Sansei Special, with spicy crab, cilantro, cucumber, and avocado, dusted with *furikake*). Entrees like grilled *opah* over fresh *nalo* greens, roasted Japanese jerk chicken, or duck breast in a foie gras demi-glaze, cost $18–40. Order before 6pm for reductions of 25 percent (Tues–Sat), or even 50 percent (Sun & Mon). Best of all, the $80 "Omakase" tasting menu for two is an amazing bargain, giving a balanced feast of seafood, sushi, and sashimi. The adjoining karaoke bar gets going when the restaurant closes. Daily 5.30–10pm; late-night sushi Fri & Sat until 2am.

Shore Bird Beach Broiler *Outrigger Reef*, 2169 Kalia Rd ☎808/922-2887. Perennially popular, cheap-and-cheerful open-air hotel restaurant, right on the beach, where the sumptuous views make up for less-than-inspiring food. The breakfast buffet costs $13, for lunch there's a $10 "healthy buffet" or entrees at $8–15, and dinner with an open salad bar is $18–25, depending on your choice of entree. Guests can cook their own meat or fish at a communal grill; kids adore it. Daily 7am–3pm & 4.30–10pm.

Singha Thai Cuisine 1910 Ala Moana Blvd ☎808/941-2898, ⓦwww.singhathai.com. Bright, elegant, dinner-only spot serving delicious Thai food with a Hawaiian tinge, including fresh fish and scallop dishes ($20 and up), plus curries and pad Thai (both around $16), and hot-and-sour soups ($6). Signature entrees, including spicy Siamese fighting fish, cost $20–32. Thai dancers perform nightly 7–9pm. Daily 4–11pm.

Todai Seafood Buffet 1910 Ala Moana Blvd ☎808/947-1000, ⓦwww.todai.com. Large, bustling outlet of a superb Japanese chain, in western Waikīkī. Lunch costs $15 (Mon–Fri) or $18 (Sat & Sun), while dinner is $29 (Mon–Thurs) or $30 (Fri–Sun), and for range and quality it's a real bargain. Delicious seafood dishes at the 160ft buffet bar include handmade sushi rolls, *ahi poke*, sashimi, shrimp, oysters, and scallops on the half-shell; cooked noodle dishes; and chicken teriyaki and pork for diehard carnivores. Even the desserts are good. Mon–Thurs 11.30am–2pm & 5.30–9.30pm, Fri 11.30am–2pm & 5–10pm, Sat 11.30am–2.30pm & 5–10pm, Sun 11am–2.30pm & 5–10pm.

Honolulu

No single district of **Honolulu** quite matches Waikīkī for its sheer concentration of eating options. Although **downtown** is all but deserted at night, nearby **Chinatown** abounds in inexpensive Chinese and Vietnamese places, with the Maunakea Market-place a total delight for fans of Asian-style fast food, while the malls along the **waterfront** hold plenty of alternatives. Both the Honolulu Academy of Arts (see p.74) and the Contemporary Museum (see p.80) have good cafés.

Alan Wong's 1857 S King St ☏808/949-2526, ⓦwww.alanwongs.com. Though expensive and hard to find – it's tucked away on the third floor in a nondescript area southwest of the University – *Alan Wong's* is one of Honolulu's most fashionable gourmet rendezvous, thanks to its fantastic contemporary Hawaiian cuisine. Besides changing daily specials, $12–20 appetizers always include the signature "da bag," a giant foil bag holding clams steamed with *kalua* pig, *shiitake* mushrooms, and spinach, and "poki-pines," crispy *ahi poke* wontons with avocado and wasabi. Typical entrees ($30–55) include ginger-crusted *onaga* (snapper) and oil-poached lamb rib-eye with three sauces. The nightly tasting menus cost $75 (five courses) and $95 (seven courses). Valet parking only. Daily 5–10pm.

Alan Wong's Pineapple Room Macy's, Ala Moana Center, 1450 Ala Moana Blvd ☏808/945-5529, ⓦwww.alanwongs.com. For dinner, this department-store offshoot of Honolulu's top gourmet restaurant – see above– is pretty much as pricey as the original, but earlier in the day it offers a much more affordable opportunity to sample Wong's delicious fusion cuisine, including his $12–18 take on local staples such as *loco moco* or *kalua* pork sandwiches. Mon–Fri 11am–8.30pm, Sat 8–10.30am & 11am–8.30pm, Sun 8–10.30am & 11am–3pm.

Cafe Laniakea YWCA, 1040 Richards St ☏808/524-8789. Lunch-only downtown cafeteria, very close to 'Iolani Palace, promising "local first, organic whenever possible, with Aloha always." Lots of inexpensive vegetarian dishes, with $10 salads and sandwiches and daily specials such as a half-chicken or grilled salmon ($12–15). Mon–Fri 11am–2pm.

Chai's Island Bistro Aloha Tower Marketplace, 101 Ala Moana Blvd ☏808/585-0011, ⓦwww.chaisislandbistro.com. Beautifully decorated pan-Asian restaurant, half indoors and half out, at the inland side of the Aloha Tower Marketplace. Though it's owned by the same chef as Waikīkī's *Singha Thai* (see p.93), the food can be a bit hit or miss and is not the main reason to visit: *Chai's* books the absolute crème de la crème of Hawaiian musicians to perform live, as detailed on p.96. Miss the show, scheduled for 7–8.30pm, and you'll be paying well over the norm for entrees like crispy whole snapper ($37) or grilled Mongolian lamb chops ($39). Lunch is significantly cheaper. Mon, Sat & Sun 4–10pm, Tues–Fri 11am–10pm.

Chef Mavro 1969 S King St ☏808/944-4714, ⓦwww.chefmavro.com. Despite his restaurant's unfashionable Mānoa location, Greek-born chef George Mavrothalassitis stands out in Honolulu's gourmet dining scene for his seasonally changing prix fixe menus (three courses $69, four $78, six $120, eleven-course "dégustation" $165). The menu sounds fussy – roasted loin of *kurobuta* pork with sansho jus, apple quinoa and savoy cabbage gribiche, say, or kobe-style roasted bavette and braised short rib with pancetta Brussels sprouts, truffle-accented celery-root purée and Pinot Noir sauce – but the food itself, a fusion of nouvelle contemporary Hawaiian, is delicate and delightful. Tues–Sat 6–9.30pm.

Grand Café & Bakery 31 N Pauahi St ☏808/531-0001. Airy Chinatown restaurant, established in the 1920s, where the appealingly old-fashioned feel extends to the menu. Choose from comfort food – pot roast, meat loaf – or more modern choices like grilled asparagus and poached-egg salad and tasty pastries and desserts. Breakfasts are particularly fine, based on tempting dishes like Banana Foster French toast. Tues–Thurs 7.30am–2pm, Fri 7.30am–2pm & 5.30–8.30pm, Sat 8am–1pm & 5.30–8.30pm, Sun 8am–1pm.

Gyotaku Japanese Restaurant 1824 S King St ☏808/949-4584, ⓦwww.gyotakuhawaii.com. In the morning, this is a hot spot for locals grabbing bento boxes – butterfish, teriyaki beef, tempura – for around $8. The dining room offers more bento, as well as a fine range of sushi and tempting noodles, wa-zen and *kamameshi*, from $12. The *poke don teishoku* ($16) is particularly tasty, with the fresh *poke* served over rice. No reservations. Bento takeout daily 10am–1pm; restaurant Sun–Thurs 11am–9pm, Fri & Sat 11am–10pm.

Hakkei 1436 Young St ☏808/944-6688, ⓦwww.hakkei-honolulu.com. Specializing in *washoku* cuisine, with unfussy dishes like *oden* (a flavorful hotpot cooked with anything from turnips and pumpkin to tofu and Japanese fish cake), crispy rice, home-made pickled vegetables and fresh veggies. $10–12 daily lunch specials – deep-fried butterfish, mushroom and soybean hotpot, scallop *kamameshi* – represent the best value. Opening hours can be irregular; call ahead to make sure. Daily except Mon 11am–2pm & 5–10.30pm.

Hiroshi Eurasian Tapas Waterfront Plaza, 500 Ala Moana Blvd ☏808/533-4476, ⓦwww.hiroshi hawaii.com. Anyone familiar with Spanish tapas shouldn't expect the same experience here; they profess to offer small plates, but these are more like largish appetizers, at prices ($9–16) that swiftly mount to a substantial check. As expected from the folks behind the superlative *Sansei* restaurants, the food, combining Mediterranean and pan-Asian cuisines – foie gras sushi, truffled crab cake, miso butterfish, Portuguese sausage potfillers – is across the board delicious, and the atmosphere contemporary and vibrant. Larger

plates – *onaga* with cauliflower purée, wilted tatsoi and fresh basil, for example – cost $24–28. Daily 5.30–9.30pm.

Indigo Eurasian Cuisine 1121 Nu'uanu Ave ⊤ 808/521-2900, Ⓦ www.indigo-hawaii.com. Chinatown's classiest option, a lovely space with indoor and outdoor seating, serves delicious nouvelle "Eurasian" crossover food, and is a favorite with President Obama. In addition to the good-value $16 lunch buffet, you can select from a broad range of dim sum ($7–12), including "thousand loved crab cakes", and entrees like wokked "Buddhist" vegetables ($16). Dinner entrees ($20–35) include sizzling fish and Mongolian lamb chops. The adjoining late-night *Green Room Lounge* has live music and dancing Tues–Sat. Tues–Fri 11.30am–2pm & 6–9.30pm, Sat 6–9.30pm.

Kaka'ako Kitchen Ward Center, 1200 Ala Moana Blvd ⊤ 808/596-7488. Cheery mall restaurant that dishes up home-cooking, Hawaiian style. The presentation is no-frills – after ordering at the counter, you eat with plastic cutlery from styrofoam boxes – but the food is healthy and excellent. Everything from the tempura catfish to the island-style chicken linguine or deli sandwiches costs $9–13, with daily specials for carnivores (meat loaf, pot roast, curry) and veggies (stir-fry tofu, eggplant parmesan) alike. Breakfast options include mahimahi with eggs for $8. Mon–Thurs 8am–9pm, Fri & Sat 8am–10pm, Sun 8am–5pm.

La Mariana Sailing Club 50 Sand Island Access Rd ⊤ 808/848-2800. Atmospheric old-time restaurant on an obscure stretch of Honolulu's industrial waterfront. The decor, original 1950s tiki-lounge styling mixed with South-Seas thrift-store kitsch, is the real thing, and the ambience – created by a crowd of eccentric locals and in-the-know tourists – decidedly surreal. Hearty fish appetizers like *taco poke* (marinated octopus) cost $7–15, while full dinners such as seafood brochette or *ahi* Cajun go for around $20. The main draw, however, is the impromptu live Hawaiian music on Friday evenings, from 6pm until 9pm; see p.97. Daily 11am–3pm & 5–9pm.

Legend Seafood Restaurant 100 N Beretania St ⊤ 808/532-1868. Chinatown seafood specialist in a modern building whose big plate-glass windows look out over the Nu'uanu Stream. The lunchtime dim sum trolleys are piled with individual portions at $3–5; full Chinese meals, with entrees including whole lobster or crab at $10–20, are served at both lunch and dinner. Mon–Fri 10.30am–2pm & 5.30–9pm, Sat & Sun 8am–2pm & 5.30–9pm.

Legend Vegetarian 100 N Beretania St ⊤ 808/532-8218. Bright, lunch-only Chinese vegetarian restaurant in the heart of Chinatown.

The menu features beef balls, cuttlefish, pork ribs, and tenderloin, but all the dishes, priced well under $10, are actually tofu or other vegetarian ingredients shaped and flavored to resemble meats and fishes. There's also a wide selection of vegetarian dim sum, plus conventional vegetable dishes. No alcohol. Daily except Wed 10.30am–2pm.

Little Village Noodle House 1113 Smith St ⊤ 808/545-3008. Smart and friendly restaurant in the heart of Chinatown, offering a perfectly prepared range of delicious Chinese dishes from Singapore noodles ($8) through salt-and-pepper pork ($9.50) to clams in black-bean sauce ($13.50). The special Hong Kong menu has congees and noodle soups from $5. Sun–Thurs 10.30am–10.30pm, Fri & Sat 10.30am–midnight.

Mei Sum 1170 Nu'uanu Ave ⊤ 808/531-3268. No-frills, high-quality dim sum restaurant, recently moved to bright and clean new premises. The trolleys are heaving all day with tasty $2–4 snacks. Tasty options include seafood or mushroom chicken dumplings, turnip cake, deep-fried scallops in taro leaves, and *char siu* buns. Noodle, rice, and wonton entrees, featuring chicken, prawns, scallops, or calamari, are also available for $7–12 per plate. A full dinner for four is just $40. Daily 7am–8.45pm.

Olive Tree Café 4614 Kīlauea Ave ⊤ 808/737-0303. Simple, understated Greek deli, adjoining but not technically within Kāhala Mall, with some outdoor seating. The value is unbeatable, and the food is great, ranging from refreshing tomato and feta cheese salads to a lovely ceviche of New Zealand mussels ($8), or souvlaki skewers of chicken or fish ($9–12). No credit cards. Daily 5–10pm.

Pavilion Café Honolulu Academy of Arts, 900 S Beretania St ⊤ 808/532-8734. With its zestful Mediterranean sandwiches and salads at $12–20, this appealing little lunch-only courtyard bistro makes the perfect midday stop while exploring downtown. Tues–Sat 11.30am–2pm, plus third Sun of each month 11.30am–2pm.

Phô 97 176 Maunakea Marketplace, Maunakea St ⊤ 808/538-0708. This large Chinatown restaurant, technically in the Maunakea Marketplace but entered direct from Maunakea Street, is the best place to sample Vietnamese *phô* (noodle soup). Also lots of Cambodian, Thai, and Vietnamese noodle and rice dishes, plus barbecued pork, simmered catfish, and crab-meat soup. The portions are huge, and almost nothing costs more than $10. Daily 8am–9pm.

Sam Choy's Breakfast, Lunch and Crab 580 N Nimitz Hwy ⊤ 808/545-7979, Ⓦ www.samchoy .com. A mile or two west of downtown, tightly sandwiched between the west- and east-bound sides of the Nimitz Highway, this garish Hawaiian

diner looks unenticing from the outside. Inside you'll find a full-sized sampan fishing boat, the gleaming *Big Aloha* microbrewery, and crowds of diners eager to gorge on celebrity chef Choy's trademark local cuisine. Crab is a feature, of course, along with hefty breakfasts (from $6) – go for the Hawaiian specialties, like *kalua* pork *loco moco* – and plate lunches ($9–17) that come very big indeed – the fried *poke* ($12.50) is a must. Evening entrees ($18–32) include fresh fish, paella, crabs' legs, and roasted or steamed whole crabs and lobsters. Restaurant Mon–Thurs 7am–2pm & 5–9.30pm, Fri 7am–2pm & 5–10pm, Sat 8am–2pm & 5–10pm, Sun 8am–2pm & 5–9.30pm; brewery daily 10.30am until late.

Summer Frappé 1120 Maunakea St, store 192 ☏808/728-3180. Hole-in-the-wall juice and snack bar in the courtyard behind Chinatown's Maunakea Marketplace food hall. With shaded outdoor seating, it's a great place to restore yourself with a delicious fresh exotic-fruit smoothie, or a fruity bubble tea studded with tapioca pearls. Daily 7.30am–6pm.

Yakiniku Camellia Buffet 2494 S Beretania St ☏808/946-7955. Authentic Korean buffet restaurant a mile north of Waikīkī, just south of the University. The few non-Korean speakers who venture in have to fend for themselves, joining families and hungry locals heaping their plates again and again. Whether at lunch ($14) or dinner ($21), the food is a treat; you select slices of marinated beef, chicken, or pork from refrigerated cabinets and grill them yourself at the gas-fired burners set into each table. There are also lots of vegetables, as well as super-fresh salads, including octopus, seaweed, *ahi poke*, pickles, and delicious tiny dried fish. Daily 10.30am–10pm.

Entertainment and nightlife

Tourists staying in Waikīkī will find plenty of resort **entertainment**, with (often free) **Hawaiian music** performances as well as live gigs in other genres and theatrical spectaculars. Waikīkī also holds plenty of **clubs**, geared more towards younger tastes in music. Nightlife elsewhere in Honolulu is more diverse, ranging from upscale clubs frequented by urban professionals to a grungier scene for surfers and students who wouldn't be seen dead in Waikīkī. Magazines and papers to keep you abreast of what's going on include the free *Honolulu Weekly* newspaper (Ⓦwww.honolulu weekly.com), and the *TGIF* section of Friday's *Honolulu Advertiser* (Ⓦwww.honolulu advertiser.com). See p.31 for a calendar of festivals and events on Oahu.

Hawaiian entertainment

It's not hard to find **Hawaiian entertainment** in Waikīkī; many of the grander hotels feature accomplished Hawaiian musicians most evenings. Although some are very good indeed, it's well worth looking out for events arranged for Hawaiian, rather than tourist, audiences, such as the one-off performances and benefit concerts at downtown's beautiful Hawaii Theater (see p.76).

Away from the hotels, the best regular **free shows** of Hawaiian music are given by the **Royal Hawaiian Band** (Ⓦwww.royalhawaiianband.com), which, throughout the year except August, gives hour-long performances on Fridays at noon on the lawns of 'Iolani Palace downtown, and Sundays at 2pm in Waikīkī's Kapiolani Park.

For more on hula and Hawaiian music, see p.438.

Banyan Veranda *Moana Surfrider*, 2365 Kalākaua Ave, Waikīkī ☏808/922-3111. Open-air beach bar that was home to the nationally syndicated *Hawaii Calls* radio show from the 1930s to the 1970s. Steel guitar and hula dancers nightly 6–8pm, followed by small Hawaiian ensembles 8–10.30pm. No cover, but a one-drink minimum.

Chai's Island Bistro Aloha Tower Marketplace, 101 Ala Moana Blvd ☏808/585-0011, Ⓦwww.chaisislandbistro .com. Fine Hawaiian musicians perform for diners at this expensive Thai/pan-Asian restaurant (see p.94) nightly 7–8.30pm. Precise schedules vary, but currently include long-term residencies by Robert Cazimero (Tues), the Brothers Cazimero (Wed), Sista Robi Kahakalau (Thurs), and regular appearances by Na Palapalai.

Lū'aus

If you want to go to a **lū'au** (a commercial approximation of a traditional Hawaiian feast) while you're in Waikīkī, the best option is the lavish **'Aha 'Aina** at the *Royal Hawaiian Hotel* on Monday at 5.30pm ($145, $65 ages 5–12; ☏808/931-8383). Making the most of its romantic Waikīkī Beach setting, this "Royal Celebration" includes a fine spread of food and a high-quality open-air show of music and performance from Hawaii and beyond, rooted in the history of the *Royal Hawaiian* itself, as well as super-abundant cocktails.

The two biggest *lū'aus* on Oahu are **Germaine's** (nightly 6pm; $72, ages 14–20 $62, ages 6–13 $52; ☏808/949-6626 or 1-800/367-5655, ⓦ www.germainesluau.com) and **Paradise Cove** (nightly 6pm; $80, ages 13–20 $70, ages 4–12 $60; deluxe options available; ☏808/842-5911 or 1-800/775-2683, ⓦ www.paradisecove.com). What their ubiquitous ads may not make clear is that both take place thirty miles from Waikīkī, in the far southwestern corner of the island. The price – activity centers offer cheaper rates – includes an hour-long bus trip each way (singalongs compulsory), and you're rewarded at the end with tacky souvenirs, bland food, weak cocktails, and third-rate entertainment.

Finally, as detailed on p.113, there's also a *lū'au* at the **Polynesian Cultural Center**, near Oahu's northeastern tip (Mon–Sat 5.15–6.30pm; ☏808/293-3333 or 1-800/367-7060, ⓦ www.polynesia.com). That's a more "educational" experience, as you can only attend as part of a longer visit to the center, but it's still basically a stage show accompanied by an unremarkable (and alcohol-free) buffet dinner. The cheapest admission price for *lū'au* visitors is $88 for adults, $64 ages 3–11, plus a minimum of $19 per person for transportation from Waikīkī.

Duke's Canoe Club *Outrigger Waikīkī*, 2335 Kalākaua Ave, Waikīkī ☏808/922-2268, ⓦ www .dukeswaikiki.com. Oceanfront cocktail bar/restaurant that hosts big-name "Concerts on the Beach" Fri–Sun 4–6pm. No cover charge.

🏃 **Honey's at Ko'olau** *Ko'olau Golf Club*, 45-550 Kionaole Rd, Kāne'ohe ☏808/236-4653. You'll need a car and a good map to find this unlikely, windward hangout. Cross the mountains on the Pali Hwy, turn left onto Kamehameha Hwy, and then left again immediately north of H-3; *Honey's* is downstairs in the clubhouse. The reason to make the effort? Genial aa wizard Eddie Kamae, founding member of the Sons of Hawaii, presides over a hugely enjoyable afternoon jam session on Sundays 3.30–6pm. Arrive early to get a good seat; full food menu available. No cover.

🏃 **House Without a Key** *Halekūlani*, 2199 Kālia Rd, Waikīkī ☏808/923-2311. Waikīkī Beach's loveliest venue to watch the sunset, this very romantic, very spacious open-air beach bar was named after a Charlie Chan mystery. The evening cocktail hour (5–9pm) is an unmissable bargain, with very gentle, old-time Hawaiian classics performed under an ancient *kiawe* tree and hula dancing by a former Miss Hawaii. You're led to your seats, which avoids the scrum for an oceanfront spot at other beach bars. Drinks prices are very reasonable and service is friendly and courteous, and they also serve a delicious snack and sushi menu all day. Daily 7am–9pm, no cover.

🏃 **La Mariana Sailing Club** 50 Sand Island Access Rd ☏808/848-2800. An extremely quirky waterfront restaurant – reviewed on p.95 – with an authentic 1950s ambience, hidden away amid the docks of Honolulu. The week's high point is Friday evening, from 8.30pm onwards, when pianist Ron Miyashiro and a group of semi-professional singers work their way through a nostalgic set of classic Hawaiian songs, but there's also live piano music nightly except Mon 5–9pm. Not to be missed, as it's practically the last of a dying breed. No cover.

🏃 **Moana Terrace** *Waikīkī Beach Marriott*, 2552 Kalākaua Ave, Waikīkī ☏808/922-6611. A consistently good roster of Hawaiian musicians perform each night at this lively, open-air, third-story cocktail bar, across the road from the beach; starts 8pm Sun, 6.30pm otherwise. No cover.

Bars, live music, and dancing

There's rarely a clear distinction between **bars**, **live music venues**, and **nightclubs** in Honolulu – for that matter, many restaurants get in on the act as well. The biggest

touring acts tend to appear at Pearl Harbor's Aloha Stadium (☎808/483-2500, ⓦwww.alohastadium.hawaii.gov) or downtown's Blaisdell Center (☎808/527-5400, ⓦwww.blaisdellcenter.com), while the Waikīkī Shell (also ☎808/527-5400, ⓦwww.blaisdellcenter.com) hosts more local events. All the venues listed below have a cover charge, unless otherwise noted.

Anna Bannanas 2440 S Beretania St, Honolulu ☎808/046 6100. Univoroity diotriot bar with reasonable prices, live R&B and reggae most nights, and a hectic weekend atmosphere. Daily 9pm–2am.

Hank's Cafe 1038 Nu'uanu Ave, Honolulu ☎808/526-1410, ⓦwww.hankscafehonolulu.com. Small art gallery-cum-bar in Chinatown, with an appealing retro feel, staging regular live music jams, some Hawaiian, some not. On the second floor, in what was once a tattoo parlor – hence the impressive mural – you'll find *The Dragon Upstairs*, which puts on live jazz Thurs–Sun. Mon 3–10pm, Tues–Sun 3pm–2am.

Lewers Lounge *Halekūlani*, 2199 Kālia Rd, Waikīkī ☎808/923-2311. Sophisticated nightspot that looks more like an English drawing room than a Waikīkī bar, and offers the finest cocktail menu in town. Live jazz Wed–Sat 8.30pm–midnight, at its best Wed & Thurs, when bass player Bruce Hamada performs.

Nashville Waikīkī 2330 Kūhiō Ave, Waikīkī ☎808/926-7911, ⓦwww.nashvillewaikiki.com. If you're hankering to hoe-down in Hawaii, this country-music club below the *Ohana West* has plenty of room to show off your rhinestones. Check

ahead: it also hosts DJ nights. Pool tables and darts, too. Daily 4pm 4am.

Oceans 808 Waterfront Plaza, 500 Ala Moana Blvd ☎808/531-8444, ⓦwww.oceanclubonline.com. Big, loud, and glitzy bar/nightclub that's a major hangout for downtown's after-work crowd. No under-23s allowed Fri & Sat; ages 21 & 22 also welcome Tues–Thurs. The short snack menu is half-price before 8pm; after that, there's a $5 cover charge, and the dancing continues late into the night. Tues–Fri 4.30pm–4am, Sat 9pm–4am.

Pipeline 805 Pohukaina St, Honolulu ☎808/589-1999, ⓦwww.pipelinecafehawaii.com. Just behind the Ala Moana Center, this is a favorite with the surf set, who come for DJ music most nights, comedy on Wednesdays, and perhaps one rock or reggae gig per week. Door policy varies nightly between over-20s and over-17s; call to check. Mon–Thurs 9pm–4am, Fri & Sat 10pm–4am.

Zanzabar WaikīkīTrade Center, 2255 Kūhiō Ave, Waikīkī ☎808/924-3939, ⓦwww.zanzabarhawaii.com. Extremely opulent nightclub, bursting with Egyptian motifs, and pumping out dance music to the well-heeled youth of Honolulu. Nightly except Mon 8pm–4am.

Gay Honolulu

While Honolulu's **gay scene** focuses largely on **Kūhīo Avenue** in central Waikīkī, the obvious first step for gay travelers is an evening at the legendary *Hula's Bar and Lei Stand* on Waikīkī's eastern fringe. Pacific Ocean Holidays (☎808/545-5252 or 1-800/735-6600, ⓦwww.gayhawaiivacations.com) organizes all-inclusive **package vacations** in Hawaii for gay and lesbian travelers, and maintains the useful ⓦwww.gay hawaii.com **website**. A gay **hiking** club, Likehike (☎808/455-8193, ⓦwww.gayhawaii.com/likehike), organizes group hikes on alternate Sundays.

Gay bars and clubs

Fusion 2260 Kūhiō Ave, Waikīkī ☎808/924-2422, ⓦwww.fusionwaikiki.com. Wild, split-level nightclub, with male strippers, drag acts, free karaoke Mon & Tues, and special drink discounts. Sun–Thurs 10pm–4am, Fri & Sat 8pm–4am.

Hula's Bar and Lei Stand *Waikīkī Grand Hotel*, 134 Kapahulu Ave, Waikīkī ☎808/923-0669, ⓦwww.hulas.com. Waikīkī's most popular and long-standing gay club occupies a suite of ocean-view rooms on the second floor of the *Waikīkī Grand*, across from the Honolulu Zoo. In addition to a state-of-the-art dance bar equipped with giant video screens, there's a more casual lounge area. Daily 10am–2am.

In-Between 2155 Lau'ula St, Waikīkī ☎808/926-7060. Local gay karaoke bar in the heart of Waikīkī, open Mon–Sat 4pm–2am, Sun 2pm–2am.

Shopping

Virtually all the shops in both Honolulu and Waikīkī are in purpose-built **malls**. For many years, Honolulu's **Ala Moana Center** held undisputed sway as the city's premier mall for serious shoppers, but it has been so successful in attracting big spenders that new rivals are springing up all the time. Even Waikīkī has made a definite move away from its traditional emphasis on souvenirs and beach accessories, with the **Beach Walk** the most prominent of several new or revamped malls.

Waikīkī shopping

If you want to buy a T-shirt, a beach mat, or a monkey carved out of a coconut, Waikīkī is definitely the place for you. Kalākaua and Kūhiō avenues especially are lined with cut-price souvenir stores; there are almost forty shops in the ABC chain alone, all open daily from 7am to midnight and selling basic groceries along with postcards, sun lotions, and other tourist essentials.

Waikīkī's largest malls, the monolithic **Royal Hawaiian Shopping Center** and the **DFS Galeria**, across the street at 330 Royal Hawaiian Ave, are aseptic, upmarket enclaves, packed with designer-clothing shops, jewelry stores and sunglasses emporiums. They've recently been joined by a similar array of stores at the **Beach Walk** nearby. By way of contrast, the venerable 1950s-style open-air **International Marketplace**, 2330 Kalākaua Ave (daily 10am–10.30pm), is still clinging on. With its simple wooden stalls scattered among the trees, it has a lot more atmosphere than the malls, though the "crafts" on sale tend to be made in Taiwan, while the "psychic readers" are as a rule devoid of paranormal powers. In addition, the two largest hotels, the *Hyatt Regency* and the *Hilton Hawaiian Village*, also hold their own upscale shopping.

While modern imitations and reproductions are available everywhere you look, it's harder than you'd expect to find that quintessential emblem of old Hawaii, the authentic **aloha shirt**. Whether you're prepared to spend thousands of dollars for an original, or happy to settle for a well-priced replica, head to Bailey's, 517 Kapahulu Ave (☎808/734-7628).

Honolulu shopping

The **Ala Moana Center** (Mon–Thurs 9.30am–9pm, Fri 9.30am–10pm, Sat 8am–10pm, Sun 10am–7pm; ☎808/955-9517, ⓦwww.alamoana.com), a mile west of Waikīkī, has since 1959 been Hawaii's main shopping destination; neighbor-island residents fly to Honolulu specifically in order to shop here. One of the largest open-air malls in the world, and still growing year on year, it holds several major department stores, including Sears, Macy's, and Neiman Marcus, as well as an Apple store and a small Barnes & Noble bookstore. Couture designers are represented by the likes of Burberry, Gucci, and Jimmy Choo, and upscale street-style by DKNY, Diesel, and Shanghai Tang. Be sure to explore the Japanese department store Shirokiya, which has a fabulous upstairs food-hall, piled high with sushi and *poi*, and also stocks a great array of bargain electronics.

The various **Ward** malls – the Centre, Warehouse, Farmers Market, Gateway Center, and Village Shops – spread themselves across four blocks along and behind Ala Moana Boulevard, starting a couple of blocks west of the Ala Moana Center. Accessible, like the Ala Moana Center, on both TheBus and the Waikīkī Trolley pink line ($2), this complex, in particular the Ward Centre, has become a serious rival to its bigger neighbor, with a more intimate atmosphere and some distinctive, locally owned stores. Highlights include the large Borders book and music store in the Ward Centre (Mon–Thurs 9am–11pm, Fri & Sat 9am–midnight,

Sun 9am–10pm; ☎808/591-8995); the excellent Native Books/Na Mea Hawaii in the Ward Warehouse (Mon–Sat 10am–9pm, Sun 10am–6pm; ☎808/596-8885, Ⓦwww.nativebookshawaii.com), which stocks great local crafts products, along with Hawaiian books and CDs; and the very feminine jewelry, home furnishings and gifts in Cottage by the Sea, again in the Ward Warehouse (Mon–Sat 10am–9pm, Sun 10am–5pm; ☎808/591-9811, Ⓦwww.cottagehawaii.com).

Downtown's **Aloha Tower Marketplace** (Mon–Sat 9am–9pm, Sun 9am–6pm; ☎808/566-2337, Ⓦwww.alohatower.com; see p.77) has failed to lure significant numbers of tourists away from Ala Moana, and is looking a little tired, verging on the downmarket, but the dockside setting makes it a fun place to wander around. Most of the seventy or so stores are one-of-a-kind rather than chain outlets.

Only a couple of miles from Waikīkī, *mauka* of Diamond Head, the **Kāhala Mall**, 4211 Waialae Ave (Mon–Sat 10am–9pm, Sun 10am–5pm; Ⓦwww.kahalamallcenter .com), is almost as chic as – though smaller and far less frenzied than – Ala Moana. As well as Macy's, Longs Drugs, an Apple store, Banana Republic, Reyn's aloha wear, Compleat Kitchen, an eight-screen movie theater, and an assortment of restaurants, it holds an excellent Barnes & Noble bookstore.

It's also well worth strolling the streets and markets of **Chinatown**, which hold all sorts of unexpected and one-of-a-kind stalls and stores. At Xin Xin's Fashion, 1011C Maunakea St (Mon–Sat 9.30am–5pm, Sun 9.30am–3pm; ☎808/531-8885), you'll find a fine selection of satin *cheong sams*, pretty parasols, and exquisite little paper ornaments.

Finally, for distinctive Hawaiian gifts, head to the stores at the Honolulu Academy of Arts (see p.74) and the Contemporary Museum (see p.80).

The rest of Oahu

Assuming you're based, like almost all visitors to Oahu, in Waikīkī, you're only likely to see the rest of the island on day-trips. The first thing you need to know, then, is that it's too big to see in a single day. Realistically, there are two obvious itineraries. A loop around **southeast Oahu** can include highlights such as famed snorkel destination **Hanauma Bay**, the Sea Life Park, and the gorgeous beach at **Kailua**, while crossing the mountains from Honolulu straight to Kailua gives you time to drive up the glorious and remarkably unspoiled **windward coast**, and return via the **North Shore** surfing beaches. Linger any length of time at destinations like the hugely popular theme-park **Polynesian Cultural Center**, the more natural **Waimea Valley**, or funky **Hale'iwa** town, and you'll need to plan at least another day's exploring into the bargain.

Southeast Oahu

The high crest of the Ko'olau Mountains curves away to the east beyond Honolulu, providing Oahu with its elongated **southeastern promontory**. The built-up coastal strip is squeezed ever more tightly between the hills and the ocean, but not until you reach **Koko Head**, eight miles out from Waikīkī and eleven from downtown,

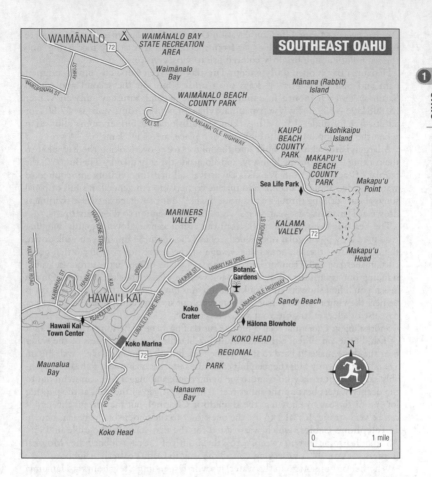

WAIMĀNALO

WAIMĀNALO BAY
STATE RECREATION
AREA

Waimānalo
Bay

WAIMĀNALO BEACH
COUNTY PARK

KALANIANA'OLE HIGHWAY

Mānana (Rabbit)
Island

KAUPŪ
BEACH
COUNTY
PARK

Kāohikaipu
Island

MAKAPU'U
BEACH
COUNTY
PARK

Sea Life Park

Makapu'u
Point

MARINERS
VALLEY

KALAMA
VALLEY

72

Makapu'u
Head

HAWAI'I KAI DRIVE

Botanic
Gardens

Koko
Crater

Hālona Blowhole

Sandy Beach

HAWAI'I KAI

Hawaii Kai
Town Center

Koko Marina

72

KOKO HEAD
REGIONAL
PARK

N

Maunalua
Bay

Hanauma
Bay

Koko Head

0   1 mile

do you really feel you've left the city behind. Thereafter, however, the shoreline is magnificent, punctuated by towering volcanoes, sheltered lagoons, and great beaches.

H-1 ends at the Kāhala Mall, just beyond Diamond Head (see p.69), to become Hwy-72, or **Kalaniana'ole Highway**. Both **Kāhala** itself, and **Hawaii Kai** further along, are upmarket residential communities that have little to attract visitors, and no desire to encourage them. Hawaii Kai spreads back inland to either side of the large Kuapa Pond, an ancient fishpond that has been remodeled to create the Koko Marina.

Hanauma Bay

Beautiful **Hanauma Bay** is barely half a mile beyond Hawaii Kai, just across the volcanic ridge of Koko Head. So curved as to be almost round, the bay was created when part of yet another volcano – southeast Oahu is one long chain of minor volcanic cones – collapsed to let in the sea. This spellbinding spot, where a thin strip of palms and sand nestles beneath a green cliff, is famous as Oahu's best place to **snorkel**. As a result, it receives almost a million visitors per year, which in turn poses a constant threat to the fragile underwater environment. In fact, overuse has killed off much of the coral reef near the shore, and since the 1960s, Hanauma

Bay has been a Marine Life Conservation District where organized tour parties are banned. While the reef itself is far from spectacular, it is slowly recovering, and the sea holds enough brightly colored fish to satisfy visitors.

Hanauma Bay is open **daily except Tuesday** between 6am and 7pm in summer, 6am and 6pm in winter; it stays open until 10pm on the second and fourth Saturday of each month in summer, and the second Saturday only in winter (☎808/396-4229, ⓦwww.hanaumabayhawaii.com). Admission is $7.50 for adults, free for under-13s, with parking an additional $1. Drivers aren't allowed in when the parking lot is full; to be sure of a place, arrive by 9am.

A large **visitor center** is built into the hilltop rocks overlooking the bay, next to the parking lot just off the highway, and alongside the stop used by TheBus #22, the regular "Beach Bus" from Waikīkī. On arrival, all first-time visitors are required to watch a video about Hanauma and marine conservation in general. It's full of banal songs about "drifting through a turquoise dream," but an average of twelve swimmers drown at Hanauma each year, so it's worth paying attention to the safety tips.

The beach is five minutes' walk from the visitor center, down a gently winding road used only by a regular open-sided trolley (75¢ down, $1 up). As you walk down, the ridge that is the sole remaining vestige of the crater rim rises like a rich green curtain ahead of you. From up here you can see patches of reef in the turquoise water, standing out against the sandy seabed, and swarms of fish are clearly visible. On the beach you'll find showers and drinking fountains but no food – the only snack bar is up near the visitor center. A pavilion here rents out **snorkel equipment**, at $6–11 per day; use of a locker to store your valuables costs $5.

Snorkeling at Hanauma feels a bit like snorkeling in an aquarium. You'll see a lot of fish, but it can all feel rather tame and predictable. The shallowness of the water near the shore makes it hard to stay off the reef, but it's essential to try – walking on a coral reef not only kills the reef, but can cause cuts that take weeks to heal. Reasonably skilled swimmers who want to see living coral, and bigger fish, can swim out to the deeper waters beyond the inner reef. The largest gap in the reef, at the parking lot end of the bay, is known as the **Backdoor Channel**, but the current through it can be very strong. It's safer to use the one closer to the middle of the beach, known as **Telephone Cables**, which was blasted for the first trans-Pacific cable in 1956. Another fearsome current sweeps across the mouth of the bay; dubbed the "Molokai Express," it's capable of carrying you all the way to Oahu's easterly neighbor.

Whether or not you go in the water, it's worth spending a few hours at Hanauma Bay no matter how crowded it is. The crisp green lawns along the foot of the *pali*, dotted with banyan trees, are ideal for picnics. Due to landslides, however, you cannot walk along the rocky ledge at either end of the beach, just above sea level.

Koko Head and Koko Crater

A dirt road leads away immediately right after the highway turnoff for Hanauma Bay – before the parking lot – to climb straight along the bare ridge above the beach. While the road is closed to drivers, whether it's open to hikers seems to vary. Take it if you can – there are great views from the 642ft summit of **Koko Head**, roughly fifteen minutes' walk away. From there you can see back to the similar peak of Diamond Head above Waikīkī, and also walk down a footpath around the lesser of its two craters to peek into the southern end of Hanauma Bay.

Koko Head Regional Park, which covers Koko Head and Hanauma Bay, extends another couple of miles northeast to take in **Koko Crater**. The youngest – and thus the largest and most completely formed – of southeastern Oahu's volcanic cones, this is considerably higher than Koko Head and makes a very impressive spectacle. Like its neighbor, it is topped by a double crater. However, it's not possible to walk up to or around the crater rim.

Hālona Blowhole

A couple of miles beyond Hanauma Bay, where Kalanianaʻole Highway squeezes between Koko Crater and the ocean, a roadside parking lot enables round-island drivers – and a *lot* of tour buses – to take a look at the **Hālona Blowhole**. The coastline here consists of layer upon layer of flat lava, each sheet set slightly back from the one below to form a stairway up from the sea. At the Hālona Blowhole, the waves have carved out a cave below the visible top layer, and as each new wave rushes in, it's forced out through a small hole to create a waterspout that can reach up to 50ft high. The blowhole itself does not go straight down, but is stepped; if you fall in – and people do – it's almost impossible to get out.

Little **Hālona Cove**, right of the Blowhole overlook and sheltered by tall stratified cliffs, holds enough sand to make a welcome private beach, if you're lucky enough to have it to yourself. Only swimming within the cove itself is at all safe, and even then only in summer.

Sandy Beach

Avoiding the crowds is not at all the point at **Sandy Beach**, half a mile further on as the shoreline flattens out between Koko Crater and Makapuʻu Head. Kids from all over Oahu meet up here most weekends for the best **body-surfing** and **boogie-boarding** in Hawaii; Barack Obama famously remains a devotee. This is also one of the few places on the island where the waves remain high enough in summer to tempt pro surfers. Tourists who try to join in soon find that riding surf of this size takes a lot of skill and experience; the beach itself is notorious for serious injuries. If you just want to watch, settle down in the broad sands that lie southwest of the central lava spit. There are normally several kite-flyers around as well. Swimming is never safe at Sandy Beach, but beyond the spit it's all but suicidal.

Makapuʻu Point

The rising bulk of Oahu's easternmost point, **Makapuʻu Head**, pushes Hwy-72 away from the coastline as it swings round to run back up the island's windward flank. Shortly before it finishes climbing up the last low incline of the Koʻolau Ridge, there's just about room to park beside the road at **Makapuʻu State Wayside**. A dirt road here snakes off to the right, soon curving south towards the hillock of Puʻu O Kipahulu. An hour-long round-trip hike wends around the hill and back north along the coastal cliffs to **Makapuʻu Point**. From the viewing platform at the end you can look straight down the cliffs to the Makapuʻu lighthouse below, out to Molokai, back to Koko Head, and up along the spine of eastern Oahu.

Rounding Makapuʻu Point on the highway is an equally memorable experience. The coastal *pali* suddenly soars to your left, while straight out to sea a couple of tiny islands, off-limits to visitors, stand out in misty silhouette. The larger of the two, Manana – also known as **Rabbit Island** – was named for its population of wild rabbits, who share their home only with sea birds.

Makapuʻu Beach County Park

Few drivers can resist stopping to drink in the views as they descend from Makapuʻu Point. The first proper parking lot, however, is down below, at **Makapuʻu Beach County Park**. In summer, this is a broad and attractive strip of sand; in winter, pounded by heavy surf, it's a rocky stretch. Swimming is rarely safe even at the best of times – ask the lifeguards if you're in doubt. Like Sandy Beach (see above), however, it's a much loved **body-surfing** and **boogie-boarding** site, with a similar propensity to lure unwary tourists into the water, and dismal record of fatalities.

Sea Life Park

Immediately opposite the Makapu'u Beach parking lot, **Sea Life Park** tends to hold greater appeal for children than for their parents (daily 10.30am–5pm; adults $30, ages 4–12 $20; ⊤1-866/365-7466, ⓦwww.sealifeparkhawaii.com). Along with the predictable dolphin and porpoise shows, it holds a giant Reef Tank, a penguin enclosure, and a hospital for injured monk seals. You can also have your own close-up encounter with the dolphins, for a fee of up to $200, depending on the degree of contact. In addition, the park raises rare green sea turtles for release into the ocean, and has even bred a **wholphin** – half-whale, half-dolphin. A couple of snack bars, and a bar run by the Gordon Biersch Brewery, make it all too possible to spend an entire day here.

Waimānalo

WAIMĀNALO, four miles on from Makapu'u, holds one of the highest proportions of native Hawaiians of any town on Oahu, and was home to the late singing superstar Israel Kamakawiwo'ole (see p.442). The main drag, lined with fast-food joints, is far from picturesque, but as long as you take care not to intrude, you can get a real glimpse of old-time Hawaii by exploring the back roads. The small family-run farms and nurseries along Waikupanaha Street, which runs inland along the base of the *pali*, are particularly rural and verdant.

The most compelling reason to come to Waimānalo, however, is its **beach**. At over three miles long, it's the longest stretch of sand on Oahu, and the setting, with high promontories at both ends and a green cradle of cliffs behind, is superb. The most accessible place to park, and also the safest swimming spot, is **Waimānalo Beach County Park** at its southern end, but wherever you start you're likely to feel tempted to stroll a long way over the seemingly endless sands.

About a mile further north, where the fir trees backing the beach grow thicker again beyond a residential district, you come to the **Waimānalo Bay Beach Park**. The waves here are a little rougher than those at the county park, but it feels even more secluded, and you can **camp** for up to five days with a permit from the county parks office in Honolulu (free; closed Wed & Thurs; see p.52).

Further on still, and reached by a separate road off the highway, lies **Bellows Field Beach Park**. Access to this pristine spot, ideal for lazy swimmers and novice body-surfers, is controlled by the adjoining Air Force base; the public is only allowed in between noon on Friday and 8am on Monday. The county parks office runs a **campground** here too, which is also open on weekends only.

Windward Oahu

Less than ten miles separate downtown Honolulu from Oahu's spectacular **windward coast**. Climb inland along either the **Pali Highway** (see p.84) or **Likelike Highway** (see p.86), and at the knife-edge crest of the Ko'olau Mountains you're confronted by amazing views of the serrated *pali* (cliff) that sweeps from northwest to southeast. As often as not, the abrupt transition from west to east is marked by the arrival of **rain** – it has, after all, been raining on this side of the island for several million years, cutting away at the cliffs to create a long, sheer wall.

The mountain highways drop down to the twin residential communities of **Kailua** and **Kāne'ohe**. Both are large towns by Hawaiian standards, and neither holds much to appeal to visitors. However, the adjacent **beaches** are quite superb –

Kailua Beach County Park in particular is a sun-kissed, sparkling-watered strand that's idyllic for swimming. If quality beach time is your major vacation priority, it's well worth coming to Kailua for the whole day, or even basing yourself in a local B&B rather than in Waikīkī.

If, on the other hand, you're trying to see as much of Oahu as possible on a single day's driving tour, you'd probably do better to avoid Kailua and Kāne'ohe altogether, and head straight off north on **Hwy-83**. Sandwiched between a tempting fringe of golden sand and a ravishing belt of well-watered farmland and tree-covered slopes, this clings to the coastline all the way up to Oahu's northernmost tip. On most Hawaiian islands, the windward shore is too exposed to be safe for swimming, but here a protective coral reef makes bathing possible at a succession of narrow, little-used **beaches**. All are open to the public, but use proper paths to reach them. Oahu is also exceptional among the Hawaiian islands in having picturesque little **islets** just offshore; you're unlikely to set foot on any of them, but they provide a lovely backdrop.

Though driving through such luscious scenery is a real joy, there are few specific reasons to stop. The **Byōdō-In Temple**, testament to the importance of the Japanese presence in Hawaii, is a tranquil stop, while further north the very different **Polynesian Cultural Center** attracts a million visitors each year. Otherwise you might want to spend an hour or two hiking in the backcountry, in places like **Kahana Valley** or **Hau'ula**.

Kailua

The shorefront town of **KAILUA** stretches along Kailua Bay roughly four miles down from the Nu'uanu Pali lookout (see p.85), and four miles north from Waimānolo. Now little more than an exclusive suburb of Honolulu, it was once a favorite dwelling place for the chiefs of Oahu, surrounded by wetlands and rich soil ideal for growing taro; more recently it's become famous as the favored winter retreat of **President Obama**, who rents a home near the stunning beach.

Almost the only remaining vestige of Kailua's past is **Ulupō Heiau**, an ancient *luakini* temple dedicated to human sacrifice (see p.427). This long, low platform of rounded lava boulders looks out across the Kawainui Marsh from a hillock just to the left of Kailua Road. To get there, take Uluo'a Road, the first left turn after Kailua Road breaks away from Kalaniana'ole Highway, and then turn right.

Maunawili Falls Trail

The best way to enjoy the spectacular rainforest around Kailua is to take a half-day hike along the **Maunawili Falls Trail**. To reach the trailhead, follow the Pali Highway down from Honolulu. Opposite the point where Kamehameha Highway branches to the left, you'll see a right turn onto Auloa Road; don't take that, but keep going down the Pali Highway to the *next* intersection on the right, which confusingly is also Auloa Road. Follow that, forking left soon to join Maunawili Road. The trailhead is just over a mile along, close to the junction with Kelewina Road.

The trail itself starts on an unpaved road, but soon becomes a muddy footpath through the lush vegetation that lines the Maunawili Stream. After ten minutes, you ford the broad stream for the first of four times; you may be able to use stepping stones each time, but don't depend on it. It's a lovely hike in itself, with plentiful views of the wild hills all around, with the bonus at the far end, an hour or so from the road, of the low, wide and pretty **Maunawili Falls**. The water beneath the pools is usually shallow enough to wade right under the flow, but don't try to climb the slippery stream-bed to the top.

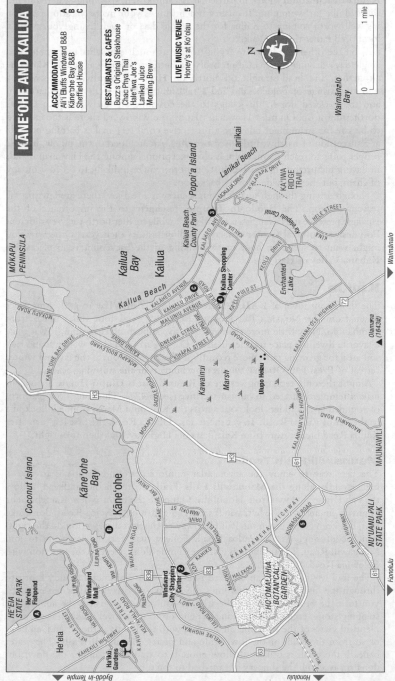

KĀNEʻOHE AND KAILUA

ACCOMMODATION
Aliʻi Bluffs Windward B&B	A
Kāneʻohe Bay B&B	B
Sheffield House	C

RESTAURANTS & CAFÉS
Buzzʻs Original Steakhouse	3
Chac Phya Thai	2
Haleʻwa Joeʻs	1
Lanikai Juice	4
Morning Brew	4

LIVE MUSIC VENUE
Honeyʻs at Koʻolau	5

0   1 mile

N

Kailua Beach

Kailua Beach County Park, which fills the colossal main curve of the bay, is utterly gorgeous – it's the prettiest beach on the whole island – and makes an ideal family swimming spot year-round. The soft wide sands slope down into turquoise waters much used by **windsurfers** and kitesurfers. You can rent windsurfing equipment, as well as **kayaks**, from vans and stalls along the park approach road or on the beach itself, or through Hawaiian Watersports (T 808/262-5483, W www.hawaiianwatersports.com) or Kailua Sailboards and Kayaks (T 808/262-2555, W www.kailuasailboards.com). Just be sure to keep away from the area around the Ka'elepulu Canal, which is often turned into a lagoon by a sandbar across its mouth, and can be unpleasantly polluted.

Head north from here, and once past the park you're on what's simply called **Kailua Beach**, where the waves hit a little harder, so there's less sand, but swimming conditions are generally safe.

Lanikai

Walking south from the county park beyond Alāla Point brings you within a few hundred yards to the very similar but less crowded **Lanikai Beach**. **LANIKAI** itself consists of just a few short streets of priceless homes, all but cut off from the rest of Kailua by Ka'iwa Ridge. The coastal road beyond the beach park becomes a one-way loop immediately south of the ridge, forcing you to turn slightly inland on A'alapapa Road. Take the second right here (Ka'elepulu Street), park near the gate of the Mid-Pacific Country Club, and you'll see the **Ka'iwa Ridge Trail** leading away to the left. Just a few minutes' steep climbing is rewarded with superb views up and down the coast and out to the tiny islands in the bay.

Practicalities

There are no hotels in Kailua, but **B&Bs** are scattered throughout the area. Contact Lanikai Beach Rentals (T 808/261-7895, W www.lanikaibeachrentals.com), or specific properties like the very hospitable *Sheffield House*, just two minutes' walk from Kailua Beach at 131 Ku'ulei Rd (T 808/262-0721, W www.hawaiisheffield house.com; ④).

The most atmospheric places to **eat** in Kailua are by the beach. While the food at *Buzz's Original Steakhouse*, 413 Kawailoa Rd (daily 11am–3pm & 5–10pm; T 808/261-4661), is nothing amazing – wood-grilled steaks, fresh fish, salad bar and cocktails – its location, among the palms across from Kailua Bay, with a wraparound *lāna'i*, is irresistible. Around the intersection of Kailua and Ku'ulei roads, a few hundred yards inland from the beach park, Kailua has the feel of a genuine little community, holding assorted neighborhood stores as well as the **Kailua Shopping Center** mall at 572 Kailua Rd. *Morning Brew* here (Mon–Thurs 6am–9pm, Fri & Sat 6am–10pm, Sun 6am–7pm; T 808/262-7770) is a friendly local coffee house, serving healthy sandwiches, salads, and bistro meals, while *Lanikai Juice* (Mon–Fri 6am–8pm, Sat & Sun 7am–7pm; T 808/262-2383) prepares great drinks and $6 "smoothie bowls" of fruit and granola.

Kāne'ohe

Slightly smaller than Kailua, and boasting a far less robust economy, as well as considerably fewer visitor amenities, **KĀNE'OHE** is seldom seen as an exciting destination in its own right. That's largely because its silty beaches are unsuitable for swimming. However, seven-mile **Kāne'ohe Bay**, reaching northwards from the Mōkapu Peninsula, is the largest bay in Hawaii and also, once you're beyond the main built-up strip, one of the most beautiful. If you want to join the local

pleasure-boaters out on the calm waters of the bay, take a one-hour **cruise** from He'eia Kea Pier on the veteran glass-bottomed *Coral Queen* (Mon–Sat 10am, 11am, noon & 1.30pm; adults $15, under-13s $7; ☎808/292-8470).

He'eia State Park, on the headland immediately before the pier, is a landscaped area set aside largely for its views of the adjoining **He'eia Fishpond**. Ancient Hawaiians built the low curving stone walls that enclose this saltwater lagoon, which is once again being used to raise mullet. Tiny **Coconut Island**, out to sea, is used for marine research by the University of Hawaii, but is better known to many from the credits sequence of *Gilligan's Island*.

Among the quietest and most relaxing of several attractive public **gardens** in inland Kāne'ohe is the **Ho'omaluhia Botanical Garden** (daily 9am–4pm; free), at the top of Luluku Road, which loops back into the hills off Kamehameha Highway between Pali and Likelike highways. Take any of the pleasant short trails away from the visitor center, and you'll soon be out in the wilderness. If you'd prefer a more commercial display of flowers, fruits, and orchids, head instead for **Senator Fong's Plantation**, near the tiny, nominally distinct community of Kahalu'u in northern Kāne'ohe (daily 10am–2pm; adults $14.50, under-13s $9; ☎808/239-6775, ⓦwww.fonggarden.com). The smaller, free **Ha'ikū Gardens**, just off Hwy-83 at the entrance to glorious Ha'ikū Valley, is an attractive little lily pond that serves mainly to lure diners into the on-site *Hale'iwa Joe's* restaurant (☎808/247-6671, ⓦwww.haleiwajoes.com; Mon–Thurs 5.30–9.30pm, Fri & Sat 5.30–10.30pm; for a review of the branch in Hale'iwa, see p.118).

Byōdō-In Temple

Just beyond central Kāne'ohe, a side road *mauka* of Hwy-83 (Kahekili Highway) leads to the interdenominational cemetery known as the **Valley of the Temples** (daily 8.30am–4.30pm; free, except for Byōdō-In Temple). Several religions have chapels and monuments here, but the one that draws in casual visitors is the Japanese Buddhist **Byōdō-In Temple** ($2), built in the 1960s to celebrate a hundred years of Japanese immigration to Hawaii. This unexpected replica of a nine-hundred-year-old temple at Uji in Japan looks absolutely stunning, its red roofs standing out from the trees at the base of the awesome *pali*.

▲ Byōdō-In Temple

Having parked outside the temple gates, you cross an arching footbridge to stroll through the peaceful gardens, passing a fishpond bursting with orange, gold, and mottled carp. Before reaching the main pavilion, you're encouraged to ring a three-ton brass bell. Once inside, you're confronted by a nine-foot meditating Buddha made of gilded, lacquered wood. Japanese visitors pay quiet tribute, while excited tourist groups take quick photos of themselves with the Buddha before dashing back to the bus; it's worth sitting for a while before you leave, allowing the tranquility of the place to touch you.

Practicalities

Like Kailua, Kāne'ohe has a number of small-scale private **B&Bs**. Both the beautifully sited *Kāne'ohe Bay B&B*, 45-302 Pu'uloko Place (reserve through Hawaii's Best B&Bs; ☎808/235-4214 or 1-800/262-9912, ⓦwww.bestbnb.com; ❺), and *Ali'i Bluffs Windward B&B*, 46-125 Ikiiki St (☎808/235-1124 or 1-800/235-1151, ⓦwww.hawaiiscene.com/aliibluffs; ❸), offer two guest rooms overlooking Kāne'ohe Bay, with en-suite facilities and swimming pools. Apart from *Chao Phya Thai*, in the Windward City mall where Likelike and Kamehameha highways meet (Mon–Sat 11am–2pm & 5–9pm, Sun 5–9pm; ☎808/253-3355), which sells tasty Thai food at bargain prices, the **eating** options are plentiful but unexciting.

Kualoa Point and Mokoli'i

At **Ka'alaea** a mile north of the Byōdō-In Temple, Kahekili Highway joins Kamehameha Highway on its way up from He'eia State Park, and the two run on together as Kamehameha Highway. The tumbling waterfalls at the heads of the Waihe'e and Waiahole valleys, visible inland, are superb, but the next point worthy of a halt is at the northern tip of Kāne'ohe Bay.

From the verdant lawns of **Kualoa Point**, out on the headland, you can look through a straggle of windswept coconut palms to conical **Mokoli'i Island**. To ancient Hawaiians, this picturesque little outcrop was the tail of a dragon killed by Pele's sister Hi'iaka as she made her way to Kauai (see p.379); its more banal modern nickname is "Chinaman's Hat." At low tide, you can wade out to it along the reef – the water should never rise more than waist high, and reef shoes are an absolute must – to find a tiny hidden beach on its northern side. Otherwise, content yourself with a swim back at the point from the thin shelf of sand at Kualoa Park.

Kualoa Ranch

Roughly two hundred yards north of Kualoa Park, a driveway leads inland, into the expansive grounds of **Kualoa Ranch**. Formerly a cattle ranch, this now plays host to flocks of Japanese tour groups, though individual travelers can sign up for a wide range of activities, including horseriding, kayaking, a gun range, and all-terrain-vehicle excursions. For full details, contact ☎808/237-7321 or ⓦwww.kualoa.com. An hour on a horse or all-terrain vehicle costs $63, two hours $93, or you can come for a whole day and join four activities for $145.

Ka'a'awa

Several more good beaches lie immediately north of Kāne'ohe Bay, in the area broadly known as **KA'A'AWA**. There's no danger of failing to spot them: in places the highway runs within a dozen feet of the ocean. So long as the surf isn't obviously high, it's generally safe to park by the road at any of the consecutive **Kanenelu**, **Kalae'ō'io**, and **Ka'a'awa** beaches, and head straight into the water. Only **Swanzy Beach County Park**, a little further along, really demands caution on account of

its unpredictable currents. It became a beach park thanks to a rich Kailua resident of the 1920s, who donated this land on condition that no other public parks be created nearer her home. Across from the park, *Uncle Bobo's* (T808/237-1000, Wwww .unclebobos.com) is a simple shack selling barbecue, smoothies, and espressos.

Kahana Valley

The whole of the deeply indented **Kahana Valley**, tucked in behind a high serrated *pali* around the corner from the roadside "Crouching Lion" rock formation, is officially known as **Ahupua'a O Kahana State Park**. In ancient Hawaii, the fundamental economic and geographical unit was the *ahupua'a*, a wedge of land reaching from the high mountains down to a stretch of coastline; Kahana is now the only *ahupua'a* to be entirely owned by the state. Still farmed by native Hawaiian families, it aims to be a "living park," though what that means isn't all that clear. In theory, the residents educate visitors in Hawaiian traditions, but while they still grow traditional crops, they don't dress up or pretend to *be* ancient Hawaiians. Even when the small **visitor center** (officially Mon–Fri 7.30am–4pm; T808/237-7766), just back from the highway as it curves around Kahana Bay, is closed, as it often seems to be, you should be able to pick up maps of the valley's **hiking trails**. Bring waterproof clothing if you plan to hike; upper Kahana Valley receives 300 inches of rain per year.

The beach at **Kahana Bay**, straight across from the park entrance, hangs onto an ample spread of fine sand all year round, and is very safe for swimming. It's possible to **camp** in the woods that line its central section; permits are issued by the park visitor center.

Kahana trails

The easiest of Kahana Valley's attractive trails, the half-hour **Kapa'ele'ele Ko'a Trail**, ascends the northern flank of the bay for great ocean views. It starts by following the dirt road that heads to the right in front of the visitor center. After passing a few houses, it leads into a lush meadow scattered with fruit trees, then veers left at a far-from-obvious junction to climb into the woods. It soon reaches a clearing where you can gaze across the valley to the high walls on the far side, and watch as it recedes away inland. Not far beyond, a few weather-worn stones mark the site of the **Kapa'ele'ele Ko'a** itself, an ancient fishing shrine. A steep climb then leads up to **Keaniani Kilo**, a vantage point from which keen-eyed Hawaiians would watch for schools of fish (usually *akule*, or big-eyed scad), and signal waiting canoes to set off in pursuit. There's nothing here now, and young trees have partially obscured the beach, but it's a lovely spot. The trail then drops down to the highway, and you can make your way back along the beach.

To take the **Nakoa Trail**, which heads for the back of the valley, park roughly half a mile inland from the visitor center, at the edge of the small residential area. Assuming that it hasn't been raining (in which case the valley streams will be too high to cross), you can then keep walking along the main valley road for another fifteen minutes, before the trail sets off to ramble its way up and around the valley walls. It runs for roughly four miles, with some great views and plenty of mosquitoes to keep you company. For a shorter adventure, head left instead from the start of the trail, and you'll soon come to an idyllic little swimming hole in **Kahana Stream**.

Hau'ula and Punalu'u

Beyond Kahana Valley, the highway continues to cling to every curve of the coastline, and traffic moves slowly. Island maps show **HAU'ULA** and **PUNALU'U** as distinct towns, but on the ground it's hard to tell where one ends and the next begins. Both are quiet little communities that barely reach a hundred yards back from the shore.

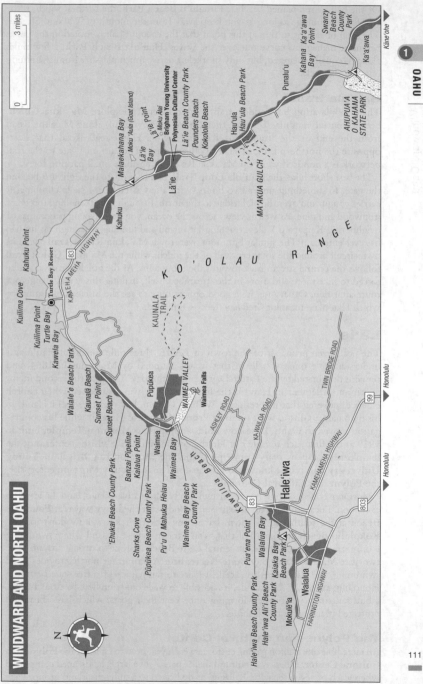

WINDWARD AND NORTH OAHU

N

0   3 miles

Ka'ena Point ►

Kāne'ohe ►

Honolulu ►

Honolulu ►

Swanzy Beach County Park
Ka'a'awa Point
Ka'a'awa
Kahana Bay
AHUPUA'A O KAHANA STATE PARK
Punalu'u
Hau'ula
Hau'ula Beach Park
MA'AKUA GULCH
Kokololio Beach
Pounders Beach
Lā'ie Beach County Park
Polynesian Cultural Center
Brigham Young University
Moku Auia
Lā'ie Point
Lā'ie Bay
Moku 'Auia (Goat Island)
Malaekahana Bay
Kahuku
Lā'ie
KO'OLAU RANGE
KAUNALA TRAIL
WAIMEA VALLEY
Waimea Falls
Kahuku Point
Kuilima Cove
Kuilima Point
Turtle Bay
Turtle Bay Resort
KAMEHAMEHA HIGHWAY
Kawela Bay
Waiale'e Beach Park
Kaunalā Beach
Sunset Point
Pūpūkea
Waimea
Waimea Bay
ASHLEY ROAD
KAWAILOA ROAD
TWIN BRIDGE ROAD
KAMEHAMEHA HIGHWAY
'Ehukai Beach County Park
Banzai Pipeline
Sharks Cove
Kalalua Point
Pūpūkea Beach County Park
Pu'u O Mahuka Heiau
Waimea Bay Beach County Park
Kawailoa Beach
Hale'iwa
Pua'ena Point
Waialua Bay
Kalaka Bay Beach Park
Waialua
Mokulē'ia
Hale'iwa Beach County Park
Hale'iwa Ali'i Beach County Park
FARRINGTON HIGHWAY

83

99

803

Of the half-dozen named beaches, **Punaluʻu Beach Park**, the furthest south, is the best for swimming, so long as you keep away from the mouth of Waiʻono Stream. The strip of sand is so thin at this point that the coconut palms rooted in the lawns behind it manage to curve out over the waves. **Hauʻula Beach Park**, a few miles along, is equally sheltered, but only snorkelers derive much pleasure from swimming out over the rocks.

Hauʻula trails

Three exhilarating but muddy trails enable hikers to explore **Maʻakua Gulch**, behind central Hauʻula. To reach them, head *mauka* (inland) along Maʻakua Road from the end of the straight stretch of Hauʻula Homestead Road that starts opposite the northern limit of Hauʻula Beach Park. The entrance gate to the trail network is a hundred yards up Maʻakua Road, alongside a small parking lot.

The best short hike, the **Hauʻula Loop Trail**, branches off to the right just beyond the gate. In something under two hours, with a few stretches of steep climbing, it carries you up and over the high ridge to the north, through sweet-smelling forests of ironwood and pine. As well as views across the ocean, you get amazing panoramas of neighboring Kaipapaʻu Valley, reaching far inland and looking as though no human has ever entered it. The similar but more overgrown **Maʻakua Ridge Trail** twists its own circuit around the southern wall of the gulch, while the **Maʻakua Gulch Trail** follows the central stream back towards the mountains. As the gulch narrows, you're forced to hike more and more in the streambed itself, making this a very dangerous route after rain. Otherwise, it's a good opportunity to see the luscious blossoms for which Hauʻula – meaning "red *hau* trees" – is named.

Lāʻie

The neat, even prim, air of the town of **LĀʻIE**, three miles on from Hauʻula, is understandable once you learn that it was founded by Mormons in 1864, and remains dominated by the Latter Day Saints to this day. This was the second major Mormon settlement in Hawaii; the first, on Lanai, was abandoned when church elders discovered that its president, William Gibson, had registered all its lands in his own name. Gibson went on to be Prime Minister of Hawaii, while his congregation moved to Oahu. Lāʻie now holds an imposing **Mormon Temple**, built in 1919 as the first such temple outside the continental US (a visitor center, not the temple itself, opens daily 9am–9pm), and the Mormon-run **Brigham Young University**, but is best known to visitors for a less obviously Mormon enterprise, the **Polynesian Cultural Center**.

Mormon colleges tend not to spawn lively alternative scenes, and Lāʻie is no exception. Local students do at least get to body-surf the heavy waves at **Pounders Beach** at the south end of town, but if you lack their know-how don't join in. **Kokololio Beach**, just south of that, is an attractive curve of sand where swimming is only safe in summer, while the central **Lāʻie Beach** is prone to strong currents. The two-part **Mālaekahana Bay State Recreation Area** further north provides good swimming, and also makes an excellent place to camp (pick up a free state permit in Honolulu; see p.52). At low tide, it's possible to wade out from here to **Goat Island**, a bird sanctuary where the Mormons once kept their goats, which has a beautiful protected beach on its north shore.

The Polynesian Cultural Center

An incredible one million paying customers each year head to Lāʻie for the **Polynesian Cultural Center**. Billed as a "cultural theme park," it's a large, landscaped compound where each of seven separate "villages" is dedicated to a different island group. Each

Visiting the Polynesian Cultural Center

There's no cheap way to visit the **Polynesian Cultural Center** (Mon–Sat noon–9pm; ☎808/293-3333 or 1-800/367-7060, ⓦ www.polynesia.com). Each of the various options, which start with basic admission at $45 for adults, $35 for ages 3–11, entitles you to explore the villages, take a canoe ride and tram tour, and see an Imax movie. The **Admission/Show/Dinner Package** ($60/$45) offers seating at the show and a buffet dinner; with the **Ali'i Lū'au Package** ($88/$64) you get a flower *lei*, a *lū'au* ticket, and better show seating; the **Ambassador Ali'i Lū'au Package** ($120/$85) gives you a guided tour, a fancier *lei*, and even better seating at the show, and various other fripperies; and the **Super Ambassador Package** ($225/$175) buys "fine dining" rather than the *lū'au*, plus loads of extra behind-the-scenes tours. With each of those packages, you can return to the center within the next three days to explore any villages you've missed, but the only show you're entitled to see is the IMAX film. Finally, the center also offers round-trip **transportation** from Waikīkī, at $19 per person (no reductions) for a seat in a motorcoach, or $28 for a minibus. It costs $6 to park your own vehicle at the center.

village includes a few typical structures, with space for demonstrations of traditional crafts and activities, ranging from food production or wood-carving to music, dances, fire-walking and games. In addition to Hawaii, Tahiti, and the Marquesas, the further-flung cultures of Fiji, Tonga, Samoa, and New Zealand are represented. As an introduction to the enormous diversity of the Pacific, it's stimulating and enjoyable, though the emphasis is very much on entertainment, and kids are likely to appreciate it more than adults.

To see anything of note, you need to time each individual village tour to coincide with the intricate daily schedule of presentations, so be prepared to spend at least half a day here. As well as stopping by each village, you can ride up and down the central lagoon in a large canoe, or take a tram trip into neighboring Lā'ie. The compound also holds an IMAX cinema, free to all visitors, and countless souvenir and gift stores, snack bars and restaurants (none of which serve alcohol). These all remain open into the evening, but the main reasons visitors stay after the villages close around 5.30pm are the **lū'au**, a seated buffet dinner accompanied by Hawaiian music and dance that runs 5.15 to 6.30pm, and **Hā Breath Of Life**, a spectacularly staged song-and-dance extravaganza that starts at 7.30pm and ends at 9pm.

The center is largely staffed by students from the adjoining university, who don't necessarily come from the relevant parts of the Pacific. The information presented is laced with Mormon theology, and can thus be wildly divergent from conventional cultural and academic beliefs. Thus the Polynesians are said not to have migrated east to west across the Pacific from Southeast Asia, but to be descended from one of the lost tribes of Israel, and to have arrived from Central America under the leadership of a certain Hagoth.

Kahuku

KAHUKU, a couple of miles on from Lā'ie, may look run-down by comparison, but is considerably more atmospheric. Though the plantation it served went out of business in 1971, the rusting hulk of the **Kahuku Sugar Mill** still overshadows this small town. Assorted outbuildings now house a half-hearted shopping mall, but it's all in a sorry state. Lumps of machinery are dotted around the courtyard, painted in peeling pastel blues and yellows, and most of the old mill workings remain in place. The *Kahuku Grill* (Mon–Sat 9am–5pm; ☎808/293-2110) serves up shrimp and barbecue, and you can also pick up freshly cooked shrimp from a couple of white

trucks stationed permanently beside the highway; of the two, *Giovanni's*, just south of the mill, serves the spicier food. Behind the sugar mill a few dirt lanes hold tin-roofed plantation homes. The long **beach** beyond is not suitable for swimming, but stretches a full five miles up to Turtle Bay if you fancy a solitary, bracing hike.

Beyond Kahuku, the highway veers away from the shore to run alongside a series of ponds, used for raising fresh shrimp that's sold by more trucks stationed along the highway. The Walsh Farms complex of small, brightly painted shacks and funky vans at the far end sells fresh fruit, shrimp, and an entertaining mixture of antiques and junk.

Turtle Bay

Just before Kamehameha Highway rejoins the ocean on the North Shore, an obvious spur road leads *makai* past some expensive condos and private homes to end at **Turtle Bay**. Photogenic **beaches** lie to either side of **Kuilima Point** here – long, wave-raked Turtle Bay to the west, and the sheltered artificial lagoon of Kuilima Cove to the east, which stays safe for swimming all through the winter – but apart from surfers the only visitors likely to head this way are those staying at the luxury hotel on the point itself.

The thousand-acre **Turtle Bay Resort**, 57-091 Kamehameha Hwy (☎808/293-6000, ⓦwww.turtlebayresort.com; ❽), holds almost five hundred ocean-view rooms, as well as three swimming pools, a luxury spa, horseriding facilities, two golf courses, ten tennis courts, a surf school, and three restaurants. Priced far beyond the pockets of most of the surfing crowd, its presence is not very welcome with North Shore residents, who are forever campaigning to prevent its further expansion. If you can afford it, though, it offers a truly fabulous resort experience, and makes a great escape from Waikīkī. The resort's signature **restaurant**, *21 Degrees North* (Tues–Sat 6–10pm), is reached via a kitschy enclosed walkway of artificial waterfalls. Both its indoor and outdoor seating offer great views of the foaming North Shore surf, spotlit at night, while the pricey but flavorful New Hawaiian menu features appetizers like a seafood medley of *ahi* and oysters ($19) and entrees ($27–42) such as crab-crusted sea bass.

Run by separate management, and open to the warm ocean breezes on the sands of Kuilima Cove, the effortlessly stylish *Ola* is the perfect island restaurant (Mon–Thurs & Sun 11am–3pm & 5.30–9.30pm, Fri & Sat 11am–3pm & 5.30–10pm; ☎808/293-0801, ⓦwww.olaislife.com). Its contemporary Hawaiian cuisine is exceptional, based on fresh ingredients and regional specialties, while the laidback atmosphere makes it hard to leave. For lunchtime it's a real bargain, with $10–12 burgers, salads and sandwiches, and specials like baby octopus at up to $20; dinner entrees include the fabulous $29 slow-poached *togarashi* smoked salmon with sweet potato and edamame succotash.

The *Turtle Bay Resort* marks the spot where TheBus #55 from the south becomes #52 as it heads west, and vice versa.

Central Oahu

Thanks to the island's slender central "waist," much the quickest route from Honolulu to the North Shore lies across the flat agricultural heartland of **central Oahu**. Cradled between the mountains, the **Leilehua Plateau** was created when lava flowing from the Ko'olau eruptions lapped against the older Wai'anae Range. Until relatively recently, sugar cane and pineapples raised in its rich soil were the foundation of the Hawaiian economy; these days, however, the area has a somewhat

dejected atmosphere. More people than ever live in towns such as **Waipahu** and **Wahiawā** – many of them personnel from the military bases tucked into the hillsides – but there's very little here to interest tourists. If you plan to drive around Oahu in a single day, you'd do better to press straight on to Hale'iwa (see p.117).

'Aiea and Pearl City

Whichever road you follow, you have to drive a long way **west of Honolulu** to reach open countryside. H-1, the main "interstate," curves past the airport and Pearl Harbor, while Hwy-78 sticks closer to the Ko'olau foothills, but they eventually crisscross to run through the nondescript communities of **'AIEA** and **PEARL CITY**. Neither town has a center worth stopping for.

Keaīwa Heiau State Park

Only **Keaīwa Heiau State Park**, on a hilltop above 'Aiea proper, merits a detour from the highway, and even that appeals more to local residents than to outsiders. 'Aiea Heights Drive, the road up, heads right from the second stoplight after the Aloha Stadium turnoff on Hwy-78, then twists for almost three miles through a sleepy residential area.

Keaīwa Heiau, whose ruined walls are on the left as soon as you enter the park, was a center where *kahuna lapa'au* healers practiced herbal medicine, using plants from the surrounding gardens. The most famous such healer was Keaīwa – "the mysterious" – himself. *Ti* plants, together with a few larger *kukui* trees, still grow within the well-maintained precinct, which also holds a little shrine and a central ring of stones. This layout is largely conjectural, however, as the *heiau* was severely damaged during the plantation era.

There are no views from the *heiau*, but a mile-long **loop road** circles the ridge that lies beyond, where the ironwood forest is punctuated with meadows and picnic areas looking out over Pearl Harbor. Halfway around, you'll come to the trailhead for the **'Aiea Loop Trail**, a five-mile circuit through the woods with views of the interior valleys as well as Honolulu. The highlight is the wreckage of a World War II cargo plane that crashed into a remote gully.

Should you plan to stay, **camping** at the park's cool, secluded campground (closed Wed and Thurs) costs $18 per site, with a state permit (see p.52).

Waipahu

Just beyond Pearl City, both H-2 and Kamehameha Highway (Hwy-99) branch away to head north across the central plateau. Only a mile or so west, however, the small town of **WAIPAHU** holds one of Hawaii's best historical **museums**, an evocative memorial to the early days of immigration. It's also home to the unexpectedly upmarket **Waikele Center** shopping mall, with its Borders bookstore and discount "factory outlets."

Hawaii's Plantation Village

A mile south of H-1 on Waipahu Street in Waipahu, just below the sugar mill to which it owes its existence, stands **Hawaii's Plantation Village** (hourly guided tours Mon–Sat 10am–2pm; $13, seniors $10, under-12s $5; ☎808/677-0110, ⓦhawaiis plantationvillage-info.com). It's a loving re-creation of the living conditions of the almost 400,000 agricultural laborers who migrated to Hawaii between 1852 and 1946, and were largely responsible for the ethnic blend of the modern state.

Enthusiastic local guides lead visitors around a small museum and then through a "time tunnel" onto the former plantation estate. Simple houses – some from this site, others brought in from elsewhere – contain personal possessions, illustrating

how much the migrants brought with them, and how much different groups shared with each other in creating a common Hawaiian identity. Cumulatively, the minor domestic details – pots, pans, buckets, family photographs, even the tiny boxing gloves used to train Filipino fighting cocks – make you feel the occupants have merely stepped out for a minute. The most moving artifacts are the *bangos*, the numbered metal badges that helped the *lunas* (whip-cracking Caucasian plantation supervisors) to distinguish each worker from the next. Goods were obtained in the company store by showing your *bango*, and the cost deducted from your next pay packet.

Wahiawā

All routes across central Oahu – whether you take H-2 or Kamehameha Highway from Pearl City, or the more scenic **Kunia Road** (Hwy-750) that leads up through the fields from Waipahu – pass through the large town of **WAHIAWĀ**. The main drag holds the dismal array of bars, fast-food outlets, and gun stores that you'd expect to find this close to the **Schofield Barracks**, Oahu's largest military base.

A couple of mildly diverting sites lie just outside the town. The **Wahiawā Botanical Gardens** (daily 9am–4pm; free), a mile east, is a reasonably attractive enclave of tropical trees and flowers that's welcome if you live here but nothing special by Hawaiian standards. To the north, on Whitmore Avenue off Kamehameha Highway, faintly marked reddish-brown lava boulders beneath a cluster of palm trees in a pineapple field constitute an archeological site known as **Kukaniloko**, or more colloquially as the **Birthing Stones**. Tradition had it that any chief hoping to rule Oahu had to be born here.

Dole Plantation

The single-story modern building of the **Dole Plantation** stands east of Kamehameha Highway a mile north of Wahiawā (daily 9am–5.30pm; free, but includes several paying attractions; Ⓦ www.dole-plantation.com). Growing ever larger year upon year, this centers on a large mall-cum-marketplace that sells tacky pineapple-related souvenirs and craft items, as well as fresh pineapples and pineapple products such as juices and frozen "whips." You can also, should you wish, pose for uproarious photographs with your head poking through a cardboard cutout of a pineapple playing a 'ukulele.

Behind the mall, extensive gardens of pineapples and more authentic Hawaiian plants can be explored either on foot ($4, under-13s $3.25) or on half-hourly excursions on the Pineapple Express motorized "train" ($8/$6). A separate section holds what's said to be the world's largest **maze** ($6/$4), again composed of Hawaiian plants. The aim here is not to reach the center, let alone escape; instead you're expected to traipse around in the hot sun to find six separate color-coded "stations."

The North Shore

Although the surfing beaches of Oahu's **North Shore** are famous the world over, the area as a whole is barely equipped for tourists. **Waimea**, **Sunset**, and **'Ehukai** beach parks are all laidback roadside stretches of sand, where you can usually find a quiet spot to yourself. In summer, the tame waves may leave you wondering what all the fuss is about; see them at full tilt in winter, between October and April, and you'll have no doubts. If you plan to surf – and this is no place for casual amateurs – then you'd do best to base yourself in **Pūpūkea** (see p.119). Otherwise, you can see all there is to see in an easy day-trip from Waikīkī, with a pause to shop and snack in **Hale'iwa**.

Hale'iwa

The main North Shore town stands where Kamehameha Highway reaches the ocean, 24 miles north of Honolulu. For most visitors, **HALE'IWA** (pronounced "ha-lay-eve-a") comes as a pleasant surprise. It's one of the very few Oahu communities whose roots have not been obscured by rebuilding and development, even though tourists have been coming here ever since a direct rail route from Honolulu was launched in 1899.

For fifty years, the town has been a gathering place for **surfers** from all over the world. Many of the first arrivals, lured from California by the cult movie *Endless Summer*, seem to have remained not only in Hawaii, but also in the 1960s. Hale'iwa is still bursting with businesses like surf shops, tie-dye stores, wholefood restaurants, and galleries of ethnic knick-knacks. Add those to a scattering of upfront tourist traps, and local stores and diners, and you've got an intriguing, energetic blend that entices many travelers to stay for months.

That said, there's precious little to see in Hale'iwa. Its main street, **Kamehameha Avenue**, runs for a mile from the Paukauila Stream to the Anahulu River, well back from the ocean, passing a succession of funky, low-rise malls. In the largest, the North Shore Marketplace, the storefront **Surf Museum** (daily except Mon noon–6pm; free) traces the history of Hawaiian surfboards from the hollow wooden boards of the 1930s through early fiberglass models from the 1950s, and holds shrines to Duke Kahanamoku in particular, and the 1960s in general.

Only as you approach the river do you finally come to the heart of Hale'iwa, a short stretch of old-fashioned boardwalk lined with false-front wooden buildings. One of these houses Matsumoto's, a Japanese grocery store so renowned for its shave ice – the Hawaiian equivalent of a sno-cone, a mush of ice saturated with sickly sweet syrup – that it's an all-but-obligatory stop on round-island tours.

Beyond that, narrow Rainbow Bridge crosses Anahulu River, affording great views upstream towards the green slopes of Anahulu Valley. The small bay at the rivermouth is **Waialua Bay**, with Hale'iwa Harbor sheltered by a breakwater on its southwestern side. Southwest of the harbor, **Hale'iwa Ali'i Beach Park** is a favorite place for local kids to learn to surf – there are **free surfing lessons** on weekend mornings in winter – but inexperienced outsiders who have a go are taking their lives in their hands. That was the pretext for making this the fictional location of TV's *Baywatch Hawaii*, a short-lived, state-subsidized experiment in relocating the Californian show to Hawaii that cost Hawaiian taxpayers dear.

Just to reach the waves at Hale'iwa Ali'i, you have to pick your way across a tricky shallow coral reef; once you're out there, you're at the mercy of strong crosscurrents. Swimming is much safer at **Hale'iwa Beach Park**, on the northeast shore of the bay.

Practicalities

There's nowhere to stay in Hale'iwa itself. Visiting surfers either put up at the *Backpacker's Vacation Inn* in Pūpūkea (see p.119), or find a room or a home to rent

Hale'iwa watersports equipment

The best-known **surf outfitter** in Hale'iwa, Surf 'n' Sea, is based in a large, ramshackle store immediately north of Rainbow Bridge (62-595 Kamehameha Hwy; daily 9am–7pm; ☎808/637-9887 or 1-800/899-7873, ⓦwww.surfnsea.com). As well as renting surfboards ($7 per hour, $30 per day), body-boards ($5/$20), paddle boards ($20/$60), and snorkel equipment ($7 half-day, $10 all day), they organize quality dive trips (shore dives one tank $75, two tanks $100; two-tank boat dives $110), offer surfing lessons ($85 for 2–3hr), and sell new and used boards and souvenirs.

as close to the beaches as they can. Bulletin boards in surf shops and coffee bars list short-term rentals, from around $1000 per month for a one-room apartment. With a free county permit (see p.52), you can **camp** under the ironwoods of **Kaiaka Bay Beach Park**. A mile out of town along a loop drive off Hale'iwa Road, the beach itself is too near the murky mouth of Kaiaka Bay to be of much use for swimmers.

Places to eat, including plenty of vegetarian options, line Kamehameha Avenue. In the North Shore Marketplace, *Cholo's Homestyle Mexican* (daily 8am–9pm; ☎808/637-3059) is a festive, very lively Mexican joint with outdoor seating. The long menu offers the usual favorites – and a few more local choices, including *ahi* quesadillas – for $8–12, plus icy mojitos. Also in the marketplace, *Coffee Gallery* (☎808/637-0085) has a cool dark-wood gallery to enjoy espresso drinks, fruity smoothies and fresh juices; they also serve wraps and burritos. Further west, the friendly, all-vegetarian *Paradise Found Café* consists of a few colorful booths at the back of the Celestial Natural Foods store, 66-443 Kamehameha Hwy (Mon–Sat 9am–5pm, Sun 9am–4pm; ☎808/637-4540), where you can pick up delicious breakfasts from $6.50, humungous lunches for $7–10, and thirst-quenching smoothies from $4.50. *Hale'iwa Eats*, closer to the ocean at 66-079 Kamehameha Hwy (Tues–Sun noon–8pm; ☎808/637-4247), is a glass-fronted diner that serves good, simple Thai curries and noodle dishes for under $10.

The pick of the more conventional steak houses and tourist haunts clustered near the harbor is *Hale'iwa Joe's*, at the mouth of the Anahulu River (Mon–Thurs & Sun 11.30am–9.30pm, Fri & Sat 11.30am–10.30pm; ☎808/637-8005, ⓦwww .haleiwajoes.com), which has an outdoor terrace. At lunchtime, sandwiches or salads cost $10–12, and most of the items on the dinner menu are also available; in the evening, sushi or *poke* appetizers cost around $10 and steamed fish more like $23.

Waimea Bay

Long **Kawailoa Beach** stretches for almost five miles northeast of Hale'iwa, interrupted repeatedly by rocky reefs and swept by fierce currents. Driving along the highway, however, virtually the first glimpse you get of the ocean is as you crest a small promontory to look down on **Waimea Bay**. This is perhaps the most famous **surfing** spot in the world, thanks to what are generally believed to be the biggest rideable waves on the planet. During the summer, it's often calm as a lake, but in winter the break off its craggy headlands can remain over 20ft high for days at a time. Anywhere else, even the waves right on the beach would count as monsters, and lethal rip currents tear along the shoreline. While entering the ocean at Waimea in winter is extremely dangerous for anyone other than expert surfers, the beautiful sands of **Waimea Bay Beach County Park** are usually crowded with swimmers, snorkelers, and boogie-boarders in summer.

Waimea Valley

Access to beautiful **Waimea Valley**, stretching inland of the bridge across Waimea River, is controlled by the Office of Hawaiian Affairs (daily 9am–5pm; $13, ages 4–12 $6; ☎808/638-7766, ⓦwww.waimeavalley.net). It was purchased by Honolulu City Council in 1966 after a troubled history that included several years as an "Adventure Park" which uneasily combined cultivating rare Hawaiian plant species with entertaining bus-loads of tourists with ATV rides and cliff-diving shows. These days it's primarily a botanical center showcasing scrupulously maintained **gardens** of Polynesian flowers and trees, and also featuring demonstrations of Hawaiian crafts and cultural traditions.

The most prominent of several **archeological sites** is the restored Hale O Lono or "House of Lono," an ancient *heiau* whose three stone terraces rise next to the main gate; in fact you can take a look without paying to enter. Once inside the center proper, you can wander for roughly a mile along stream-side walkways that pass the fenced-off ruins of further *heiaus* and ancient burial sites, as well as a mock-up of a Hawaiian village. Just be sure you wear repellent to deter the ever-present mosquitoes. Following the path to the far end, a lovely walk even if you have no great interest in learning about plants, brings you to the double, 60ft **Waimea Falls** at the head of the valley.

The *Waimea Valley Grill*, a café close to the main entrance, serves good inexpensive snacks, such as *ahi* tuna and avocado sandwiches; you don't have to pay the admission fee to reach it.

Pūpūkea

Immediately beyond Waimea Bay, Kamehameha Highway starts to cruise beside magnificent surfing beaches. Driving demands patience; at the best of times, vehicles pull off without warning, while during competitions traffic slows to a virtual standstill. **Pūpūkea Beach County Park**, which, like Hanauma Bay (see p.101), is a Marine Life Conservation District, stretches for well over a mile from the mouth of Waimea Bay. At its western end, the Three Tables surf break is named after three flat-topped chunks of reef, where many an unwary swimmer has come to grief, while **Shark's Cove** to the east, riddled with submarine caves, is popular with snorkelers and scuba-divers in summer.

PŪPŪKEA itself is a low-key community, with a few stores and no restaurants. While real-estate prices here have been rising for years, steadily pushing out its large population of international surf bums, political campaigns have so far kept it free of large-scale development. Pūpūkea holds by far the best **accommodation** along the North Shore. The rambling main building of the *Backpacker's Vacation Inn, mauka* of the highway at 59-788 Kamehameha Hwy (☎808/638-7838, ⓦwww .backpackers-hawaii.com; ❶–❼), offers dorm beds for $27 per night, while the low oceanfront buildings across the street hold good-value studio apartments with great views, costing from $120. The associated *Plantation Village*, a hundred yards down the road, across from the sea, consists of nine restored plantation cabins, with more $27 dorm beds, plus private rooms at $72, and larger cabins at anything up to $290 for eight people. Communal buffet dinners on Tuesday, Wednesday, Friday, and Sunday cost $7, and there's a $5 bus service to Honolulu Airport and Waikīkī. They also provide free snorkeling equipment and boogie-boards, rent out bicycles at $5 per day, and arrange island tours, plus whale-watching in winter and scuba diving in summer.

Puʻu O Mahuka Heiau State Monument

For a superb view of Waimea Valley and the bay, head up to **Puʻu O Mahuka Heiau**, perched on the eastern bluff above the river mouth. As Oahu's largest temple of human sacrifice, this was home at the time of the earliest European contact to a terrifying brotherhood of *pahupu* warrior-priests. A group of these "cut-in-two" warriors, who tattooed half their bodies – either top to bottom, or their entire heads – completely black, killed three members of the crew of the *Daedalus* in 1792.

To reach the *heiau*, turn off the coastal highway at the Foodland supermarket, a few hundred yards beyond the bay. Having climbed the hill on twisting Pūpūkea Road, turn right onto a narrow paved track that skirts the cliff edge for just under a mile, to end at a parking lot alongside the higher of the temple's two tiers. The meadow that appears to lie just beyond the *heiau* is in fact on the far side of the deep cleft of Waimea Valley. **Trails** lead around and through the old stone walls, within which it's easy to make out the outlines of several subsidiary structures; most were originally paved with

water-worn stones carried up from Waimea Bay. The main "altar" at the *mauka* end, usually covered with offerings of flower *leis*, pineapples, vodka, and water, probably bears little resemblance to its original configuration. From the little loop path around the java plum trees nearby, you can see along the North Shore to Ka'ena Point in the western distance; beacon fires at the *heiau* could signal to Wailua on Kauai.

Kaunala Trail

Beyond the *heiau* turnoff, Pūpūkea Road heads inland for another two miles, to a Boy Scout camp. From here, the five-mile **Kaunala Trail**, open on weekends only, runs along the thickly wooded crest of a high mountain ridge. As well as views of the deep and inaccessible gorges to either side, if the clouds clear you'll eventually see Oahu's highest peak, **Mount Ka'ala** (4020ft), far across the central plains.

Sunset Beach

With its wide shelf of yellow sand, lined by palm trees, **Sunset Beach**, northeast of Pūpūkea, is perhaps the most picture-perfect beach on Oahu. Only occasional gaps between the oceanfront homes allow access, but once there you're free to wander for two blissful miles of paradise-island coastline. Unless you come on a calm and current-free summer's day (ask the lifeguards), it's essential to stay well away from the water; the "Sunset Rip" can drag even beachcombers out to sea.

In winter, when the waves are stupendous, Sunset Beach fills with photographers in search of the definitive surfing shot, while reckless pro surfers perform magazine-cover stunts out on the water. Each break here has its own name, the most famous being the **Banzai Pipeline**, where the goal is to let yourself be fired like a bullet through the tubular break and yet manage to avoid being slammed down onto the shallow, razor-sharp reef at the end. To watch the action, walk a few hundred yards west (left) from **'Ehukai Beach County Park**, to where a small patch of lawn separates the beach from the road.

Sunset Beach proper, a mile past 'Ehukai, was where North Shore surfing first took off, following advances in surfboard technology in the early 1950s, and remains the venue for many contests. The break known as **Backyards** is renowned for being especially lethal, though it's a popular playground for windsurfers. **Kaunala Beach** beyond that, the home of the **Velzyland** break, is the last major surf spot before the highway curves away towards Turtle Bay (see p.114) and the windward coast. Velzyland offers reliable rather than colossal waves, but riding them with any degree of safety requires immense precision.

Practicalities

No formal overnight accommodation is available beyond Pūpūkea. As for **eating**, short-lived fruit stands, shrimp shacks and snack bars come and go along the *mauka* side of Kamehameha Highway, especially in the little cluster of buildings and tents alongside the giant totem pole dedicated to Maui Pōhaku Loa, six miles north of Hale'iwa between Sunset and 'Ehukai beaches.

West from Hale'iwa

The coast of northern Oahu **west of Hale'iwa** lacks suitable surfing beaches, and is so rarely visited that most people don't really count it as part of the North Shore at all. The area's principal landmark is the **Waialua Sugar Mill**, slowly rusting away at the foot of the Wai'anae Mountains. A moderately interesting driving tour leads down the back roads of the village of **Waialua** and along oceanfront Crozier Drive to even smaller **Mokulē'ia**, but while that gives you attractive views of Hale'iwa in the distance, you might as well go straight to Hale'iwa itself.

Ka'ena Point

Oahu's westernmost promontory, **Ka'ena Point**, is only accessible on foot or mountain bike; it's not possible to drive all the way around from the North Shore to the leeward shore. As Farrington Highway runs west of Waialua and Mokulē'ia, the landscape grows progressively drier, and the road eventually grinds to a halt a couple of miles beyond **Dillingham Airfield**, where Honolulu Soaring offers **glider flights** (from $79; daily 10am–5.30pm; ☎808/637-0207, ⓦwww .honolulusoaring.com).

On the far side of the gate, you can follow either a bumpy, dusty dirt road beside the steadily dwindling Wai'anae Ridge, or a sandy track that straggles across the coastal rocks. The only sign of life is likely to be the odd local fisherman, perched on the spits of black lava reaching into the foaming ocean.

After roughly an hour of hot hiking, the ridge vanishes altogether, and you squeeze between boulders to enter the **Ka'ena Point Natural Area Reserve**. This largely flat and extremely windswept expanse of gentle sand dunes, knitted together with creeping ivy-like *naupaka*, is a winter nesting site for Laysan **albatross**. At the very tip, down below a rudimentary lighthouse – a slender white pole topped by flashing beacons – tiny little beaches cut into the headland. Winter waves here can reach more than 50ft high, the highest recorded anywhere in the world, and way beyond the abilities of any surfer, though humpback whales often come in close to the shore.

From Ka'ena Point, you can see the mountains curving away down the leeward coast, as well as the white "golfball" of a military early-warning system up on the hills. Just out to sea is a rock known as **Pōhaku O Kaua'i** ("the rock of Kauai"); in Hawaiian legend, this is a piece of Kauai, which became stuck to Oahu when the demi-god Maui attempted to haul all the islands together.

If you'd prefer to try the slightly longer hike to Ka'ena Point from the end of the road on the western coast, see p.124.

The leeward coast

The **west** or **leeward coast** of Oahu, cut off from the rest of the island behind the Wai'anae Mountains, is only accessible via **Farrington Highway** (Hwy-93), which skirts the southern end of the ridge. Customarily dismissed as "arid," the region may not be covered by tropical vegetation, but the scenery is still spectacular. As elsewhere on Oahu, the mountains are pierced by high green valleys – almost all of them inaccessible to casual visitors – while fine beaches such as Mākaha Beach Park line the shore.

However, the traditionally minded inhabitants of towns such as **Nānākuli** are not disposed to welcome the encroachment of hotels and golf courses, and visitors tend to be treated with a degree of suspicion. The further north you go, the stronger the military presence becomes, with soldiers lurking in the hillsides, and helicopters flying overhead. Farrington Highway once ran all the way around Ka'ena Point, at the northwest corner of the island – that's why it has the same name on both coasts – but it's no longer possible to drive right to the point.

The southwest corner

The strip development that characterizes both sides of Hwy-1 from Honolulu to Waipahu finally comes to an end as you enter Oahu's southwest corner. Though long-cherished plans by the state authorities to turn this region into a major tourism and residential center have still not quite reached fruition, the former

plantation settlement of **'Ewa** has become ever more overshadowed by the burgeoning community of **Kapolei**.

'Ewa

A couple of miles south of Farrington Highway along Fort Weaver Road, **'EWA** is a picturesque hamlet of wooden sugar-plantation homes arranged around a well-kept village green. Other than snapping a few photos along the back lanes, the only reason to visit is to take a **train excursion** with the Hawaii Railway Society, based west of town along Renton Road. The restored *Waialua #6* locomotive sets out on its ninety-minute round-trip journeys, westwards to Kahe Point, on Sunday afternoons only (1pm & 3pm; adults $10, seniors and under-13s $7; ☎808/681-5461, ⓦwww.hawaiianrailway.com). On the second Sunday of each month, at the same times, you can have a private narrated tour in the comfort of a restored luxury parlor car ($20).

'Ewa Beach Park, three miles south, is an attractive oceanfront park popular with sailors from the nearby base. It has plenty of sand, and views across to Diamond Head, but the water tends to be too murky for swimming, and there's an awful lot of seaweed.

Kapolei

Until recently, the name **KAPOLEI** did not appear on even the most detailed maps of Oahu. Now, however, it's the island's fastest-growing town, stretching alongside H-1 as the road approaches its end in the southwest corner of the island. Homes, movie theaters, and shopping malls have sprung up, but the new town has only one tourist attraction, the **Hawaiian Waters Adventure Park**, at 400 Farrington Hwy just off Hwy-1 exit 1 (adults $42, ages 3–11 $32; ☎808/674-9283, ⓦwww.hawaiianwaters.com). Hawaii's first water-park holds lots of swirling plastic tubes for visitors to raft or simply slide down, children's play areas, and an exhilarating wave pool. It's all great fun, though with so many wonderful beaches on the island, it hasn't yet succeeded in attracting great numbers of visitors. In principle, it's open daily from 10.30am until dusk, but it often seems to shut its gates as early as 4pm, and it's closed altogether some days in winter; call ahead before you make the drive.

Ko Olina Resort

A great deal of money was poured during the 1980s into landscaping the **Ko Olina Resort**, just north of **Barbers Point** at the southwest tip of the island. Four successive artificial lagoons were blasted into the coastline, each a perfect semicircle and equipped with its own crescent of white sand. Work also began on creating a marina for luxury yachts at the Barbers Point Harbor. Apart from the *Ihilani Resort*, the other projected developments, scheduled to include residential estates, condo buildings, shopping centers, and more hotels, have taken a long time to materialize. However, things may finally take off with the construction of Disney's new **Aulani Resort**, a themed, child-oriented beachfront complex of hotel rooms and rental villas that had yet to open when this book went to press.

The **Marriott Ihilani Resort and Spa**, 92-1001 Olani St (☎808/679-0079, ⓦwww.ihilani.com; ❼–❾) is a largely successful attempt to mimic the resort hotels of the outer islands. It's an absolute idyll if you can afford it; its fifteen stories of state-of-the-art rooms are equipped with every high-tech device imaginable, while the adjoining spa boasts thalassotherapy and sauna facilities, and there are also rooftop tennis courts and a top-quality golf course. Even at the least expensive of the excellent in-house restaurants, the poolside *Naupaka Terrace*, a meal will set you back at least $50, though its delicate Pacific Rim fish dishes are well worth trying.

Nānākuli

Farrington Highway reaches the Wai'anae coast at **Kahe Point Beach Park**. As well as being a small but pretty strip of sand, this is Oahu's most popular year-round **surfing** site. The waves offshore remain high (but not overpoweringly so) even in summer, and break much closer to the shore than usual. Since the bay itself is relatively sheltered, swimming usually only becomes dangerous in the depths of winter.

A couple of miles further on, **NĀNĀKULI** is the southernmost of a string of small coastal towns. Its population is largely Hawaiian, and there's little attempt to cater to outsiders. **Nānākuli Beach County Park**, which runs alongside the highway all through town, is another good summer swimming beach, while **Zablan Beach** at its southern end is much used by scuba-divers. The beach immediately north of Nānākuli is called **Ulehawa** or "filthy penis," after a particularly unsavory ancient chief.

Wai'anae

WAI'ANAE, five miles up the coast, centers on curving **Poka'i Bay**. Thanks to the breakwaters constructed to protect the boat harbor at its northern end, the main sandy beach here is the only one on the leeward coast where swimming can be guaranteed safe all year round. The high-walled valley behind provides an irresistible backdrop.

Beyond a flourishing coconut grove at the tip of the flat spit of land that marks the southern end of Poka'i Bay stand the ruined walls of **Kū'ilioloa Heiau**. Unusual in being virtually surrounded by water, this three-tiered structure is said to mark the place where the first coconut tree to be brought from Tahiti was planted in Hawaiian soil. Kamehameha offered sacrifices here before launching his first invasion attempt against Kauai (see p.338).

Mākaha

MĀKAHA, or "savage," the last of the leeward towns, was once the hideout of a dreaded band of outlaws. Now famous for the savagery of its **waves**, it began to attract surfers in the early 1950s. Before that, virtually all Oahu surfing was concentrated in Waikīkī. When changes in the ocean conditions there led surfers to start looking elsewhere, Mākaha was the first place they hit on. The waves at its northern end offer the largest consistently reliable surf in Hawaii, and major contests still take place at **Mākaha Beach Park** each year. In summer, when sand piles up in mighty drifts, it's often possible to swim here in safety, and Mākaha retains enough sand to remain a beautiful crescent beach even in winter. You'll probably notice what look like hotels along the oceanfront near Mākaha Beach, but they're long-term rental condos intended for local families. With a county permit, however (see p.52), it's possible to **camp** at **Kea'au Beach Park**, in an attractive but somewhat exposed location another couple of miles up the coast, in view of Ka'ena Point. Swimming in the rocky sea here, with its pounding surf, is not recommended, but the numbered campsites are pleasant enough.

A couple of miles back from the ocean in Mākaha Valley – follow Mākaha Valley Road inland beyond the defunct *Sheraton Mākaha Resort* – the private driveway of the Mauna Olu Estates leads to **Kāne'āki Heiau**. Hawaii's most thoroughly restored ancient temple, it was excavated by Bishop Museum archeologists in 1970 and can now be visited with permission from the security guards at the gate (Tues–Sun 10am–2pm; free). Its principal platform of weathered, lichen-covered stones is topped once more by thatched structures such as the *anu'u* ("oracle tower"), as well

as carved images. The *heiau* originated as an agricultural temple to the god Lono in the fifteenth century. Two hundred years later, it was converted into a *luakini*, where human sacrifices were dedicated to the god Ku – a typical progression indicating that the valley now supported a large enough population to have its own chief.

The road to Ka'ena Point

Beyond Mākaha, the highway traces a long, slow curve up the coast to Yokohama Bay. Barely populated, and splendidly bleak, this region attracts very few visitors other than a handful of daredevil surfers prepared to risk its sharks, currents, and mighty waves. Inland, the rolling green slopes of **Mākua Valley** also conceal dangerous secrets. Used for bombing practice during and after World War II, the valley is still barred to the public owing to unexploded ordnance.

Not even the sturdiest four-wheel-drive vehicle could negotiate the dirt road that continues from the end of the highway. In any case, the dunes beyond were designated as the **Ka'ena Point Natural Area Reserve** to help repair damage done by military jeeps and motorbikes. However, an exposed one-hour **hike** – similar to the corresponding trail along the North Shore, described on p.121 – along the old railroad tracks will bring you to the very tip of the island.

The Big Island

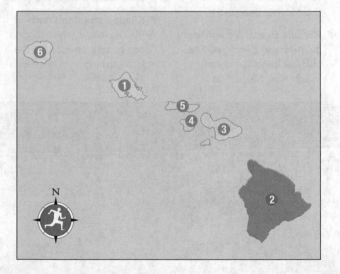

CHAPTER 2 # Highlights

* **The Coffee Shack** Simple roadside café, serving up fresh Kona coffee to go with its stupendous ocean views. See p.147

* **Pu'uhonua O Hōnaunau** Atmospheric "place of refuge" that conjures up vivid images of life in ancient Hawaii. See p.150

* **Kona Village Resort** The oldest of the Big Island's luxury resorts remains the most idyllic. See p.154

* **Hāpuna Beach** A magnificent palm-fringed beach with the calmest turquoise waters imaginable. See p.159

* **Hwy-250** The drive along the pastoral flanks of Kohala Mountain is among the most beautiful in all Hawaii. See p.167

* **Mauna Kea** Join the locals in gathering snowballs from the Pacific's highest peak to take to the beach. See p.187

* **Kehena Beach** Wild parrots and naturists share the pleasures of this little-known black-sand beach. See p.192

* **Kīlauea eruption** Watch as the Big Island grows bigger day by day, courtesy of the lava gushing from Kīlauea. See p.203

▲ Pu'uhonua O Hōnaunau

The Big Island

All the Hawaiian islands were formed by volcanic action, but only on the island officially named **Hawaii** are those volcanoes still active – which is why it's larger than all the other Hawaiian islands put together, and is universally known as the **Big Island**. Visitors flock here to watch the fiery eruptions that shape the youngest land on earth. Such sheer rawness might make the island seem an unlikely tourist destination, but it also offers everything you could want from a tropical vacation – sunshine, sandy beaches, warm turquoise waters, swaying coconut palms, and pristine rainforest.

Though **tourism** is crucial to its economy, the Big Island lags well behind Oahu and Maui in terms of annual visitors, and nowhere has seen development on the scale of Waikīkī or the south or west Maui shoreline. In the 1960s the island was expected to emerge as the first serious rival to Oahu. A highway system was built to cope with the anticipated influx, and **luxury resorts** shot up on bare lava, while more reasonably priced hotels appeared in the Kailua area. As things turned out, however, it was Maui that mushroomed, to become plagued by traffic problems and overcrowding. Save for the immediate vicinity of **Kailua**, the Big Island remains relatively stress-free.

The entire island has the population of a medium-sized town, with 176,000 people spread across its four thousand square miles; it has its fair share of restaurants, bars, and so on, plus a few budget inns and hostels to complement its hotels and resorts, but basically it's a rural community. There's plenty of opportunity to be active – **hiking** in the state and national parks, **snorkeling** in Kealakekua Bay, deep-sea **fishing** off the Kona coast, **golfing** in the Kohala resorts – but most visitors are content to while away their days meandering between beach and brunch.

As befits the birthplace of **King Kamehameha**, the first man to rule all the Hawaiian islands, the Big Island maintains strong links with its Polynesian past. Little more than two centuries have passed since the isolation of its original inhabitants came to an end, and their *heiaus*, petroglyphs, and abandoned villages are scattered throughout the island. Otherwise, though many of its smaller towns have an appealing air of the nineteenth-century West about them, with their false-front stores and wooden boardwalks, few historical attractions are likely to lure you away from the beaches. Any time you can spare to go sightseeing is better spent exploring the waterfalls, valleys, and especially the volcanoes that were so entwined with the lives of the ancient Hawaiians.

A brief history of the Big Island

Most of the seminal moments of Big Island history are recounted in the general history of Hawaii at the end of this book; before the Europeans changed everything, the island was so significant that it would be impossible to disentangle its own history from that of the whole archipelago.

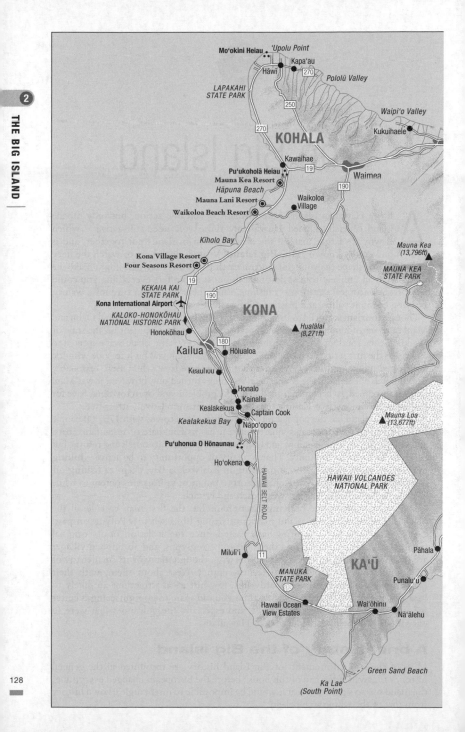

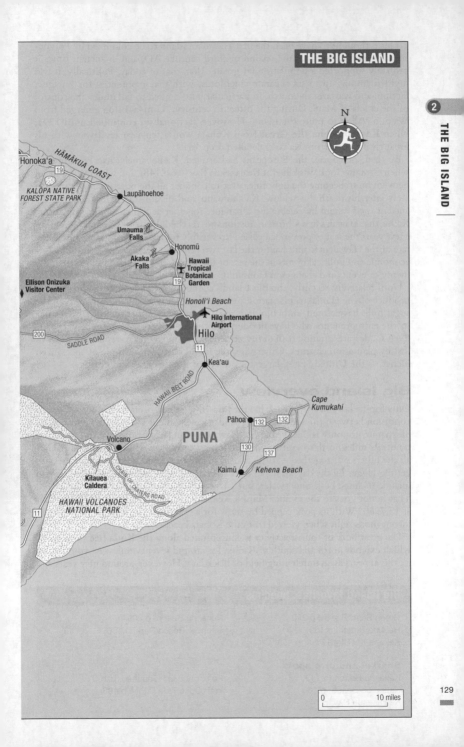

THE BIG ISLAND

N

Honoka'a
HĀMĀKUA COAST
19
KALŌPA NATIVE
FOREST STATE PARK
Laupāhoehoe

Umauma
Falls
Honomū
Akaka
Falls
Hawaii
Tropical
Botanical
Garden
19
Ellison Onizuka
Visitor Center

Honoli'i Beach
Hilo International
Airport
200
SADDLE ROAD
Hilo
11
Kea'au

HAWAII BELT ROAD
Cape
Kumukahi
Pāhoa
132
132
PUNA
130
Volcano
137
Kīlauea
Caldera
Kaimū
Kehena Beach
CHAIN OF CRATERS ROAD
HAWAII VOLCANOES
NATIONAL PARK
11

0   10 miles

This is thought to have been the first Hawaiian island to be colonized by Polynesian voyagers, as early as the second or third century AD, and in ancient times it probably supported a population far greater than that of today. Politically, it was divided among up to six separate chiefdoms, with major potential for intrigue, faction, and warfare; the north, in particular, also tended to fall under the control of the chiefs of Maui. During the fifteenth century, **'Umi-a-Liloa** emerged from Waipi'o Valley to unite the island. However, factionalism continued until 1791, when **Kamehameha the Great** from Kohala won a ten-year civil war with his great rival Keōua from Ka'ū, as detailed on p.161.

By then, of course, the Europeans had arrived. Kamehameha had been present when Captain Cook was killed at Kealakekua Bay (see p.148), and with European aid he went on to become the only ruler ever to conquer all the other islands. Immediately after his death, his widow, Ka'ahumanu, and his son Liholiho destroyed the ancient *kapu* system by celebrating a banquet together at Kailua, and it was also at Kailua that Hawaii's first Christian missionaries reached the islands. However, within a few years the seat of power had passed irreversibly to the island of Oahu. Just as the fate of the Hawaiian islands has for the last two centuries been largely determined by economic and political events in the rest of the world, the Big Island has been at the mercy of events and changes in Honolulu.

Until relatively recently, the Big Island's economy depended largely on the rich produce of the Hāmākua plantations, traded through Hilo. Now, however, all the sugar mills have closed, and Hilo finds itself regarded as something of a backwater by the entrepreneurs who have flooded into the sunny spots along the Kona coast. Even so, despite a frantic rush of investment, tourism has yet to replace all the jobs lost by plantation closures. Otherwise, the island occupies a couple of specialized niches, as the United States' largest producer of both **ginger** and **coffee**.

Big Island overview

Only for the last sixty years or so has the title "Big Island" been widely used, to avoid confusion between the state and the island whose name it took. It's an appropriate nickname: not only is this the biggest Hawaiian island – measuring at its maximum points 92 miles north to south, and 76 miles east to west, it would comfortably hold all the others put together – but thanks to **Mauna Loa** and **Kīlauea** volcanoes, it's getting bigger by the day. Mauna Loa may be the largest mountain on earth if you include its huge bulk underwater, but it's not the highest mountain on the island. That honor goes to the extinct **Mauna Kea**, slightly north and around 100ft taller at 13,796ft. With its peak capped by snow for a few months each year, it makes an incongruous sight when viewed from the Kohala beaches.

The great bulk of tourist activity is concentrated along the **Kona** (leeward) coast, which extends north and south of **Kailua** for around seventy miles. As you first fly in, this appears as an unrelenting field of black lava. However, around fifty years ago

---

Big Island favorites: beaches

Green Sand Beach, p.210
Hāpuna Beach, p.159
Kekaha Kai State Park, p.156

Punalu'u Beach, p.208
Spencer Beach Park, p.160

Snorkel and dive spots
Kahalu'u Beach, p.142
Kauna'oa Beach, p.160
Kealakekua Bay, p.147

Pu'uhonua O Hōnaunau, p.150
Wai 'Ōpae Tide Pools, p.193

its virtues of being consistently dry and hot began to be appreciated. Resort development took off, and this became one of Hawaii's prime tourist destinations. Although the five-mile stretch from Kailua south to Keauhou has acquired an unbroken succession of hotels and condos, Kailua itself remains recognizable as the sleepy little town where Kamehameha the Great had his palace. To the **south**, reached by a gorgeous road through lush coffee groves, lies **Kealakekua Bay**, where Captain Cook met his end, with the nearby **Puʻuhonua O Hōnaunau**, or "Place of Refuge," bearing witness to a vanished Hawaiian way of life and death.

The **northernmost** spur of the Big Island is its oldest segment, named after the first of its five volcanoes to appear above the ocean – the long-extinct **Kohala Mountain**. The Big Island's largest **coral reefs** – albeit small by most standards – lie just offshore, and its only sizeable **white-sand beaches** have been washed into nearby sheltered coves. Although the landscape gets more dramatic the further north you go, facilities for tourists are almost entirely restricted to **South Kohala**. This region, too, consists of barren lava flats, but lavish resorts such as the Disney-esque *Hilton Waikoloa Village* are tucked into inlets all along the coastline.

Continuing around the island, beyond the upland cattle country of **Waimea** – home to the Parker Ranch and generations of lasso-toting *paniolo* cowboys – you reach the magnificent **Hāmākua coast**, to be confronted by archetypal South Seas scenery. Even before the emergence of commercial agriculture, these rain-drenched slopes formed the fertile heartland of Hawaii: broad, green **Waipiʻo Valley** was capable of feeding the entire island. After a century of growing sugar, however, the small towns here are reeling from the closure of the plantations. So is the Big Island's only city, its capital, **Hilo**, where attempts to attract tourists have always been thwarted by the rainfall. Nonetheless it's an attractively low-key community, renowned for spectacular flowers and orchids.

Finally, the **south** of the island is dominated by the exhilarating wilderness of **Hawaii Volcanoes National Park**. Apart from the steaming craters and cinder cones of Mauna Loa and Kīlauea, its terrain ranges from arctic tundra and sulphurous desert to lowland rainforest and remote Pacific beaches. This is a thrilling hiking destination, holding trails that run through still-active craters. Here and there along the shore the volcanoes have deposited beaches of jet-black sand, while near **South Point** – the southernmost point of the United States – you can hike to a remote beach composed of green(ish) sand. Otherwise, the southern coastline is now sparsely populated, and few visitors bother to leave the highway in the time-forgotten regions of **Puna** and **Kaʻū**.

Getting to the Big Island

The only way to get to the Big Island is to **fly**. Of the two main airports, **Kona International Airport** is on the west coast, seven miles north of Kailua (see p.135), and **Hilo International Airport** on the outskirts of Hilo (see p.172), on the east coast. Most tourists arrive at Kona, but Hilo is kept busy with local travelers, and the two airports receive similar numbers of flights each day. The vast majority of each day's arrivals come from Honolulu. As detailed on p.19, the only **nonstop flights** to the Big Island from the US mainland are to Kona; United, American, Delta, Aloha, and ATA currently offer services. It's also possible to fly direct to **Waimea** from Honolulu and Maui on tiny Pacific Wings (☎808/887-2104 or 1-888/575-4546, ⓦwww.pacificwings.com).

Getting around the Big Island

The only practicable way to explore the Big Island is to **drive**. All the major car rental chains are represented at both main airports. In a sense, there's just one main road, the **Hawaii Belt Road**, which circles the entire island. Other than in and around Kailua, traffic problems are all but nonexistent, and if you have to, you can get from anywhere on the island to anywhere else pretty quickly. It's possible to sleep in Kailua and catch a plane out from Hilo the next day, while a nightly exodus of cars drive the hundred-plus miles from the volcanoes back to Kona. Unlike all the other islands, however, the Big Island is too big to make it worth attempting a complete circuit in one day, and visiting the volcanoes as a day-trip from Kona won't give you enough time at the park.

You should also keep a close eye on your fuel gauge. **Gas stations** are common around Kailua and Hilo, but in several regions, including the National Park, you can drive up to fifty miles without seeing one.

Some of the national chains forbid drivers to take ordinary vehicles onto lesser roads such as **South Point Road** (see p.210) or the high-altitude **Saddle Road** (see p.186). If you're determined to explore those areas, or drive to the summit of Mauna Kea, you can rent a **four-wheel-drive vehicle** from Harper Car & Truck in Hilo or Kailua (☎1-800/852-9993 or 808/969-1478, ⓦ www.harpershawaii.com), whose rates start from $100 per day.

As for **public transport**, Hele On (Mon–Sat only; ☎808/961-8744, ⓦ www .heleonbus.org) run **free buses** between Hilo and Kailua, and between Hilo and the volcanoes (Mon–Fri, daily; see p.197), though they're much more useful for local commuters than for visitors.

Details on seeing the island by **air** are given below; for **boat tours** see p.141; and for getting around by **motorbike** or **bicycle**, see p.135. Otherwise, the only alternatives to driving are the **minibus tours** run by companies such as

Big Island flight-seeing

Unlike the other Hawaiian islands, the Big Island is too large to see in a single **air tour**, but it has the incomparable attraction of the unpredictable Kīlauea **eruption**. If it's the volcano you want to see, opt for a flight from Hilo or Volcano; many of the cheaper ones on the Kona side go up the Kohala coast and miss Kīlauea, while if you do want to reach the volcano from Kona you'll find yourself paying for a *long* flight.

Prices generally start at around $160 for a 45min flight, and can reach $500 for a full circle-island flight with a good, long stare at the eruption. If you're traveling in a group of four or more, it makes sense to charter a helicopter by the hour, and devise your own flight path.

Helicopters

	Number	Web (ⓦwww.)	Departs
Blue Hawaiian	☎808/961-5600	bluehawaiian.com	Hilo, Waikoloa
Paradise	☎808/969-7392	paradisecopters.com	Hilo, Kona
Safari	☎808/969-1259	safarihelicopters.com	Hilo
Sunshine	☎808/270-3999	sunshinehelicopters.com	Hilo, Hāpuna
Tropical	☎808/961-6810	tropicalhelicopters.com	Hilo, Kona

Fixed-wing

	Number	Web (ⓦwww.)	Departs
Big Island Air	☎808/329-4868	bigislandair.com	Kona
Iolani Air Tours	☎808/329-0018	iolaniair.com	Hilo, Kona

Roberts Hawaii (☎808/329-1688 or 1-866/898-2519, ⓦwww.robertshawaii
.com), who do a volcano tour from Hilo and a circle-island tour from Kailua,
both costing $79.

The best **adventure tour** operator is Hawaii Forest & Trail (☎808/331-8505
or 1-800/464-1993, ⓦwww.hawaii-forest.com). From their base near Kona
International Airport, they take half- and full-day van tours to all corners of
the island, including hiking trips to places like Volcanoes National Park and
Pololū Valley, and a tour to the top of Mauna Kea. Prices range from $150 to
$180 per person.

Where to stay

Where you **stay** depends on what sort of vacation you're planning. If most of
your time will be spent on the beach, the prime oceanfront areas of the **Kona**
and **Kohala coasts** are filled with upscale hotels, condos, and self-contained
resorts. Many of the cheapest options on this side of the island are in **Kailua**,
though that town, too, has its share of luxury properties. Elsewhere, **Hilo**
offers small, attractive inns that are far preferable to its faded old hotels, while
both the **National Park** area and **Waimea** have some medium-scale lodges and
abundant **B&Bs**.

Bear in mind when you book that it's barely possible to see the entire island from
a single base. Even if you plan to concentrate on the Kona or Kohala coasts, reckon

For state park **camping permits**, contact the Division of State Parks, 75 Aupuni St, Hilo
(rates vary; ☎808/974-6200, ⓦwww.hawaiistateparks.org). **County park permits**, at $5
per day, are administered by the Department of Parks and Recreation, 101 Pauahi St,
Hilo (Mon–Fri 7.45am–4.30pm; ☎808/961-8311, ⓦwww.hawaii-county.com), which has
subsidiary offices at Yano Hall in Captain Cook (Mon–Fri noon–2pm), and Waimea
Community Center in Waimea (Mon–Fri 8.30–10.30am).

on spending at least a night or two in the National Park area, or possibly in Hilo. It may even be worth simply not using a pre-paid Kona-side room for one night, to give yourself time at the volcanoes.

When to go

Throughout the year, sea-level **temperatures** rarely drop below the low seventies Fahrenheit (around 22°C) in the daytime, or reach above the low eighties (around 28°C); at night the thermometer seldom falls below the low sixties. Average daily temperatures in Hilo range from 71°F in February to 76°F in August, while Kailua fluctuates between 72°F and 77°F. Waimea has similar daily maximums, but drops to the low fifties (around 11°C) at night. Volcano Village, too, can get cold at night, while temperatures at the summit of Mauna Kea, which receives snow in winter, range from 31°F up to 43°F.

In principle the **rainiest** months are from December to February, but where you are on the island makes far more difference than what time of year it is. Hilo is the wettest city in the US, with an annual rainfall of 128 inches, and Volcano Village is even wetter, but the Kona coast, and especially the Kohala resort area, receive very little rain at any time. Kawaihae in Kohala gets a mere ten inches each year.

As in the rest of Hawaii, the state of the **ocean** varies with the seasons. It's possible to swim all year round in more sheltered areas, but the high surf between October and April makes certain beaches (identified throughout this chapter) extremely dangerous.

Mention should also be made of a unique Big Island phenomenon. While the summits of Mauna Loa and Mauna Kea are renowned for having the clearest air on earth, down below, when the tradewinds drop, the island is prone to a choking haze of sulphurous volcanic emissions known as **"vog."** The pollution on such days hits levels worse than those in Los Angeles or London; the only spot on the island that is consistently downwind of Kīlauea, the Ka'ū Desert, is a lifeless wasteland.

Nightlife and entertainment

Most of what limited **nightlife** the Big Island has to offer is arranged by the major hotels, and many feature live musicians every night. In a typical week, the biggest events are the various *lū'aus* listed on p.143, but visiting artists from the other islands or the mainland also make regular concert appearances. Most such activity happens in the prime tourist areas of Kona and Kohala, but Hawaiian performers with strong local followings also schedule appearances in Hilo.

Big Island favorites: eating

These restaurants are in ascending order of price, not quality

The Coffee Shack, Captain Cook, p.147

Ocean Sushi Deli, Hilo, p.178

Hilo Bay Café, Hilo, p.178

Thai Thai, Volcano, p.207

Sansei, Waikoloa, p.163

Bamboo Restaurant and Bar, Hāwī, p.168

Merrimans, Waimea, p.165

Roy's, Waikoloa, p.162

Brown's Beach House, Fairmont Orchid, p.162

Coast Grille, Hāpuna Beach Prince, p.162

Bike and motorbike rental and tours

For general advice on **cycling** in Hawaii, see p.24.

Bike Volcano ☎808/934-9199 or 1-888/934-9199, ⓦwww.bikevolcano.com. Daily guided bike tours of Volcanoes National Park and/or the current eruption site from $99.

Bike Works Kailua ☎808/326-2453, ⓦwww.bikeworkskona.com. Mountain or road bikes from $40 per day or $140 per week.

Hawaii Harley Rental Kailua ☎808/241-7020 or 1-877/212-9253, ⓦwww.hawaiiharley rental.com. Harley-Davidson motorcycles for rent from $139 per day.

Orchid Isle Bicycling Kailua ☎808/327-0087 or 1-800/219-2324, ⓦwww.orchid islebicycling.com. The widest program of cycling tours on the island; one-day tours (4–8hr) cost from $125, or you can take the multi-day circle-island "Tour de Paradise" for $2495.

Kailua

The largest town on the Kona side of the Big Island, **KAILUA** is also Hawaii's oldest Western-style community. Even before the first Christian missionaries arrived here from New England in 1820, it was a favorite home of Kamehameha I. However, it didn't expand significantly beyond its picturesque harbor, home to a royal palace, until the 1980s' tourist boom suddenly made this the island's busiest holiday area. Since then, its original core has been swamped, with a ribbon of high-rise hotels and sprawling condos stretching south along the coast for several miles, and ugly shopping malls climbing ever further up the hillside. Some locals disparagingly refer to it as "Kona-fornia," decrying the loss of its former Hawaiian identity.

In fact, though, Kailua's heyday as a resort seems to be over. What new tourism investment is still taking place is concentrated further north, and Kailua feels as though it has reverted towards being a less frenzied and more likeable destination, recognizable as the town Mark Twain called "the sleepiest, quietest, Sundayest looking place you can imagine."

If you've come to relax, you'll probably find its low-key pleasures appealing. At least one local beach is bound to suit you, and there are plenty of alternative activities. In particular, sitting on the *lānai* of a waterfront café or bar, for a morning blast of Kona coffee or a sunset cocktail, is enough to make anyone feel that all's well with the world.

Incidentally, although the town's official name is Kailua, tourists in particular often mistakenly call it "Kona," and the post office hyphenates it to "Kailua-Kona" to distinguish it from the Kailuas on Oahu and Maui.

Arrival and information

Kona International Airport, the Big Island's busiest airport, is a laidback and largely open-air affair that sprawls across the lava seven miles north of Kailua. It holds a **tourist information** desk, open to coincide with flights; there's no visitor center in Kailua itself.

Most arriving passengers rent a **car** immediately from the usual outlets, or arrange to be picked up by their hotels. **Taxis** from the airport rank cost around $30 to Kailua, $50 to Waikoloa; the multi-passenger shuttle vans run by **Speedi Shuttle** (☎808/329-5433 or 1-877/242-5777, ⓦwww.speedishuttle.com) charge slightly less per person.

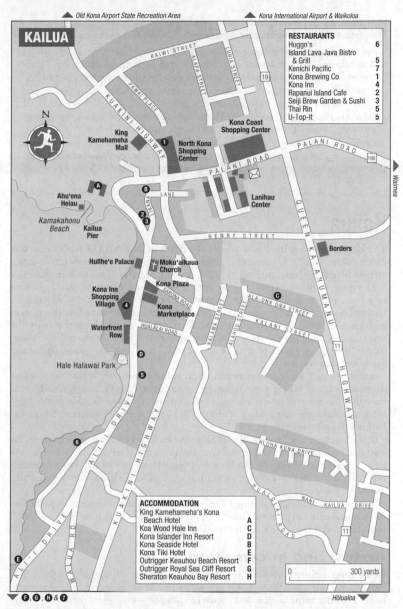

KAILUA

▲ Old Kona Airport State Recreation Area   ▲ Kona International Airport & Waikoloa

RESTAURANTS

Huggo's	6
Island Lava Java Bistro & Grill	5
Kenichi Pacific	7
Kona Brewing Co	1
Kona Inn	4
Rapanui Island Cafe	2
Seiji Brew Garden & Sushi	3
Thai Rin	5
U-Top-It	5

ACCOMMODATION

King Kamehameha's Kona Beach Hotel	A
Koa Wood Hale Inn	C
Kona Islander Inn Resort	D
Kona Seaside Hotel	B
Kona Tiki Hotel	E
Outrigger Keauhou Beach Resort	F
Outrigger Royal Sea Cliff Resort	G
Sheraton Keauhou Bay Resort	H

0 ────── 300 yards

▼ **F**, **G**, **H** & **7**   Hōlualoa ▼

Regular **free buses**, run by Hele On (Mon–Sat only; ☎808/961-8744, ⓦ www .heleonbus.org), ply Ali'i Drive in Kailua; several continue south to Captain Cook, while one service daily goes north to Waimea, and another follows the Belt Road around the northern part of the island all the way to Hilo. In addition, the Honu Express (daily 7.30am–7.15pm; ☎808/822-3000, ⓦ www.keauhoushoppingcenter .com) is a free **shuttle bus** that loops all day between Kailua Pier and the Keauhou Shopping Center (see p.140), with stops along Ali'i Drive.

Accommodation

Well over half the Big Island's **hotel** and **condo** rooms are in or near Kailua, almost all along the five-mile oceanfront stretch of Ali'i Drive. While the area is generally less luxurious than the resorts to the north, attractive and good-value accommodation can still be found, and if you prefer to spend your vacation in a real town rather than a self-contained resort, Kailua is still the island's best option.

Although Ali'i Drive also holds a handful of **B&Bs**, for a traditional B&B experience you're better off choosing a more rural location among the options listed under "South Kona accommodation" on p.146.

King Kamehameha's Kona Beach Hotel 75-5660 Palani Rd ☏ 808/329-2911 or 1-800/367-2111, ⓦ www.konabeachhotel.com. Guest rooms at this veteran resort hotel have been beautifully renovated, making it great value for such a superb oceanfront location, facing picturesque Kamakahonu Beach (see p.142) in the very heart of Kailua. The public areas retain an appealing "Hawaiian" feel, while the gardens are an attractive setting for *lū'aus* (Tues–Thurs & Sun 5pm; $70). Although there's no full-scale restaurant, abundant dining options lie within easy walking distance. Check online for special deals. ❹

Koa Wood Hale Inn 75-184 Ala-Ona Ona St ☏ 808/329-9633, ⓦ www.alternative-hawaii.com /affordable/kona. Clean, welcoming budget hostel, a few hundred yards from the town center – reached by taking Kalani Street up from Kuakini Highway at *McDonald's*, and then the second turn on the left. Popular with backpackers and surfers, it offers dorm beds for $25, or basic private doubles for $65, with mountain bikes for rent, and wi-fi; no alcohol allowed. ❶–❷

Kona Islander Inn Resort 75-5776 Kuakini Hwy ☏ 808/329-3333 or 1-800/244-4752, ⓦ www .konaislanderinnhotel.com. These centrally located 1960s condos, just behind the Coconut Grove Marketplace, may not seem the height of style from the outside, but they're perfectly adequate and offer good rates. Kitchen facilities are minimal. ❸

Kona Seaside Hotel 75-5646 Palani Rd ☏ 808/329-2455 or 1-800/560-5558, ⓦ www .seasidehotelshawaii.com. Long-established 225-room property, sprawling across central Kailua. No resort-style amenities, simply small, far-from-fancy but good-value air-conditioned rooms, clustered around two separate pools. Discount rates online. ❸

Kona Tiki Hotel 75-5968 Ali'i Drive ☏ 808/329-1425, ⓦ www.konatiki.com. This simple, old-fashioned, three-story, fifteen-room property, inches from the ocean a mile south of central Kailua, is a gem for budget travelers. All the clean, comfortable rooms have private oceanfront balconies or patios; some slightly more expensive ones also have kitchenettes, and rates include breakfast beside the small pool. No TVs or phones, and credit cards aren't accepted; three-night minimum stay, often booked up years in advance. ❸

Outrigger Keauhou Beach Resort 78-6740 Ali'i Drive ☏ 808/322-3441 or 1-866/326-6803, ⓦ www.outrigger.com. Seven-story hotel jutting into the sea on a black-lava promontory at the southern end of Kahalu'u Beach Park, five miles south of central Kailua. Very well equipped rooms, some directly above the ocean, plus pool, tennis courts and Hawaiian archeological sites. Free buffet breakfasts at the nice open-air *Kamaaina Terrace*, and live Hawaiian music at the *Verandah Lounge*. ❹

Outrigger Royal Sea Cliff Resort 75-6040 Ali'i Drive ☏ 808/329-8021, ⓦ www.outrigger.com. White, multilevel condo complex of luxurious studios and one- and two-bedroom suites, dropping down to the ocean a mile south of central Kailua; the public areas are nothing special, though there's a lush courtyard garden. You can't swim in the sea here, but it has fresh- and saltwater pools, plus a sauna and hot tub. ❹

Sheraton Keauhou Bay Resort 78-128 Ehukai St ☏ 808/930-4900 or 1-866/716-8109, ⓦ www .sheratonkeauhou.com. The most upscale resort along Kailua's coastal strip, in a spectacular oceanfront location five miles south of central Kailua. It's heavily geared towards families, with a pool complex and waterslide to compensate for the lack of a beach, and the rooms are enormous and luxurious. ❻

The Town

Central Kailua still retains something of the feel of a seaside village. Every visitor should take a leisurely oceanfront stroll along the old Seawall, whose scenic route runs for a few hundred yards around the bay from the **Ahu'ena Heiau**, jutting into the ocean in front of the *King Kamehameha* hotel, to the **Hulihe'e Palace** and **Moku'aikaua Church**.

At its heart is the small jetty of **Kailua Pier**, which up until the 1960s was still a cattle port, but is now given over to tourism. Popular with anglers, romantic couples, and surf bums alike, it's also used by a handful of boat-tour operators, although most commercial boats leave from Honokōhau Harbor, three miles north (see p.155). At least the time-honored tradition of fishermen displaying their catches in the early evening persists, with the biggest fish of all weighing in during August's International Billfish Tournament. More gleaming flesh is on show in mid-October each year, when the pier is the starting point of the 2.4-mile swimming leg of the **Ironman Triathlon**, which also requires its participants to cycle 112 miles and run a marathon on the same day.

The resort area stretches away to the south, while up from the seafront a plethora of **shopping malls** cater more to the needs of local residents, and less to those of tourists, the higher you climb from the shoreline.

Ahuʻena Heiau

The **Ahuʻena Heiau** guards the mouth of Kailua Bay in a too-good-to-be-true setting beside a sandy little beach, in front of the *King Kamehameha* hotel. Kamehameha the Great held sway from this ancient temple, dedicated to Lono, between his return from Honolulu in 1812 and his death here on May 8, 1819. Soon afterwards, his son Liholiho, spurred on by Kamehameha's principal queen, Kaʻahumanu, broke the ancient *kapu* system by hosting a banquet here, and thereby inadvertently cleared the way for the missionaries.

Thanks to detailed drawings made in 1816, archeologists have been able to restore the *heiau* to its original appearance, but because it still possesses great spiritual significance, all access to the platform is forbidden. You can get a close-up view by walking to the end of the King Kamehameha beach – officially Kamakahonu Beach (see p.142) – or by swimming out a short way. The *heiau* itself is small, but follows the conventional Hawaiian template, consisting as it does of three distinct structures set on a *paepae* (platform) of black volcanic rock. The largest hut is the *hale mana* ("house of spiritual power"), a place of prayer and council. The smaller *hale pahu* ("house of the drum") alongside is thatched with *hala* leaves, while the ramshackle, tapering structure nearby is the *anuʻu*, or "oracle tower," used by the priests to intercede with the gods. In addition, half a dozen *kiʻi akua*, carved wooden images, stand on the platform. The tallest, a god of healing, has a golden plover on his head, in honor of the migratory bird credited with having first guided Polynesian voyagers to Hawaii.

After his death, Kamehameha's bones were prepared for burial on a similar rock platform adjacent to the *heiau*, then interred in a location that remains secret to this day (though recent research has suggested it may lie on the adjoining property to the north, which now holds the home of Microsoft co-founder Paul Allen). The platform still exists, though the *hale pohaku* that stood upon it, in which the ceremonies took place, has long since disappeared.

Huliheʻe Palace

Though the four-square, two-story **Huliheʻe Palace** (Wed–Sat 10am–3pm; $6; ☏808/329-1877, ⓦwww.huliheepalace.org), facing out to sea from the center of Kailua, was built in 1838 for Governor John Adams Kuakini, it soon passed into the hands of the Hawaiian royal family. Feeling more like a quaint Victorian private residence than a palace, it was constructed using lava rock, coral, and native hardwoods, but you wouldn't know that from a glance at its coffee-colored modern exterior.

The palace is still recovering from heavy earthquake damage sustained in 2006, but has reopened for full tours, enabling visitors to admire its massive *koa*-wood furniture, photos, and ancient Hawaiian artifacts. Pleasant *lānais* run the full length

of the ocean side of both the first and second floors. Visitors are free to wander into the well-maintained gardens, which play host to free Sunday-afternoon music and hula performances once each month, to no fixed schedule.

Moku'aikaua Church

The original **Moku'aikaua Church**, immediately inland from the palace, was the first church to be built on the Hawaiian islands. When constructed in 1820 for the use of Reverend Asa Thurston, who had arrived in Kailua Bay on April 4 of that year, it closely resembled a *heiau*, being just a thatched hut perched on a stone platform. The current building was erected immediately before Hulihe'e Palace by the same craftsmen, and incorporates large chunks of lava into a design clearly related to the clapboard churches of New England. Open daily from dawn to dusk, it's free to visitors, and welcomes worshippers to its Congregational services (Sun 8am & 10.30am).

The church itself is not of great interest, though a section serves as a museum of the early days of Hawaiian Christianity. Displays include a large model of the *Thaddeus* – the first missionary ship – and an exhibition on traditional Polynesian navigational techniques featuring, among other things, a fascinating Micronesian "stick chart," in which an intricate latticework of twigs and cowrie shells depicts ocean currents, swells, and islands. Such charts were committed to memory rather than carried on board, and guided canoes across thousands of miles on the open Pacific.

South along Ali'i Drive

Heading south from both church and palace, **Ali'i Drive** is at first fringed with modern malls housing T-shirt stores, boutiques, and restaurants. Beyond Kailua proper, it stretches five miles along a rugged coastline scattered with tiny lava beaches and lined all the way with hotels and condos. The only thing you could call a "sight" along here is the tiny, blue, and highly photogenic **St Peter's Church**, built in 1880. It takes perhaps a minute to admire its waterfront setting, on a tiny patch of lawn at the north end of Kahalu'u Bay, and to glance in through the open door at the etched glass window. A bare platform of lava boulders alongside is all that remains of the Kue'manu Heiau (see p.142).

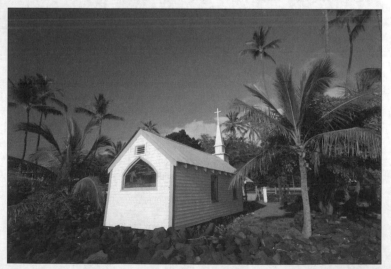

▲ St Peter's Church

Ali'i Drive comes to an end in what's nominally the distinct community of **Keauhou**, which isn't a "town" in any sense of the word. Apart from the **Keauhou Shopping Village**, set a long way up from the ocean, it simply consists of yet more seafront hotels.

Kailua's beaches

Central Kailua is surprisingly short of **beaches**. There are enough patches of sand along Ali'i Drive to satisfy those who like the convenience of being able to walk to and from their hotels, but most visitors tend to drive north when they fancy a swim. The Big Island's best beaches – such as Kekaha Kai State Park (p.156), Hāpuna Beach (p.159), and Spencer Beach Park (p.160) – start ten miles or more up the coast, but a good nearby alternative is the Old Kona Airport park, just a few minutes from town.

Snorkel Bob has a branch of his inimitable **snorkel equipment** rental service opposite *Huggo's*, near the *Royal Kona Resort* (daily 8am–5pm; ☏808/329-0770, Ⓦwww.snorkelbob.com), and another just south of the airport, behind Home Depot, at 73-4976 Kamanu St (same hours and website; ☏808/329-0770).

None of the beaches covered in this section permits **camping**.

Boat trips on the Kona coast

Snorkel cruises are extremely popular on the Kona and Kohala coasts, supplemented in season (Dec–April) by **whale-watching** expeditions. Most boats depart from Honokōhau Harbor, though some also leave from Kailua Pier and Keauhou Bay.

Snorkel cruises

The prime destination for snorkel cruises is the underwater state park of **Kealakekua Bay** (see p.147). The shallowest and most sheltered spot here is in the immediate area of Captain Cook's monument, where the reef provides perfect conditions for snorkelers. Swarms of yellow butterfly fish and tangs, plus parrotfish, triggerfish, and hundreds of other species can always be found circling near the edge. As passengers are forbidden to set foot ashore, snorkeling rather than sightseeing has to be your priority. Many Kealakekua boats start from Honokōhau Harbor (see p.155), but that's a *long* way away; you'd do better to choose a boat from Keauhou.

Body Glove ☏808/326-7122 or 1-800/551-8911, Ⓦwww.bodyglovehawaii.com. A complex schedule of cruises that conveniently leave from Kailua Pier. Snorkel cruises head two miles north to the excellent spot in Pawai Bay (4hr 30min morning cruise $120, ages 6–17 $78; 3hr afternoon cruise $78/58), with scuba diving as an optional extra. They also offer 2hr 30min whale-watching trips (Dec–April; $78/58); historical dinner cruises to Kealakekua Bay (Tues, Thurs & Sat 4pm; $94/58); and sunset cocktail cruises (Wed & Fri 5.30pm; $94/58).

Captain Zodiac ☏808/329-3199, Ⓦwww.captainzodiac.com. Daily 4hr cruises in a rubber raft from Honokōhau to Kealakekua Bay (8.15am & 1pm; $100, ages 4–12 $84), plus some 5hr trips (Mon & Tues 10am; same price), and 3hr whale-watching trips in winter (Jan–April Tues & Thurs 9am; $65/59).

Dolphin Discoveries ☏808/322-8000, Ⓦwww.dolphindiscoveries.com. Snorkel tours from Keauhou Bay to Kealakekua (8am 4hr cruise also includes Pu'uhonua O Hōnaunau; $93/78; noon 3hr trip, $78, no reductions), plus 4hr "dolphin swims" at Kealakekua ($130).

Fair Wind ☏808/345-0268 or 1-800/677-9461, Ⓦwww.fair-wind.com. All trips depart from Keauhou Bay. Schedules vary, but as a rule, the large *Fair Wind II* catamaran sails on 4hr 30min trips at 9am daily ($125, ages 4–12 $75) plus 2pm around three days per week in summer ($109/69), while the faster *Hula Kai* hydrofoil operates a 5hr

Old Kona Airport State Recreation Area

When Kona International Airport opened in 1970, it replaced a small airport on the northern outskirts of Kailua whose site was then set aside for public use as the **Old Kona Airport State Recreation Area** (daily dawn–8pm). Though it's not all that attractive, it's now Kailua's most extensive and popular beach. Driving in along the long former runways, which run parallel to the sea, is either hair-raising or fun depending on your state of mind, as no one ever seems sure which, if any, of the plentiful road markings to follow.

A strip of coarse, whitish sand lies beyond the fringe of low palm trees, while the shoreline itself consists almost entirely of flat, smooth *pāhoehoe* lava, indented with calm shallow pools that are ideal for children to splash in. Sheltered pavilions and barbecue facilities are scattered all the way along, and despite the lack of food and drink outlets, there are usually plenty of people around, especially at weekends.

If you walk north across the lava beyond the end of the beach for ten to fifteen minutes, you'll come to **Pawai Bay**, a prime **snorkeling** spot often used by boat trips, which holds no amenities for visitors. The intricately sculpted rocks immediately offshore shelter many interesting species of fish, but when the waves are at all strong it's safer to swim a little further out, where the visibility is generally superb.

cruise daily at 9.30am ($155), with scuba diving for an additional $46, and after-dark manta ray encounters (snorkelers $99, divers $145).

Sea Paradise ☎808/322-2500, ⓦwww.seaparadise.com. Spacious Kealakekua catamaran that heads from Keauhou to Kealakekua (4hr; daily except Sun 8.30am; $99, ages 4–12 $59) and also offers night-time manta ray snorkeling ($89/59).

Sea Quest ☎808/329-7238, ⓦwww.seaquesthawaii.com. Bouncy six-person Zodiac rafts without any shade that leave for Kealakekua from Keauhou at 8am ($92, ages 6–12 $75; 4hr) and 1pm ($724/$62; 3hr).

Sightseeing cruises

Atlantis Submarines ☎1-800/548-6262, ⓦwww.atlantisadventures.com. Cramped but fascinating hour-long ocean-floor cruises, with foolhardy divers trying to entice sharks alongside. Daily at 10am, 11.30am & 1pm from Kailua Pier ($99, under-13s $45).

Captain Dan McSweeney's Whale Watch ☎808/322-0028, ⓦwww.ilovewhales.com. Between Christmas and March, 3hr tours depart 7.30am & 11.30am daily from Honokōhau. In April, July, Aug & Nov to Christmas, the only tours are Tues, Thurs & Sat at 7.30am. $80, children under ninety pounds $70).

Dive boats

Two-dive cruises tend to cost $115–150, with a $25–40 surcharge for unqualified divers, and equipment rental costing $7–10 per item. Most operators offer certification courses for upwards of $500. Kailua offers the particular treat of **night dives** to see the massive manta rays attracted by artificial lights around the *Sheraton Keauhou Bay Resort*; prices are similar to those for day-dives.

The following is a selective list of recommended operators.

Big Island Divers	☎808/329-6068	ⓦwww.bigislanddivers.com
Dive Makai	☎808/329-2025	ⓦwww.divemakai.com
Jack's Diving Locker	☎808/329-7585	ⓦwww.jacksdivinglocker.com
Kohala Divers	☎808/882-7774	ⓦwww.kohaladivers.com
Kona Honu Divers	☎808/324-4668	ⓦwww.konahonudivers.com
Pacific Rim Divers	☎808/334-1750	ⓦwww.pacificrimdivers.com

Kamakahonu Beach

Many visitors to Kailua glance at pretty little **Kamakahonu Beach** and assume that it belongs to the *King Kamehameha* hotel. However, non-guests are entirely at liberty to sunbathe here or to swim out for a closer look at the Ahu'ena Heiau (see p.138), and it's also a popular launching point for kayaks and canoes. While it's a delightful spot, swimming beyond the mouth of the tiny inlet is not recommended, and in terms of size, calmness, and crowds, it can often resemble a swimming pool.

Ali'i Drive beaches

The coast along Ali'i Drive south of central Kailua predominantly consists of black lava flats interspersed with the odd sandy cove. Few hotels or condos have adjacent beaches, so the designated beach parks tend to be the only places where it's possible to swim.

If you visit in winter or early spring, you probably won't even be able to find the small **White Sands Beach**, immediately north of St Peter's Church (see p.139), four miles south of central Kailua. Long renowned as an exhilarating surfing beach – the pile of black boulders near the church are the ruins of the Kue'manu *heiau*, the only Hawaiian temple devoted exclusively to surfing – this remains Kona's most popular venue for boogie-boarders and body-surfers. However, the dramatic waves are capable of washing the beach away altogether – hence the name by which it's more commonly known, **Magic Sands**. For most of the year, bathing is safe for children in the inshore area, while experienced divers will enjoy investigating a network of submarine lava tubes. So long as the beach is not devoid of sand, the snorkeling, too, is superb – especially if you head off to the right.

The largest of the beaches along Ali'i Drive, and even better for snorkeling, is **Kahalu'u Beach**, just south of St Peter's Church. It's more of a slight indentation in the coastline than a bay, but that's enough for it to hang on to a fair-sized spread of white sand. Children play in the lava hollows to either side, snorkelers explore deeper but still sheltered pools, and strong swimmers and scuba-divers use the shelving sand to reach the open waters of the bay. Large segments remain of a long breakwater, which originally protected the whole area and was constructed to aid fish-farming by early Hawaiians.

Generally this is a safe spot, but high surf conditions can create a devastating rip current. Don't venture into the water if you're in any doubt; if you get caught by the current, your best strategy, as ever, is to allow yourself to be swept out beyond its reach rather than exhaust yourself trying to fight it.

Eating and drinking

Though Kailua is packed with places to **eat**, and each of its many malls holds at least a couple of restaurants, with Asian cuisines strongly represented, there's little that could be considered fine dining. Strolling the waterfront, you'll find some determinedly old-fashioned, inexpensive diners, several of which also hold open-air, ocean-view **bars**.

Huggo's 75-5828 Kahakai St ☎ 808/329-1493, ⓦ www.huggos.com. Large open-sided oceanfront restaurant, where lunch includes salads, burgers, and sandwiches, for $10–15. The dinner menu features Pacific Rim dishes such as fish stuffed with prawns, at $25–39. Prices owe as much to the lovely location as to the food, so come while there's light to enjoy the views. For breakfast, the nominally distinct *Java On The Rocks* espresso bar takes over the location. There's often live evening entertainment, usually with Hawaiian music 6.30–8pm and a local easy-listening band later on. Daily 6.30–11am & 11.30am–10pm, bar open until midnight.

🏃 **Island Lava Java Bistro & Grill** Ali'i Sunset Plaza, 75-5799 Ali'i Drive ☎ 808/327-2161, ⓦ www.islandlavajavakona.com. Seafront mall café, with several open-air

tables, and offering delicious Kona coffee, plus exotic juices, fresh-baked breads, $10 sandwiches, salads up to $12.50, and pizzas at $15–19. The perfect place for a light ocean-view breakfast or inexpensive lunch or dinner, with wi-fi. Daily 6.30am–9.30pm.

Kenichi Pacific Keauhou Shopping Village ☎808/322-6400. Smart sushi/Pacific Rim place in an upscale but anonymous mall, well up from the ocean five miles south of central Kailua. Pricey but excellent food, with appetizers like fried squid priced at $9, fish and meat entrees at $23–38, and sushi rolls at $6–11. Daily 5–9.30pm.

Kona Brewing Co 75-5629 Kuakini Hwy ☎808/334-2739, ⓦwww.konabrewingco.com. If you're wondering where everybody is, chances are they're in this large, friendly, and always lively brewpub, hidden away in an unexciting mall behind the *King Kamehameha* hotel, which offers lots of outdoor seating but no views. As well as home-brewed beers ("Liquid Aloha," they call them) like Longboard Lager, they sell inventive salads and sandwiches ($12), and tasty pizzas for $18–24. Food service stops an hour before closing time. Sun–Thurs 11am–10pm, Fri & Sat 11am–11pm.

Kona Inn Restaurant Kona Inn Shopping Village, 75-5744 Ali'i Drive ☎808/329-4455. Conventional waterfront fish place, on an open-air *lānai* facing the ocean across tranquil lawns, and divided into two sections. The *Café Grill* sells bar snacks, salads, and sandwiches, while the more formal dinner-only restaurant serves appetizers from clam chowder to sashimi, and $20–35 entrees that concentrate on seafood, but also include steaks. *Café Grill* daily 11.30am–9.30pm, dinner daily 5–9pm.

Rapanui Island Cafe 75-5695 Ali'i Drive ☎808/329-0511. Dinner-only pan-Polynesian restaurant, at the back of a tiny central mall. Run by a friendly New Zealand couple, it has no views but a pleasant atmosphere. The food is generally spicy, with *sate* meat and fish plus vegetarian alternatives, and delicious coconut rice. Mon–Sat 5–9pm.

Seiji Brew Garden & Sushi 75-7699 Ali'i Drive ☎808/329-7278. Ramshackle little sushi place where handmade rolls cost well under $10, and substantial noodle or rice entrees are $10–12. It's not the best you'll ever taste, but the service is friendly, and the prices low. Daily noon–2.30pm & 5–9pm.

Thai Rin Ali'i Sunset Plaza, 75-5799 Ali'i Drive ☎808/329-2929. Smart, somewhat minimalist Thai restaurant, facing the sea in front of a modern mall, with outdoor seating. Weekday lunch specials go for $8–9; for dinner, try *satay* or *poocha* (crab and pork patties) to start, for $8–9, followed by either tom yum soup or a Thai curry ($10–17). Daily 11.30am–9pm.

U-Top-It Ali'i Sunset Plaza, 75-5799 Ali'i Drive ☎808/329-0092. What do you top? A "taro pancrepe," as in a purple pancake made with taro flour. And what do you top them with? Whatever you fancy, from egg, spam, or sausage to banana, whipped cream, and mac nuts (that one's called a Hula Girl). All cost under $10 and taste pretty good; burgers and other fast-food snacks are also served. Daily except Mon 7.30am–2pm.

Big Island lū'aus

All seven of the regular **lū'aus** on the Big Island are based at Kona-side hotels. The *Kona Village Resort*'s *lū'au* wins hands down for atmosphere, due in part to its remote location.

Firenesia *Sheraton Keauhou Bay Resort* ☎808/326-4969, ⓦwww.islandbreezeluau .com; Mon 4.30pm; $80.

Gathering of the Kings *Fairmont Orchid* ☎808/326-4969, ⓦwww.islandbreezeluau .com; Sat 4.30pm; $99.

Island Breeze *King Kamehameha's Kona Beach Hotel* ☎808/329-8111, ⓦwww .islandbreezeluau.com; Tues–Thurs & Sun 5pm; $70.

Kona Village Lū'au *Kona Village Resort* ☎808/325-4214, ⓦwww.konavillage.com; Wed & Fri 5.15pm; $98.

Lava Legends and Legacies *Royal Kona Resort* ☎808/329-3111, ⓦwww.royalkona .com; Mon, Wed & Fri 5pm; $75.

Legends of the Pacific *Hilton Waikoloa Village* ☎808/886-1234, ⓦwww.hilton waikoloavillage.com; Tues, Fri & Sun 5.30pm; $95.

Royal Lū'au *Waikoloa Beach Marriott* ☎808/886-6789, ⓦwww.marriott.com; Wed & Sun 5.30pm; $80.

South Kona

South of Kailua and Keauhou, the Belt Road, as **Hwy-11**, sets off on its loop around the island by rising away from the sea through attractive verdant uplands. Trees laden with avocados, mangos, oranges, and guavas stand out from the general greenery, but the route is characterized above all by its **coffee** industry, with the blossom of coffee bushes everywhere apparent, and the aroma of the mills wafting through the air.

Kealakekua Bay, along the South Kona coast, is where Captain Cook chose to anchor in 1779, as it was then both the best harbor and the main population

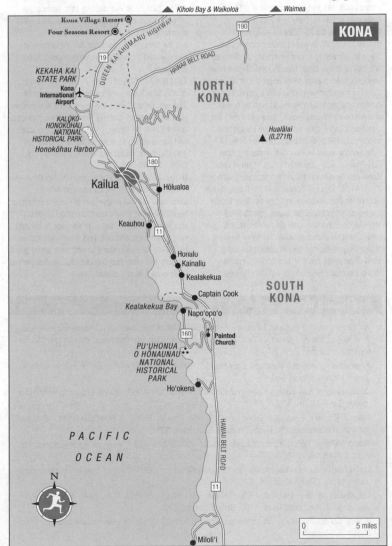

Kona coffee

Succulent, strong-smelling **Kona coffee** has been grown on the Kona coast since the first seedlings arrived from Brazil in 1828. Strictly speaking, the Kona name only applies to beans grown between 800ft and 2000ft up the western slopes of Hualālai and Mauna Loa. This narrow strip, extending from Hōlualoa to Hōnaunau, offers perfect greenhouse conditions: bright sunny mornings, humid rainy afternoons, and consistently mild nights.

Though Kona boasts an enviable reputation, and demand always outstrips supply, the work of planting and tending the coffee bushes and harvesting the ripe red "cherry" from the tangled branches is too labor-intensive to appeal to large corporations, and the business remains in the hands of around eight hundred small-scale family concerns. Something over two thousand acres are currently under cultivation in Kona, with the long-standing Japanese farmers having been joined by an influx of back-to-the-land *haoles*.

Independent farmers have long campaigned to restrict the label "Kona" to coffee consisting of one hundred percent pure Kona beans. Hawaiian state law, however, which allows any coffee containing at least ten percent Kona-grown beans to be sold as Kona coffee, has had the unfortunate effect of encouraging bulk buyers to use a smattering of Kona beans to improve lesser coffees and sell them at inflated prices.

Coffee **prices** in the area range from around $20 per pound for the lowest ("prime") grade up to as much as $50 for a pound of the gourmets' favorite, Peaberry. Roadside outlets, serve fresh Kona coffee in whatever form you desire. Beside a huge, rusty old roasting mill on Nāpo'opo'o Road, a mile or so up from the ocean, the **Kona Pacific Farmers Cooperative** runs a small store that gives out free sample coffees and also has a paying espresso bar (daily 9am–4.30pm; ☎808/328-2411, ⓦwww.kpfc.com).

Visitors are welcome at working coffee farms such as the **Bay View Farm** on Painted Church Road, half a mile north of the Painted Church (daily 9am–5pm; free; ☎808/328-9658 or 1-800/662-5880, ⓦwww.bayviewfarmcoffees.com), and **Greenwell Farms**, just off the highway in Kealakekua (Mon–Fri 8am–4pm, Sat 8am–3pm; free; ☎808/323-2295 or 1-888/592-5662, ⓦwww.greenwellfarms.com). In addition, the **Kona Historical Society** offers regular tours of the old Uchida coffee farm, restored to illustrate agricultural life during the 1920s and 1930s (Mon–Thurs 10am–2pm; $20; ☎808/323-3222, ⓦwww.konahistorical.org).

center on the island. Within a century, however, the seafront slopes were largely abandoned, and these days even the area higher up tends to be inhabited only by assorted farmers and New Age newcomers. Most tourists scurry through, put off perhaps by the lack of beaches and the dilapidated look of the small towns that sprawl along the highway. However, many of these hold one or two welcoming local cafés or intriguing stores, and it's certainly worth dropping down to visit the restored **Puʻuhonua O Hōnaunau**, or "Place of Refuge."

The coffee towns

HŌLUALOA, the first and nicest of the South Kona coffee-growing towns, is the only one that's not located on Hwy-11, the main Belt Road circling the island. Instead, you'll only see it if you choose to detour inland and upwards from Kailua. Though located barely three miles from central Kailua, it's a sleepy little village that feels a long way removed from the hurly-burly below. It consists of a single quiet road (Hwy-180) that meanders across the flanks of Hualālai, 1400ft up from the ocean, and is lined on either side with little stores, as well as orchards brimming with tropical blooms.

A few years back, Hōlualoa established a reputation as an artistic community, but most of its former artists and galleries have been driven away by rising real-estate prices, and little locally produced art is on show here any more.

South of both Hōlualoa and Kailua, there are officially four separate towns within the first four miles south of the junction of Hwy-180 and Hwy-11. However, where one ends and the next begins is far from obvious. Any points of interest can be easily spotted as you drive through, be they wayside coffee stalls, antiquated general stores, local diners, or simply junkyards.

If you want to sample the atmosphere, the best stop comes just south of tiny Honalo, in the shape of **KAINALIU**'s still-active 1930s Aloha Theater. As well as performances by local drama groups and visiting musicians, and the occasional movie, this holds an appealing café, reviewed opposite.

In **KEALAKEKUA**, a couple of miles south of Kainaliu, the **Kona Historical Society Museum** is set back from the highway in a former general store known as the Greenwell Home (Mon–Thurs 10am–2pm; $7; ☏ 808/323-3222, ⓦ www.kona historical.org). The low-key collection of photographs and heirlooms documents Kona's history from the perspective of its immigrant farmers, and also offers walking tours of a restored old coffee farm nearby (see p.145).

Immediately beyond Kealekekua, a minor road branches off the highway to lead down to Nāpo'opo'o Beach (see p.150), at the southern end of Kealakekua Bay. Stay on the main road, however, and you soon find yourself in the small community of **CAPTAIN COOK**, which is most noteworthy as the site of the venerable *Manago* hotel and restaurant, reviewed below.

Accommodation in the coffee towns

Small-scale **accommodation** options are scattered throughout the various "coffee towns," ranging from simple village hotels to luxurious B&Bs. Not all are conspicuous from the main road; several distinctive properties are hidden away from view on the lush South Kona slopes.

B&Bs

Aloha Guest House 84-4780 Māmalahoa Hwy, Captain Cook ☏ 808/328-8955 or 1-800/897-3188, ⓦ www.alohaguesthouse.com. Comfortable, spacious guest rooms, all en suite, on a German-owned farm a mile up from the highway near mile marker 104, 17 miles south of Kailua. The more expensive upper rooms have tremendous panoramic views, and rates include fresh fruits and coffee; check online for bargain discounts. ④–⑦

🏃 **Hōlualoa Inn B&B** 76-5932 Māmalahoa Hwy, Hōlualoa ☏ 808/324-1121 or 1-800/392-1812, ⓦ www.holualoainn.com. Exquisite B&B just below the main road through Hōlualoa, three miles and 1400ft up the hill from Kailua. The six tasteful en-suite guest rooms are arranged around a Japanese-style open-plan living room, plus there's a pool, hot tub, and homegrown coffee. A crow's-nest seating area atop the small, central wooden tower looks down on the rest of Kona, enjoying incredible views. ⑧

Pomaika'i "Lucky" Farm B&B 83-5465 Māmalahoa Hwy, Captain Cook ☏ 808/328-2112 or 1-800/325-6427, ⓦ www.luckyfarm.com.

Inexpensive, pleasantly furnished B&B accommodation on this working coffee and macnut farm beside the main highway ranges from farmhouse rooms to four-person suites and a converted former barn. Two-night minimum stay. ③–④

Rainbow Plantation 81-6327B Māmalahoa Hwy, Captain Cook ☏ 808/323-2393 or 1-800/494-2829, ⓦ www.rainbowplantation.com. Appealing en-suite B&B accommodation on a working coffee plantation, off Hwy-11 a quarter of a mile north of the top of Nāpo'opo'o Rd. Two guest rooms in the main house, two more in a separate cottage. ③

Hotels and hostels

Kona Hotel 76-5908 Māmalahoa Hwy, Hōlualoa ☏ 808/324-1155. Extremely basic, very old-fashioned (and very pink) family-run hotel in the attractive village of Hōlualoa, three miles up-slope from Kailua. The plainest of double rooms go for $40 a night, and the shared bathrooms are very dingy. ②

🏃 **Manago Hotel** Māmalahoa Hwy, Captain Cook ☏ 808/323-2642, ⓦ www.manago hotel.com. Century-old wooden hotel beside the

main highway in the center of Captain Cook, offering some of the best-value and most charmingly "local" lodging on the island. Cheaper rooms, in the main building, share bathrooms and have minimal facilities, but those in the newer three-story motel-like wing behind, where the rates rise floor by floor (and the first floor allows smoking), enjoy magnificent ocean views. Each of the conventional suites has a small *lānai*, and a strong hot shower, but no phone; there's also one deluxe Japanese room, costing $78 per night, and a good-value restaurant, described below. ❶–❸

Pineapple Park 81-6363 Māmalahoa Hwy, Kealakekua ☎ 808/323-2224 or 1-877/800-3800, ⓦ www.pineapple-park.com. Part hostel, part hotel, part kayak rental outlet, on Hwy-11, halfway between mileposts 110 and 111. While it's on a free bus route (see p.136), you'll likely feel very stranded without your own transport. Bunks in the rudimentary downstairs dorms cost $25, while en-suite rooms start at $65 per night. The nicest private rooms enjoy far-reaching views, as does the upstairs *lānai*, only open to guests in those rooms. The same owners run another budget hostel in Hilo; see p.172. Dorms ❶, rooms ❷–❸

Eating and drinking in the coffee towns

Most of the places to **eat** in the coffee towns are aimed at day-trippers and lunching locals, so they're busier in the middle of the day than the evening. Not surprisingly, many of course also specialize in serving fresh local **coffee**.

Aloha Theater Café 79-384 Māmalahoa Hwy, Kainaliu ☎ 808/322-3383, ⓦ www.alohatheatre cafe.com. Friendly local gathering spot, spreading through the lobby and *lānai* of the 1930s Aloha Theater, which serves coffees, salads, sandwiches, cooked breakfasts, and pastries. The dinner menu, served only when there's something on at the theater, includes fish tacos for $16, tofu curry for $18, and steak and seafood for up to $25. Mon–Sat 7.30am–2.30pm, plus events nights.

The Coffee Shack Captain Cook ☎ 808/328-9555, ⓦ www.coffeeshack.com. The quintessential South Kona café, a mile south of Captain Cook's minimal "downtown," perched above gorgeous gardens on the ocean side of the highway just north of mile marker 108, and enjoying staggering views all the way down to Kealakekua Bay. As well as wonderfully fresh coffee, they make sensational smoothies, plus cooked breakfasts, pizzas, salads, and the colossal $10 sandwiches using fresh-baked breads like the "Greek Isle," made with olives, feta, and yoghurt. Daily 7.30am–3pm.

Hōlualoa Gardens and Café Māmalahoa Hwy, Hōlualoa ☎ 808/322-2233. Welcoming "slow food establishment," with lots of sheltered outdoor seating, at the north end of Hōlualoa village. The Mediterranean-influenced menu focuses on organic and locally sourced ingredients, with appetizers at $7–12 and entrees from grilled *ahi* (tuna) to

beef tenderloin ranging from $17 to $32. The adjoining *Café* sells coffees and snacks from early morning, and has its own little garden. *Gardens* Tues 10am–2.30pm, Wed–Fri 10am–2.30pm & 5.30–8.30pm, Sat 9am–2.30pm & 5.30–8.30pm, Sun 9am–2.30pm; *Café* Mon–Fri 6.30am–3pm, Sat & Sun 6.30am–3pm.

Keei Café 79-7511 Māmalahoa Hwy, Kainaliu ☎ 808/322-9992. High-quality local café that has been so successful that it's repeatedly relocated along the highway, each time closer to Kailua and in smarter premises. In a bright, breezy, upstairs dining room that's unfortunately a little close to the traffic, its wide-ranging menu emphasizes home-grown produce, with lunchtime sandwiches and noodles for $10–12, and dinner entrees like half a roasted chicken, fresh catch, or Thai red curry for $18–22. Mon 10.30am–2pm, Tues–Fri 10.30am–2pm & 5.15–9pm, Sat 5.15–9pm.

Manago Hotel Māmalahoa Hwy, Captain Cook ☎ 808/323-2642, ⓦ www.managohotel.com. Cooled by whirring fans and ocean breezes, the paneled dining room in this venerable old hotel (see above) is a major local hangout. Full breakfasts for $7, while later in the day specialities include lightly breaded pork chops for $10.50, or a tangy fried butterfish for $12. Note the early closing time. Daily except Mon 7–9am, 11am–2pm & 5–7.30pm.

Kealakekua Bay

KEALAKEKUA BAY may be familiar because of Captain Cook's fatal encounter with the rulers of old Hawaii – as well as the *Little Grass Shack* of the song – but it's a surprisingly inaccessible spot. Very few visitors make it as far as the actual

site of Cook's death, on the north shore of the bay, and most of those who see the obelisk to the navigator's memory do so from the south side, across a mile of sea. **Nāpo'opo'o Beach** is the only point that can be reached by car; to see the bay otherwise, you either have to undertake a strenuous hike, or come by boat.

The name Kealakekua, which means "pathway of the god," refers to the 500ft cliff that backs the sheltered crescent bay. It was said that this *pali*, which slopes from north to south, was used as a slide by the god Lono when he needed to leave his mountain home in a hurry. The cliff was created by a massive landslide 120,000 years ago, which in turn generated an enormous tsunami that washed clean over the island of Kaho'olawe and reached three thousand feet up the more distant island of Lanai. When Cook was here, around eighty thousand Hawaiians are thought to have lived on the coastal lava plain that extends to the north and south. Though the mummified bodies of their chiefs, and possibly that of Cook as well, remain entombed in lava-tunnel "caves" high on the cliff face, all that remains below are overgrown walls and ruined *heiaus*.

Although Kealakekua Bay is officially a "State Historical Park," plans to restore the area around Cook's monument, and build a visitor center atop the cliffs, have yet to come to fruition. The waters of the bay itself are more formally protected as a Marine Life Conservation District, and offer some of the best snorkeling on the island – **snorkel cruise** operators are listed on p.140. Most of the bay is very deep, as the sheer *pali* drops straight down beneath the surface of the ocean.

The death of Captain Cook

When **Captain James Cook** sailed into Kealakekua Bay on January 17, 1779, he was on his second visit to the Hawaiian islands, on his way home after a year spent searching in vain for the fabled Northwest Passage. His ship, the *Resolution*, had circled the Big Island for seven weeks, trading with canoes that came alongside but not allowing anyone ashore. Finally Cook anchored in this sheltered bay, where a vast crowd of Hawaiians had gathered to greet him. For three weeks he was feasted by Chief Kalaniopu'u and his priests, attending temple ceremonies and replenishing his supplies.

The departure of the *Resolution*, amid declarations of friendship, might have been the end of things, had it not been forced to return just a week later, following a violent storm. This time the islanders were less hospitable, and far from keen to part with further scarce resources. On February 14, Cook led a landing party of nine men in a bid to kidnap Kalaniopu'u and force the islanders to return a stolen small boat. In an undignified scuffle, surrounded by thousands of warriors, including the future Kamehameha the Great, Cook was **stabbed** and died at the water's edge. His body was treated as befits a dead chief: the skull and leg bones were kept, and the rest cremated (though supposedly his heart was eaten by children who mistook it for a dog's).

The **interpretation** of Cook's death has always been controversial. It became widely believed by Europeans that the Hawaiians had taken Cook to be the great god Lono. The legend goes that, by chance, Cook had arrived at the temple of Lono at the height of the Makahiki festival, a major annual celebration in honor of Lono. The billowing sails of the *Resolution* were taken to be Lono's emblems, while the ship itself was believed to be the floating island of tall trees on which he was expected to voyage around Hawaii.

Some argue, however, that this story is rooted in a European view of Cook and of primitive people in general, rather than on Polynesian perceptions of the man. The European mentality of the time assumed that a noble Enlightenment figure such as Cook must appear god-like to the superstitious "natives." His voyage was perceived by the British as bringing civilization and order to heathen lands, while Cook saw himself

Walking to the bay

Walking down to the site where Cook was killed – or, more accurately, walking back up again – is a serious undertaking, though well worth it for keen hikers. With no facilities at the bottom, not even water, you have to carry everything you need; allow a total walking time of at least four hours for the round-trip.

The unmarked trail starts a hundred yards down Nāpoʻopoʻo Road, which leaves Hwy-11 a quarter-mile before Captain Cook. Park where you can here, then set off hiking down a dirt road that drops to the right, and keep going straight when that road veers off to the right within a couple of hundred yards. A rutted track, fringed with bright purple and red flowers, continues to drop for about a mile through open pastureland and avocado orchards. Eventually the vegetation thins out, and you find yourself picking your way over jagged and very exposed black lava fields. Avoid climbing this stretch in the midday sun.

From this high vantage point you can discern the worn path of the old King's Trail that once encircled the entire island, paved with river-rounded boulders. The trail then drops abruptly to the foot of the hill, before pushing into the tangled undergrowth at the bottom. Soon you can make out the ruined black walls of the long-vanished Hawaiian village of **KAʻAWALOA**, half submerged by twisted pandanus trees. Somewhere here stood the house of the high chief Kalaniopuʻu, whose attempted kidnapping by Captain Cook precipitated the final drama of Cook's life (see below).

as a stern father forever having to chastise the islanders who were his "insolent" children. His last recorded words are "I am afraid that these people will oblige me to use some violent measures; for they must not be left to imagine that they have gained an advantage over us." Cook would have been shocked had he realized that the Hawaiians surmised that "Brittanee" must be suffering from a severe famine, judging by the hunger of its sailors.

Cook may have wanted to be seen as the representative of a superior civilization and creed, but to Pacific islanders his superiority was largely a matter of **firepower**. A common theme in European contacts with the peoples of Polynesia is the attempt to draw well-armed foreigners into local military conflicts. Ironically, in 1777 Cook had sailed away from Tonga, having named it one of "the Friendly Islands," without realizing that he had narrowly avoided a plot to kill him and seize his ships. It's impossible now to say whether the elaborate ceremonies at Hikiau Heiau in Kealakekua Bay (see p.150), during which Cook was obliged to prostrate himself before an image of the god Kū, were designed to recognize him as Lono, or simply an attempt to incorporate him into the *kapu* system (see p.428) as a man of equal ranking with the high chiefs.

The major anomaly in the Cook-as-Lono legend is quite why the Hawaiians would have killed this "god." Some say it was a ritual sacrifice, while others argue that the man who struck the fatal blow had only just arrived from upcountry, and didn't know that Cook was a "god." The usual explanation, that it was simply an accident, both perpetuates the idea of Hawaiians as "innocent" savages, and absolves Cook himself of any responsibility for his fate. Though the British version of the dismantling of Hikiau Heiau has the priests eager to cooperate in return for iron trinkets, other sources, including Hawaiian tradition, have Cook's peremptory behavior seen as sacrilegious enough to merit his death. That suggests that while the chiefs may well have seen Cook as a valuable potential ally, the priests and commoners viewed him as a blasphemer, and when he antagonized the chiefs by seizing Kalaniopuʻu, deference gave way to defiance.

The trail reaches the sea at the precise spot where Cook died; a bronze **plaque** lies in a rocky pool under a couple of inches of water. Fifty yards to the left, on what is legally a small patch of England, a white marble **obelisk**, 27ft high, was raised to Cook's memory in 1884. No one is allowed to stand on the monument, but visiting ships traditionally set their own small plaques in the cement at its base.

Snorkelers from visiting cruise boats (see p.140) will ensure that you don't have the place to yourself, although they're not allowed to leave the water. There's no beach here, so if you want to swim out and join them, you just have to scramble in as best you can.

Nāpo'opo'o Beach County Park

To drive to the south shore of Kealakekua Bay, follow Nāpo'opo'o Road down from just before Captain Cook as it twists for four miles around the great *pali*. It reaches sea level at the small, usually crowded, parking lot of **Nāpo'opo'o Beach County Park**, and then continues a few yards north to dead-end at the "beach" itself, which thanks to 1992's Hurricane Iniki now consists of a jumble of black lava boulders rather than sand.

The **snorkeling** at Nāpo'opo'o remains as good as ever, however, once you've eased across the rocks at the water's edge. Fish congregate in greater numbers on the far side, near the conspicuous obelisk, but you may be swimming with the sharks for a mile to get there. Many visitors make the crossing by **kayak** instead; it's only legal to launch into the water from the ramp beside the jetty at the parking lot. Unlicensed operators here usually offer rental kayaks, and there are plenty of official outlets in Kailua and on the upper highway around Kealakekua town.

The waters here are a favorite haunt of **"spinner" porpoises**. Though marine biologists can't explain why, the porpoises gather in schools of up to a hundred individuals to while away the afternoons arching in and out of the water. Mark Twain described them as "like so many well-submerged wheels," but they do vary their routines by spinning vertically and even flipping the occasional somersault. At the end of the day, they head out once more to the open sea, to feed on the deep-water fish that come to the surface at night.

Stone steps beside the end of the road climb the stout black-lava tiers of **Hikiau Heiau**, the temple where Captain Cook was formally received in January 1779. During a baffling ceremony that lasted several hours, he was fed putrefied pig, had his face smeared with chewed coconut, and was draped with red *tapa* cloth. Shortly afterwards, it was also the site of Hawaii's first Christian service – the funeral of William Whatman, an elderly member of Cook's crew who died of a stroke. Nothing remains of the structures that once stood on the temple platform – indeed, Cook may well have precipitated his death by dismantling its wooden palings for use as firewood. Visitors are not allowed onto the platform, but it is possible to clamber your way around the perimeter, to get a sense of its scale and atmosphere.

Pu'uhonua O Hōnaunau

A featureless one-lane road runs south from Nāpo'opo'o for four miles, across the scrubby coastal flatlands, before meeting another road down from the main highway. The two converge at the entrance to the most evocative historical site in all the Hawaiian islands, **PU'UHONUA O HŌNAUNAU NATIONAL HISTORICAL PARK** (daily 7.30am–5.30pm; $5 per vehicle; ☎808/328-2288, ⓦwww.nps.gov /puho; US National Park passes are sold and valid).

This small peninsula of jagged black lava, jutting into the Pacific, holds the preserved and restored remains of a royal palace, complete with fishpond, beach, and private canoe landing, plus three *heiaus*, guarded by carved effigies of gods.

Cities of Refuge

Pu'uhonuas used to be promoted as **"Cities of Refuge"** because of their alleged parallels with the cities mentioned in the Bible. However, these were not cities but **sacred precincts**, which unlike the Jewish model served not to protect the innocent but to absolve the guilty. The idea was that any condemned criminal who succeeded in reaching a *pu'uhonua* would undergo a **ritual** lasting a few hours – at the very most, overnight – and then be free to leave. The snag was, *pu'uhonuas* always stood near strongly guarded royal enclaves, so the condemned had first to run a gauntlet of armed warriors by land, or dodge canoeists and sharks by sea.

The survival of the fittest was a fundamental principle of ancient Hawaiian law, in which might was generally considered to be right. Determined by gods, not men, the laws were concerned not with acts such as theft and murder but with infractions of the intricate system of *kapu* (taboo) – for which the penalty was always death. Besides providing a sort of safety valve to spare prime citizens from summary execution, *pu'uhonuas* also served other purposes. In times of war, noncombatants, loaded with provisions, could go to the nearest one to sit out the conflict, while defeated armies might flee to a *pu'uhonua* to avoid death on the battlefield. Each island had at least one, and the Big Island had six. Other **sites** included Waipi'o Valley and Coconut Island in Hilo. In addition, certain high chiefs, such as Kamehameha's wife, Queen Ka'ahumanu, were considered to be living, breathing *pu'uhonuas*.

However, it is most famous for the **pu'uhonua** sanctuary that lies firmly protected behind the mortarless masonry of its sixteenth-century Great Wall.

Visiting the park

From the information desk beside the Pu'uhonua O Hōnaunau parking lot, visitors descend along paved walkways, through the black lava field, into a grove of rustling giant palms. A couple of replica structures have been erected on lava platforms here – a small tent-like shelter for storage, and a larger house, as used by the *ali'i* (chiefs). To one side is a small but perfect sandy **beach** that once served as the royal canoe landing. You can swim or snorkel here, but not picnic, sunbathe, or smoke. Away to the left is the King's Fishpond, as placid as a hotel swimming pool but much less enticing. Lava boulders nearby were hollowed out by early Hawaiians to serve as bowls or salt pans; one was leveled to create a playing surface for *kōnane*, a game in which black and white pebbles were used as counters.

A thatched carving shed nearby usually holds one or two idols on which work is still in progress, or outrigger **canoes**, fashioned by master craftsmen from mighty trunks of beautiful dark *koa* wood.

Beyond the royal area, the L-shaped **Great Wall** – 10ft high and up to 17ft wide – runs across the tip of the promontory, sealing off the sanctuary itself. Its northern end is guarded by the **Hale O Keawe Heiau**, which once housed the bones of powerful chiefs, possibly even those of Captain Cook. When dismantled and stripped by Lord George Byron in 1825, this was the last Hawaiian *heiau* to remain in perfect condition. It has now been reconstructed; all the fearsome wooden *ki'i* idols that surround it are modern reproductions, but they're still eerie in their original setting.

Few buildings now stand beyond the wall. Apart from a couple of bare *heiau* platforms, there's just a scattering of trees on the rippling *pāhoehoe* lava that runs into the ocean. One large gray stone, supposedly the favorite spot of the chief Keōua, is surrounded by six holes that may have held the wooden poles of a canopy. Black crabs scuttle across the waterfront rocks, and countless pools are alive with tiny, multicolored fish.

You can't linger on the beach in the main part of the park, but stretches of **public beach** lie both north and south. The northern section, within sight of the sanctuary, is a renowned snorkeling spot, while a short walk either from the parking lot or the Great Wall brings you to the more attractive southern section. Even here there's very little sand along the shoreline, which consists of a broad expanse of black lava scattered with pools, but the shady grove beneath the coconut palms makes a great place for a picnic. Visitors who come for the beach alone are not obliged to pay the *pu'uhonua* admission fee.

In ancient times, the coastal flatlands to the south were densely populated, and traces remain everywhere of house-sites and other structures.

St Benedict's Painted Church

When you visit the *pu'uhonua*, make the slight detour north from Hwy-160, the spur road to Hwy-11, to see **St Benedict's Painted Church** (Ⓦ www.thepainted church.org). This small wooden church, an intriguing hybrid of medieval Europe and Hawaii, was decorated between 1899 and 1904 by a Belgian priest, Father John Velge, with Biblical and allegorical scenes. Columns with Hawaiian texts erupt into palm leaves on a vaulted ceiling depicting a tropical sky, and the walls behind the altar are painted with a *trompe l'oeil* Gothic cathedral. Orchids and leis festoon the altar and statuary within, while purple bougainvilleas fill the lush gardens outside. Spectacular views down the hillside look out over the flat expanse of trees that line the coast between Hōnaunau and Nāpo'opo'o.

Ho'okena Beach

Continue south along Hwy-11, for just under three miles from the Hwy-160 turnoff, and another small road leads to the sea at **Ho'okena Beach**. The vegetation thins out as you drop the two miles down the hillside, but the park itself is pleasant enough. It consists of a genuine, if grayish, sandy beach, pressed against a small *pali*, and shaded with coconut palms and other trees. Getting in and out of the water across the sharp lava can be a bit grueling, but the **snorkeling** is excellent.

This sheltered, south-facing bay was once a regular port of call for inter-island steamers, but it now houses very few buildings. As a county park, it does have toilets and a picnic area, and also allows camping; permission must be obtained from the Department of Parks and Recreation in Hilo (☎ 808/961-8311), for $5 per day. You'll find public showers and a little snack stand at the foot of the road.

Miloli'i

The last point in South Kona from which access to the sea is practicable is another twelve miles beyond Ho'okena, where a very tortuous five-mile single-lane road winds down the steep, exposed ridge of Mauna Loa. Having reached the sea at **Ho'opuloa** – no more than a few houses on bare rock – the road follows the coastline south, to drop to the small bay of **MILOLI'I**. The tiny stretches of beach here are mere indentations in the black lava, filled with a scattering of white coral and black pebbles, and backed by groves of coconut palms. The thick tongue of a lava flow that obliterated Ho'opuloa in 1926 can be seen spilling over the sparse slopes above.

At the south end of the cove there's another county beach park, with a thatched picnic shelter and a rest room, near an especially sheltered pond that's a favorite with children. Camping is once again permitted, but this is too public a spot for that to hold much appeal, and most visitors content themselves with snorkeling around the rocks. A short way back from the sea, the Miloli'i Grocery Store sells snacks and sodas. The road ends next to the pastel-yellow, red-roofed Hau'oli Kamana'o Church.

North Kona and South Kohala

Though the whole of the western seaboard of the Big Island tends to be referred to as the Kona coast, its most famous resorts are concentrated to the north, in the districts of **North Kona** and, starting roughly 25 miles north of Kailua, **South Kohala**. Until the 1970s, it was barely possible to travel overland along the coast here – and few people had any reason to do so. Then Queen Ka'ahumanu Highway, Hwy-19, was laid across the bare lava slopes, serving the new airport and granting access to previously remote beaches. To this day, with the road running on average a mile in from the ocean, the beaches remain occasional, distant bursts of greenery in an otherwise desolate landscape.

South Kohala is the sunniest area in all Hawaii, and also boasts the finest of the Big Island's few **white-sand beaches**, with **Hāpuna Beach** as the pick of the crop. Since the mid-1960s, when entrepreneur Laurance Rockefeller established the pattern by erecting the *Mauna Kea Beach Hotel* beside lovely Kauna'oa Beach, the terrain has undergone an amazing transformation. Holes large enough to hold several more giant hotels have been blasted into the rock, and turf laid atop the lava to create lawns and golf courses. Multi-property resorts appeared in quick succession at **Waikoloa, Mauna Lani**, and most recently **Ka'ūpūlehu**, closer to Kailua.

Kohala Mountain itself, the oldest and now at around 5000ft high also the smallest of the Big Island's five volcanoes, forms only the northern-most spur of the island, known as North Kohala (see p.166). South Kohala as it exists today was created by lava flowing from the newer peaks of Mauna Kea and Hualālai; the only vestiges of the original mountain to survive here are the offshore **coral reefs** with which it was once ringed.

Since it's illegal for anyone to deny access to the Hawaiian shoreline, both locals and visitors not staying at the Kohala resorts are entitled to use all the beaches. Some hotels make things difficult by restricting parking facilities for non-guests, but so long as you can get to the sea, you're entitled to stay there.

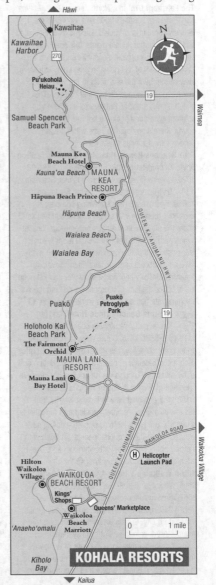

KOHALA RESORTS

Accommodation in North Kona and South Kohala

The huge **resorts** that punctuate the Kona and Kohala coasts are on a scale that beggars belief, and charge prices to match. Each is effectively an oasis amid a desert of black lava, offering wonderful oceanfront accommodation and very imaginable luxury, but very much isolated from the actual life of the island. Unless otherwise indicated, the hotels and resorts in this section are marked on the map on p.153.

The Fairmont Orchid 1 North Kaniku Drive, *Mauna Lani Resort* ☎ 808/885-2000 or 1-866/540-4474, ⓦ www.fairmont.com/orchid. The most sophisticated and elegant of the Kohala giants, this spacious complex of six-story buildings was originally a *Ritz-Carlton*. All 539 of its opulent rooms enjoy extensive views either over the sea or up to the volcanoes across one of the resort's two golf courses. The beach here is artificial, but as well as a lovely seafront swimming pool and hot tub, and ten tennis courts, there's an open-air "spa without walls." Garden view ⑧, ocean view ⑨.

Four Seasons Resort Hualālai 72-100 Ka'ūpūlehu Drive, Ka'ūpūlehu ☎ 808/325-8000 or 1-888/236-3026, ⓦ www.fourseasons.com/hualalai. See map, p.144. Open since 1996, but still the Big Island's newest major resort, this sprawling complex of two-story "bungalows," set on an exposed headland, offers the ultimate in luxurious accommodations, at a minimum of $750 per night. Each room holds a four-poster bed plus a bath and shower, and many have an additional outdoor, lava-lined shower. An oceanfront infinity pool and a saltwater snorkel pond make up for the lack of a proper beach, and there's also a private golf course and world-class spa. ⑨

🏃 **Hāpuna Beach Prince Hotel** 62-100 Kauna'oa Drive, Kohala coast ☎ 808/880-1111 or 1-866/774-6236, ⓦ www.hapunabeach princehotel.com. Few resorts in the world can offer such a combination of opulent accommodation and idyllic situation. Though it's an undeniably intrusive presence at the north end of Hāpuna Beach (see p.159), the prospect as you look outwards from this low-slung luxury hotel, molded into the hillside, is superb. The giant lobby is open to cooling sea breezes, while the turquoise pool is set flush with a broad patio, complete with whirlpool spa. Great rates can often be found online. ⑥

Hilton Waikoloa Village 425 Waikoloa Beach Drive, Waikoloa ☎ 808/886-1234 or 1-800/445-8667, ⓦ www.hiltonwaikoloavillage.com. This giant 1240-room, eight-restaurant resort is almost a miniature city. Guests travel between its three seven-story towers on a light rail system, in canal boats, or along a mile-long network of walkways lined with works of art. While there's no access to the coastline, it boasts a beach of imported sand lined by coconut palms, and a four-acre artificial lagoon, complete with waterfalls and a "swim with a dolphin" program (from $205 for 30min; reserve in advance, with Dolphin Quest ☎ 808/886-2875, ⓦ www.dolphinquest.org). Staying at the *Hilton* feels more like staying in a theme park than in Hawaii, so it appeals most to families with young children. Rates are more affordable than you might expect, though the lowest don't include necessities like parking at $15 per day. ⑥

🏃 **Kona Village Resort** 1 Kahuwai Bay, Ka'ūpūlchu ☎ 808/325-5555 or 1-800/367-5290, ⓦ www.konavillage.com. See map, p.144. The Big Island's oldest luxury resort, built in the black Kona desertscape in 1961 – there was no road then, so guests and employees alike had to be flown in – remains an idyllic vision of paradise. Supposedly it's a re-creation of the Polynesian past, but its main appeal lies in the very fact that it bears so little relation to reality of any kind. The 125 thatched *hales* (huts), have no phones, TVs, or radios, but each has a private *lānai*, a hammock, and a coffee-grinding alarm clock. Daily rates of $605 to $1250 for two include all meals at the *Hale Moana* and *Hale Samoa* restaurants (also open to non-guests), plus use of beach gear like masks, fins, and even kayaks and outrigger canoes. Most outsiders visit on *lū'au* nights – Wed & Fri – when $98 buys an atmospheric beachside feast plus Polynesian entertainment; advance reservations are essential. ⑨

Mauna Kea Beach Hotel 62-100 Mauna Kea Beach Drive, Kohala coast ☎ 808/882-7222 or 1-866/977-4589, ⓦ www.maunakeabeachhotel .com. The one major casualty of the Big Island's 2006 earthquake, this venerable resort has been comprehensively rebuilt on its exact original "footprint," and is once more poised in splendor immediately above the stupendous curve of Kauna'oa Beach, much closer to the ocean than current planning regulations would allow. Newly enlarged, colorful, modern, and very comfortable rooms feature spacious balconies, and bath tubs with ocean views. Garden view ⑧, ocean view ⑨

Mauna Lani Bay Hotel 68-1400 Mauna Lani Drive, *Mauna Lani Resort* ☎ 808/885-6622 or 1-800/327-2323, ⓦ www.maunalani.com. With its gleaming white central building thrusting like

an arrow into the Pacific, and an oceanfront golf course to either side, this is a classic, unabashed resort hotel. Lavish rooms are accessed via a waterfall- and lagoon-filled atrium, and offer wide ocean views. Sandy beaches and ancient fishponds line the waterfront, while historic sites are scattered on the extensive grounds. Garden view ⑧, ocean view ⑨.
Waikoloa Beach Marriott 69-275 Waikoloa Beach Drive, Waikoloa ☎808/886-6789 or 1-888/236-2427, ⓦwww.marriotthawaii.com.

Originally a budget alternative to the *Hilton*, as a *Marriott* this has become a classy and very elegant hotel, which unlike its flamboyant neighbor, enjoys access to the ocean, via lovely 'Anaeho'omalu Beach (see p.158). Sadly, however, the process of upgrading the resort lost almost all its former appealing Hawaiian touches, so it can feel a little soulless. All of the 500-plus well-equipped rooms have private balconies, most with ocean views, and since the recession, rates have dropped to very reasonable levels. ⑤

Honokōhau Harbor

A couple of miles north of Kailua, a short avenue leads down to narrow **Honokōhau Harbor**, which provides safe moorings for most of the local pleasure, fishing, and cruise boats. The only reason to come here is to take one of the many boat trips that leave from the far end of the quay, as listed on p.140. The most appealing spot to sit and watch the proceedings is the open-air deck of the *Harbor House* (Mon–Sat 11am–7pm, Sun 11am–5.30pm; ☎808/326-4166), a bar in the central Kona Marina complex that sells reasonably priced snacks and sandwiches. To its left is a line of **fishing charter** vessels, together with an information kiosk, the Charter Desk (☎808/326-1800 or 1-888/566-2487, ⓦwww .charterdesk.com); trips cost from $100 per person for a half-day to $750-plus for the entire boat for a full day.

If you have an hour or two to kill before or after an excursion, you can hike south for ten minutes across the lava to small, secluded, and sandy **'Alula Beach**, which is ideal for snorkeling, or take a five-minute walk around to the north of the harbor, which will bring you to the southern access of the Kaloko-Honokōhau National Historical Park.

Kaloko-Honokōhau National Historical Park

Kaloko-Honokōhau National Historical Park, north of the harbor and south of the airport (daily 8.30am–4pm; free; ☎808/329-6681, ⓦwww.nps.gov/kaho), preserves one of the state's last surviving natural **wetlands**. The National Park Service is attempting to achieve the contradictory objectives of restoring the area to its pre-contact appearance, making it accessible to visitors, and keeping it unchanged to protect endangered Hawaiian water birds.

As described above, it's possible to walk directly into the oceanfront portion of the park, which most visitors see as its most appealing part, from Honokōhau Harbor. Indeed, there's no real point accessing the park via its main entrance, which stands just off the main highway, half a mile north of the harbor turnoff and immediately south of milepost 97; the **visitor center** here holds little of interest, and your car will be locked in when the gate closes. That said, if you do come this way, the lava landscape that lies towards the ocean may look forbidding, but the trail that drops from the parking lot is surprisingly shady. A pleasant ten-minute stroll leads through assorted native vegetation, with a raised boardwalk that circles some ancient petroglyphs.

The coastal frontage of the park is both beautiful and fascinating. At its southern end, which is the point where you walk in from Honokōhau Harbor, alongside the pleasant **'Ai'opio Beach**, an ancient *heiau*, the Hale O Mono, stands guard over a succession of tiny sandy coves. In the water immediately in front of the *heiau*, shallow walls across the lava form the boundaries of the small 'Ai'opio Fishtrap,

in which fish would be deposited at high tide. Walking north along the shore brings you to more sophisticated relics of ancient Polynesian aquaculture, in the form of large artificial **fishponds** used to raise species such as mullet. The first, the 'Aimakapa Fishpond, is now largely the preserve of **water birds** like the *ae'o* (Hawaiian black-necked stilt) and the *alae ke'oke'o* (Hawaiian coot). Beyond that, the massive dry-masonry wall of the tranquil Kaloko Fishpond is being rebuilt so that fish can be harvested here once again.

Elsewhere in the mostly trackless expanse of the park, several more *heiaus* as well as a *hōlua* ("land-surfing") slide and fields of petroglyphs lie scattered. Descendants of Kamehameha the Great took pains to reserve this area for themselves, which suggests that one of its countless caves may still hold his bones.

Kekaha Kai State Park

One of the Big Island's least-known but most beautiful beaches, designated as **Kekaha Kai State Park** but also widely known by its old name of Kona Coast State Park, lies a couple of miles north of Kona International Airport (daily except Wed 9am–7pm; free). You need to keep your eyes peeled to spot the driveway, halfway between mileposts 90 and 91, and then be prepared to bump your vehicle for 1.5 miles over rippling *pāhoehoe* lava, on a virtually unsurfaced but just about passable track that takes a good fifteen minutes to drive each way.

From the parking lot at the bottom of the track, an obvious path sets off northwards across 200 yards of bare lava towards a dense grove of coconut palms. When you come to two portable toilets, you can either cut in through the trees to reach the beach directly, or follow the path round until it emerges in the middle of a perfect horseshoe-shaped bay. All around you is an exquisite beach of coarse golden sand, lightly flecked with specks of black lava – what the locals call "salt and pepper" sand. Each of the headlands jutting to either side is a spur of rougher *'a'ā* lava, topped with its own clump of palms. Immediately behind the beach is the looming bulk of Hualālai, and at this point Mauna Kea becomes visible far inland, as does Haleakalā across the sea on Maui. The calm waters of the bay are ideal for swimming, or boogie-boarding when they get a bit rougher in winter. Local surfers ride the tumbling waves offshore, while divers delve into submarine caves and tunnels.

A separate section of Kekaha Kai State Park, two miles further north and known as both **Manini'ōwali Beach** and Kua Bay, can be accessed via a much better road that leaves the highway at the crest of the hill halfway between mileposts 88 and 89. Open the same hours, it's not nearly as pretty, but consists instead of a smallish cove with a big shorebreak that makes it very popular with local boogie-boarders. While normally sandy, it's regularly washed bare by high winter surf.

Neither section of the park offers food or drink facilities for visitors.

Ka'ūpūlehu

The area known as **KA'ŪPŪLEHU**, five miles north of the airport, consists of a forbidding expanse of rough, jet-black lava that was deposited by an eruption of the Hualālai volcano in 1801. Its utter inaccessibility led it to be chosen as the site of the *Kona Village Resort* in 1961 – at first, in the absence of a road, all guests and employees alike had to be flown in – though since the appearance of the *Four Seasons* it has felt significantly less secluded.

While the *Four Seasons* has no beach of its own, the *Kona Village Resort* sits on sandy **Ka'ūpūlehu Beach**, which is superb for snorkeling; stately turtles cruise by, and manta rays billow in at night. Anyone is entitled to visit this isolated strand, though the resort's security guards do their best to discourage non-residents.

Kīholo Bay

Bit by bit, as road construction increases along the Kona and Kohala coasts, spots that were previously hidden are coming to the attention of tourists. Among the finest is the superb lagoon at **KĪHOLO BAY**, which until recently most visitors merely glimpsed from a tantalizing Hwy-19 overlook halfway between mileposts 82 and 83.

Kīholo Bay is now easy to reach by car, and it's a magical spot, which remains relatively unvisited. To get there, look out for an unmarked gravel road that heads *makai* (oceanward) from the highway just south of the highway overlook, immediately before a small hill. The gravel road itself is an easy 0.8-mile drive; don't stop at the gate on the right near the bottom, but keep going straight, and don't fork left.

From the parking lot at the end of the road, walk to the ocean and head right, and views will soon open up to the north. Three hundred yards along, before a lovely little bay dominated by a private home, you reach a natural freshwater swimming pool known as **Queen's Bath**, just inland from the beach. Created from a lava tube and entered via a short ladder, it offers a chance for a cooling salt-free dip.

Another twenty minutes or so along the shoreline lies the major reason for coming here: a spellbinding crescent lagoon, dotted with black-lava islets that are studded with coconut palms. This idyllic landscape was shaped by an unusual succession of events. First came a lava flow from Hualālai in 1801; then came a huge communal effort by the Hawaiians to enclose the bay to form a shallow fishpond; and finally another lava flow in 1859 breached the walls, filled in much of the pond, and let the sea back in. As well as looking utterly magnificent, the shallow turquoise waters here provide some of the finest swimming and snorkeling in all Hawaii – the only snag is that there's no beach to enter from, so you have to clamber over the rocks instead.

Waikoloa

For the ancient Hawaiians, the fundamental division of land was the *ahupua'a*, a wedge-shaped "slice of cake" reaching from the top of the mountain down to a stretch of coastline. The name "Waikoloa" referred to such a division, which is why visitors are often confused as to where exactly **WAIKOLOA** is. As a tourist,

▲ A 'ukulele lesson at the Kings' Shops, Waikoloa

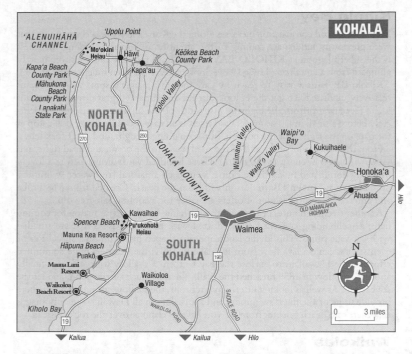

it's **Waikoloa Beach Resort** you're looking for, down by the sea and accessed via a road that leaves the highway a little way south of mile marker 76, 25 miles north of Kailua. Don't get sidetracked up to **Waikoloa Village** instead, a dormitory community six miles uphill from the highway.

There's very little to the beach resort beyond two huge hotels, the *Hilton* and the *Marriott* (both reviewed on p.154), a handful of condo developments, and two shopping malls close to the highway. Both the **Kings' Shops** and the **Queen's Marketplace** hold a reasonable assortment of generally upscale clothing and luxury-good stores, and the Queen's Marketplace also has a good grocery store, Island Gourmet Markets, but they're most likely to be of interest for fine restaurants such as *Roy's* and *Sansei*, reviewed on p.162.

While the *Hilton* is a self-contained resort with no ocean access, the delightful, sheltered white-sand beach in front of the *Marriott* is well worth visiting. Shelving very gradually out to sea, and lined with coconut palms, **'Anaeho'omalu Beach** is a favorite spot with snorkelers and windsurfers, and bathing is generally considered safe; watersports available via the hotel include snorkeling, kayaking, scuba diving, and excursions in glass-bottomed boats and catamarans. To reach the beach, follow the landscaped walkways beyond the hotel that skirt the two ancient fishponds to which this area owes its name. 'Anaeho'omalu means "protected mullet," as the mullet raised in these ponds were reserved for the use of chiefs alone.

Mauna Lani Resort

A mile or so north of the Waikoloa Village turnoff, another approach road *makai* of Queen Ka'ahumanu Highway heads through lurid green lawns down to the plush **Mauna Lani Resort**. Two major resort hotels, the *Mauna Lani Bay* and the *Fairmont Orchid* (both reviewed on p.154), face the sea here in splendid isolation, sharing the

use of two golf courses. Each has its own small artificial beach, not worth visiting unless you're a guest. There's also a shopping mall close to the highway, the **Shops at Mauna Lani**, which as well as a couple of expensive restaurants holds the Foodland Farms grocery store, where the deli counter offers high-class takeout sandwiches and sushi.

An impressive array of ancient **petroglyphs** is located between the *Orchid* and the small residential community of **PUAKŌ**. You can see them along the exposed, mile-long Malama Trail, which heads inland from the *mauka* end of the parking lot of **Holoholo Kai Beach Park**. (The beach itself here, a mixture of black lava and white coral, is not particularly good for swimming.)

Beyond its first 150 yards, the trail plunges into a tinderbox-dry *kiawe* forest. The main group of petroglyphs lies half a mile on, across an unpaved track, where a fenced-off viewing area faces a sloping expanse of flat, reddish rock that's covered with simple stick figures, most a couple of feet tall, still lying where they were left to bake centuries ago. Laboriously etched into bare *pāhoehoe* lava, the petroglyphs range from matchstick warriors to abstract symbols and simple indentations where the umbilical cords of newborn babies were buried. They're most visible early in the morning or late in the evening.

Waialea, Hāpuna, and Kauna'oa beaches

South Kohala's finest **white-sand beaches** are just south of Kawaihae Harbor. Such beaches are formed from the skeletal remains of tiny coral-reef creatures; they're found in the most sheltered areas of the oldest part of the island, because that's where reefs have had the longest time to grow.

Of the three best-known beaches, which are separated by short stretches of *kiawe* forest, only the southernmost, **Waialea**, remains in anything approaching a pristine state. Comparatively small, and sheltered by jutting headlands, it's a perfect base for recreational sailing, while the gentle slope into the sea makes it popular with family groups.

Hāpuna Beach

With its gentle turquoise waters, swaying palm groves, and above all its broad expanse of pristine white sand, **Hāpuna Beach**, just north of Waialea and a total of six miles north of Mauna Lani, has often been called the most beautiful beach in the United States. Though in summer it's the widest beach on the Big Island, it always seems to retain an intimate feel, thanks in part to the promontory of black lava that splits it down the middle and cuts it entirely in two when the sands retreat in winter. However, its northern end is dominated by the giant *Hāpuna Beach Prince Hotel* (see p.154), which opened in 1994 despite bitter opposition from campaigners who treasured Hāpuna's status as an unspoiled state recreation area.

Although hotel guests inevitably dominate the sands north of the promontory, Hāpuna Beach remains a delightful public park, well equipped with washrooms and pavilions. To protect body-surfers, who consider this the best spot on the island, surfboards are forbidden. However, Hāpuna has the worst record for spinal injuries in the entire state, most frequently suffered by novice body-surfers as the surf rises at the start of the winter. Pay serious attention to any warning flags posted along the beach, and ask lifeguards for current advice.

A simple kiosk sells burgers, shave ice, and other snacks (daily 10am–5pm) and rents out boogie-boards and snorkel sets (daily 9am–4pm). Tent **camping** is not permitted, but six simple A-frame shelters, set well back from the beach itself and capable of holding up to four people, can be rented for $20 per night through the state parks office in Hilo (☎808/974-6200).

②

Kauna'oa Beach

A mile north of Hāpuna Beach, barely a hundred yards beyond the turn for the *Hāpuna Beach Prince*, and a mile south of the point where Hwy-19 meets Hwy-270, a separate approach road cuts down to reach the ocean at **Kauna'oa Beach**. Like its neighbors, it offers superb conditions for much of the year, but is exposed to very strong winds and high surf in winter, when much of the sand is washed away and swimming becomes very hazardous. The construction here in 1965 of the *Mauna Kea Beach Hotel* (see p.154) was almost as controversial as the more recent development on Hāpuna Beach. Although locals won an eight-year legal battle to have their rights of access respected, Kauna'oa Beach swiftly became in effect the hotel's own exquisite private beach.

Kawaihae

For the ancient Hawaiians, the natural harbor at **KAWAIHAE**, a couple of miles north of Hāpuna Beach, was one of the most important landing points along the coast of the Big Island. Over the last seventy years, massive earthmoving projects have destroyed any beauty that it once possessed, but in terms of population it remains no more than a tiny settlement.

Samuel M. Spencer Beach County Park

The last significant beach along the Kohala coast, **'Ohai'ula Beach**, is one of the few still geared toward low-tech, low-budget family fun. Better known as **SPENCER BEACH PARK**, it offers the best oceanfront **campground** on the island, as well as full day-use facilities, but it can get very crowded, and with the access road extending along its full length it's seldom peaceful either. No cabins are available: campers are expected to bring their own tents or trailers and to obtain permits in advance from the Hawaii County Parks office in Hilo ($5 per day; ☎808/961-8311, ⓦwww.co.hawaii.hi.us).

The beach itself, sheltered by a long reef and backed by some amazing gnarled old trees, is popular with recreational swimmers as well as more serious snorkelers and scuba-divers, but kayaks are forbidden. It takes a major storm to render bathing unsafe.

Pu'ukoholā Heiau National Historic Site

The colossal, three-tiered **PU'UKOHOLĀ HEIAU**, just north of Spencer Beach Park, is the single most dramatic and imposing Hawaiian temple still standing on any of the islands (daily except hols 7.45am–4.55pm; free; ☎808/882-7218, ⓦwww.nps.gov/puhe). Its construction between 1790 and 1791 by the future Kamehameha I is one of the greatest – and most horrific – epics of Big Island history, and it's well worth allowing an hour of your time to explore the site.

An impressive new **visitor center**, largely open-air and in full view of the *heiau*, stands near the foot of the approach road to the park. Displays in English and Hawaiian explain the temple's history and significance, and fascinating short films are shown in rotation.

As you follow the trail beyond, around "the hill of the whale" for which the *heiau* was named, the vast temple platform – 224ft long by 100ft wide – looms above you, commanding a long stretch of coastline. Disappointingly, this is as close as you'll get; access is forbidden, as it remains a sacred site. No traces survive of the thatched houses and other structures that originally stood upon it – the Hale Moi, the smaller Hale Kahuna Nui for the priest, the oracle tower and drum house, and the lava altar that once held the bones of human sacrifices are all gone.

A little further toward the sea stands the subsidiary **Mailekini Heiau**. Narrower but longer, and much older, it too is inaccessible to visitors. Both *heiaus* loom large above **Pelekane Beach**, which you are free to walk along, although nowadays it's

The last of the luakinis

Puʻukoholā Heiau was the last *luakini* – a "war temple" fed by **human sacrifice** – to be erected in all Hawaii. Its story began in 1782, when the young warrior **Kamehameha** seized control of the northwest segment of the Big Island. Over the next few years, he conquered Maui, Lanai, and Molokai, but failed to defeat his rivals on the rest of his home island of Hawaii. Eventually, when he heard that his cousin **Keōua** wanted to expand out from Kaʻū, in the southwest of the Big Island, Kamehameha sent his aunt to consult the prophet Kapoukahi of Kauai, who suggested that building a **luakini** at Puʻukoholā and dedicating it to his personal war god Kūkāʻilimoku would guarantee success in the coming conflict.

Kapoukahi himself oversaw the construction of the new temple, on the site of a ruined *heiau* erected two centuries before by the legendary Lonoikamakahiki. The process was accompanied throughout by exacting ritual: in the words of an old Hawaiian proverb, "the work of the *luakini* is like hauling *ohia* timber, of all labor the most arduous." First of all, the entire island had to be purified, by means of clearing the circle road and erecting altars at regular intervals.

For Kamehameha's rivals, the start of work was a clear announcement of impending **war**. They set out to sabotage the project, knowing that its completion would give Kamehameha irresistible *mana*, or spiritual power. Not only Keōua, but also the defeated chiefs of Maui, Lanai, and Molokai, and even the rulers of Kauai and Oahu, joined forces to attack, but Kamehameha held them all off and pressed on with construction.

When the *heiau* was completed, in the summer of 1791, the prophet ordained a great feast, involving the **sacrifice** of four hundred pigs, four hundred bushels of bananas, four hundred coconuts, four hundred red fish, four hundred pieces of *oloa* cloth, and plenty of human beings, preferably those possessing considerable *mana*. Kamehameha therefore invited Keōua to attend the dedication and make peace. Like a figure from Greek tragedy, Keōua accepted the invitation.

The moment Keōua stepped ashore on the beach, he was **slain** with a spear thrust by Kamehameha's trusted warrior, Keʻeaumoku (the father of Queen Kaʻahumanu). All his companions were also killed before Kamehameha, who later insisted that he had not sanctioned the slaughter, called a halt upon recognizing the commander of the second canoe as his own son Kaoleioku. Keōua's body was the main sacrifice offered, together with those of ten of his associates (the war god did not like blood on his altar, and preferred his victims to have been killed elsewhere).

As sole ruler of the Big Island, Kamehameha went on to reconquer first Maui, Lanai, and Molokai, then Oahu, all of which had been recaptured by their original rulers during the building of the temple. Finally he exacted tribute from Kauai, whereupon the whole archipelago took on the name of Kamehameha's native island, and thus became known as Hawaii.

The altar and idols at Puʻukoholā were destroyed in 1819 on the orders of Kamehameha's successor, Liholiho, shortly after the breaking of the ancient *kapu* system (see p.417).

---

not all that spectacular. In Kamehameha's era the beach was far longer, and a royal compound stood in the palm grove just back from the sea. The land that now lies immediately to the north is infill created during the construction of Kawaihae Harbor, when the beach itself was largely obliterated.

Breeding sharks still circle the **Haleokapuni Heiau**, dedicated to the shark deities, which was built underwater and still lies beneath the waves around a hundred feet out. The voracious beasts would devour offerings beneath the watchful gaze of the king. Swimming is neither permitted nor particularly desirable: if the sharks aren't enough to put you off, the water is also clogged with gritty silt.

Kawaihae Harbor

Despite remaining without a wharf until 1937, **KAWAIHAE HARBOR** has long been the most important anchorage on the leeward coast of Hawaii. It was always the major port for the cattle of the Parker Ranch (see p.165); in the old days, intrepid cowboys would swim both cows and horses from the beach out to sea, then lasso them in the water and lash a dozen to the outside of flimsy whaleboats, which in turn rowed them to larger vessels anchored offshore.

The bay was finally dredged by the military during the 1950s. Casualties of the process included an assortment of grassy islands, each of which held a thatched shack or two, and most of the Big Island's best coral reef. Nevertheless, the port has long remained relatively low-key, poorly protected from occasional violent storms, and with few services nearby. Its biggest flurry of activity for many years came with the much-troubled filming of the Kevin Costner blockbuster *Waterworld* in 1994–95, during which the movie's centerpiece, a floating "slave colony," sank at least once to the bottom of the harbor.

Beside the port at the junction of Hwy-19 and Hwy-270, the small, two-story **Kawaihae Shopping Center** holds a few stores and galleries, and a couple of restaurants.

Eating and drinking in North Kona and South Kohala

Each of the Kona and Kohala hotels holds at least a couple of fine-dining **restaurants** plus a **bar** or two, so there's little encouragement for guests to venture out in search of eating and drinking alternatives – especially if you don't like driving at night on unlit roads. That said, the malls of Waikoloa, in particular, are home to some great Pacific Rim restaurants.

Brown's Beach House *The Fairmont Orchid*, 1 North Kaniku Drive, *Mauna Lani Resort* ☎808/885-2000. The *Orchid*'s gloriously breezy signature restaurant, set in the open air right by the beach, serves excellent Pacific Rim cuisine, for dinner only, with live music Tues–Sat. Typical entrees cost $35–50, with highlights including crispy kampachi with couscous. Daily 5.30–8.30pm.

Café Pesto Kawaihae Shopping Center ☎808/882-1071, ⊛www.cafepesto.com. This friendly Italian restaurant, serving the same menu of delicious calzones and pizzas as the branch in Hilo (see p.178), makes a handy stop if you're touring the island or nearby beaches. Daily 11am–9pm.

CanoeHouse *Mauna Lani Bay Hotel*, 68-1400 Mauna Lani Drive ☎808/881-7911. This flamboyant open-air Polynesian-style restaurant, close to the sea and surrounded by fishponds, serves some of Hawaii's finest but most expensive Pacific Rim cuisine, for dinner only, with typical entrees priced at $40–60. Daily 5.30–9pm.

Coast Grille *Hāpuna Beach Prince Hotel*, 62-100 Kauna'oa Drive, Kohala coast ☎808/880-3023. This dinner-only "American bistro" enjoys a great location, down by the pool in a very stylish two-tier circular building. The menu varies widely, from a burger for $15 to roasted mahimahi for $26, and a $35 set menu is served 6–6.30pm. Daily except Fri 6–9pm.

Merriman's Market Café Kings' Shops, Waikoloa ☎808/886-1700, ⊛www.merrimansmarketcafe.com. Casual bistro and deli, run by a pioneer of "Hawaii Regional Cuisine," where $20–30 entrees like tagine roasted mahimahi with lemon couscous have a strong Middle Eastern and Mediterranean flavor. *Merriman's* has plenty of outdoor seating, so it makes a good lunch spot, with a short menu of salads and sandwiches at $10–14; tapas snacks are served in the afternoon. Daily 11am–9pm.

Pahui'a *Four Seasons Resort Hualālai*, 72-100 Ka'upulehu Drive ☎808/325-8000. Gorgeous resort restaurant, comprising several interlinked wooden pavilions with sliding panels that open them to the ocean; sea breezes waft in, and spotlights play on the surf. The food itself is excellent, with a wide range of Asian and American dishes. The buffet breakfast costs $32, dinner appetizers such as spicy scallops cost around $20, entrees average $40, and on Saturdays they have a beach barbecue. Daily 6.30–11.30am & 5.30–9.30pm.

Roy's Waikoloa Bar & Grill Kings' Shops, Waikoloa ☎808/886-4321, ⊛www.roysrestaurant.com. Flamboyant Pacific-Rim dinners at

the Big Island's only outlet of *Roy's* gourmet chain are best enjoyed in the moonlight on the lakeside terrace. Dim-sum-style appetizers, designed to share, are around $10–15, while entrees such as *shutome* (swordfish) with lemongrass and Thai curry, and Waikoloa roast duck cost $30–40. Daily 5–9.30pm.

🏃 **Sansei** Queens' Marketplace, Waikoloa ☎808/886-6286, ⓦwww.sanseihawaii.com. Chef DK Kodama's Hawaiian take on Japanese cuisine makes for a superb dining experience. Despite its mall location, this restaurant is every bit as buzzy and exciting as the *Sanseis* on the other islands, though it's a bright and dynamic spot rather than a romantic one. Delicious specialty sushi rolls like mango crab or *moi* sashimi cost $11–14; the crab ramen is succulently rich; and the *omakase* tasting menu, at $80 for two, is fabulous value. Sun–Thurs 5.30–10pm, Fri & Sat 5.30pm–1am.

Waimea

The only town of any size in Kohala, **WAIMEA** is poised between north and south, a dozen miles up from the sea on the cool green plains between Kohala Mountain and Mauna Kea. For many of the visitors who climb inland from Kawaihae on Hwy-19, the interior of Hawaii comes as a surprise. These rolling uplands are cowboy country, still roamed on horseback by the *paniolos* of the United States' second-largest private cattle ranch, the **Parker Ranch**. Only when you look closely at the rounded hills that dot the landscape do you spot signs of their volcanic origin; many are eroded cinder cones, topped by smoothed-over craters.

Waimea is no longer the company town it used to be; the Parker Ranch now employs just one hundred of its eight thousand inhabitants. While still proud of its cowboy past, it has become more of a sophisticated country resort and is now home to a diverse community that includes astronomers from the Mauna Kea observatories. Halfway between the Kohala and Hāmākua coasts, Waimea has "wet" and "dry" sides of its own; it's the drier Kohala side, not surprisingly, where real estate is at a premium.

Waimea is also known as "Kamuela" – by the post office, for example – to avoid confusion with other Waimeas on Kauai and Oahu. Neither older nor more authentic, this name is simply a nineteenth-century corruption of "Samuel," one of the many scions of the house of Parker.

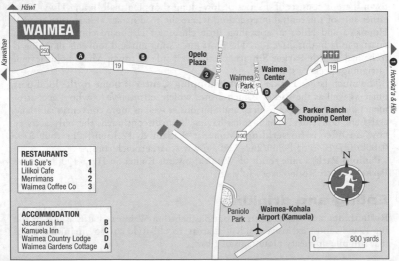

Arrival and accommodation

Waimea's tiny **airport**, in the rolling ranchlands just south of town, sees very little use. The only airline offering scheduled service is **Pacific Wings** (☎ 808/887-2104 or 1-888/575-4546, ⓦ www.pacificwings.com), which operates daily flights to Honolulu and Kahului on Maui.

Few visitors spend the night in Waimea, although it's one of the most pleasant towns on the island; the chief drawback is that the nights are significantly colder here than down by the ocean. For Hawaii residents, that's a plus point, so accommodation is often booked well in advance.

Jacaranda Inn 65-1444 Kawaihae Rd ☎ 808/885-8813, ⓦ www.jacarandainn.com. Once the home of a Parker Ranch manager, this century-old house is now a charming luxury B&B, with eight en-suite guest rooms and a lavish, separate three-bedroom cottage. Rooms ❺, cottage ❽
Kamuela Inn 65-1300 Kawaihae Rd ☎ 808/885-4243 or 1-800/555-8968, ⓦ www .hawaii-bnb.com/kamuela.html. Former motel, set back from the road a half-mile west of the central intersection. Refurbished and given an extra wing, it holds adequate budget rooms, all with private baths, and some "penthouse suites" with kitchenettes. Rates include basic continental breakfast. The same owners also operate the five-room *Log Cabin B&B*, a lovely rural lodge (shared bath ❷, en-suite ❸) just outside Āhualoa on the Old Māmalahoa Highway (see p.166). Rooms ❷, suites ❸

Waimea Country Lodge 65-1210 Lindsey Rd ☎ 808/885-4100 or reserve through Castle Resorts ☎ 1-800/367-5004, ⓦ www.castle resorts.com. Simple motel backing onto the Kohala slopes, at the start of the road down to Kawaihae. It may look a little shabby from the outside, but the rooms themselves are large and perfectly acceptable. There's a run-of-the-mill steakhouse on-site. ❹
Waimea Gardens Cottage PO Box 563, Kamuela HI 96743 ☎ 808/885-4550, ⓦ www.waimea gardens.com. Upmarket and extremely hospitable B&B two miles west of central Waimea, with two large and comfortable antique-furnished guest cottages; one has kitchen facilities, and both have private bathrooms and views toward the rolling Kohala hills. Three-night minimum stay; reservations essential. ❺

The town

There's not all that much to Waimea as a destination; most visitors simply while away an afternoon or so enjoying its dramatic setting between the volcanoes. What town there is consists of a series of low-slung shopping malls lining Hwy-19 to either side of the central intersection, where the road makes a sharp turn toward Honoka'a and Hilo; an appealing little cluster of clapboard churches stands a quarter-mile in this direction. The most interesting gift and souvenir shopping is to be had at little **Parker Square**, on the west side of town, which holds several intriguing specialty stores.

The much larger **Parker Ranch Shopping Center** is home to the local post office as well as the Parker Ranch Store, which sells *paniolo* (cowboy) accoutrements like belts, checked shirts, and Stetsons as well as more conventional island crafts and souvenirs. Ranch tours having been discontinued, the only activity now on offer is **horseriding** (Mon–Sat 8.15am & 12.15pm; 2hr tour $79; ☎ 808/887-1046 or 1-800/262-7290, ⓦ www.parkerranch.com).

Paniolo Park, a mile south of Waimea towards Kailua on Hwy-190, hosts the **Parker Ranch Rodeo** every July 4.

Eating and drinking

Restaurants range from gourmet options befitting Waimea's status as one of the Big Island's most exclusive residential areas, to old-style cowboy **drinking** holes that still pile up meaty mountains of ribs.

The Parker Ranch

At its largest, in the nineteenth century, the **Parker Ranch** spread across more than half a million acres of the Big Island. It still covers around ten percent of the island, currently holding around fifty thousand cattle on over 150,000 acres. The bulk of the land is divided into three huge parcels: one takes up most of North Kohala, one curves around the higher Hāmākua reaches of Mauna Kea, and the largest runs for forty miles up the western slopes of Mauna Kea from the ocean at Kawaihae.

It all dates back to **John Palmer Parker**, a ship's clerk from Massachusetts, who jumped ship in Kawaihae Harbor in 1809 and soon came to the attention of King Kamehameha, who gave him the job of maintaining the fishponds at Hōnaunau (see p.150).

In February 1793, Captain George Vancouver of the *Discovery* had presented Kamehameha with six cows and a bull and suggested that a *kapu* be placed on the cattle to allow a population to grow. By 1815, wild cattle had become a serious problem, destroying crops and terrorizing villages, and wild mustangs, too, were roaming unchecked. Kamehameha gave Parker permission to shoot the cattle, and from a base near Pololū he set out to impose discipline on the unruly beasts. With the decline of the sandalwood trade, the supply of fresh beef and hides to visiting whalers became crucial to the Hawaiian economy. Parker managed the business for the King, and by taking his pay in live animals built up his own herds. Marrying Kamehameha's granddaughter **Kipikane**, he integrated into local society and moved to the village of Waimea in 1835.

The ponchos, bandanas, and rawhide lassos of the Mexican, Native American, and Spanish *vaqueros* who were brought to work here were adopted by the Hawaiian cowboys they recruited and trained. They called themselves **paniolos** (from *Españoles*, or Spaniards).

Like many outsiders, Parker seized his opportunity in the Great Mahele of 1847, when private land ownership was first allowed (see p.420). He was granted two acres, and his wife, Kipikane, received 640 more. Soon he was in a position to buy another thousand acres and to lease the entire *ahupua'a* (see p.425) of Waikoloa.

Although attempts to diversify into sugar production and beekeeping came to nothing, the cattle ranch continued to thrive throughout the twentieth century. The last Parker to control the operation, the sixth-generation **Richard Smart**, died in 1992, having chosen to leave just one percent of his holdings to his family. The ranch now belongs to a charitable trust, with assorted local schools and health-care facilities among the beneficiaries of its profits.

Having suffered heavy financial losses from 2006 onwards, the ranch announced in late 2009 that it was re-focussing on the core business of cattle raising, and cut back its previously extensive program of tours for visitors.

Huli Sue's 64-957 Māmalahoa Hwy ☎ 808/886-1888, ⓦ www.hulisues.com. Funky, popular old barn, well out of town on the road east towards Honoka'a, where they pride themselves on buying ingredients from local farmers, and specialize in tasty barbecue. "St Louis Pork Ribs" with your choice of sauce cost $16; a large plate from the salad bar, $10. Daily 11am–9pm.

Lilikoi Cafe Parker Ranch Center ☎ 808/885-1686. Clean, busy deli around the back of the mall, which serves salads and sandwiches for $7–11, and daily lunch specials such as meatloaf for $10. Mon–Sat 7.30am–4pm.

Merrimans Opelo Plaza, 65-1227A Opelo Rd ☎ 808/885-6822, ⓦ www.merrimanshawaii.com. This gourmet restaurant, with its emphasis on organic produce, has regularly been voted the Big Island's best. Lunches are simple, with a burger, Chinese short-rib or other sandwich for around $13. Dinner entrees, at $20–37, tend to be much richer, but the signature wok-charred *ahi* is superb. Check the website for details of farm tours, combined with tastings. Mon–Fri 11.30am–1.30pm & 5.30–9pm, Sat & Sun 5.30–9pm.

Waimea Coffee Co Parker Square ☎ 808/885-4472. Lively café where the fresh coffee is complemented by inexpensive soups, salads, and sandwiches, all priced at $7–9. Mon–Fri 6.30am–5.30pm, Sat 8am–4pm, Sun 10am–3pm.

Onwards from Waimea

Whichever direction you head from Waimea, there's spellbinding scenery just a few miles down the road. Heading east toward Hilo on Hwy-19 brings you to Honoka'a in less than twenty minutes, with Waipi'o Valley not far beyond (see p.183). From an intersection just six miles south of Waimea, the **Saddle Road** starts its dramatic climb across the heart of the island between Mauna Kea and Mauna Loa – a journey covered in detail on p.186. The most attractive drive of all is Hwy-250 along Kohala Mountain to Hāwī.

However, the transition from the dry to the wet side of the Big Island can be experienced at its most pronounced if you make a slight detour off Hwy-19 three miles east of Waimea and follow the atmospheric and little-used **Old Māmalahoa Highway**. Once part of Kamehameha's round-island trail, this was notorious to ancient Hawaiians as a site where *'oi'o*, or processions of the souls of the dead, might be encountered at night as they headed for the underworld said to lie below Waipi'o Valley. Now it's a minor road, somewhat slow and sinuous, but not difficult, even for cyclists.

It heads first through treeless volcanic uplands where the rolling meadows, misty when they're not windswept, are grazed by horse and cattle. After eight miles, you abruptly plunge into a magnificent avenue of stately old ironwoods. Thereafter, the vegetation is tropical and colorful, and homes with glorious gardens dot the hillside. Soon after passing through residential **Āhualoa**, you rejoin the Belt Road near Honoka'a.

North Kohala

The district of **North Kohala**, which starts four miles or so north of Kawaihae, largely comprises the low-rise flanks of Kohala Mountain itself. Spreading across both sides of the mountain, it's a microcosm of the whole island, with its dry leeward side separated by rolling uplands from the precipitous wet valleys to the east. The road that curves around the north comes to an end at **Pololū Valley**, the northernmost of a chain of valleys that begins with Waipi'o (see p.183). Like Waipi'o, Pololū was home to generations of ancient taro farmers; two centuries ago this region was the power base of Kamehameha the Great, and several sites associated with Hawaii's first monarch can still be seen. The traditional Hawaiian way of life came to an end in

---

Kohala Mountain adventures

To take a guided **four-wheel-drive tour** into the unique backcountry of Kohala Mountain, contact ATV Outfitters in Kapa'au (closed Sun; ☎808/889-6000 or 1-888/288-7288, ⓦwww.atvoutfittershawaii.com). Prices range from $129 for 1hr 30min up to $249 for an all-day expedition.

You can also see the mountain on **horseback**. Na'alapa Stables (☎808/889-0022, ⓦwww.naalapastables.com) sets off daily into the uplands from the ironwoods of Kahua Ranch on Hwy-250 (2hr 30min ride at 9am, $90 per person; 1hr 30min ride at 1.30pm, $70). Paniolo Riding Adventures (☎808/889-5354, ⓦwww.panioloadventures .com), based at Ponoholo Ranch on Hwy-250, offers similarly priced rides. Dahana Ranch, on the Old Māmalahoa Highway outside Waimea (☎808/885-0057, ⓦwww .dahanaranch.com), features 1hr 30min rides for $70, plus the more unusual experience, on demand, of joining a 2hr 30min cattle drive for $130.

Big Island Eco Adventures offers **zip-line** adventures in the hills above Hāwī (daily, $159; ☎808/889-5111, ⓦwww.bigislandecoadventures.com).

1906, when the waters from Pololū were diverted for irrigation. By 1975, the last of the sugar plantations had closed down, and these days the area is relatively unpopulated, scattered with tiny communities.

Though North Kohala holds beautiful scenery, few visitors take the time to explore it. Its major drawback is that access to the sea is restricted on both the leeward side, which is almost entirely devoid of beaches, and the rugged windward coast. While little accommodation is available, there are a number of appealing restaurants and snack bars.

Across the mountain: Hwy-250

With a maximum elevation of 5408ft, Kohala Mountain is considerably lower than its younger Big Island rivals. Its summit is always green, never covered by snow, and its smooth velvet knobs betray few traces of their violent volcanic past. This landscape might not conform with what's usually thought of as Hawaiian, but the varying views you get of it from a trip along **Hwy-250** are among the most sublime in the entire state.

For the first four miles or so out of Waimea, as the highway climbs the west flank of Kohala Mountain, a panorama of the Kohala coast gradually unfolds. At first the rolling lava landscape is covered with wiry green turf. Then scattered trees start to appear, together with clumps of flat-bladed cactus, often growing straight out of bare black lava. Higher still you enter ranching country; for a while the road becomes an avenue lined with splendid ironwood trees, the undulating pastureland beyond which is grazed by sleek horses. Vivid green turf-covered cinder cones bulge from the meadows, speckled with black and brown cattle.

Along the coast: Hwy-270

The only alternative to Hwy-250, the coastal **Hwy-270**, heads north from Kawaihae Harbor. Most visitors drive a circular route that takes in both; the shoreline road is not as immediately attractive, but it does offer a handful of interesting historic sites, the occasional beach park, and, in winter, the possibility of spotting humpback whales out in the 'Alenuihaha Channel.

Lapakahi State Historical Park

Fourteen miles north of Kawaihae, **Lapakahi State Historical Park** (daily 8am–4pm; free) marks the site of the ancient village of Koai'e, which was inhabited for more than five hundred years until it was abandoned during the nineteenth century.

A hot, exposed, but fascinating one-mile-long trail leads past the villagers' dwelling places – not necessarily roofed, their low walls served primarily as windbreaks – as well as assorted traces of their day-to-day life. Most are simply hollowed-out rocks; some were used to hold lamps, others served as salt pans, while one little indented stone, holding black and white pebbles, was used to play the game *konane*. Beside a fish shrine, a carved decoy rests on an open net; the shy *ahu* fish was captured when it attempted to make friends with its wooden counterpart. Sustaining a population on such barren land must always have been hard, but Hawaiians probably chose this site because of its white coral beach and lack of cliffs, which made it the safest year-round canoe landing for many miles.

The **beach** at Lapakahi is composed of medium-sized boulders rather than fine sand. This is a marine conservation area and the water is very clear, with parrotfish and darting yellow shapes visible in its turquoise depths. The one place visitors are allowed to enter the water is north of the ancient village, and even there the use of sunscreen and towels is forbidden. Strictly speaking, you're only permitted to snorkel, not swim, though how to do one without the other is not specified.

Moʻokini Heiau and the Kamehameha Birthplace

At the island's northernmost tip, a long, straight road drops down to the perimeter fence of ʻUpolu's military airport. From there, an unpaved road, highly unlikely to be passable in an ordinary rental car, winds west along the coastline, degenerating frequently into pools of mud. There are no trees along this exposed and windy stretch, where the rolling meadows halt a few feet up from the black lava shoreline.

One of Hawaii's remotest but most significant ancient temples, **Moʻokini Heiau**, is roughly two miles from the airport. In the center of a large green lawn, the *heiau* is a ruined but impressive pile of lichen-covered rocks; you can enter the structure and discern the traces of separate rooms, as well as a boulder on which victims were prepared for sacrifice.

Two conflicting legends make the temple's origins obscure. Its current guardians state that it was built between sunset and sunrise on a single night in 480 AD by Kuamoʻo Moʻokini, using water-worn basalt stones passed from hand to hand along a fourteen-mile human chain from Pololū Valley. Alternative sources suggest it was created by the Tahitian warrior-priest Paʻao seven centuries later, as a temple to Kū, the god of battle. The most likely explanation, though, is that Paʻao simply rededicated an existing temple to Kū; it may even have been the site where the practice of human sacrifice was first introduced to Hawaii. The Kahuna Nui, the hereditary priesthood of Kū, has maintained an unbroken descent; the traditional *kapu* barring female priests has long since been broken, however, and the current Kahuna Nui, Leimomi Moʻokini Lum, is the seventh woman to hold the position.

A few hundred yards further along, the low, double-walled **Kamehameha Akahi Aina Hanau** slopes down a little closer to the sea. Kamehameha the Great was born here in 1758, at a time when his parents were in the retinue of King Alapaʻi, who was preparing to invade Maui. Whisked away in secret and brought up in Waipiʻo Valley, he returned to live in Kohala in 1782. A rock marks his precise birth-site; visitors still leave offerings to Hawaii's greatest ruler on the walls nearby.

Hāwī

Over thirty years after the closure of its *raison d'être* – the Kohala Sugar Company mill – tiny **HĀWĪ**, a mile beyond the ʻUpolu turnoff, is hanging on as one of the nicest little towns in Hawaii. It's an attractive place, with its all-purpose stores, galleries, and snack outlets connected by old creaking boardwalks, and every yard bursting with bright flowers.

There's nothing to see or do in Hāwī beyond strolling across the village green and along the hundred yards of its main street. However, the spacious ⚘ *Bamboo Restaurant and Bar* (Tues–Sat 11.30am–2.30pm & 6–8pm, Sun 11.30am–2.30pm; ☎ 808/889-5555, ⓦ www.bamboorestaurant.info) ranks as one of the Big Island's best **restaurants**, serving "island-style" cuisine in a bamboo-furnished dining room. A lunchtime salad, burger, or plate of stir-fried noodles costs $8–15, while dinner entrees ($28–34) include fish cooked to your specification in a range of styles such as "Hawaii Thai," as well as chicken, beef, and lamb from local farms. There's live Hawaiian music on Friday and Saturday evenings, and a store-cum-gallery selling attractive *koa*-wood gifts and other crafts. A few yards further up the street, in the Hāwī Hale building, *Sushi Rock* is a tiny, funky **sushi** restaurant (daily except Wed noon–3pm & 5.30–8pm; ☎ 808/889-5900), where rolls like the ten-piece Pele's Revenge, containing *ahi* and white fish and chili, cost $8–19. If you're just after a light snack, the *Kohala Coffee Mill* (Mon–Fri 6.30am–6pm, Sat & Sun 7am–5.30pm; ☎ 808/889-5577), across the street, has fresh Kona coffee plus burgers, bagels, and ice cream.

Hāwī also holds a very well-priced **accommodation** option, in the appealing shape of the ✦ *Kohala Village Inn*, 55-514 Hāwī Rd (☏808/889-0404, ⓦwww .kohalavillageinn.com; rooms ❸, suites ❹). Tucked away just off the highway intersection, it's a single-story, timber "plantation-style" building, which means that all the simple but tastefully furnished rooms, all of which have en-suite facilities, open onto an internal veranda and open courtyard. The two-bedroom suites are especially good value. The large, adjoining *Luke's Place* restaurant (☏808/889-1155), run by the same management, is a real social hub, serving straightforward but tasty food such as Korean chicken ($11), with live music in its *Tiki Lounge* most nights.

Kapaʻau

The main feature in the even smaller hamlet of **KAPAʻAU**, a couple of miles east of Hāwī on Hwy-270, is its **statue** of King Kamehameha. The original of the one facing ʻIolani Palace in Honolulu (see p.73), it was commissioned from an American sculptor in Florence for the coronation of King Kalākaua in 1883, lost at sea, and then miraculously recovered after the insurance money had paid for a replacement. As Kamehameha had established his headquarters near here in 1782, this sleepy town seemed a reasonable alternative location for the surplus statue.

Immediately behind the statue, the former courthouse now serves as the **Kohala Information Center** (Mon–Fri 10am–4pm). Staffed by local senior citizens, it holds a few rudimentary exhibitions, but it's basically a place to hang out. *The Snack Shack*, opposite (daily 10am–6pm; ☏808/889-6126), serves sandwiches and sodas.

A huge wayside boulder at a tight curve in the road on from Kapaʻau is known as **Kamehameha Rock**, as the future king is said to have demonstrated his right to rule by having sufficient *mana*, or spiritual power, to raise it above his head. Immediately beyond, a lane leads down to **Kēōkea Beach County Park**. Here, in the center of a rocky bay, a small stream flows into the ocean, and the surrounding hillsides have been pounded to pieces by high surf; despite the name, there's no beach.

A short way along the side road to the bay, *Kohala's Guest House* (☏808/889-5606, ⓦwww.kohalaguesthouse.com; ❷) doubles as both a **B&B** for short visits and a longer-term vacation rental. Each of the two separate houses has three clean and comfortable guest rooms, fruit trees fill the yard, and there's also a separate studio with kitchenette.

Pololū Valley

As Hwy-270 reaches its dead end at a tiny parking lot, you get a view over one final meadow to the open cliff-face that abuts the sea. Stretching away into the distance, it's punctuated by a succession of valleys, only accessible on foot and each therefore progressively less frequented and wilder than the last. The last of the chain, not visible from here, is Waipiʻo (see p.183); the first, spread out beneath you, is **POLOLŪ VALLEY**.

If not quite on the scale of Waipiʻo, Pololū was also once heavily planted by taro farmers. Regular tsunamis did little to encourage a stable population, however, and the death knell came when the valley's previously plentiful water supply was drained off for use on the nearby sugar plantations.

Pololū Valley remains a magnificent spectacle, and nowhere more so than from the initial overlook. If you take the time to explore it close up you may well find the hike down less strenuous, and more private, than its better-known equivalent further east. The pedestrian-only trail from the parking lot takes twenty minutes without ever being steep, but when it's wet – which is almost always – it's a quagmire of gloopy brown mud. Conditions are at their worst at the start, where

the trail drops immediately into dense, head-high grasses. From there you wind down the hillside among ironwood, guava, and *hala* trees. Occasionally the trees yield to stretches of loose lava pebbles, a welcome relief from the prevailing mud, with glimpses of the shore below.

Once on the valley floor, the trail remains thoroughly mucky as it approaches the broad river-cum-lake that meanders across the terrain, surrounded by marshy reeds. You can't venture inland.

Though Pololū's **beach**, like the one at Waipi'o, is commonly referred to as being black sand, it's basically gray grit, littered with pulverized flotsam. In winter, the shore is prone to strong winds and heavy surf; there's no question of swimming even at the best of times. Depending on whether rocks are blocking its mouth, you may have to wade across the shallow but fast-flowing stream to reach the longer segment of the beach; take care if so, as high water is capable of carrying hikers out to the sharks offshore. On the far side of the stream, the beach is lined by gentle woodlands of pine-needle-covered hillocks, grazed by mules and horses.

Hilo

Although it's the Big Island's capital, and the second-largest community in the state, **HILO** is more like a small town than the "city" it claims to be. Tourism has never quite taken off on this wetter, windward side of the island, and the large hotels that were constructed along the oceanfront south of downtown decades ago have long since fallen into shabby disrepair.

Which is a shame, because Hilo is actually a very nice place to visit, relaxed and attractive, spread over a surprisingly large area but with an appealingly old-fashioned downtown district where you can stroll between friendly cafés, street markets, and historic sites. The snag, quite simply, is that it **rains** too much. Hilo averages 130 inches of rainfall annually, with fewer than ninety rain-free days per year. Most mornings, however, start out clear and radiant; the rain falls in the afternoon or at night, leaving America's wettest city ablaze with wild orchids and tropical plants.

Hilo does have some pretty **beaches**, though none as sandy or good for swimming as those in Kona and Kohala. Tourists who come here are drawn instead either by the scenic beauty of the nearby Hāmākua coast, or the relative proximity of Volcanoes National Park. The fifty-mile excursion up to Waipi'o Valley is hard to resist, but nearer at hand you can enjoy the delightful Pepe'ekeo Scenic Drive, or the mighty 'Akaka and Rainbow falls.

Hilo stands where the Wailuku and Wailoa rivers empty into an enormous curving bay, named "Hilo" by ancient Hawaiians in honor of the first crescent of the new moon. In principle, the bay is calm and sheltered, but its funnel shape means that during great storms it can channel huge waves directly into the center of town. Cataclysmic **tsunamis** killed 96 people in April 1946, and an additional 61 in May 1960.

In 1796, Kamehameha the Great chose this superb natural harbor to build his *peleleu*, a fleet of eight hundred war canoes. These hybrid Western-influenced vessels carried mighty armies of warriors into battle against the other Hawaiian islands; some say they were never destroyed and still lie hidden in caves along the Kona coast. Thanks to a strong **missionary** influence, the port prospered in the nineteenth century as a clean-living alternative to dissolute Honolulu. Hilo also became the center of the Big Island's **sugar** industry, shipping out raw cane and serving as the arrival point for immigrants from around the world.

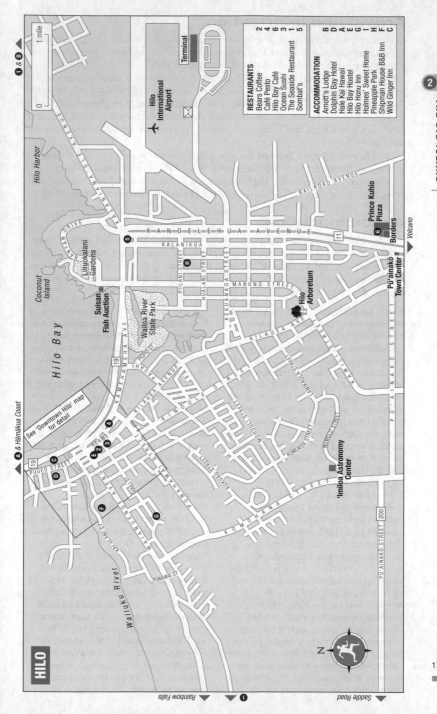

HILO

RESTAURANTS
Bears Coffee	2
Café Pesto	4
Hilo Bay Café	6
Ocean Sushi	3
The Seaside Restaurant	1
Sombat's	5

ACCOMMODATION
Arnott's Lodge	B
Dolphin Bay Hotel	D
Hale Kai Hawaii	A
Hilo Bay Hostel	E
Hilo Honu Inn	G
Holmes' Sweet Home	I
Pineapple Park	H
Shipman House B&B Inn	F
Wild Ginger Inn	C

171

Arrival and information

Served by direct flights from the other Hawaiian islands, but not the US mainland, **Hilo International Airport** is on the eastern outskirts of town. Rental cars are available, while a taxi downtown will cost around $12.

Free **buses**, primarily intended for commuters and seldom at times convenient for visitors, are operated by Hele-On Bus (Mon–Sat only; ☏808/961-8744, ⓦwww .heleonbus.org) from the **Mooheau Bus Terminal** on Kamehameha Avenue downtown. As well as city routes, they circle the island northwards towards Waimea, Waikoloa, and Kailua, and southwards towards the national park; all timetables are detailed online.

The **Hawaii Visitors Bureau** has a helpful information office at 250 Keawe St downtown (Mon–Fri 8am–4.30pm; ☏808/961-5797, ⓦwww.bigisland.org).

Helicopter and fixed-wing **flight-seeing** operators based at Hilo International Airport are listed on p.132, while lava-viewing **boat trips** are described on p.192.

Accommodation

The accommodation situation in Hilo is rather strange. With a fine array of **inns**, **B&Bs**, and **hostels** in the appealing downtown area, there's simply no point recommending that you stay in the large **hotels** that line the oceanfront crescent of **Banyan Drive**, a mile southeast, all of which have steadily deteriorated over the last few decades.

Arnott's Lodge 98 Apapane Rd ☏808/969-7097, ⓦwww.arnottslodge.com. Laidback, somewhat run-down budget accommodation in a two-story motel-style lodge a couple of miles east of downtown. Shared dorms hold twelve beds for $25 each, while they also have semi-private double rooms, sharing bathrooms, for $60, and fancier en-suite rooms for $70, plus camping for $10. There's a tree house and bar, free wi-fi or paid internet access, but no food except free pizza on Saturdays. Free morning airport shuttle, bike rental, and assorted van day-trips; guests pay $85 for excursions to the lava flows, $80 for the summit of Mauna Kea, non-guests pay considerably more. ❶–❸

Dolphin Bay Hotel 333 Iliahi St ☏808/935-1466 or 1-877/935-1466, ⓦwww.dolphinbayhilo.com. Very friendly little hotel, just across the Wailuku River from downtown, set out like a motel on two levels. All the spotlessly clean studios and one- and two-bedroom suites have TV, bathroom, and kitchen, but not phones. No pool or restaurant, but free papayas and bananas dangle enticingly, and the owner is a mine of useful advice. ❹

Hale Kai Hawaii 111 Honoli'i Pali ☏808/935-6330, ⓦwww.halekaihawaii.com. Small, comfortable B&B, perched above the ocean a couple of miles north of downtown. Each of the three rooms in the main building has its own bath and shares a living room; the adjacent guest cottage has a living room and kitchenette. All share use of pool and hot tub. Reservations essential; two-day minimum stay. ❹

Hilo Bay Hostel 101 Waiānuenue Ave ☏808/933-2771, ⓦwww.hawaiihostel.net. Smart, clean, safe, and very welcoming hostel, upstairs in an attractive and extremely central, historic building. Dorm beds $25, private room with no bathroom $65, more comfortable en-suite room $75. Discounts on car and jeep rentals and local tours. ❶–❷

Hilo Honu Inn 465 Haili St ☏808/935-4325, ⓦwww.hilohonu.com. Gloriously comfortable B&B in a beautifully restored, historic home above downtown Hilo, with one double en-suite room, a larger suite capable of sleeping three, and the upstairs floor given over to a Japanese-style two-bedroom suite. Great tropical breakfasts. ❹ ❼

Holmes' Sweet Home 107 Koula St ☏808/961-9089, ⓦwww.hilohawaiibandb.com. Two simple but comfortable en-suite rooms in a friendly B&B with extensive views, three miles up from downtown Hilo. ❸

Pineapple Park 454 Kalanikoa St ☏808/968-8170 or 1-877/800-3800, ⓦwww.pineapple-park.com. Budget hostel in a spruce, clean bungalow a mile from the airport, too far from downtown to walk. Bunks in six-person dorms for $25 each, plus semi-private rooms, sharing bathrooms, for $65. There's another *Pineapple Park* in South Kona (see p.147). ❶/❷

Shipman House B&B Inn 131 Kai'ulani St ☏808/934-8002 or 1-800/627-8447, ⓦwww.hilo-hawaii.com. Magnificent, turreted Victorian mansion, in a quiet but central location, converted by descendants of the original owners

into a plush B&B. Three grand antiques-furnished en-suite rooms in the main house, which has a lovely *lānai*, and two more in a guest cottage. Beautiful polished wooden floors, no TVs or private phones. Rates include gorgeous breakfast and afternoon tea. Two-night minimum stay. **6**

Wild Ginger Inn 100 Pu'u'eo St ☎808/935-5556 or 1-800/882-1887, ⓦ www.wildgingerinnhilo.com. Pink-painted, somewhat spruced-up inn in a quiet

residential area just across the Wailuku River from downtown. While second-best to the nearby *Dolphin Bay*, it remains a good-value option for budget travelers. About thirty basic but adequate en-suite rooms arranged around attractive gardens, plus a few slightly more secluded "deluxe" rooms with TVs. Those closest to the main highway, with its traffic noise, sleep four. Rates include a simple breakfast buffet. **2–3**

The city

Compact and walkable, **downtown Hilo** focuses on the junction of seafront Kamehameha Avenue and Waiānuenue Avenue. There's a simple and tragic reason why its modest streets and wooden stores seem so low-key: the whole town center, on the ocean side of Kamehameha Avenue, was destroyed by the tsunamis of 1946 and 1960. Indeed, the inundation of 1946 literally cut the city in two, and all hope of rebuilding it was abandoned after the waters returned in 1960. Instead, the devastated area around the Wailoa River was cleared as a "buffer zone," and a new administrative complex was laid out above the high-water mark.

Little in central Hilo today bears witness to its long history, but it's a pleasant place to amble around. Regular influxes of cruise passengers keep a myriad small novelty and souvenir stores open, especially along Keawe Street a block up from the highway. By far the best downtown store, indeed the finest source of **aloha wear**

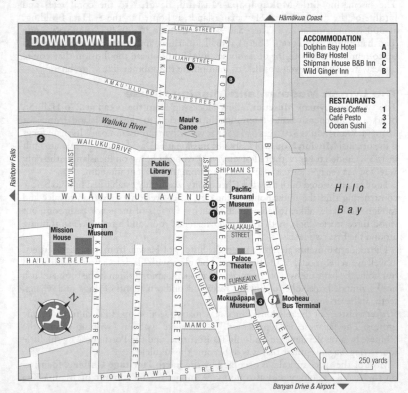

▲ *Hāmākua Coast*

DOWNTOWN HILO

ACCOMMODATION	
Dolphin Bay Hotel	A
Hilo Bay Hostel	D
Shipman House B&B Inn	C
Wild Ginger Inn	B

RESTAURANTS	
Bears Coffee	1
Café Pesto	3
Ocean Sushi	2

Hilo Bay

▼ *Banyan Drive & Airport*

in the entire state, is Sig Zane's, 122 Kamehameha Ave (☎808/935-7077, Ⓦwww
.sigzane.com), where the clothing designs are inspired by native Hawaiian plants.
Look out too for the **Palace**, 38 Haili St (Ⓦwww.hilopalace.com), a restored 1925
theater that puts on regular movies and concerts.

On Wednesdays and Saturdays a mouthwatering and colorful **open-air market**
takes place on Mamo Street, across the highway from the ocean. As you wander
past stalls selling orchids, tropical fruits, and coffee fresh from the farm, it's hard
to believe you're still in the USA.

The Pacific Tsunami Museum

The high-tech **Pacific Tsunami Museum** is housed downtown in a former bank at
the corner of Kamehameha Avenue and Kalākaua Street (Mon–Sat 9am–4pm; adults
$8, under-18s $4; Ⓦwww.tsunami.org). Although its primary emphasis is on the
causes and effects of Hilo's two lethal tsunamis, and of similar and potential events
throughout the Pacific, it also documents the town's entire history. A scale model,
complete with a running train, shows Hilo before the 1946 disaster; contemporary
footage and personal letters bring home the full impact of the tragedy. The section
devoted to the wave of 1960 is even more poignant. It was caused by an earthquake
off Chile, so locals had several hours' warning that it was on its way. Many flocked
to the seafront to watch it come in; photos show them waiting excitedly for the
cataclysm that killed 61 of their number.

The Mokupāpapa Museum

The fascinating little **Mokupāpapa Museum**, devoted to the coral reefs and
birdlife of the northwestern Hawaiian islands, is housed in the S. Hata Building,
at 308 Kamehameha Ave (Tues–Sat 9am–4pm; free; ☎808/933-8195, Ⓦwww
.papahanaumokuakea.gov). There's a small aquarium, and one tiny room is mocked
up to represent the interior of a submersible. Films create the illusion that you're
underwater, and it's even possible to manipulate the submersible's "grabber."

The Lyman Museum and Mission House

The two-part **Lyman Museum**, a few blocks up from the ocean at 276 Haili St,
offers a comprehensive and interesting introduction to the Big Island (Mon–Sat
10am–4.30pm; adults $10, ages 6–17 $3; Ⓦwww.lymanmuseum.org). Its main focus
is the original **Mission House** of Calvinist missionaries David and Sarah Lyman, built
in 1839. Guided tours of the oldest surviving wooden house on the island – the only
way you can see it – start at 11am and 2pm from the adjacent museum.

The Lymans waited until they felt Christianity was firmly established in Hilo before
constructing this, the finest home in the city, fit to welcome Hawaiian royalty and
foreign dignitaries alike. It had neither kitchen – for fear of fire – nor bathroom, but
stood three stories high, with a towering thatched roof, and a roomy *lānai* running
around the first two levels.

The modern museum alongside traces the history of Hawaii from its earliest settlers,
as well as a relief model of the Big Island, complete with black lava flows. A thatched
hut holds the basic utensils of the ancient Hawaiians, among them stone tools and fish
hooks, rounded calabashes of *kou* and *koa* wood, and ornaments of dogs' and whales'
teeth, and even human bone.

After a history of the missions comes a fascinating section on Hilo's different ethnic
groups. The Japanese are represented by an ornate wooden "wishing chair," the
Chinese by a resplendent red-and-gilt Taoist shrine, and the Portuguese by the little
four-string *braginha* guitar that was to become the 'ukulele.

Most of the space upstairs is occupied by the **Earth Heritage Gallery**, focusing
on the island's geology and astronomy. A model of the summit of Mauna Kea

shows the international observatories, while a brief account of Polynesian techniques of stellar navigation mentions that the Ahua'umi Heiau on Mauna Kea, now badly damaged, was probably the first observatory to be built up there. A huge sonar map of the entire archipelago shows how alarmingly prone Hawaii is to massive landslides, and pinpoints the fiery submarine volcano of Lo'ihi thrusting its way to the surface just off the southeast coast of the Big Island. Another collection contains corals, shells (including those of some unique indigenous land snails), a few stuffed birds and fossils, and colorful minerals from around the world, some of which glow in the dark.

'Imiloa Astronomy Center of Hawaii

A five-minute drive from downtown Hilo – turn left onto Komohana Street a couple of miles up Waiānuenue Avenue – brings you to the gleaming **'Imiloa Astronomy Center of Hawaii**, at 600 'Imiloa Place (Tues–Sun 9am–4pm; adults $17.50, ages 4–12 $9.50; ⓦwww.imiloahawaii.org). A lavish museum complex for such a small, out-of-the-way city, 'Imiloa is designed to meet a rather strange brief, and one that may puzzle visitors from beyond Hawaii.

Whereas scientists see the summit of the Mauna Kea as the world's finest location to build astronomical observatories, many argue that according to traditional Hawaiian beliefs such observatories desecrate a sacred site. Largely funded by NASA, this museum is an attempt to reconcile those two views. Thus it combines highly informative displays on the Hawaiian creation chant, the Kumulipo, and the ongoing practice of burying the *piko* or umbilical cord of newborn infants in a secret family location, with computerized updates of the latest readings from the mountaintop telescopes. It's all very fascinating, and when the scientific and traditional viewpoints dovetail convincingly, as for example in the stargazing techniques used by Polynesian navigators, it makes a lot of sense; elsewhere, though, it feels like a chalk-and-cheese museum, vainly attempting to persuade visitors that the two are actually one and the same.

The museum also incorporates a **planetarium**, which besides daytime astronomy lectures reopens for Friday-night music shows like Laser Beatles (Fri 7.30pm; $8) or Hypnotica, featuring 90s' electronica (Fri 9pm; $8).

Wailuku River and Rainbow Falls

The **Wailuku River**, at the western limit of downtown Hilo, is at eighteen miles the longest river in the Hawaiian archipelago. Now safely channeled and crossed by three road bridges, it once had a fearsome reputation; *wailuku* means "destroying water," as it was considered extremely dangerous during periods of high rain.

A large rocky outcrop in the river bed, upstream from the bridge that connects Pu'u'eo and Keawe streets, is known as **Maui's Canoe**. In legend, it was abandoned by the mighty warrior after he'd raced it back from Haleakalā on his namesake island (with just two paddle strokes). Maui was hurrying to rescue his mother, Hina, who lived in a cave further up the river and had become trapped by rising waters engineered by a dragon.

Maui's route is now followed by Waiānuenue ("rainbow seen in the water") Avenue, and the site of Hina's cave, two miles from downtown, is known as **Rainbow Falls**. Sightseers drive out to admire this broad waterfall from a safe distance; you can't get anywhere near the actual water. A fenced-off viewpoint to the right of the parking lot faces the falls square-on, as they shoot over a thick shelf of hard rock. In the pool below, the water has scooped out the hollow that was home to Maui's mother. Climbing a small but often very muddy staircase off to the left brings you level with the streambed at the top of the falls, behind which the summit of Mauna Kea looms high in the distance.

Almost two miles on up the road, the **Boiling Pots** are a succession of churning, foaming pools in the river as it drops toward the ocean, accompanied by another, smaller, set of falls. A treacherous ungraded path to the right of the viewing area allows you to approach the maelstrom, but you'd be crazy to swim.

Banyan Drive

Green, semi-rural **Banyan Drive**, a mile east of downtown Hilo, became the city's prime hotel district after being spared by the tsunamis. Though the hotels themselves have deteriorated, it's an attractive area, graced by curving rows of the eponymous, giant drooping banyan trees. Incredibly, these magnificent specimens are little more than seventy years old, having been planted in the 1930s by the celebrities after whom they're named – Franklin Roosevelt, Babe Ruth, and King George V among others.

The best place for a stroll among the trees is **Lili'uokalani Gardens**, an ornamental Japanese park built to honor Japanese migrants to Hawaii. A slender footbridge stretches out to **Coconut Island**, now just a green speck on the edge of the bay but once, as Mokuola ("healing island"), the site of a *pu'uhonua* or "place of refuge," like that at Hōnaunau (see p.150). There was also a *luakini*, where human offerings were killed by having huge stones dropped on their chests while lying bound to a rock.

A small, covered market area next to the quayside on Lihiwai Street is the site (daily except Sun) of the **Suisan Fish Auction**. You have to arrive by 7am to be sure of seeing anything; a nearby coffee stall will help wake you up. Suisan is a large operation, and fishing vessels from all over the island sell their catches here. Most of the trays are packed with glistening tuna, but you can also see red snapper, parrotfish, squid, ripped-up multicolored reef fish speared by scuba-divers, and the occasional shark. Though it's a hectic and lively spectacle, there's no dramatic shouting: buyers simply inspect the shiny rows of fish and write down their bids.

Panaewa Rainforest Zoo

Panaewa Rainforest Zoo, just after mile marker 4 on Hwy-11, south of Hilo (daily 9am–4pm; free; ☏808/959-9233, Ⓦwww.hilozoo.com), is home to a relatively small menagerie of animals, few of them all that unusual. The main pleasure of stopping here en route to the volcanoes is the chance to roam beneath the zoo's canopy of tropical vegetation.

The Merrie Monarch festival

Since 1963, Hilo has celebrated the week-long **Merrie Monarch hula festival** in the week that follows Easter Sunday. The festival's centerpiece is a royal parade in honor of the "Merrie Monarch" himself, King David Kalākaua. He was largely responsible for the revival of hula following decades of missionary disapproval, when, at the time of his coronation in 1883, he staged a performance of women dancers and male drummers on the lawns of Honolulu's 'Iolani Palace.

Performers from around thirty different hula *halau* (schools) – of which eighteen tend to be female and twelve male, and not all are necessarily from Hawaii – compete for awards in both *kahiko* (ancient) and *'auana* (modern) styles of hula. Official events take place in the evenings at the six-thousand-seat **Kanaka'ole Stadium**, named after Auntie Edith Kanaka'ole, one of the Big Island's best-loved twentieth-century *kumu hulas* (hula teachers). In addition, informal demonstrations and other events are held during the daytime in the *Hilo Hawaiian* and *Naniloa Volcanoes Resort* hotels.

For full schedules see the website Ⓦ www.merriemonarchfestival.org or call ☏808/935-9168. Tickets go on sale each year on January 1 but sell out almost immediately.

Hiking in Hawaii

From the soaring cliffs of Kauai's North Shore and the rainforest waterfalls of Maui to the active volcanoes of the Big Island, Hawaii is an absolute paradise for hikers. Thanks to the mighty volcanoes that formed them, even the smaller islands hold barely explored wildernesses, while the dramatic effects of erosion have produced some of the most majestic scenery on the planet. Well-maintained but nonetheless demanding trails enable visitors to escape the crowds and see Hawaii in something approaching its original pristine state.

Awaʻawapuhi Trail, Kauai ▲

Waiheʻe Ridge Trail, Maui ▼

Choosing your trail

Hawaii's two finest **hiking** destinations are the youngest of the islands, the **Big Island**, where you can watch new land forming daily as lava spills from the Kīlauea volcano, and the oldest, **Kauai**, where breathtaking trails penetrate remote North Shore valleys that no road could ever reach.

Kauai's legendary **Kalalau Trail**, which clings precariously to the Nā Pali cliffs for eleven unforgettable miles, is often hailed as the greatest in the world, and offers the reward of camping beside the golden sands of Kalalau Valley at the far end. Three thousand feet up from there, in Kōkeʻe State Park, the **Awaʻawapuhi Trail** runs along a perilous mountain ridge to reach an incredible bird's-eye view of yet another verdant hidden valley.

Hawaii's top ten trails

The following hikes are listed in ascending order of length. In addition, there's the hike to wherever the current **eruption site** may be on the Big Island, which may be anything up to four or five miles (see p.203).

▸▸ **Mānoa Falls** (Oahu); 1hr; see p.83
▸▸ **Kīlauea Iki Trail** (Big Island); 2hr; see p.201
▸▸ **Waipiʻo Valley** (Big Island); 2hr; see p.183
▸▸ **Awaʻawapuhi Trail** (Kauai); 3hr; see p.409
▸▸ **Waiheʻe Ridge Trail** (Maui); 3hr; see p.242
▸▸ **Pēpēʻōpae Trail** (Molokai); 4hr; see p.321
▸▸ **Hālawa Valley** (Molokai); 5hr; see p.318
▸▸ **Alakaʻi Swamp Trail** (Kauai); 6hr; see p.408
▸▸ **Sliding Sands Trail** (Maui); 7hr; see p.275
▸▸ **Kalalau Trail** (Kauai); 2 days; see p.382

Sliding Sands Trail, Maui ▼

Rainforest trails

Several great trails explore Hawaii's lush **rainforests**, filled with unique flora and fauna – and entirely devoid of nasty reptiles or dangerous predators. Two of the finest, the **Alaka'i Swamp Trail** on Kauai and the **Pēpē'ōpae Trail** on Molokai, follow boardwalks across strange stunted swamplands at the very top of the islands, where patches of dense jungle-like vegetation are interspersed with eerie marshes scattered with orchids and twisted shrubs. Both offer alert hikers tantalizing glimpses of some of the rarest birds on earth, and culminate with fabulous views across remote, inaccessible, and quintessentially Polynesian valleys.

On Maui, the **Waihe'e Ridge Trail** climbs a steep ridge on the eastern flank of the West Maui mountains, ascending beyond pine and eucalyptus groves en route to a remote and colorful rainforest. Much lower down, starting from sea level in eastern Maui, the **Pīpīwai Trail** climbs up into the Kīpahulu section of Haleakalā National Park, crisscrossing streams on precarious bridges, to reach two spectacular waterfalls high in the rainforest.

You have to join a guided hike to see the waterfalls of glorious **Hālawa Valley** on Molokai, but this was among the very first places to be settled by humans in all Hawaii, and learning its history and traditions from a true native makes for a totally compelling experience.

The **Hāmākua coast** of the Big Island too holds abundant waterfalls, with 'Akaka Falls, for example, accessible on a short forest loop, as well as magnificent **Waipi'o Valley** with its sea-level taro fields. Even on Oahu, on the edge of Honolulu, lovely rainforest trails lead through **Makiki** and **Mānoa valleys**, on President Obama's home turf.

▲ Pēpē'ōpae Trail, Molokai

▼ Hālawa Falls, Molokai

Kīlauea Iki ▲

Kīlauea eruption ▼

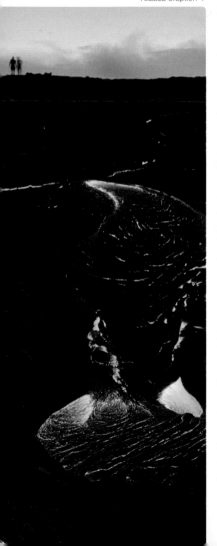

The lure of lava

The most exciting hike Hawaii has to offer is the chance to watch the ongoing **eruption of Kīlauea** on the Big Island, in Hawaii Volcanoes National Park. Whereas every other hike detailed in this book follows a well-defined trail, there's no predicting where or how far you'll have to walk to see it; the current flow might be anywhere in the desolate, ten-mile-wide lava field that stretches along the island's southeastern shoreline. As if the thrill of close-up views of torrents of molten lava were not enough, it's often possible to hike out there at night, when the hillside is alive with glowing red fire.

Even if the eruption turns out to be beyond your reach, further great hikes in the national park enable you to explore Kīlauea's summit caldera. The **Kīlauea Iki** trail ventures out across a desolate, still-steaming crater floor, while the aptly named **Devastation Trail** skirts recent cinder cones where the rainforest is clawing its way back. The longer Halemaʻumaʻu Trail, which crosses the heart of the main crater, was forced to close by a spurt of activity in 2010, but may have reopened by the time you read this.

On Maui, Haleakalā may not be active these days, and technically what looks like its summit crater is simply an eroded hilltop, but it too offers superb hiking. The wonderful day-hike that combines the **Sliding Sands** and **Halemaʻumaʻu** trails is a real test of stamina, being at least eleven miles long, and a wearying ten thousand feet above sea level. Unlike on the Big Island, it's also possible to **camp** atop Haleakalā, either in tents or in a rudimentary cabin – as memorable a spot as you're ever likely to spend the night, and perfectly sited to catch the sunrise over the crater the next morning.

On weekdays you may find that you're the rarest species of all, and that the animals will go out of their way to have a closer look at you. Walkways through the dense, steamy undergrowth lead past enclaves inhabited by a giant anteater, iguanas from South America, and wide-eyed lemurs and bushy-tailed colobuses from Madagascar. Impressive peacocks wander the grounds at will, displaying their plumage, while rare Hawaiian owls and hawks are confined in cages. The largest, lushest enclosure holds a white Bengal tiger, though the vegetation is so thick that you may not spot him unless you're here for his indoor feed at 3.30pm or are prepared for a long wait by his watering hole.

Hilo's beaches

If neither sharks nor pollution bother you, you could in theory swim out among the canoes and fishing boats from the **Hilo Bayfront Park**, across the highway from downtown Hilo. This was a fine black-sand beach before the dredging of the harbor in 1913. Now it's a pleasant place for a picnic, but the only spot nearby where you might be tempted to swim is at Coconut Island, off Banyan Drive (see opposite).

All Hilo's **beach parks** lie southeast of downtown, facing Mauna Kea across the bay and reached by following Kalaniana'ole Avenue beyond Banyan Drive. As few have any sand – they consist of shallow pools in the black lava at the ocean margin, usually backed by small grass clearings ringed with coconut palms – they attract local families rather than tourists, and so are only crowded on weekends.

The best spot for family groups is **Onekahakaha Beach Park**, a mile and a half down Kalaniana'ole Avenue. Here a solid breakwater of boulders has created a calm lagoon for swimming, while the spacious lawns alongside are good for picnics. The open ocean beyond the breakwater can, however, be extremely dangerous, while fifty yards or so back from the sea the park acquires from time to time a sizeable population of homeless locals. That's the main reason why none of Hilo's beach parks currently allows camping.

Leleiwi Beach Park, a couple of miles further along, is a little more exposed, with no sandy beach and some dangerous currents. Away from the open sea, the lagoon is so supremely still and tranquil as to appeal primarily to anglers, who stand in quiet contemplation almost entirely undisturbed by bathers.

Just beyond Leleiwi, four miles from downtown, Kalaniana'ole Avenue dead ends at **Richardson Ocean Park**, where a tiny black-sand beach among the coconut groves is very popular with young children. Some venture out to play in the surf as it sweeps into the bay, beyond the snorkelers exploring the rock pools. Behind the sea wall there's a larger "beach" area – more of a sandpit, really – while the adjacent gardens are laid out around ancient fishponds.

One other beach that's well worth visiting is located a couple of miles **north** of downtown Hilo. **Honoli'i Beach** is a beautiful curve of black sand at the mouth of the Honoli'i Stream. Though not safe for swimming, it's as spectacular a spot for **surfing** as you can imagine, and thus throngs with locals at weekends. The northern side of the bay is flanked by a steep wall of deep-green vegetation, making a great backdrop for action photos.

Eating and drinking

Hilo offers an unusually varied assortment of **restaurants**, most of which are aimed more at locals than at visitors. **Downtown** is at its busiest during the working week, however; the **bars** are pretty full in the early evening on weekdays, but you may be surprised at how quiet things are on weekends.

Bears Coffee 110 Keawe St ☏ 808/935-0708. Breakfast hangout, one block from the ocean downtown. All kinds of coffee, plus bakery goodies, freshly squeezed juices, and specials like soufflèd eggs on a muffin with spinach ($5). Lunch consists of $5–8 burgers, sandwiches, salads, and simple fish and chicken dishes. Mon–Fri 5.30am–4pm, Sat 5.30am–1pm.

Café Pesto S. Hata Building, 130 Kamehameha Ave ☏ 808/969-6640, ⓦ www.cafepesto.com. Large, Pacific-influenced Italian restaurant at southern end of downtown. For a substantial snack, the lunchtime sandwiches, such as the Japanese eggplant Sandalwood and the shrimp Miloliʻi, are excellent value ($11–15). As well as pizzas and calzones, with tasty, inventive fillings such as lime-marinated fish, the dinner menu features $19–27 entrees like fresh fish, or risotto with lobster, shrimp, and scallops. There's another *Café Pesto* at Kawaihae Harbor; see p.162. Mon–Thurs & Sun 11am–9pm, Fri & Sat 11am–10pm.

Hilo Bay Café 315 Makaʻala St ☏ 808/935-4939, ⓦ www.hilobaycafe.com. Smart, good-value mall café, well south of the ocean, serving much the same deli-style menu for lunch and dinner, plus lunchtime salads and sandwiches and a full-service bar. Most dishes are pretty rich, from the French onion soup ($7) and the "Blue Bay Burger" ($9) to entrees like lemon-grass pork tenderloin or seared scallops ($16–24). Mon–Sat 11am–9pm, Sun 5–9pm.

Ocean Sushi 250 Keawe St ☏ 808/961-6625. Large and very popular Japanese cafeteria, serving good and inexpensive sushi (from $2.50 for two pieces) and great-value bento meals to the downtown crowd. Mixed sushi plates start at $11, sashimi at $17. Mon–Sat 10.30am–2pm & 5–9pm.

The Seaside Restaurant 1790 Kalanianaʻole Ave ☏ 808/935-8825, ⓦ www.seaside restaurant.com. The full name of this plain but lively restaurant continues "and Aqua Farm," which has to be a good sign. Just over two miles out, opposite Kealoha Beach, it's almost entirely surrounded by water, with its thirty-acre fishponds full of trout, mullet, and catfish. Beyond the bare-bones main dining room, there are a few outdoor tables. The fish is great, whether steamed or fried as an entree, or sushi-style as an appetizer, and you'd be hard pressed to spend much over $20 on a full fish supper. Tues–Thurs 5–8.30pm, Fri & Sat 5–9pm.

Sombat's 88 Kanoelehua Ave ☏ 808/969-9336, ⓦ www.sombats.com. Hilo's best and freshest Thai cuisine, with $7 lunch special, appetizers like basil rolls for $9, and all curry entrees, including the delicious green kang kiew warn, with eggplant and basil, costing $13 with chicken, $16 with fish or shrimp. Mon–Fri 10.30am–2pm & 5–8.30pm, Sat 5–8.30pm.

The Hāmākua coast

The **Hāmākua coast** extends for fifty ravishing and colorful miles north and west from Hilo up to Waipiʻo Valley. This spectacular landscape has been carved by the torrents of rain unleashed when the trade winds hit Mauna Kea after crossing two thousand miles of open ocean. Countless streams and waterfalls cascade down the cliffs and gullies, nourishing jungle-like vegetation filled with multicolored blossoms and iridescent orchids. Hāmākua farms formerly fueled the economy of the Big Island, but the last sugar mill closed in 1994, and agribusiness has all but pulled out.

For most of this stretch of shoreline, Hwy-19 follows the original route of the sugar-company railroad, which carried local produce to ships waiting in Hilo. Barely rising or falling, the highway clings to the hillside, crossing ravines on slender bridges. Damage to these bridges in the 1946 tsunami put the railroad out of business, but they were sufficiently repaired to be able to carry the road instead. Each little bridge offers its own glimpse of the verdant scenery – sometimes close to the ocean but high above it, sometimes winding further in to follow the contours of the gorges and passing babbling streams and waterfalls.

At first, the fields are crammed into narrow, stream-carved "gulches," and there are few places to stop and enjoy the views. The two most popular off-road sight-seeing spots are the **Hawaii Tropical Botanical Garden**, just a few miles north of Hilo, and the impressive **ʻAkaka Falls**, another ten miles on.

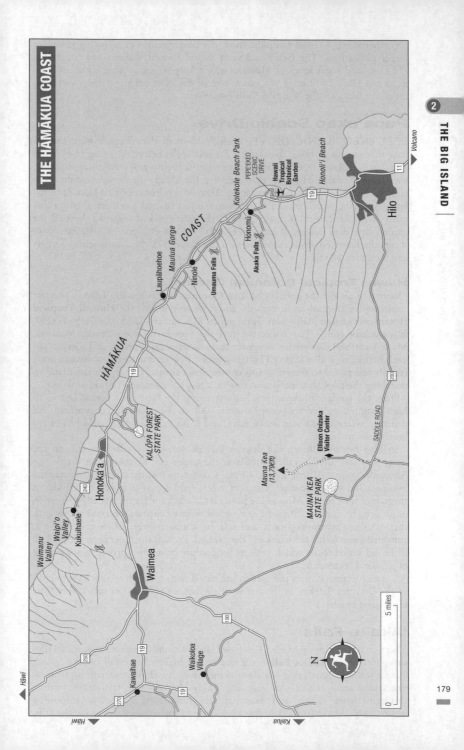

THE HĀMĀKUA COAST

Further north, beyond **Laupāhoehoe**, the land spreads out, allowing room for larger plantations. The Belt Road veers inland toward Waimea just before the old-fashioned sugar town of **Honoka'a**, but keeping on another eight miles on dead-end Hwy-240 brings you out at one of the most unforgettable viewpoints on all the islands – the **Waipi'o Valley** overlook.

Pepe'ekeo Scenic Drive

PEPE'EKEO SCENIC DRIVE, a small side-road that drops toward the sea four miles north of Hilo, then curves for four miles before rejoining Hwy-19 at Pepe'ekeo, makes a worthwhile detour from the highway. It once formed part of the Old Māmalahoa Highway that encircled the island – hence its most dramatic stretch, a superb avenue of overhanging Alexandra palms imported from Queensland, Australia, which make their appearance just beyond a delightful gorge that bursts with African tulip trees. Close to the north end of the road, beyond the garden described below, *What's Shakin* (daily 10am–5.30pm; ☎808/964-3080) serves the best fresh-fruit **smoothies** on the island ($7), plus sandwiches, burgers and wraps for $8–10.

Hawaii Tropical Botanical Garden

Occupying almost the entirety of lush **Onomea Bay** is the Big Island's premier showcase for tropical trees, orchids, and flowering plants, the **Hawaii Tropical Botanical Garden** (daily 9am–5pm; adults $15, under-17s $5; ☎808/964-5233, ⓦwww.htbg.com). The collection includes specimens from Brazil, Malaysia, Madagascar, and Guatemala, alongside endemic Hawaiian species, and is garnished with flamingos and macaws. Though a major stop on the tour-bus circuit, with crowds and prices to match, it still comes closer than anywhere on the island to matching the popular conception of what a tropical rainforest should look like.

From the garden headquarters, halfway along the Pepe'ekeo Scenic Drive, an hour-long self-guided trail drops around 500ft to the ocean. Insect repellent and drinking water are on sale at the start, and if it's raining you should be able to borrow an umbrella.

Striking features during the descent include views of a tall waterfall, on the innermost wall of the valley, visible at the upper end of the "palm jungle" of Alexandra palms. A little lower, a huge Cook pine is surrounded by spectacular heliconia and vast, spreading "travelers' trees," said always to hold a little water at the base of their leaves. Most of the plants are labeled, and there's a heady succession of gingers, bromeliads, dramatic orange and yellow heliconia, coconut palms with their writhing worm-like roots, and *hala*, or pandanus trees, whose roots serve as stilts that seem to lift the trunk off the ground. Perhaps the most prominent of all is the red-leafed *obake*, which with its lurid white or yellow "prong" is something of an island trademark.

A state footpath crosses the garden halfway down; turn left to reach the mouth of the Onomea Stream, in the center of the bay, or right to get to a lovely little black-sand beach.

'Akaka Falls

Three or four miles up Mauna Kea from Hwy-19, and fifteen miles out of Hilo, the photogenic **'Akaka Falls** may not be the highest waterfall on the island, but its setting is unrivaled – a sheer drop through a chasm overrun by tropical vegetation and orchids. An easy and enjoyable half-mile trail leads visitors through a dense "jungle" and past other falls, culminating at a viewpoint looking upstream to 'Akaka itself. You don't get close to the riverbed, let alone the falls,

so the only dangers to contend with are the steamy heat and persistent mosquitoes. If possible, come in the morning, when the sunshine, assuming there is any, directly hits the falls.

Follow signs off the highway, through Honomū (see below) and up Hwy-220 via a small belt of meadowland, to reach the parking lot. If you're pressed for time, head left from the trailhead here for a shorter round-trip hike that will only take you to 'Akaka Falls. Otherwise, follow the signs and descend a narrow staircase that swiftly plunges you into dense tropical foliage, where thickets of bamboo soar from the gorge below to meet high above your head. Few plants along the route are native to Hawaii, and the whole forest is a battleground of vivid blossoms. Among the most lurid are the fiery "lobster-claw" heliconia and birds of paradise, bedecked in either orange and blue, or white.

Shortly after you cross a narrow stream, the canopy opens up and you reach an overlook facing across a gorge to spindly **Kapuna Falls**. Mighty trees stand alongside the path, festooned with thick green mosses, fern, and creepers, with all kinds of parasitic plants sprouting from their branches and trunks. To the left, a vast banyan drips with tendrils.

Across the next bluff, you get your first view of 'Akaka Falls itself, foaming through a narrow channel to plunge around 450ft down a mossy cliff-face and disappear in a cloud of spray into the pool below. After leaving the viewing area, you recross the stream at a higher point, where a small waterfall bubbles beneath another overhanging bamboo grove.

Honomū

Were it not for the steady flow of visitors to 'Akaka Falls, tiny **HONOMŪ**, on the *mauka* side of Hwy-19, would probably have been swallowed up by the rainforest by now. As it is, the village consists of a row of little timber-framed galleries and crafts stores, a couple of which sell sodas, juices, and snacks as well as run-of-the-mill souvenirs. Stop by Ishigo's General Store, an authentic plantation store run by the same family since 1910.

Umauma Falls

Heading inland from Hwy-19 along any of the little access roads around milepost 16, roughly two miles north of Kolekole Beach Park (which lacks a beach, and is used predominantly by local surfers), enables you to join the minor road, parallel to the main highway, that leads to **Umauma Falls**. Visitors who drop in at the relatively unenthralling **World Botanic Gardens** here (daily 9am–5.30pm; adults $13, ages 13–17 $6, ages 5–12 $3; ☎808/963-5427, ⓦwww.wbgi.com), and pay the high admission fee, are given directions for reaching an overlook beside the Umauma Stream that commands a superb prospect of the triple-tiered falls themselves. They're not nearly as dramatic as 'Akaka Falls, but are still an impressive sight.

Laupāhoehoe

For most of the Hāmākua coast, the shoreline cliffs are too abrupt to leave room for settlements by the sea. Hence the significance of **LAUPĀHOEHOE**, ten miles along from Umauma Falls, where a flow of lava extruding into the ocean has created a flat, fertile promontory (*lau* means leaf, and *pāhoehoe* is smooth lava).

As the best canoe-landing between Hilo and Waipi'o, Laupāhoehoe has long been home to a small community; the location has its perils, however. On April 1, 1946, a ferocious tsunami destroyed the school at the tip of the headland, killing 24 teachers and children.

As the approach road to Laupāhoehoe rounds the first tight corner on its way to the sea, you're confronted by a stunning view of the green coastal cliffs stretching away to the south. After rain, countless small waterfalls cascade from crevices in the rock. The narrow road winds down past the **Jodo Mission**, a temple built by Japanese immigrants in 1899, and arrives at a flat spit of land at the foot of the cliffs. Most of the space here is taken up by a large lawn, fringed with tall coconut palms. Assorted seafront parking lots are squeezed in before the forbidding black-lava coastline and its pounding surf, in which swimming is definitely not advisable.

Until the tsunami of 1946, the main coastal road passed through Laupāhoehoe at sea level. Part of the village had already relocated higher up the hillside in 1913, however, when the sugar company **railroad** reached this far up the Hāmākua coast. Both the lower road and the railroad were destroyed by the tsunami, and the whole community subsequently shifted to the top of the cliffs.

Since the last of the local sugar mills closed, Laupāhoehoe has been facing an uncertain future. There's no town for visitors to explore, and no accommodation is currently available. The one concession to tourism is the little **Laupāhoehoe Train Museum**, housed in the former ticket-agent's residence alongside the highway (Mon–Fri 9am–4.30pm, Sat & Sun 10am–2pm; $4; Ⓦwww.thetrainmuseum.com). Enthusiastic volunteers explain the history of the railroad, aided by a plethora of photos and artifacts, and can tell you how far they've got with their schemes to restore some of the rusted-up old machinery.

On the little residential road that runs parallel to the highway, the *50s Highway Fountain Diner* (closed Mon; ℡808/962-0808) makes an enjoyable **lunch** spot, with its burgers, local foods, and 1950s memorabilia.

Honoka'a

The largest and most appealing of the Hāmākua towns is rough-and-tumble **HONOKA'A**, forty miles north of Hilo where the Belt Road curves west to run across the island to Waimea (see p.163). Consisting largely of a row of quaint timber-framed stores set on the wooden boardwalks of Mamane Street, selling antiques, crafts, and just plain junk, it stands a couple of miles back from the ocean and is surrounded by rolling meadows.

Just over two thousand people live in Honoka'a, whose economy depended on a mill belonging to the Hāmākua Sugar Company from 1873 until it finally shut down in 1994. However, this is one of several Big Island communities to have been spruced up and revitalized by federal funding, and its historic downtown district makes it an appealing port of call.

The most conspicuous landmark along Mamane Street is the Art Deco **Honoka'a People's Theater**, built as a movie theater in 1930. Restored and repainted, it is now used for occasional movie performances and musical events, including a "Jazz Getaway" in May and November's **Hāmākua Music Festival**, which focuses on Hawaiian performers (Ⓦwww.hamakuamusicfestival.com).

Practicalities

The only **accommodation** in central Honoka'a, the *Hotel Honoka'a Club*, on Mamane Street at the Hilo end of town, divides travelers' opinions (℡808/775-0678 or 1-800/808-0678, Ⓦwww.hotelhonokaa.com; ❶–❹). Some love this rambling, thin-walled, and spartan old wooden structure, and particularly the en-suite rooms on the upper floor, which have sweeping ocean views; others feel it's all a bit too spartan for the price, and balk at more basic hostel-style dorms downstairs (beds $20). Two miles out of Honoka'a toward Waipi'o, the *Waipi'o Wayside* **B&B** (℡808/775-0275 or 1-800/833-8849, Ⓦwww.waipiowayside.com; ❹) offers five themed en-suite rooms in an attractive old plantation house.

The best place to **eat** in Honoka'a is *Jolene's Kau Kau Korner* (Mon & Wed 10.30am–3.30pm & 5–8pm, Tues & Thurs–Sun 10.30am–3.30pm; ☎808/775-9498), next to the Lehua–Mamane intersection in the center of town. A lunchtime burger or stir-fry in this attractive Hawaiian-style diner will set you back $4–11; more substantial dinner entrees, such as the tasty seafood platter of breaded fish, cost $12–17. A decent Italian place opposite, *Café Il Mondo* (Tues–Sat 11am–8pm; ☎808/775-7711), serves soup and focaccia ($5) and calzones ($11), plus substantial lasagnas and pizzas, while an excellent health-food deli nearby at 45-3625 Mamane St, *Simply Natural* (Mon–Sat 8am–3.30pm; ☎808/775-0119), sells fabulous sandwiches.

Kukuihaele

The village of **KUKUIHAELE**, on a looping spur road off Hwy-240, less than a mile short of the Waipi'o overlook, is the nearest community to the valley. Its name, meaning "traveling light," is a reference to the lights carried by the ghostly nocturnal processions that head for the underworld below Waipi'o (see p.184). As well as the Waipi'o Valley Art Works (☎808/775-0958), the appealing crafts store and snack bar that serves as the base for the Waipi'o Valley Shuttle and other tours described on p.186, it's home to a delightful **B&B**, *Hale Kukui*, at 48-5460 Kukuihaele Rd (☎808/775-1701 or 1-800/444-7130, ⓦwww.halekukui.com; ❹–❺). Set in lush gardens above the ocean, with views of the valley mouth, the guest cottage here stands a couple hundred yards off the loop road as you head toward Waipi'o. Accommodation is in a one-bedroom studio or a two-room unit; they insist on a two-night minimum stay.

Waipi'o Valley

Beyond Honoka'a, Mamane Street continues north as Hwy-240, and comes to an abrupt end after nine miles at the edge of **WAIPI'O VALLEY**. The southernmost of a succession of deeply indented, sheer-walled valleys stretching away up the coast to Pololū (see p.169), Waipi'o is the only one accessible by road. It's as close as

▲ Waipi'o Valley

the Big Island gets to the classic South Seas image of an isolated and self-sufficient valley, sparkling with waterfalls, dense with fruit trees, and laced by footpaths leading down to the sea. More dramatic examples of this kind of scenery abound on older islands such as Kauai, but as the Big Island is the newest in the chain, it's only here on the flanks of Kohala – its oldest volcano – that rainwater has had the necessary eons to gouge out such spectacular chasms.

Between its high walls, the valley has a surprisingly broad floor, filled with rich silt carried down by the meandering **Waipi'o Stream**. Such large areas of prime agricultural land are surprisingly rare in the Hawaiian islands. This was probably the leading taro-farming valley of the entire archipelago; its produce alone could feed the whole population of the island in times of famine. The valley is now far more overgrown than it was in its heyday, and inhabited by just a few farmers who squelch their way across paddy-like taro fields.

Only a small proportion of the steady trickle of visitors who admire the view from the Waipi'o overlook make their way down into the valley itself. It's a very strenuous hike, so most of those who do join a motorized or horseback tour (see below for details). Facilities at the bottom are minimal; there's nowhere to eat or sleep, and **camping** is no longer permitted. However, it's a magical spot, and one that deserves to figure on even the most breakneck Big Island itinerary.

The history of Waipi'o

Beautiful and enormously productive, Waipi'o Valley occupies a crucial place in Big Island history. The Hawaiian word for "law," *kanawai*, literally means "the equal sharing of water," and the system to which it refers was instigated here in the fifteenth century by **'Umi-a-Liloa**. The first ruler to unite the entire Big Island, he was responsible as a taro farmer for the development of the valley's highly complex network of irrigation channels. 'Umi also had his nastier side, as one of the first major practitioners of large-scale human sacrifice. Victims, such as his rival high chief and half-brother Hakua-a-Liloa, were baked in an *imu* pit and their remains placed on the altar of Waipio's Moa'ula Heiau.

Another Waipi'o legend states that a pit at the mouth of the valley marked the entrance to the **underworld** known as Kapa'aheo, the Hawaiian equivalent of ancient Greece's Hades. This insubstantial and barren wasteland was said to be populated by famished ghosts gnawing on lizards and butterflies; dead souls could occasionally be seen making their way to it at night, in stately processions along the Old Māmalahoa Highway (see p.166).

Waipi'o was also the boyhood home of **Kamehameha the Great**. It was here that chief Kalaniopu'u granted Kamehameha custody of the war god Kūkā'ilimoku in 1780, thereby sanctioning his ambitions to become ruler. Eleven years later, his warriors fought Kahekili of Maui just offshore in the inconclusive but bloody "Battle of the Red-Mouthed Gun," in which, for the first time, Hawaiian fleets were equipped with cannons, operated by foreign gunners.

All sorts of estimates have been made of the population of Waipi'o in different eras. In Kamehameha's day, there may have been as many as 7500 inhabitants; within a century that was down to more like 2000, but you may still meet people brought up in the valley who can point out overgrown spots where Catholic, Protestant, and Congregational churches, and a Chinese temple, were thriving as recently as the 1930s.

However, large-scale settlement of Waipi'o came to an end after the tsunami of April 1946 scoured the valley from end to end. No one died, but few felt much inclination to rebuild their devastated homes. The busiest Waipi'o has been since then was during the 1960s, when Peace Corps volunteers were trained here. These days, sixty percent of the land is owned by Kamehameha Schools, and leased to

private farmers. So far, all threats to "develop" Waipiʻo have come to nothing – tourists, and golfers in particular, don't like the rain.

Exploring the valley

If you just want to say you've seen Waipiʻo, the view from the **overlook** is more comprehensive than any you get down below. Drivers must in any case leave their vehicles at the top. A few yards down from the parking lot, a pavilion stands in a small grassy area on the very lip of the cliff, 900ft above the sea; a friendly **information officer** is stationed here to answer visitors' questions (daily 9am–5pm). Off to your left is the green floor of Waipiʻo, with terraced fields but barely a building in sight as it reaches back toward misty Kohala Mountain. As you look straight up the coast, across the beach at the mouth of the valley, you should be able to make out three distinct headlands, the furthermost of which is up in North Kohala, near the town of Kapaʻau on the road route to Pololū (see p.169). Unless you are the hardiest of hikers or kayakers or take a flight-seeing tour, you'll never see the hidden valleys that lie in between. On clear days, Maui is visible in the far distance.

A paved road heads down the side of the *pali* from the parking lot, but don't try to drive it yourself. Without four-wheel-drive it's suicidal, and even with it you need to know exactly what you're doing. That leaves you with the choice of either taking a **tour** – see below – or **hiking** down. It takes little more than fifteen minutes to reach the floor, but be warned, the 25 percent gradient makes the return trip heavy going, and you need to have at least two hours to make it worth the effort.

One thing the tour operators don't mention is that they're not allowed to take visitors to the seashore. On foot, however, you're free to make your own way there. As soon as you come to the yellow warning sign at the bottom of the slope, well before you reach the stream, double back onto what swiftly becomes a muddy lane. Don't stray off this path; the taro fields to either side are strictly private.

It takes about five minutes, walking through a fine avenue of ironwood trees, to reach the flat **beach** of gray sand that's fronted by small black lava boulders. The wide mouth of Waipiʻo Stream cuts the beach in two; usually it's not too difficult to wade across, but don't attempt it if the water is any deeper than your thighs. Neither should you drink it, as it's liable to carry diseases. **Leptospirosis** in particular is a major problem here, so don't let the water come into contact with the smallest open wound (see p.36). Surfers and boogie-boarders while away days on end playing in the white breakers, but it's no place for a casual dip.

If, instead of heading for the beach, you keep going at the foot of the slope, toward the back of Waipiʻo, you soon come within sight of the 1200ft **Hiʻilawe waterfall**, with the parallel but slimmer **Nani** cascade plummeting to its left. Both were restored to full strength in 2004, after a century of having their waters diverted to quench the thirst of the sugar plantations, and once more feed Waipiʻo Stream as it emerges into the heart of the valley. Hiʻilawe is further away than it looks; walking to its base takes an hour and a half and involves scrambling up a channel of giant boulders.

Waipiʻo tours

Various **organized tours** take visitors around the floor of Waipiʻo Valley, offering the chance to learn more about the valley from local people. Many of the guides were born in Waipiʻo and are eager to share stories of the old days. However, regulations as to what each operator is allowed to do tend to change from year to year. As the beach is off-limits and the waterfalls are too remote, most tours consist of anecdotal rambles through the taro fields and along the riverbank.

The Waipiʻo Valley Shuttle, which runs ninety-minute **van trips** from the overlook, is based at the Waipiʻo Valley Art Works (see p.183) in Kukuihaele, a mile from the end of the road. They prefer that you call ahead to reserve a trip, but there's often a driver hanging around the overlook itself waiting to fill up his vehicle (Mon–Sat, departures usually at 9am, 11am, 1pm, & 3pm; $55, under-12s $28; ☎808/775-7121). Likewise working out of the Waipiʻo Valley Art Works, Waipiʻo Naʻalapa Trail Rides runs two-hour **horseback expeditions** around the valley (Mon–Sat 9am & 12.30pm; $90; ☎808/775-0419, ⓦwww.naalapastables.com). The Last Chance Store, also in Kukuihaele, is the headquarters for Waipiʻo Valley Wagon Tours, which takes groups of up to twelve people down into the valley for hour-long **covered-wagon excursions** (Mon–Sat 10.30am, 12.30pm & 2.30pm; $55, under-12s $25; ☎808/775-9518, ⓦwww.waipiovalleywagontours.com).

In addition, various tours explore the backcountry close to and along the upper rim of Waipiʻo, without making the descent into the valley itself or necessarily even offering more than the occasional glimpse. Waipiʻo Ridge Stables (☎808/775-1007 or 1-877/757-1414, ⓦwww.waipioridgestables.com) offer both **horse rides** ($85 for 2hr 30min, $165 for 5hr) and, as Ride The Rim (☎808/775-1450, ⓦwww.ridetherim.com), **off-road vehicle tours** in individual all-terrain buggies ($159 for 3hr). Hawaiian Walkways organizes none-too-strenuous **guided hikes** ($119 for 4–5hr; ☎808/775-0372 or 1-800/457-7759, ⓦwww.hawaiianwalkways.com), as do Hawaii Forest & Trail, with expeditions starting from their headquarters near Kailua ($149 for 8hr tour; ☎808/331-8505 or 1-800/464-1993, ⓦwww.hawaii-forest.com).

The Saddle Road

From a glance at the map, the **SADDLE ROAD** looks the quickest route from one side of the Big Island to the other. What no map can convey, however, is quite how high and remote it is, involving a long, slow haul to an altitude of well over 6000ft in order to cross the "saddle" of land that lies between **Mauna Kea** to the north and **Mauna Loa** to the south. The fifty-mile stretch from Hilo to the point where it rejoins the Belt Road, Hwy-190 – six miles south of Waimea, and more than thirty northeast of Kailua – is one of the bleakest stretches of road imaginable, utterly unlike anything you'd expect to encounter in the middle of the Pacific Ocean.

Even if the Saddle Road is not much use as a short cut, it is an enjoyable adventure in its own right. Despite the elevation, it passes a long way below the summits of the two mountains, so you probably won't see the snowcaps, but there's some memorable scenery en route.

Until recently, the Saddle Road was so poorly surfaced, and so narrow in places, that all the car-rental chains forbade drivers to take their vehicles along it. It has now been extensively improved, indeed in parts entirely re-routed along newly constructed segments, and some rental companies no longer insist you avoid it. However, certain dangers remain: the road serves the military bases in the high stretches, and still sees a lot of uncompromising military traffic – it's frequently closed to non-military vehicles for hours at a time – and also the weather is often atrocious, so visibility can be very bad. Above all, there are no facilities of any kind for the entire 85 miles from Hilo to Kailua, so if you do get stuck or break down, rescuing you is a difficult and expensive job. If you choose to risk it, fill up with gas, take it slowly, and be sure to allow time to complete your journey in daylight.

Leaving Hilo, along Pūʻāinakō Street, the Saddle Road seems to go on climbing forever, straight from the ocean. Beyond the suburbs, with their tropical gardens, it heads up into the clouds, winding through a moist and misty heathland of spindly trees, then undulating across bare lava fields, until with any luck it emerges into the sun, on what feels like a wide grassy plain between Mauna Loa and Mauna Kea.

Gradually the road then curves to the north, circling Mauna Kea and bringing Hualālai into view. Only on the **Kona side** of the island is the going at all rough, with several one-lane bridges, and even here reconstruction should soon straighten things out. Within the next few years, it's expected that the road will follow a new course down to Hwy-190, cutting perhaps twenty miles of the total driving distance between Kailua and Hilo, and quite possibly it will also be extended down to meet the coastal Hwy-11 near Waikoloa.

Mauna Kea

For the moment, **MAUNA KEA** is, at 13,796ft, the highest mountain in the entire Pacific. Being extinct, however, and therefore already eroding away, it's steadily losing ground to still-active Mauna Loa, 25 miles southwest. Nonetheless its height and isolation make Mauna Kea one of the very best sites for **astronomical observatories** on earth. Its summit is an otherworldly place, not just because of the surreal ring of high-tech telescopes, but because it's so devoid of life, its naked hillocks composed of multicolored minerals. A spur road ascends to the summit from the Saddle Road, though its last nine miles are most safely attempted with a four-wheel-drive vehicle, and the observatories are seldom open to casual visitors.

Ancient Hawaiians named Mauna Kea the "white mountain," as it's capped by snow for over half the year. That didn't deter them from climbing right to the top, however. Like Mauna Loa, Mauna Kea is a shield volcano (see p.196), so most of its slope is very gentle. It differs from its neighbor in having been here during the last Ice Age, making it the only spot in the central Pacific to have been covered by **glaciers**. The ice chilled its molten lava to create the best basalt in the islands, and, incredibly, there's an ancient **adze quarry** 12,400ft up the mountain. From 1100 AD onwards, it was the major source of the stone used for all the islanders' basic tools.

Ellison Onizuka Visitor Center

The turnoff to the summit of Mauna Kea comes at mile marker 28 on the Saddle Road. At first the road passes through grazing land, covered with wiry grass but devoid of trees. Most of this land is open cattle range – a broad swathe of this flank of Mauna Kea, just like the northern side, belongs to the Parker Ranch (see p.165). The road surface is good for the nine miles to the **Ellison Onizuka Visitor Center**, a small facility that houses displays about the observatories and also has its own much more basic telescope, used for the nightly stargazing sessions (center open daily 9am–10pm; stargazing daily 6–10pm; free; ☎808/961-2180, Ⓦwww.ifa.hawaii.edu/info/vis). Every Saturday, there's a special program of some kind, perhaps an astronomer describing the observatories' work, or a cultural talk.

Whether or not you plan to continue on to the summit, the eerie views here, at 9000ft, make it worth coming this far. Bizarre reddish cinder cones and other volcanic protrusions float in and out of the mists that swathe the grasslands. In any case, to help prevent **altitude sickness** and related problems, you should remain for at least an hour at this level before going any higher. Drink as much water as possible – and don't come this high within 24 hours of **scuba diving**.

The road to the summit

The road on from the visitor center is kept in reasonably good condition; the astronomers who work at the top have to commute this way. Adverse weather conditions can close it altogether for days at a time, but otherwise, although it's much safer to drive it in a **four-wheel-drive vehicle**, ordinary cars are not forbidden. The surface is unpaved for the first five miles, largely to deter visitors; for its final four miles the road is paved once more, in order to avoid churning up dust that might interfere with the telescopes.

Locals delight in driving to the top of Mauna Kea to fill their pick-up trucks with snow. Most tourists, however, are keen to see the inside of the observatories. If that's your goal, the best day to come is either Saturday or Sunday, when staff at the visitor center coordinate **free summit tours** (minimum age 16; you mustn't have respiratory or heart problems, or be pregnant). Participants are required to bring their own four-wheel-drive vehicles. If you don't have one, you could try to hitch a ride, but you can't arrange it in advance and it's a big favor to ask, as you'll be dependent on your new friend for several hours. The tour parties assemble at 1pm to watch a video presentation, then set off in a convoy at 2pm.

In addition, several operators run **guided tours** to the summit of Mauna Kea, which usually include the after-dark stargazing sessions and therefore require afternoon pick-ups at either Kona-coast or Waimea hotels. A typical tour lasts around eight hours and costs around $200 per person; operators include Hawaii Forest & Trail (☎808/331-8505 or 1-800/464-1993, ⓦwww.hawaii-forest.com), Mauna Kea Summit Adventures (☎808/322-2366 or 1-888/322-2366, ⓦwww .maunakea.com), and the much cheaper *Arnott's Lodge* in Hilo (☎808/969-7097, ⓦwww.arnottslodge.com; see p.172), which charges hostel guests $80.

Alternatively, if you're feeling *really* energetic, you can **hike** up. This involves a grueling haul up six miles of exposed road, with an elevation increase of 4000ft, before you're rewarded with your first glimpse of the summit.

Weather conditions at and near the summit can be absolutely atrocious. Wind speeds of over 170 mph have been measured, twelve feet of snow has fallen in a single night, and visibility is always liable to drop to zero. It's essential to bring very warm, windproof clothing, sunscreen, and sunglasses.

The observatories

When you finally reach the top of Mauna Kea, it's far from obvious which of the many rusty red and gold cinder cones in the vicinity is the actual summit. In fact, out of deference to Hawaiian sensibilities, all the gleaming golf-ball-shaped **observatories** are clustered on slightly lesser eminences; the highest mound of all is topped only by a small Hawaiian shrine.

Mauna Kea was first opened up to astronomical use in the 1960s and now holds thirteen observatories, all under the auspices of the University of Hawaii. No further telescopes will be built, though existing ones can be replaced as they become outdated.

Some observatories are remote-controlled by technicians in Waimea and Hilo, while others require human operators to be on hand. Working at this altitude brings unique problems; however often you come here, the thin air is liable to render you light-headed and greatly affect your ability to concentrate. As a result, the weekend guided tours (see above) tend to be rather surreal, with guides and visitors alike unable to string coherent thoughts together. Those tours take you into three or four different observatories; if you arrive alone, the only ones you can visit are Keck I, the original of the two identical domes of the **Keck** observatories (Mon–Fri 10am–4pm; free; ⓦwww.keckobservatory.org),

and the giant **Subaru Observatory** (reservations essential, check website for upcoming tours; ⓦ www.subarutelescope.org), which boasts the world's largest glass mirror, at 8.2 meters (about 27ft 5inches) across.

Don't expect to able to peer through the eyepieces of the telescopes; all information is digitally processed and can only be seen on computer screens. Astronomers from all over the world, including amateur hobbyists, can, however, submit proposals to use the telescopes for their pet projects, at typical fees of around $1 per second.

The summit of Mauna Kea

The summit of Mauna Kea, the cinder cone officially known as **Puʻu Wōkiu**, to the right of the observatory access road, can only be reached via a short, steep hike up the crumbling slope. Alongside the geodesic plate at the top you'll find a simple cairn of rocks, erected as a Hawaiian shrine. The view is awesome, with natural cones and craters nearby and the mighty shapes of Mauna Loa and Haleakalā on the horizon. If there's any snow on the ground, you may well be sharing this magnificent spot with groups of teenagers, rendered silly by the altitude, who come up here to **snowboard** down the rough surrounding slopes.

Mauna Kea holds one last surprise. Reached by a ten-minute hiking trail that leaves the main road at a hairpin bend just below the summit, **Lake Waiʻau** is a permanent lake set in a cinder cone 13,020ft above sea level. Some visitors swim in its icy waters, which are replenished by thawing permafrost from the thirty-foot layer that starts three feet below the surface.

Mauna Kea State Park

Once past the summit approach road, the Saddle Road starts to head slightly north, and views begin to open up of the whole Kona coast. Close to mile marker 35, a short but very tiring two-mile **hike** in **Mauna Kea State Park** can bring you to superb views of the island's three largest volcanoes.

From the parking lot, head past the wooden cabins – available for rent through the state parks office in Hilo ($55 per night; ⓣ 808/974-6200) – and follow a jeep track toward Mauna Kea. Having made your way as far as three pale-blue water towers, continue along the track until just before you reach an older tower. So far the trail has all been flat, but now a footpath leads straight up a small-looking mound to the right. The next few hundred yards are chest-thumpingly steep. Climbing across a loose surface of powdery brown dust, you pass a wide range of brittle high-altitude plants, including desiccated shrubs and a few native silverswords. Though far below the top of Mauna Kea, the crest of the mound makes a perfect vantage point for views of the entire slope of Mauna Loa across the saddle, Hualālai away to the west, and the sprawling army camp below.

Puna

With the compelling attractions of Hawaii Volcanoes National Park nearby, few tourists bother to leave the highway as they pass through the district of **PUNA**, which takes up the southeastern corner of the Big Island. The county government, too, seems to see it as a land apart, a quirky enclave that doesn't quite fit in with the rest of the island. In the 1960s and 1970s, large portions of the region were rezoned for residential development, but it still lacks the infrastructure that you – and the thirty-thousand-plus people who live here – would expect.

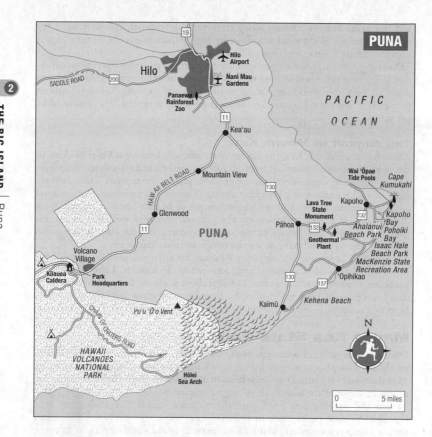

The volcanoes haven't helped matters either, incinerating newly built homes and cutting the coastal road to leave poor, traffic-ridden **Kea'au** as the only point of access to the whole region.

Although the eleven-mile stretch of oceanfront highway that has so far survived the volcanoes makes an attractive drive, unless lava is currently flowing here (see p.192) there's no great reason to spend more than a couple of hours in Puna. Stop for lunch in the self-consciously outlaw town of **Pāhoa**, dominated by hippies and back-to-the-landers, but don't expect to swim from any of Puna's photogenic but dangerous beaches.

Kea'au

The town of **KEA'AU** lies just south of Hwy-11 as it climbs toward the volcanoes, little more than three miles beyond Hilo's city limits. As a dormitory for Hilo's workers, and the gateway to Puna, it's choked morning and evening by huge traffic jams.

Kea'au consists of little more than the large parking lot for the **Kea'au Shopping Center**. This low-key wooden shopping mall holds a funky grocery store, Kea'au Natural Foods, as well as a farmers' market, a laundromat, a raucous sports bar, and a couple of small Asian fast-food diners.

Pāhoa

With its false-front stores and rudimentary timber boardwalks, tiny **PĀHOA**, a dozen miles southwest of Keaʻau, is a distinctive blend of Wild West cowboy town and Shangri-la. Life here moves so slowly that it hasn't quite kept up with the rest of America; the streets seem to be filled with refugees from the 1960s – even if most of them were born a decade or two later – watched by occasional, and equally incongruous, groups of aloha-shirted tourists. The only building of any size is the venerable Akebono Theater, founded in 1917, where the parking lot is the scene of a lively Sunday-morning flea market.

Practicalities

Pāhoa holds a couple of budget **accommodation** options, both at the north end of town. The *Island Paradise Inn* (T 808/990-0234, W www.islandparadiseinn.com; 3-day minimum stay; ❶) consists of a group of simple but very neat and clean one- and two-bedroom wooden cottages, rented at exceptionally low rates; while *JoMamas Pāhoa Town Hostel* (T 808/430-1573, W www.jomamahawaii.com; ❶/❷), is a clean, new hostel in a private home, with single-sex dorm beds for $30 and private doubles for $60.

The handful of **restaurants** in Pāhoa are complemented by an ever-changing cast of coffee-house hangouts filled with barefoot, tie-dyed locals. The best food around is served at *Ning's*, a small Thai diner on the boardwalk (daily except Wed noon–8.30pm; T 808/965-7611), which offers the same delicious menu at both lunch and dinner, with tom yum soup ($7–12) in vegetarian or seafood versions, and red, green, and yellow curries for around $10. *Sirius Coffee Connection*, also on the main village road opposite the 7-Eleven (Mon–Fri 7am–7pm, Sat 7am–10pm, Sun 8am–6pm; T 808/965-8555), is a **cybercafé** that serves good coffee and smoothies.

Lava Tree State Monument

Set back in the rainforest just off Hwy-132, almost three miles out of Pāhoa, **Lava Tree State Monument** (daily dawn–dusk; free) preserves the petrified record of a double catastrophe that took place two centuries ago. First a fast-flowing lava stream destroyed the underbrush and lapped against the *ʻōhia* trees of the forest, clinging to their trunks and cooling as it met resistance. Then an earthquake opened fissures in the ground into which the liquid rock quickly drained. That left the landscape scattered with upright columns of lava, hollow inside where the trees themselves had burned away.

It takes around half an hour to walk the level, paved trail that loops around the finest specimens, which look like black termite mounds or gnarled old candles. While this landscape may be unusual and striking, if your time is limited it's best to push on to the main attractions of Hawaii Volcanoes National Park.

The Puna coast

A thick layer of shiny black lava, unceremoniously dumped by Kīlauea in 1988, brings Hwy-130 to a halt close to mile marker 21, just under ten miles from Pāhoa. Some trees are still visible beyond, and new plant growth has appeared, but barely a trace survives of the extensive Royal Gardens residential area that once stood here.

Almost all of the coastal village of Kalapana, to which the highway originally led, has also been destroyed. Fortunately, however, roughly half a mile short of its own dead end, Hwy-130 still joins up with Puna's main coast road, Hwy-137, enabling you to complete an enjoyable loop-drive back to Pāhoa.

Kaimū

Hwy-137 reaches the ocean slightly east of the former site of **KAIMŪ** black-sand beach, which until it was obliterated in 1990 was one of the most photographed spots on the island. Only *Verna's* grocery and deli, alongside, was spared by the lava, though some of the coconut palms from the beach were rescued and airlifted to the *Hilton Waikoloa* hotel in Kohala.

Kehena Beach

Driving east along Hwy-137 takes you through scenery that varies one minute to the next, depending on the age of the lava flow you're crossing. In places the undergrowth thins out to bare black rock, but most of the route is dripping with tropical vegetation. From time to time you get glimpses of the ocean and successive palm-bedecked headlands, but only rarely is it possible to get down to the seashore.

The best spot to do so is **Kehena Beach**, close to the 19-mile marker, where a cluster of parked cars usually betrays the presence of a small path down the cliffs. At the bottom you'll find an absolutely stupendous little **black-sand beach**, created by an eruption in 1955, backed by coconut palms that are home to a colony of wild parrots, and forever battered by spectacular crashing surf. Boogie-boarding and body-surfing can only be recommended if you know exactly what you're doing – locals do both naked – while from the jet-black shoreline it's often possible to watch dolphins at play in the water.

Isaac Hale Beach Park

Just north of where Hwy-137 meets a minor road from Pāhoa, **Isaac Hale Beach Park** finally lets you get down to the sea. Set in Pohoiki Bay, with a small beach of black and white pebbles, overhanging green vegetation, and high surf, the park is popular with surfers, anglers, and picnickers, though it's not a place for family bathing or for anyone inexperienced in the ways of rough Hawaiian seas. A small

---

Lava viewing in Puna

As explained on p.195, **lava flows** from the Kīlauea eruption can often be best seen by approaching from Puna rather than from the national park. Whenever active flows are accessible from the end of Hwy-137 – which was the case, for example, throughout 2009, but was no longer so when this book went to press – the county authorities set up facilities and safeguards to help visitors.

A county parking lot has been established a mile's rough but passable driving beyond the end of the paved road at Kaimū. As and when there are flows within walking distance, and dangerous fumes are not blowing, the county controls access to the area, usually between 5pm and 10pm nightly. For the latest information, call ☎808/961-8093, access ⓦwww.lavainfo.us, or contact the national park (see p.195).

Do not attempt to walk beyond the road without getting up-to-date local advice. Unless you know exactly where you're going, which in this ever-changing lavascape is all but impossible, you could easily get yourself into very serious danger. Several visitors attempting short strolls from the road have become totally disoriented and ended up stranded all night in the wilderness.

In addition, and again only when lava is entering the ocean, various operators have in recent years run after-dark **boat trips** that approach the eruption site. These typically cost $150–200 per person, and start from Isaac Hale park nearby (see above), with coach connections to and from Hilo and Kailua. No such trips were running at the time of publication, but no doubt operators like Lava Ocean Adventures (☎808/966-4200, ⓦwww.lavaocean.com) and C Big Island (☎808/640-7474 or 1-800/901-0468, ⓦwww.cbigisland.com) will spring into action again if conditions change.

boat ramp, protected by an army-built breakwater, is used by local vessels, and particularly by the **lava-viewing boat tours** described opposite.

Not far from Pohoiki Bay, the *Pamalu Hawaiian Country House* (T 808/965-0830, W www.apeacefulenclosure.net; 3-night minimum stay; ❹–❺) is a gay-friendly **B&B**. The five-acre property offers four en-suite guest rooms and has its own swimming pool.

Ahalanui Beach Park

A mile past Isaac Hale Park, **Ahalanui Beach Park** is a spot that can sound perfect on paper – a sheltered oceanfront lagoon, filled with water that's naturally heated to 90°F, and surrounded by coconut palms. In reality, it feels more like an open-air swimming pool, having been shaped into a neat rectangle and surrounded by walls of cemented black-lava boulders, complete with several small staircases into the water and attendant lifeguards. Strangely enough, when the construction work was done the water was cold; only later did the volcano step in to heat things up. At weekends, Ahalanui gets very crowded with local families. There have also been alarming reports of dangerous bacteria in the hot water; at least one bather has died, so at the very least don't go in the water if you have an open wound.

Wai 'Ōpae Tide Pools

As a paved road, Hwy-137 comes to an end four miles on from Pohoiki Bay, where it meets Hwy-132 from Pāhoa. To reach this spot, you pass over the site of Kapoho, yet another town swallowed up by the lava, this time in 1960. A great **snorkeling** spot can be found if you turn oceanwards on Kapoho Kai Drive, just over a mile south of the intersection, where "Vacationland" is spelled out on a row of coconuts. Turn left at the far end of Kapoho Kai Drive, and you'll come within a few yards to the **Wai 'Ōpae Tide Pools Marine Life Recreation Area**. Natural lava-walled lagoons here offer safe fish-viewing, though they're much too shallow to swim in for pleasure.

Hawaii Volcanoes National Park

HAWAII VOLCANOES NATIONAL PARK may well be the most dynamic, unpredictable place you'll ever visit, and it's one where normal rules just don't seem to apply. It's almost impossible to set out in a guidebook what you'll see or how to go about seeing it; the raw power of an active volcano is not something that can be tamed and labeled to suit those who like their scenery to stay still and their sightseeing to run to schedule. **Kīlauea**, at the heart of the park, is often called the "drive-in volcano"; it's said to be the only volcano in the world where news of a fresh eruption brings people flocking *toward* the lava flows. Only very rarely does the lava claim lives, but much of the excitement stems from the ever-present whiff of danger.

The park's sole entrance is roughly a hundred miles southeast of Kailua, thirty miles southwest of Hilo, and ten miles (as the crow flies) from the ocean. Driving from the west of the island takes at least two hours, with the last thirty miles spent ascending through a barren lava landscape. The road from Hilo, on the other hand, climbs more steeply through thick, wet rainforest.

You arrive at the park headquarters, beside the caldera (summit crater) of Kīlauea, with no real sense of being on top of a mountain. That's because Kīlauea, at only 4000ft high, is a mere pimple on the flanks of **Mauna Loa** (13,677ft), which, despite its deceptively gentle incline, stands almost ten thousand feet taller. Furthermore, for

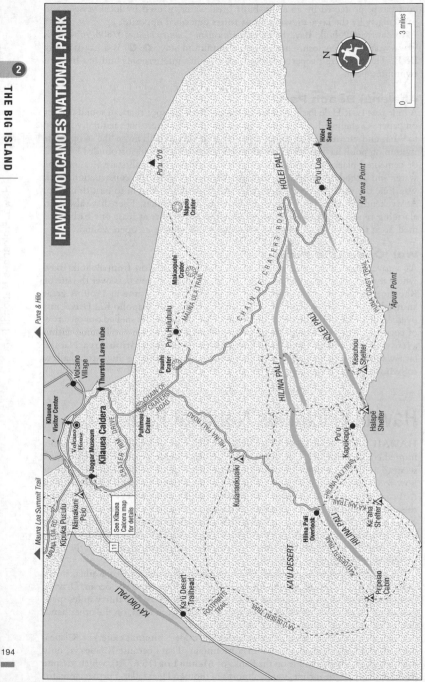

HAWAII VOLCANOES NATIONAL PARK

Park information

Hawaii Volcanoes National Park (visitor center ☎808/967-7311, ⓦwww.nps.gov/havo) is open 24 hours daily, 365 days a year; $10 per vehicle, $5 for cyclists, motorcyclists, and hikers (valid for seven consecutive days). An annual pass that also grants admission to the Big Island's Puʻuhonua O Hōnaunau park and Haleakalā on Maui costs $25, and system-wide national-parks passes are sold and valid. For the latest eruption information, check ⓦhvo.wr.usgs.gov.

all its trails and overlooks, the crater area is a long way from the park's most compelling attraction. Somewhere down the side of the mountain, molten lava is bursting out of the ground and cascading down to the sea – assuming that the eruption that has been going nonstop ever since 1983 has not died down by the time you visit.

The irregular boundaries of the national park take in around 550 square miles, including Kīlauea Caldera plus the summit craters and most of the eruption-prone rift zones of both volcanoes, an area that is largely desert but includes scattered pockets of rainforest and even one or two beaches. From being solely devoted to geology, the park's brief has expanded to cover responsibility for preserving vestiges of pre-contact occupation and protecting indigenous wildlife such as the Hawaiian goose, the **nēnē**. Although the most recent lava flows have been beyond the official park boundaries, its rangers still control public access to the danger spots.

Ever since the early missionaries, with their images of the fires of hell, Western visitors have tended to see the volcanoes as purely destructive. The ancient Hawaiians, whose islands would never have existed without them, were much more aware of the volcanoes' generative role, embodied in the goddess **Pele**. It may take longer to create than it does to destroy, but fresh lava is rich in nutrients, and life soon regenerates on the new land. On a single visit to the park, it's impossible to appreciate the sheer rapidity of change. What is a crackling, flaming, unstoppable river of molten lava one day may be a busy hiking trail the next. Come back twenty years later, and you could find a rich, living forest.

Planning a visit

Visiting Hawaii Volcanoes National Park normally involves several components; what exactly you do will depend on conditions on the day you arrive. Your top priority should be to see the **current eruption**, assuming that it's still active (which it has been since 1983) and that it's somewhere within reach (which it may not be).

Lava is most likely to be flowing southeast of Kīlauea Caldera, somewhere in the ten-mile stretch of coastline that lies between the end of **Chain of Craters Road** inside the park, and the small community of **Kaimu** – see p.192 – which lies outside the park and can only be reached by road via the **Puna** district. At any one time, several separate flows may well be active, but most are likely to be too far from any road, for example way up the hillside, or simply too dangerous to reach. To be accessible to visitors, they need to lie within hiking distance of a road (which generally means about two miles, as walking across fresh lava is a slow and tricky business), and thus either close to, or actually entering, the ocean.

As the active eruption is best seen **after dark**, when the glow of lava is much more spectacular, you'll probably have time to explore the park's more permanent attractions, concentrated **around Kīlauea Caldera**, the summit crater of the volcano. Potential stops here include the park **visitor center**, as well as the **Jaggar Museum** of vulcanology, and various hiking trails. In the last few years, volcanic activity has started up again in **Halemaʻumaʻu Crater**, inside the caldera itself.

The shield volcanoes of Hawaii

According to the classic popular image, a volcano is a cone-shaped mountain, topped by a neat round crater that's filled with bubbling lava and spouts columns of liquid fire.

Hawaiian volcanoes aren't like that. Although you may be lured to the park by photos of pillars of incandescent lava, you're unlikely to see any such thing. These are **shield volcanoes**, which grow slowly and steadily rather than violently, adding layer upon layer as lava seeps out of fissures and vents all along the **"rift zones"** on their sides. The result is a long, low profile, supposedly resembling a warrior's shield laid on the ground.

Mauna Loa and Kīlauea are simply the latest in the series of volcanoes that created the entire Hawaiian chain. Like all the rest, they're fueled by a **"hot spot,"** way below the sea floor, which has been channeling magma upwards for seventy million years. As the continental plates drift northwest, at around three inches per year, that magma has found its way to the surface in one volcano after another. Each island in turn has clawed its way up from the depths, emerged above the waves, and then ceased to grow as its volcanoes moved away from the life-giving source. In time, erosion by rain and sea wears away the rock, sculpting the fabulous formations seen at their most dramatic on Kauai, and eventually the ocean washes over it once more, perhaps leaving a ring of coral – an **atoll** – to bear witness. The oldest Hawaiian islands are by now 3500 miles away, mere specks in the Emperor chain, off the coast of Japan.

Look at the gentle slope of **Mauna Loa**, project that gradient down through almost twenty thousand feet of ocean, and you'll see why its Hawaiian name, "long mountain," is so appropriate. It's the most massive single object on earth; its summit is, at 13,677ft, very slightly lower than Mauna Kea, but its volume of ten thousand cubic miles makes it a hundred times larger than Washington's Mount Rainier. It took two million years for Mauna Loa to reach the open air, and for another million years it has continued to climb. In the last 150 years, the world's highest active volcano has erupted every three or four years – in a single hour in 1984, it let forth enough lava to pave a highway from Honolulu to New York. Geologists predict that every spot on its surface will receive at least one more coating of fresh lava before the fires die down.

Of late, however, the younger upstart **Kīlauea** – its name means "much spewing" – has been grabbing the attention, having been in a record-breaking continuous state of eruption since 1983. Although fed by a separate conduit from the fires below, Kīlauea emerged as a lump on the side of Mauna Loa, so you can hardly tell it's a separate mountain. Its lava tends to flow consistently in the same direction, down toward the ocean. Since 1983, it has added well over five hundred acres of new land to a nine-mile stretch of the Puna coastline.

Meanwhile the next volcano is on its way. Were you to stay around for three thousand years, you might see the submarine "seamount" of **Lo'ihi** poke its head from the ocean twenty miles southeast of the Ka'ū coast. One day it may seem no more than a blemish on the vast bulk of Mauna Loa – or it may be destined to overrun its older sisters altogether.

Further afield, you may choose to drive the fifty-mile round-trip down **Chain of Craters Road** to the ocean; to explore the harshly beautiful moonscape of the **Ka'ū Desert**, away to the west; or to drive the first 3000ft of the route up **Mauna Loa**, although reaching the summit itself involves a four-day hike.

Few people allow enough time to see the park properly. Ideally, you should spend a night nearby, either at the *Volcano House* hotel in the park itself (see p.199), in a B&B in the village of Volcano (p.206), or at the park campgrounds (p.199 &

p.202). Failing that, at least base yourself in Hilo, thirty miles away, rather than distant Kailua or Kohala.

It is possible to reach the park visitor center by free **public bus** from Hilo (Mon–Sat only; 1hr 20min; departs Mooheau Bus Terminal 5am & 4.40pm; departs visitor center 6.10am & 5.50pm; ⊤808/935-8241, ⓦwww.heleonbus.org), though to see the park itself, or the eruption, you really need your own vehicle. Alternatively, you could opt for an organized **bus tour** (see p.132), but generally these are not a good idea. They'll show you Kīlauea Caldera from above, but are unlikely to give you the flexibility to approach the eruption.

Kīlauea Caldera

The **park entrance** is just off Hwy-11, the Belt Road, a mile west of the village of **Volcano** (see p.206); the visitor center is just inside the park. If you're coming from the Kona side you can visit the park without ever passing through Volcano, though as it holds the only gas station for miles, you may well have to.

This area of the park focuses around **Kīlauea Caldera**, the summit crater of the volcano. Looking from a distance like a large oval of predominantly gray lava, roughly three miles long by two miles wide, the caldera is flanked on two sides by a steep *pali*, around 400ft high. On those sides, and in places down below the wall as well, patches of rainforest have escaped the fires; off to the south and east, however, the cliff dwindles to almost nothing, and strong-smelling sulphur drifts across the plains to ensure that nothing living can find a foothold.

Out in the middle of the caldera lies a further deep indentation, known as **Halema'uma'u Crater**. Until recently, it was possible to stand right above it and look down into its gray depths, but since volcanic activity re-started here in 2008 all access has been barred. When this book went to press, only distant plumes were visible to visitors, but the crater was for the hundred years up to 1924 filled with an incandescent lake of fire, and it's conceivable that by the time you read this it may once more have become the park's principal attraction.

In principle, you can circle Kīlauea Caldera on foot, along **Crater Rim Trail**, and by car along **Crater Rim Drive**. Both are approximately eleven miles long, and neither literally follows the edge the whole way around. As of 2010, however, both trail and road were partially closed, because of fumes from Halema'uma'u Crater. It's still possible nonetheless to visit various spots along Crater Rim Drive, including the worthwhile **Jaggar Museum**.

Kīlauea Visitor Center

Though **Kīlauea Visitor Center**, on the right within a few yards of the main park entrance, does not overlook the crater of Kīlauea, call in as soon as you arrive to pick up the latest information on the eruption and advice on hiking trails (daily 7.45am–5pm; ⊤808/967-7311, ⓦwww.nps.gov/havo). The center also has a bookstore and a small museum, and provides excellent free literature. Frequent films and lectures explain aspects of local geology, botany, and environmental issues; at 7pm on most Tuesdays, the center reopens for a series of talks called "After Dark in the Park." Ranger-led hikes include a free, four-hour **lava tube hike** once a week (Wed noon); reserve well in advance. Note that if you plan to camp in the backcountry, you must register here.

Just beyond the visitor center, set a little way back from the road, the **Volcano Art Center** (daily 9am–5pm; ⊤808/967-7565) is a nonprofit gallery and crafts store that sells the work of local artists. Prices are slightly higher than elsewhere, but the standard of the artwork – ranging across sculpture, prints, paintings, and photographs, and not all volcano-related – tends to be much higher as well.

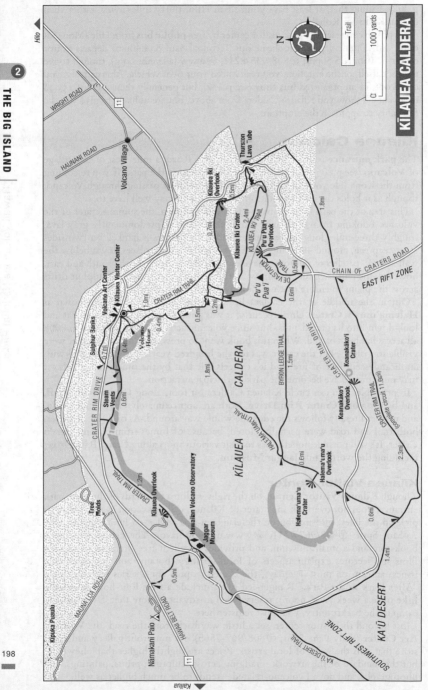

KĪLAUEA CALDERA

N

Trail

0   1000 yards

Hilo

WRIGHT ROAD

HAUNANI ROAD

11

Volcano Village

Kīlauea Iki Overlook

Thurston Lava Tube

0.7mi

Kīlauea Iki Crater

0.5mi

2.4mi

Kīlauea Visitor Center

Volcano Art Center

KĪLAUEA IKI TRAIL

Puʻu Puaʻi Overlook

Sulphur Banks

0.7mi

CRATER RIM TRAIL

1.0mi

CHAIN OF CRATERS ROAD

Puʻu Puaʻi

EAST RIFT ZONE

Volcano House

0.4mi

0.5mi

0.2mi

DEVASTATION TRAIL

0.6mi

Steam Vents

0.6mi

CRATER RIM DRIVE

0.5mi

BYRON LEDGE TRAIL

1.5mi

Keanakākoʻi Crater

Keanakākoʻi Overlook

CRATER RIM DRIVE

1.8mi

CALDERA

1.8mi

Kīlauea Overlook

1.2mi

CRATER RIM TRAIL

HALEMAʻUMAʻU TRAIL

KĪLAUEA

CRATER RIM TRAIL
(complete circuit 11.6mi)

2.3mi

Tree Molds

MAUNA LOA ROAD

Hawaiian Volcano Observatory

Jaggar Museum

1.4mi

Halemaʻumaʻu Overlook

0.6mi

Halemaʻumaʻu Crater

0.6mi

Kīpuka Puaulu

0.5mi

Nāmakani Paio

HAWAIʻI BELT ROAD

1.4mi

KAʻŪ DESERT TRAIL

KAʻŪ DESERT

SOUTHWEST RIFT ZONE

11

Kailua

Volcano House

Pride of place on the lip of Kīlauea Caldera belongs to the **Volcano House** hotel (T 808/967-7321, W www.volcanohousehotel.com), which has in various incarnations stood near this spot since 1846. When Mark Twain was a guest, in 1866, it was a four-roomed thatched cottage; now it consists of two separate motel-style buildings.

As this book went to press, the entire complex was **closed** for renovation, and was due to reopen in 2011. It will definitely be upgraded, and may be run by a different concessionaire; access the park or hotel websites for the latest news on rates and facilities. It's safe to assume, however, that *Volcano House* will continue to have a **restaurant**, open for all meals, and that as before, very few of its **guest rooms** will offer views of the volcano.

Even if the hotel remains closed, it's still worth walking across to it from the visitor center, for the views of the caldera from the footpath on its far side.

Sulphur Banks and Steam Vents

The first two stops on the Crater Rim Drive, on opposite sides of the road a few hundred yards and a mile respectively beyond the visitor center, are natural phenomena with the self-explanatory names of **Sulphur Banks** and **Steam Vents**. Both these unspectacular spots are characterized by white fumes that drift from cracks in the ground across open meadows; the difference is that the Sulphur Banks stink to high heaven, while the vapor from the Steam Vents is, once it condenses, in theory pure enough to drink. Unbelievably, two people have died after getting stuck when they climbed into similar steam vents nearby in the hope of experiencing a "natural sauna"; instead, they were poached alive.

Jaggar Museum

A little less than three miles from the visitor center, and sited here for the good reason that it has the clearest, highest view of the caldera, is the fascinating **Thomas A. Jaggar Museum** (daily 8.30am–5pm; T 808/967-7643, W http://hvo.wr.usgs .gov). Its primary aim is to explain the work of the adjacent **Hawaiian Volcano Observatory**, which is not open to the public. Videos show previous eruptions and panel displays illustrate Hawaiian mythology and historical observations by travelers. You can also visit the former laboratory of Dr Jaggar himself, who founded the observatory in 1911 (daily 9am).

The museum is the place to get the distinction clear between the kinds of lava known as *'a'ā* and *pāhoehoe* (used by geologists throughout the world, these are among the very few Hawaiian words to have been adopted into other languages). Chemically the two forms are exactly the same, but they differ owing to the temperature at which they are ejected from the volcano. Hotter, runnier *pāhoehoe* is wrinkled and ropy, like sludgy custard pushed with your finger, but with a sandpaper finish; cooler *'a'ā* does not flow so much as spatter, creating a sharp, jagged clinker. Other volcanic by-products on display include **Pele's hair** – very fine filaments made of glass that really do look like hair – and the shiny droplets called **Pele's tears**.

Outside, a viewing area looks down into Kīlauea, and Halemaʻumaʻu Crater in particular, which is 360ft deep at this point. By now you're on the fringes of the Kaʻū Desert, so there are no trees to block the view. The trade winds have for millennia blown the noxious emissions from the crater southwest, so despite receiving large quantities of rainfall the land in this direction supports no growth.

Nāmakani Paio

A ten-minute walk from the Jaggar Museum parking lot, away from the caldera, brings you to the only **campground** in the main area of the park, **Nāmakani**

Paio. It's actually just across the Belt Road, so if you're driving straight to it you don't enter the park proper. The pleasant wooded sites are free and available on a first-come, first-served basis for maximum stays of seven nights (in any one year).

The campground also holds some basic **cabins**, which have long been rented for $50 per night through *Volcano House* (see above). These too, like *Volcano House*, were closed for restoration as this book went to press; check the park website to see whether they've reopened, and with what facilities.

Thurston Lava Tube

Heading in the opposite direction from the park entrance, south through the rainforest towards Chain of Craters Road, brings you after a mile to the **Thurston Lava Tube**. As soon as you cross the road from the parking lot here, you're faced by a large natural basin bursting with huge *'ōhi'a* trees. Beneath it is the tube itself, created when the surface of a lava stream hardened on exposure to the air and the lava below was able to keep flowing with only a slight loss of temperature. When the lava eventually drained away, it left behind a damp, empty tunnel, an artificially lit portion of which is now open to the public. If you've ever descended into a subway system, the basic concept and appearance will be familiar.

Pele: The volcano goddess

Every visitor to Hawaii soon hears the name of **Pele**, the "volcano goddess" of the ancient Hawaiians. The daughter of Haumea the Earth Mother and Wākea the Sky Father, she is said to have first set foot in the Hawaiian chain on Kauai. Pursued by her vengeful older sister, the goddess of the sea, she traveled from island to island and finally made her home in the pit of **Kīlauea**. As well as manifesting herself as molten lava, she appeared sometimes as a young woman, sometimes as an elderly crone. Small acts of charity to her human forms could spare the giver a terrible fate when she returned as fire.

Imbued as they are with poetry, legend, history, and symbolism, it's impossible now to appreciate all that the tales of Pele meant to those who once recounted them by the distant glow of Kīlauea. Certainly these were people who studied the volcanoes carefully; specific places appear in the chants describing Pele's progress through the archipelago in the exact order of age agreed by modern experts. However, the **destructive** power of the volcanoes was just one small aspect of the goddess; she was also associated with the **hula**, with fertility, and with creation in general.

Talk of Hawaiian religion as a single system of belief ignores the fact that different groups once worshipped different gods. The god **Kū**, to whom human sacrifices were made in the *luakinis* (see p.427), was probably the chosen deity of the warrior elite; Pele may have been far more central to the lives of most of the islanders. She seems to have been a Polynesian deity whose worship became prominent in Hawaii around the thirteenth century. That may be because, together with Kū, she was brought to the islands by migrants who arrived then from **Tahiti**, or it may be that that was when Kīlauea entered the period of high activity that still continues today.

The earliest Christian **missionaries** to the Big Island were disconcerted to find that even after the old ways were supposedly abandoned, belief in Pele endured. They made great play of an incident in 1824, when **Queen Kapiʻolani**, a recent convert to Christianity, defied the goddess by descending into the caldera, reading aloud from her Bible, eating the *kapu* red *'ōhelo* berries and throwing their stones into the pit. Less fuss was made in 1881, when an eight-month flow from Mauna Loa had reached within a mile of central Hilo, Christian prayers had elicited no response, and **Princess Ruth Keʻelikōlani** was called in from Oahu to help. Under the gaze of journalists and missionaries, she chanted to Pele at the edge of the molten rock and offered her red silk handkerchiefs and brandy. By the next morning, the flow had ceased.

It takes less than ten minutes to walk to and through the main section of the tube, which is remarkable only for the smoothness of its walls and its conveniently flat natural floor. Occasionally roots from the gigantic ferns that grow up above have worked their way through cracks in the rock to dangle from the ceiling. If you've brought a flashlight, it's worth continuing beyond the official exit at the end of the illuminated portion, to explore a few hundred yards more of the tube, in a much rawer state. Back outside, the native red-billed 'i'iwi bird can always be heard, if not seen.

If visiting the Thurston Lava Tube whets your appetite, try to join the free, four-hour ranger-led **lava tube hike** mentioned on p.197; it's much more dramatic.

Devastation Trail

A bare, rust-colored cinder cone known as **Pu'u Pua'i**, formed by lighter debris thrown up by the 1959 Kīlauea Iki eruption (see above), can be reached along the half-mile **Devastation Trail**, which connects two parking lots on Crater Rim Drive.

If you set out from the Devastation parking area, opposite the top of Chain of Craters Road, you start by following the old route of Crater Rim Drive, which was severed at this point by the eruption. A paved pathway snakes through low, light-pink undergrowth – a favorite haunt of the park's population of **nēnē** geese. Most of what you see is new growth, though a few older trees survived partial submersion in ash by developing "aerial roots" some way up their trunks. Pu'u Puai itself is just a heap of reddish ash, while the barren land around it is scattered with bleached branches.

The Kīlauea Iki Trail

The recent eruptions within Halema'uma'u Crater have closed the **Halema'uma'u** and **Byron Ledge** hiking trails, which formerly crossed the main floor of Kīlauea Caldera. As a result, the two-hour, four-mile **Kīlauea Iki Trail**, which traverses the subsidiary crater of **Kīlauea Iki** ("little Kīlauea") immediately east of Kīlauea Caldera, offers the best opportunity to hike this spectacular volcanic landscape.

Kīlauea Iki took on its current shape during a gigantic eruption in 1959. Prodigious quantities of lava, shooting 1900ft high, raised the crater floor by around 350ft; some of it is still thought to be red-hot, a few hundred feet below the surface.

The loop trail is most easily done as a counterclockwise hike from the **Thurston Lava Tube** (see opposite), a mile south of the visitor center. Start by following the Crater Rim Trail for about a mile, as it circles close to the lip of the gulf. At a three-way junction with the now-closed spur to Byron Ledge, signs point left to the Kīlauea Iki Trail proper. Now the rainforest becomes especially dense, with startled wild game birds running along the path ahead, and songbirds overhead.

Soon you glimpse the far wall of Kīlauea Iki, tinged with pastel greens and yellows against the general darkness. Views of the crater floor thus far have made it appear smooth, but after a half-mile or so the path drops abruptly down to reach a primeval mess of jagged 'a'ā lava. Follow the line of cairns for a few hundred yards before arriving at the vent where the 1959 eruption took place. This sudden, gaping maw in the hillside, filled like an hourglass with fine reddish-orange sand, is seen across an open scar in the lava; do not approach any closer.

The trail then descends slightly to a more even, but no less alarming, expanse of undulating pāhoehoe, punctuated by white- and yellow-stained cracks that ooze stinking plumes of white vapor. As you step across the fissures, it takes an act of faith to follow the scattered cairns that mark the way. Eventually, however, you pass through a final chaos of rocks into the dripping, dank bosom of the rainforest. The path then zigzags back up to the rim; the gradient is never steep, but it's a fair walk and can get pretty muddy.

Chain of Craters Road

CHAIN OF CRATERS ROAD winds down to the ocean from the south side of Crater Rim Drive, sweeping around cones and vents in an empty landscape where only the occasional dead white tree trunk or flowering shrub pokes up. From high on the hillside, the lava flows look like streams of black tarmac, joining in an ever-widening highway down to the Pacific. Long **hiking trails** and the minor **Hilina Pali Road** lead to sites of geological and historic interest all the way down, but the real reason to head this way is to see what may be at the end – the ongoing **eruption of Kīlauea**.

Chain of Craters Road used to run all the way to Puna, then loop back up to the highway. The scale of the damage since 1983 has been too great to repair, however, so now it's a dead end, and getting shorter year by year. One by one, landmarks along its seafront stretch such as Wahaʻula Heiau, and the black-sand beach at Kamoamoa, have been destroyed, and before long the road may not follow the shoreline at all.

Check current conditions at the visitor center when you arrive and make sure you have enough gas. The end of the road is a fifty-mile round-trip from the park entrance, and there are no facilities of any kind along the way, while it's impossible to buy gas even in Volcano after 7.30pm.

Hilina Pali Road

Four miles down Chain of Craters Road, a sign to the right points out **Hilina Pali Road**. This crosses the bleak Kaʻū Desert for nine miles, to reach an overlook above the main 1200ft drop of Hilina Pali. *Pali* is the Hawaiian word for cliff; you may be used to hearing it applied to the lush razorback hills of the Hāmākua coast, but Hilina is much starker and rawer than that, being the huge wall left behind when a piece of the island dropped into the sea. The views are immense, but desolate in the extreme. Infrequent clusters of battered palms in the distance show the locations of former coastal villages; the hillock of Puʻu Kapukapu, near the shore to the southeast, however, obscures the most popular of the park's backcountry campgrounds, at Halapē.

Halfway along the road, **Kulanaokuaiki** is one of the park's two fully equipped, drive-in **campgrounds**. Smaller and somewhat more basic than *Nāmakani Paio* (see p.199), it's free and available on a first-come, first-served basis for up to seven nights in any one year.

All **hiking** in this area involves extended periods of walking across barren, exposed, and baking-hot lava flats. If you want to get to the shoreline, it makes more sense to hike the **Puna Coast Trail** (see p.204) than to climb up and down the *pali* as well. However, gluttons for punishment have a choice of two trails to the sea. Both the **Hilina Pali** and **Kaʻaha trails** start by zigzagging down the cliff along the same poorly maintained footpath; the Kaʻaha leads for just under four miles to **Kaʻaha Shelter**, while the Hilina Pali covers the eight miles to the **Halapē Shelter**, joining the **Halapē Trail** from Kīpuka Nēnē.

Mauna Ulu Trail and Puʻu Huluhulu

Another three miles along Chain of Craters Road beyond the Hilina Pali turnoff, a small approach road on the left leads to the **Mauna Ulu Trail**. In theory this leads for ten miles to the open **Puʻu ʻŌʻō** vent, far out along Kīlauea's East Rift Zone, but the only section currently open to visitors is the three-mile round-trip to **Puʻu Huluhulu**, an ancient cinder cone that has somehow escaped inundation for several millennia. It owes its name (*huluhulu* means "very hairy") to the dense coating of unspoilt, old-growth rainforest that surrounds it as a result. Following the footpath to the top of this small mound enables you to peer into its inaccessible hollow

interior, circled by craggy red rocks and filled with primeval-looking green ferns and darting birds. The sensation of being in a real-life "lost world" is enhanced by the wasteland visible all around.

Pu'u 'Ō'ō itself is extremely unstable; gaping holes regularly split its sides to release floods of liquid rock, and there have been several major collapses. With luck, you should be able to spot its smoldering cone from Pu'u Huluhulu, while views to the south are dominated by the miniature shield volcano of **Mauna Ulu**, created between 1971 and 1974 and already home to native trees and shrubs like the *'ōhi'a* and *'ōhelo*.

Pu'u Loa petroglyphs
Ten miles beyond Mauna Ulu, just after its descent of the 1000ft Holei Pali, Chain of Craters Road passes within a mile of the most extensive field of **petroglyphs** – ancient rock carvings – on the island.

From a roadside parking lot, a level hiking trail leads east to Pu'u Loa, ending at a circular raised boardwalk. Most of the petroglyphs visible from here are no more than crude holes in the lava, and only inspire any wonder if you're aware that each was probably carved to hold the umbilical cord of a newborn infant. *Pu'u loa* means "long hill," and by extension "long life," so this was considered a lucky spot for the traditional ceremony. The purpose of the boardwalk is not to display the most elaborate petroglyphs, but to discourage you from exploring further, for fear that you might damage such irreplaceable works of art as the images of pre-contact **surfers**, said to lie somewhere in the area.

Hōlei Sea Arch
Chain of Craters Road currently comes to an end just beyond mile marker 20, with the small parking lot near **Hōlei Sea Arch** used as a turn-around point for all vehicles. Less than two miles survive of the road's previous eleven-mile shoreline route to Kalapana, and soon it may not reach the coast at all.

Until recently, few visitors bothered to pause at the sea arch; now it's the only named feature left in what was once a very scenic area. From the parking lot, cross a few yards of sparsely grassed lava and you'll see a chunky pillar of basalt blocks to your right, tenuously connected to the rest of the island by the top slab. The thudding of the waves against the cliffs makes the ground reverberate beneath your feet – clear evidence of the fragility of this coastline, most of which is too dangerous to approach.

Approaching the eruption
It's impossible to do more than generalize as to what might lie beyond the end of Chain of Craters Road. Assuming that the eruption is still continuing, somewhere high on the hillside one or more fissures in the earth will be spilling out large quantities of molten lava, which then sets off toward the ocean. En route it may or may not have to pour over fault scarps (cliffs formed by minor earthquakes), and its surface may or may not harden to create an underground stream. You can only view the lava itself if the nearest active flow has reached a point you can walk to from the road; if it is flowing directly into the ocean, which is easy to spot because the contact produces great plumes of steam; or if it is crossing or flowing along the road itself.

Find out if any of these scenarios apply by calling the **Volcano Update line** (☎808/985-6000) or Hawaii county's equivalent information line (☎808/961-8093); calling or visiting the park visitor center (see p.197); or accessing websites such as ⓦhvo.wr.usgs.gov, www.nps.gov/havo, or www.lavainfo.us.

The park service maintains a wooden **information shack** (on wheels, for obvious reasons) at the end of the road, where they hand out alarming leaflets explaining that new lava is unstable and may collapse at any time, and that it's best to avoid clouds of hydrochloric acid. When safety permits, rangers lead **guided hikes** to the site of the eruption. A daily schedule is posted at the visitor center; as a rule they start in the early afternoon, in order to get back to the road before nightfall.

The description and **safety advice** below applies whether you attempt to approach the eruption from the end of Chain of Craters Road, within the park, or from the foot of Hwy-130 in Puna, as described on p.191.

Since the early 1990s, at least twelve visitors have died in separate incidents, and many more have had to be rescued after becoming stranded out on the lava at night. The most dangerous situation occurs when lava flows directly into the **ocean**, when there's a risk of inhaling toxic fumes that contain not only acids but even tiny particles of glass. In addition, new land is extremely unstable; it may be no more than a thin layer of solidified lava resting on sea water – a "bench" – and thus liable to collapse at any moment. Swirling mists can make it hard to keep your bearings and can also mean that only occasionally do you see the actual lava.

Walking across flaky, crumbling, new lava is an extraordinary experience. Every surface is like sandpaper, a fall can shred your skin and, even far from the apparent center of activity, the ground can be too hot to touch. Heavy rain dries off without penetrating your clothing. The sight of liquid rock oozing towards you, swirling with phlegmy gobbets and destroying all it touches; the crackle as it crunches across previous layers of lava; the sudden flash as a dried-out tree bursts into flame: all leave you with a disconcerting sense of the land itself as a living, moving organism.

After dark, the orange glow of the eruption becomes even more apparent. Pinpoint incandescent lights become visible all across the slopes and leave the mountain looking like the proverbial city on a hill. Without official sanction or approval, and heedless of the immense risks, many visitors stay out all night to marvel at the glowing rivers of molten rock. If you try it, be sure to carry a flashlight for the walk back across the lava.

Finally, it's only fair to warn you that when current activity is occurring several miles beyond the end of the road, as it often is, you may well feel a profound sense of **anticlimax** at the little you see. Children in particular, excited by photographs of lava fountains, are liable to be very disappointed by the reality. On the other hand, they may see something that one day they will tell their own kids about.

Puna Coast Trail

The **southern coastline** of the Big Island is now very sparsely populated; the villages that once stood along its central section were abandoned in the mid-nineteenth century, following a succession of devastating tsunamis. Underground upheavals make this region extremely prone to **earthquakes**; in 1960 the entire south coast dropped by three feet, and campers in backcountry sites were washed out to sea after another major landslide in 1975.

The only way to explore the area is on foot, by means of the **Puna Coast Trail**. This starts roughly a mile up from the sea, at the Pu'u Loa parking lot (see p.203), setting off west, away from the eruption area, towards the coastal campgrounds at **Keauhou**, almost ten miles along, and **Halapē**, a couple of miles beyond.

Also known as the **Puna Ka'ū Trail**, this long and very challenging hike is only worth attempting if you have several days to spare. It's possible to get to 'Āpua

Point and back in a single day, but that's a thirteen-mile round-trip that still stops a long way short of the more interesting spots along the trail. If you plan to camp out, you must register at the Kīlauea visitor center, as this area is prone to landslides and tsunamis. Collected rainwater is available at the shelters, but carry plenty more yourself. All three shelters consist of three-walled primitive huts, so you'll need a tent as well.

From Chain of Craters Road, the trail makes its way across a patchwork of lava flows, the new ones glistening in the sun and crunchy underfoot, the older ones worn and smooth. Roughly four miles along, you reach the low seafront cliffs, which you follow for a couple more miles to **'Āpua Point**. From a distance it's a welcome flash of green against the relentless grays and blacks of the lava; when you arrive it turns out to have just a few coconut palms emerging from a tangled carpet of the ivy-like native *naupaka* shrub.

With no water, shelter, or other facilities at 'Āpua, you either have to turn back to the road or continue along the coast. Heading west, you're faced by the massive fault scarp of Hilina Pali looming ever larger inland. As well as releasing cascades of rock and even lava toward the ocean, landslides like those that created the *pali* also produce tsunamis that flood the coastal plains, so little is left standing along this stretch of the shoreline. The **Keauhou** and **Halapē** campgrounds lie three and five miles respectively from 'Āpua. Halapē in particular has the feel of a little oasis beside the sea, though so many campers trek out to its white-sand beach that the cabins at both campsites are infested with ants and cockroaches. The tidal pools are excellent for snorkeling, but the open sea can be very dangerous.

Mauna Loa

If you're interested in seeing a bit more of **Mauna Loa**, as opposed to Kīlauea, leave the caldera area by the park's main entrance and head west for a couple of miles. The third turning on the right, **Mauna Loa Road**, winds up toward the summit from there, although it stops a long way short and only very rarely allows you views either up the mountain or down toward Kīlauea and the sea.

Kīpuka Puaulu

Most visitors take the drive of less than a mile up Mauna Loa Road to see the enchanting little forest sanctuary of **Kīpuka Puaulu**. Known as the "bird park," this enclave is an utter contrast to the raw landscape elsewhere in the national park. A *kipuka* is a patch of land that has been left untouched by lava, and thus forms a sort of island in a sea of lava. Kīpuka Puaulu's well-preserved rainforest serves as a sanctuary for rare native birds such as the *'elepaio* flycatcher and the *'amakahi* honey-creeper.

A woodland stroll around the two-mile loop path takes you past some huge old *koa* trees and through sun-dappled clearings, with birds audible on all sides. However, unless you have a lot of patience – and binoculars – you may not manage to see more than the odd flash of color. Your best bet is to walk slowly and quietly and hope to surprise a group on the ground. At lunchtime, the covered **picnic area** makes this a popular stop for park visitors.

The Mauna Loa Summit Trail

Beyond Kīpuka Puaulu, Mauna Loa Road climbs through thick woodland virtually all the way to the end, fourteen miles up, crossing only a single stray lava flow. Its width varies between one and two lanes, but it's driveable if not exactly conducive to a quick journey. The surrounding tree-cover gradually changes from tropical to high-altitude before the road finally stops in a small clearing, 6662ft up.

The parking lot here is the trailhead for the **Mauna Loa Summit Trail**. As the very explicit signs in the small pavilion explain, this is no trail to attempt on a whim. The summit is a gradual but exhausting nineteen miles further on across bleak, barren lava, with a round-trip usually taking four days. There's no shelter along the way except for two crude cabins – check with the Park Service, with whom you must register anyway, to see whether they are stocked with water. Hypothermia is a very real threat, as the higher slopes are prone to abominable weather. If you make it to the top, you're confronted by the **Moku'āweoweo Caldera**, similar to Kīlauea's, which last erupted in 1984.

The Ka'ū Desert

All the land in the national park that lies to the south and west of Kīlauea Caldera is officially known as the **Ka'ū Desert**. By the conventional definition of a desert, it should therefore receive no rain: in fact it receives almost as much as the rainforest to the east, but here it falls as a natural acid rain, laden with chemicals from Kīlauea. Only a few desiccated plants ever managed to adapt to this uncompromising landscape, and most of those have now been eaten away by ravenous wild goats.

Trails in this area, too, were closed as this book went to press. The eighteen-mile **Ka'ū Desert Trail** is unlikely to reopen in its entirety, but it's possible the short **Footprints Trail**, which starts at an inconspicuous roadside halt ten miles west of the park entrance, may be accessible when you visit. It leads due south for just under a mile across rough 'a'ā lava to a small shelter, at what might seem like a random spot. In fact it covers a bunch of depressions in the rock, which popular legend says are human footprints. Whether or not you agree, the factual basis for the story is bizarre.

In 1790, Keōua, a rival of Kamehameha, was returning to his own kingdom of Ka'ū after two major battles in Puna. As his armies, complete with attendant women and children, traversed this stretch of desert, he divided them into three groups. The first group got safely across; then Kīlauea erupted, and the third group found the members of the second strewn across the pathway. All were dead, poisoned by a cloud of gas from the volcano. Supposedly, their footprints in the falling ash solidified and can still be seen, alternately protected and exposed as sand blows across the desert.

Keōua himself, incidentally, met a no less dramatic end: see p.161.

Volcano village

Unless you stay in *Volcano House* (p.199) or the park-service campgrounds (p.199 & p.202), the village of **VOLCANO** offers the only **accommodation** in the vicinity of the park. Though it's just a mile or so east of the park entrance, toward Hilo, it would be easy to drive straight past it without realizing it's there. The main street runs parallel to the highway, on the *mauka* (uphill) side, but it's well hidden by a roadside fringe of trees. Along it you'll find little apart from a small post office, a handful of stores and restaurants, and two gas stations, both of which close by 7.30pm nightly.

Accommodation

The strange thing about staying in Volcano is that there's nothing to suggest you're anywhere near an active volcano – only *Volcano House* in the park (see p.199) can offer crater views. Instead, the village's crop of small-scale **bed and breakfasts** are tucked away in odd little corners of a dense rainforest. Be warned that it rains a *lot* in Volcano.

Hale Ohia Hale Ohia Rd 96785
☏ 808/967-7986 or 1-800/455-3803,
ⓦ www.haleohia.com. Very attractive and tastefully furnished accommodation, ranging from studio apartments in a lovely converted water-tank (really) to a three-bedroom cottage. The buildings are scattered across the ravishing rainforest gardens of a former plantation estate, south of the highway across from the village. ❹

Holo Holo In 19-4036 Kalani Honua Rd
☏ 808/967-7950, ⓦ www.enable.org/holoholo. Volcano's cheapest option, this HI-AYH-affiliated "Japanese-style" hostel consists of a rambling rainforest home, half a mile up from the highway, that offers beds in rudimentary but adequate single-sex dorm rooms for $19, and one private double for $45. ❶–❷

Inn at Volcano 19-4178 Wright Rd ☏ 808/967-7786 or 1-800/937-7786, ⓦ www.volcano-hawaii .com. Very plush, lavishly furnished B&B, well north

of the highway, with themed individual rooms in the main house and separate cottages, including a "tree house," on the grounds. The owners also run the *Chalet Kīlauea Collection*, a wide assortment of B&Bs and vacation rentals, for all budgets. ❸–❽

Kīlauea Lodge 19-3948 Old Volcano Rd
☏ 808/967-7366, ⓦ www.kilaualodge.com. Imposing former YMCA on the main street, converted into an upmarket B&B, with some of its seventeen en-suite bedrooms in secluded chalets and cottages dotted across the grounds. The central lodge building holds a good restaurant (see below). ❺

My Island PO Box 100, Volcano, HI 96785
☏ 808/967-7216, ⓦ www.myislandinnhawaii.com. Several different grades of accommodation in individual buildings set amid dense tropical vegetation. The friendly owner, an island expert, lives in the central lodge; guests can use his library and a communal TV lounge. ❸–❺

Eating and drinking

Although *Volcano House* (see p.199) holds the only **restaurant** within the national park itself, Volcano village offers a few good alternatives, plus a couple of stores where you can pick up picnic supplies.

Kīlauea Lodge 19-3948 Old Volcano Rd
☏ 808/967-7366. Large inn dining room, with rich wooden furnishings and a blazing log fire. Inexpensive sandwich lunches, and for dinner a full range of strong-flavored European-style meat and game entrees for $20–40, including *Hasenpfeffer*, a braised rabbit dish not found on many Big Island menus, plus specialties such as Seafood Mauna Kea (seafood and mushrooms on pasta). Non-residents should reserve well in advance. Daily 7.30am–2pm & 5–9pm.

Lava Rock Café 19-3972 Old Volcano Rd
☏ 808/967-7969. Funky local café, behind the

Aloha gas station on Volcano's main street, which serves inexpensive snacks, plate lunches, and espresso, and also offers internet access. Mon 7.30am–5pm, Tues–Sat 7.30am–9pm, Sun 7.30am–4pm.

Thai Thai 19-4084 Old Volcano Rd
☏ 808/967-7969. Unassuming but high-quality Thai place on the main village road. Lunch specials $8–10; dinner entrees, which include salads as well as green and yellow curries, a tasty Masaman curry with coconut and peanut, and pad Thai noodles, cost around $15. Daily except Wed noon–9pm.

Ka'ū

The district of **KA'Ū** occupies the southern tip of the Big Island, which is also the southernmost point of the United States. Stretching for fifty miles along the southern side of the immense west flank of the "long mountain," Mauna Loa, it ranges from the bleak Ka'ū Desert, across fertile, well-watered hillsides, to the windswept promontory of **South Point** itself. Situated downwind of the acrid fumes emitted by both Mauna Loa and Kīlauea, it's far from being the most enticing area of the island. Nonetheless, it may well have been home to the first Polynesian settlers, and remains one of the last bastions of anything approaching the traditional Hawaiian way of life.

Ka'ū was a separate kingdom right up to the moment of European contact. Its last independent ruler was Kamehameha the Great's arch-rival, Keōua, some of

whose warriors met a bizarre end in the Kaʻū Desert (see p.206) and who was himself killed during the dedication of Puʻukoholā Heiau (see p.161).

As the main local employer, the sugar mill at Pāhala, closed in 1996, the population today is very sparse. All the local towns are tiny; on the map the grid of streets at **Hawaiian Ocean View** may look impressive, but this fifty-year-old residential development is still only minimally occupied, even if the real-estate boom in the rest of the island has finally pushed up land values here as well.

Although it has a handful of accommodation options, few people spend more than a day at most exploring Kaʻū. Access to the sea is limited, as the highway curves around the ridge of Mauna Loa roughly ten miles up from the shoreline. The two most obvious stops are **South Point**, to admire the crashing waves and perhaps hike to **Green Sand Beach**, and **Punaluʻu**, which since the demise of Kalapana boasts the island's finest black-sand beach.

As you pass through Kaʻū, look out for the strange, eroded cinder cones that dot the landscape. Some of these craters are so steep-sided as to have been forever inaccessible to man or beast, and paleobotanists are intrigued by the pre-contact vegetation that is thought to survive within.

Huge **Kahuku Ranch**, which stretches inland from the Belt Road near South Point Road almost to the summit of Mauna Loa, was in 2003 incorporated into Hawaii Volcanoes National Park. Much of it is scheduled to remain as wilderness, but some of the areas immediately up from the highway may well open up to hiking and backcountry exploration.

Pāhala and Wood Valley

As the vegetation reasserts itself after the bleak Kaʻū Desert, 23 miles west of the national park entrance, little **PĀHALA** stands just *mauka* of the highway. Apart from its tall-chimneyed sugar mill, a gas station, and a small shopping mall that's home to an outlet of the *malasada* (donut) specialist *Tex Drive-In* (Mon–Sat 7am–8pm, Sun 7am–6pm; ☎808/928-8200), there's nothing to catch the eye here, but a drive back up into the hills to the northwest takes you through some appealing agricultural scenery.

Just when you think the road is about to peter out altogether, it enters a grove of huge eucalyptus trees and you're confronted with one of the Big Island's least likely buildings: on top of a hill, and announced by streamers of colored prayer flags, stands a brightly painted Tibetan temple. Originally built by Japanese sugar laborers, the **Wood Valley temple** (or Nechung Dryung Ling) was rededicated by the Dalai Lama in 1980 and now serves as a retreat for Tibetan Buddhists from around the world (☎808/928-8539, ⓦwww.nechung.org; ❸). Priority is given to religious groups, but when there's room, travelers can stay in simple private rooms.

Punaluʻu

Five miles beyond Pāhala, at the point where the highway drops back down to sea level, **PUNALUʻU** has been flattened by tsunamis so often that it's given up trying to be a town any more. A single road loops from the highway to the ocean and back, running briefly along what is now the largest **black-sand beach** on the island.

Black sand is a finite resource, as it's only created by molten lava exploding on contact with the sea, and at any one spot that happens very rarely. Even those beaches not destroyed by new lava usually erode away within a few years. Each time the coastline of Punaluʻu Bay gets redrawn, however, its black sand washes in again, piling up to create a new beach. At the moment it's gorgeous,

a crescent of jet-black crystals surrounding a turquoise bay and framed by a fine stand of coconut palms.

Swimming in the rough waters here, however, is out of the question, but many people come to Punalu'u to **camp**. Hawksbill turtles drag themselves ashore on the main beach at night, so camping on the sand is forbidden, but there's a pleasant, if incredibly windy, campground tucked into the rolling meadows of Punalu'u Beach Park, immediately to the south. Permits can be obtained from the Department of Parks and Recreation in Hilo ($5 per day; ☎808/961-8311).

The dilapidated complex of pseudo-Polynesian buildings behind the palms in the center of the beach, facing the sea across its own private lagoon, holds a restaurant that has been closed since the early 1990s downturn in tourism. Plans have repeatedly been announced to construct **new hotels** here; the latest scheme, unveiled in 2007 with the participation of Jean-Michel Cousteau, envisaged the construction of an eco-tourism center, and up to 350 hotel rooms, but it has been bitterly opposed locally and seems unlikely to materialize.

For the moment, the only **accommodation** nearby is in the *SeaMountain at Punalu'u* condo complex, a few hundred yards from the beach on the southern segment of the loop road (☎808/928-6200 or 1-800/333-1962, ⓦwww .vrivacations.com/resorts/seamountain; 2-night minimum stay; ❹–❺). It's an incredibly remote and often very windy place to stay, but most of its studios and one- and two-bedroom apartments, arrayed along what looks like a typical suburban residential street, are well equipped and comfortable. The name "Sea Mountain," incidentally, refers to the underwater volcano of Lo'ihi, just twenty miles offshore (see p.196).

Nā'ālehu

You can't miss **NĀ'ĀLEHU** as you drive through Ka'ū. Eight miles south of Punalu'u, it lines each side of the highway for around half a mile, without stretching very far away from the central ribbon. Although it bills itself as "America's southernmost town," Nā'ālehu offers little to induce drivers to stop. Whittington Beach Park, a couple of miles outside it to the north, is not so much a beach as a picnic ground, and the only reason to call in at Nā'ālehu is for a quick lunch.

Nā'ālehu holds a handful of **restaurants**, which change names with monotonous regularity. The best of the bunch is the *Hana Hou Bakery*, 95-1148 Spur Rd (☎808/929-9717), open for all meals daily and serving high-quality diner food as well as fresh baked goods. The *Shaka Restaurant* is a reasonable alternative (daily except Mon 10am–9pm; ☎808/929-7404, ⓦwww.shakarestaurant.com).

Wai'ohinu

Having climbed away from the sea for two miles west of Nā'ālehu, the highway makes a sweeping curve around the small settlement of **WAI'OHINU**. This held a dozen houses when Mark Twain passed through in 1866, and boasts barely more than that today. Twain planted a monkey-pod tree here, but even that has now been dead for fifty years. Alongside what may or may not be its descendant, a few hundred yards east of the center, Mark Twain Square is a gift shop that also sells sandwiches, cakes, and coffee (☎808/929-7550). Nearby, the run-down *Shirikawa Motel* (☎808/929-7462, ⓦwww.shirakawamotel.com; ❷) is gradually being overwhelmed by trees, while just around the highway bend you pass a pretty chapel, the white-and-green clapboard 1841 **Kauaha'ao Church**.

Half a mile south of the church, *Macadamia Meadows Farm*, 94-6263 Kamaoa Rd (☎808/929-8097 or 1-888/929-8118, ⓦwww.macadamiameadows.com; ❹), is

a large modern home that offers four comfortable, spacious **B&B** rooms. Guests have use of the on-site pool and tennis courts.

South Point Road

As you circle the southern extremity of the Big Island on the Belt Road, you're too far up from the ocean to see where the island comes to an end. It is possible, however, to drive right down to the tip along the eleven-mile **SOUTH POINT ROAD**, which leaves the highway six miles west of Wai'ohinu.

Car rental agencies forbid drivers from heading to South Point because vehicle damage is more likely on the poor road surfaces and providing emergency recovery is inconvenient. It's not a difficult or dangerous drive, however. Most of the way it's a single-lane paved road, with enough room on either side for vehicles to pass comfortably.

The road heads almost due south, passing at first through green cattle-ranching country. As it starts to drop, the landscape takes on a weather-beaten look, with pale grass billowing and the trees bent double by the trade winds. It comes as no surprise to encounter the giant propellers of the Kamoa wind farm, though you're unlikely to see many of them turning: the winds have proven too gusty and violent for the farm to be a commercial success.

Ka Lae

Ten miles past the wind farm, the road forks 100 yards beyond a sign announcing the **Ka Lae National Historic Landmark District**. The right fork ends a mile later at a red-gravel parking lot perched above a 30ft cliff. Many locals still come here to fish over the edge. Watch out for the large, unfenced hole in the middle of the parking lot, which plummets all the way down to the sea.

Walk a couple of minutes south and you come to **Ka Lae**, or **South Point**, where you can ponder the fact that everyone in the United States is to the north of you. The earliest colonizers of Hawaii battled against the winds to reach this spot long before the Pilgrims crossed the Atlantic, and in doing so traveled a far greater distance from their homes in the distant South Seas. Abundant bone fishhooks found in the area are among the oldest artifacts unearthed in Hawaii, dating as far back as the third century AD. At the restored **Kalalea Heiau**, at the very tip, offerings wrapped in *ti* leaves are still left by native Hawaiians. Beyond that is a ledge of black lava, steadily pounded by high surf.

The deep waters offshore were renowned not only for holding vast quantities of fish, but also because they're prey to such fierce currents that it can take days on end for human- or sail-powered boats to negotiate the cape.

Among the rocks at the headland, you can still see holes drilled for use as **canoe moorings**. In ancient times, fishermen would tie their canoes to these loops by long cords so that they could fish in the turbulent waters without having to fight the sea. Looking inland, you can follow the grey outline of Mauna Loa in the distance; on a cloudless day, you might even make out its snow-capped peak. Nearer at hand, across a foam-flecked sea to the northwest, is the stark shoreline cinder cone of **Pu'u Waimānalo**.

As you head back to the fork, a side turning toward the ocean leads swiftly to more dramatic views up the coast. Don't drive too fast here though; the road ends almost immediately where it simply crumbles with no warning into the sea.

Green Sand Beach

GREEN SAND BEACH, a couple of miles northeast of Ka Lae, doesn't quite live up to its name. It is a beach, and it is greenish in a rusty-olive sort of way, but if

you're expecting a dazzling stretch of green sand backed by a coconut grove you'll be disappointed. The only reason to venture here is if you feel like a hot, shadeless, four-mile hike along the oceanfront, with a mild natural curiosity at the end. Without great expectations, and on a rain-free day, it's worth the effort.

If you want to try it, start from the junction on South Point Road a mile short of Ka Lae, and drive down the left fork as far as a loop parking lot. You'd have to have a very high-clearance four-wheel-drive vehicle to follow the rutted mud tracks that continue a hundred yards or so down to a boat landing at the foot of the slope, let alone the two-mile onwards track from there to the beach.

Apart from one or two heavily rutted sections, the walk itself is easy, and takes about an hour each way. On the way out, you can expect to be pushing into a stiff tradewinds breeze. For most of the route you cross rolling, pastel-green meadows – an oddly pastoral landscape considering the mighty surf pummeling at the lava rocks alongside.

Your destination comes in sight after more than a mile – the crumbling **Puʻu O Mahana** cinder cone that forms the only significant bump on the line of the coast. As you approach you can see that half the cone has eroded away, and the resultant loose powder has slipped down the cliffs to form a long sloping beach. You can admire it all from up above, but with the help of a short fixed ladder it's straightforward to scramble down to the seashore and examine handfuls of the "green sand." Close inspection reveals shiny green-tinged crystals of various sizes – this is in fact a mineral called **olivine**, which once formed part of a lava flow. Depending on surf conditions, most visitors venture into the sea from the beach, but it's not safe to swim beyond the small bay.

Hawaiian Ocean View Estates

West of South Point Road, you can't get down to the sea again in the twelve miles before the Belt Road reaches South Kona. The road does, however, run past a few isolated buildings and communities where you can get a snack or fill up with gas.

The residential zone of **HAWAIIAN OCEAN VIEW ESTATES**, also known as "Ocean View" or "HOVE," was designated for development during the 1960s. Intricate grids of roads were planned, and some sites were sold that were no more than patches of bare lava. People have slowly moved in, but only a small proportion of the lots have been built on, and many of the roads still don't exist. The center of Ocean View consists of two small malls, in one of which the friendly little *Desert Rose* (daily 7am–7pm; ☎808/939-7673) serves simple **breakfasts** and highly recommended lunchtime sandwiches and salads.

The four-roomed *Bougainvillea* **B&B** stands two blocks down from the *Desert Rose* (☎808/929-7089 or 1-800/688-1763, ⓦ www.bougainvilleabedand breakfast.com; ❸).

Manukā State Park

Kaʻū comes to an end half a dozen miles west of Ocean View, as you finally cross the long ridge of Mauna Loa. The former royal lands on the border with Kona, once the *ahupuaʻa* of **MANUKĀ**, remain set aside to this day as the **Manukā Natural Area Reserve** – at 25,000 acres, the largest natural reserve in the state.

Only a small segment of the reserve is open to the public – **Manukā State Park**, three miles west of Ocean View. From its leafy roadside parking lot, equipped with a picnic pavilion, restrooms, benches, and rolling lawns, the one-hour, two-mile **Manukā Nature Trail** leads into peaceful woodlands. Almost all the

terrain is *'a'ā* lava, and although there's no great climb, the path can be very rough underfoot. Humans aren't the only ones who find it hard to cross lava flows, so pigs and exotic plants alike are relatively scarce, and the area remains a haven for native plants. The trail's only dramatic feature is a collapsed lava pit, whose sides are too steep to permit access to wild pigs (see p.434), and which gathers enough moisture to feed plants such as the *'ie 'ie* vine, which normally only grows in much wetter areas.

Free maps, available at the trailhead, explain how the vegetation varies with the age of the lava flow. Some of the ground is new and barren, and some is around two thousand years old, but those areas that date back four thousand years have managed to develop a thick coating of topsoil.

About eight miles beyond Manukā, as the road heads due north toward Kailua, you come to the turnoff down to **Miloli'i Beach** – see p.152.

3

Maui

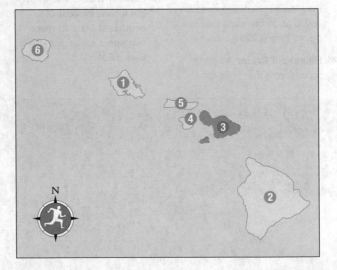

CHAPTER 3 # Highlights

✳ **Molokini snorkel cruises**
A daily flotilla of small boats
ferries snorkelers out to see
the abundant marine-life
around this tiny submerged
crater. See p.223

✳ **Sunset in Lahaina** Best
admired from the seafront of
this West Maui town, the setting
sun sinks behind the russet
island of Lanai. See p.227

✳ **The Feast at Lele** This
sumptuous banquet of
Polynesian specialties beats
any *lū'au* in the state hands
down. See p.233

✳ **Haleakalā Crater** An eerie
moonscape that feels far

removed from the bustle of
modern Maui. See p.269

✳ **Ho'okipa Beach Park** The
world's premier windsurfing
destination hosts the sport's
top competitive events.
See p.280

✳ **The Road to Hāna** Legendary
day-trip drive that twists its
way past dozens of hidden
waterfalls and verdant valleys.
See p.281

✳ **Pīpīwai Trail** Climb through
the lush rainforest of
southeast Maui to reach
two spectacular waterfalls.
See p.291

▲ Windsurfing at Ho'okipa Beach Park

3

Maui

Widely trumpeted, not least by its own inhabitants, as the world's most glamorous vacation destination, the island of **Maui** has long proclaimed its charms with the slogan *Maui Nō Ka 'Oi* – "Maui is the Best." Although it ranks a distant second behind the Big Island in terms of size, and behind Oahu for its number of visitors, Maui does indeed have a lot to boast about, starting with the quality of its **beaches**, the sheer variety of its **landscapes**, and the vast range of **thrills** it offers to adventurous travelers.

Above all, Maui is a **beautiful** island. The windward flanks of both its two volcanoes are ravishingly scenic, as typified by the winding, fifty-mile **road to Hāna** on the eastern shore, while cool, green **Upcountry Maui** is an unexpected pastoral idyll, and the volcanic desert on top of **Haleakalā** offers an unforgettable spectacle at sunrise. The drier western coastlines of the island hold some of Hawaii's most popular and attractive **beaches**, perfectly suited to the needs of tourists who come specifically for sun, sand, and swimming. In West Maui, you can walk the streets of old **Lahaina**, once the capital of Hawaii and rendezvous for the hell-raising Pacific whaling fleet, while atmospheric smaller towns elsewhere, such as **Makawao** and **Hāna**, evoke the island's plantation and ranching heritage.

Aside from its natural attractions, Maui entices a younger, more dynamic crowd than Waikīkī by offering Hawaii's most exhilarating range of vacation **activities**, including surfing, windsurfing, diving, sailing, snorkeling, cycling, hiking, and horseriding. That sense of energy helps to explain why Maui appears to be weathering the latest recession better than its neighbours, and remains the most vibrant destination in the state.

A brief history of Maui

Ancient Maui was not the fertile island it is today; both the central isthmus and the upcountry slopes were arid wastelands, and the population was crowded into scattered coastal valleys. For its first thousand years of human occupation, the island consisted of several independent regions, each constantly at war with the rest. Both the two main centers were in **West Maui** – one was the northwestern shoreline, the other stretched northwards from 'Īao Valley – while remote Hāna on the east coast was a lesser chiefdom, prone to fall under the control of Big Island invaders.

The first chief to rule over all of Maui was **Pi'ilani**. During the fifteenth or sixteenth centuries, he conquered all the way from Hāna to West Maui, and even extended his kingdom to include Kaho'olawe, Lanai, and Molokai. Pi'ilani also started work on the first road to encircle a Hawaiian island, wide enough to hold eight men abreast. Parts of the modern Pi'ilani Highway follow the ancient route, and in places, such as beyond La Pérouse Bay, the original stones can still be seen.

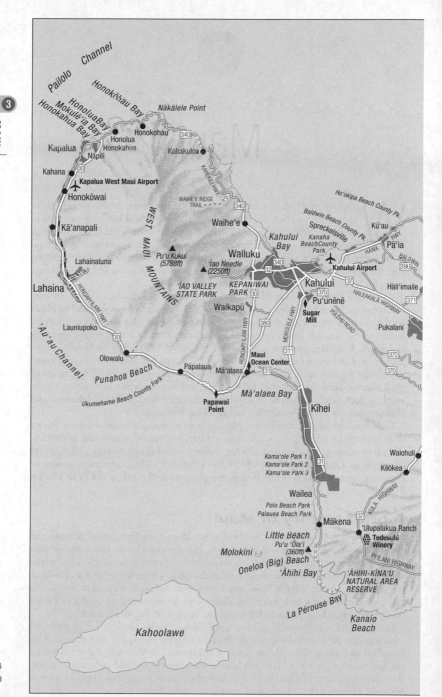

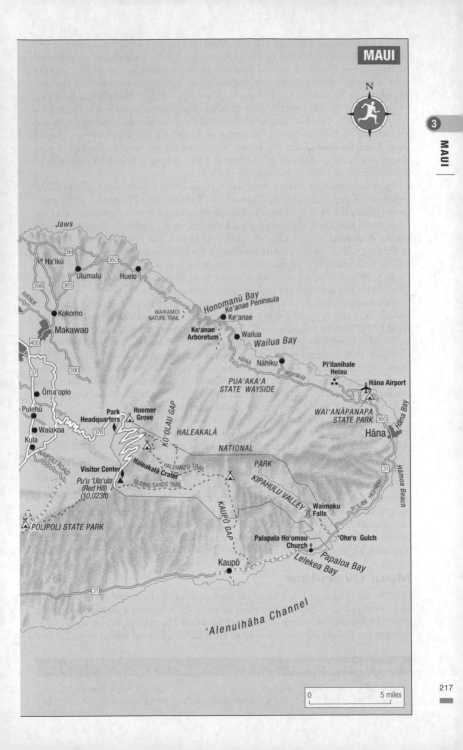

MAUI

N

Jaws

Ha'ikū

36

360

Ulumalu   Huelo

398   365

AVENUE

Kokomo

Makawao

400

37   390

'Ōma'opio

Pulehū

Waiakoa

Kula

WAIPOLI ROAD

WAIKAMOI
NATURE TRAIL

Honomanū Bay

Ke'anae Peninsula

Ke'anae

Ke'anae
Arboretum

Wailua

Wailua Bay

HĀNA   Nāhiku

HIGHWAY

Pi'ilanihale
Heiau

Hāna Airport

PUA'AKA'A
STATE WAYSIDE

WAI'ĀNAPANAPA
STATE PARK   360

Park
Headquarters

Hosmer
Grove

378

Visitor Center

Pu'u 'Ula'ula
(Red Hill)
(10,023ft)

Haleakalā Crater

HALEMAU'U TRAIL

SLIDING SANDS TRAIL

KŌ'OLAU GAP

HALEAKALĀ

NATIONAL

PARK

KIPAHULU VALLEY

Waimoku
Falls

Hāna

Hāna Bay

Hāmoa Beach

31

PI'ILANI HIGHWAY

POLIPOLI STATE PARK

KAUPŌ GAP

Palapala Ho'omau
Church †

'Ohe'o Gulch

Papaloa Bay

Kaupō

Lelekea Bay

31

'Alenuihāha Channel

0   5 miles

With a population of around 120,000, Maui held perhaps a quarter as many people as the Big Island of Hawaii by the time the Europeans arrived, but its warriors' military prowess and its central position in the archipelago made it a worthy rival. The eighteenth century saw endless battles for supremacy between the two neighbors. From around 1736 onwards, Maui was ruled by **Kahekili**, a ferocious *pahupu* or "cut-in-two" warrior, half of whose body was tattooed black. During his sixty-year reign, Kahekili conquered almost all the other islands, invading Oahu and establishing his half-brother on the throne of Kauai. His nemesis, however, proved to be **Kamehameha** of the Big Island, who some suggest was his illegitimate son. Kamehameha successfully invaded Maui in 1790, defeating Kahekili's chosen heir, Kalanikūpule, in a bloody battle at 'Iao Valley.

Meanwhile, the first foreign ships had reached Hawaii. Although Captain Cook welcomed Kahekili aboard the *Discovery* off Wailuku in 1778, another eight years passed before the French admiral La Pérouse became the first outsider to set foot on Maui. Soon the island was swamped with visitors, starting with fur and sandalwood traders. **Lahaina**, by now a favored chiefly residence, was the capital of all Hawaii in the first half of the nineteenth century. It attracted such an intensive missionary effort, enthusiastically supported by the island's devoutly Christian Governor Hoapili, that, within a few years of opening its first school and printing press in 1831, Maui had achieved the highest rate of literacy on earth.

After Hoapili died in the early 1840s, and the seat of government shifted to Honolulu, Lahaina spent twenty raucous years as the "**whaling capital of the world**." When the whaling trade finally died down (see p.421), Maui was left high and dry, with its population reduced to a mere twelve thousand. However, the lands that had been used to grow food for the sailors turned toward other crops, especially **sugar**. Thanks to the frenzied efforts of entrepreneurs such as the German-born Claus Spreckels, Samuel Alexander, and Henry Baldwin, irrigation channels were built to carry water from East Maui to the isthmus, and immigrants from all over the world were shipped in to work the fields.

Agriculture was the mainstay of Maui's economy until after World War II, when state-wide labor unrest finally broke the power of Hawaii's "Big Five" (see p.420), and in doing so, sent the plantations into permanent decline. Maui still has one working sugar plantation, but pineapple production has ended, and **tourism** dominates all else. In 1927, 428 tourists came to the island; even in 1951 there were just fourteen thousand visitors, and the *Hotel Hāna-Maui* (see p.287) was Maui's only purpose-built tourist hotel. Then came the idea of turning cane fields into luxury resorts, which was pioneered at Kā'anapali in the 1950s and continues to this day, luring some 2.4 million tourists to the island each year. Many of those tourists have chosen to settle permanently on Maui, raising the population towards 150,000 and triggering a real-estate boom that has forced many young locals to leave the island.

Maui overview

As a "volcanic doublet," the island of Maui consists of two originally separate but now overlapping volcanoes. The older of the two, which has eroded to become a serrated ridge usually referred to as the **West Maui Mountains**, is now dwarfed by the younger **Haleakalā** to the southeast. Haleakalā itself stood several thousand feet

Maui favorites: hikes		
Halemau'u Trail, p.201	Pīpīwai Trail, p.291	Waihe'e Ridge Trail, p.242
Kaupō Trail, p.278	Sliding Sands Trail, p.275	Waikamoi Nature Trail, p.282

Maui favorites: beaches

Swimming beaches
Kā'anapali Beach, p.235
Kapalua Beach, p.238
Oneloa (Big) Beach, p.262

Polo Beach, p.261
Wai'ānapanapa Beach, p.285

Snorkel spots
Honolua Bay, p.241
Kā'anapali Beach, p.235

La Pérouse Bay, p.263
Molokini, p.223

Surfing and windsurfing
Honolua Bay, p.241
Honomanū Bay, p.282
Ho'okipa Beach, p.280

Jaws, p.280
Kanahā Beach, p.246
Mā'alaea Bay, p.252

3

MAUI

taller around 400,000 years ago, and dominated the landmass of Maui Nui, which took in what are now Kaho'olawe, Molokai, and Lanai. Although the ocean has flowed in to create four distinct islands, the channels between them are the shallowest, and the calmest, in Hawaii. That's one reason why the western coastlines of both parts of Maui are its most popular tourist playgrounds, with safe, sandy beaches and good sailing conditions – and why so many whales come here in winter.

When you've tired of resorts such as **Lahaina** and **Kā'anapali** in West Maui, or **Kīhei** in South Maui, there's plenty to explore elsewhere on the island. The central isthmus, or "neck," between the volcanoes can be so flat in places that you fear the waves will wash right over it. It holds **Kahului**, the main commercial center, and the faded but appealing older town of **Wailuku**, standing guard over once-sacred **'Iao Valley**.

To the east, **Upcountry Maui**, on the lower slopes of Haleakalā, is a delight, its meadows and flower farms offering a pastoral escape from the bustle below. Higher up, beyond the clouds, you can look out across the many-hued volcanic wasteland of the vast **Haleakalā Crater** or dwindle into cosmic insignificance by hiking down into it.

Tortuous, demanding roads wind right around the **windward coasts** of both halves of the island. The countless waterfalls and ravines along the better known of the two, the **road to Hāna** in the east, make for a wonderful day-trip, culminating at lush **'Ohe'o Gulch**. West Maui's equivalent, **Kahekili Highway**, offers a glimpse of how Maui must have looked before the tourists arrived.

Getting to Maui

Kahului (see p.245) is by far the largest airport on Maui, and the only one capable of handling trans-Pacific flights. For full details of flights to and from Hawaii, and contact details for the airlines mentioned below, see pp.19–22.

The route between **Honolulu** and Kahului is the busiest domestic route in the entire US, with over three million passengers per year. Hawaiian Airlines flies this way around twenty times every day, and also operates nonstop flights between Kahului and both Kona (2 daily) and Hilo (1 daily) on the Big Island. Go! connects Kahului with all the other islands, while Island Air flies between Kahului and Kona, Kauai, and Molokai at weekends only (1 daily Fri–Mon). In addition, Pacific Wings (☏808/873-0877 or 1-888/575-4546, ⓦwww.pacificwings.com) operates scheduled flights that connect Molokai, and Waimea on the Big Island, with Kahului.

219

Kapalua in West Maui – see p.238 – receives around five Island Air and four Go! flights from Honolulu each day, plus one from Molokai, while the only scheduled flights to Maui's third, tiny airport at **Hāna** are Pacific Wings services from Kahului.

As the Superferry between Honolulu and Kahului no longer operates, the only **ferries** to serve Maui connect Lahaina with Lanai and Molokai; see p.229.

Getting around Maui

Although you can't really make the most of a Maui vacation without renting your own vehicle, the island does offer a **public transport** network. Maui Bus (T808/871-4838, W www.mauicounty.gov/bus) operates scheduled **bus** services from the Queen Ka'ahumanu Center in Kahului to both Lahaina – where you can connect with separate services on to Kā'anapali, as detailed on p.235 – and South Maui (see p.254). Both routes run via the Maui Ocean Center at Mā'alaea, meaning that with one change of bus you can get from Lahaina to Wailea. Another route connects **Kahului Airport** with downtown Kahului and Pā'ia and Haikū. In addition, Speedishuttle (T808/661-6667 or 1-877/242-5777, W www.speedishuttle.com) run **shuttle vans** on demand from the airport; typical rates start at $18 to Kīhei, $30 to Lahaina, and $40 to Nāpili.

All the national **rental car** chains are represented at Kahului Airport and at or near Kapalua Airport. **Traffic** on Maui is consistently bad, with the worst area being the narrow **Honoapi'ilani Highway** around West Maui, where drivers make sudden stops in winter to watch whales in the ocean. At least the snail's pace along the **Haleakalā** and **Hāna** highways is owing to the natural obstacles en route, and gives you a chance to appreciate the scenery.

The most popular **bus tours** on the island run around East Maui to Hāna (typically costing around $100), and up the volcano to Haleakalā Crater ($75–100). Operators include Polynesian Adventure Tours (T808/833-3000 or 1-800/622-3011, W www.polyad.com) and Ekahi Tours (T808/877-9775 or 1-888/292-2422, W www.ekahi.com).

Flight-seeing tours

All the **helicopter** companies listed below operate from Kahului Airport. Maui is large enough for a full round-island flight to take more than an hour and cost over $200; a shorter 20–30min loop over West Maui will cost more like $90, while it's also possible to fly over to Molokai or Lanai as well. Visibility is almost always best in the early morning.

It's also possible to take an **airplane** or "fixed-wing" tour with Volcano Air Tours (T808/877-5500, W www.volcanoairtours.com), which flies across to the active volcano on the Big Island from Kapalua ($395) or Kahului ($355).

Helicopter tour operators

Air Maui	T808/877-7005 or 1-877/238-4942	W www.airmaui.com
Alexair Helicopters	T808/871-0792 or 1-888/418-8455	W www.helitour.com
Blue Hawaiian Helicopters	T808/871-8844 or 1-800/745-2583	W www.bluehawaiian.com
Sunshine Helicopters	T808/270-3999 or 1-866/501-7738	W www.sunshinehelicopters.com

Horseriding

Ironwood Ranch ☎808/669-4991, ⓦwww.ironwoodranch.com. Riding excursions up to the forest above Kapalua, at $60 per hour.

Lahaina Stables ☎808/667-2222, ⓦwww.mauihorse.com. Horseback adventures on the slopes above Lahaina; $110–135.

Mākena Stables ☎808/879-0244, ⓦwww.makenastables.com. Morning or evening rides (2–3hr) along the South Maui coastline; $145–170.

Maui Horseback Tours ☎808/248-7799, ⓦwww.mauistables.com. Riding tours (3hr) with a strong Hawaiian emphasis, in East Maui's beautiful Kīpahulu district; $150.

Mendes Ranch ☎808/871-5222, ⓦwww.mendesranch.com. Trail rides on cattle ranch in East Maui's Waiheʻe Valley, with barbecue lunch; $130 per person or $280 with helicopter flight.

Pony Express Tours ☎808/667-2200, ⓦwww.ponyexpresstours.com. Tours of Haleakalā Ranch, Maui's largest cattle ranch ($95–110), or 4hr descent to Ka Moa O Pele junction in Haleakalā Crater ($182).

Two specialist **food tours** offer insights into Maui's culinary traditions. Local expert Bonnie Friedman's explorations of central and Upcountry Maui include a "Lunch Like A Local" tour focusing on the ethnic restaurants in Wailuku (☎808/242-8383, ⓦwww.tourdafoodmaui.com), while Oʻo Farm in Kula offers gourmet lunch tours twice weekly ($50; ☎808/667-4341, ⓦwww.oofarm.com).

Among companies renting out **bikes**, typically at $25–30 per day or up to $120 per week, are South Maui Bicycles, 1993 S Kīhei Rd, Kīhei (☎808/874-0068, ⓦwww .southmauibicycles.com); West Maui Cycles, 1087 Limahana Place (☎808/661-9005, ⓦwww.westmauicycles.com); and Island Biker, 415 Dairy Rd, Kahului (☎808/877-7744, ⓦwww.islandbiker.com). For details of **downhill bike rides** on Haleakalā, see p.270.

Where to stay

The majority of Maui's hotels and condos are located either along the leeward coast of **West Maui**, in the highly developed strip that runs from Lahaina up to Kapalua, or on the southwest shoreline of the eastern half of the island, between Kīhei and Mākena in what's known as **South Maui**. If beaches or golf are your main priority, you'll be well situated in these areas; many of Maui's historic sites and most attractive landscapes, however, are a long way away.

Travelers looking for a paradise-island hideaway would do better to consider one of the many plush **B&Bs** tucked away in the meadows of Upcountry Maui and in the rainforests around Hāna in the east. If you're not planning on renting a car, **Lahaina** is the only place where you can stay in a real town with sightseeing, beaches, and restaurants within easy walking distance. For **budget travelers**, the cheapest options of all are in faded downtown Wailuku.

Opportunities to **camp** on Maui are very limited, with the best sites in **Haleakalā National Park**, up near the crater (see p.273), and also at Kipahulu on the southeast shore (see p.291). Cabins and tent camping are also available at Maui's two **state parks**, Polipoli (see p.267) and the much nicer **Waiʻānapanapa** (see p.285); permits are issued online, or at 54 S High St, Wailuku (Mon–Fri 8am–3.30pm; ☎808/984-8109, ⓦwww.hawaiistateparks.org). For information on camping at **Kanahā Beach County Park** outside Kahului – see p.246 – contact the Department of Parks and

Recreation, 1580 Ka'ahumanu Ave, Wailuku (Mon–Fri 8am–4pm; ☎808/270-7389, ⓦ www.co.maui.hi.us).

When to go

Maui basks in the usual balmy Hawaiian **climate**, rarely experiencing temperatures along the coast below the mid-seventies Fahrenheit or higher than the mid-eighties. The busiest tourist season, between December and February, coincides with the "rainiest" time of year. You can be unlucky, but as a rule the main leeward tourist areas seldom receive more than the occasional light shower even then.

Unless you have specialized interests, there's no overriding reason to visit the island at one time rather than another. To avoid the crowds and take advantage of lower room rates, come between March and June or from September through November. The best **swimming** conditions are between April and September, but the peak **surfing** season arrives with the higher winter waves, from November through March – which is also the time when there's every chance you'll see humpback **whales**. The **flowering trees** along the Hāna Highway reach their peak in June, while July and August are the best months to see the extraordinary blossoming **silversword** plants of Haleakalā.

Watersports and other activities

From the moment you arrive on Maui, you'll be inundated with handouts and free magazines that detail the island's vast range of tours and activities. **Activities operators** in all the tourist areas offer **cut-price deals** well below the advertised rates, but most are also trying to sell time-shares. Tom Barefoot's Tours run a website detailing every imaginable island activity, along with the latest prices (☎1-800/7709-6305, ⓦ www.tombarefoot.com).

In addition to the activities detailed below, you'll find lists of Molokini **snorkel cruises** on p.223; downhill **bike rides** on p.270; **helicopter tours** on p.220; and **horseriding** trips on p.221.

Diving

Maui and its immediate neighbors offer probably the best **scuba diving** in the Hawaiian islands. The most popular spots are in the vicinity of **Molokini Crater**, off South Maui. Learners and inexperienced divers start by exploring the sheltered, shallow "Inside Crater" area, and eventually progress to the "Back Wall," with its huge drop-offs. There's also good **shore diving** at Black Rock in Kā'anapali, while the most spectacular dives of all lie off southern Lanai, within easy reach of a day's boat-trip.

For full listings of the many local operators see p.224. **Prices** generally start at around $130 for two tanks, with equipment rental costing an additional $30 or so. Almost all offer multi-day packages for beginners, leading to PADI certification. Bear in mind that many of the Molokini snorkel cruises listed below actually offer diving as well as snorkeling.

Be sure not to dive within 24 hours of flying, or ascending to any significant altitude. The summit of Haleakalā is certainly out of bounds, while you should ask your dive operator for advice before even driving into the Upcountry.

Snorkeling

Maui offers some of the finest conditions for **snorkeling** in all Hawaii. The most unusual and compelling destination is the tiny crescent islet of **Molokini**, three miles off Mākena. Created by a volcanic eruption some 230,000 years ago, it rises about 500ft from the underwater flank of Haleakalā, though only the southern half of the circular crater still pokes above the waves, to a maximum height of 162ft. There's no beach or landfall, but it's a real thrill to enter the water, and see the steep crater wall dropping into the abyss beneath you, and you're certain to see a staggering array of multicolored fish, including deep-water species.

Strong ocean currents off the South Maui coast render it too dangerous to try to swim or kayak to Molokini, so the only way to experience it is on a **snorkel cruise**, most of which depart from **Mā'alaea Harbor** (see p.252). Prices depend on the size and comfort of the boat and the refreshments offered, and typically cost around $60–120 for a five- to six-hour early-morning trip, or $40–60 for a shorter afternoon trip. Recommended **boats** include *Four Winds II* (T808/879-8188 or 1-800/736-5740, W www.mauicharters.com), and the smaller *Paragon II* (T808/244-2087 or 1-800/441-2087, W www.sailmaui.com). It's also possible to take a significantly longer and more expensive cruise from Lahaina, while the very shortest crossing departs from South Maui's *Mākena Beach and Golf Resort* (see p.259). Note that between November and April many companies stop running Molokini trips and concentrate on lucrative **whale-watching** cruises instead; for full details, see p.224.

Plenty of great snorkeling can, of course, also be enjoyed from Maui's beaches. When conditions are calm, the turquoise waters of magnificent **Honolua Bay**, at the northern tip of West Maui, are teeming with fish, but even in the major resorts the snorkeling can be wonderful, as for example at **Kā'anapali** and **Wailea** beaches.

Surfing

Surf aficionados rate several Maui sites as equal to anything on Oahu's fabled North Shore, with **Honolua Bay** on the northern tip of West Maui, and **Jaws** off Ha'ikū in the east, as the greatest of all. You need to be a real expert to join the locals who surf there, however – beginners would do better to start out at Lahaina and Kā'anapali beaches. The peak **season** is between November and March.

Companies that offer surfing and paddleboarding lessons in the Lahaina area include the Goofy Foot Surf School (T808/244-9283, W www.goofyfootsurfschool.com) and the Nancy Emerson School of Surfing (T808/244-7873, W www.mauisurf clinics.com). South Maui instructors include Hawaiian Style Surf School (T808/874-0110), while Maui Waveriders (T808/875-4761, W www.mauiwaveriders.com) operate in both locations.

Windsurfing and kitesurfing

Maui is renowned as the world's most sublime **windsurfing and kitesurfing** destination. Legendary **Ho'okipa Beach Park**, just east of Pā'ia on the central

Dive operators
Ed Robinson's Diving Adventures Kīhei ☎808/879-3584, ⓦwww.mauiscuba.com
Extended Horizons Lahaina ☎1-888/348-3628, ⓦwww.scubadivemaui.com
Maui Dive Shop island-wide ☎1-800/542-3483, ⓦwww.mauidiveshop.com
Maui Dreams Kīhei ☎1-888/921-3483, ⓦwww.mauidreamsdiveco.com
Mike Severn's Kīhei ☎808/879-6596, ⓦwww.mikeseversdiving.com
Pacific Dive Lahaina ☎808/667-5331, ⓦwww.pacificdive.com
Prodiver Kīhei ☎808/875-4004, ⓦwww.prodivermaui.com
Trilogy Lahaina ☎1-888/225 6284, ⓦwww.sailtrilogy.com

Boat tours
For details of snorkel trips to **Molokini**, see p.223.
Atlantis Submarines ☎1-800/548-6262, ⓦwww.atlantisadventures.com. Underwater excursions off Lahaina (1hr; $99; look for discounts online).
Hawaiian Sailing Canoe Adventures ☎808/281-9301, ⓦwww.mauisailingcanoe .com. Hugely enjoyable excursions in an outrigger canoe that sails from Polo Beach, in front of Waimea's *Fairmont Kea Lani* resort, and focuses on whale-watching in winter, snorkeling otherwise, with an emphasis on Hawaiian culture and traditions (2hr; $99).
Maui Princess ☎808/661-8397 or 1-877/500-6284, ⓦwww.mauiprincess.com. Dinner ($87) and whale-watching ($24 and $29) cruises from Lahaina, plus one-day excursions to Molokai (from $108).
Pacific Whale Foundation ☎808/249-8811 or 1-800/942-5311, ⓦwww.pacificwhale .org. This nonprofit organization offers 2–3hr whale-watching cruises from Lahaina or Māʻalaea (Nov–April; around $30), plus snorkeling and dolphin-watching tours to Molokini ($55–80) or Lanai ($80).
Reefdancer ☎808/667-2133, ⓦwww.mauiglassbottomboat.com. Cruises in a semi-submersible from Lahaina (1hr at $35, 1hr30min at $45); passengers view the reef from an underwater cabin.
Trilogy Ocean Sports ☎808/661-4743 or 1-888/225-6284, ⓦwww.sailtrilogy.com. Day-long sailing trips from Lahaina to Lanai, including snorkeling, beach barbecue, and Lanai van tour ($189). They also offer diving and snorkeling at Molokini and off Lanai.

Kayak tours and rentals
Kelii's Kayak Tours ☎1-888/874-7652, ⓦwww.keliiskayak.com. Kayak tours (2hr; $54) from Lahaina, plus several more options in West, North and South Maui.
South Pacific Kayaks ☎808/875-4848 or 1-800/776-2326, ⓦwww.southpacifickayaks .com. Kayak rentals in Mākena, plus an extensive range of kayaking tours, from 2hr 15min whale-watching trips ($65; in season only) via 3hr guided excursions at Mākena or Lahaina, up to extended tours in South or West Maui for up to $99.

Equipment rental
Auntie Snorkel 2439 S Kīhei Rd, Kīhei ☎808/879-6263 or 1-877/256-4248, ⓦwww .auntiesnorkel.com. Snorkels and kayaks.
Boss Frog's Dive Shop 1215 S Kīhei Rd, Kīhei (☎808/891-0077, ⓦwww.bossfrog .com) and six other Maui locations. Activity center that also rents out scuba, snorkeling and surf gear.
Maui Dive Shop 1455 S Kīhei Rd, Kīhei (☎808/879-3388), and six other Maui locations; ⓦwww.mauidiveshop.com. Dive specialists who rent scuba and snorkeling equipment.
Snorkel Bob's 1280 S Kīhei Rd, Kīhei (☎808/875-6188); 2411 S Kīhei Rd, Kīhei (☎808/879-7449); 180 Dickenson St, Lahaina (☎808/661-4421); and Nāpili Village Hotel, 5425C Lower Honoapiʻilani Rd, Nāpili (☎808/669-9603); ⓦwww.snorkelbob .com. Snorkel gear that can be returned on any island.

Maui favorites: eating

These are not so much the ten best restaurants on Maui as ten very good places to eat, drawn from all price categories and arranged in ascending order of price.

Soup Nutz and Java Jazz, Honokōwai, p.240
Cilantro Fresh Mexican Grill, Lahaina, p.233
Fresh Mint, Pā'ia, p.281
AK's Café, Wailuku, p.250
Sansei Seafood Restaurant, Kīhei, p.257
Hula Grill, Kā'anapali, p.237
Roy's Kahana Bar and Grill, Kahana, p.240
Hali'imaile General Store, Hali'imaile, p.266
Merriman's, Kapalua, p.240
The Feast at Lele, Lahaina, p.233

isthmus, is a mecca for devotees and plays host to major championships throughout most of the year. Strong winds are of greater importance to windsurfers than high surf, so summer is the peak season for the sport. Between December and February the winds tend to drop for days on end, but even then conditions are usually good enough somewhere on the island; **Mā'alaea Bay** on the south shore of the isthmus is the likeliest spot.

The best place to **learn** to windsurf is Kanahā Beach near Kahului, a few miles west of Ho'okipa. Expect to pay $80–90 for a 2hr 30min lesson (including equipment rental) with operators such as Action Sports Maui (T 808/871-5857, W www .actionsportsmaui.com), or Alan Cadiz's HST Windsurfing School (T 808/871-5423 or 1-800/968-5423, W www.hstwindsurfing.com). Maui Windsurfari specializes in putting together all-inclusive **packages** for windsurfers (T 808/871-7766 or 1-800/736-6284, W www.windsurfari.com).

Nightlife and entertainment

Although it can't compete with the big-city atmosphere of Honolulu, and island residents jokingly refer to the hour of 10pm as "Maui midnight," by Hawaiian standards Maui offers visitors a reasonably lively **nightlife**.

As ever, most of the activity is confined to the tourist enclaves, and the resort hotels in particular, but if you enjoy wandering the streets from bar to bar the oceanfront at **Lahaina** provides almost the same buzz as Waikīkī. The south coast, from **Kīhei** on down, is too spread out to have the same intensity, but it's always party time somewhere along the strip.

Lovers of traditional **Hawaiian music** should head to the *Nāpili Kai Beach Resort* in West Maui (see p.239), which stages a superb series of weekly slack-key guitar concerts, masterminded by virtuoso George Kahumoku, Jr (Wed 7.30pm; $40; T 808/669-3858 or 1-888/669-3858, W www.slackkey.com). Each week sees a different guest star, from the very biggest names of the genre – regulars include Cyril Pahinui, Led Ka'apana, and Dennis Kamakahi – and live recordings drawn from the concerts have four times won Grammies.

Away from the resorts, the local community of rock exiles and ex-Californians makes *Casanova's* in upcountry **Makawao** an amazingly happening venue for such a tiny town, while assorted venues in **Pā'ia** stage numerous weekend gigs, especially reggae. There's also the Maui Arts and Cultural Center by the harbor in **Kahului**, which attracts big-name touring bands.

West Maui

Over the eons, the older of Maui's two volcanoes has eroded away to create a long, curving ridge known collectively as the **West Maui Mountains**. The highest point – Pu'u Kukui – is deluged by around four hundred inches of rain per year and is almost always obscured by clouds. However, the leeward (western) slopes are consistently dry, and West Maui has therefore become a major resort destination.

Though tourism focuses especially on the one genuine town here, historic **Lahaina**, most of the **accommodation** options lie along the sun-baked beaches to the north. A seamless succession of hotels and condos stretches for around eight miles, in purpose-built resorts such as **Kā'anapali**, **Honokōwai**, and **Kapalua**. None of these communities holds the slightest interest in its own right, but all offer superb facilities for family vacations, even if room rates tend to be too high for budget travelers.

No road crosses the mountains themselves; in fact, parts of the all-but-impenetrable wilderness of the interior have never been explored. The main road to Lahaina from central Maui, **Honoapi'ilani Highway**, is forced to loop laboriously around the southern end of West Maui. As development is only allowed on its *makai* (oceanward) side, it's an attractive drive, with views of inland hills and valleys left largely untouched; it's also a very slow one, thanks to horrendous and ever-growing traffic problems.

At the northern end of West Maui, beyond Kapalua, the weather becomes progressively wetter; the coast is more indented with bays; and driving conditions grow increasingly difficult. Honoapi'ilani Highway eventually gives up altogether around Nākalele Point. Although sinuous, undulating **Kahekili Highway** beyond narrows to a single lane for several miles, it's possible to complete a full circuit back to Wailuku. Driving that whole loop in one go would take around three hours – not that there'd be any point doing so without stopping.

Maui lū'aus

The **lū'aus** listed below charge anything from $60 to $110 per adult and $35–80 per child; you can buy discounted tickets (perhaps $10 off the usual price) from activities operators all over the island. While *The Feast at Lele* offers the best food (see p.233), it's not quite a *lū'au* in the usual sense of the word, so the *Old Lahaina Lū'au*, in a splendid oceanfront setting, is generally considered to be the best value.

Drums of the Pacific *Hyatt Regency Maui*, Kā'anapali ☏808/661-1234. Daily 5pm.

The Feast at Lele 505 Front St, Lahaina ☏808/667-5353, ⓦwww.feastatlele.com. April–Sept daily 6pm, Oct–March daily 5.30pm.

Honua'ula Lū'au *Marriott Wailea*, Wailea ☏808/875-7710. Mon & Thurs–Sat 5pm.

Maui Sunset Lū'au *Mākena Beach and Golf Resort*, Mākena ☏808/871-1111. Tues & Thurs 5.30pm.

Old Lahaina Lū'au Lahaina Cannery Mall, Lahaina ☏808/667-1998 or 1-800/248-5828, ⓦwww.oldlahainaluau.com. April–Sept daily 5.45pm, Oct–March daily 5.15pm.

Royal Lahaina Lū'au *Royal Lahaina Resort*, Kā'anapali ☏808/661-9119, ⓦwww.royal lahaina.net. Daily 4.45pm.

Lahaina

Seen from a short distance offshore, **LAHAINA**, the only true town in West Maui, is one of the prettiest communities in all Hawaii. During the early nineteenth century it served as capital of the entire Kingdom of Hawaii, but it has barely grown since then and could almost be mistaken for a peaceful, tropical village. Its main oceanfront street is lined with timber-frame buildings; yachts bob in the harbor; coconut palms sway to either side of the central banyan tree; surfers swirl into the thin fringe of beach to the south; and the mountains of West Maui dominate the skyline, ringed as often as not by beautiful rainbows.

Although Lahaina is not quite as enticing up close – **Front Street** holds rather too many tacky themed restaurants and T-shirt stores, not to mention crowds reminiscent of Waikīkī – it still makes an attractive base, sandwiched between the spectacular ocean and spellbinding hills. Early evening is especially unforgettable, with the sun casting a rich glow on the mountains as it sets behind the island of Lanai. Lahaina is lively and by Maui standards inexpensive, with a huge range of activities and little rainfall, but above all it's the only town on Maui to offer lodging, sightseeing, dining, and nightlife, all within easy walking distance of each other.

A brief history of Lahaina

Lahaina boasts a colorful past. By the time the first foreigners came to Hawaii, it was already the residence of the high *ali'i* (chiefs) of Maui. **Kamehameha the Great** sealed his conquest of Maui by sacking Lahaina in 1795, while his successors made it their **capital** between the 1820s and 1840s, ruling from the island of **Moku'ula**, in a lake in what is now Malu 'Ulu o Lele Park, south of downtown.

When **whaling** ships started to put in during the 1820s, fierce struggles between the sailors and Lahaina's Christian **missionaries** became commonplace. By the 1840s, it was a lawless and rip-roaring frontier town, characterized as "one of the breathing holes of Hell." Surprisingly, though, it was never a true deep-water port. Its prosperity was based on its calm, shallow roadstead, sheltered by Molokai and Lanai. Sailing ships simply anchored well offshore, and sent their crews ashore by rowboat. During the nineteenth century, a long covered marketplace lined the banks of a canal parallel to the seafront, enabling seamen to buy all they needed without ever leaving their boats. To this day, cruise ships still anchor a considerable distance out to sea.

Devastated by a huge fire in 1919 and by the state-wide tsunami of 1946, Lahaina remained a sleepy backwater until the 1970s, when the successful resort development at neighboring **Kā'anapali** triggered its return to prominence as a tourist destination.

Arrival and information

Although Lahaina is served by Maui's fairly basic public transport system, the only way to **reach** it from either of the island's airports is by renting your own **vehicle** or taking a taxi-style **shuttle bus** (see p.245). Once you get to town, a car can be a real nuisance; the cramped streets make **parking** a terrible business. The only free public parking is at Front and Prison streets, or you can usually leave your car at one of the larger malls, such as the Lahaina Shopping Center.

Walk along Front Street and you'll be deluged with brochures and leaflets hawked by the various activity kiosks. Somewhat more dispassionate advice can be obtained at the **Lahaina Visitor Center** (daily 9am–5pm; ☎808/667-9175 or 1-888/310-1117, ⓦwww.visitlahaina.com), inside the Old Lahaina Court House on Banyan Tree Square, though even that is more of an official souvenir store than a useful resource.

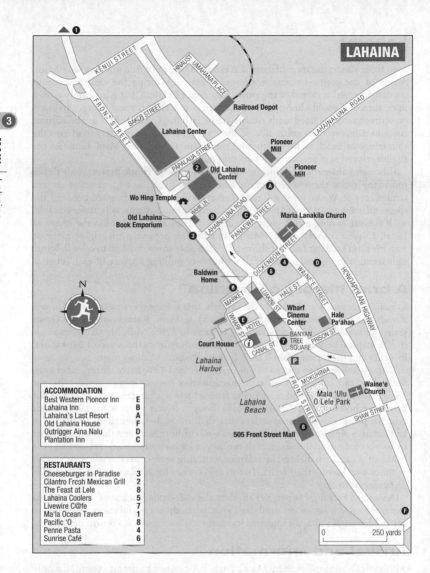

Map: LAHAINA

ACCOMMODATION

Best Western Pioneer Inn	E
Lahaina Inn	B
Lahaina's Last Resort	A
Old Lahaina House	F
Outrigger Aina Nalu	D
Plantation Inn	C

RESTAURANTS

Cheeseburger in Paradise	3
Cilantro Fresh Mexican Grill	2
The Feast at Lele	8
Lahaina Coolers	5
Livewire C@fe	7
Ma'la Ocean Tavern	1
Pacific 'O	8
Penne Pasta	4
Sunrise Café	6

0   250 yards

Accommodation

In terms of **accommodation**, Lahaina has nothing to rival the opulence of Kā'anapali and Kapalua, further north up the coast. However, the *Pioneer Inn* harks back romantically to the old days of Hawaiian tourism, and there are also a couple of classy B&B inns, plus a few central but quiet hotel-cum-condos.

Best Western Pioneer Inn 658 Wharf St ☎808/661-3636 or 1-800/457-5457, ⓦwww.pioneerinnmaui.com. Maui's oldest hotel, splendidly positioned on the seafront in the very center of Lahaina, makes a historic and highly

atmospheric place to stay, even if it's nothing like as luxurious as the modern resorts. All the tastefully furnished rooms have private baths and a/c, and open onto lovely *lānais*; the quieter ones face an inner courtyard, while those overlooking Banyan

Tree Square can be noisy. There's a small pool, but no on-site parking. ⑤

Lahaina Inn 127 Lahainaluna Rd ☎808/661-0577 or 1-800/669-3444, ⓦwww.lahainainn.com. Set slightly back from Front Street, this sumptuous, antique-furnished re-creation of how a century-old inn ought to look was actually built as a store in 1938. The twelve rooms of varying sizes have a/c, private bathrooms (most with showers rather than baths) and phones, but no TV. No children under 15 years. ⑤

Lahaina's Last Resort 252 Lahainaluna Rd ☎808/661-6655, ⓦwww.lahainaslastresort.com. Friendly, well-run budget hostel, in a noisy location beside the main through-highway, and open to out-of-state visitors only. As well as (rather smelly, if truth be told) co-ed six-bed dorms, they have some nicer private rooms, with and without en-suite facilities. ①–③

Old Lahaina House 407 Ilikahi St ☎808/667-4663 or 1-800/847-0761, ⓦwww.oldlahaina.com. Good-quality B&B

accommodation in a friendly private home with pool, a few hundred yards south of downtown Lahaina. There's one guest room in the house and four more in a separate garden wing; all are en suite, with refrigerators, TVs, and a/c. Rates include breakfast on the *lānai*. ③–⑤

Outrigger Aina Nalu 660 Waine'e St ☎808/667-9766, 1-800/688-7444, ⓦwww.outrigger.com. This sprawling but low-key condo complex, a couple of blocks from the sea in central Lahaina, has been through many incarnations over the years. It currently offers smart, well-equipped rooms in two X-shaped blocks, though with no beach and just a small pool, it's not a place to linger all day. ⑤

Plantation Inn 174 Lahainaluna Rd ☎808/667-9225 or 1-800/433-6815, ⓦwww.theplantationinn.com. Luxury B&B hotel, not far back from the sea and styled after a Southern plantation home, complete with columns and verandas and a 12ft-deep pool. All nineteen rooms have bathrooms and *lānais*, while the suites also have kitchenettes. Guests get a discount at the downstairs restaurant, *Gerard's*. ⑤

Downtown Lahaina

Almost all the activity of modern Lahaina is concentrated along **Front Street**, where a few historic buildings, such as the Baldwin Home and Wo Hing Temple, hang on amid an awful lot of shopping malls, souvenir stores, and fast-food outlets. The very heart of town is **Banyan Tree Square**, an attractive public space that's often rendered too busy for comfort by busloads of tourists.

For respite, locals and visitors alike gravitate toward the **waterfront**. The views are superb, whether you look straight across to the island of Lanai, where you'll probably be able to make out the crest of Norfolk pines along its topmost ridge, or north toward Molokai, where the west-end mountain of Mauna Loa is visible on a clear day. Closer at hand, fishermen angle for sand fish in the inshore waters, boats

Public transport from Lahaina

Maui Bus (☎808/871-4838, ⓦwww.mauicounty.gov/bus; see also p.220) run hourly **buses** between Lahaina and **Kahului** ($1; departs Queen Ka'ahumanu Center in Kahului daily 5.30am–7.30pm, Wharf Cinema Center in Lahaina daily 6.30am–8.30pm). All those services call at Mā'alaea, where you can change for buses to Kīhei and Wailea. They also offer frequent connections between Lahaina and **Kā'anapali**, leaving from Lahaina Harbor hourly from 6.30am until 8.30pm daily.

In addition, Lahaina Harbor is home to a couple of **inter-island ferry services**. *Expeditions* (☎808/661-3756 or, from outside Maui, 1-800/695-2624, ⓦwww.go-lanai .com) sails from in front of the *Pioneer Inn* to Manele Bay on **Lanai** daily at 6.45am, 9.15am, 12.45pm, 3.15pm, and 5.45pm. Departures from Lanai are at 8am, 10.30am, 2pm, 4.30pm, and 6.45pm; the adult fare is $30 each way, while under-12s go for $20. The trip takes approximately fifty minutes.

It's also possible to make a 1hr 30min ferry crossing between Maui and **Molokai** on the *Molokai Princess* (departs Lahaina Mon–Sat 7.15am, daily 6pm; departs Molokai Mon–Sat 5.15am, daily 4pm; adults $54 one-way, under-12s $27; ☎808/662-3535 or 1-877/500-6284, ⓦwww.mauiprincess.com).

The Sugar Cane Train

The **Lahaina Kā'anapali Railroad** (adults $22.50 round-trip, under-13s $15.50; ☎808/667-6851 or 1-800/499-2307, ⓦwww.sugarcanetrain.com), also known as the **Sugar Cane Train**, is a restored locomotive (complete with "singing conductor") that runs a six-mile, half-hour-long excursion through the cane fields from Lahaina to Kā'anapali, and then half a mile beyond to turn around at Pu'ukoli'i. For anyone other than a small child, it's not an exciting trip. The first departure from Lahaina is at 11.05am daily and the last at 4pm; from Kā'anapali, the first is at 10.25am daily, the last at 3.25pm. There's also a weekly dinner train, setting off from Pu'ukoli'i at 5pm on Thursday (adults $60, under-13s $46). Free shuttle buses connect the Lahaina and Kā'anapali stations with the Wharf Cinema Center and the Whaler's Village, respectively.

and yachts rock beyond the placid roll of white surf fifty yards out, and parasailers peer down upon all this activity from on high.

Banyan Tree Square

A magnificent banyan tree, planted on April 24, 1873, almost completely fills **Banyan Tree Square**. It consists of at least twenty major trunks, plus any number of intertwined tendrils pushing back down into the ground. A phenomenal number of chirruping birds congregate in the branches, while portrait artists tout for customers in the shade below.

Here and there on the surrounding lawns, outlines mark the former extent of **Lahaina Fort**, built in 1832. Its walls once held as many as 47 cannons, salvaged from shipwrecks throughout Hawaii; a drum was beaten on its ramparts at nightfall as a signal for all foreign seamen to return to their ships. The fort was demolished in 1854, but one small corner has been reconstructed, at the southwest end of the square.

The stolid, four-square **Court House**, on the harbor side of Banyan Tree Square, was constructed in 1859 after a storm had destroyed most of Lahaina's official buildings. Downstairs, you'll find the small local visitor center (see p.227), as well as the Banyan Tree Gallery, which hosts interesting, free **art exhibitions** (daily 9am–5pm). Up on the second floor, the town's former courtroom, last used in 1987, now serves as the **Lahaina Heritage Center** (same hours; $2 suggested donation), where the displays and photographs on local history include illuminating sections devoted to the whaling and plantation eras.

Across Hotel Street from the Court House, the **Pioneer Inn** has, since it was moved en masse from the island of Lanai in 1901, been the main social center of Lahaina. Its original owner, a Canadian "Mountie" who had pursued a criminal all the way to Maui, decided to stay on and go into the hotel business, catering to passengers on the Inter-Island Steamship line. It makes an atmospheric – and busy – place to stop in for a beer.

Immediately north of the *Pioneer Inn*, Lahaina Public Library stands on the site of the former royal taro patch, personally tended by the first three Kamehamehas. A line of bricks set into the grass on its seaward side traces the foundations of the **Brick Palace**, the first Western-style building in Hawaii. Two stories high and measuring 20ft by 40ft, it was built for Kamehameha the Great in 1798 by an English convict who had managed to escape from Australia; the palace survived until the 1860s.

Lahaina Harbor

On the waterfront, across from the *Pioneer Inn*, a simple and modern white structure has replaced what was the oldest **Pacific lighthouse**, built to serve the whaling fleet in 1840. Shielded by a breakwater of boulders, **Lahaina Harbor** now serves as an overworked pleasure-boat marina, and is also the base for ferries to Molokai and Lanai

(see p.229). Although the harbor wall has kiosks for most local **boat operators**, it's not much of an area to stroll around, and you can usually get better prices from the activity centers along Front Street.

Lahaina Beach

Immediately south of the marina, **Lahaina Beach**, with its shallow water, sandy bottom, and gentle breaks, is where companies such as the Goofy Foot Surf School (☎808/244-9283, ⓦ www.goofyfootsurfschool.com) and the Nancy Emerson School of Surfing (☎808/244-7873, ⓦ www.mauisurfclinics.com) teach their clients the rudiments of **surfing**, and beginners and old-timers alike swoop back and forth. The beach itself is too narrow for long days of family fun, but it's fine for a stroll.

Baldwin Home

The **Baldwin Home**, on Front Street just north of Banyan Tree Square, is the oldest surviving house in Lahaina. Dating from the days when this was Hawaii's royal capital, it was built as the Maui base of the Sandwich Islands Mission and is now a reasonably interesting museum of missionary and local history (daily 10am–4pm; adults $3, couples $5, under-13s free; ⓦ www.lahainarestoration.org). The admission price includes a brief narrated tour, after which visitors are free to take a closer look around.

Constructed in 1834, with 24-inch-thick walls made of plastered lava and coral, the house is named for Reverend Dwight Baldwin, who took it over when his predecessor fell sick three years later. Baldwin remained as pastor of Lahaina's Waine'e Church until 1871, and much of his original furniture is still in place. Oddly frivolous touches among the chairs, quilts, and memorabilia include an inlaid *koa* gaming table and a table-top croquet set.

The Baldwin Home reopens on Friday nights for atmospheric **candlelit tours** (Fri 6–8.30pm; adults $4, couples $6).

Wo Hing Temple

The distinguished-looking building with the unmistakably Oriental facade, a short walk north of downtown Lahaina on Front Street, is known as the **Wo Hing Temple** (daily except Fri 10am–4pm, Fri 1–8pm; $2). It was built in 1912 as the

▲ Baldwin Home

meeting place for the Wo Hing Society, a mutual-aid organization established in China during the seventeenth century. Until the 1970s it housed elderly members of the society, but it's now a fine little museum devoted to Chinese immigration to Hawaii, with a small Taoist altar on its second story.

Amid the faded signs and battered pots and pans in the decrepit adjacent **cookhouse**, you can watch scratchy film footage shot by Thomas Edison in Hawaii in 1898, shown in a continuous loop.

Waine'e Church

The first church on Maui, built in 1828 after five years of open-air services, was Waine'e Church, one block back from the sea. Twice destroyed by hurricanes, and burned down in 1894 amid protests against the overthrow of the Hawaiian monarchy, this less-than-enthralling edifice was officially renamed Waiola Church when it was last rebuilt in 1953, but is still widely referred to by its old name.

Tombs in the sun-scorched graveyard alongside include some great names in early Hawaiian history. A simple monument commemorates the last king of Kauai, **Kaumuali'i**, who was buried here in 1825 after being kidnapped by Liholiho and forced to live in exile (see p.338). Nearby are **Queen Keopuolani**, one of the many wives of Kamehameha the Great, who was of such distinguished *ali'i* blood that her husband could only enter her presence naked on all fours; the governor of Maui, **Hoapili Kane**, who died in 1840; and his widow and successor **Hoapili Wahine**, who passed away two years later.

Lahainaluna

High above Lahaina town, reached by a winding two-mile climb up Lahainaluna Road past the Pioneer Sugar Mill, **Lahainaluna Seminary** was founded by American missionaries in 1831. Its goal was to teach Hawaiians to read and write, in the hope of producing future teachers and ministers. In 1850, however, the seminary passed into government control, and it eventually became Hawaii's most prestigious public **high school**. Although when it was built Hawaii did not belong to the US, it's regarded as being the first American educational institution west of the Rockies, and during the Gold Rush years many Californians sent their children here rather than risk the long journey east.

Visitors are welcome to take a quick look around the high school grounds; pause to identify yourself at the gate first. The only building you can enter is the seminary's small printing house, **Hale Pa'i** (Mon–Fri by appointment only; free; ☎808/661-3262). Dating from 1837, it holds some of Hawaii's first printed books, as well as a replica of the press that produced them.

Eating and drinking

Dozens of places to **eat** line the waterfront in Lahaina, with sophisticated gourmet **restaurants** mingling with national and local chain outlets and takeout places, so you should find something to suit you within a few minutes' wandering. Almost all offer **bars** as well, busy at sunset. For a quick snack, the best local **fast-food court** is in the Lahaina Cannery mall, a mile north of downtown, while the more central Old Lahaina Center holds some cheap Asian diners.

For a full listing of Maui's *lū'aus*, see p.226. Otherwise, for a fun night out in Lahaina, head to *Warren and Annabelle's Magic Show*, in the oceanfront Lahaina Center, 900 Front St (☎808/667-6244, ⓦwww.warrenandannabelles.com; Mon–Sat 5pm & 7.30pm; adults only, $58, or $96 with food and two cocktails). The full four-hour experience combines a spell in a "haunted" cocktail bar with a wonderful display of sleight-of-hand magic.

Cheeseburger in Paradise 811 Front St ☎808/661-4855. Busy, crowded seafront restaurant, perched on stilts above the water. Great views, buzzing ambience, and seafaring bric-a-brac are more of a draw than the food, though in addition to meaty $9–16 cheeseburgers they have fish sandwiches and tofu nut-burgers at similar prices. Live music nightly. Daily 8am–midnight.

Cilantro Fresh Mexican Grill Old Lahaina Center, 170 Papalaua Ave ☎808/667-5444. Simple but clean and very appetizing Mexican diner, where you order at the counter in front of the open kitchen and either take it away or eat on site with plastic utensils. The food is uniformly tasty and fresh, with enchiladas, burritos and so on for $7–15, whole rotisserie chickens for $15, and specials like a chicken or fish taco plate for just over $10. There's no liquor license, but you can bring a bottle from the nearby supermarket. Mon–Sat 11am–9pm, Sun 11am–8pm.

The Feast at Lele 505 Front St ☎808/667-5353 or 1-866/244-5353, ⓦwww.feastatlele .com. An inspired cross between a *lū'au* and a gourmet restaurant that, for once, lavishes as much care on the food as on the entertainment. Among the Polynesian specialties are *kalua* pork from Hawaii, *fafa* (steamed chicken) and *e'iota* (marinated raw fish) from Tahiti, and grilled fish in banana leaves from Samoa. Each of the five excellent and unusual courses consists of at least two dishes, while the very romantic beachfront setting features individual tables facing the ocean at sunset. Music and hula performances punctuate the evening, culminating in a Samoan fire dance. Though steep, the $110 adult charge includes unlimited cocktails and other beverages; for children, it's $80. Reservations are essential. April–Sept daily 6pm, Oct–March daily 5.30pm; schedules may vary.

Lahaina Coolers 180 Dickenson St ☎808/661-7082, ⓦwww.lahainacoolers.com. Central bistro serving eggy breakfasts for around $10, then lunch specials like *kalua* pig tacos for $10–16, and an extensive dinner menu of pizzas from $13, and entrees like fresh fish or steak for $18–29. A couple of blocks from the sea, but it's open and breezy, with a pleasant atmosphere, and serves dinner until midnight. Live English soccer games shown regularly. Daily 8am–1am.

Livewire C@fe 612 Front St ☎808/661-4213. The staff can be a little ditzy, but this roomy, tidy café, just south of Banyan Square, serves good coffees, snacks, and excellent smoothies, and is a handy place to check your email. Mon–Sat 6am–8pm, Sun 7am–8pm.

Ma'la Ocean Tavern 1307 Front St ☎808/667-9394, ⓦwww.malaoceantavern.com. Gourmet restaurant, part Pacific Rim, part Mediterranean, at the sleepy northern end of the Lahaina oceanfront; outdoor tables mean you can watch turtles as you dine. Breakfast and lunch are the best value; typical dinner appetizers, like a mixed plate of hummus and other middle Eastern specialties, cost $13–18, while entrees such as seared sashimi or wok-fried fish range from $28 to $38. Mon–Fri 11am–9.30pm, Sat 9am–9.30pm, Sun 9am–9pm.

Pacific 'O 505 Front St ☎808/667-4341, ⓦwww.pacificomaui.com. Attractive ocean-front mall restaurant, serving Pacific Rim cuisine on a beach-level terrace with indoor dining above. Lunch offerings ($10–16) include a bleu burger, a chicken wrap, salads, and delicious sesame fish. In the evening, try appetizers ($9–16) such as the shrimp won tons in Hawaiian salsa, and entrees like roast rack of lamb with aioli ($36) – or tempura blocks of fish ($30). For vegetarians, the "leaning tower of tofu" costs $13.50 at lunch, and there's blackened tofu at $30 for dinner. Leave room for the huge, delicious chocolate desserts. Daily 11am–4pm & 5.30–10pm; live jazz Fri & Sat from 9pm.

Penne Pasta 180 Dickenson St ☎808/661-6633, ⓦwww.pennepastacafe.com. Cheerful Italian café, with sidewalk and indoor seating, serving straight-forward but tasty pastas, salads, and pizzas for under $10. The thin, crispy flatbread topped with olives, capers, basil, oregano, and roasted peppers is particularly good. Mon–Fri 11am–9.30pm, Sat & Sun 5–9.30pm.

Sunrise Café 693A Front St at Market St ☎808/661-8558. Small, laidback, and very central café-cum-restaurant, with outdoor seating beside its own tiny patch of beach. Coffees, smoothies, and full cooked breakfasts are served from dawn onwards, plus $7–9 sandwiches, plate lunches, and salads later on. No credit cards. Daily 6am–6pm.

South of Lahaina

Few people live along the parched coastline to the **south of Lahaina**, where ditches in the hillside still irrigate extensive green cane-fields. There are no significant settlements, but the only road, Honoapi'ilani Highway, is prone to hideous traffic

The Olowalu Massacre

Olowalu was the site of the worst **massacre** in Hawaiian history, perpetrated by **Captain Simon Metcalfe** of the American merchant ship *Eleanora* in 1790. After Hawaiians killed a member of his crew as they stole a ship's boat off East Maui, Metcalfe set fire to the nearest village and sailed for Olowalu, which he was told was the home of the chief culprit. Offering to continue trading, he lured two hundred canoes out to the *Eleanora*, many of them filled with children coming to see the strange ship, then bombarded them with his seven cannons. More than a hundred Hawaiians died.

Ironically, Captain Metcalfe's 18-year-old son, **Thomas**, was to pay for his father's sins. Metcalfe had previously antagonized a Big Island chief, Kame'eiamoku, who vowed to kill the next white man he met. Ignorant of events at Olowalu, Thomas Metcalfe landed his tiny six-man schooner *Fair American* on the Big Island a few days later and was killed when it was stormed by Kame'eiamoku and his men. Of its crew, only **Isaac Davis** was spared, for putting up such valiant resistance.

When the *Eleanora* arrived on the Big Island searching for the younger Metcalfe, first mate **John Young** was sent ashore to investigate, and was prevented by Kamehameha the Great from rejoining his vessel with the news of the killings. Concluding that his envoy had been killed, Captain Metcalfe sailed away. He was killed soon afterwards and never learned of the death of his son; both Davis and Young, however, remained on the islands, and became valued royal advisors. They were responsible for teaching the Hawaiians to fight with muskets and cannon, and personally directed Kamehameha's armies at battles such as 'Iao Valley on Maui (see p.251) and Nu'uanu Pali on Oahu (see p.85).

congestion, especially as it narrows to climb around Papawai Point in the far south and head back to **Mā'alaea** (see p.252).

Launiupoko State Wayside Park

While always scenic, the beaches immediately south of Lahaina are not nearly as appealing as those to the north, consisting as a rule of narrow strips of sand deposited atop sharp black rocks. The first one you come to, Puamana Beach County Park, offers no visitor facilities, but **Launiupoko State Wayside Park**, three miles out, makes an attractive picnic spot. Coconut palms lean out from the shoreline, while larger trees shade the tables on the lawn; the only snag is that it's very much in earshot of the highway. From the center of the park, boulder walls curve out to enclose a shallow artificial pool, suitable for small children, with two narrow outlets to the sea. South of that is a small beach of gritty sand, while to the north the lava rocks create a sea wall, alive with scuttling black crabs.

Olowalu

There's little more to **OLOWALU**, six miles south of Lahaina, than a tiny row of storefronts *mauka* of the highway. The most noteworthy of these now holds *Chez Paul* (☎ 808/661-3843, ⓦ www.chezpaul.net), an incongruous and very expensive French bistro set behind a pretty little brick wall. It's open for dinner only, nightly except Sunday, with two seatings, at 6.30pm and 8.30pm. Most of the appetizers cost around $15, and there's caviar for $95, while entrees such as fish poached in champagne or duck *à l'orange* are well over $40.

There's no public access to the ocean on the promontory across the road, but you can take a short hike toward the mountains to a cluster of ancient **petroglyphs**. Start by heading round to the left behind the stores and then continue inland, following the dirt road that starts immediately left of the nearby water tower.

After about ten minutes' walk through the cane fields, you'll notice that the nearest side of the cinder cone straight ahead of you has sheared off, leaving behind a flat wall of red rock. Fresh-painted red railings a few feet up the rock mark the site of the petroglyphs, but the stairs and walkways that once enabled visitors to climb up to them have largely vanished. So too have many of the petroglyphs, and others have been vandalized. However, you should still spot several wedge-shaped human figures etched into the rock, together with a sailing canoe or two, characterized by their "crab-claw" sails. Looking back, you'll also get good views across to Lanai.

Ukemehame and Pāpalaua

South of Olowalu the cane fields come to an end, and Hwy-30 skirts the shoreline only a few feet above sea level. It's possible to park just about anywhere, and in whale-watching season that's exactly what people do – often with very little warning.

Ukemehame Beach County Park, three miles along, consists of a very small area of lawn between the highway and the ocean, with picnic tables and portable restrooms, fringed by a small strip of sand.

Pāpalaua State Wayside, which leads south from Ukemehame, is a long dirt strip used as a parking lot, separated from the sand by a thin line of scrubby trees. Local surfers and snorkelers set up tents among the trees, but there are virtually no facilities.

Immediately beyond Pāpalaua, the highway starts its climb over (and through) the headland of **Papawai Point**, where a roadside lookout is one of Maui's best **whale-watching** sites. From there it's less than two miles to Mā'alaea (see p.252) and the isthmus.

North from Lahaina: Kā'anapali

When American Factors (Amfac), the owners of Lahaina's Pioneer Sugar Mill, decided in 1957 to transform the oceanfront cane fields of **KĀ'ANAPALI** into a luxury tourist resort, they established a pattern that has been repeated throughout Hawaii ever since. There had never been a town at Kā'anapali, just a small wharf served by a short railroad from the sugar mill. What Kā'anapali did have, however, was a superb white-sand **beach** – far better than anything at Lahaina – backed by a tract of land that was ripe for development and more than twice the size of Waikīkī.

Kā'anapali's first hotel opened in 1963 and has been followed by half a dozen similar giants. Their four thousand rooms now welcome half a million visitors each year, but there's still no town here, just a couple of small shopping malls. Kā'anapali is a pretty enough place, with its two rolling **golf courses** and sunset views of the island of Lanai filling the western horizon, but there's little to distinguish it from any number of similar purpose-built tropical resorts around the world.

As for **Kā'anapali Beach**, it's divided into two separate long strands by the forbidding, 300ft cinder cone of Pu'u Keka'a, known as the **Black Rock**. The sand shelves away abruptly from both sections, so swimmers soon find themselves

Public transport from Kā'anapali

Maui Bus (☎808/871-4838, ⊛www.mauicounty.gov/bus; see also p.220) run hourly **buses** from Kā'anapali both south to **Lahaina** ($1; departs Whalers Village daily 6am–9pm) and northwards to **Honokōwai**, **Kahana**, and **Nāpili** ($1; departs daily 6am–8pm).

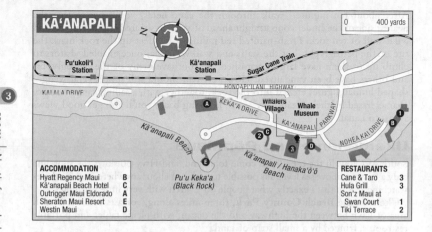

KĀʻANAPALI

0   400 yards

Puʻukoliʻi Station

Kāʻanapali Station

Sugar Cane Train

HONOAPIʻILANI HIGHWAY

KALALA DRIVE

KEKAʻA DRIVE

Whalers Village

Whale Museum

Kāʻanapali Beach

KAʻANAPALI PARKWAY

NOHEA KAI DRIVE

Kāʻanapali / Hanakaʻōʻō Beach

Puʻu Kekaʻa (Black Rock)

ACCOMMODATION

Hyatt Regency Maui	B
Kāʻanapali Beach Hotel	C
Outrigger Maui Eldorado	A
Sheraton Maui Resort	E
Westin Maui	D

RESTAURANTS

Cane & Taro	3
Hula Grill	3
Son'z Maui at Swan Court	1
Tiki Terrace	2

in deep water, but bathing is usually safe outside periods of high winter surf. The rugged lava coastline around the Black Rock itself is one of the best **snorkeling** spots on Maui.

Whether or not you're staying at one of Kāʻanapali's hotels, you're free to use the main beach, but there are also a couple of **public beach parks** just around the headland to the south, alongside Hwy-30. Swimming is generally safer at **Wahikuli**, but the facilities and general ambience are more appealing at **Hanakaʻōʻō**.

Accommodation

Kāʻanapali is far from being a budget destination, but its lavish **hotels** do offer cut-price deals on rental cars or longer stays, and all feature kids' activities. Be warned that many hotels add a daily "resort charge" of up to $20 to their room rates, and quite possibly a $15 parking fee on top of that.

Hyatt Regency Maui 200 Nohea Kai Drive ☏808/661-1234 or 1-800/554-9288, ⓦwww.maui.hyatt.com. Kāʻanapali's grandest hotel, with opulent gardens, a palm-filled atrium with a pool of live penguins, and a vast labyrinth of swimming pools including a swinging rope bridge and bar. A ten-story main tower and subsidiary wings house a total of eight-hundred-plus luxurious rooms, four restaurants, including the sumptuous *Son'z at Swan Court* (see opposite), and a full-service oceanfront spa; a nightly *lūʻau* is held alongside (see p.226). Mountain view ⑧, ocean view ⑨

Kāʻanapali Beach Hotel 2525 Kāʻanapali Parkway ☏808/661-0011 or 1-800/262-8450, ⓦwww.kbhmaui.com. This low-rise property, somewhat faded and the least expensive on Kāʻanapali Beach, has a fine stretch of beach plus a whale-shaped swimming pool complete with tiki bar. All of its large, well-equipped rooms, arrayed around attractive oceanfront lawns, have balconies or patios, though some offer showers rather than a bath. A strong commitment to preserving Hawaiian culture

is reflected in regular classes and performances. Garden view ⑥, ocean view ⑦

Outrigger Maui Eldorado 2661 Kekaʻa Drive ☏808/661-0021 or 1-888/339-8585, ⓦwww.outrigger.com. Condo property consisting of several low buildings ranged up the hillside, well back from the shoreline; shuttle buses run to the resort's private beachfront area. All units offer a/c, *lānai*, maid service, washer/dryer, and a kitchenette or full kitchen. Garden view ④, ocean view ⑤

Sheraton Maui Resort 2605 Kāʻanapali Parkway ☏808/661-0031 or 1-866/716-8109, ⓦwww.sheraton-maui.com. This large luxury resort was the first to open at Kāʻanapali, in 1963, and has been almost entirely rebuilt, with five tiers of rooms dropping down the crag of Black Rock and separate oceanfront wings, plus a colossal and lovely pool and lagoon, all at the broadest end of Kāʻanapali Beach. ⑨

Westin Maui 2365 Kāʻanapali Parkway ☏808/667-2525 or 1-866/500-8313, ⓦwww.westinmaui.com. High-rise hotel in the center of

Kā'anapali Beach, immediately south of Whalers Village, where the five swimming pools are fed by artificial waterfalls and feature great waterslides, and there's a lagoon of live flamingos to match the predominantly pink decor. Not surprisingly, it's a major favorite for families with young children, so other guests can find it too noisy and hectic. Bright, modern, luxurious hotel rooms, all with private *lānai*. Mountain view **➐**, ocean view **➒**

Whale Museum

A pavilion at the main (inland) entrance to the Whalers Village mall shelters the articulated skeleton of a sperm whale, whose vestigial "fingers" are visible in its flippers. Nearby, a mock-up of a small nineteenth-century whaleboat is labeled with its esoteric components and gadgets. Both serve to introduce the gripping, if somewhat grisly, **Whale Museum**, which spreads through a couple of rooms on the mall's uppermost floor (daily 9am–10pm; free).

Devoted to Maui's former heyday as a whaling center, the exhibition illustrates the tedium and terror of the seamen's daily routine through scrimshaw, shellwork valentines, logbooks, tools, letters, and bills. The largest exhibit is a cast-iron "try pot"; used for reducing whale blubber at sea, such pots gave rise to the stereotyped image of cannibals cooking missionaries in big black cauldrons. Contrary to what you might imagine, no actual killing of whales took place in Hawaiian waters. Hawaii was simply the place where the whaling ships came to recuperate after hunting much further north in the Pacific.

Eating and drinking

Away from Kā'anapali's hotels, each of which holds at least one flagship **restaurant**, the only alternative is to eat at the **Whalers Village** mall. In addition to its formal oceanfront restaurants, each equipped with its own **bar**, it holds a **food court**, set back on the lower level.

Cane & Taro Whalers Village ☎808/662-0668. Pick your way carefully through the stunningly complicated menu at this strange hybrid restaurant, and you're in for a real treat, as well as tremendous sea views from both terrace and covered but open-sided main dining room. Run by D.K. Kodama of *Sansei* fame (see p.240 and p.257), it offers resort staples like burgers or seafood fettuccine alongside his trademark cutting-edge Japanese cuisine; some dishes literally combine the two, serving a succulent shrimp cake and crispy noodles stuffed into a burger bun with fries, for example. Lunch specials are a real bargain at around $10. Daily 8am–10pm.

Hula Grill Whalers Village ☎808/667-6636. Large, long, oceanfront restaurant, open to the sea breezes and offering great views, with live Hawaiian music nightly. Chef Peter Merriman, known for his distinctively Hawaiian take on things, offers lunchtime sandwiches ($10–$15) and a more interesting dinner menu: interesting appetizers include a Hawaiian ceviche, marinated in coconut milk ($9), along with dim sum and sashimi, while among the entrees are a $27 coconut seafood chowder, or fresh fish in various styles – even tandoori. Daily 11am–9.30pm.

Son'z Maui at Swan Court *Hyatt Regency Maui*, 200 Nohea Kai Drive ☎808/667-4506. Sublimely romantic restaurant, laid out around a lagoon populated by live swans and flamingos, revamped to serve "classic cuisine for the next generation." The predominantly Pacific Rim menu features $15–20 appetizers like tiger-eye sushi and New Zealand mussels, and some great fish entrees at $35–45, plus Mediterranean staples like *coq au vin* ($36) or steak. Sun–Thurs 5–10pm, Fri & Sat 5–10.30pm.

Tiki Terrace *Kā'anapali Beach Hotel*, 2525 Kā'anapali Parkway ☎808/667-0124. This unassuming hotel restaurant attempts to serve traditional Hawaiian foods, meaning plenty of fish, plus local ingredients like taro and sweet potato, and much of it steamed in *ti*-leaf parcels. The breakfast buffet is good value at $16. In the evening, when there's somewhat cheesy entertainment, a set Hawaiian dinner menu costs $26, or you can order more Westernized entrees like BBQ ribs or New York steak ($20–50). However, the open-air "tiki grill" section is a favorite with young kids, and tends to be both hectic and messy. Daily 7–11am & 6–9pm.

North of Kā'anapali: from Honokōwai to Kapalua

A mile or so out of Kā'anapali, Lower Honoapi'ilani Road branches down toward the ocean from the main highway, to undulate its way through **Honokōwai**, **Kahana**, and **Nāpili**. None of these barely distinguishable, purpose-built communities holds an ounce of interest for casual visitors. Even though they do have some great **beaches** – **Nāpili Bay** in particular is well worth seeking out – you'll hardly glimpse them unless you're staying at one of the innumerable condo buildings that line the entire road. There are few shops or restaurants nearby, so the highway is always busy with traffic heading south to the hot spots of Lahaina and beyond.

KAPALUA, at the end of Lower Honoapi'ilani Road in Maui's far northwest corner, is a pristine and very upscale enclave much like Wailea in South Maui (see p.258). A perfect little arc of white sand, set between two rocky headlands, **Kapalua Beach** is frequently voted the best beach in the US. Besides being pretty, it's also one of Maui's safest beaches, especially good for snorkeling and diving, and even receives occasional visits from monk seals. The one drawback to Kapalua is that the climate is undeniably worse even this short distance north of Lahaina, with rain and cloud more likely to drift in from the northeast.

Accommodation

The **condo** properties along Lower Honoapi'ilani Road make reasonable cut-price alternatives to the

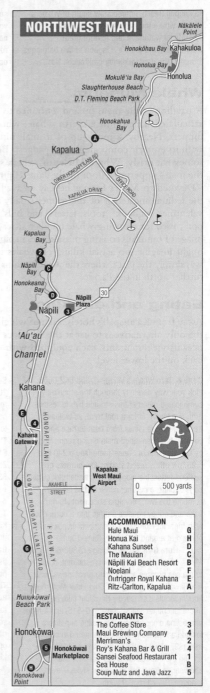

NORTHWEST MAUI

Nākālele Point
Honokōhau Bay Kahakuloa
Honolua Bay
Mokulē'ia Bay
Slaughterhouse Beach Honolua
D.T. Fleming Beach Park
Honokahua Bay
Kapalua
LOWER HONOAPI'ILANI RD
OFFICE ROAD
KAPALUA DRIVE
Kapalua Bay
Nāpili Bay
Honokeana Bay
Nāpili Nāpili Plaza 30
'Au'au Channel
Kahana
HONOAPI'ILANI
Kahana Gateway
LOWER HONOAPI'ILANI ROAD
Kapalua West Maui Airport
AKAHELE STREET
0   500 yards
Honokōwai Beach Park
HIGHWAY
Honokōwai
Honokōwai Marketplace
Honokōwai Point

ACCOMMODATION

Hale Maui	G
Honua Kai	H
Kahana Sunset	D
The Mauian	C
Nāpili Kai Beach Resort	B
Noelani	F
Outrigger Royal Kahana	E
Ritz-Carlton, Kapalua	A

RESTAURANTS

The Coffee Store	3
Maui Brewing Company	4
Merriman's	2
Roy's Kahana Bar & Grill	4
Sansei Seafood Restaurant	1
Sea House	B
Soup Nutz and Java Jazz	5

Tiny **Kapalua Airport** – a short distance above Hwy-30, halfway between Kapalua and Kāʻanapali – is too small to be served by anything other than commuter flights, principally Island Air service from Honolulu. For details of flight frequencies, see p.220. All the major car-rental chains have outlets at the airport – see p.23 – but there's no public transport.

Kāʻanapali and Kapalua resort hotels, though if you don't rent a car you could feel very stuck indeed.

Hale Maui 3711 Lower Honoapiʻilani Rd, Honokōwai ☎808/669-6312, ⓦwww.halemaui vacationrental.com. Small family-run "apartment hotel" in Honokōwai, offering one-bedroom suites that sleep up to five guests, with kitchens, washer-dryers, and *lānais*, but no phones; maid service is limited. Three-night minimum stay. ④

Honua Kai 130 Kai Malina Parkway, North Kāʻanapali ☎808/662-2800 or 1-888/718-5789, ⓦwww.honuakaimaui.com. This ultra modern luxury resort, Maui's newest, opened in 2009, having been controversially constructed in an area that had previously been spared development, in front of a lovely stretch of beach. All rooms and suites have huge glass balconies, and can sleep up to four. ⑧

Kahana Sunset 4909 Lower Honoapiʻilani Rd, Kahana ☎808/669-8700 or 1-800/669-1488, ⓦwww.kahanasunset.com. Luxury condos, spacious inside but squeezed close together, in lush gardens by a lovely sandy beach that's effectively restricted to guests only. Only the larger two-bedroom units have ocean views. Garden view ⑤, ocean view ⑥

The Mauian 5441 Lower Honoapiʻilani Rd, Nāpili ☎808/669-6205 or 1-800/367-5034, ⓦwww.mauian.com. Very friendly, laidback little resort, in vintage 1950s architectural style, right on ravishing Nāpili Beach. Extensively upgraded to a high standard, it consists of three two-story rows of tastefully furnished rooms, with very comfortable beds; most are studio apartments with kitchenettes, some are a little smaller and lack ocean views, but are very competitively priced. The only phone and TV are in the communal lounge and library, where a complimentary breakfast is served. ⑤

Nāpili Kai Beach Resort 5900 Lower Honoapiʻilani Rd, Nāpili ☎808/669-6271 or 1-800/367-5030, ⓦwww.napilikai.com. This sprawling 1960s resort was built much closer to the ocean than would be allowed these days, so guests can enjoy breathtaking Nāpili Bay right on their doorstep. Now thoroughly renovated, it's an independent property with a friendly old-time feel and a wonderful location; the on-site *Sea House* restaurant is reviewed below. ⑦

Noelani 4095 Lower Honoapiʻilani Rd, Kahana ☎808/669-8374 or 1-800/367-6030, ⓦwww .noelani-condo-resort.com. Fifty great-value condo apartments of all sizes, set on a promontory, so all units enjoy views across to Molokai. Amenities include two oceanfront pools, a hot tub, and laundry facilities. ④

Outrigger Royal Kahana 4365 Lower Honoapiʻilani Rd, Kahana ☎808/669-5911 or 1-800/447-7783, ⓦwww.outrigger.com. This oceanfront condo building, standing twelve stories high in central Kahana, enjoys views of Molokai and Lanai. While it's less intimate than the family resorts of Nāpili, it's undeniably smart, and all the a/c units, which include studios as well as one- and two-bedroom suites, have kitchens, washer-dryers, and private *lānais*. ④

Ritz-Carlton, Kapalua 1 Ritz-Carlton Drive, Kapalua ☎808/669-6200 or 1-800/241-3333, ⓦwww.ritzcarlton.com. The opulent, marble-fitted *Ritz-Carlton* was totally revamped in 2008 to give it a more intimate Hawaiian feel; it's a little far back from the beach, but there's no disputing the level of comfort, with its bright spacious rooms, multi-level swimming pool, nine-hole putting green, and lavish spa. ⑨

Eating and drinking

Considering its number of visitors, the Honokōwai-to-Kapalua stretch of northwest Maui is notably short of places to **eat** and **drink**. Barely any of the hotels and condos have restaurants, so the few options are largely concentrated in three highway-side **malls** – the Honokōwai Marketplace, the Kahana Gateway, and the Nāpili Plaza.

The Coffee Store Nāpili Plaza, 5095 Nāpili Hau St, Nāpili ☎808/669-4170, ⓦwww.mauicoffee.com. Small espresso bar, busy with active locals, offering pastries, sandwiches and internet access. Daily 6.30am–11pm.

Maui Brewing Company Kahana Gateway, 4405 Honoapi'ilani Hwy ☎808/669-3474, ⓦwww.maui brewingco.com. Large mall browpub, serving pilsners, stouts, and wheat beers brewed on the premises, plus a full bar menu ranging from $12 burgers and sandwiches to $17–20 entrees like pork ribs, jambalaya or shrimp pasta. Daily 11am–12.30am.

Merriman's I Bay Drive, Kapalua ☎808/669-6400, ⓦwww.merrimanshawaii .com. Exquisite "Hawaii Regional" restaurant in an absolutely sumptuous setting at the tip of an ocean-front promontory, best appreciated as the sun goes down. The food is out of this world, though so too are the prices, with entrees like wok-charred *ahi* or the succulent Maui beef fillet typically available at $30 "smaller" and $40 "full" sizes. Mixed sampler plates, at $32 for appetizers and $48 for entrees, are the way to go for larger groups. Daily 5–9pm; open for happy-hour cocktails 3–5pm.

Roy's Kahana Bar & Grill Kahana Gateway, 4405 Honoapi'ilani Hwy ☎808/669-6999, ⓦwww.roysrestaurant.com. Celebrity chef Roy Yamaguchi's Maui showcase is open for dinner only – which is just as well, given its lack of views. The aromas of its superb "Euro-Asian" food waft from its open kitchen as soon as you walk in. Signature dishes such as hibachi salmon, "butterfish" (black cod) steamed with *miso*, and "Roy's 'Original' Blackened Rare *Ahi*" appear on the menu as both appetizers (around $12) and entrees ($25–30); there are also mouthwatering specials each night. Daily 5.30–10pm.

Sansei Seafood Restaurant 600 Office Rd, Kapalua ☎808/669-6286, ⓦwww .sanseihawaii.com. Top-quality, dinner-only seafood specialist, which also has outlets in Kīhei (see p.257), and on Oahu and the Big Island. *Sansei* is fundamentally Japanese, though there's a strong Pacific Rim element as well. The fresh sushi selection includes a mouthwatering mango crab salad roll ($8), while entrees include a delicious prawn and scallops pasta ($20) and daily fish specials ($25). Karaoke until 1am on Thursday and Friday nights. Mon–Wed, Sat & Sun 5.30–10pm, Thurs & Fri 5.30pm–1am.

Sea House *Nāpili Kai Beach Resort*, 5500 Lower Honoapi'ilani Rd, Nāpili ☎808/669-1500, ⓦwww .napilikai.com. Very popular seafront restaurant, right on Nāpili Beach at the most upscale of the oceanside hotels. The food is good without being exceptional – conventional American breakfasts for around $10; lunchtime soups, salads, sandwiches, or sushi rolls for $10–15; and steak or seafood dinner entrees costing $24–34 – but the views from the oceanside tables are fabulous. Mon & Wed–Sun 8–10.30am, 11.30am–2pm & 6–9pm; Tues 5.30–9pm.

Soup Nutz and Java Jazz Honokōwai Marketplace, 3350 Lower Honoapi'ilani Rd ☎808/667-0787, ⓦwww.javajazz.net. At first glance, you'd think this funky, arty mall hangout is just a juice and espresso bar, but it actually serves pretty good food throughout the day, and with lots of comfy seating and a steady jazz soundtrack you may well feel tempted to linger despite the lack of views. The menu includes omelets ($8–12); falafel and other lunchtime sandwiches ($11–13); and evening specials that range up to steak and lobster ($21–35). Daily 6am–9pm.

Beaches beyond Kapalua

Honoapi'ilani Highway sweeps down beyond Kapalua to rejoin the ocean at **D.T. Fleming Beach Park**, in Honokahua Bay. The dunes here, knitted together with ironwood trees, drop sharply into the sea, and swimming can be dangerous, though surfers love the big waves. Full park amenities, including showers, restrooms, picnic tables, and the presence of lifeguards, make this a popular desti-nation for local families.

From here, the highway climbs again to cross a rocky headland. You can't see it from the road, but **Mokulē'ia Bay** lies at the foot of the cliffs. At several points along the highway, the landowners, Maui Pineapple, have built fences to stop people from clambering down through the undergrowth to shaded, sandy **Slaughterhouse Beach**. Keep your eyes peeled instead for the top of the concrete stairway that provides safe access; look for cars parked on the verge. Winter conditions usually preclude bathing, but nude sunbathing carries on year-round.

Both Mokulōʻia Bay and **Honolua Bay**, just past the point, have been set aside as a Marine Life Conservation District, and in summer offer some of the island's best **snorkeling**. Honolua's major claim to fame, however, is as Maui's most heralded **surfing** spot, and between September and April the waters regularly swarm with surfers. As long as the swell remains below five feet, intermediate surfers can enjoy some of the longest-lasting and most predictable waves in all Hawaii. By the time they exceed ten feet, however, only absolute experts can hope to survive; perils include not only a fearsome cave that seems to suck in every passing stray, but cut-throat competition from other surfers. Parking for surfers is at several ad hoc lots along the graded dirt roads that line the fields covering the headland on the far side of the bay. Large galleries of spectators assemble on the clifftop to watch the action, while the surfers themselves slither down to the ocean by means of treacherous trails.

To reach the **beach** at Honolua, park instead beside the road at the inland end of the bay and walk down. The access path is the width of a road, but the surface is terrible and driving on it is illegal. Taking it will lead you through a weird, lush forest with the feel of a Louisiana bayou, where every tree has been throttled by creeping vines. Across a (usually dry) streambed lies the neat, rocky curve of the beach itself, consisting largely of dark black rocks, with the eastern end of Molokai framed in the mouth of the bay.

The **snorkelers** who congregate at Honolua whenever the waves die down generally ease themselves in from the beach, but then have to swim a fair way out beyond the clear turquoise inshore waters to reach the coves and coral on the left side of the bay. Beyond here Honoapiʻilani Highway runs past one final beach, at **Honokōhau Bay**. You're still only five miles out of Kapalua here, but it feels like another world. The entire valley is swamped by a dense canopy of flowering trees; there's a hidden village in there, but it's hard to spot a single building. The beach itself is a small crescent of gray pebbles, used only by fishermen.

Kahekili Highway

Although on the map the **Kahekili Highway** looks like a good route to continue around northwest Maui and back to Wailuku, rental car companies generally advise their customers not to use it. Those warnings should be taken seriously: it's unquestionably a dangerous drive. And it's certainly not a short cut; Wailuku is little more than twenty miles beyond Honokōhau Valley, but you have to allow well over an hour for the journey.

While not quite on a par with the road to Hāna (see p.281), the Kahekili Highway can be exhilaratingly beautiful, and it provides a rare glimpse of how Maui must have looked before the advent of tourism. Often very narrow, but always smoothly surfaced, it appears to wind endlessly along the extravagantly indented coastline, alternating between scrubby exposed promontories, occasionally capable of supporting a pale meadow, and densely green, wet valleys.

Nākālele Point

Kahekili Highway begins at Maui's northernmost limit, **Nākālele Point**, 6.5 miles out of Kapalua, at milepost 38. This rolling expanse of grassy heathland fell victim a few years ago to a bizarre craze that swept most of Hawaii. In remote spots all over the islands, people started erecting miniature stone cairns, under the impression that they were maintaining an ancient tradition. Stacks of perhaps a dozen small rocks are still dotted all over the landscape.

Various deeply rutted dirt roads drop away from the highway toward the sea in this area, starting both from the parking lot at milepost 38 and from another more makeshift lot half a mile further on. Hiking in that direction enables you to inspect the small **light beacon** that warns passing ships of the rocky headland, and an impressive natural **blowhole** in the oceanfront shelf. Be exceedingly wary of approaching the water, however; several hikers have been swept off the rocks by rogue waves in recent years.

Kahakuloa

A few miles after Nākālele Point, the huge and very un-Hawaiian crag of **Kahakuloa Head** towers 636ft above the eastern entrance to Kahakuloa Bay. The name means "tall lord," on account of its supposed resemblance to a chieftain wearing a feathered cape; alongside it stands his attendant, a lesser peak known as Puʻu Kāhuliʻanapa. The verdant valley that stretches back from both once ranked among the most populous on Maui, and still looks like a classic *ahupuaʻa* – the fundamental ancient land division, reaching from the sea to the mountain via low-lying taro terraces and groves of palms and fruit trees.

The perfect little village of **KAHAKULOA** is poised just behind its beach of black and gray boulders. Close to the green clapboard church as you drive in, a couple of fruit stands, laden with fresh pineapples and other goodies, make tempting places to stop. The streambed nearby is lined with trees, while dirt roads crisscross the valley between the fields and the ramshackle houses. A little further back nestles the **St Francis Xavier Mission**, built in 1846.

Waiheʻe Ridge Trail

One of Maui's most enjoyable hikes, the **Waiheʻe Ridge Trail**, starts a mile up a spur road that branches *mauka* (inland) from Kahekili Highway at milepost 7, opposite the Mendes Ranch and roughly seven miles south of Kahakuloa. Signposted to *Camp Maluhia*, a scout camp, the dirt road is 2.8 miles north of the village school in **Waiheʻe**, which is in turn four miles north of Wailuku, the logical way to come if you're driving from central or South Maui.

This gorgeous climb, best done in the morning before the clouds set in, takes you as deep into the West Maui mountains as it's possible to go; allow at least two hours, and preferably three, for the round-trip. From the parking lot where the road makes a sharp curve right towards the camp itself, the trail starts off as a clear cement path beyond a barred gate. This is its steepest section, but soon comes to an end, when you turn left to enter a pine and eucalyptus forest. Before long you emerge from that in turn, to enjoy views down into Waiheʻe Valley, over to a double waterfall embedded in the next ridge to the north, and back across the isthmus to Haleakalā Highway snaking up the volcano.

For all this first stretch of the trail, which totals 1.5 miles, it looks as though you're heading for the crest of the ridge ahead. Ultimately, however, the path sidesteps across a brief razorback to reach an unexpected high mountain valley. The terrain here is extremely marshy, but you're soon climbing again, this time through tree-less uplands filled with native Hawaiian plants and shrubs, including some spectacular orchids and also stunted red- and orange-blossomed *lehua* trees.

The trail ends at an unsheltered picnic table in a clearing 2.25 miles up. By now you're probably well up into the clouds, but if you're lucky enough to be here on a clear morning, you can see most of northern Maui from this spot, which is the summit of Lanilili ("Small Heaven") Peak but still well short of the overall summit of West Maui. Towering cliffs and waterfalls lie ahead, while as you look north towards the ocean, Molokai is clearly visible beyond the rocky pinnacle of Kahakuloa.

Waihe'e Valley

Beyond Waihe'e Ridge, the road drops steadily down to Waihe'e, by which time you're clearly out of the backwoods. The traffic picks up again, and the highway broadens for the final four miles to Wailuku.

At times during the past few years, it has been possible to drive half a mile inland from Waihe'e on Waihe'e Valley Road, and then take a two-hour hike up into the rainforest of **Waihe'e Valley** itself. It's one of Maui's finest trails, but it crosses private land, and at the time this book went to press it was only accessible on **guided hikes** run by Maui Eco-Adventures (daily 8am & 2.30pm; adults $125, under-13s $62.50; ⓣ 808/661-7720, ⓦ www.ecomaui.com).

Central Maui: the isthmus

The plains of **central Maui**, overshadowed by mighty Haleakalā to the east and the West Maui mountains to the west, were formed as a narrow "neck" when eroded rock washed down the slopes of the island's two volcanic massifs and fused them together. Measuring just seven miles north to south, this is the economic heartland of Maui. In ancient times, only **Wailuku**, on the western fringes, held much of a population. From a royal enclosure at the mouth of the stunning **'Iao Valley**, its chiefs ruled a region known as Nā Wai 'Ōha, watered by four rivers that flowed down from the West Maui mountains.

The rest of the isthmus was described by the nineteenth-century British traveler Isabella Bird as "a Sahara in miniature, a dreary expanse of sand and shifting sand hills, with a dismal growth of thornless thistles and indigo." Only since the sugar barons created irrigation channels to carry water from the eastern flanks of Haleakalā has the land been capable of supporting the agriculture that now makes it green. As a result, Wailuku and its upstart neighbor **Kahului** are now home to nearly half of Maui's 140,000 inhabitants – the workers who keep this fantasy island going.

Kahului

KAHULUI may be the largest town on Maui, and hold the island's principal harbor and airport, but it's not an interesting, let alone historic, place to visit. There's next to nothing to see, and you could miss it altogether with a clear conscience.

Having started the nineteenth century as a cluster of grass shacks, Kahului grew in tandem with the expansion of commercial agriculture. At first it was an unsanitary place: an outbreak of plague in 1900 forced the authorities to burn down the oceanfront Chinatown district and ring the whole town with rat-proof fences. When it was rebuilt, the harbor was greatly expanded and dredged to provide the only deep-water anchorage on the island. Kahului has remained Maui's main port to this day. It was further boosted after World War II, when new, low-cost housing lured laborers away from plantation towns such as Pā'ia.

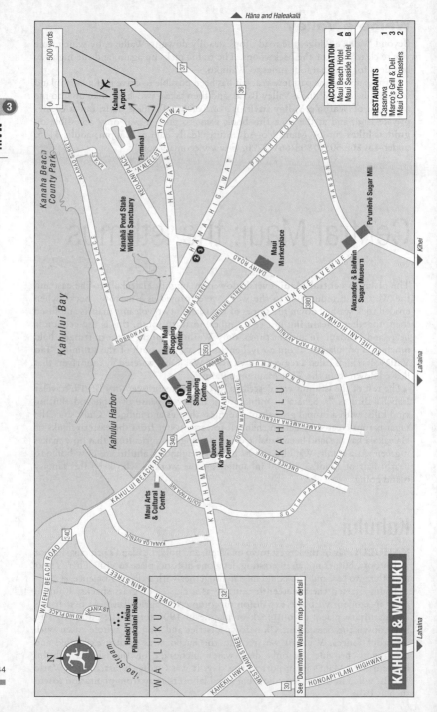

Hāna and Haleakalā

500 yards

0

Kahului Airport

Terminal

Kanaha Beach County Park

Kanahā Pond State Wildlife Sanctuary

Kahului Bay

Kahului Harbor

AMALA PLACE

ALAHAO STREET

KA'A ST

ALIHIO STREET

KEOLANI PLACE

'A'ALELE STREET

HALEAKALĀ HIGHWAY

37

36

HANA HIGHWAY

PULEHU ROAD

HANSEN ROAD

Pu'unēnē Sugar Mill

Maui Marketplace

Alexander & Baldwin Sugar Museum

DAIRY ROAD

HUKILIKE STREET

SOUTH PU'UNĒNĒ AVENUE

380

WEST PAPA AVENUE

KŪIHELANI HIGHWAY

Kīhei

Lahaina

ACCOMMODATION
Maui Beach Hotel   A
Maui Seaside Hotel   B

RESTAURANTS
Casanova   1
Marco's Grill & Deli   3
Maui Coffee Roasters   2

2 3

HOBRON AVE

Maui Mall Shopping Center

Kahului Shopping Center

350

KAHAWAHINE ST

KANE ST

KAILAWAHINE ST

LONO AVENUE

KAMEHAMEHA AVENUE

SOUTH WAKEA AVENUE

ONEHEE AVENUE

KAHULUI

B A

1

Queen Ka'ahumanu Center

340

KA'AHUMANU AVENUE

KAHULUI BEACH ROAD

340

Maui Arts & Cultural Center

SOUTH PAPA AVE

KANALOA AVENUE

SOUTH PAPA AVENUE

WAIEHU BEACH ROAD

340

KU HIO PLACE

KANIA ST

LOWER MAIN STREET

WEST MAIN STREET

KAHEKILI HWY

32

30

HONOAPI'ILANI HIGHWAY

WAILUKU

'Īao Stream

Halekiʻi Heiau
Pihanakalani Heiau

N

See 'Downtown Wailuku' map for detail

KAHULUI & WAILUKU

Lahaina

Arrival

Almost all visitors to Maui arrive at **Kahului Airport**, a couple of miles east of town. See p.19 for details of trans-Pacific flights; inter-island services are summarized on p.22. All the national **rental car** chains (see p.24) have offices immediately across from the terminal. In addition, Speedishuttle (☎808/661-6667 or 1-877/242-5777, ⓦwww.speedishuttle.com) run **shuttle vans** on demand to all the resorts. Typical rates start at around $18 to Kīhei, $30 to Lahaina, and $40 to Nāpili.

Maui Bus (☎808/871-4838, ⓦwww.mauicounty.gov/bus; see also p.220) run frequent **buses** between the Queen Ka'ahumanu Center in downtown Kahului and the airport, with alternate services continuing either to Pā'ia or to Makawao. The same company also offers hourly buses from the Queen Ka'ahumanu Center to **Lahaina**, and to both **Kīhei** and **Wailea** ($1; departures daily 5.30am–7.30pm), in both instances via Mā'alaea.

Accommodation

If you plan to spend most of your time on Maui touring the island or windsurfing at Ho'okipa just down the coast (see p.280), Kahului's pair of aging **hotels** may suit your needs. Although both are right in the center of town, Kahului is not a place you'd choose to stroll around and doesn't make a lively overnight stop.

Maui Beach Hotel 170 W Ka'ahumanu Ave ☎808/877-0051, ⓦwww.mauibeachhotel.net. Although it's right on the oceanfront, this veteran hotel is also in the middle of Kahului's downtown business district, and following a long-overdue renovation now sensibly pitches itself at bargain-conscious business travelers rather than tourists. Its 150 rooms are small and simple, but adequate. ➍

Maui Seaside Hotel 100 W Ka'ahumanu Ave ☎808/877-3311 or 1-800/560-5552, ⓦwww.mauiseasidehotel.com. Bland but reasonably well-kept waterfront hotel, with a swimming pool and its own artificial beach. The location, across from the shopping malls, is hardly romantic, but at least it is by the sea and makes a convenient and relatively inexpensive base. ➌

The Town

Central Kahului is dominated by a characterless sprawl of aging shopping malls along **Ka'ahumanu Avenue**. Only the **Queen Ka'ahumanu Mall** itself is worth visiting, for its generic upmarket stores and a few more distinctive crafts outlets. There's no point trying to get close to the **waterfront**, though, which is lined with factories and warehouses. Further out, the **Maui Marketplace** mall, on Dairy Road, is noteworthy as the home of a Borders **bookstore**.

Maui Arts and Cultural Center

Just off the busy Kahului Beach Road, which curves around Kahului Harbor, the **Maui Arts and Cultural Center** (☎808/242-7469, ⓦwww.mauiarts.org) is Maui's premier venue for the visual and performing arts. In addition to a four-thousand-seat open-air amphitheater, it houses two separate indoor theaters and an art gallery. Those big-name musicians who make it as far as Maui play here, and the Maui Symphony Orchestra puts on half a dozen concerts each winter.

Kanahā Pond State Wildlife Sanctuary

Half a mile west of Kahului Airport, just before Hwy-36A meets Hwy-36, a tiny roadside parking lot marks the only public access to the **Kanahā Pond State Wildlife Sanctuary**. This marshy saltwater lagoon – used as a fishpond until it was choked by the mud dredged up from Kahului Harbor – is now set aside for endangered bird species, among them the black-necked *ae'o* stilt and the *'auku'u* (night heron).

There are no official opening hours; visitors simply make their way through the gate and follow a pedestrian causeway for fifty yards out to a windy, open-sided viewing shelter. Although it's not a very prepossessing spot, with the factories of Kahului Harbor clearly visible to the left, and planes passing low overhead, it's surprisingly peaceful, and waterfowl do indeed seem to like it. Wading birds can almost always be spotted picking their way through the shallow waters, though when it comes to smaller species you're likely to hear more than you actually see.

Kanahā Beach County Park

Due east of central Kahului, Amala Place runs through an industrial area behind Kanahā Pond. Even on the ocean side of the airport, before the road joins Alahao Street, you'll find plenty of places where you can park beside the road and walk through the trees to find a long strip of empty beach.

However, the most popular oceanfront spot is the large **Kanahā Beach County Park** which, despite its proximity to the runways, is completely undisturbed by the comings and goings. Its shallow, choppy turquoise waters are ideal for novice **windsurfers**, who come from all over the world to swirl back and forth against the backdrop of ʻĪao Valley and the West Maui mountains. Among companies offering windsurfing lessons here (at $80–90 for 2hr 30min, including equipment rental) are Action Sports Maui (☎808/871-5857, ⓦwww.actionsportsmaui.com), and Alan Cadiz's HST Windsurfing School (☎808/871-5423 or 1-800/968-5423, ⓦwww .hstwindsurfing.com). Windsurfers ready for the big time graduate to **Hoʻokipa**, just a few miles east but light-years away in terms of difficulty; see p.280.

For its full, considerable length, the beach is fringed by pine trees, with fallen needles creating a soft carpet just behind. Local clubs keep their outrigger canoes here, and you're likely to see them practicing. The lawns under the trees have picnic tables.

A **campground** here, administered by the county parks office (see p.221), holds seven individual sites ($3 per night; three-night maximum stay), but being so near to the airport it's not really a location to recommend.

Alexander & Baldwin Sugar Museum

There's no missing the rusty red hulk of the **Puʻunēnē Sugar Mill**, alongside Hwy-350 a mile south of Kahului. Still belching smoke as it consumes cane from the surrounding fields, this was the largest sugar mill in the world when it was built in 1902, and is the only one still operating in Hawaii. Easily overlooked, however, is the smaller building just across from the mill that houses the **Alexander & Baldwin Sugar Museum** (Mon–Sat 9.30am–4.30pm; adults $7, under-13s $2; ⓦwww.sugar museum.com).

The museum relates the history of sugar production on Maui, a tale of nineteenth-century scheming and skullduggery that may not be capable of holding your interest for very long. Alexander & Baldwin was one of the original "Big Five" companies at the heart of the Hawaiian economy – see p.420 – and remains a prominent island name to this day. **Samuel T. Alexander** and **Henry Baldwin** started growing sugar at Pāʻia in 1869 and constructed the first irrigation channel in 1878 to carry water from East Maui to the central isthmus. Their great rival was **Claus Spreckels**, who used his royal connections to acquire land and water rights at "Spreckelsville" near Pāʻia, and all but controlled the Hawaiian sugar industry before losing favor with the king and being forced to return to California. Alexander and Baldwin were then free to expand their operations across Maui, centered on the processing facilities at Puʻunēnē.

Scale models in the museum include a whirring but incomprehensible re-creation of the main mill machinery, and a relief map of the whole island. More illuminating displays focus on the lives of the plantation laborers, showing the thick clothes they

wore to protect against the dust and poisonous centipedes, and the numbered *bango* tags by which they were identified in place of names. No bones are made of the fact that the multi-ethnic workforce was deliberately, but ultimately unsuccessfully, segregated to avoid solidarity. The museum store is well stocked with books on ethnic and labor history, as well as souvenir packets of raw sugar.

Eating and drinking

Kahului is disappointingly short of **restaurants**, and few people would choose to drive here from elsewhere on Maui in search of a good meal. There are, however, a few possibilities scattered around the town's lesser malls, while the breezy **Queen's Market** area, upstairs at the Queen Ka'ahumanu Center, holds a wide assortment of fast-food counters and a couple of **bars**, and there's a smaller food court at the Maui Marketplace.

Bistro Casanova 33 Lono Ave ☎808/873-3650. Smart, citified offshoot of Makawao's long-standing Italian stalwart (see p.265), suited to upscale local appetites but lacking the views or ambience tourists might want. Lunchtime sandwiches, paninis, and pasta specials for $9–14; dinner entrees range through the same pasta dishes to fancier options such as bouillabaisse for $26, paella for two at $28, or *osso buco* at $36. Mon–Sat 11.30am–2.30pm & 5.30–11pm.

Marco's Grill & Deli 395 Dairy Rd ☎808/877-4446. Lively Italian restaurant, in a modern mall not far from the airport. Once the breakfast omelets, pancakes, and espressos have finished, the lunch and dinner menus feature deli sandwiches, pizzas (from $12), and rich meat and seafood pastas, including rigatoni with prosciutto in a vodka sauce ($20). Daily 7.30am–10pm.

Maui Coffee Roasters 444 Hāna Hwy ☎808/877-2877, ⓦwww.mauicoffeeroasters.com. This relaxed, daytime-only espresso bar with hand-painted tables is a popular hangout for windsurfers from the nearby beaches. Vegetarian wraps and sandwiches, like focaccia with mozzarella, are $6–8; try the fabulous raspberry-and-white-chocolate scones. Mon–Fri 7am–6pm, Sat 8am–5pm, Sun 8am–2.30pm.

Wailuku

The center of **WAILUKU** is barely two miles west of Kahului, and there's no obvious dividing line to mark where one town ends and the other begins. However, Wailuku, located at the mouth of the fertile and spectacular 'Īao Valley, has a very different geography and a much more venerable history. This lush area was what might be called the *poi* bowl of Maui, at the heart of the largest taro-growing area in Hawaii, and was home to generations of priests and warriors in ancient times.

Well into the twentieth century, Wailuku was the center of the island's nascent tourist industry, housing the few visitors Maui received and equipping their expeditions up Haleakalā. Much of its administrative and commercial role was then usurped by Kahului, and Wailuku went into decline. These days, it holds a handful of new county offices, but it remains a sleepy sort of place, easily seen in less than half a day. Nonetheless, it's one of the few towns on Maui that still feels like a genuine community, and can serve as a welcome antidote to the sanitized resorts elsewhere.

Information

The Maui office of the **Hawaii Visitors Bureau**, tucked away half a mile northeast of central Wailuku at 1727 Wili Pa Loop (Mon–Fri 8am–4.30pm; ☎808/244-3530 or 1-800/525-MAUI, ⓦwww.visitmaui.com), stocks lots of printed material.

Camping permits for Maui's state parks, also available online, are issued by the Department of Land and Natural Resources, opposite Ka'ahumanu Church at 54 S

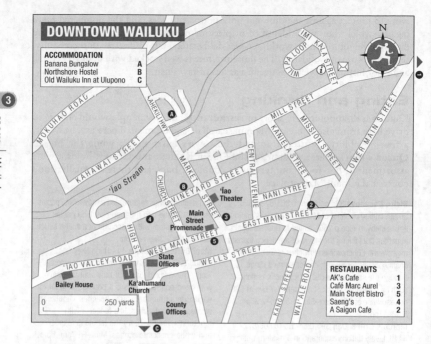

DOWNTOWN WAILUKU

ACCOMMODATION
Banana Bungalow   A
Northshore Hostel   B
Old Wailuku Inn at Ulupono C

RESTAURANTS
AK's Cafe   1
Café Marc Aurel   3
Main Street Bistro   5
Saeng's   4
A Saigon Cafe   2

High St (Mon–Fri 8am–3.30pm; ☎808/984-8109, ⓦwww.hawaiistateparks.org), while the county parks office is at Baldwin High School, just east of central Wailuku at 1580 Ka'ahumanu Ave (Mon–Fri 8am–1pm & 2.30–4pm; ☎808/270-7389, ⓦwww.co.maui.hi.us). For more details of camping on Maui, see p.221.

Accommodation

As Wailuku has Maui's two best-known **hostels** – and no hotels – the only people who spend the night here tend to be backpackers and surfers. One drawback for budget travelers is that the nearest beaches are several miles away, but the *Banana Bungalow* runs inexpensive minivan trips to them.

Banana Bungalow 310 N Market St ☎808/244-5090 or 1-800/846-7835, ⓦwww.mauihostel.com. Friendly independent hostel, open to non-Maui residents only, in a run-down light-industrial area not far from central Wailuku. Beds in four- and six-bed dorms are $25, while basic private rooms, without en-suite facilities, cost from $59 single, $68 double. Guests can hang out in the gardens and living rooms. There's a free shuttle service to the airport, plus a changing rotation of free excursions to all parts of the island, free internet access, and use of a hot tub. ①–②

Northshore Hostel 2080 Vineyard St ☎808/986-8095 or 1-866/946-7835, ⓦwww.northshorehostel .com. Refurbished budget accommodation in downtown Wailuku, with communal kitchen facili-ties. Beds in plain four- and six-bed dorms cost

$25, or $20 with leaflets available at the airport, while equally plain private rooms – each with just a bed or two bunks, and a closet – go for $50 single, $65 double. Popular with European travelers, who leave their surfboards propped against the giant banyan in the courtyard. Free shuttles to the airport and Kanahā Beach. ①–②

Old Wailuku Inn at Ulupono 2199 Kaho'okele St ☎808/244-5897 or 1-800/305-4899, ⓦwww.mauiinn.com. Spacious plantation-style home, in landscaped gardens a short walk south of central Wailuku, that's now a luxurious B&B. All ten rooms have tasteful 1930s-era furnishings, DVD players, private *lānais* and baths; some also have whirlpool spas. Guests share use of a living room and veranda. Two-night minimum stay. ⑤

Central Wailuku

The heart of Wailuku is where **Main Street**, the continuation of Ka'ahumanu Avenue, crosses **Market Street**. Both streets hold a small assortment of shops, the most interesting of which are the faded **antique** and **junk stores** along Market Street to the north, just before it drops down to cross the 'Īao Stream. Also look for the 1929 **'Īao Theater**, an attractive little playhouse on Market Street that typically puts on six Broadway-type shows each year (Sept–June; ☎ 808/242-6969, ⓦ www .mauionstage.com).

Ka'ahumanu Church, at the intersection of Main and High streets just west of the center, was founded in 1832. Naming it after Queen Ka'ahumanu, a convert to Christianity who was largely responsible for the destruction of the old Hawaiian religion (see p.288), was the idea of the Queen herself. The current building, whose four-story white spire has a clock face on each side, dates from 1876. It's not usually open to visitors, but you're welcome to attend the Hawaiian-language services at 9am on Sunday mornings.

Bailey House

The **Bailey House**, to the left of Main Street as it climbs west out of Wailuku as 'Īao Valley Road, is the best museum of general history on Maui (Mon–Sat 10am–4pm; adults $7, ages 7–13 $2, under-7s free; ⓦ www.mauimuseum.org). The oldest house on the island, it sits on what was once Maui's most highly prized plot of land, the site of a royal compound that controlled access to the sacred 'Īao Valley. Local chiefs donated it during the 1830s so the Central Maui Mission could build day-schools to teach adults and children to read. From 1837 until 1849, it was also the site of the **Wailuku Female Seminary**, a boarding school designed to produce "good Christian wives" for the male graduates of the Lahainaluna Seminary (see p.232).

The first occupant of the house was Reverend Jonathan Green, who resigned from the mission in 1842 to protest against the fact that the American Board of Commissioners for Foreign Missions accepted money from slave-owners. For the next fifty years, it was home to Edward Bailey and his wife Caroline Hubbard Bailey. He was a minister, schoolmaster, carpenter, and amateur painter, while she is remembered in the name of the long "Mother Hubbard" dresses, also known as *mu'umu'us*, that she made for local women.

After an entertaining introductory talk, visitors wander through rooms filled with period furniture. The largest room focuses on ancient Hawaii; finds from Maui, Lanai, and Kaho'olawe include bones, clubs, shark's-tooth weapons, and *leis* of shells and feathers. One large wooden platter was used for serving boiled dog – popular with Hawaiian women, who were forbidden to eat pork. There's also a copy of the only carved temple image ever found on Maui, a likeness of the pig-god Kamapua'a discovered in a remote sea cave. As the label points out, both the Baileys and the ancient Hawaiians alike would be appalled to see such a sacred item on public display.

A separate gallery downstairs is reserved for local landscapes painted by the white-bearded Edward Bailey in his old age, while the upstairs rooms are preserved more or less as the Baileys would have known them, though presumably they'd disavow the opium pipe and paraphernalia. A very solid wooden surfboard that once belonged to Duke Kahanamoku (see p.67) hangs in the garden.

Haleki'i and Pihanakalani heiaus

A mile from central Wailuku – but over three miles by road – the twin ancient temples of **Haleki'i** and **Pihanakalani** guard the Wailuku Plain from two separate

hillocks near the mouth of the 'Iao Stream (both open daily 7am–7pm; free). They can only be reached via a very convoluted route; follow Kahekili Highway all the way out of Wailuku to the north, double back south along Waiehu Beach Road, turn inland at Kuhio Place, and take the first left, Hea Place.

With rows of low-budget housing to the north and the industrial area of Kahului to the south, this is not the most evocative of sites, but raising your gaze toward the horizon provides fine views of the ocean, while, in the early morning, mighty Haleakalā can often be seen in its entirety. The short trail from the parking lot leads through scrubby soil to **Haleki'i Heiau**. Maui's ruling chief, Kahekili, lived at this "house of images" during religious ceremonies in the 1760s, when its uppermost platform would have held thatched huts interspersed with carved effigies of the gods. The hilltop is now bare, and the only remnants of the *heiau* are the lower stone terraces dropping down toward Kahului.

Both Haleki'i and **Pihanakalani Heiau**, on the far side of the gulch to the west, were *luakinis*, or temples used for human sacrifices. Pihanakalani was originally constructed sometime between 1260 and 1400 AD, and reoriented to face toward the Big Island during the eighteenth century. When Kamehameha the Great's Big Island warriors finally conquered Maui, they celebrated their victory at 'Iao Valley (see opposite) with a rededication ceremony at Pihana that included its final human sacrifice. Like all ancient Hawaiian temples, it was stripped of its images and largely dismantled after the death of Kamehameha. Significantly more traces survive than of Haleki'i, however, so it's worth continuing this far, by following the main path to the far side of the gulch.

Maui Tropical Plantation

The **Maui Tropical Plantation**, two miles south of Wailuku below the entrance to Waikapū Valley, may be a principal stop on round-island bus tours, but it's of minimal interest (daily 9am–5pm; free; ⓦ www.mauitropicalplantation.com). Visitors are free to walk into the main "Marketplace," where the stalls are piled with plants, fruits, and souvenirs, and then pass into the lackluster gardens beyond to explore pavilions describing the cultivation of macadamia nuts, sugar, coffee, and other local crops. You can see a few more unusual plants on forty-minute **tram tours** (daily 10am–3.15pm, every 45min; adults $14, under-13s $5), then take in the spectacular orchids in the nursery before you leave.

Eating and drinking

Wailuku holds a fine array of inexpensive **restaurants** and **cafés**. Most are downtown, including some funky little **takeout** options in the **Main Street Promenade** at 2050 Main, with the rest – too far to walk to from the center – strung along Lower Main Street as it loops down toward Kahului Harbor. For details of the "Lunch Like A Local" tour of Wailuku, see p.221.

AK's Cafe 1237 Lower Main St ☏ 808/244-8774, ⓦ www.akscafe.com. Bright, clean, and highly recommended little restaurant, well away from downtown on the road up from Kahului Harbor, with a mission to improve local health, via an emphasis on steaming or grilling. Great-value lunch specials at $7–9, such as the succulent baked *ono*, and $12–16 dinner entrees like crab cakes or lemon-grass duck breast, come with two sides. Tues–Fri 11am–1.30pm & 5.30–8.30pm, Sat 5.30–8.30pm.

Café Marc Aurel 28 N Market St ☏ 808/244-0852, ⓦ www.cafemarcaurel.com. Smart and very popular sidewalk café, serving espressos, smoothies, and pastries, and a bistro menu of $10 sandwiches and salads, plus pizzas and deli plates. Mon–Sat 7am–9pm.
Main Street Bistro 2051 Main St ☏ 808/244-6816, ⓦ www.msbmaui.com. The chef/owner of this simple, roomy café has an impressive track record, and now prepares good-value, healthy but filling meals for appreciative locals. Salad choices

include an *ahi tataki* fresh tuna salad for $13, Southern fried chicken costs $9, and daily specials like Thursday's beef brisket run $8–15; later in the afternoon they serve $12 burgers, and tapas-sized portions of dishes like beef brisket or grilled peppers. Mon–Fri 11am–7pm.
Saeng's 2119 Vineyard St ☎808/244-1567. Pleasant Thai restaurant, serving high-quality food at bargain prices. Plate lunches, on weekdays only, include honey-lemon chicken and garlic shrimp for $7–10, while selections from the full dinner menu cost a few dollars more. Mon–Fri 11am–2.30pm & 5–9.30pm, Sat & Sun 5–9.30pm.

A Saigon Cafe 1792 Main St ☎808/243-9560. Friendly, quirky, and very "local" Vietnamese restaurant with a wide-ranging and unusual menu, most of it very tasty. Hot and cold $10 noodle dishes and soups, a lot of curries and seafood stews at more like $20 – even a "Vietnamese bouillabaisse" – plus simpler steamed fish specials, and plenty of vegetarian options. Though the address is on Main Street, it's below the raised section of the highway; approach via Central Ave. Mon–Sat 10am–9.30pm, Sun 10am–8.30pm.

'Īao Valley

Main Street heads due west out of Wailuku to enter the high-walled cleft carved by 'Īao Stream into the West Maui mountains, with waterfalls dropping down pleated grooves in the rock on either side. For ancient Hawaiians, the gorgeous **'Īao Valley** (pronounced "ee-ow") was the equivalent of Egypt's Valley of the Kings: they buried their royal dead in the long-lost Olopio cave, and access was barred to commoners.

Kamehameha the Great conquered Maui in a battle here in 1790. The local armies were driven back into the valley from the shoreline, where they could be bombarded with impunity by the great cannon *Lopaka*, directed by John Young and Isaac Davis (see p.234). While the defeated general, Kalanikupule, the son of Maui's chief Kahekili, fled across the mountains, the corpses of his men choked 'Īao Stream. Hence the name by which the battle became known – **Kepaniwai**, "the water dam."

'Īao Valley is now one of Hawaii's most famous beauty spots, easily explored along a three-mile road that dead-ends at the stunning **'Īao Needle**, a 1200ft pinnacle of green-clad lava. The needle itself cannot be climbed, but you can admire it from various short trails that meander around its base.

Kepaniwai County Park

Just after the road crosses 'Īao Stream, a couple of miles out of Wailuku, **Kepaniwai County Park** is an attractive public garden set amid dramatic, curtain-like folds in the mountains (daily dawn–dusk; free). Its lawns and flowerbeds are laid out in themed areas paying tribute to Maui's Japanese, Chinese, and Portuguese immigrants, among others. Wandering the grounds you'll come upon a traditional thatched *hale*, ornamental pavilions, and miniature pagodas, as well as statues of anonymous sugarcane workers and even Dr Sun Yat Sen.

Hawaii Nature Center

The **Hawaii Nature Center**, adjoining Kepaniwai County Park, is largely an educational facility for schoolchildren and holds simple exhibitions on Hawaiian flora, fauna, and handicrafts (daily 10am–4pm; adults $6, under-13s $4; ☎808/244-6500, ⓦwww.hawaiinaturecenter.org). In addition, however, staff members conduct guided **hikes** in the 'Īao Valley area (Mon–Fri 11.30am & 1.30pm, Sat & Sun 11am & 2pm; adults $30, ages 5–12 $20). As the high-mountain trails are otherwise closed to visitors, these provide the only access to the wilderness beyond the Needle; the fee includes admission to the center.

ʻĪao Valley State Park

ʻĪao Valley Road meanders to a dead end three miles out of Wailuku, at the parking lot for **ʻĪao Valley State Park** (daily 7am–7pm; free). Although you can clearly see ʻĪao Needle from here, a short but steep footpath crosses the stream and climbs up a nearby knoll for even better views from a covered rain shelter. Two very short trails, paved but potentially slippery, loop down to the stream from the main footpath, one on either side of the stream. Gardens laid out with native plants line the one closer to the parking lot, and the small waterlogged taro patch here, similar to a paddy field, offers a great angle for photographs, as you look up past the footbridge toward the Needle itself.

Despite appearances, the velvety **ʻĪao Needle** is not freestanding, but simply a raised knob at the end of a sinuous ridge. Towering, head usually in the clouds, at the intersection of two lush valleys, it's what geologists call an "erosional residual" – a nugget of hard volcanic rock left behind when the softer surrounding rocks were eroded away. From this side, the Needle is an impressive 1200ft tall, but no higher than the ridges that surround it. The ancient Hawaiians, with their usual scatological gusto, named it Kukaʻemoku, which politely translates as "broken excreta."

This whole area owes its existence to the phenomenal amount of rain that falls on West Maui; the 5788ft peak of **Puʻu Kukui**, just over two miles from here, receives more than four hundred inches per year. Unless you come early in the morning, it's likely to be raining in ʻĪao Valley, but even when it's pouring you can usually look straight back down the valley to see the dry sunlit plains of the isthmus. The **trails** that lead beyond ʻĪao Needle can only be seen on the Hawaii Nature Center's guided hikes (see p.251).

Māʻalaea

The direct road south from Wailuku, **Honoapiʻilani Highway** (Hwy 30), is joined as it crosses the isthmus by highways from Kahului and Kīhei, all heading for Lahaina and the West Maui resorts. At the point where it reaches the south coast, six miles out of Wailuku, the little harbor at **MĀʻALAEA** is the preferred marina of Maui's cruise and pleasure boats. The largest contingent are the **Molokini** snorkel boats (see p.223), which collectively bring Māʻalaea to life very early in the morning, when the day's passengers assemble. At this time it also offers great views of Haleakalā, whose summit pokes out above the ring of clouds that usually obscures it from Kīhei.

Swimming anywhere near Māʻalaea is not recommended, but there are good **surfing** breaks just to the south, while **windsurfers** hurtle out into Māʻalaea Bay from the thin and unexciting strip of sand that stretches all the way east to Kīhei.

Maui Ocean Center

While Māʻalaea is not a town in any meaningful sense, it has acquired a center of sorts, in the form of the **Māʻalaea Harbor Village** mall. That in turn focuses on the **Maui Ocean Center**, a state-of-the-art **aquarium** providing a colorful introduction to the marine life of Hawaii (daily: Sept–June 9am–5pm; July & Aug 9am–6pm; adults $25.50, ages 3–12 $18.50; ☏808/270-7000, ⓦwww.maui oceancenter.com). It's not quite as large as you might expect from the size of the entrance fee, but the exhibits are well chosen and very well displayed, and this is Maui's most-visited paying attraction.

The most spectacular section comes first. The coral groves of the **Living Reef** (some of them fluorescent) hold such species as camouflaged scorpionfish, seahorses, octopuses, and bizarre "upside-down jellyfish." Eerie garden eels poke

▲ Maui Ocean Center

like blades of grass from the sandy sea-bed, but the star, of course, is the little *humuhumunukunukuapua'a* – literally, "the triggerfish with a snout like a pig."

Open-air terraces perched above the harbor hold tanks of huge rays and green sea turtles; as a rule, each turtle is kept at the aquarium for just a few months before being fitted with a tracking device and released into the ocean. Further on, additional displays cover the life cycle of **whales**, and the relationship between **Hawaiians and the sea**, illustrating traditional fishing techniques and equipment. A final huge tank holds **pelagic**, or open-ocean, sea creatures; its walk-through glass tunnel means that you can stand beneath mighty sharks and rays as they swim above your head. Certified scuba-divers can arrange to take an accompanied **dive** into the tank for a one-on-one shark encounter (Mon, Wed & Fri 8.15am; $200); some divers have even been married in the tank.

Practicalities

Half-a-dozen characterless **condo** buildings line up beyond Mā'alaea Harbor, along Hau'oli Street, but it's not recommended as a place to stay. There are a couple of ordinary **restaurants**, aimed at snorkel-cruise passengers, in the Harbor Village mall, while *Kylie's Aloha Deli* (☎808/249-8078) sells good-value snacks and coffee. The best place to eat is the large, scenic, and very expensive *Mā'alaea Waterfront Restaurant*, nearby at 50 Hau'oli St (daily 5–9.30pm; ☎808/244-9028, ⓦwww.waterfrontrestaurant.net), where the menu focuses on freshly caught fish, with a cioppino stew priced at $46. You can also buy fish for yourself at the Mā'alaea Fish Market (Mon–Sat 10am–4pm), just around the harbor.

253

South Maui

The area generally referred to as **South Maui** is in fact the western shoreline of East Maui, stretching south of Māʻalaea Bay. Until well after World War II this was one of the island's least populated districts, a scrubby, exposed, and worthless wasteland. Since then, a largely unattractive and almost unchecked ribbon of resort development has snaked down the coast, with the mass-market hotels and condos of **Kīhei** in the north being joined more recently by far more exclusive luxury properties at **Wailea** and **Mākena**.

Almost all the way down, narrow strips of white sand fill each successive bay, so most hotels are within easy walking distance of a good stretch of **beach**. The development stops just short of the largest beach of all, **Oneloa** or **Big Beach**, while the coastal highway peters out not far beyond. This final stretch, and the oceanfront trail to secluded **La Pérouse Bay**, is the only part of South Maui worth visiting on a sightseeing tour of the island; none of the resort communities holds any interest in itself.

Kīhei

Stretching for seven miles south from Māʻalaea Bay, **KĪHEI** is a totally formless sprawl of a place, whose only landmarks consist of one dull mall or condo building after another. That said, it can be a perfectly pleasant place to spend your vacation, with abundant inexpensive lodging and dining options and plentiful **beaches**. Just don't come to Kīhei expecting a town in any sense of the word.

During the 1960s, Kīhei spread for just a hundred yards to either side of the point where the cross-island highway reached Māʻalaea Bay. **North Kīhei Road** is still a hundred yards long, but **South Kīhei Road** now keeps going for around five miles. It's not totally built up, but only occasional gaps of unused land remain undeveloped; Kīhei was in the 1990s ranked as the second-fastest-growing community in the United States. Traffic congestion is so rife that for all journeys of any length, you'd do better to follow the parallel **Piʻilani Highway**, half a mile or so up the hillside.

Accommodation

There's little difference between Kīhei's countless **condos** and **hotels**, with standards in even the cheapest options tending to be perfectly adequate. Very few visitors

---

South Maui public transport

As ever, renting a vehicle is by far the most convenient way for South Maui visitors to explore the island. However, Maui Bus (☏ 808/871-4838, ⓦ www.mauicounty.gov/bus; see also p.220) runs hourly **buses** between the Queen Kaʻahumanu Center in Kahului and both **Kīhei** and **Wailea**, via **Māʻalaea** ($1; departs Kahului daily 5.30am–7.30pm, the Shops At Wailea daily 6.30am–8.30pm), and also a separate loop between Kīhei's Piʻilani Shopping Center and Māʻalaea ($1; departs Kīhei daily 4.53am–7.53pm). There's no direct service to Kahului Airport, but you can change buses at the Queen Kaʻahumanu Center to get there.

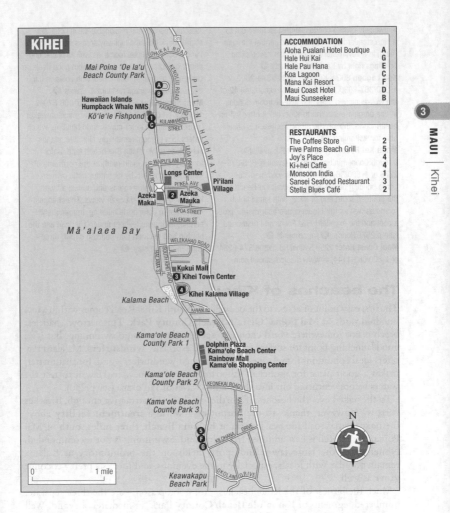

KĪHEI

Mai Poina 'Oe Ia'u Beach County Park

Hawaiian Islands Humpback Whale NMS
Kō'ie'ie Fishpond

Longs Center

Azeka Makai
Azeka Mauka

Pi'ilani Village

Mā'alaea Bay

Kukui Mall
Kīhei Town Center
Kīhei Kalama Village

Kalama Beach

Kama'ole Beach County Park 1

Dolphin Plaza
Kama'ole Beach Center
Rainbow Mall
Kama'ole Shopping Center

Kama'ole Beach County Park 2

Kama'ole Beach County Park 3

Keawakapu Beach Park

0   1 mile

N

ACCOMMODATION

Aloha Pualani Hotel Boutique	A
Hale Hui Kai	G
Hale Pau Hana	E
Koa Lagoon	C
Mana Kai Resort	F
Maui Coast Hotel	D
Maui Sunseeker	B

RESTAURANTS

The Coffee Store	2
Five Palms Beach Grill	5
Joy's Place	4
Ki+hei Caffe	4
Monsoon India	1
Sansei Seafood Restaurant	3
Stella Blues Café	2

simply pass through for a single night; there are no rock-bottom budget alternatives or B&Bs, and most places insist on a minimum stay of at least three nights. Rates on the whole are low, but Kīhei is more seasonally sensitive than most destinations, and in peak season (mid-Dec to March) you can expect to pay perhaps $50 over the price code given below.

Aloha Pualani Hotel Boutique 15 Wailana Place ☎808/875-6990 or 1-866/870-6990, ⓦwww.alohapualani.com. Five two-story suites across from Ma'alaea Bay at the north end of Kīhei, providing luxurious personalized accommodations. Each suite has a living room, kitchen, bedroom, and *lānai*, and they're clustered around a central pool and bar. On-site owners provide breakfast and advice. No under-16s; two-night minimum stay. ➏

Hale Hui Kai 2994 S Kīhei Rd ☎808/879-1219 or 1-800/809-6284, ⓦwww.halehuikaimaui.com. Comfortable, spacious oceanfront condos facing Keawakapu Beach at Kīhei's southern end. Each sleeps up to four, not all have a/c; pick the one you fancy from the website. They don't take credit cards, which can be a problem for international visitors; five-night minimum stay. ➎

Hale Pau Hana 2480 S Kīhei Rd ☎808/879-2715 or 1-800/367-6036, ⓦwww.hphresort.com.

Individually owned condos, almost all fitted out to a high standard and sharing good central management, in a seven-story block or two lower-slung buildings right by Kama'ole 2 beach. ❻

Koa Lagoon 800 S Kīhei Rd ☎808/879-3002 or 1-800/367-8030, ⓦwww.koalagoon.com. All 42 of the well-equipped one- and two-bedroom condos in this bargain priced north-Kīhei block offer full-on ocean views, though the attractive beach is unsuitable for swimming. ❹

Mana Kai Resort 2960 S Kīhei Rd; available through Condominium Rentals Hawaii ☎808/879-2778 or 1-800/367-5242, ⓦwww.crhmaui.com. Large building beside lovely Keawakapu Beach at the grander, south end of Kīhei, with small hotel rooms as well as full-blown condo apartments, plus a pool and the excellent *Five Palms* grill restaurant (see p.257). Rooms ❹, apartments ❻

Maui Coast Hotel 2259 S Kīhei Rd ☎808/874-6284 or 1-800/663-1144, ⓦwww.mauicoasthotel.com.

Tasteful, upscale, and reasonable-value hotel, set slightly back from the highway across from Kama'ole Park 1. Standard hotel rooms, as well as pricier one- and two-bedroom suites; no views, but good deals on car rental, plus an attractive pool with poolside bar, and an above-average restaurant, *Spices*. ❻

Maui Sunseeker 551 S Kīhei Rd ☎808/879-1261 or 1-800/532-6284, ⓦwww.mauisunseeker.com. This small hotel-cum-condo building, which caters to a predominantly gay clientele, stands very close to Mā'alaea Bay beach (and, unfortunately, also the main road) at the north end of Kīhei. As renovated by its enthusiastic owners, it offers great-value rooms and suites, all with kitchen facilities and ocean views. The cheapest rooms are in a separate building, immediately behind; all guests (except under-18s) can use the hot tub and deck on that building's roof; three-night minimum stay. ❹

The beaches of Kīhei

The first easy point of access to the ocean along South Kīhei Road comes within a few hundred yards, at **Mai Poina 'Oe Ia'u Beach County Park**. This narrow, shadeless beach is not somewhere you'd choose to spend a day, or to go swimming, but it's a good launching point for surfers, kayakers, and especially **windsurfers**. Mā'alaea Bay offers ideal conditions for relatively inexperienced windsurfers – and, for that matter, makes a good place for proficient sailboarders who are new to Hawaii to test the waters before venturing out into the mighty waves of Ho'okipa (see p.280).

To the naked eye, the beaches of northern Kīhei look attractive enough, if rather narrow. However, thanks to the output of a **sewage treatment facility** above the next formal roadside beach park, at **Kalama Beach**, three miles south of Mai Poina, this stretch is best admired from dry land. Swimming is not recommended. Nonetheless, the large lawns and sports fields on the promontory at Kalama remain popular with locals, especially in the evenings, and there's a pretty coconut grove as well.

Much the busiest of the Kīhei beaches – for good reason – are the three separate, numbered segments of **Kama'ole Beach County Park**, immediately beyond. Well past the reach of the sewage, they all boast clean white sand and are generally safe for swimming, with lovely views across the bay to West Maui, and all are constantly supervised by lifeguards. Most of beautifully soft **Kama'ole 1** beach is very close to the road, but it also curves away out of sight to the north, which is where you're likely to find the best snorkeling conditions. Little **Kama'ole 2**, cradled between two headlands, is a bit short on shade, and very near a large concentration of condos, which leaves long, broad **Kama'ole 3** as the pick of the bunch. Families gather under the giant trees on its wide lawns, while the beach itself, which is especially popular with boogie-boarders, is shielded from the road at the bottom of a ten-foot grassy slope.

In high season, **Keawakapu Beach Park**, at the far south end of South Kīhei Road, makes an inviting and less crowded alternative. Swimming is best in the center, while there's good snorkeling off the rocks to the south, thanks to an artificial offshore reef made up mostly of old automobile parts that were submerged to boost the fish population.

Hawaiian Islands Humpback Whale National Marine Sanctuary

At the northern end of Kīhei, squeezed onto a minor headland not far south of Mai Poina 'Oe Ia'u Beach, a compound at 726 S Kīhei Rd serves as the headquarters of the **Hawaiian Islands Humpback Whale National Marine Sanctuary** (☎808/879-2818 or 1-800/831-4888, ⓦwww.hawaiihumpbackwhale.noaa.gov). The organization was created to protect and study the estimated three thousand humpback whales that annually winter in Hawaiian waters. Enthusiastic volunteers can explain its work and talk you through the displays in the **Sanctuary Learning Center** (Mon–Fri 10am–3pm; free). Though the blue office building on the seafront is not open to the public, its spacious veranda makes an ideal spot for watching whales in Mā'alaea Bay.

A six-acre tract of ocean immediately offshore is enclosed by the ancient lava walls of the **Kō'ie'ie Fishpond**, which dates originally from the sixteenth century. This area was then the site of the village of **Kalepolepo**, whose inhabitants left after the fishpond became silted up during the 1860s.

MAUI | Kīhei

Eating and drinking

The **restaurants** listed below represent just a small selection of what's available in Kīhei. Virtually all the malls also hold at least one budget **diner** or takeout place, and most have an **espresso bar**, too.

The Coffee Store Azeka Mauka, 1279 S Kīhei Rd ☎808/875-4244, ⓦwww.mauicoffee.com. Cheery mall café serving espressos of all kinds, plus breakfast pastries, lunch salads, pizzas, and sandwiches. Mon–Sat 6am–5pm, Sun 6am–3pm.

Five Palms Beach Grill *Mana Kai Resort*, 2960 S Kīhei Rd ☎808/879-2607, ⓦwww.fivepalms restaurant.com. Beachfront restaurant in a spectacular setting on the ground floor of a condo building, with open terraces within earshot of the waves, and live music nightly. An à la carte brunch menu is served until 2.30pm daily, including a crabcake-eggs Benedict for $18, or salad or lunch specials for $13–20. Dinner items – mostly Pacific Rim, along with standard ribs and steaks – are delicious and beautifully presented, with appetizers such as coriander-seared Cajun seared scallops ($18) and entrees like fresh *opah* (moonfish), and Kaho'olawe rack of lamb ($28–43). Daily 8am–9pm.

Joy's Place 1993 S Kīhei Rd ☎808/879-9258. Organic, predominantly vegetarian, takeout that's ideal for budget-conscious beach-goers; delicious soups and sandwiches, and legendary collard-green wraps. Daily except Sun 10am–3pm.

Kīhei Caffe 1945 S Kīhei Rd ☎808/879-2230. Friendly café offering espressos, flavored lattes, and smoothies, plus breakfast eggs and pancakes and $7 lunchtime sandwiches or burgers, to take out or eat at a shaded roadside gazebo. Daily 5am–3pm.

Monsoon India 760 S Kīhei Rd ☎808/875-6666, ⓦwww.monsoonindiamaui.com. Surprisingly good Indian restaurant, with full-on ocean views. Meat- or

fish-based curries and kebabs cost around $20, vegetarian options like roasted eggplant more like $15, and there's a Sunday brunch buffet. Mon–Sat 11.30am–2.30pm & 5–9pm, Sun 11am–3pm & 5–9pm.

Sansei Seafood Restaurant Kīhei Town Center, 1881 S Kīhei Rd ☎808/669-6286, ⓦwww.sanseihawaii.com. Sensational Japanese–Hawaiian, dinner-only restaurant, also in Kapalua (see p.240). Individual appetizers and entrees are invariably delicious, but the special Omakase Tasting Menu, at $70 for two, is fabulous value, offering copious portions of signature dishes such as *miso* butterfish and the Asian rock-shrimp cake. It's all pretty hectic, so don't expect to linger over a romantic dinner, and there are no views, but it's a dynamic spot and the food is out of this world. Laser karaoke until 2am at weekends. Mon–Wed & Sun 5.30–10pm, Thurs–Sat 5.30pm–1am.

Stella Blues Café Azeka Mauka, 1279 S Kīhei Rd ☎808/874-3779, ⓦwww.stellablues.com. California-style café, complete with ponytailed waiters and Grateful Dead posters, and centering on a huge wood-burning grill. Locals regularly vote it Maui's best restaurant, though that owes more to the live music (especially Saturdays) and general ambience than the food, which is dependably good but not exceptional. The menu includes continental and cooked breakfasts ($7–12); burger, salad, and sandwich lunches ($10–16 (try the special of grilled and roasted vegetables on herb bread); and dinners like fettuccini Alfredo, Cajun chicken, crab cakes, and ribs ($18–28). Daily 7.30am–11pm.

Wailea and Mākena

Both South Kīhei Road and Piʻilani Highway end on the southern fringes of Kīhei. The only road south from here, branching off Okolani Drive halfway between the two, is **Wailea Alanui Drive**, which becomes **Makena Alanui Drive** after a couple of miles. It's forced to run several hundred yards inland by half a dozen colossal resort hotels, on a scale to rival any in Hawaii. Neither Wailea nor Mākena is a town as such; were it not for the resorts, the names would not even appear on island maps. The only **shops** are congregated in the very upmarket **Shops at Wailea** mall, whose target audience can be guessed from the presence of Louis Vuitton, Cartier, and Dolce & Gabbana stores.

Until the 1950s, what is now **WAILEA** was just barren ocean-front acreage belonging to the ʻUlupalakua Ranch (see p.268). It was then bought by Matson Cruise Lines, who planned to turn it into the "City of Roses," but nothing happened until control of Matson passed to Alexander & Baldwin in the 1970s.

MĀKENA, which blends imperceptibly into the south end of Wailea, was developed even more recently: its first hotel appeared at the end of the 1980s. During the late nineteenth century, however, it ranked as Maui's second port after Lahaina, thanks to the comings and goings at ʻUlupalakua Ranch, just two miles higher up the gentle slope of Haleakalā. These days, in the absence of any direct road, getting to the ranch requires a forty-mile drive.

Wailea and Mākena together constitute a luxurious enclave of velvet golf courses and pristine beaches, where non-guests feel distinctly unwelcome. That said, outsiders are free to use any of the

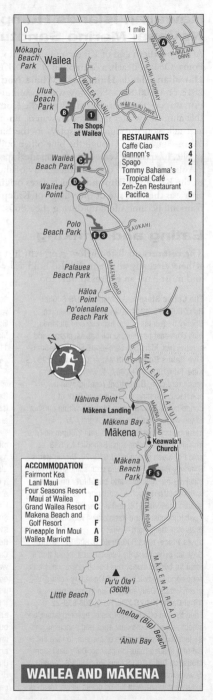

RESTAURANTS

Caffe Ciao	3
Gannon's	4
Spago	2
Tommy Bahama's Tropical Café	1
Zen-Zen Restaurant Pacifica	5

ACCOMMODATION

Fairmont Kea Lani Maui	E
Four Seasons Resort Maui at Wailea	D
Grand Wailea Resort	C
Makena Beach and Golf Resort	F
Pineapple Inn Maui	A
Wailea Marriott	B

WAILEA AND MĀKENA

beaches, and glorious strands like **Polo**, **Mākena Beach Park**, and magnificent **Oneloa Beach** (see p.262) just beyond Mākena, really should not be missed.

Accommodation

The moment you see the manicured lawns of Wailea, let alone its gleaming resorts, it will become clear that you need a lot of money to **stay** at this end of South Maui. There are one or two little B&Bs nearby, but otherwise rooms can rarely be found for under $250 a night.

Fairmont Kea Lani Maui 4100 Wailea Alanui Drive, Wailea ☎ 808/875-4100 or 1-866/540-4456, ⓦ www.kealani.com. Dazzling white resort, resembling something from the *Arabian Nights*. Despite its flamboyant domed silhouette, the interior is characterized by smooth unadorned curves, and you can see through the lobby to lily ponds and the lagoon-cum-pool, crossed by little footbridges. Two huge wings of plush rooms, 37 garden villas, and some excellent restaurants are all focused on lovely Polo Beach; every conceivable extra is available, at inconceivable prices. ❾

Four Seasons Resort Maui at Wailea 3900 Wailea Alanui Drive, Wailea ☎ 808/874-8000 or 1-800/819-5053, ⓦ www.fourseasons.com/maui. Lavish resort property at the south end of Wailea, with a large, beautiful, white-sand beach on view beyond the open lobby, and a gorgeous, palm-ringed pool. The huge rooms have private *lānais*, bamboo furnishings, and 24-hour room service, and you can choose from several restaurants, including *Spago* (see p.261). ❾

Grand Wailea Resort 3850 Wailea Alanui Drive, Wailea ☎ 808/875-1234 or 1-800/888-6100, ⓦ www.grandwailea.com. Large and very ostentatious tropical-themed resort hotel, where minimalism is a dirty word. The five-level swimming pool ("Wailea Canyon") is linked by waterslides and features a swim-up bar, hot-tub grottoes, and even a water elevator back to the top; just renting a poolside cabana costs $300. There's also a luxurious spa, half a dozen restaurants, a nightclub, and tropical flowers everywhere. ❾

Mākena Beach and Golf Resort 5400 Mākena Alanui Drive, Mākena

☎ 808/874-1111 or 1-800/321-6284, ⓦ www.makenaresortmaui.com. South Maui's southernmost resort, formerly the *Maui Prince*, is a stylish low-rise facing gorgeous, sandy Maluaka Beach. Less ostentatious and flamboyant than its neighbours, but still quintessentially luxurious, its seclusion is a delight. All the spacious and elegant rooms open off a vast open-air courtyard, but the ocean views are utterly magnificent, and there are trickling ponds filled with *koi* carp everywhere you look. Top-quality restaurants, golf packages, pilates, and yoga on the beach, and early-morning snorkel cruises to nearby Molokini. Since the recession, the best rates have been truly extraordinary. ❺

Pineapple Inn Maui 3170 Akala Drive ☎ 808/298-4403 or 1-877/212-6284, ⓦ www.pineappleinnmaui.com. Small, luxurious purpose-built inn, high on the Wailea hillside, that makes a wonderfully affordable alternative to the giants down below. The pastel-yellow main building holds four guest rooms with private baths and ocean-view *lānais*, and there's a separate two-bedroom cottage. Rooms ❹, cottage ❻

Wailea Marriott 3200 Wailea Alanui Drive, Wailea ☎ 808/879-1922 or 1-888/859-8262, ⓦ www.marriott.com. Wailea's first resort hotel retains its original open-air appeal, while now also backing onto the Shops at Wailea. It's set at the tip of an oceanfront promontory, but despite the ravishing views from the lobby, the nearest beach is ten minutes' walk away, so guests content themselves with a fine array of pools. The overall feel is more of a generic resort than anything particularly Hawaiian, but the rooms are spacious and comfortable, the *Mala* restaurant is recommended, and there are four weekly *lū'aus* (see p.226). ❽

The beaches

Five separate little bays indent the coastline of Wailea, with two more at Mākena. All hold crescent beaches of white sand that, in all but the worst winter conditions, are ideal for swimming.

A short access road just past the *Renaissance Wailea* leads down to **Ulua Beach**, where the surf is usually at its highest along this stretch of coast and which is therefore popular with body-surfers and boogie-boarders. There's also great snorkeling around the rocky point that separates it from **Mōkapu Beach**, a short walk to the north.

Kahoʻolawe

The uninhabited island of **Kahoʻolawe** is clearly visible from all along Maui's south and west coasts, and especially around Wailea and Mākena. Measuring just eleven miles by six, and a maximum of 1477ft above sea level, it's the eighth-largest Hawaiian island, with its nearest point a mere eight miles off Maui. From a distance, Kahoʻolawe looks like a barren hillock; at sunset it glows red, thanks to a haze of red dust lifted by the winds. Trapped in the rainshadow of Haleakalā, it receives thirty inches of rain a year. Agriculture is now all but impossible, but a few green valleys, invisible from the other islands, cut into the central plateau.

For the fifty years up to 1994, Kahoʻolawe was used for target practice by the **US Navy**. Whether the island had ever held much of a population was a deeply controversial issue during the protracted campaign by **native Hawaiians** to claim it back. Both sides marshaled archeologists and anthropologists, and Kahoʻolawe was more thoroughly probed and excavated than anywhere else in Hawaii. The conclusion was that, although it served principally as a seasonal fishing base, it also held permanent agricultural settlements. In addition, Kealaikahiki Point at its southwest corner was a marker for navigators sailing to and from Tahiti. A "navigator's chair" of shaped boulders still stands atop the island's second-highest peak, the 1444ft Moaʻulaiki, which is thought to have served as a school and observatory for apprentice navigators.

The whole island was probably covered by forest until 1450 AD, when it was swept by a bushfire. The trees have never grown back, and Captain Cook's expedition described Kahoʻolawe as "altogether a poor Island" in 1779. The process of erosion was completed by sheep and goats imported during the nineteenth century. For a short period during the 1840s, Kahoʻolawe was a penal colony; several ranchers then eked out a living, until the Navy summarily evicted the last of them after the 1941 attack on Pearl Harbor.

After World War II, the military declined to give Kahoʻolawe back. President Eisenhower granted the Navy control over the island in 1953, stipulating that it should be cleaned up at Federal expense and returned when no longer needed. For forty more years, Kahoʻolawe was blasted by thunderous explosions that could be seen and heard from Maui.

Intermittent Hawaiian efforts to reclaim Kahoʻolawe crystallized in 1975 with the formation of the **Protect Kahoʻolawe ʻOhana**, a group of young activists who saw Kahoʻolawe as a unifying cause for all native Hawaiians, the most obvious symbol of the way in which Hawaiian lands had been seized and desecrated by the United States. Following a series of illegal occupations of the island, the PKO eventually turned to the courts. Accusing the Navy on several fronts – water, noise, and air pollution; the threat to endangered marine mammals and historic sites; and the infringement of religious freedoms – they won restrictions on bombing and gained "visiting rights." President George H.W. Bush finally called a halt to the bombing in 1990, but even after Kahoʻolawe was handed back in 1994, the Navy continued to control access for ten more years, while it struggled to fulfill its commitment to remove all unexploded ordnance. In the end, when control passed to the state in 2003, seventy percent of the island's surface had been cleared, although only ten percent had also been checked for explosive materials buried beneath the soil. Open access to native Hawaiians, let alone casual visitors, is still a long way off, though there are plans to develop a safe "perimeter trail" around the shoreline, and a program of reforestation is achieving some success.

Although **Wailea Beach** itself, reached by a spur road between the *Grand Wailea* and the *Four Seasons*, is more thoroughly overshadowed by the resorts than any other local beach, the hotels are here for a reason. A superb broad expanse of curving sand, it offers safe swimming virtually year round, with a gentle ripple at

the southern end to please first-time boogie-boarders, and easy snorkeling around the rocks at either extremity. The views are great too, looking across the bay with its busy pleasure-boat traffic and whales in winter to East Maui on the far side.

Polo Beach, the next along, is the best for swimming. A pleasant, paved coastal trail connects it to Wailea Beach, while there's plenty of parking just off Kaukahi Street, on the south side of the *Fairmont Kea Lani*. The path down from the parking lot hits the sand at Polo Beach's northern end, which, being right beneath the hotel, can feel rather a goldfish bowl, crammed with loungers and short on shade. Double back south, however, and you'll come to two much less crowded stretches, which in winter become distinct beaches.

Ten minutes' walk south from Polo Beach, **Palauea Beach** is Wailea's quietest beach, well away from the built-up areas. Surfers and boogie-boarders predominate, but it's also a good spot for a family day by the sea and for snorkeling.

Mākena Road, which leaves Mākena Alanui Drive a little over a mile south of the *Kea Lani*, skirts the shoreline of **Mākena Bay**. This was once the site of busy **Mākena Landing** harbor, superseded by Kahului's new docks in the 1920s. The jetty has now gone, leaving behind a sleepy black-lava bay with little sand.

A little further on, the **Keawalaʻi Congregational Church** stands on an oceanfront patch of lawn that doubles as a graveyard, surrounded by trees with multicolored blossoms. It's a plain cement structure, topped by a pretty, wood-shingled belfry, and painted with a neat green trim; the coconut palms beyond front a tiny beach. Visitors are welcome to the 7.30am and 10am Sunday services, which incorporate Hawaiian language and music.

Keawalaʻi Church is opposite the parking lot for **Maluaka Beach** – also known as **Mākena Beach Park**, which naturally leads to confusion with Mākena State Park, described on p.262 – a hundred yards down the road. A delightful little half-moon beach, it offers reasonable snorkeling, and is adjacent to the *Mākena Beach and Golf Resort* (see p.259). Its combination of relative tranquility and superb sunset views over to Molokini and Kahoʻolawe also makes it a favorite spot for wedding ceremonies.

Eating and drinking

Neither Wailea nor Mākena holds many alternatives to the resort hotels' own **bars** and **restaurants**, but there are enough excellent places to choose from, provided you don't mind paying $60 per head per night for dinner. For cheaper dining, you'll just have to head back to Kīhei (see p.257).

Caffe Ciao *Fairmont Kea Lani Maui*, 4100 Wailea Alanui Drive, Wailea ☎808/875-2225. Very good, if pricey, Italian bakery/deli/trattoria, downstairs and to the left of the *Kea Lani*'s imposing lobby. The deli section sells pastries and espressos all day, plus massive $10 wraps and sandwiches, while the trattoria serves more formal meals on an open-air terrace, with lunchtime sandwiches or pasta specials for $15–22, and dinners ranging from $20 pizzas up to a $40 *cioppino* seafood stew. Daily 6.30am–10pm.

Gannon's 100 Wailea Golf Club Drive, Wailea ☎808/875-8080. Grand terrace restaurant in the clubhouse of the Wailea Golf Club, a few hundred yards uphill from the highway. Owned by the same top-notch team as the *Haliʻimaile General Store* (see p.266), it's open daily for all meals, and enjoys stupendous ocean views during daylight hours.

Lunch is the best time to come, perhaps for eggs Benedict ($10) or prosciutto bruschetta ($12), though the dinners are very tasty, with entrees such as herb gnocchi with squash ($26) or tandoori lamb ($38). Daily 8am–3pm & 5.30–9pm.

Spago *Four Seasons*, 3900 Wailea Alanui Drive, Wailea ☎808/879-2999. Celebrity chef Wolfgang Puck spreads himself a little thin these days, but as befits the stunning ocean-view location in this grandest of resorts, the buzzy *Spago* pulls out all the stops. It serves dinner only, with an assured and irresistible Pacific-Rim menu that includes a great scallop *ceviche* with Kula onions ($25), and $40–50 entrees like whole steamed *hapuʻupuʻu* (sea bass). Daily 6–9.30pm.

Tommy Bahama's Tropical Café The Shops at Wailea, 3750 Wailea Alanui Drive, Wailea ☎808/875-9983. Pricey but pretty good bar and restaurant

adjoining the upscale clothes store. At lunch, you can tuck into huge fishy sandwiches or pasta specials for $15–20 while enjoying sweeping (if distant) ocean views from the terrace. Dinner entrees are more overtly Caribbean, including Tobago tandoori or Trinidad tuna, at $26–40. Sun–Thurs 11am–11pm, Fri & Sat 11am–midnight.

🏃 Zen-Zen Restaurant Pacifica *Mākena Beach and Golf Resort*, 5400 Mākena Alanui Drive, Mākena ☎ 808/874-1111. Dinner-only Japanese-cum-Pacific-Rim restaurant, with tastefully minimal decor – but for the odd framed vintage Aloha shirt – and no views. Full sushi or sashimi dinners cost $32–45, but it's more fun to pick from the fine sushi menu or delicious entrees like sautéed *opah* ($26). On Saturdays, there's also a $48 dinner buffet. Wed–Sat 6–9pm.

Beyond Mākena

Once past the *Mākena Beach and Golf Resort*, you're finally clear of South Maui's resorts and can enjoy some of the island's finest beaches and most unspoiled scenery, though the road gives out altogether before long.

Oneloa Beach – "Big Beach"

Maui's most spectacular sweep of golden sand stretches for over half a mile south of the landmark cinder cone of Pu'u 'Ōla'i, just south of Mākena. There's not a building in sight at **Oneloa Beach** (literally "long sand," and widely known as **Big Beach**), just perfect sands and mighty surf, backed by a dry forest of *kiawe* and cacti. During the 1970s, it was home to a short-lived hippy commune; nowadays it's officially **Mākena State Park**, with two paved access roads.

The very first turn off the main road south of Mākena, though labeled "Mākena State Park," is a dirt track that leads via an orange gate to a scrubby gray-sand beach. Instead, keep going on a little further along the main road until you reach the paved turnoff to Oneloa. A footpath from the parking lot here leads through the trees to a cluster of portable toilets and picnic tables, and then emerges at the north end of Big Beach. While the clear blue ocean across this broad expanse of deep, coarse sand is irresistible, Big Beach is actually extremely **dangerous** because it faces straight out to sea and lacks a reef to protect it. Huge waves crash right on to the shoreline, and fearsome rip currents tear along the coast just a few feet out. It's been the scene of many drownings, so check with lifeguards before you enter the water.

Despite its perils, Big Beach remains busy most of the time with enthusiastic swimmers, boogie-boarders, and even snorkelers. Non-locals tend to congregate at its northern end, where in calmer periods the red-brown cliffs provide enough shelter to create a little turquoise "lagoon" of relatively placid water.

From the north end of the beach, a crude "stairway" leads up a natural cleft to the top of the rocky headland, and thus offers access to the much smaller, and significantly safer, **Little Beach**. Thanks to recent rockfalls, however, this is now quite a scramble, which in winter will almost certainly require you to wade thigh-deep in the sea. Those rockfalls have also precluded any attempt to climb the crumbling **Pu'u 'Ōla'i** cinder cone here.

Shielded by the headland, and shaded by the adjacent trees, Little Beach is perhaps the most idyllic swimming spot on Maui, with views of Molokini and Lanai. The winter surf can still get pretty high, however, and here too there have been drownings in winter, when it's more suitable for bodysurfing than swimming. One relic of the hippy days is that it's still widely known as an (illegal) **nudist** beach; even if you don't go naked yourself, some of your fellow beachgoers certainly will. As a result, they can be extremely sensitive to intruders carrying, let alone using, cameras.

La Pérouse Bay

Mākena Road continues for three miles south from Big Beach, as a narrow, undulating road that often narrows to a single lane. During the initial stretch, it runs right beside the ocean, clinging to the coastline of **'Āhihi Bay** around several small coves lined by very rough, jagged *'a'ā* lava, before setting out across a wide, desolate field of yet more chunky lava. **La Pérouse Bay** lies beyond.

Most visitors either park or turn around at what looks like the end of the road, where a cairn bearing a bronze plaque commemorates the voyages of the French Admiral Jean-François Galaup, Comte de la Pérouse. In fact, however, you can turn right at the cairn and continue for another couple of hundred yards to the shoreline, where there's much more parking space.

By spending three hours ashore here on May 30, 1786, La Pérouse became the **first foreigner** to set foot on Maui. He was under orders to claim the island for the King of France but, unusually for a European, considered that he had no right to do so. As he put it, "The customs of Europeans on such occasions are completely ridiculous." His ships, the *Astrolabe* and the *Boussole,* simply sailed away, and were lost with all hands in the Solomon Islands two years later.

La Pérouse encountered a handful of coastal villages in this area. Its inhabitants knew it as *Keone'ō'io,* or "bonefish beach," and told how Chief Kalani'opu'u of the Big Island had landed a fleet of canoes here during an attempted invasion of Maui a few years earlier. However, the villages were destroyed just four years after La Pérouse's visit by the last known eruption of Haleakalā. A river of lava two miles wide flowed into the sea at the center of what had been one long bay, to create the two separate bays seen today. Look inland to see several russet cinder cones that are relics of the eruptions.

The waters around the headland at the east end of La Pérouse Bay, popular for some reason with dolphins, are set aside as the **'Āhihi-Kīna'u Natural Area Reserve**. All fishing is forbidden; snorkeling is allowed, but it's easier to enter the water in the inlets around La Pérouse Bay itself than to go in off the sharp rocks of the headland. In 2008 the state greatly **restricted access** to the area, and at the time this book went to press it was no longer possible to hike any distance from the end of the road, and thus to reach the best snorkeling sites. A ranger is usually posted beside the parking lot, and can advise on current regulations.

Upcountry Maui

The lower western slopes of Haleakalā, which enjoy a deliciously temperate climate a couple of thousand feet above the isthmus, are known as **Upcountry Maui**. Most visitors simply race through on their way up the mountain, but the upcountry is among the most attractive regions in all Hawaii. A narrow strip that stretches for at most twenty miles, it varies from the wet, lush orchards and rainforests around **Makawao** in the north to the parched cattle country of **'Ulupalakua Ranch** twenty miles south. While the region holds few towns and even fewer tourist attractions, it's laced with quiet rural lanes that make for relaxing explorations. Although commuter traffic up and down Haleakalā Highway attests to its status as a popular residential district, accommodation for visitors is limited to a handful of pretty, small-scale **B&Bs**.

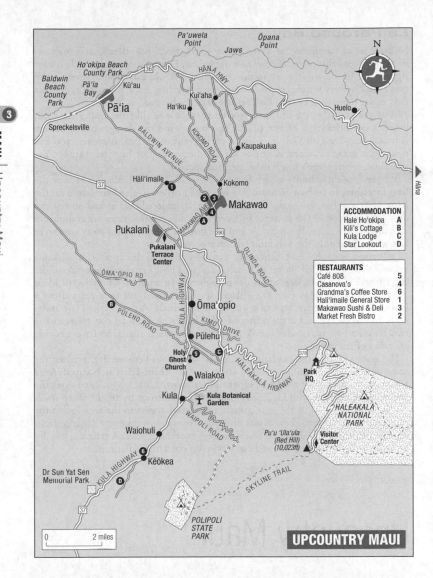

ACCOMMODATION

Hale Ho'okipa	A
Kili's Cottage	B
Kula Lodge	C
Star Lookout	D

RESTAURANTS

Café 808	5
Casanova's	4
Grandma's Coffee Store	6
Hali'imaile General Store	1
Makawao Sushi & Deli	3
Market Fresh Bistro	2

UPCOUNTRY MAUI

At this altitude, the pineapple and sugar plantations of the isthmus give way to smaller private farms. In the past these grew the white potatoes that first lured the whaling fleet to Maui, as well as coffee, cotton, and Maui onions, but the most conspicuous crop now is flowering plants, especially dazzling **protea blossoms**.

If you expect a nonstop riot of greenery and color, however, you may be disappointed to find that much of the upcountry is dry and desolate. It takes irrigation to render this land fertile, and the many gulches that corrugate the flanks of Haleakalā only manage to support sparse grass, dry stunted trees, and even cacti. That becomes ever more true as you head further south, where bare slopes are scattered with the rounded knolls of ancient cinder cones.

There's often talk that a new stretch of highway, or possibly a whole new road, will be constructed to connect Kīhei directly with Upcountry Maui. For the moment, however, the only route up from the island's south or west coasts is via Kahului.

Makawao

The small town of **MAKAWAO**, seven miles up from coastal Pā'ia (see p.279), represents Maui at its best. Still recognizable as the village built by plantation workers and *paniolo* cowboys in the nineteenth century, it's now home to an active artistic community dominated by exiles from California. When they're not giving each other classes in yoga, feng shui, belly dancing, and Hawaiian healing, they make its galleries, crafts stores, and coffee bars some of the liveliest hangouts on the island.

Makawao barely existed before Kamehameha III chose it as the site of Hawaii's first experiment in private land ownership in 1845. Almost a hundred Hawaiians acquired small homesites, but most of the area was grabbed by outsiders when they were permitted to buy land by the Great Mahele of 1848 (see p.420). Local timber-yards, harvesting the rainforest east of town, provided the dark *koa* wood used in Honolulu's 'Iolani Palace, while Portuguese immigrants flocked in to work on the neighboring cattle ranches.

The moment when Makawao's lawless cowboy past gave way to the outlaw chic of today can be pinned down to July 30, 1970, when **Jimi Hendrix** played one of his last concerts, barely a month before he died, to eight hundred people gathered in a field above Seabury Hall private school. The occasion was immortalized in the turgid movie *Rainbow Bridge*.

Although Makawao extends for well over a mile, only its central intersection – where **Baldwin Avenue**, climbing from Pā'ia, meets **Makawao Avenue** from Pukalani – holds any great interest. Baldwin here points straight up Haleakalā, toward the lush green meadows on the slopes above town. Its timber-frame buildings, painted in fading pastel hues, are connected by a rudimentary boardwalk and hold half a dozen quirky art galleries. The real artistic epicenter of town, however, is the **Hui No'eau Visual Arts Center**, a country estate a mile south at 2841 Baldwin Ave (Mon–Sat 10am–4pm; ☎808/572-6560, ⓦwww.huinoeau.com). As well as offering classes in practical arts and crafts, it houses its own small store and a gallery for temporary exhibitions.

Makawao's *paniolo* days are commemorated on July 4 each year by the Makawao Rodeo, which includes a parade through town as well as competitive events at the Oskie Rice Arena.

Eating and drinking

There's very little **accommodation** in or near Makawao; see the accommodation listings for the Upcountry as a whole, on p.266, for B&Bs within a few minutes' drive. The town does, however, boast an excellent selection of friendly **restaurants**, good for inexpensive lunch stops, as well as lively **nightlife** focused on *Casanova's*.

Casanova's 1188 Makawao Ave ☎808/572-0220, ⓦwww.casanovamaui.com. The 1970s Art Nouveau–style lettering and faded exterior of this single-story wooden building in the heart of Makawao belies its status as one of Maui's hottest nightspots. There's a dancefloor and bar just inside the door, a romantic Italian restaurant stretches further back, and the breakfast deli/espresso bar is alongside. Lunchtime salads, pastas, and sandwiches range from $7 to $8, while in the evening wood-fired pizzas or pasta entrees are $12–18, and specials are $22–36. Portions are huge. The $5 cover charge on dance nights (unless you dine) can rise to $10 when there's live music (typically Fri and Sat). Mon & Tues 5.30am–12.30am, Wed–Sun 5.30am–1am.

Hali'imaile General Store 900 Hali'imaile Rd ☎ 808/572-2666, ⊛ www.bevgannon restaurants.com. One of Maui's very best restaurants, serving gourmet Hawaiian food in a large, bright and smart former store in the village of Hali'imaile, which is two miles down Baldwin Avenue from Makawao and then a mile west towards Haleakalā Highway. Appetizers (up to $20) include an Asian pear and duck taco, and fresh island fish cakes; typical entrees, like Asian bouillabaisse or rack of lamb Hunan style, cost over $30; and there's also a raw bar. Mon–Fri 11am–2.30pm & 5.30–9pm, Sat & Sun 5.30–9pm.

Makawao Sushi & Deli 3647 Baldwin Ave ☎ 808/573-9044. This smart little place on the main drag started out as a coffee bar, and still serves panini, espressos, and smoothies, but these days it's better known for its good, inexpensive sushi, with individual rolls from $3, eight-piece specialty rolls at $16–20, and sashimi plates from $19. Good-value lunches include a *miso* butterfish plate or chef's bento box for $9. Daily 11.30am–9pm.

Market Fresh Bistro 3620 Baldwin Ave ☎ 808/572-4877. Pleasant off-street café in the Courtyard Mall, serving espressos, pastries, salads, and sandwiches, for around $10, plus entrees such as crab cakes or lamb ragu for a little more, to eat at shaded garden tables or indoors. Sun–Wed 11.30am–4pm, Thurs–Sat 11.30am–3pm & 5.30–9pm.

Kula and the heart of the Upcountry

Immediately beyond the unenthralling dormitory town of Pukalani, Hwy-37 changes its name to **Kula Highway**, while **Haleakalā Highway**, now Hwy-377, branches off up the mountain. It meets the route to the summit, **Haleakalā Crater Road**, after six miles, and then, as **Kekaulike Highway**, swings back to rejoin Kula Highway.

This general region is known as **Kula**. None of the four separate communities – from north to south, **Ōma'opio**, **Pūlehu**, **Waiakoa**, and **Kula** itself – amounts to very much, but the views they afford are superb. Far below, the curve of the ocean bites into either side of the flat, green isthmus, while on the horizon, clouds squat on the West Maui mountains. In the light of the morning sun, you can make out the condo buildings lining the Kīhei coast, but by afternoon, apart from the odd glint from a car, the long gentle slopes seem predominantly rural.

Accommodation

Driving across the Kula district, you probably won't notice any **accommodation** apart from the *Kula Lodge*, but tucked away on the back roads are a wide assortment of lovely little B&Bs. All require advance reservations, and some can only be booked through specialist B&B agencies.

Hale Ho'okipa 32 Pakani Place, Makawao ☎ 808/572-6698, ⊛ www.maui-bed-and -breakfast.com. Tucked away on a quiet residential street, this lovely timber-built plantation-style home abounds in tasteful architectural detail. Three well-furnished, en-suite B&B rooms share a common living room, where good breakfasts are served in a friendly atmosphere, and there's also a separate two-bedroom suite. ❹–❺

Kili's Cottage Kula; reserve through Hawaii's Best B&B ☎ 808/263-3100 or 1-800/262-9912, ⊛ www .bestbnb.com. A real bargain: a comfortable three-bedroom, two-bathroom house, set in beautiful upland gardens below Pūlehu, with full kitchen, and rented for less than the price of most Maui hotel rooms. Three-night minimum stay. ❹

Kula Lodge 15200 Haleakalā Hwy ☎ 808/878-1535 or 1-800/233-1535, ⊛ www.kulalodge. com. Upmarket board and lodging in a Hawaiian approximation of an Alpine inn, just before the Haleakalā Crater Rd turnoff. Accommodation is in five chalets, four of which can sleep family parties; all are comfortably furnished, though they don't have phones or TV. ❹–❺

Star Lookout 622 Thompson Rd, Kula ☎ 808/878-6730, reservations on ☎ 907/346-8028, ⊛ www.starlookout.com. Gorgeous rental cottage perched high on the green Upcountry slopes just above Kula, offering comfortable accommodation for four for $200 per night. There's a full kitchen, and a long *lānai*, with stupendous views. Two-night minimum stay. ❻

Holy Ghost Church

Five miles south of the point where it branches away from the route up to Haleakalā, the lower Upcountry road, the Kula Highway, passes just below the white octagonal **Holy Ghost Church**. Portuguese Catholics came to Maui from 1878 onwards, and by 1894 were prosperous enough to construct their own church, shipping the hand-carved high-relief gilt altar from Austria, and capping the structure with a gleaming silver-roofed belfry. The interior is very light, with pink-painted walls, and features the Stations of the Cross labeled in Portuguese. Not surprisingly, this was the only octagonal structure built in nineteenth-century Hawaii; it's thought to be eight-sided either because the crown of the Portuguese Queen Isabella was octagonal, or because the German parish priest came from near Aachen, the site of a similar octagonal chapel built by Charlemagne.

Kula Botanical Garden

A couple of miles beyond the foot of Haleakalā Crater Road, at 638 Kekaulike Highway, the **Kula Botanical Garden** offers self-guided tours through large and colorful landscaped gardens (daily 9am–4pm; adults $10, kids 6–13 $3; ⓦwww.kulabotanicalgarden.com). Among its broad range of plants are proteas, hydrangeas, lurid yellow and red cannas, and spectacular purple and yellow birds of paradise from South Africa. Many of its species betray their Pacific origins by bearing the Latin name *banksia*, in honor of Sir Joseph Banks, the pioneering botanist who sailed with Captain Cook; perhaps the finest is the red and white "Raspberry Frost" from Australia.

Polipoli State Park

Although Maui residents rave about thickly wooded **Polipoli State Park**, set high above the Upcountry, visitors from beyond Hawaii may feel that as an "ordinary" temperate forest it has little they can't see at home. The park stands at the top of the ten-mile Waipoli Road – *not* nearby Polipoli Road, oddly enough – a fun drive that climbs away from Kekaulike Highway just south of the Kula Botanical Garden. The first six miles, in which you do all the climbing, are paved, passing through tough, springy ranchland where cattle graze on the open range. This is Maui's best launching spot for **hang gliders**, which you may see sharing the winds with circling Hawaiian owls (unique in that they fly by day, rather than night).

It shouldn't be too difficult to coax a rental car along the rough, but level, dirt road that meanders along the hillside above the ranch. After three miles, the road surface improves; drop right at the fork half a mile further along, and after another half a mile you'll come to Polipoli's **campground** in a grassy clearing, which offers neither showers nor drinking water. Tent camping here ($18 per site), and overnight stays in the simple cabin nearby (permits for up to four people $60 for HI residents, $90 otherwise; closed Tues) can be obtained either online at ⓦwww.hawaiistateparks .org/camping, or from the state parks office in Wailuku (see p.221).

The entire Polipoli area was planted with Californian redwood trees during the 1930s. The **Redwood Trail**, which leads down from a hundred yards before the campground, burrows through such thick forest that the persistent rain can barely penetrate it, and very little light does either. It comes as a huge relief when the trail emerges from the bottom-most strip of eucalyptus after 1.5 miles to show expansive views across the ranchlands.

Various other trails crisscross throughout Polipoli, including some to lava caves hidden in the woods, but the one most likely to interest visitors from outside Hawaii is the **Skyline Trail**. This epic thirteen-mile trek follows the southwest rift zone of Haleakalā right the way up to Science City, at the summit (see p.274). It climbs a

dirt track that heads off to the left two miles along the left fork from the junction 9.5 miles up Waipoli Road, described above. Unless you arrange a pick-up at the far end, it's too far for a day-hike, and the higher you get the more exposed to the biting winds you'll be. Alternatively, you can take a **mountain bike** along the trail.

Kēōkea

A couple of miles south of the intersection of the Kekaulike and Kula highways, the village of **KĒŌKEA** consists of a small cluster of roadside stores, together with the green-and-white **St John's Episcopal Church**. All were built at the end of the nineteenth century to serve the local Chinese community, which also supported three Chinese-language schools and, it's said, a number of opium dens. Alongside *Grandma's Coffee Store* (see below), one room of Henry Fong's general store houses the appealing little **Kēōkea Gallery** (Tues–Sat 9am–5pm, Sun 9am–3pm; Ⓦwww .keokeagallery.com), where you'll find arts and crafts displayed.

The wife and children of Sun Yat Sen, the first president of China, stayed on his brother's ranch here during 1911 and 1912, while Sun was away fomenting revolution. Hence the statue of Sun, guarded by Chinese dragons, which looks out over Wailea and Kahoʻolawe from the somewhat neglected **Dr Sun Yat Sen Memorial Park**, where Hwy-37 meets Kealakapu Road, less than two miles beyond Kēōkea.

Eating and drinking

Although the Kula region holds very few **eating** and **drinking** options, there's no need to bring a picnic if you're touring the area.

Café 808 4566 Lower Kula Rd ☎808/878-6874. Hidden away above the Holy Ghost Church with just a few plastic tables and chairs scattered across its large, bare floor, this friendly café feels much like a village hall. Upcountry residents gather all through the day; breakfast pancakes are $5, while later on, local favorites – "island grinds" like *loco moco* or *saimin* – cost under $10. Daily 6am–8pm.

Grandma's Coffee Store 9232 Kula Hwy, Kēōkea ☎808/878-2792, Ⓦwww.grandmascoffee.com. You're unlikely to see "Grandma" at this little café, where an open-air deck enjoys panoramic views, but there's plenty of her fresh Maui-grown coffee, plus avocado sandwiches, salads, macnut pesto,

taro burgers, and killer home-made cookies and desserts. Daily 7am–5pm.

Kula Lodge 15200 Haleakalā Hwy ☎808/878-1535, Ⓦwww.kulalodge.com. The wood-furnished dining room of *Kula Lodge* (see p.266) is busiest at the start of the day, when customers are already on their way back down Haleakalā after watching the sunrise. The food is American, with a Pacific Rim tinge; the lunch menu ranges across sandwiches and a few specials ($12–20), while evening offerings include a *miso* oysters Rockefeller appetizer ($16), and $25–35 entrees like lavender-balsamic rack of lamb. Protea blossoms adorn the tables, and the views are immense. Daily 6.30am–9pm.

'Ulupalakua Ranch

Six miles on from Kēōkea, the six tin-roofed, single-story wooden buildings of the **'Ulupalakua Ranch** headquarters nestle into a shady bend in the road. Comings and goings are overseen by the three carved wooden cowboys stationed permanently on the porch of the *'Ulupalakua Ranch Store* (daily 9.30am–5pm; Ⓦwww.ulupalakua ranch.com); inside, you can buy sodas, *paniolo* hats, and T-shirts, plus deli supplies and lunchtime takeout.

'Ulupalakua Ranch started out in the middle of the nineteenth century as **Rose Ranch**, owned by an ex-whaling captain, **James McKee**. Originally its main business was sugar, but the focus soon shifted to cattle, and it employed expert *paniolo* cowboys such as Ike Purdy, a former world rodeo champion. In his

huge mansion, McKee played host to Robert Louis Stevenson and King David Kalākaua among others, who took advantage of Hawaii's first-ever swimming pool. Spotting ships arriving at Mākena Landing (see p.261), McKee would fire a cannon to signal that he was sending a carriage down to meet his guests. The mansion burned down during the 1970s, but the ranch itself is still going, with a permanent herd of over two thousand brood cows.

Tedeschi Winery

Around the corner beyond 'Ulupalakua Ranch, one of the ranch's co-owners has established the **Tedeschi Winery** as a successful sideline on the site of James McKee's original Rose Ranch. It uses two annual grape harvests from a small vineyard in a fold below the highway, a mile to the north, to produce thirty thousand cases a year of white, red, and rosé wines, as well as Maui Brut champagne and a "sparkling pineapple" wine. They're sold in the **King's Cottage**, which also houses an entertaining little museum of ranch and cowboy history and serves as the assembly point for fifteen-minute guided **tours** (store and museum daily 10am–5pm, free tours daily 10.30am, 1.30pm & 3pm; ☎1-877/878-6058, ⓦwww.mauiwine.com). The converted and imitation ranch buildings used for processing and bottling are less than enthralling, but you do at least get to see some amazing trees, including a pine drowning in multicolored creeping bougainvillea, and a giant camphor.

Pi'ilani Highway

South of 'Ulupalakua, Kula Highway confusingly becomes the **Pi'ilani Highway**, despite having no connection with the parallel road of the same name that runs through Wailea and Mākena down below. For all the strictures of the rental companies – see p.220 – it takes appalling weather to render it unsafe, and in principle, for most of the year, it's possible to drive all the way along the south coast to Hāna, 37 miles away. The road is often closed for months at a time due to rockfalls, however, so check before you set out. A detailed description of the route, coming in the opposite direction, begins on p.292.

Haleakalā

Although the briefest glance at a map shows the extent to which mighty **Haleakalā** dominates Maui, it's hard to appreciate its full majesty until you climb right to the top. Hawaiian-style shield volcanoes (see p.196) are not as dramatic as the classic cones of popular imagination, and with its summit often obscured by clouds, Haleakalā can seem no more than a gentle incline rising a short distance above the rest of Maui.

By ascending more than ten thousand feet above sea level in just 38 miles from Kahului, **Haleakalā Highway** is said to climb higher, faster than any road on earth. En route, it crosses a bewildering succession of terrains, equivalent to a drive from

Downhill biking

For many years, one of Maui's most unusual and popular tourist activities was to ride in a minivan to the top of Haleakalā – especially at dawn – and then climb onto a **bike** and ride, or rather roll, all the 39 miles back down the mountain to the sea.

Since 2007, however, the authorities no longer allow operators to start bicycle descents at the crater. Companies still take their passengers up to see the sunrise, but the actual cycling segment now has to begin several thousand feet lower, at the park boundary. Similarly, most no longer take groups all the way to the ocean, preferring to end their tours somewhere in the Upcountry.

As a result, downhill bike tours are no longer either as enjoyable or as popular. If you still fancy the idea, expect to pay $120–150; wear plenty of warm clothing; and be prepared to be picked up at your hotel as early as 2am.

Cruiser Phil's ☏ 808/893-2332 or 1-877/764-2453, ⊛ www.cruiserphil.com

Maui Downhill ☏ 808/871-2155 or 1-800/535-2453, ⊛ www.mauidownhill.com

Mountain Riders ☏ 808/242-9739 or 1-800/706-7700, ⊛ www.mountainriders.com

Mexico to Alaska. Beyond the exclusive homes and clapboard churches of Upcountry Maui, it leads through purple-blossoming jacaranda, firs, and eucalyptus to reach open ranching land, then sweeps in huge curves to the volcanic desert and the awe-inspiring **Haleakalā Crater** itself. Almost eight miles across, this eerie wasteland would comfortably hold Manhattan.

To the ancient Hawaiians, Haleakalā was "the House of the Sun." They told of how at one time the sun crossed the sky much faster than it does today, until the demi-god Maui captured it here in a web of ropes, and only released it on the condition that it travel slowly enough to give his mother time to dry her *tapa* (bark-cloth). Pre-contact Hawaiians trekked to the summit in search of basalt for adzes, to hunt birds, and to bury their dead; traces have even been found of a paved trail that crossed the crater and led down through the Kaupō Gap (see p.278).

The higher reaches of the mountain joined with the volcanoes of the Big Island to form Hawaii Volcanoes National Park in 1921, and became the independent **Haleakalā National Park** in 1961. It now ranks as the tenth most visited national park in the US, with around a million people a year reaching the summit. The most popular time to come is for sunrise – described by Mark Twain as "the sublimest spectacle I ever witnessed" – but don't get the impression that it's not worth coming later in the day. The views of the crater itself are at their best in mid-afternoon, when the sun lights up its staggering array of russet cinder cones, ashen slopes, pockmarked craters, and craggy cliffs, and you can enjoy superb views from the roadside lookouts along the way up whatever time you arrive. It's also possible to hike into the crater, and even to spend the night there.

Officially, Haleakalā National Park also includes Kīpahulu Valley and 'Ohe'o Gulch, on Maui's southeast coast (see p.290). However, no hiking trail, let alone direct road, connects those areas with Haleakalā Crater.

Haleakalā Crater Road

From all the major accommodation centers on Maui, the quickest route to the top of Haleakalā is to head for Kahului, and then follow **Haleakalā Highway** into the Upcountry (see p.263). Also known from there on as **Haleakalā Crater Road**, it continues all the way to the summit, entering the park after a twisting

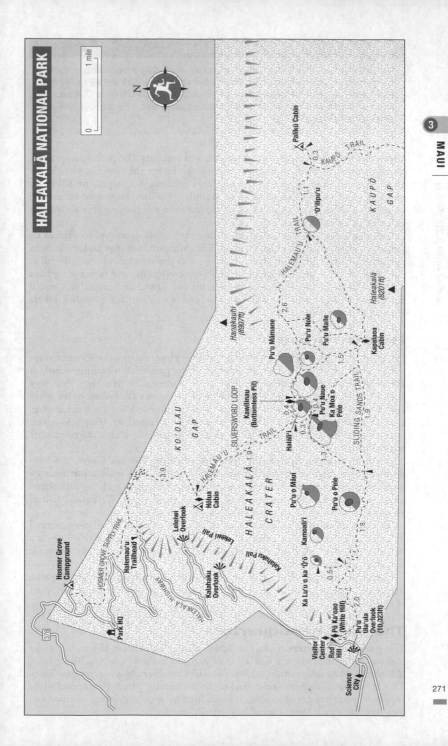

HALEAKALĀ NATIONAL PARK

0   1 mile

N

Paliku Cabin

KAUPŌ TRAIL

0.3

1.1

'Ō'ilipu'u

HALEMAU'U TRAIL

KAUPŌ GAP

2.6

Hanakauhi (8907ft)

Pu'u Māmane

Haleakalā (8201ft)

Pu'u Nole

Pu'u Malie

1.5

Kapalaoa Cabin

KO'OLAU GAP

3.9

1.9

HALEMAU'U TRAIL

SILVERSWORD LOOP

Kawilinau (Bottomless Pit)

TRAIL

Pu'u Māmane

Halāli'i

0.4

Pu'u Naue

0.3

Ka Moa o Pele

1.3

SLIDING SANDS TRAIL

1.9

Hōlua Cabin

HALEAKALĀ CRATER

Pu'u o Māui

Pu'u o Pele

1.8

Leleiwi Overlook

Kamoali'i

HOSMER GROVE SUPPLY TRAIL

Halemau'u Trailhead

Leleiwi Pali

Hosmer Grove Campground

Kalahaku Overlook

Kalahaku Pali

Ka Lu'u o ka 'Ō'ō

0.5

HALEAKALĀ HIGHWAY

Park HQ

Visitor Center

Pō Ka'oao (White Hill)

Red Hill

Pu'u 'Ula'ula Overlook (10,023ft)

2.0

Science City

378

3

Haleakalā National Park hours and fees

Haleakalā National Park remains open around the clock; $5 per pedestrian or cyclist, $10 per vehicle, valid for three days in both sections of the park; $25 for Tri-Parks Annual Pass, which also covers Hawaii Volcanoes National Park, and Puʻuhonua O Hōnaunau National Historic Park on the Big Island; national passes (see p.36) are sold here and are valid for admission.

twelve-mile climb through the meadows, and reaching the park headquarters shortly after that. With another ten miles to go before the summit, you should allow two full hours to get to the top from Lahaina, Kāʻanapali, or Kīhei, or one and a half hours from Kahului or Wailuku. The last gas station before the summit is at Pukalani, 28 miles below; the last food and lodging is at *Kula Lodge* (see p.268), 22 miles short.

Assuming you join the majority in attempting to drive up to Haleakalā Crater to witness the **sunrise** (around 5.50am in midsummer and 6.50am in midwinter) – and don't feel that you have to, as the views can be wonderful at any time of day – you'll need to make a very early start, and face a long hard drive in the dark. If you do end up late for the dawn, be warned that you'll be driving straight into the dazzling sun, and watch out for downhill bikers coming the other way.

Hosmer Grove

Just beyond the **park entrance** – the gates never close, though there's not always a ranger on duty – a short road leads left to the park's main **campground**, at **Hosmer Grove**. Set almost exactly at the mountain's tree line, this may look like a pleasant wooded copse, but in fact it marks the failure of an early twentieth-century experiment to assess Maui's suitability for timber farming. Out of almost a hundred different tree species planted by Ralph Hosmer, only twenty survived, though that's enough to provide a nice thirty-minute **nature trail**.

By way of contrast, **Waikamoi Preserve**, adjoining Hosmer Grove, is a five-thousand-acre tract of upland rainforest that's home to a wide assortment of indigenous Hawaiian **birds**. You can only hike through it with an authorized guide, so check to see when the Park Service's regular free **Waikamoi Cloud Forest Hikes** are scheduled (currently Mon & Thurs 9am).

There's **tent camping** in a soft sloping meadow surrounded by tall pines; a small open pavilion holds basic washing facilities. The fifty sites are available free on a first-come, first-served basis. No advance reservations are taken, and no permit is required, but there's a three-night maximum stay.

It's possible to walk all the way into Haleakalā Crater from Hosmer Grove; a supply trail up the mountain meets the Halemauʻu Trail after 2.5 miles, just short of the crater rim.

The park headquarters

The **park headquarters** looks out across central Maui from the right of the highway, three quarters of a mile up from the park entrance (daily 6.30am–4pm; ☎808/572-4400 information, ☎808/871-5054 weather; ⓦwww.nps.gov/hale). This is where to inquire about backcountry camping places (see opposite) or register if you've reserved a cabin. It holds little by way of exhibits, but you can pick up a basic park brochure and buy detailed maps.

Backcountry camping and cabins at Haleakalā

Hosmer Grove is the only Haleakalā campground accessible by car, and the only one for which campers do not need to obtain permits. Backcountry camping, in the sense of simply pitching your tent in some remote spot, is not permitted anywhere in the park. There are, however, three rudimentary, but sound, **backcountry cabins** within Haleakalā Crater, which can only be reached on foot. All are on the grassy fringes of the crater, sheltered by the high surrounding cliffs, and are padlocked to deter casual backpackers from wandering in. Each is rented to one group only per night, and has twelve bunk beds, with no bedding, plus a kitchen, a stove for heating, and an outhouse. **Hōlua** and **Palikū** cabins offer **tent camping** in the adjacent meadows – the 25 free daily permits are issued on a first-come, first-served basis at the park headquarters, between 8am and 3pm daily – but **Kapalaoa Cabin** does not. Water is normally available, but it's up to you to purify it before you drink it.

Permits to stay in the cabins are limited to three days in total, with no more than two days at any one cabin. For each specific day, they become available exactly ninety days in advance, online at ⓦ www.fhnp.org or by phone on ☏ 808/572-4400 (Mon–Fri 1–3pm Hawaiian time only). Each cabin costs $75 per night, or $60 should it happen still to be available 21 days in advance.

The roadside lookouts

Beyond the park headquarters, Haleakalā Crater Road zigzags for another ten miles up the mountain, repeatedly sweeping toward the lip of the crater then doubling back. The three closest approaches are each marked by a roadside parking lot.

The first, 2.5 miles up from the park headquarters, is the **Halemau'u Trailhead**. One of the park's two main hiking trails begins its long descent into the crater from here, as described on p.275, but the edge of the *pali* is almost a mile away; there's nothing to see at the parking lot.

Another 4.5 miles up the road, **Leleiwi Overlook** is set a couple of hundred yards beyond its parking lot. It offers views across the isthmus to West Maui, as well as a first glimpse into Haleakalā Crater, but you'll probably have seen enough of West Maui from the Crater Road, and better vantage points over the crater lie ahead.

It's only legal to stop at the **Kalahaku** or **"Silversword" Overlook**, a couple of miles short of the visitor center, as you drive *down* rather than up the mountain; in fact it's easy to pass by without noticing it at all. That's a shame, because this sheltered viewpoint provides perhaps the best overall prospect of Haleakalā Crater. Mauna Kea on the Big Island is often visible through the Kaupō Gap in the ridge to the right, and when the clouds clear you can also see down to the north coast of Maui. Unless you hike into the crater, this may be the only place you see any **silverswords** (see p.276); there are a few in the small enclosure below the parking lot, across from the overlook.

Haleakalā Visitor Center

Although the highway continues beyond it, most visitors consider they've reached the top of Haleakalā when they get to the **Visitor Center**, eleven miles up from the park entrance (daily 5.15am–3pm; no phone). The railed open-air viewing area beside the parking lot commands great views of Haleakalā Crater. In the pre-dawn chill, however, many people prefer to admire the procession of red-brown cinder cones, marching across the moonscape far below, through the panoramic windows

of the small visitor center itself. If you're feeling more energetic, follow the short paved trail to the right instead, which leads up **Pa Ka'oao**, or White Hill, for 360° views.

There's a good 3-D model of Haleakalā inside the visitor center to help you get oriented. Park rangers also provide hiking tips and lead free **guided hikes**, such as the **Cinder Desert** walk, which sets off from here along the Sliding Sands Trail (see opposite) and the **Waikamoi Cloud Forest Hike** from Hosmer Grove.

Pu'u Ula'ula (Red Hill)

A few hundred yards further up the highway, a smaller parking lot at a final loop in the road stands just below **Pu'u Ula'ula**, or **Red Hill** – at 10,023ft, the highest spot on Maui. A circular shelter at the top of a short stairway offers what feel like aerial views of Haleakalā Crater. In clear conditions – soon after dawn is the best bet – you may be able to see not only the eighty miles to Mauna Loa on the Big Island, but even the 130 miles to Oahu.

Science City

The road beyond Pu'u Ula'ula is closed to the public, but leads in a few more yards to the gleaming white domes of **Kolekole**, or **Science City**. This multinational astronomic research facility, perched at the top of the House of the Sun, monitors the earth's distance from the moon by bouncing laser signals off a prism left there by the Apollo astronauts.

The geology of Haleakalā

Dramatic, multicolored **Haleakalā Crater**, 10,023ft above sea level at the summit of Haleakalā, and measuring more than seven miles long, two miles wide, and half a mile deep, is often hailed as the largest extinct volcanic crater in the world. As far as geologists are concerned, however, it's none of these things. They insist that not only is the "crater" not a crater at all – in shape, size, origin, and location it bears no relation to any summit crater Haleakalā may once have possessed – but strictly speaking it's not even volcanic, having been created by erosion rather than eruption.

Fueled by the same "hot spot" that has created all the volcanoes of Hawaii, Haleakalā originally thrust its way from the ocean 800,000 years ago. In the 400,000 years that followed, it first fused with, and eventually dominated, the West Maui mountains. At its highest, it may have stood 15,000ft tall, and towered over the land mass geologists call "**Maui Nui**," or Big Maui, which also incorporated the present-day islands of Kaho'olawe, Molokai, and Lanai.

The volcano then slumbered, while for several hundred thousand years torrential rainfall eroded away its topmost six thousand feet and sculpted vast canyons into its flanks. Two of these valleys, **Keanae** to the north and **Kaupō** to the east, cut so deeply into the mountain that they met in the middle, creating a huge central depression. When the "hot spot" beneath Haleakalā finally reawakened, a series of smaller eruptions poured another three thousand feet of lava into that cavity, and gushed out of the Ko'olau and Kaupō gaps to refill the valleys. Peppering the summit with raw red cones of cindery ash, it made it look to the untrained eye like the sort of crater you might expect to find at the top of a volcano.

Although the "hot spot" today directs most of its energy into Kīlauea on the Big Island, Haleakalā is merely **dormant**. It has erupted at least ten times in the last thousand years, with its most recent volcanic activity being in 1790 (see p.263). That it's been peaceful for two hundred years doesn't mean it always will be – in 1979, for example, it was thought more likely to explode than Mount St Helens.

Hiking in Haleakalā Crater

The best way to get a sense of the beauty and diversity of Haleakalā Crater is by hiking down into it. Although there are just two principal trails – the **Sliding Sands** and **Halemau'u** trails – the terrain varies far more than you can tell from the crater-edge viewpoints, ranging from forbidding desert to lush mountain meadows.

The obvious problem is that, once you've descended into the crater, you'll have to climb back out again, which at an altitude of 10,000ft is never less than grueling. That said, reasonably fit hikers should be able to manage a **day-hike** that takes them down one trail and back up the other – a minimum distance of eleven miles, which is likely to take at least seven hours. More ambitiously, you could aim to take in *Kapalaoa Cabin* along the way, for a total of thirteen miles and more like eight hours, but heading any further east would be unrealistic. The easier route is to go down Sliding Sands and back on Halemau'u, though since the trailheads are several miles apart, you'll need to arrange a pick-up or hitch a ride between the two. A parking lot near the Halemau'u Trailhead makes the ideal spot for hitch-hikers hoping to get a lift back up the mountain.

If you arrange to stay overnight in the crater (see p.273), you can see the whole thing in two days, although most hikers spend longer. It takes a hardy and very well-prepared backpacker, however, to trek out via the **Kaupō Trail** to the south (see p.278).

Don't underestimate the effects of the **altitude**. Allow an hour in the summit area to acclimatize before you set off on the trails; that will prepare you for the effort ahead, and also mean that you're still close to the road if you start to feel ill. By far the most effective treatment for altitude sickness is to descend a few thousand feet. **Scuba-divers** should not go up Haleakalā within twenty-four hours of a dive. You should also be prepared for the **cold**. Temperatures at the summit at dawn are likely to be around freezing, while rain clouds can drift into the crater at any time, and seriously chill anyone without warm, waterproof clothing.

Finally, Haleakalā is an ecologically delicate area where it's essential to practice **minimum-impact hiking**. Carry out everything you carry in, take all the water you need (reckon on six pints a person a day, and check whether there's water available to filter at the wilderness cabins), and stick to established trails. Above all, never walk on the cinder soil surrounding a silversword plant (see p.276).

For details of companies that organize **horseriding** expeditions in Haleakalā Crater, see p.221.

Route 1: The Sliding Sands Trail

From the visitor center parking lot, the **Sliding Sands Trail** – which you may also see called the **Keonehe'ehe'e Trail** – briefly parallels the road to skirt White Hill. It then starts its leisurely switchback sweep into the crater, down a long scree slope of soft red ash. While the *pali* north of the visitor center is scattered with buttresses of rock and patches of green vegetation, this side is almost completely barren, the smooth crumbling hillside only interrupted by an occasional bush. Far ahead, mists and clouds stream into the crater through the Ko'olau Gap.

For most of the way down, the ground beneath your feet is made of tiny fragments of rock with different colors and textures; hard-baked pink clay is interspersed with tiny brown gravel and little chunks of black basalt. It takes a while to appreciate the immensity of the crater; for the first mile, you expect to arrive at the crater floor at a group of multicolored rocks in the middle distance, but when you reach them you find a longer descent ahead.

Two miles down, the trail passes between a clump of 20ft-high 'a'ā rock outcroppings. A spur trail from here leads 0.4 miles, by way of a miniature "garden" of silverswords, to the smooth lip of the **Ka Luʻu O Ka ʻŌʻō Crater**. This full round cinder-cone, glinting with pink, red, yellow, and ochre highlights in the bright sun, cradles a hollow core filled with tumbled boulders. From the trail above, you can see long clinker flows extending for two miles north of it, eating away at the neighboring Kamaoliʻi Crater.

Continuing on the main trail, you wind down through a rough field of 'a'ā lava. In season, the silverswords that almost line the path shoot up above head height. For the final stretch of the total 3.8-mile descent, the desolate crater floor spreads out broad and flat ahead of you, punctuated by heaped mounds of ash.

Route 2: The Halemauʻu Trail

The alternative route down into the crater, the switchbacking **Halemauʻu Trail**, starts at a trailhead half a dozen miles down Haleakalā Crater Road from the visitor center. Toward the end of the relatively featureless 0.75-mile descent from the parking lot to the crater rim, the main trail is joined by a side trail up from Hosmer Grove (see p.273). It then passes through a gate, to run parallel to the wire fence that marks the park boundary. After a few more minutes, the trail crosses a high, narrow ridge; provided the afternoon clouds aren't passing over it, you'll get staggering views down to the North Maui coastline, as well as south into the crater.

Silverswords

Not far from the ragged edge of the crater, we came upon what we were searching for; not, however, one or two, but thousands of silverswords, their cold, frosted silver gleam making the hill-side look like winter or moonlight. They exactly resemble the finest work in frosted silver, the curve of their globular mass of leaves is perfect, and one thinks of them rather as the base of an épergne for an imperial table, or as a prize at Ascot or Goodwood, than anything organic.

Isabella Bird, May 1873

Haleakalā is a treasure-trove of unique plants and birds, but the most distinctive of all its species is the **silversword**. A distant relative of the sunflower, presumably descended from a lone seed that wafted across the Pacific from America, this extraordinary plant has adapted perfectly to the forbidding conditions of Haleakalā Crater.

Known by the ancient Hawaiians as the *ʻāhinahina*, or "silvery-gray," it consists of a gourd-shaped bowl of curving gray leaves, a couple of feet across, and cupped to collect what little moisture is available. Slender roots burrow in all directions just below the surface of the low-quality cinder soil; merely walking nearby can crush the roots and kill the plant.

Each silversword takes between three and twenty years to grow to full size, and then blossoms only once. Between May and June of the crucial year, a central shaft rises like a rocket from the desiccated silver leaves, reaching a height of from three to eight feet, and erupting with hundreds of reddish-purple flowers. These peak in July and August, releasing their precious cargo of seeds, and the entire plant then withers and dies.

The slopes of Haleakalā no longer glow with the sheer abundance of silverswords, thanks to depredation by wild goats. In recent years a new threat has been posed by the appearance of Argentinean ants, which prey on the Hawaiian yellow-faced bee that's responsible for pollinating the silversword. However, the park authorities have so far managed to reverse the decline, and clusters of silverswords can be seen at many places along the crater trails.

▲ Silversword, Haleakalā National Park

Only the first few switchbacks cross back and forth between the north and south sides of the high bluff. Here at the tip of the **Leleiwi Pali**, it's very obvious how the landscape below has simply poured down through the Koʻolau Gap, from the crater toward the ocean. Soon, however, the trail narrows to drop sharply down the south side of the *pali*; it never feels too dangerous, though the drop-offs are enormous. The tiny shape of the overnight *Hōlua Cabin* comes into view a couple of miles ahead, a speck at the foot of the mighty cliff.

The trail eventually levels out beyond a gate at the bottom of the final switchback, then undulates its way through a meadow filled with misshapen and overgrown spatter-cones toward **Hōlua Cabin**, just under four miles from the trailhead. A slight detour is required to reach the cabin itself, where the lawns are often filled with honking *nēnē* geese (for camping regulations, see p.273). Beyond it, the trail climbs on to a much more rugged *aʻā* lava flow, the youngest in the crater area. Indentations in the rocky outcrops are scattered with red-berried *ʻnhelo* bushes, nurtured by the wet clouds that drift in through the Koʻolau Gap.

As you climb slowly toward the heart of Haleakalā Crater, you can branch away to the left to follow the brief **Silversword Loop**, which holds the park's greatest concentration of silversword plants.

The crater floor

At the point where the **Halemauʻu Trail** reaches the **crater floor**, almost six miles from its start, a bench enables weary hikers to catch their breath while contemplating the onward haul around the north side of the **Halāliʻi** cinder cone. If you continue south, and turn right after 0.3 miles, you'll come to the foot of the Sliding Sands Trail 1.3 miles after that.

Keep going to the left, however, and within a couple of hundred yards the Halemauʻu Trail follows the crest of a low ridge to make a serpentine twist between Halaliʻi and the nameless cinder cone to the north. Known as **Pele's Paint Pot**, this gorgeous stretch is the most spectacular part of Haleakalā Crater, the trail standing out as a lurid red streak of sand against the brown and yellow mounds to either side. You can tell that Halāliʻi is of relatively recent origin by the fact that its rim has not

yet worn smooth; looking back you'll see the park visitor center framed far away on the crater rim.

It's possible to loop right around Halāliʻi and head back along either trail, but the Halemauʻu Trail continues east for another four miles. Immediately north of the junction where you're forced to decide, you'll see the fenced-off hole of **Kawilinau**, also known, misleadingly, as the **Bottomless Pit**; in fact, this small volcanic vent is just 65ft deep. Spatters of bright-red rock cling to its edges, but it's not especially remarkable. Ancient Hawaiians are said to have thrown the bones of important chiefs into it, to insure their remains would never be disturbed. Half a mile further east, you have the additional option of cutting south across the crater, between Puʻu Naue and Puʻu Nole, to meet the Sliding Sands Trail near *Kapalaoa Cabin* (see p.273).

Those hikers who choose, on the other hand, to take the **Sliding Sands Trail** down from the visitor center know they've reached the crater floor when they reach the south end of the clearly marked spur trail that connects the two main trails. Turning left toward the Halemauʻu Trail involves a fairly stiff climb across the flanks of the ruddy **Ka Moa O Pele** cinder cone; over to the right, the triangular mountain peak of **Hanakauhi** can be seen rising beyond Puʻu Naue.

If instead you continue east along the Sliding Sands Trail, you enter a landscape that resembles the high mountain valleys of the western United States. The trail runs at the foot of a steep *pali*, on the edge of a delightful alpine meadow carpeted with yellow flowers, including the primitive native *moa*. Two miles along – shortly after two successive turnoffs to the left, both of which join to cut across to the Halemauʻu Trail – you come to **Kapalaoa Cabin**. This small, wood-frame, green-roofed cabin, on a slight mound tucked beneath the peak that's officially named Haleakalā, is the only overnight shelter in the crater that doesn't have its own campground (see p.273 for details).

East of Kapalaoa, the Sliding Sands Trail has two more miles to run before it finally merges with the Halemauʻu Trail at the ʻOʻilipuʻu cinder cone, and the two then run together a further 1.4 miles to **Palikū Cabin**. Only press on if you've arranged to stay overnight; the hike all the way here from the crater rim and back up again is too far to attempt in a single day. The last three miles along either trail involve a gentle descent through sparsely vegetated terrain that turns progressively greener as you approach Palikū. There are actually two cabins at Palikū, one for public use and one for rangers; both nestle beneath a sheer cliff, where an attractive, but generally dry, meadow gives way to a well-watered strip of forest.

Kaupō Trail

The very demanding, nine-mile **Kaupō Trail** heads south from *Palikū Cabin*, first through the Kaupō Gap to the edge of the park, and beyond that all the way down to meet the Piʻilani Highway on Maui's remote south coast. It takes a couple of miles to escape the pervasive cindery dryness of the crater floor, but once past it you find you've crossed to the rain-drenched eastern side of the island.

As the walls of the Kaupō Gap rise to either side, the trail drops through dense forest, then, once out of the park, descends steeply through lush grazing land. Now that you're on Kaupō Ranch land, be scrupulous about staying on the correct trail; free-ranging bulls roam on the other side of many of the fences. After several hours of extravagant switchbacks, you finally reach the highway two hundred yards east of the Kaupō Store (see p.292). Unless you've arranged to be picked up, your problems may just be beginning – little traffic passes this way.

Some people make the entire hike from the summit to Kaupō in a single day, on the basis that doing so means that they don't have to reserve a cabin or campsite or carry heavy equipment. That's a very, very long and demanding day-hike, however, and not one you should attempt without prior experience of hiking in Haleakalā.

East Maui

Exposed to the full force of the trade winds and sculpted by rainwater flowing back down the northern slopes of Haleakalā, Maui's **northeast coast** holds the most inspiring scenery on the island. From Kahului, the **Hāna Highway** takes fifty miles to wind its way round to the time-forgotten hamlet of **Hāna** at the easternmost tip. This memorable drive forms an essential part of most Maui itineraries, but is almost always done as a day-trip. Devoid of safe beaches, and too wet to build resorts, East Maui has very little overnight accommodation, and thus remains the **least spoiled** region of the island.

Pā'ia

PĀ'IA, four miles east of Kahului on the Hāna Highway, is a friendly, laidback town that's a center for windsurfers, alternative types and beach bums, and is also kept busy with day-trippers heading for the Road to Hāna. Pā'ia started life in the 1870s, divided into two distinct sections that both served the sugar plantations. The town familiar to visitors today was originally **Lower Pā'ia**, set up at sea level by freebooting entrepreneurs who opened stores, theaters, and restaurants, to entice the plantation laborers who lived and worked in **Upper Pā'ia**, concentrated around the sugar mill half a mile inland.

The local **beach** is not especially attractive, but neighbouring **H.A. Baldwin Beach County Park** is much more inviting, while **Ho'okipa Beach County Park**, a couple of miles east of town, offers the best windsurfing on the island.

Accommodation

While Pā'ia is not a resort destination, it does hold a handful of small-scale **accommodation** options. Windsurfers on a tight budget tend to stay at the *Banana Bungalow* in Wailuku (see p.248), while long-term visitors can find rooms through the **bulletin boards** outside *Mana Foods Deli* on Baldwin Avenue, which advertises rates from around $250 per week, or $700–1000 per month. There's no **camping** nearby.

Aloha Maui Cottages 101 Loomis Rd
☏ 808/572-9820, ⊛ www.alohamauicottages.com. Very rural B&B, not far off Hwy-360 and thirteen miles east of Pā'ia, consisting of two separate cottages plus a bedroom in the main house. All accommodation is en suite, and the rates are very reasonable, especially for longer stays. Three-night minimum stay. ❹

The Inn at Mama's Fish House 799 Poho Place ☏ 808/579-9764 or 1-800/860-4852, ⊛ www.mamasfishhouse.com. Nine fully equipped, tropically styled rental suites and cottages, right beside Kū'au Beach, and alongside a popular restaurant. The two-bedroom oceanfront units are quite beautifully located, but the others, set slightly

back in lush gardens, can cost less than half the price. ❺–❾
Nalu Kai Lodge 18 Nalu Place ☏ 808/384-4344 or 1-888/574-8666, ⊛ www.nalukailodge.com. Pleasant little budget inn, in the heart of Pā'ia, and furnished in an attractive retro-Hawaiian style; rooms lack phones and TVs. Two-night minimum stay. ❹

Pā'ia Inn 93 Hāna Hwy ☏ 808/579-6000 or 1-800/721-4000, ⊛ www.paiainn.com. Very lovely, very comfortable boutique hotel, right in the middle of town but still peaceful, and offering a hip modern take on traditional Polynesian style, with plush beds and tiled bathrooms, and a couple of larger suites. ❺–❾

The Town

The charming, paint-peeling wooden buildings that cluster around the intersection of the Hāna Highway with Baldwin Avenue, which climbs up towards Makawao (see p.265), now abound in good-value cafés and restaurants, along with gift stores and galleries. Look out in particular for **Alice in Hulaland**, 19 Baldwin Ave (T 808/579-9922, W www.aliceinhulaland.com), which is by far the best store on Maui to buy *tiki*-themed gifts and novelties.

Narrow footpaths thread their way toward the ocean from the Hāna Highway, passing between ramshackle houses with colorful gardens, to reach a short, tree-lined, and sandy **beach**. Swimming here in Pā'ia Bay is rarely appealing, however, thanks to shallow, murky water and abundant seaweed, so locals head instead to the H.A. Baldwin Beach County Park, a mile west.

H.A. Baldwin Beach County Park

Named after Harry Baldwin, son of Henry Baldwin of Alexander & Baldwin fame (see p.246), the **H.A. Baldwin Beach County Park** was once the official sugar-company beach, and the chimneys of the defunct sugar mill remain visible a few hundred yards off the highway, across the cane fields. The beach itself is reached by a short road lined by a graceful curve of palm trees. Perfect bodysurfing waves crash onto its long stretch of sand, with safer swimming areas at either end.

Ho'okipa Beach County Park

The best **windsurfing** site in Maui, if not the world, is **Ho'okipa Beach County Park**, just below the highway two miles east of Pā'ia. Thanks to a submerged rocky ledge that starts just a few feet out, the waves here are stupendous, and so are the skills required to survive in them – this is no place for beginners. The peak season for windsurfing is summer, when the trade winds are at their most consistent. By long-standing arrangement, sailboarders can only take to the water after 11am each day. In the early morning, and on those rare winter days when the wind dies down, expert **surfers** flock to Ho'okipa to ride the break known as "Pavilions" near the headland to the east.

As a beach, Ho'okipa is not hugely attractive. There's little shade for most of its length, apart from a nice big grove of trees at the western end. Picnic shelters, showers, and restrooms are ranged along a platform of lava boulders raised above the small shelf of sand. In summer, the surf can be low enough for swimming, but you still have to negotiate the seaweed-covered ledge to reach deep enough water.

Ho'okipa is so busy that you can only approach it along a one-way loop road, which starts beyond its far eastern end; the auxiliary parking lot on the headland here is a great place from which to watch or photograph the surf action.

Jaws

Thanks to mouthwatering photo-spreads in many a surfing magazine, Maui's most famous **surf site** is Jaws, a highly inaccessible spot east of Pā'ia where 70ft waves are recorded on perhaps ten days each winter. Surfing there has only become at all practicable since the advent of **tow-in surfing**, using jet skis, in the early 1990s, and when weather conditions are right Hawaii's premier surfers now flock here to do battle with monsters. If you want to watch the action, you can reach Jaws by turning left toward the ocean five miles east of Ho'okipa, between mileposts 13 and 14 on Hwy-36, following Hanaha Road until your vehicle can take no more, which will probably be soon in an ordinary rental, and then hiking oceanwards between the pineapple fields.

Eating and drinking

As far as **restaurants** are concerned, Pā'ia comes up trumps. Though fresh fish is the local specialty, there's something for all tastes, even including vegetarians. For once there's also a lively **drinking** scene, focused around the bars and restaurants near the main highway intersection.

Anthony's Coffee Co 90C Hāna Hwy ☎808/579-8340. Small, early-opening coffee bar just west of central Pā'ia, fitted with a churning coffee-roaster and serving espressos, pastries, soups, omelets, and deli sandwiches at a handful of indoor tables, plus $5 smoothies and a wide range of ice creams to go. Daily 5.30am–6pm.

Cafe Mambo 30 Baldwin Ave ☎808/579-8021. Pale orange diner, just off the highway, serving espressos plus $7–10 burger or sandwich lunches; picnics to go cost from $8.50 per person, $15 for two. The Spanish owner prepares tapas and paella in the evening, as well as a crispy duck – even a crispy duck burger – and they hold regular cinema nights. Daily 8am–9pm.

The Flatbread Company 89 Hāna Hwy ☎808/579-8989. If you suspect "flatbread" is a fancy way of saying "pizza," you're dead right. Call them what you will, these ones, cooked in a wood-fired clay oven, are delicious, courtesy of a small New England-based chain that places its emphasis on free-range and organic ingredients. The restaurant itself is lively but unhurried. Twelve-inchers cost $11–14, and toppings include *kalua* pork and mango BBQ. Daily 11.30am–10pm.

Fresh Mint 115 Baldwin Ave ☎808/579-9144. Smart, cool, vegetarian Vietnamese restaurant. Lots of delicious noodles, stir-fries, soups, or curries, some with soy chicken or soy fish, others with tofu or just eggplant. All entrees cost around $10. Daily 5–9pm.

Haz Beanz 103 Baldwin Ave ☎808/268-0149. Friendly, spacious, laidback coffee-bar-cum-wi-fi hangout, serving espresso, smoothies, and cheap burritos. Part of the premises is given over to a store selling authentic hula accessories. Mon–Fri 6am–2pm, Sat 6am–1pm, Sun 6am–noon.

Mama's Fish House 799 Poho Place ☎808/579-8488, ⓦwww.mamasfishhouse.com. Upmarket fish restaurant, in breezy beachfront gardens a mile east of downtown Pā'ia. At lunch, you can opt for $13–17 fish sandwiches and burgers, or go for full-scale fish entrees, each identified with the name of the fisherman who caught it. Dinner offers similar choices, along with even more fancy gourmet-Hawaiian dishes like mahimahi steamed in a *ti* leaf with coconut milk, costing anything from $30 upwards. While the views are sublime, if you come after sunset you may feel you're paying premium prices for little added value. Daily 11am–3pm & 4.15–9pm.

Moana Bakery & Cafe 71 Baldwin Ave ☎808/579-9999. Smart, tasteful café/sushi bar/restaurant not far off the main highway, with mosaic tables and large windows. Fancy breakfasts, lunchtime *saimin* or sandwiches ($9–12), and dinner entrees ($15–44) that range from green or red Thai curries to chilli-seared *ahi* or an entire rack of lamb. Daily 8am–9pm.

Pā'ia Fish Market 110 Hāna Hwy at Baldwin Ave ☎808/579-8030. Informal, inexpensive place with wooden benches, where fresh fish – sashimi or blackened – is $15, while scallops, shrimp, and calamari cost a bit more, and a fish or meat burger is just $9. Fish'n'chips is $12 for lunch, $14 for dinner. Pasta entrees include chicken ($15) and seafood ($16), and there's a sideline in quesadillas, fajitas, and soft tacos. Daily 11am–9.30pm.

The road to Hāna

The endless rains that fall on Haleakalā cascade down Maui's long windward flank, covering it with jungle-like vegetation. Ancient Hawaiians allowed up to two days for the canoe trip from the isthmus round to the far-eastern settlement of **Hāna**. Now the **Hāna Highway**, hacked into the coastal cliffs by convicts during the 1920s, is a major attraction in its own right, twisting tortuously in and out of gorges, past innumerable waterfalls and over more than fifty tiny one-lane bridges. All year round, and especially in June, the route is ablaze with color from orchids, rainbow eucalyptus, and orange-blossomed African tulip trees, while little fruit stands and flower stalls make tempting places to stop. Many people make a big point of taking a **picnic** with them, but it's more fun to pick up food along the way.

The usual day's excursion is roughly fifty miles each way, from Pā'ia to **'Ohe'o Gulch** beyond Hāna. While not as hair-raising as legend would have it, driving is slow going, taking three hours each way, and demands serious concentration. If you'd prefer to keep your eyes on the scenery rather than on the road, consider taking an **organized tour** with the operators detailed on p.220.

Huelo

Although the coastal road around East Maui is called Hāna Highway from the moment it leaves Kahului, it changes from Hwy-36 to Hwy-360 ten miles east of Pā'ia, at the foot of Hwy-365 from Makawao, and that's where you'll find **mile marker 0**.

The first potential distraction on the drive to Hāna is the unsigned turnoff, marked by a double row of mailboxes at a bend in the highway roughly 3.5 miles along, that leads down to the village of **HUELO**. The dirt road soon passes the plain **Kaulanapueo** ("resting-place of the owl") **Church**, built of coral cement on a black-lava base and usually kept locked. It continues for a couple of miles, but neither it nor its many side roads offer access to the sea. Like many local communities, Huelo has become an uncertain mixture of Hawaiians and wealthy *haoles*.

Not far beyond the road down to Huelo, the picnic table immediately below the *Huelo Lookout* fruit stand offers an opportunity to stop and admire the views of the forested slopes and the ocean beyond.

Waikamoi Nature Trail

Your one opportunity to explore the forested ridges above the Hāna Highway comes just over half a mile beyond the mile-9 marker, where the short but enjoyable **Waikamoi Nature Trail** sets off from a roadside pull-out. The one-mile loop trail starts beyond a small picnic shelter, gently zigzagging up a muddy ridge. Despite the stone benches along the way, there are no views – it's barely possible to see beyond the tight-packed *hala* trees and green rustling bamboos hemming the track – but sunlight dapples down through the overhead canopy to magical effect. Here and there, you pass eucalyptus trees whose bark peels like fine tissue paper. The trail tops out at a smooth grassy clearing, with another picnic shelter, and a large mosquito population. It makes little difference whether you return by the same route, or down the adjacent jeep road that drops directly to the parking lot.

A little further along the highway, **Waikamoi Falls** tumbles down toward the road at a tight hairpin bend. If you want a closer look, the only place to park is immediately before the bridge – a spot that's all too easy to overshoot. Not far beyond Waikamoi Falls, at mile 10.5, the small and privately owned **Garden of Eden Arboretum** (daily 8am–3pm; $10; ⓦwww.mauigardenofeden.com) displays colorful flowers and orchids. It also offers a slightly distant waterfall view, and has picnic tables with a panoramic prospect of the coastline.

Honomanū Bay

Shortly after mile marker 13, the highway drops down to sea level for the first time since Ho'okipa Beach, and you finally start to get the long coastal views for which it's famous. The Ke'anae Peninsula appears on the horizon, but much closer at hand – where the gorgeous, uninhabited **Honomanū Valley**, lit up by tulip trees, gives way to the ocean – you'll see the black-gravel beach at **Honomanū Bay**. Swimming and snorkeling here is only advisable on the calmest of summer days, but it's a popular site with local **surfers**.

Two separate dirt tracks cut down to the shore from the road as it sweeps around the narrow valley. The first, at 13.5 miles, leads down to the north shore of the

stream; the second, just after the mile-14 marker on the far side of the stream, is paved for the first few yards, but then becomes steeper and muddier. It comes out at the longer side of the beach.

Ke'anae Arboretum

From a wooded bend in the road a few hundred yards before the mile-17 marker, a paved, level trail heads inland to the attractive public gardens of the **Ke'anae Arboretum** (daily dawn–dusk; free). Following the course of a stream you can hear but not see, it leads into a lush, narrow valley and reaches the arboretum within a quarter of a mile.

Fifty-foot-high clumps of "male bamboo" guard the entrance, with tropical plants beyond including Hawaiian species such as torch ginger and wet and dry taro. Beyond the taro fields, a mile into the park, the trail becomes a wet scramble through the rainforest, crossing up and over the valley ridge by way of tree-root footholds. Along with lots of small waterfalls and swarms of tiny flies feasting on fallen guava and breadfruit, there's a good chance of spotting rare forest birds and even wild boar.

Ke'anae Peninsula

Not far beyond the arboretum, a side road twists down to the flat **Ke'anae Peninsula**, the site of a small, and still predominantly Hawaiian, village. It's said that this windswept promontory consisted of bare rock until a local chief forced his followers to spend two years carrying baskets of soil down the mountainside; thereafter it became a prime taro-growing region, and supported a large population.

The taro fields are still here, surrounded by abundant banana trees and birds of paradise, and there's also a fine old **church** among the tall palms. The edge of the ocean is as bleak as ever, with *hala* trees propped up along the shoreline and the surf crashing onto headlands of gnarled black lava; swimming here is out of the question. A small pavilion nearby holds the best **public restrooms** on the whole route to Hāna.

Practicalities

Almost the only **food** and **lodging** along the main stretch of the Hāna Highway is in the Ke'anae area. *YMCA Camp Ke'anae*, on the highway shortly before the arboretum, was originally a prison, but now offers **cabin** accommodation and also has its own grassy **campground** (T 808/248-8355, W www.mauiymca.org/campk.htm). Whether you stay in your own tent or in a cabin, it costs $17 per person or $35 per family. Not surprisingly, the facilities tend to be reserved way in advance.

Simple **snacks** are sold at two roadside kiosks – *Halfway to Hāna* and *Uncle Harry's*, before and after the mile-18 marker respectively. The specialty at *Halfway to Hāna* (which has its own ATM machine) is the banana bread; at *Uncle Harry's*, opposite a dazzling bed of flowers, try the banana and pineapple smoothie. Neither keeps very regular hours, but both claim they're open daily for lunch.

Wailua

Within a mile of Ke'anae, as the highway veers inland, the arrow-straight Wailua Road plunges down to another traditional village, **WAILUA**. Unlike Ke'anae, its ancient rival, Wailua has always been fertile and still holds extensive taro terraces.

The lower of the two churches that stand a short way down from the turnoff is known as the **Coral Miracle**. Local legend has it that in 1860, just as its builders were despairing of finding the stone to complete it, a freak storm washed up exactly enough coral on the beach below. It's a simple but attractive chapel, painted white, with turquoise stenciling around the porch and windows. Look back across the valley

as you leave the building for a superb view of the high **Waikani Falls**, garlanded by flowering trees at the head of the valley.

Wailua Road ends just above the tranquil mouth of Wailua Stream, which makes a sharp contrast with the ocean pummeling the beach of black pebbles beyond. Don't drive down to the stream – there's no room to turn round – and don't even consider a swim.

Wailua viewpoints

Lookouts on either side of the highway beyond the Wailua turnoff offer scenic views up and down the coastline. From the inconspicuous *mauka* parking lot of **Wailua Valley State Wayside**, steps climb through a tunnel of trees to a vantage point overlooking Wailua Valley as it reaches the sea, and also inland across Keʻanae Valley, to towering waterfalls, undulating ridges, and endless trees.

A little further on, immediately after the mile-19 marker, Wailua Valley spreads like a little oasis beneath **Wailua Lookout**. The taller of Wailua's two churches, **St Gabriel's**, pokes its head above the sea of trees, while the thickly wooded gorge stretches away to the right. At the next bend, just around the corner, a big cascade roars beside the road; you have to react quickly to stop.

Puaʻakaʻa State Wayside

The spacious parking lot of **Puaʻakaʻa State Wayside**, 22.5 miles along Hāna Highway, is every bit as big as the park itself. In fact, this is a favorite stop for bus tours, because so little effort is required to negotiate the park's few yards of paved trails. If you brave the crowds, you'll see a pretty but far from spectacular sequence of small waterfalls, with picnic tables dotted on either side of a stream.

Nāhiku

Not far after the mile-25 marker, a narrow unmarked road takes about three miles to wind down to the ocean. The few houses along the way constitute **NĀHIKU**, though there's no town, just a jungle of trees and vines, some of which all but engulf the abandoned vehicles left here. The road comes out at **Ōpūhano Point**, from where you can look back toward Wailua atop the tree-covered cliffs reaching down into the water.

Early in the twentieth century, Nāhiku was the site of the first, albeit unsuccessful, rubber plantation in the US. Subsequently, ex-Beatle George Harrison had a home here, but in his later years he only visited occasionally, following a bitter legal dispute with his neighbors that centered on the construction of a beach-access footpath.

Just before the mile-29 marker, the ⚚ *Nāhiku Fruit Stand* (daily 6.30am–4.30pm) is a funky, friendly roadside shack that sells delicious espressos and smoothies, along with home-made lunches such as banana bread and fish specials. There's a small crafts gallery alongside, as well as an open-air grill, *Up In Smoke BBQ*, that serves baked breadfruit and smoked fish to no discernible schedule.

Kahanu Garden

The first sign that you're finally approaching Hāna is when you pass **Hāna Gardenland**, a commercial nursery, on the right. Immediately afterwards, **ʻUlaʻino Road** drops away to the left of the highway. Three-quarters of a mile down, where the road crosses a minor ford, the paved surface gives out. On the far side, you'll find the entrance to **Kahanu Garden**, a nonprofit facility belonging to the National Tropical Botanical Garden (Mon–Fri 10am–2pm; adults $10, under-13s free; guided tour Sat 10am, $25; ☎808/248-8912 or 332-7234, ⓦwww.ntbg.org).

While Kahanu Garden holds over a hundred acres of tropical plants, it's of most significance as the site of **Pi'ilanihale Heiau**, the largest ancient *heiau* (temple) not merely in Hawaii but quite possibly in the entire Pacific. A *luakini*, or temple where human sacrifice took place, it was built in the late thirteenth century, and enlarged and re-dedicated by Pi'ilani around 1570 AD to celebrate his then-recent conquest of the entire island. It was re-built once more in the late eighteenth century, and extensively restored and reconstructed during the 1990s.

A mile-long loop trail through Kahanu Garden begins by skirting an extensive forest of splay-footed *hala* trees. A free booklet describes the traditional uses of several different species of indigenous and imported plants that have been cultivated along the way. Your first sight of the *heiau* itself presents it towering above the lush oceanfront lawns. Constructed from black-lava boulders, intricately slotted into place, and set on a natural lava flow, it's an impressive spectacle. Measuring 174m by 89m, it covers almost three acres and consists of five separate tiers on its oceanward side. As usual at such sites, however, in deference to ongoing Hawaiian religious beliefs, visitors are not allowed to set foot on the actual structure and can only admire it from a distance. As a result, you're not likely to spend more time here than the half-hour it takes to walk the trail, which also offers some gorgeous views along the coast.

You may hear talk of an oceanfront **waterfall**, popularly known as the **Blue Pool**, that lies a short walk beyond the point where 'Ula'ino Road ends, 1.4 miles beyond the garden. Sadly, local residents have become so infuriated by the sheer quantity of day-trippers who try to reach it that they've taken to intimidating would-be visitors, and making the attempt is no longer worth the hassle.

Wai'ānapanapa State Park

Within two miles of Hāna, beyond the turnoff to Hāna Airport (see p.287), a clearly signed road *makai* of the highway leads through a "tunnel" of overhanging trees to the shoreline at **Wai'ānapanapa State Park**. To reach the main parking lot, perched above a tiny **black-sand beach**, turn left when you reach the park cabins at the end of the first straight stretch of road. A short and easy trail descends from the parking lot to this beautiful little cove, where the beach changes from shiny black pebbles to fine black sand as it shelves into the ocean. It looks wonderful, and barely has room to hold its daily crowd of sunbathers, but swimming is deadly, with heavy surf and deep water just a few yards out.

At the right-hand side of the beach as you face the sea, look for a hollow cave in the small cliff that you just walked down. Squeeze your way through its narrow entrance and you'll find that not only does it widen inside, but that it is, in fact, a **tunnel**. The far end, where it's open to the ocean, is a truly magical spot.

By contrast, a very short loop trail to the left of the parking lot back at the top leads down and through **Wai'ānapanapa Cave**. A few yards back from the sea, this "cave" is actually a collapsed lava tube, holding two successive grotto-like pools. It's slightly stagnant and smells rather like a public restroom, but you do see some nice clinging flowers.

Coastal **hiking trails** in both directions make it easy to escape the throngs at the beach. Heading **northwest** (left), you're soon clambering over a headland of black lava through a forest of *hala* and *naupaka*. Inlets in the jagged shoreline harbor turquoise pools, while the surf rages against the rocks; in places, where the sea has hollowed out caverns, you can feel the thud of the ocean beneath you. A painting of a natural "lava bridge" here, executed in 1939 by Georgia O'Keeffe, now hangs in the Honolulu Academy of Arts. A mile or so along, the trail ends at the fence of Hāna Airport.

Southeast of the beach, the footpath crosses smoother, firmer lava, passing the park campground, a cemetery, and an impressive blowhole. After around a mile, it reaches the ruined **Ohala Heiau**, the walls of which remain clear despite ivy-like *naupaka* growing inside. You can continue four miles on to Hāna; the scenery is invigorating all the way, but the trail gets progressively harder to follow.

Wai'ānapanapa is by far the nicest place on Maui to **camp** beside the ocean. In addition to tent camping ($18 per site), it has basic cabins, each holding up to four people, at $60 per cabin for HI residents, $90 otherwise. Permits are available online at ⓦ www.hawaiistateparks.org, or from the state parks office in Wailuku (see p.221); the cabins are usually reserved far in advance.

Hāna

For some visitors, the former sugar town of **HĀNA** comes as a disappointment after the splendors of the Hāna Highway. Certainly, the point of driving the road is to enjoy the scenery en route, rather than to race to Hāna itself. Having said that, it's one of the most relaxing places on Maui to spend a few days, short on swimmable beaches and golf, perhaps, but very long indeed on character, history, and beauty.

In ancient times, Hāna controlled a densely populated region. It's now home to just a few hundred inhabitants, who continue to resist any concept of "development," proudly viewing themselves as one of the most staunchly traditional communities in the state. When the local sugar plantation closed in 1943, most of its land was bought by **Paul Fagan**, a Californian businessman. He established not only the

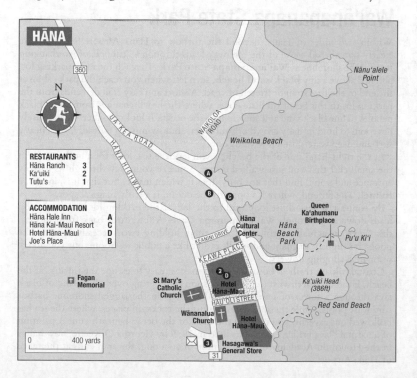

Hāna Ranch, whose cowboys still work cattle herds in the fields above town, but also modern Maui's first **hotel**, the *Hotel Hāna-Maui* (see below). Fagan died in 1959 – he's commemorated by a large white cross on the hillside – but the town remains dominated by the businesses he founded. Most of the town's central area is taken up by the *Hotel Hāna-Maui*, while the Hāna Ranch headquarters on the main highway houses its most conspicuous restaurant and other utilities.

Arrival

The principal user of Hāna's small **airport**, perched beside the ocean three miles north of town, is the tiny Pacific Wings airline (☎808/248-7700 or 1-888/575-4546, ⓦwww.pacificwings.com), which operates around four (expensive) daily round-trip flights between Kahului and Hāna. In addition, Hang Gliding Maui is a one-man operation that provides (powered) **hang-gliding lessons** at $150 for half an hour, $200 for an hour (☎808/572-6557, ⓦwww.hangglidingmaui.com).

Accommodation

More **accommodation** is available around Hāna than is immediately apparent. As well as the *Hotel Hāna-Maui*, small-scale B&Bs are scattered all over town, and many of the houses along the shoreline are for rent. You can also **camp** at Wai'ānapanapa State Park (see opposite).

🏃 **Hāmoa Bay House and Bungalow** PO Box 773, Hāna, HI 96713 ☎808/248-7884, ⓦwww.hamoabay.com. Two fabulous rental properties, splendidly isolated – even from each other – two miles south of Hāna. Perched on stilts in a jungle-like setting, and with an open-air hot tub on its wooden *lānai*, the bungalow makes an idyllic honeymoon hideaway, while the house is large enough for two couples. Both have Balinese bamboo furnishings, and require a three-night minimum stay. Bungalow ⑥, house ⑦

Hāna Hale Inn 4829 Ua'kea Rd ☎808/248-7641, ⓦwww.hanahaleinn.com. A cluster of distinctive rainforest-style timber buildings, not far up from the ocean and overlooking an attractive fishpond that actually belongs to the neighbors. All are very luxurious, with hot tubs and bamboo furnishings; the more expensive ones can comfortably sleep four. ⑤–⑦

Hāna Kai-Maui Resort 1533 Ua'kea Rd ☎808/248-8426 or 1-800/346-2772, ⓦwww .hanakaimaui.com. Small condo building, set in lovely multilevel gardens overlooking Hāna Bay, a short way north of Hāna Beach County Park. Each

well-equipped studio and one-bedroom unit has a kitchen and private *lānai*; the larger ones sleep four. Studios ⑤, apartments ⑥

Hotel Hāna-Maui 5031 Hāna Hwy ☎808/248-8211, ⓦwww.hotelhanamaui.com. This secluded luxury hotel was built in the 1940s as Hawaii's first self-contained resort and integrated into the community to create a unique atmosphere. In addition to the older rooms in the Bay Cottages near the lobby, rows of plantation-style Sea Ranch Cottages are arranged across lawns that drop down to the ocean. As the hotel was sold immediately before this book went to press, it's impossible to predict what exactly the future may hold for its facilities or affordability. Check the website for the latest details. ⑧

Joe's Place 4870 Ua'kea Rd ☎808/248-7033, ⓦwww.joesrentals.com. Joe himself passed away some years ago, but his ordinary Hāna home, opposite the *Hāna-Kai Maui Resort*, still offers eight bare-bones rooms, sharing a kitchen and communal lounge. All cost $50 except the one that has its own en-suite bath, priced at $60; there are no sea views, but this is Hāna's best option for budget travelers. ②

Downtown Hāna

None of the buildings along the main highway, which passes through Hāna a hundred yards up from the ocean, is especially worth exploring, though **Wananalua Church**, whose square, solid tower contrasts appealingly with the flamboyant gardens surrounding it, makes a photogenic landmark. Across the road, the **Hāna Ranch Center** is a dull mall, designed to feed and water the daily influx of bus tours, but given a flash of color by the odd *paniolo* cowboy. **Hasegawa's General**

Queen Kaʻahumanu: scenes from a life

No figure encapsulates the dramas and paradoxes of early Hawaiian history as completely as **Queen Kaʻahumanu**, the daughter of Nāmāhana, a chiefess from East Maui, and Keʻeaumoku from the Big Island. Her parents' strategic alliance presented such a threat to Kahekili, the ruling chief of Maui, that they were fleeing for their lives when Kaʻahumanu was born at Hāna, around 1777.

Chief Keʻeaumoku was the most trusted lieutenant of **Kamehameha the Great**; it was he who killed Kamehameha's rival Keōua at Puʻukoholā (see p.160). His daughter may have been as young as eight when she first caught the eye of the king; soon afterwards, she became the seventeenth of his twenty-two wives.

Captain Vancouver described Kaʻahumanu in 1793 as "about sixteen [she] undoubtedly did credit to the choice and taste of Kamehameha, being one of the finest women we had yet seen on any of the islands." According to nineteenth-century historian Samuel M. Kamakau, "Of Kamehameha's two possessions, his wife and his kingdom, she was the most beautiful."

Kaʻahumanu was Kamehameha's favorite wife. As a high-ranking *aliʻi*, she possessed great **spiritual power**, or *mana*; she herself was a *puʻuhonua* (see p.150), meaning that *kapu*-breakers who reached her side could not be punished. She was also an expert surfer and serial adulterer. Among her paramours was the dashing Kaiana, killed commanding the armies of Oahu against Kamehameha at Nuʻuanu Pali, in 1795.

It was after Kamehameha's death, in 1819, that Kaʻahumanu came into her own. Announcing to her son Liholiho that "We two shall rule over the land," she proclaimed herself **Kuhina Nui**, or Regent, and set about destroying the system of *kapu*. This elaborate system of rules denied women access to certain foods and, more importantly, to the real source of power in ancient Hawaii – the *luakini* war temples. At first Kaʻahumanu's goal was to break the grip of the priesthood, but in 1825 she converted to Christianity, after being nursed through a serious illness by Sybil Gingham, the wife of Hawaii's first missionary. Meanwhile, in 1821, she had married both the last king of Kauai, Kaumualiʻi, and his 7ft-tall son, Kealiʻiahonui.

Kaʻahumanu outlived Liholiho, who died in England in 1824, and remained the effective ruler of Hawaii when his younger brother Kauikeaouli succeeded to the throne as Kamehameha III. Her achievements included selecting Hawaii's first jury, presiding over its first Western-style trial, and enforcing its first law on marriage and divorce. After seven years spent proselytizing for her new faith, she died on June 5, 1832. Her last words were reported as "Lo, here am I, O Jesus, Grant me thy gracious smile."

Store, stocked with every item imaginable, is a friendly place to pick up supplies. The **Hāna Coast Gallery**, at the northern end of the lobby of the *Hotel Hāna-Maui*, sells an unusually good, if expensive, assortment of Hawaiian crafts and paintings of East Maui landscapes.

Local history is recalled by the low-key exhibits – gourds, calabashes, fish hooks, and crude stone idols – at the **Hāna Cultural Center** (Mon–Fri 10am–4pm; $3; Ⓦwww.hanaculturalcenter.org), on Uaʻkea Road, down from the highway and above the bay. It also holds art exhibitions plus a comprehensive collection of photos of past and present Hāna residents. Nearby stands a tiny nineteenth-century jail-cum-courthouse, alongside a replica living compound, with a thatched stone dwelling and a canoe house, plus garden terraces planted with taro and *ti*.

Hāna Bay

Hāna's reputation for beauty relies largely upon broad **Hāna Bay**, a short walk below the north end of the town center. Much the safest place to swim in East Maui, it's also the only protected harbor in the area.

The small gray-sand beach known as **Hāna Beach County Park** spreads to the south, at the foot of Keawa Place, backed by lawns that hold picnic tables, restrooms, and changing rooms. The park's long terraced pavilion, pressed against the curving hillside across the road, houses *Tutu's* takeout counter (see below).

Thrusting into the ocean further south, the high cinder cone of **Ka'uiki Head** is the most prominent feature of the bay. Now covered with trees, it used to be just a bare rock, and served as a fortress for the ancient chiefs of Maui; Kahekili is said to have repelled an invasion from the Big Island here in 1780. Its far side – only seen easily from the air – collapsed into the sea long ago.

A short **hiking trail** heads off around Ka'uiki Head from beyond the jetty, offering excellent views across the bay and up to Hāna itself. Soon after a tiny red-sand beach, it reaches a bronze plaque, set into a slab of rock near a couple of small caves in the base of the hill. This marks the birthplace of the great Hawaiian queen **Ka'ahumanu**, though she was probably born later than the year it says, 1768 (see box opposite). Continuing on, you discover that the rocky point beyond is in fact an island. Known as **Pu'u Ki'i**, it was once topped by a giant *ki'i* (wooden idol), erected by the Big Island chief, Umi; an automated lighthouse now stands in its place. Around the next corner, the trail is blocked by an impassable red-scree slope.

Red Sand Beach

A precarious coastal footpath leads along the south flank of Ka'uiki Head to a lovely little cove that shelters one of Maui's prettiest beaches, **Red Sand Beach**. The Hāna Ranch, which owns the land here, considers the walk so dangerous that it makes every effort to discourage visitors; the path is often closed due to serious erosion, and should only be attempted after seeking local advice as to current conditions. To find it, walk left from the south end of Ua'kea Road, below a small, neat Japanese cemetery. Approximately a five-minute walk, the path follows, and in places spans, a narrow ledge around a hillside of loose red gravel, but at this low elevation it's not too nerve-racking.

Behind a final promontory, the beach lies angled toward the rising sun, shielded by a row of black dragon's-teeth rocks, kept well flossed by the waves. Hawaiians knew this canoe landing as Kaihalulu Beach. It's only ever safe for swimming in the tiny inshore area, and even then the razor-sharp rocks beneath the surface make it essential to wear reef shoes. The origin of the beach's coarse reddish cinders – the eroded red cliffs above it – is very obvious, and it's equally obvious that you can hike no further.

Eating and drinking

For a town with so many daytime visitors and overnight guests, Hāna has remarkably few places to **eat** or **drink**.

Hāna Ranch Hāna Hwy ☎808/248-8255. Bland, quick-fire restaurant in the heart of Hāna, specializing in dull lunches for the daily hordes of bargain-seeking day-trippers. Mostly it's fries with everything – a half-pound burger made from local beef costs $15 – and they do a vegetarian taro burger too. A cheaper takeout counter sells *saimin* for $4 and plate lunches for around $8. Restaurant daily 11.30am–7pm; takeout daily 6.30am–4pm.
Ka'uiki *Hotel Hāna-Maui*, Hāna Hwy ☎808/248-8211. Though it may well change under the hotel's new ownership (see p.287) and perhaps be taken

over by the Longhi's chain of upscale seafood restaurants, this open-sided, wicker-furnished dining room ranked as this book went to press among the most expensive restaurants in Hawaii, which can make its downhome ambience and local-style service seem a little odd. The food, however, is great. Daily 7.30–10.30am & 6–9pm.
Tutu's Hāna Bay ☎808/248-8244. Beachfront takeout counter, whose indifferent sandwiches, burgers, plate lunches, sodas, and lemonades attract long queues at lunchtime. Daily 8.30am–4pm.

South of Hāna

South of Hāna, Hāna Highway gives way to **Pi'ilani Highway**, but the scenery is, if anything, even more gorgeous than before. In those stretches where the road is not engulfed by magnificent flowering trees, you can look up beyond the ranchlands to the high green mountains, while Mauna Kea on the Big Island comes into view across the 'Alenuihaha Channel.

Kōkī Beach Park

A couple of miles south of Hāna, the Haneo'o Loop Road heads left from the highway. After half a mile, it reaches the ocean alongside the white sands of **Kōkī Beach Park**. Local surfers and boogie-boarders love this spot, but unless you're a very confident swimmer and all-round watersports expert, take heed of the many signs that warn of a very dangerous rip current just offshore. It's a great place for a coastal stroll, in any case. The exposed red cinder-cone dominating the beach is named **Ka Iwi O Pele**, or "the bones of Pele," as the volcano goddess was supposedly killed here by her sister, the goddess of the sea. Oprah Winfrey has a home on a hundred-acre plot immediately north.

Just south of Kōkī Beach, tiny **Ā'lau Islet** stands just out to sea. Ancient Hawaiians reshaped the lava rocks along the promontory closest to the island to create artificial fishponds, and fishermen are still frequent visitors.

Hāmoa Bay

Not far beyond Kōkī Beach, a 1.5-mile detour down the Haneo'o Loop Road takes you to the white-sand beach at **Hāmoa Bay**, used by *Hotel Hāna-Maui* for all its oceanfront activities. A good surfing spot, it's unsafe for swimming, but holds a nice picnic area. The highway continues south through a succession of tiny residential villages, where, apart from the odd roadside fruit-stand and countless crystal-clear waterfalls, there's no reason to stop.

'Ohe'o Gulch

Almost all the day-trippers who reach Hāna press on to beautiful **'Ohe'o Gulch**, ten miles beyond, where a natural rock staircase of waterfalls descends to the oceanfront meadows at the mouth of the **Kīpahulu Valley**. This far-flung outpost of Haleakalā National Park, sometimes spuriously known as "Seven Sacred Pools," tends to be jam-packed in the middle of the day, but, as one of the few places on Maui to offer easy access to unspoiled Hawaiian rainforest, it shouldn't be missed. If you hike a mile or two into the hills, you'll soon escape the crowds to reach cool rock pools, which so long as it's not raining are ideal for swimming.

'Ohe'o Gulch remains open 24 hours a day. Anyone who pulls into the roadside parking lot will find a kiosk that collects the standard admission fee to Haleakalā National Park of $10 per vehicle. This covers access to the entire park for three days, so you need to visit 'Ohe'o Gulch and the summit crater (see p.273) within two days of each other if you want to avoid paying twice. A **ranger station** just down the slope from the lot has up-to-date information on local roads and hiking trails (daily 9am–5pm; ☏808/248-7375, Ⓦwww.nps.gov/hale), and organizes **guided hikes** to no fixed schedule. For details of **horseback** trips nearby, see p.221.

Access to the upper reaches of the **Kīpahulu Valley**, one of the most pristine and environmentally significant regions in all Hawaii, is barred to the public.

The lower trail

The paved footpath that leads **downhill** from the 'Ohe'o Gulch parking lot – officially, **Kōloa Point Trail** – is so busy that it's forced to operate as a one-way loop. Ideally, you'd get here early to enjoy it before the onslaught, but it's still worthwhile at any time of day. After ambling through the meadows for five minutes, the trail winds past ancient stone walls on the low oceanfront bluff, and then down to a tiny gray-grit beach, where the shark-infested ocean is far from tempting.

However, upwards from the ocean, a "ladder" of stream-fed **pools** climbs the craggy rocks. Several are deep and sheltered enough for swimming, and on calm sunny days the whole place throngs with bathers. It's impossible to follow the stream as far up as the high road bridge; by that point, the gorge is a slippery, narrow water chute.

The higher waterfalls

The **Pīpīwai Trail**, into the mountains above 'Ohe'o Gulch, is among the very best hikes in Hawaii (though be sure to carry mosquito repellent). Occasionally it's closed by bad weather, but the construction of two sturdy footbridges has insured that the first mile or so is almost always accessible. It starts beside the ranger station, but swiftly crosses the highway and heads uphill through steep fields, where thick woods line the 'Ohe'o Stream. After the first half-mile, which is by far the most demanding stretch, a spur trail cuts off to the right to reach a railing that overlooks the towering 200ft **Makahiku Falls**. A deep groove in the earth nearby leads to a series of shallow bathing pools just above the lip of the falls, where the stream emerges from a tunnel in the rock. As well as commanding magnificent views, it's an utterly idyllic spot for a swim.

Continuing via a gate in a fence along the main trail, you emerge into an open guava orchard and soon hear the thundering of smaller waterfalls to your right. There's no way to get to the water, but you'll see it framed through the thick jungle, together with the gaping cave mouth it has hollowed out on the far side. A little further on, you may be lured off the trail again by a pair of twin falls near a small concrete dam, which can be admired from a rocky outcrop in the streambed below.

Beyond that lies a lovely meadow, with views to the high valley walls in the distance, laced by huge waterfalls. A mile up, the trail crosses high above the stream twice in quick succession, over the bridges. It then follows a dark and narrow gap through a forest of huge old bamboo interspersed with sections of level wooden boardwalk. Eventually, two miles up from the road, you'll spot the spindle-thin 400ft **Waimoku Falls** ahead. Reaching its base requires a lot of scrambling, and close to the end you have to cross the stream itself on stepping stones. Despite the obvious danger of falling rocks, many hikers choose to cool off by standing directly beneath the cascade. Allow a good two hours to complete the entire round-trip hike.

Camping

The first-come, first-served National Park **campground** at 'Ohe'o Gulch is extremely rudimentary – it's just a field, with pit toilets and no drinking water – but it stands in the ruins of an ancient fishing village, and enjoys superb ocean views. Permits are not required, and it's free, with a three-night maximum stay.

Kīpahulu

Within a mile of 'Ohe'o Gulch, the highway passes through the village of **KĪPAHULU**. Time seems to have stood still in this attractive little spot since the local sugar mill closed down eighty years ago. The only sign of life these days comes from the occasional lunchtime fruit-stand selling the produce of the roadside orchards.

A quarter-mile beyond **milepost 41** at Kīpahulu, a paved road branches left off the highway. After a couple of hundred yards, turn left again onto a dirt road through a "tunnel" of trees, emerging near the **Palapala Hoʻomau Church**. Founded in 1864, it has whitewashed coral walls and a green timber roof, and is set in pretty clifftop gardens. The interior is utterly plain and unadorned.

Visitors make their way to this tranquil spot because the fenced-off platform of black-lava stones in the churchyard holds the grave of **Charles Lindbergh** (1902–74), who won fame in 1927 as the first man to fly the Atlantic. Lindbergh retired to Maui in his old age, and died within a couple of years.

Leading off from the cemetery, and only accessible through it, **Kīpahulu Point Park** is a small, shaded lawn, fringed with bright orange-leafed bushes, where the picnic tables command wonderful ocean views.

Along the South Maui coast

If you've driven the Hāna Highway and have a congenital aversion to going back the same way you came, it's possible in normal weather to follow the Piʻilani Highway right around the whole barren coastline of southern Maui and into the Upcountry above Wailea. Roughly five miles of the road is unpaved; it's a bumpy ride, which is not as spectacular as the Hāna Highway, and won't save you any time either, but it does offer a glorious sense of isolation. It is, however, prone to frequent, long-term **closures**, usually due to landslides – check in advance at the ʻOheʻo Gulch ranger station, and don't attempt to drive this way after dark.

Immediately beyond Kīpahulu, the countryside is lovely, dotted with exclusive homes whose owners are no doubt happy that this is not yet a standard tourist loop. After less than two miles, the road returns to sea level – for the first time in several miles – and skirts the long gray pebble beach at **Lelekea Bay**. As you climb the cliffs at the far end, look back to see water spouting out of the hillside above an overhang in the rock, forceful enough to be a gushing jet rather than a waterfall.

The pavement gives out after the second of the two little coves that follow. An overlook 2.3 juddering miles further on looks down on the small flat promontory holding the 1859 **Huialoha Church**. A mile after that, the solitary **Kaupō Store** is an atmospheric general store that's normally open on weekdays only. By now, the landscape has become much drier, and you're starting to get views up to the **Kaupō Gap**, where a vast torrent of lava appears to have petrified as it poured over the smooth lip of Haleakalā Crater. To the east, you can peek into the lushness of the upper Kīpahulu Valley, but the slopes to the west are all but barren.

Beyond **St Joseph's Church**, which stands below the highway a mile beyond the Kaupō Store, the pavement starts up again and the road begins to mount the long southern flank of Haleakalā at the gentlest of angles. There's no tree cover on the deeply furrowed hillside, so cattle gather beneath the occasional shade tree beside the road.

Naked russet cinder cones lie scattered to either side of the road, some bearing the traces of ancient stone walls, while rivers of rough black ʻaā lava snake down to the sea. An especially vast hollow cone, near the mile-20 marker, marks the spot where small huts and ranch buildings start to reappear. Soon Mākena becomes visible below, with Molokini and Lanai out to sea, and three miles on it's a relief to find yourself back in green woodlands. The Tedeschi Winery (see p.269) is a little over a mile further on, with another 23 miles to go before Kahului.

Lanai

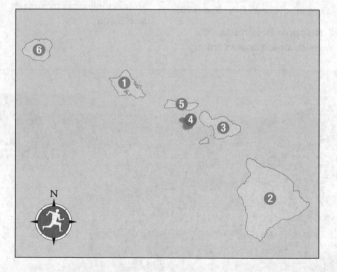

CHAPTER 4

Highlights

✳ **Expeditions Ferry** Much the best way to reach Lanai; in winter, whales are usually spotted on the ocean voyage from Maui. **See p.297**

✳ **Four-wheel-drive adventures** Careering down Lanai's sand-logged back roads in a rented jeep makes an exhilarating day's adventure. **See p.297**

✳ **Hotel Lanai** Attractive old wooden hotel-cum-restaurant, facing the tranquil "village green" of Lāna'i City. **See p.299**

✳ **Hulopo'e Beach** Beautiful sandy beach shared among

locals, campers, and guests at the adjoining *Mānele Bay Hotel*. **See p.303**

✳ **Shipwreck Beach** Flotsam and jetsam lie strewn across the sands of this atmospheric beach, where trans-Pacific voyagers have been coming to grief ever since the sixteenth century. **See p.304**

✳ **Garden of the Gods** Bizarre rock-strewn desert in the heart of the island that takes on an unearthly glow at sunset. **See p.306**

▲ Shipwreck Beach

4

Lanai

The sixth-largest Hawaiian island, and the last to open up to tourism, **Lanai** stands nine miles west of Maui and eight miles south of Molokai. Firmly in the rainshadow of its neighbors, it's a dry and largely barren place, measuring just thirteen miles wide by eight miles long. Until the twentieth century, ancient Hawaiians and modern settlers alike barely bothered with it; then began its seventy-year reign as the world's largest **pineapple** producer.

Lanai's days as the "Pineapple Island" are long over. Widely known as the "Private Island," it has become the personal fiefdom of **David H. Murdock**, a Californian businessman who in 1985 became chairman of **Castle & Cooke** and thus acquired control of 98 percent of the land on Lanai. Deciding that the island's future lay with tourism, he shut down the pineapple plantation and set about redeveloping Lanai as an exclusive resort.

Prospective visitors should not picture Lanai as the ultimate unspoiled Hawaiian island. In many ways, it's very un-Hawaiian, largely lacking both the lush scenery and the safe sandy beaches of the other islands. Instead it's a vast flat-topped mound of red dirt, with a low wooded mountain ridge running down the center as its "backbone." Almost all the island's 2200 inhabitants – half of whom are of Filipino ancestry – live in the former plantation village wildly misnamed **Lāna'i City**, 1600ft above sea level. This is also the site of all its hotels, restaurants, and other businesses, except for the *Mānele Bay Hotel*, set on the south coast near Lanai's only swimming beach.

Guests at Lanai's two major hotels tend to be either rich locals, for whom the damp upland forests make a welcome break, or mega-rich jet-setters, who either place a great premium on privacy or want to have stayed on every Hawaiian island. It's hard to imagine why an ordinary visitor from outside Hawaii would choose Lanai over the other islands, even though it does have one reasonably priced hotel, one B&B rental, and even a campground to make it affordable. Most visitors simply come for the day, on the ferry from Maui.

A brief history of Lanai

For the thousand years after the Polynesians first reached Hawaii, they gave Lanai a wide berth, as the abode of evil spirits. Its first permanent inhabitants came across from **Maui** during the fifteenth century, and the island has remained subordinate to its larger neighbor ever since. However, the population never rose much over three thousand, concentrated in fishing villages such as Kahe'a in the east and Kaunolū in the far southwest.

Although European explorers dismissed Lanai as worthless and barren, it was wetter and more fertile before imported animals deforested the hillsides. Even so, early attempts by outsiders to grow sugar ended in failure. Lanai's main nineteenth-century flurry of activity came around 1850, with the establishment of Hawaii's first

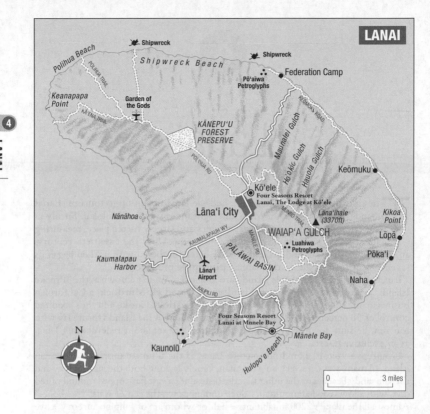

Mormon church. In 1861, a recent Mormon convert, **William Gibson**, arrived on Lanai proclaiming himself to be "Chief President of the Islands of the Sea," and galvanized the congregation into buying the entire Pālāwai Basin. Three years later, it was revealed that Gibson had registered all the ten thousand acres in his own name. He was excommunicated, while his flock moved on to Lāʻie on Oahu. Not only did Gibson hold onto the land but he went on to become the most powerful politician in the kingdom, winding up as King Kalākaua's prime minister.

Gibson's heirs eventually sold his holdings and, following abortive attempts to rear sheep and cattle, Lanai's population had dwindled to around 75 by 1920. After entrepreneur **Jim Dole** bought Gibson's Lanai Ranch in 1922, he set out to grow **pineapples**, which require remarkably little water, and housed his predominantly Filipino labor force in newly built Lānaʻi City. The Pālāwai Basin became the world's largest pineapple plantation. Its workers were expected to pick a ton of fruit per day, and well into the 1980s Lanai was shipping out a million pineapples a day. However, the statewide struggle to win decent wages for farm laborers eventually made it cheaper to grow pineapples in Thailand and the Philippines, and Lanai's last official harvest took place in 1992.

What's particularly surprising about the program to turn Lanai into a **tourist destination** is that it has focused as much on the pinewoods at **Kōʻele**, just outside Lānaʻi City, as on the shoreline. *The Lodge at Kōʻele* opened in 1990, followed by the more traditional beachfront *Mānele Bay Hotel* the next year; both hotels have since been rebranded as *Four Seasons* properties, and been surrounded by luxury condo

developments. However, although Murdock has invested well over a billion dollars, he has yet to make the slightest profit. The annual running cost of his operations on Lanai is estimated at around $100 million, whereas in 2009 tourists spent a total of only $62 million.

With tourism in decline – visitor numbers dropped by a quarter in the wake of the recession, to around 61,000 per year – Murdock has turned his attention to Lanai's potential for **wind farming**. Ambitious and very controversial proposals call for the erection of up to two hundred 400ft-tall wind turbines on the island's northern slopes, near Polihua Beach, which would supply Oahu with electricity by cable. Islanders are up in arms, not just about how the windmills would ultimately look, but about the massive network of roads that would have to be carved into the landscape to get them into place.

Getting to Lanai

Island Air (☎1-800/652-6541, ⓦwww.islandair.com) connects Lanai around six times daily with **Honolulu**, and also offers one daily flight from **Molokai** to Lanai, in that direction only; all flights can also be booked through Hawaiian Airlines. Budget airline **Go!** (☎1-888/435-9462, ⓦwww.iflygo.com) flies between Honolulu and Lanai three times daily. Perched on the western edge of the central plateau four miles southwest of Lānaʻi City, tiny **Lanai Airport** holds a small store, but no café. Guests at the major hotels are picked up by bus; for details of taxis and rental cars, see below.

It's also possible to get to Lanai by **boat**. The Expeditions ferry (☎808/661-3756 or 1-800/695-2624, ⓦwww.go-lanai.com) sails from Lahaina on **Maui** (see p.229) to Mānele Bay daily at 6.45am, 9.15am, 12.45pm, 3.15pm, and 5.45pm. Departures from Lanai are at 8am, 10.30am, 2pm, 4.30pm, and 6.45pm; the adult fare is $30 each way, while under-12s go for $20. The trip takes approximately fifty minutes.

Although Expeditions also arranges discounted golf packages and overnight stays, most ferry passengers simply come for the day. **Shuttle buses** meet each arriving ferry at the harbor and charge a $5 flat fare even for the five-hundred-yard hop to the *Mānele Bay Hotel*.

Finally, many visitors also come to Lanai on day-trips with **Trilogy Ocean Sports** (☎808/874-5649 or 1-888/225-6284, ⓦwww.sailtrilogy.com), whose **Discover Lanai** tour includes a barbecue picnic beside Hulopoʻe Beach ($189, ages 13–18 $119, ages 3–12 $79).

Getting around Lanai

Lanai has the most rudimentary road system imaginable, with less than thirty miles of paved highway, none of it along the coast. The most significant stretches are the eight-mile Mānele Road from Lānaʻi City down to Mānele Bay, and the four miles of Kaumalapau Highway between Lānaʻi City and the airport. Free **shuttle buses** ferry hotel guests along these routes. Buses between the *Mānele Bay Hotel* and *The Lodge at Kōʻele* run every half-hour until the late evening, via *Hotel Lanai* in the heart of Lānaʻi City; non-guests should have no problem hopping a ride.

Of the two **car rental** outlets, **Lānaʻi City Service**, based in Lānaʻi City (daily 7am–7pm; ☎808/565-7227 or 1-800/JEEP-808), is affiliated with Dollar but does not offer online reservations. **Adventure Lanai Ecocenter** (☎808/565-7373, ⓦwww.adventurelanai.com) doesn't have an office but will deliver a vehicle anywhere you choose. There's no point renting an ordinary car; the only way to explore the island is with a **four-wheel-drive vehicle**, along rough-hewn, mud-and-sand jeep trails. Furthermore, following heavy rain, many of those trails are closed to all traffic; both companies advise customers as to which roads they

consider open, with Lānaʻi City Service much the stricter of the two. Don't rent a vehicle until you're sure you can take it where you want to go.

A basic Wrangler jeep costs around $140 per day – the prices are high partly because repair facilities are very limited – so most visitors cram their sightseeing into a single 24-hour period. Both companies provide full instruction if you've never driven four-wheel-drive before, plus booklets of suggested routes. However, neither offers any extra insurance; you're liable for any damage to your vehicle, which can easily amount to several thousand dollars for a basic mishap in the sand.

Lānaʻi City Service also runs the island's only **taxis**, charging around $5 to the airport or Mānele Bay from Lānaʻi City, and $10 from the airport to Mānele Bay.

In addition, Adventure Lanai Ecocenter offers guided **jeep tours**, which involve some hiking, at around $100 for a half-day trip. They also arrange half-day **kayaking**, **quad-biking**, and **diving** tours, as well as **bike** rental and **surfing** lessons.

Where to stay

Apart from a **B&B** in Lānaʻi City (see p.300) and **camping** at Hulopoʻe Beach (see p.304), the only accommodation is in **three hotels**. *The Lodge at Kōʻele* (see below) is modeled on a European country inn, while the *Mānele Bay Hotel* (see p.302) is a full-fledged beach resort; both are run by Four Seasons, with rates starting at around $300. The *Hotel Lanai*, in sleepy Lānaʻi City (see opposite), is lower-key and much less expensive.

When to go

There's no real reason to visit Lanai in any particular season. Room rates stay constant all year, and rainfall is so minimal that the supposed rainy season of September to November is seldom noticeable. The only beach where swimming is safe is Hulopoʻe Beach, below the *Mānele Bay Hotel*, and it remains so in winter, barring the occasional storm. The climate, however, varies between sunny Mānele Bay and cooler Lānaʻi City, which is often overcast and can get chilly (down to 50° F) in the evenings.

Lānaʻi City

To think of **LĀNAʻI CITY** as a town requires a stretch of the imagination; that it should call itself a "city" is little short of absurd. Laid out on a basic grid in 1924 to house laborers from the newly opened pineapple plantations, this neat, pretty community of just two thousand people has barely changed since then. You have to search to find a two-story building: the leafy backstreets hold rows of simple plantation cottages, identical but for the colors they're painted and the rampant flowers in their gardens.

Accommodation

Apart from the *Mānele Bay Hotel* (see p.302), all Lanai's **accommodation** is in Lānaʻi City. In the seclusion of *The Lodge at Kōʻele*, there's little to remind you that you're in Hawaii at all, but the smaller-scale alternatives offer a real taste of the old plantation days.

Four Seasons Resort Lanai, The Lodge at Kōʻele 1 Keōmoku Hwy ☎808/565-4000 or 1-800/919-5053, ⓦwww.fourseasons.com /koele. Despite being a past winner of *Condé Nast Traveler*'s poll as the world's best tropical resort, this gorgeous luxury hotel is several miles from the ocean, 1600ft up in a pine forest reminiscent of the Scottish Highlands. The ambience is pure country-house, and most of its hundred rooms – tucked away in the low

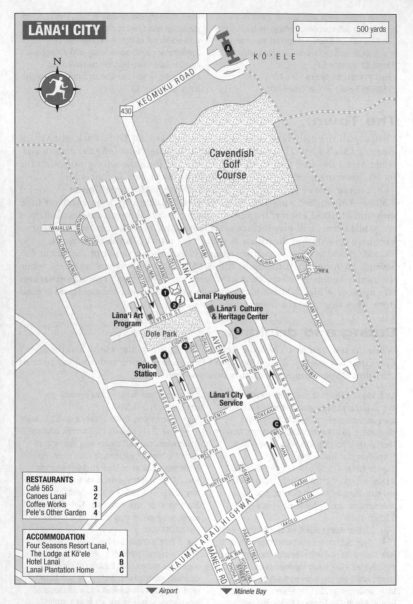

LĀNA'I CITY

0   500 yards

KŌ'ELE

KEŌMUKU ROAD

430

Cavendish
Golf
Course

THIRD

FOURTH

WAIALUA

CALDWELL AVENUE

HOOKIO CIRCUS

FIFTH

SIXTH

SEVENTH ST

EIGHTH

NINTH

TENTH

ELEVENTH

TWELFTH

THIRTEENTH

HOUSTON

GAY

ILIMA

JACARANDA

KŌ'ELE

LĀNA'I

MĀNAKŌ

MANI

ALPA

LAUHALA

NININIWAI SIDES

'ŌHI'A

PU'ULANI PLACE

KONAWAI

QUEEN'S AVENUE

1 ✉

2 ⓘ

Lanai Playhouse

**Lāna'i Culture
& Heritage Center**

**Lāna'i Art
Program**

Dole Park

3

4

**Police
Station**

FRASER AVENUE

TENTH

AVENUE

KIELE ST

DALES ST

TENTH

NOKEAHA

TWELFTH

**Lāna'i City
Service**

Ⓑ

Ⓒ

JASMINE

'AKAHI

KUALUA

'AKOLU

'AHA

HŌ'AI

HUALĀINA

PĀKALĪ STREET

HŪNA WAI

MĀNELE RD

'ŌHUA STREET

KAUMALAPAU HIGHWAY

AWALUA ROAD

▼ Airport   ▼ Mānele Bay

RESTAURANTS
Café 565	3
Canoes Lanai	2
Coffee Works	1
Pele's Other Garden	4

ACCOMMODATION
Four Seasons Resort Lanai,	
The Lodge at Kō'ele	A
Hotel Lanai	B
Lanai Plantation Home	C

bungalows around the "executive putting course"
and croquet lawns – are comfortably furnished
rather than opulent. The surrounding landscaping
is magnificent, with an ornamental lake encircled
by rolling gardens and statuary. Guests have full
privileges at the *Mānele Bay Hotel*, while special
offers can include a third night free. ⑦

Hotel Lanai 828 Lāna'i Ave ☎808/565-
7211, ⓦwww.hotellanai.com. Delightful
wooden bungalow hotel, perched at the edge of
the woods above Dole Park. Built in the 1920s,
it's now run as an inexpensive, low-key alternative to the resorts, and consists of a long
central veranda flanked by two wings of tasteful

299

en-suite rooms, each with lavishly comfortable beds, plus a self-contained cottage. Rates include a self-service continental breakfast abounding in pineapple, and there's also a good restaurant. Rooms ❹, cottage ❺
Lanai Plantation Home 1168 Lāna'i Ave ☎808/565-6961 or 1-800/566-6961,

Ⓦwww.dreamscometruelanai.com. This restored plantation home, set in nice gardens a short walk southeast of Dole Park, has four very comfortable guest rooms, each with a luxurious en-suite bathroom, that can be rented out individually, or you can also rent the entire house. Room ❹, house ❾

The Town

Virtually all the daily business of Lanai revolves around **Dole Park**, the village green of Lāna'i City. The main road, **Lāna'i Avenue**, runs along the eastern end, while over a hundred 90ft Cook Island pines rise from the wiry grassland in the center, towering over the stores, cafés, and offices that line all four sides.

On the east side of the park, the **Lāna'i Culture & Heritage Center** (Mon–Fri 8.30am–3.30pm, Sat 9am–1pm; free; Ⓦwww.lanaichc.org) is an excellent little **museum** of island history. Its walls are adorned with photos from the plantation era, while items on display include some remarkable everyday artifacts thought to have been carved from the ballast of sixteenth-century Spanish shipwrecks.

Lanai's small but friendly **visitor center** is just off the north side of the park at 431 Seventh St (Mon–Fri 10am–2pm; ☎808/565-7600, Ⓦwww.visitlanai.net), while the local government offices are at its western end. The island's two **supermarkets** take up most of Eighth Street, along the park's south side; like old-fashioned general stores, they stock just about everything.

Eating and drinking

While the restaurants at *The Lodge* set out to match any in the world, and the *Lāna'i City Grille* is a worthy alternative, Lāna'i City's other eating and drinking options offer down-home atmosphere rather than gourmet cuisine.

Café 565 408 Eighth St ☎808/565-6622. As well as pizzas and calzones, this small café, with open-air seating alongside Dole Park, serves sandwiches, plate lunches, and even sushi. Mon, Thurs & Fri 10am–3pm & 5–8pm, Tues & Wed 10am–8pm, Sat 10am–3pm.

Canoes Lanai 419 Seventh St ☎808/565-6537. A local-style diner, complete with swivel stools and soda fountain, serving burgers, *loco moco*, plate lunches, and big breakfast fry-ups. Daily 6.30am–1pm.

🏃 **Coffee Works** 604 Ilima St ☎808/565-6962 Spacious coffee bar a block north of Dole Park, behind the post office. Besides the espressos, they also sell a few cheap sandwiches and ice cream, which you can enjoy on the large *lāna'i*. Mon–Sat 6am–4pm, Sun 7am–noon.

Dining Room *The Lodge at Kō'ele* ☎808/565-4580. Extremely formal restaurant, with a lofty reputation and silver-service treatment. Reserve early and savor the presentation as much as the food, which is a richer, meatier version of the usual upscale Hawaiian resort cuisine. Typical appetizers include seared venison ($23) and foie gras ($28); entrees, upwards of $46, include lamb loin, steak,

and seafood; and the chocolate desserts are amazing. Daily 6–9.30pm.

🏃 **Lāna'i City Grille** *Hotel Lanai*, 828 Lāna'i Ave ☎808/565-7211. Friendly, intimate dining room, open for dinner only, but with an adjoining bar that's open late each night. Run under the auspices of Maui chef Bev Gannon (see p.266), it features her trademark contemporary Hawaiian dishes like barbecued ribs or Joe's meatloaf, with entrees at $28–42 and appetizers such as crab cakes for around $15. Daily 5.30–9pm.

🏃 **Pele's Other Garden** Eighth Street and Houston ☎808/565-9628, Ⓦwww .pelesothergarden.com. Bustling wholefood café with attached deli, and plenty of outdoor seating. After serving juices and wholesome $8 sandwiches to take out or eat in at lunchtime, it turns into a full-fledged Italian restaurant in the evening, with entrees like a gnocchi pasta special priced at $17–20. Mon–Fri 11am–3pm & 4.30–8pm, Sat 4.30–8pm.

The Terrace *The Lodge at Kō'ele* ☎808/565-4580. *The Lodge*'s somewhat less formal restaurant, with indoor and outdoor seating overlooking the lawns,

serves health-conscious food, but still at quite high prices: even an egg-and-ham breakfast costs $14. Lunch is the best value, with $10 freshly made soups and $16–21 sandwiches. Typical dinner entrees include roasted lamb with white bean stew ($30) or half a roasted chicken ($23). Daily 6am–9.30pm.

The Munro Trail

The only way to explore the mountainous ridge that forms Lanai's "backbone" is along the ill-defined **Munro Trail**, as a loop trip from Lāna'i City. This rutted track climbs through the forest to the 3370ft summit of **Lāna'ihale**, which when clear is the only spot in Hawaii from which you can see five other islands.

The trail was named after New Zealand naturalist **George Munro**, who calculated that a single tall tree on Lanai can collect forty gallons of water per hour that would not otherwise fall as rain, and planted the island with Cook Island and Norfolk Island pines around 1917. Although it's often promoted as a **hiking** trail, even the shortest possible route is at least twelve miles long. Most visitors prefer to see it from a rented **four-wheel-drive vehicle**, which allows for detours while making it much easier to reach the summit before the clouds set in.

Even the start of the trail is far from obvious. Basically, you head east into the woods from the main road as it heads north beyond *The Lodge*. If you're driving, it's easiest to wait until the road curves east, and turn right after a mile onto the paved Cemetery Road. Otherwise, simply turn right as soon as you get the chance, and then, once on the ridge, turn right again. Either way, you should come to a Japanese cemetery, where the only sign on the whole route sets you off. Turn left soon after and then follow your nose; fork left whenever you're in doubt, look for the most-used path, and don't worry about dropping down because you'll soon head back up again. As you climb through the fresh pine forest, look up to see if clouds are sitting on the ridge; if they are, consider coming back on a day when you'll be able to make the most of the view.

The first major viewpoint comes after three miles, where a short spur road leads to the head of the bare, red **Maunalei Gulch**. A few sparse trees sprinkle the top of the ridge at its western edge, while far below a jeep road winds along the greener valley floor. Molokai should be obvious on the northern horizon, and you may even see Oahu too, to the left.

Continuing on the main trail, you pass some tall communications towers. Road and ridge narrow to the width of a single vehicle, and you find yourself driving between rounded "parapets" of mud, overhung by dense thickets of strawberry guava. Any turkeys and other game birds you may startle – in the absence of mongooses, they thrive here – are forced to run shrieking up the road ahead of you.

After five miles, a clearing on the right looks out over the high, green **Waiapa'a Gulch**. For the clearest views of Lāna'i City, keep going for another muddy mile, to the very summit. It's another two miles, however, before you finally see across the ocean to West Maui, dwarfed beneath the misty silhouette of Haleakalā, while Lanai's central Pālāwai Basin spreads out behind you.

From here on, the soil reverts from dark brown mud to Lanai's more usual red earth. As the Munro Trail drops ever more steeply, clearings on the left frame views of Kaho'olawe, with Mauna Kea on the Big Island potentially visible in the endless ocean beyond.

Drivers can follow more or less any of the countless red-dirt roads that branch off at the southern end of the trail, and thread their way back to town. If hiking, you'll want to take the shortest route back to Lāna'i City, so head as directly as you can along the base of the ridge, which means generally following right forks.

South and west Lanai

The southern half of Lanai used to be the main pineapple-growing region, but now all activity revolves around the tourist industry. **Hulopo'e Beach** is the island's one safe swimming beach, while **Mānele Bay**, next door, is its only pleasure-boat harbor. That's as much as visitors usually bother with; **Kaunolū** in the remote southwestern corner is a well-preserved ancient village site, but the road down is so bumpy that even a normal four-wheel-drive can't reach it.

Lanai's **west coast** is the one leeward shoreline in Hawaii to have sea cliffs, some of which rise over a thousand feet. These have been shorn away by wintertime *kona* storms, while the rest of the island is sheltered by Maui and Molokai. No road runs along the coast, though it is possible to drive down to Kaumalapau Harbor.

The Pālāwai Basin

It would be easy to drive repeatedly through the shallow **Pālāwai Basin**, immediately south of Lāna'i City, without noticing what it is. Once it's pointed out, however, it's glaringly obvious that you're in the collapsed caldera of the volcano that built Lanai. The entire fifteen-thousand-acre basin – until a few years ago the largest pineapple field on earth – is a bowl-shaped depression. The high mountain ridge on its eastern side stands thousands of feet taller than the low rise to the west, while the bowl spills over altogether to flow down to the ocean on the southern side. Nothing is planted in the fields, but the occasional vivid flowering tree lights up the highway.

Luahiwa Petroglyphs

On the eastern edge of the Pālāwai Basin, a grove of trees a short way up the hillside marks the site of the **Luahiwa Petroglyphs**. It's hard to find, so ask for directions at your hotel or car rental outlet. Etched into boulders embedded in the soil – once part of a *heiau* dedicated to prayers for rain – these carvings were created during several separate eras. The earliest examples, which may be five hundred years old, show simple stick figures, sometimes superimposed on each other. A couple of centuries later, the Hawaiians began to depict wedge-shaped bodies, and thereafter the human shapes have muscles and wield oars or weapons. Animals also start to appear, with images of horses produced after European contact.

Mānele Bay

Just under five miles from Lāna'i City, Mānele Road drops from the southern lip of the Pālāwai Basin to wind for three more miles down to **Mānele Bay**. The word *mānele* refers to the Hawaiian equivalent of a sedan chair, but no one knows why the long-vanished fishing village that once stood here bore that name.

As parched and barren as a Greek island, the bay is protected from the open ocean by the high flat-faced cliff on its eastern side, which glows red when it's hit by the setting sun. Its main function is as the port used by the Expeditions ferry from Maui (see p.297). People fish from the rocks or picnic nearby, but there's little else here apart from the Plantation Store, which sells light snacks. Day-trippers usually head straight for Hulopo'e Beach, around to the left, or up to Lāna'i City.

Mānele Bay Hotel

Despite its name, the *Four Seasons Resort Lanai at Mānele Bay*, 1 Mānele Bay Rd (T 808/565-2000 or 1-800/919-5053, W www.fourseasons.com/manelebay; terrace view **7**, garden view **8**, ocean view **9**), is not actually at Mānele Bay, although its jade-tiled roof is visible from the harbor. It spreads instead across the hillside above

the much nicer Hulopoʻe Beach, a few hundred yards west. The *Mānele Bay* conforms far more closely than *The Lodge* to what most visitors want from Hawaii: a lovely beach, ocean views, marble terraces, cocktails by the pool and plenty of sun. Its 250 lavishly appointed rooms (some come with their own private butler) are arranged in two-story terraced buildings, engulfed by colorful gardens, with a golf course alongside. The whole property is themed towards Hawaiian and Pacific history, and centers on a wonderful pool. There's also a luxury spa, offering Hawaiian treatments such as *lomi lomi* massage or ti-leaf wraps (from $165 for 50min).

At the lovely, breezy ⚓ *Hulopoʻe Court* **restaurant** (daily 7–11am & 6–9.30pm), breakfast buffets cost $31 (full) or $22 (continental), while the dinner menu reflects Lanai's culinary traditions from Portuguese to Japanese, with entrees costing $20–34. The dinner-only *Ihilani Dining Room* serves "Mediterranean Gourmet" cuisine with a strong Italian tinge, featuring $40 entrees like *osso buco*. At lunchtime, your choice is restricted to sandwiches and gourmet snacks, like a $20 burger, at the *Ocean Grill* beside the pool.

Hulopoʻe Beach

Only accessible by road from Mānele Bay – it's just a couple of hundred yards further along, at the end of Mānele Road – but also reached via a footpath down from the *Mānele Bay Hotel*, curving, sandy **Hulopoʻe Beach** is by far the best swimming beach on Lanai. What's more, it's far enough from the hotel to retain its own character; apart from a small equipment kiosk at the west end, the hotel maintains no snack bars or other facilities.

The beach was set aside by Castle & Cooke as a beach park in 1961, and the main users, especially at weekends, still tend to be local families rather than tourists. They come to swim, picnic, and explore the **tide pools** at the foot of **Mānele Cone**, the extinct cinder cone dividing Hulopoʻe Bay and Mānele Bay. Both the tide-pool area and the bays form a Marine Life Conservation Area. **Spinner dolphins** are regular visitors, and in the morning, especially, the **snorkeling** here can be excellent.

The waters off Lanai's south coast rank among the best **diving** sites in Hawaii. Dive trips are organized by **Trilogy Ocean Sports** (☎808/874-5649 or 1-888/225-6284, ⓦ www.sailtrilogy.com), whose day-trips from Maui (see p.297) include a picnic beside **Hulopoʻe Beach**.

▲ Hulopoʻe Beach

The beach park maintains showers and restrooms just back from the sand, and it's also possible to **camp**, for up to a week, at a tiny, peaceful, six-pitch campground under the *kiawe* trees ($10 per person per night, plus $25 registration fee per group; T808/565-3982).

The black-lava walls of a Hawaiian village that was occupied intermittently during the last five centuries are clearly visible around the hotel and beach. Sometimes it held permanent residents, who grew gourds and sweet potatoes, while during other periods it served as a seasonal fishing camp. A rough coastal footpath, the **Lanai Fishermen's Trail**, runs both east and west from the hotel, with signs explaining how the whole place used to look.

Pu'u Pehe

Although you can't quite see it from either Hulopo'e Beach or Mānele Bay, Mānele Cone curves around to protect a tiny, inaccessible pocket beach, with the islet of **Pu'u Pehe** just offshore. Technically, this isolated rock is a sea stack, a rocky column that was formerly part of a cliff but has become cut off. It's also known as Sweetheart Rock because, according to legend, a jealous warrior once hid his Maui-born wife (Pehe) in a cave here; when she was killed by a storm, he threw himself from the top of the rock. Pu'u Pehe is best seen from a boat entering or leaving Mānele Bay.

Kaumalapau Harbor

West of Lanai's airport, Kaumalapau Highway winds for four miles down the coastal cliffs. En route, it offers views northwards to the sea stacks – tall, thin islands – known as the **Nānāhoa**, a bird sanctuary that can't be approached more closely.

The highway ends at **Kaumalapau Harbor**, built in the 1920s to ship Lanai's pineapples to a waiting world, but now used only by local fishermen and the once-weekly ships that bring in almost all of Lanai's food supplies. It's a functional rather than a scenic port, where there's no temptation even to get out of your car.

The east coast

Most visitors who rent four-wheel-drive vehicles set out to drive down as many of Lanai's roads as they can. The longest, **Keōmuku Road**, runs the full length of Lanai's **east coast**, a forty-mile round-trip from Lāna'i City that on maps may appear to offer plentiful beaches, sleepy long-lost towns, and ocean views. In reality it's a long, hard drive for very little reward, and you'd be better off simply driving its paved section as far as the sea, taking the detour north to **Shipwreck Beach**, and skipping the jeep road south altogether.

Keōmuku Road heads briefly north from *The Lodge*, then veers east to enter the forest and cross Lanai's central ridge. As soon as it leaves the plateau, it enters a barren but spectacular landscape, meandering down a long, red, desolate hillside. For much of its eight-mile descent, you'll get views of the giant, ragged **Kaimuhoku meteor crater**, but the road never approaches the rim. Whichever way you turn when the pavement runs out, four-wheel-drive is essential.

Shipwreck Beach

Just over a mile after you take the obvious left turn at the foot of Keōmuku Road, the bumpy track passes the tumbledown shacks of **Federation Camp**. This recreational weekend "village," built by Filipino plantation workers in the 1950s,

Blue Hawaii

Defined and shaped, wooed and caressed by the Pacific Ocean, the Hawaiian islands make an irresistible destination for anyone who loves the sea. Some set out to master it atop a surfboard; some simply play in it, swimming or boogie-boarding; and some snorkel on the surface, or dive to explore coral caverns. Others are happy to admire it from a distance, strolling the golden sands of long, empty beaches. All have to share it with other species, like the mighty migrating humpback whales that spend their winters here, and the spinner dolphins that wheel in and out of the water.

Kailua Beach County Park, Windward Oahu ▲

Polihua Beach, Lanai ▼

Punalu'u black-sand beach, Big Island ▼

Hawaii's best beaches

Whether you're a swimmer, a snorkeler, or just a snoozer, Hawaii has the perfect beach for you. For safe swimming, pick a beach with a sandy, slowly shelving floor and gentle waves; obvious examples are resort beaches such as Waikīkī on Oahu, and Kā'anapali and Wailea on Maui, but they can get very crowded. Quieter alternatives include gorgeous Kailua Beach on Oahu, and Kekaha Kai and Hāpuna beaches, for most of the year at any rate, on the Big Island's Kona coast. Keen snorkelers prefer to swim in shallow waters with a rocky or coral floor; both Oahu's Hanauma Bay and Kauai's Kē'ē Beach offer the perfect combination of a lovely sandy shoreline and fish-filled ocean.

The exposed western coasts of each island hold long beaches of deep golden sand, fabulous to walk on but far too dangerous for swimming; these include Mākena or Big Beach on Maui; Pāpōhaku Beach on Molokai; Polihua on Lanai; and the longest of all, Polihale on Kauai. Oahu's North Shore surfing beaches are similar, except on the calmest summer day.

Genuine black-sand beaches are created when fragments of fresh lava are washed ashore; they seldom survive for long, being either simply washed away again, or engulfed by further lava flows. The Big Island has lost some incredible jet-black strands to Kīlauea, but can still boast ravishing little Kehena Beach, deep in the Puna rainforest, and larger Punalu'u Beach further west, while Maui has lovely Wai'ānapanapa Beach. And finally, two real oddities: the tiny Red Sand Beach, reached by a precarious footpath from Hāna on Maui, and the remote Green Sand Beach near the Big Island's South Point.

Humpbacks on holiday

Around five thousand humpback whales migrate south from Alaska each year to winter off the shores of Hawaii; that's a quarter of the total North Pacific population, the rest of which head for Mexico and Japan. Measuring up to 45ft long, and weighing up to 45 tons, they eat nothing while in Hawaiian waters. Instead they come to court, and mate, and then a year later, to give birth and introduce their calves to the world. Partly because Hawaiian myth and legend make so little reference to humpbacks, experts believe they only started wintering in Hawaii in the early nineteenth century. And although Hawaii was once a gathering place for the great whaling fleets, humpbacks were never hunted here, because unlike the "right" whale their bodies sank when they were killed.

The whales are especially fond of the shallow channels between Maui, Molokai, and Lanai, at the heart of the Hawaiian Islands Humpback Whale National Marine Sanctuary. Between late November and early April they make themselves astonishingly conspicuous, through display behaviors like slapping the water with their tails and pectoral fins, or "breaching" – leaping right out of the water. During that time, whale-watching boats set off from all the islands, and on Maui in particular you're all but certain of a sighting. You'll probably see them even if you stay on shore, whether from roadside vantage points or simply from the beach. While few people get to see whales underwater – although you can spot them from a helicopter, suspended in the turquoise ocean – you may well hear them. Snorkelers at Kāʻanapali frequently hear the whistles and grunts of singing whales, whose "song" changes each year and is common to all Pacific humpbacks.

▲ Waikīkī Beach, Oahu

▼ Humpback whale breaching

Kings of the surf

Polynesian people invented *he'e nalu*, or "wave-sliding," perhaps four thousand years ago; for the ancient Hawaiians, **surfing** truly was the sport of kings. Only the *ali'i*, of noble blood, could use the largest boards – sixteen-foot, 150-pound *koa*-wood planks – or surf the finest breaks. They seldom stood erect; instead they lay on raised elbows, like modern boogie-boarders. They even had an equivalent to tow-in surfing, whereby a surfer would leap with his board from a speeding canoe.

Discouraged by the missionaries, Hawaiian surfing all but died out before being revitalized by the iconic Waikīkī Beach Boys, led by Olympic gold-medalist **Duke Kahanamoku**, at the start of the twentieth century. It took technological advances from the 1950s onwards, like the development of fins and lightweight fiberglass boards, to bring it international popularity.

Duke Kahanamoku ▲

Banzai Pipeline, North Shore, Oahu ▼

These are the breaks

Each Hawaiian island boasts its own legendary **surf sites**. Here are five of the best, strictly for **experts** – the best **beginners'** breaks are at Waikīkī (Oahu), Lahaina (Maui), and Po'ipū (Kauai).
▶▶ **North Shore, Oahu** The finest breaks of all: mighty tubular waves include the fabled Banzai Pipeline, which races in at gorgeous Sunset Beach. See p.120
▶▶ **Honolua Bay, Maui** Spectators watch the action from the fields above this magnificent bay. See p.241
▶▶ **Jaws, Maui** Colossal waves, accessible only via jet-ski. See p.280
▶▶ **Hanalei Bay, Kauai** A superb, curving crescent bay in full view of the spectacular Nā Pali cliffs. See p.375
▶▶ **Honoli'i Beach, Big Island** At this lush rivermouth north of Hilo, surfers perform against a backdrop of dense tropical vegetation. See p.177

backs onto a little crescent of sand that's fine for fishing but not swimming. This is **Kaiolohia Beach** ("tranquil sea"), but the name has also come to refer to the whole eight-mile stretch west to Polihua.

Lanai's northern shoreline, however, is more commonly known as **Shipwreck Beach**, because countless vessels have come to grief in these shallow, treacherous waters; the coast is littered with fragments, while two large wrecks remain stuck fast a few hundred yards offshore. Many historians believe that a sixteenth-century Spanish galleon was wrecked here; see p.416.

The sand road lurches to a halt at a parking lot less than half a mile beyond Federation Camp, by which time the tree cover has given out, too. Walk in the same direction for a few more yards, and from the ruined foundations of a lighthouse you'll see the rusting orange hulk of a World War II "**Liberty Ship**" propped up on the rocks, almost completely out of the water. It was probably beached here deliberately in the late 1940s.

An enjoyable **hike** heads northwards for closer views of the wreck; allow at least an hour, or make a day of it by continuing all the way to Polihua. The only viable route runs along the shorefront; set off further inland, and you're soon confronted by a succession of gullies filled with thorny *kiawe* scrub, where the only trails have been made by animals, and close over at waist height. Head instead for the mouth of the first gully you come to. A thin filament of sand, a few feet wide, runs just beyond the vegetation, but it's often so narrow that you have to sidestep the waves. Picking your way across the tide pools sunk into the odd spit of lava, you'll encounter all sorts of flotsam and jetsam.

A mile or so along, you round a final corner to find a large red refrigerated container washed onto the beach. The wreck of the ship lies a hundred yards offshore – you can easily pick out the details of its deck – while the green valleys of east Molokai rise directly behind it.

Pōʻaīwa Petroglyphs

From the parking lot where the trail to the lighthouse and Liberty Ship begins (see above), a short walk directly inland leads to a gulch where the rocks still bear a handful of ancient **petroglyphs**. As you face back down the small ramp from the lighthouse platform, follow the footpath bearing fractionally to the right, which may be marked with faint white paint. After about two hundred yards, beyond a warning sign, you drop down into the gully itself. It's filled with large red boulders; where sections have shorn off to leave smooth flat surfaces, the rocks are incised with tiny stick drawings and bird-headed figures.

South along the coast

To drive **south** along the coast, simply continue along Keōmuku Road instead of taking the left turn to Shipwreck Beach. Check first with your rental company whether the road is currently passable. Assuming it is, from this initial junction onwards, the road repeatedly divides into separate deep sandy channels, which rejoin every few hundred yards. Whichever branch you follow, you'll be deep in the woods for most of the way. Thanks to soil runoff, the shoreline pushes farther out to sea by an amazing ten feet every year; only rarely do you even glimpse the ocean. Similarly, the encroaching scrubby vegetation makes it hard to spot the long-overgrown abandoned villages en route.

The windward coasts of other Hawaiian islands are usually lush and fertile, but little rain reaches Lanai. Only the valley of **Maunalei**, a mile down the road, was wet enough to grow taro, and it still supplies most of the island's fresh water.

Six miles from the turnoff, in a small grove of coconut palms, **Mālamalama Church** is all that survives of the village of **Keōmuku**. Built to serve a new sugar plantation in 1899, the village was deserted within two years. The church is not a very evocative relic; its original wood having rotted away, it has been completely rebuilt.

Normally, the one difficult stretch on Keōmuku Road comes after ten miles, as it undulates across the headland at Kikoa Point. At **Lōpā**, immediately beyond, it twice passes within a few feet of the waves, offering views of ancient fishponds – now mostly submerged – as well as across to the island of Kaho'olawe (see p.260). By the time the road ends at **Naha**, after just over twelve miles, it has made a right-angle turn to head along Lanai's south coast, with West Maui out of sight behind you.

North Lanai

The eight-mile drive from Lāna'i City to the **north coast** is the island's best four-wheel-drive excursion. The scenery ranges from the dust bowl of the central plateau, through thick woodlands and multicolored desert, to one of Hawaii's emptiest and largest beaches. The main drawback is that **Polihua Road** is truly a dirt road; it's the filthiest drive imaginable, leaving you coated in thick, red mud even if you never wind down your windows. As the famed Garden of the Gods is best seen at sunset, make this your last stop of the day before heading home to wash off the grime.

Garden of the Gods

Lanai's extraordinary **Garden of the Gods** looks more like the "badlands" of the Wild West than anything you'd expect to find in Hawaii. Perched on a bleak, windblown plateau above the island's north coast, five miles from Lāna'i City, this small desert wilderness is predominantly a rich russet red, but its unearthly hillocks and boulders are scored through with layers of lithified sand of every conceivable hue – grays, yellows, ochres, browns, and even blues. At sunset, the whole place seems to glow, and the rocks scattered across the red sands cast long, eerie shadows.

Although the main depression at the Garden of the Gods holds the most impressive rock formations, it's worth continuing for at least a short distance beyond. Take the right fork at the only point where the route may be hard to make out, and as the hillside starts to slope down, you come to a fabulous vantage point that looks across the bare red soil toward Molokai.

Polihua Beach

A short way past the Garden of the Gods, signposts mark the junction of the Ka'ena and Polihua roads. The latter is the right fork, which gets steadily worse as it drops toward the ocean, cutting a groove into the red earth. It virtually never rains here, and the views are amazing.

At sea level, the road ends at broad **Polihua Beach**, where the red dust gives way to broad yellow sand. Over a hundred yards wide and 1.5 miles long, Polihua is a magnificent sight, and you may well have it to yourself. This remote spot used to be a favorite laying-ground for green turtles – the name means "eggs in the bosom." They rarely turn up these days, but during the winter humpback **whales** can often be seen not far offshore.

Like the similar vast, windswept beaches at the western extremities of Kauai and Molokai, Polihua is best admired from a distance. The current is always too dangerous for swimming, though there's great **windsurfing** around the headland to the east. Beyond that stretches Shipwreck Beach; as described on p.305, it's possible to hike its full eight-mile length.

Molokai

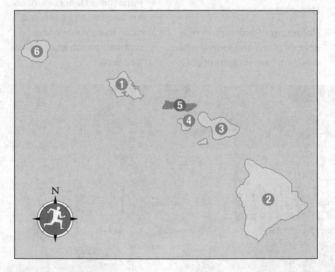

CHAPTER 5 # Highlights

✳ **Hālawa Valley** Superb guided hikes explore this lush tropical valley, at the far eastern end of the island. See p.318

✳ **Kamakou Preserve** The rainforest of eastern Molokai is home to some of Hawaii's rarest birds and plants. See p.319

✳ **Coffees of Hawaii** Gloriously relaxing plantation café in Kualapu'u that serves fresh-picked Muleskinner coffee. See p.321

✳ **Kalaupapa Peninsula** A truly special place: the former leper colony where Belgian priest Father Damien carried out his inspiring mission. See p.323

✳ **Molokai Mule Ride** Let a mule carry you down the steep trail to remote Kalaupapa – they've been doing it all their lives. See p.324

✳ **Molokai Ka Hula Piko** Atmospheric annual festival held in the upland groves where the art of hula was born. See p.331

✳ **Pāpōhaku Beach** Perhaps the largest, emptiest, and most fearsomely wave-battered beach in all Hawaii. See p.331

▲ St Philomena's Church, Kalaupapa Peninsula

Molokai

MOLOKAI is not the sort of island you'd expect to find halfway between Oahu and Maui. With a population of just eight thousand, and a mere fraction of the tourist trade of its hectic neighbors, it feels more like a small Caribbean outpost than a part of modern Hawaii. Measuring forty miles west to east, but only ten miles north to south, it doesn't have a single traffic light or elevator. No building on Molokai stands taller than a palm tree, and even the capital, Kaunakakai, is no more than a dusty street of wooden false-front stores.

Since the Molokai Ranch, which had been the main provider of visitor facilities on the island, closed down in 2008, Molokai has become less of a tourist destination than ever. With just one small hotel left in operation, visitor numbers immediately plummeted. Fewer than fifty thousand travelers came to Molokai in 2009, and collectively they spent just 25 million dollars, which is what a single medium-sized resort on Maui would expect to make.

There is in any case some truth in the criticism that there's nothing to do on Molokai. If you like to stay in plush hotels, spend lots of money in shops and restaurants, enjoy active nightlife, try out expensive sports and pastimes – or even simply swim from pretty beaches – this is probably not the place for you.

Many visitors, however, rank Molokai as their favorite island, saying it offers a taste of how Hawaii must have been fifty or sixty years ago. Until recently, Molokai was promoted under the slogan of "The Most Hawaiian Island"; now it makes more sense to think of it as "The Last Hawaiian Island." With a higher proportion of native Hawaiians than any of the major islands, it has resisted excessive development while maintaining a friendly and distinctive character. Spend any time exploring the island – even visiting "attractions" that might on paper sound too mundane to bother with – and you'll soon find yourself drawn into the life of the community. That said, Molokai holds some indisputable highlights as well, including unspoiled **scenery** to rival any in Hawaii – from ravishing **Hālawa Valley** in the east to gigantic, deserted **Pāpōhaku Beach** in the west – and the poignant historical relic of Father Damien's leprosy colony at **Kalaupapa Peninsula**.

A brief history of Molokai

Molokai may have been home to as many as thirty thousand people in ancient times. Lush **Hālawa Valley**, at its **eastern** end, was among the first regions to be settled in Hawaii, and an almost permanent state of war existed between the Kona and Ko'olau sides of the eastern mountain. The **western** end was also extensively settled, and served as a meeting place for travelers from all the islands.

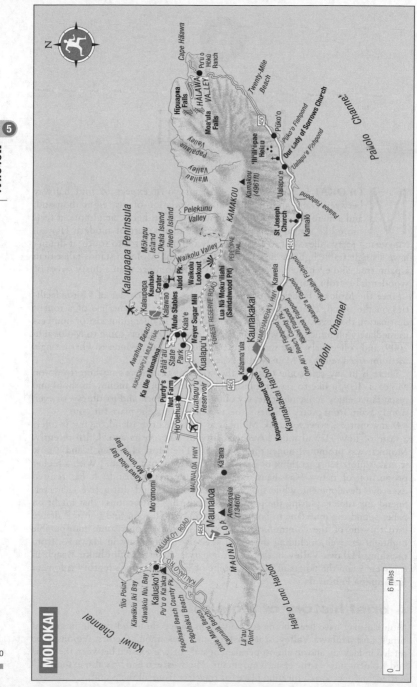

MOLOKAI

Kaiwi Channel

Kalaupapa Peninsula

Kaunakakai

Maunaloa

'Ilio Point
Kawākiu Iki Bay
Kawākiu Nui. Bay
Kalukoʻi
Puʻu o Kaʻaka
Pāpōhaku Beach County Pk.
Pāpōhaku Beach
Dixie Maru Beach
Kaunala Beach
Lāʻau Point

Kawa āoa Bay
Moʻomomi
Moʻomomi Bay

MAUNA LOA
Amikopala
(1346ft)

MAUNALOA HWY

KALUAKOʻI ROAD
KALUAKOʻI RD

Kaʻana

Hoʻolehua

Kualapuʻu Reservoir

Purdy's Nut Farm
Ka Ule o Nanahoa
Pālāʻau State Park
KUKUIOHAPUʻU MULE TRAIL

Awahua Beach
Kalaupapa
Kalawao
Kalaʻe
Mule Stables
Kauhakō Crater
Judd Pk.
Waikolu Lookout
Meyer Sugar Mill

Mōkapu Island
Ōkala Island
Huelo Island

Pelekunu Valley

Waikolu Valley
PEPEʻŌPAE TRAIL

Kualapuʻu

Lua Nā Mokuʻiliahi
(Sandalwood Pit)

FOREST RESERVE ROAD

KAMEHAMEHA V HWY

Kalama'ula

Kapuāiwa Coconut Grove
Kaunakakai Harbor

Kawela

Aliʻi Fishpond Pk.
One Aliʻi Beach County Pk.
Kaloni Fishpond
Kanoa Fishpond
Paʻakaʻu Fishpond
Pāhonāhona Fishpond

Kaunakakai

KAMAKOU
Kamakou
(4961ft)

Wailau Valley
Papalaua Valley

Hipuapapa Falls
Moaʻula Falls
HĀLAWA VALLEY

Cape Hālawa
Puʻu o Hōkū Ranch

Twenty-Mile Beach

Pūkoʻo

'Ualapuʻe

'Iliʻiliʻōpae Heiau

Puʻu o Fishpond
Our Lady of Sorrows Church
'Ualapuʻe Fishpond
Pāialoa Fishpond

St. Joseph Church
Kamalō

Kalohi Channel

Paiolo Channel

Hale o Lono Harbor

N

0   6 miles

During the eighteenth century, the fertile valleys and rich fishponds of the east attracted a succession of foreign **invaders** to Molokai. For around fifty years after the Europeans arrived, however, Molokai was largely ignored. That was partly because the coast held no safe anchorages for ocean-going ships, but also because the island had a reputation for black magic, as the home of the greatly feared **poisonwood gods** (see p.329).

The concept of Molokai as being godforsaken played a role in the decision to site a **leprosy colony** at Kalaupapa during the 1860s; the work of the Belgian **Father Damien** there gave the island its only brush with world fame (see p.326). By the time **Robert Louis Stevenson** visited in 1889, Damien was dead; so too was the vast majority of the island's native population, wiped out by imported diseases.

Meanwhile, the **Molokai Ranch** had been established, taking over the entire western end of the island for raising cattle. Constructing pipelines and tunnels to channel water from the northern valleys, the ranch prospered, producing **honey** and **pineapples**. Like everywhere in Hawaii, however, agriculture on Molokai turned unprofitable during the 1970s, and the island went into recession. Unemployment hit hard, while local resistance to development, and a perennial water shortage, thwarted plans to shift the economy toward **tourism**.

Under new owners, the Molokai Ranch started the twenty-first century by renewing its efforts to develop visitor facilities, and turned the former pineapple town of **Maunaloa** into a tourist center. However, in the face of local opposition to its plans to construct luxury housing at **Lāʻau Point**, at the far southwestern tip of the island, the ranch ceased all its operations on the island in May 2008, abruptly closing down all its accommodation options. That left **Monsanto**, who grow experimental **GM crops** on roughly half of Molokai's agricultural land – not that casual visitors are likely to spot any signs of their presence – as the island's leading employer. Whether Molokai will ever re-emerge as a significant visitor destination remains in doubt.

Molokai overview

Like Oahu and Maui, Molokai consists of two separate **volcanoes**, plus the "saddle" that lies between them. At almost 5000ft, the younger mountain to the east – sometimes named after its highest peak, Kamakou – is tall enough to capture most of the island's rain. Its **north shore** holds the world's highest sea cliffs, pierced by spectacular valleys, but it's virtually impossible to reach, and there's hardly anywhere from which you can even see it. The mountaintop rainforest, protected as the **Kamakou Preserve**, can only be explored on foot.

From Molokai's principal town, tiny Kaunakakai in the center of the south coast, a ribbon of colorful little settlements stretches east along the shoreline, all the way to sumptuous **Hālawa Valley**. To the west, the smoother, smaller, and much drier mountain of Mauna Loa offers little sign of life; its only two communities, hillside **Maunaloa** and oceanfront **Kaluakoʻi**, feel spookily abandoned since the ranch pulled out. Molokai's central plain holds a few more farming villages, while tacked on below the cliffs to the north, the isolated Kalaupapa Peninsula is still home to the island's celebrated leprosy colony.

Getting to Molokai

Despite its proximity to both Oahu and Maui, Molokai is surprisingly hard to reach. Its main **airport**, outside Hoʻolehua in the center of the island, is served by direct flights from **Oahu**, **Maui**, and **Lanai** only, though it's easy enough to connect with flights from the other Hawaiian islands.

Island Air (☎ 1-800/652-6541, ⓦ www.islandair.com) flies from Honolulu to Molokai seven to eight times daily, and from both Kahului and Lanai once daily; it code-shares with **Hawaiian**, which doesn't operate any of its own flights. Budget airline **Go!** (☎ 1-888/435-9462, ⓦ www.iflygo.com) has nonstop services between Molokai and both Honolulu and Kahului. For what are usually much higher fares, you can also fly between Maui and Molokai on tiny **Pacific Wings** (☎ 1-888/575-4546, ⓦ www.pacificwings.com).

For details of flights direct to the **Kalaupapa Peninsula** – not a sensible option if you want to see the whole island – from Oahu, Maui, and "top-side" Molokai, see p.324.

It's also possible to make a 1hr 30min **ferry** crossing between Maui and **Molokai** on the *Molokai Princess* (departs Lahaina Mon–Sat 7.15am, daily 6pm; departs Molokai Mon–Sat 5.15am, daily 4pm; adults $54 one way, under-12s $27; ☎ 808/662-3535 or 1-877/500-6284, ⓦ www.mauiprincess.com). No public transport is available at the ferry port, at Kaunakakai Harbor (see p.314).

Getting around

There is no **public transport** on Molokai, and the airport is several miles out of town. The only national **rental car** chain represented at the airport is Alamo (☎ 808/567-6042, ⓦ www.alamo.com), but Molokai Rent-A-Car (☎ 1-866/344-7612, ⓦ www.molokairentalcar.com) also offers airport pick-ups, and friendly local alternative Island Kine (☎ 808/553-5242 or 1-877/553-5242, ⓦ www.molokai -car-rental.com), based in Kaunakakai, provides free airport transfers.

As well as **taxi** service, Molokai Off-Road Tours & Taxis (☎ 808/553-3369, ⓦ www.molokai.com/offroad) run **minivan tours** for three or more passengers, costing $49 per person for "island highlights", $41 for Hālawa Valley, and $53 for a jeep tour that will take you up to, but not into, the Kamakou Preserve (see p.319).

Where to stay

Molokai holds very few **accommodation** options. Apart from the most obvious choices, the *Hotel Molokai* and the *Molokai Shores* condos in **Kaunakakai**, a handful of pretty B&Bs are scattered along the **southeastern** coast, and there are a few more upscale condo apartments in the largely defunct Kaluako'i resort at the island's western end. There's nowhere to stay in or near Molokai's most scenic spot, Hālawa Valley, while the island's most historic area, the Kalaupapa Peninsula, can only be visited on guided day-trips. The Molokai Visitors Association website (ⓦ www.molokai-hawaii .com) lists several privately owned homes for rent, and you can also contact agencies such as Molokai Vacation Properties (☎ 1-800/367-2984, ⓦ www.molokaivip.com) and Friendly Isle Realty (☎ 1-800/600-4158, ⓦ www.molokairealty.com).

As for **camping**, the county-run **One Ali'i Beach Park** (see p.315) limits campers to a three-day maximum stay; permits are issued in person only at the Mitchell Pau'ole Center on 'Āiloa Street in Kaunakakai (Mon–Fri 8am–4pm; permits Mon–Thurs $5 per person, Fri–Sun $8; ☎ 808/553-3204, ⓦ www.co.maui.hi.us). Camping is not currently allowed at **Pāpōhaku Beach Park** in the west.

When to go

In terms of **climate**, it makes very little difference what time of year you visit Molokai; the west is sunny all year round, while the higher or farther east you go, the greater the chance of rain. Only a few of the beaches are suited to swimming, even in summer. All else being equal, the best time to come to Molokai is in May, during the **Molokai Ka Hula Piko** festival (see p.331).

Molokai watersports and other activities

The main **activity operator** on the island is **Molokai Fish and Dive**. The company runs a store at 63 Ala Malama St in Kaunakakai (Mon–Sat 8am–6pm, Sun 8am–2pm; ☎808/553-5926, ⓦwww.molokaifishanddive.com), as well as offices at the *Hotel Molokai*, and serves as agents for virtually every activity available on the island. Its program of outdoor pursuits includes **sightseeing cruises** along the North Shore cliffs ($150); **whale-watching**, **kayaking** and **snorkeling** trips (all $69); and the can't-miss **Hālawa Valley hikes** described on p.318 ($75). Although **scuba diving** is also offered, the sport is not as popular on Molokai as on the other islands.

Many of these same activities are offered by **Molokai Outdoor Activities** (☎808/553-4477 or 1-877/553-4477, ⓦwww.molokai-outdoors.com), which also rents out **kayaks** and snorkel equipment. Fun Hogs Fishing (☎808/567-6789, ⓦwww.molokaifishing.com) run customized **sport-fishing** trips, and whale-watching excursions in winter. **Bike** rental is available from Molokai Bicycle, 80 Mohala St, Kaunakakai (☎808/553-3931, ⓦwww.bikehawaii.com/molokaibicycle).

At the eastern end of the island, the Puʻu O Hōkū Ranch organizes **horseback** riding amid idyllic scenery (see p.317). For hunting, deep-sea fishing, spear fishing, and kayaking trips on the remote north shore, contact Walter Naki of Molokai Action Adventures (☎808/558-8184).

Kaunakakai

KAUNAKAKAI, at the midpoint of the southern shoreline seven miles southeast of the airport (see p.311), is by far the largest settlement on Molokai. Despite being home to most of the businesses that keep island life ticking over, it's really no more than a village. There's just one main street, **Ala Malama Street**, half a mile in from the ocean. Once you've ambled its full two-hundred-yard length and scanned its array of wooden, single-story, false-front stores and the little timber-framed **St Sophia's Church**, you've seen all that central Kaunakakai has to offer. Call in at the Kanemitsu Bakery, no. 79, to pick up a loaf of sweet Molokai bread, renowned throughout the islands.

Arrival and information

Molokai's central crossroads is at milepost 0 on Kamehameha V Highway, where Ala Malama Street heads away inland. The friendly offices of the **Molokai Visitors Association** are a short way east, at 2 Kamōʻi St (Mon–Fri 8am–5pm; ☎808/553-5221 or 1-800/800-6367, ⓦwww.molokai-hawaii.com).

Accommodation

As the obvious base for exploring Molokai, Kaunakakai has the only **hotel** on the island, *Hotel Molokai*. The condos at the *Molokai Shores* are slightly smarter, while there are a few **B&Bs** as well. It's also possible to **camp** at One Aliʻi Park; see p.315.

A'Ahi Place B&B ☎808/553-8033, ⓦwww .molokai.com/aahi. Welcoming garden-set holiday cottage, on a low hill just east of Kaunakakai. The one bedroom has two large beds; there are no phones or TVs, but an ample breakfast is served each morning. The nearby "Backpackers' Cabin" is more basic but still has a decent bed and en-suite bathroom. No credit cards. Cabin ❶, cottage ❸

Ka Hale Mala 7 Kamakana Place ☎808/553-9009, ⓦwww.molokai-bnb.com. Secluded four-room garden apartment, with kitchen and *lānai*, plus bikes and snorkel equipment, a little under five miles east of Kaunakakai. Run as a B&B, with reduced rates if you don't want breakfast. Airport pick-up. ❸

Hotel Molokai ☎ 808/553-5347 or 1-877/553-5347, ⓦ www.hotelmolokai .com. Appealing beach hotel, just before milepost 2 east of town, consisting of several two-story cottages shaped like so many armored samurai, with broad shoulders and sweeping cloaks. Accommodation options range from two-person rooms up to six person suites; each apartment has private *lānai* and bath, and a separate living room. Those closest to the ocean really are *incredibly* close; a thin strand of sand, scattered with palm trees strung with hammocks, is a single step away. There's a nice pool, and a bar open daily 3–11pm; the restaurant is reviewed opposite. Garden view ❺, ocean view ❻

Molokai Shores ☎ 808/553-5954, ⓦ www .castleresorts.com. A hundred comfortable one- and two-bedroom oceanfront condos (all sleep up to four), a mile east of Kaunakakai, with big sea-view *lānais*, are arranged around a pleasant oceanfront lawn. The ocean beyond the thin strip of beach is too shallow for swimming, but there's a pool, though no restaurant. Some units are individually rented out by their owners; rates are cheaper, but the quality varies considerably. ❺

Kaunakakai Harbor and the shoreline

From the town's central intersection, **Wharf Road** leads down to **Kaunakakai Harbor**. Ancient Hawaiians knew this spot as *Kaunakahakai* ("resting on the beach"), and hauled their canoes ashore beside the nearby freshwater stream. The long stone mole, or jetty, that turned Kaunakakai into a full-fledged port was constructed in 1898 to serve the newly opened pineapple plantation; the boulders themselves came from a dismantled *heiau*.

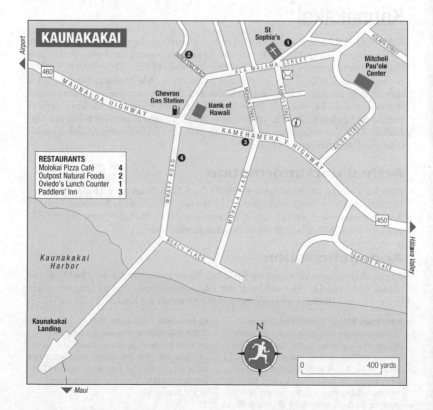

RESTAURANTS
Molokai Pizza Café	4
Outpost Natural Foods	2
Oviedo's Lunch Counter	1
Paddlers' Inn	3

The harbor facilities, used by local fishermen as well as the **ferry** service between Molokai and Maui (see p.312), are well over half a mile out from the shore, along the mole. It's usually possible to buy fresh fish from the Molokai Ice House here, a cooperative venture to which all the fishing vessels sell their catch.

None of the beaches near Kaunakakai is particularly suited to swimming, though walking along the shoreline to the east can be pleasant enough. The sea is not hazardous, but there's only a narrow strip of often rather dirty sand, and the water tends to be murky, thanks to runoff from the hills.

One Ali'i Beach Park, three miles east, is little better, but does at least offer some nice lawns and coconut palms, as well as the neighboring Ali'i Fishpond (see p.316). The original name of the beach was *oneali'i* or "royal sands," but what was once a spelling mistake has become the official name. The beach itself consists of two separate sections; the first one you come to, Number 2, is reserved for day use only, while the nicer Number 1, a little further on, holds a **campground** (see p.312).

A couple of miles **west** of central Kaunakakai, on the ocean side of Maunaloa Highway across from a neat little row of wooden chapels, the photogenic **Kapuāiwa Coconut Grove** originally held over a thousand tall palm trees, planted in the 1860s by Chief Kapuāiwa. As the coastline gradually erodes, they are toppling one by one, but they still make a fine spectacle, especially in the glow of sunset. Swimming from the park is not recommended.

Eating and drinking

Although almost all Molokai's **restaurants** and **bars** are located in Kaunakakai, the choice is far from overwhelming. The island lacks the national fast-food chains, but neither is there anything that might be called fine dining. Saturday morning sees a **farmers' market** around the central intersection.

Hula Shores *Hotel Molokai*, Kamehameha V Hwy ⊤808/553-5347. The oceanfront dining room at the *Hotel Molokai*, two miles east of town, has a romantic ambience and live nightly entertainment, including Aloha Friday with Na Kupuna on Fridays 4–6pm, when local "aunties" sing, dance, and "talk story." The food itself is pretty good, with lunch entrees at $9–15 and dinner entrees from *furikake*-crusted crab to prime rib at $18–30; you can also enjoy fresh seafood as *poke* or sashimi. Daily 7am–2pm & 6–9pm.

Molokai Pizza Café Kaunakakai Place, Wharf Rd ⊤808/553-3288. This good-value diner, near Kaunakakai's central intersection, always seems to be busy, and is still full when everywhere else has shut for the night. Different-sized pizzas range from the basic Molokai ($12) up to the Big Island ($23); at lunchtime you can get an individual Molokini for $5. The menu also features subs, ribs, and roast chicken, plus evening fresh-fish specials for $15 or so. Mon–Thurs 10am–10pm, Fri & Sat 10am–11pm, Sun 11am–10pm.

Outpost Natural Foods 70 Maka'ena Place ⊤808/553-3377. Lunch counter and juice bar in a wholefood store, just off Ala Malama Street. Tofu sandwiches and tempeh burgers $5; sensational smoothies, quite possibly the best in the world, cost $4. Shop Mon–Thurs 9am–6pm, Fri 9am–4pm, Sun 10am–5pm, closed Sat; kitchen Mon–Fri 11am–3pm.

Oviedo's Lunch Counter 145 Pauli St ⊤808/553-5014. Simple one-room Filipino restaurant in the heart of town where the owner cooks up delicious dishes like chicken stewed with papaya and local herbs ($8) as well as pork *adobo* (stew), roast pork, and turkey-neck stew. There's lots of ice cream to round things off. Daily 8am–5pm.

Paddlers' Inn Kamehameha V Hwy ⊤808/553-5256. This large restaurant-cum-sports-bar is a major drinking hangout for locals, but it's still a welcoming spot for visitors, with lots of outdoor space, including an open-air stage that regularly features live if not necessarily Hawaiian music. *Saimin* or burgers for under $10, lunch specials like *kalbi* beef around $12, and $20 steaks, plus prime rib Wed & Fri. Mon–Fri 7am–11pm, Sat & Sun 9am–11pm.

Eastern Molokai

Kamehameha V Highway runs along the coast for 28 miles **east of Kaunakakai** before reaching a dead end at one of the great Hawaiian "amphitheater valleys," **Hālawa Valley**. Molokai's equivalent to Maui's Road to Hāna on (see p.281), it ranks among the most beautiful driving routes in the state.

It takes well over an hour to drive from Kaunakakai to Hālawa, and there are no gas stations. The highway remains in good condition all the way to the end, but gets progressively narrower, as finding a foothold between the hills and the ocean becomes more difficult. Eastern Molokai is the wettest part of the island; most of the rain that falls on the mountaintop flows down to the inaccessible valleys of the North Shore, but enough feeds the streams to the south to create a verdant patchwork of fields and forest.

Tiny wayside communities hold the odd church, B&B, or ancient site, but the real attraction is the lush countryside, with flowers and orchids at every turn, and horses and cows, each with its attendant white egret, grazing in the meadows. For much of the way the road lies within a few yards of the sea, but there's no good swimming in the first twenty miles, and barely a decent stretch of sand. The coast is lined instead with pre-contact **fishponds**, now largely silted up and overgrown.

Kawela

Six miles out of Kaunakakai, a small cluster of houses constitutes **KAWELA**. Kamehameha the Great invaded Molokai here in around 1794, with a vast wave of

---

The fishponds of Molokai

Ancient Hawaiians developed aquaculture, or fish farming in artificial **fishponds**, laced around sheltered coastal areas, to standards unmatched elsewhere in Polynesia. As nineteenth-century historian Samuel Kamakau put it, "fishponds were things that beautified the land, and a land with many fishponds was called 'fat'." By that reckoning, the southeastern coast of Molokai was very fat indeed. More than fifty fishponds lie within a twenty-mile stretch – a sure sign that the area was home to many powerful chiefs.

A typical fishpond consisted of a long stone wall that curved out from the beach to enclose as much as five hundred acres of shallow ocean. Building such a wall usually took a great deal of labor, but in southern Molokai, which holds the longest contiguous coral reef system in the entire US, the inshore reef already all but encircled natural lagoons. The complete wall would have one or two gaps, or sluice gates, sealed with wooden lattices. Small fry could enter, but once they grew to full size they'd be unable to leave.

Fishponds connected to the sea always also held freshwater springs, and were used to raise fish that liked brackish water, such as 'ama'ama (mullet) and awa (milkfish). Similar freshwater ponds, usually built near rivermouths, held species like 'ōpae (shrimp) and 'o'opu (a native goby).

Although Molokai's fishponds remained in use well into the nineteenth century, most of the ponds these days, along with the coral reefs beyond them, have been submerged by sediment washed down from the hills. Overgrazing on the higher slopes allows a foot of mud per year to settle into the ocean, and many ponds have become mangrove swamps.

If you'd like to take a close-up look, drop by the **Ali'i Fishpond**, immediately west of One Ali'i Beach Park, where an 800m wall enclosing a thirty-acre pond is being cleared of mangroves and painstakingly restored by community volunteers (no fixed hours; ☎808/553-8353, ⓦwww.kahonuamomona.org).

canoes landing simultaneously along a four-mile length of beach. The remains of the dead killed in the subsequent battle lie beneath a mound to the east. Kamehameha subsequently grew taro for a year farther along the coast, before launching his invasion of Oahu in 1795 (see p.417).

Kawela's small **Kakahai'a Beach Park** makes a convenient launching-point for **kayak** expeditions, as listed on p.313. Otherwise, it is significant solely because it is adjacent to the **Kakahai'a National Wildlife Refuge**, a wetland area set aside for rare waterbirds. Its main feature, the freshwater **Kakahai'a fishpond**, stands *mauka* of the highway, obscured by palm trees; access to both pond and refuge is forbidden.

Kamalō

KAMALŌ, six miles east of Kawela, was Molokai's main port during the nineteenth century, but is now just a tiny village. Its simple white **St Joseph's Church** was built by Father Damien in 1876; his garlanded statue stands outside.

Set in superb tropical gardens across from St Joseph's, the Kamalō Plantation offers **B&B** accommodation for two in a private cottage, with its own kitchen and outdoor deck, as well as a lovely two-bedroom beach house further along the coast (☎ 808/558-8236; cottage ❹, beach house ❺).

Pūko'o

Six miles east of Kamalō, and not far beyond the point where the huge but currently inaccessible ancient temple of 'Ili'ili'ōpae Heiau stands a couple of hundred yards inland, the village of **PŪKO'O** is another nineteenth-century port that has all but withered away.

Coastal traffic is forced to slow down here by a succession of narrow curves, but sightseers are rewarded by some delightful little pocket beaches. Just before milepost 16 in Pūko'o, *Mana'e Goods & Grindz* (daily except Wed 8am–6pm; ☎ 808/558-8498) is the only place along Kamehameha V Highway where you can **eat**, serving lunches such as chimichangas ($6) or a mixed *laulau* plate ($11).

Twenty-Mile Beach

The prettiest of the south-coast beaches, and almost the only one where swimming and snorkeling are consistently safe, can be found at milepost 20. Commonly known as **Twenty-Mile Beach**, it consists of a small but sheltered strand of golden sand, with ample parking.

After that, the twin islets of **Moku Ho'oniki** and **Kanaha Rock** – both bird sanctuaries – become visible ahead, and the speed limit drops to just 5mph as the road twists in and out around the rocky headlands.

Pu'u O Hōkū Ranch

Each of the three lush little inlets beyond Twenty-Mile Beach holds a house or two and a patch of sand. As the rocky silhouette of Kahakuloa Head, at the tip of West Maui, looms into view across the water, the highway climbs into the rolling meadows of the **Pu'u O Hōkū Ranch**. The scenery by now is absolutely gorgeous, with the ranchlands stretching a long way back from either side of the road.

The ranch headquarters, near mile marker 25, sells a small array of groceries and souvenirs, and rents out two fully equipped **guest cottages** in the heart of this pastoral idyll (☎ 808/558-8109, ⓦ www.puuohoku.com; ❹). One has two bedrooms, and the other four; both cost $140 per night for two people.

Hiking in Hālawa Valley

It's only possible to hike into the depths of Hālawa Valley on a **guided tour** ($75; reserve through Molokai Fish and Dive, ☎808/553-5926, ⓦwww.molokaifishand dive.com). Don't let that put you off, however; this is the best such tour anywhere in Hawaii.

The tours are designed to raise awareness of – and funds for – an ambitious attempt to restore taro production in the valley. Spearheaded by Lawrence Aki and his extended family, some of whom lead each tour, it's part of the same process of revitalizing Hawaiian cultural traditions that's the inspiration for the reconstruction of Molokai's fishponds (see p.316).

The tours set off at 9.30am daily, reserve in advance, wear good walking shoes, plus a swimsuit beneath your clothes, and bring insect repellent and a picnic. After first being introduced to the ongoing restoration work being carried out by community volunteers on the ancient **lo'i** – the walled, and usually water-logged, patches in which taro is grown – you'll follow the trail back through the valley. It soon leaves the cultivated areas to reach magnificent tropical rainforest, crossing streams and passing numerous ruined homesites and *heiaus*. At one such temple, dedicated to Lono, the only practicable route leads straight through the most sacred area, necessitating a **chant** that asks for permission. The ultimate goal, the dramatic 250ft **Moa'ula Falls**, is said in legend to be the dwelling place of a giant lizard or *mo'o*. Swimming in the chilly pool beneath the falls is only safe if a *ti* leaf tossed into the water floats; otherwise, it is said, you'll be dragged down by the *mo'o*.

While it's barely two miles up to the falls, the round-trip hike can easily take five hours, allowing time for a swim, and lots of stops to "talk story" along the way.

Hālawa Valley

Twenty-six miles out of Kaunakakai, beyond a series of progressively wider and deeper gulches, Kamehameha V Highway reaches an overlook poised 750ft above the full spread of **HĀLAWA VALLEY**. The view from here is staggeringly beautiful, with the stream meandering far below towards the foaming ocean, the rich green valley reaching back, and distant waterfalls shimmering in the valley's innermost recesses, half-hidden by clouds.

For its final 1.5 miles the highway drops down the walls of the valley, with tremendous views at each hairpin curve, before ending on the south side of the stream. Where the road reaches the valley floor, the tiny wooden **church** of Jerusalema Hou is always unlocked and open for quiet meditation. The dirt road just beyond leads back upstream, but the only way to pass through its locked gate is on a **guided hike** (see box above).

The main road continues a couple of hundred yards to a rough parking lot by the mouth of the stream. To the right, a **beach** of grayish sand is accessible beyond a carpet of creeping flowers and barely sheltered from the force of the ocean. Off the low rocky promontory to the left, where the waves sweep in toward the river-mouth, is Molokai's most popular **surfing** site. Large numbers of local kids may be in the water, but it's seldom safe for outsiders.

Across the stream on the far side of the bay, another pretty little crescent **beach** is backed by a line of palm trees and made up of sand rendered grubby by soil washed down the valley walls. You can normally wade the stream to reach it, though you may not be made welcome by the inhabitants, and the only road access is barred.

The history of Hālawa Valley

When the Polynesians first arrived in Hawaii, they settled in each island's lush windward valleys. Its sheltered sandy inlet, abundant rainfall, and year-round

streams made Hālawa an ideal home. Remains of round-ended huts, resembling those of Easter Island and eastern Polynesia but otherwise unknown in Hawaii, have been dated to before 650 AD.

Home to perhaps a thousand people, Hālawa became the major population center of Molokai. Its fertile slopes were terraced into stone-walled fields, while the valley floor cradled over a thousand taro ponds (*lo'i*). In addition to *heiaus* dedicated to agricultural deities, it held a *pu'uhonua* (see p.150), and twelve human-sacrifice *luakinis* (see p.427), including one erected by Chief Alapa'inui of the Big Island around 1720 to celebrate his conquest of the island.

Taro production in Hālawa continued well into the twentieth century. Californian businessman Paul Fagan, based at the Pu'u O Hōkū Ranch, bought up much of the valley in 1935. His hopes of revitalizing its traditional lifestyle were dashed by the tsunami of 1946, and Fagan turned his attentions to Hāna on Maui instead (see p.286).

During the 1960s, the waterfalls flowed so fiercely that they destroyed the remaining *lo'i*, and made the river channel too deep to use for irrigation. Previously treeless, the valley floor swiftly became overgrown. Squatters moved in, planting marijuana in the backcountry, and Hālawa became a byword for lawlessness. Only recently has the situation stabilized, and the residents set about restoring the *lo'i*.

Central Molokai

West of Kaunakakai, Maunaloa Highway follows the coast for a couple of miles before turning inland to climb the "saddle" between Molokai's two volcanoes. No road follows the island's southwest shoreline, which vehicles can only reach via Maunaloa at the western end (see p.329).

The **central plain** of Molokai used to nourish extensive pineapple plantations, but apart from the island's main airport it holds little to interest visitors today. Villages such as **Kualapu'u** and **Ho'olehua** are sleepy little places, and although any stay on Molokai is likely to involve passing this way several times, there's no compelling reason to stop, other than to pause over a fortifying espresso at Kualapu'u's coffee plantation. More thrilling is the rough jeep track that heads east from Maunaloa Highway up to the **rainforest**, leading to a fine **viewpoint** and a fabulous **hiking trail**.

The rainforest

The summit of eastern Molokai remains covered by pristine **rainforest**. Owned by the Molokai Ranch, but run by the private, nonprofit Nature Conservancy of Hawaii as the **Kamakou Preserve**, it's a sanctuary for native plants and animals, the last-known haunt of rare indigenous birds such as the Molokai thrush (*olomāo*) and the Molokai creeper (*kakawahie*). Most of the area is completely inaccessible even on foot, and the authorities prefer outsiders to venture in only with experienced local guides such as those listed on p.313.

There is, however, a rough dirt road that climbs right to the top of the mountain from central Molokai. It's virtually always raining up there, and even at its best the track tends to be a deep wet furrow in the earth, where anything other than a high-clearance four-wheel-drive vehicle will slither uncontrollably. Ask for advice at the Nature Conservancy of Hawaii office, to the left of Maunaloa Highway 2.5 miles up from Kaunakakai (Mon–Fri 8am–3pm; ☎808/553-5236, ⓦwww .nature.org), which also organizes **guided hikes** (usually on the first Saturday of each month; call for details).

The Forest Reserve road

Less than four miles from Kaunakakai, just before Maunaloa Highway crosses a bridge, the **Forest Reserve jeep road** heads off to the right and soon reaches the dusty Homelani Cemetery. The long, straight, red-dirt track from here may seem innocuous at first, but it becomes heavily rutted as you climb higher.

By the time you pass the sign announcing the Molokai Forest Reserve, you'll probably have penetrated the mountain's semi-permanent cloud cover. Within half a mile, you'll spot the largely abandoned scout camp where sculptor Robin Baker carved totem poles, sharks, octopuses, and cobras into the living trees. Well beyond that, the imported eucalyptus starts to give way to a pine forest that's interspersed with bright-blossomed native *ohia* trees.

The Sandalwood Pit

In a grassy clearing on the very crest of the Kamakou ridge, a deep groove betrays the site of Lua Nā Moku 'Iliahi, or the **Sandalwood Pit**. This is one of the few surviving "*picul* pits," dug early in the nineteenth century to the exact size and shape of a ship's hull. Hawaiian commoners were sent up into the mountains by their chiefs to cut down precious sandalwood trees; once they filled a pit with logs (weighed in units called *piculs*), they then had to carry them back down to the sea on their naked backs and load them onto ships bound for China.

You're unlikely to see any living sandalwood here now, though a small stand survives somewhere nearby. It's said that the exploited laborers deliberately uprooted sandalwood saplings to ensure that their children would not have to do the same cruel work.

Waikolu Lookout

Ten miles from the highway – 45 minutes' driving on a good day – the jeep road reaches **Waikolu Lookout**. This dramatic viewpoint commands a majestic prospect of the verdant Waikolu Valley, which drops 3700ft down to the ocean. Tiny Huelo

The valleys of the North Shore

The **north coast** of Molokai boasts the world's tallest **sea cliffs**, up to 4000ft high. Geologists once believed these sheer green walls were created by gigantic landslides, perhaps along volcanic fault lines, but it's now known that they were created by the power of the Pacific alone.

Few visitors ever see the cliffs or the mighty **amphitheater valleys** – so called for the unclimbable walls that soar to either side and meet in a high encircling ridge at the head – that cut deep into them. **Hālawa** to the east is accessible by road (see p.318), while **Waikolu** in the west can technically be reached on foot from Kalaupapa (not that you'd ever get permission to do so), but **Pelekunu**, **Wailau**, and **Papalaua** valleys are sealed off from the rest of Molokai.

All of these valleys held substantial populations in pre-contact times. The name of the largest, Pelekunu, means "moldy smell" – even when it's not raining, the valley floor receives less than five hours of direct sunlight each day. Pelekunu's taro farmers abandoned the valley each winter, when the seas grew too rough to permit canoe landings, and migrated west to Mo'omomi to catch and dry fish. The last permanent population had left by 1917, though for a few years after that the valley was infested by wild water buffalo abandoned by Chinese farmers.

These days most of the land in the north-shore valleys is privately owned. Back-to-nature enthusiasts camp out on their properties in summer, but there's no formal agriculture. Meanwhile, the state is gradually buying up the area, in the hope of turning the whole shoreline into a vast nature reserve.

Island stands offshore, while the Kalaupapa Peninsula is just out of sight around the headland to the left. Most of Molokai's drinking water comes from Waikolu, flowing to the reservoir at Kualapu'u along a tunnel that pierces the valley wall almost directly below this spot.

The Pēpē'ōpae Trail

Commercial off-road tours (see p.313) tend not to go beyond Waikolu Lookout, which marks the start of the **Kamakou Preserve**. For most of the year, the jeep road beyond is impassable, but it's always possible to continue on foot. Winding through successive minor gulches, it soon leaves the dryland forest behind and plunges into the jungle.

The **Pēpē'ōpae Trail**, which starts 2.5 miles along the road, is the only track to penetrate into the heart of the preserve – and it's an absolutely wonderful hike. To protect fragile ecosystems, it consists of a slender wooden boardwalk, seldom more than a plank wide. It begins by pushing its way through thick rainforest, where every tree is festooned with dangling vines and spongy, fluorescent moss, and dazzling orchids glisten amid the undergrowth of tightly coiled ferns. Between wisps of mountaintop mist, you might just glimpse unique native birds such as the Molokai creeper or the Molokai thrush.

The trail eventually emerges into an eerie patch of windswept bog. Amazingly, the red-blossomed, stunted shrubs scattered across the desolation are *'ohia*, the same species that grows as full-sized trees in the neighboring forest. A viewpoint here enables you to look back across the island to the west end, before the trail plunges once more into the jungle. After a final steep climb, the boardwalk ends abruptly at another incredible view of the north coast, this time over **Pelekunu Valley**.

It takes over an hour to walk the full length of the Pēpē'ōpae Trail, to the overlook and back, and more like four hours to hike from the Waikolu Lookout.

Kualapu'u

The former plantation town of **KUALAPU'U** stands two miles east of Maunaloa Highway on Kala'e Highway (Hwy-470). Dole having stopped growing pineapples in this area in 1982, Kualapu'u is now concentrating on **coffee** instead. Brands such as its Muleskinner Coffee have gained a foothold as somewhat cheaper rivals to the Big Island's long-established gourmet crop.

The headquarters of the coffee estate is the *Coffees of Hawaii* **café**, on Farrington Avenue at the eastern end of Kualapu'u, just off Kala'e Highway (Mon–Fri 7am–5pm, Sat 8am–4pm, Sun 8am–6pm; ☎808/567-9490, ⓦwww.coffeesof hawaii.com). It serves free percolated coffee and inexpensive espressos, plus sandwiches and takeout lunches (and truly dreadful smoothies), while the attached Plantation Store sells Muleskinner and other coffees, plus souvenirs and local crafts. Sitting on their open terrace, looking out across Molokai, is as enjoyable and relaxing an experience as the island has to offer. To explore the plantation in more detail, join either a **walking tour** ($20; Mon–Fri 11am) or a mule-drawn **wagon tour** ($40; Tues & Fri 9am & 1pm).

A few hundred yards west, an attractive timber building houses the *Kualapu'u Cookhouse* (Mon 7am–2pm, Tues–Sat 7am–8pm, Sun 9am–2pm; ☎808/567-9655), a popular diner with indoor seating and an adjacent garden terrace. Breakfast eggs cost around $8, and burgers and plate lunches are $6–10, but the place really comes into its own in the evening, when high-quality dinner specials like stuffed shrimp, seared *ahi*, or rack of lamb are more like $20. Arrive by 6.30pm or you may well have a long wait to be seated, let alone served. On Thursdays at 5pm they serve prime rib accompanied by live Hawaiian music.

The lake-like expanse of water south of Farrington Avenue is the world's largest rubber-lined **reservoir**, holding over a billion gallons of water piped from the north-shore valleys.

Ho'olehua

There's even less to **HO'OLEHUA** – a mile west of Kualapu'u along Farrington Avenue, or a mile north of Maunaloa Highway, east of the airport – than there is to its neighbor. Anywhere else, its lone attraction, Purdy's Nut Farm, 0.4 miles up Lihi Pali Avenue, might not seem a big deal. Take the time to stop, however, and you can while away an inconsequential but thoroughly enjoyable half-hour (Mon–Fri 9.30am–3.30pm, Sat 10am–2pm; free). In a nutshell, Tuddie Purdy stands at a counter amid a small grove of macadamia nut trees, telling whoever drops by about the trees, cracking nuts with his hammer, and handing out slices of coconut to dip in honey. With any luck he'll also sell a few nuts, some fruit from his orchard, or a little honey. Because Tuddie does not use pesticides, which preclude visits to macadamia nut orchards elsewhere, you can stroll among the 75-year-old trees. They're rooted in bare red earth, which is swept clean every day, to make the fallen nuts easy to spot.

Mo'omomi Beach

Farrington Avenue heads west through Ho'olehua and out the far side almost before you'd notice. After another 2.5 miles, the road surface turns to red dirt, but usually remains in good enough condition to make it worth driving the final two miles down to **Mo'omomi Bay**. There's a little sandy **beach** to the left of the end of the road, and tide pools in the jagged sandstone to the right, formed in the rounded depressions left by long-gone lava boulders. Local kids choose this side of the bay to go surfing and boogie-boarding.

Mo'omomi Bay is one of several small indentations in the three-mile stretch of solidified sand dunes known as **Mo'omomi Beach**. The shallow offshore waters were once highly prized fishing grounds, and countless ancient octopus lures and fishhooks have been found nearby, but the dry coastline has probably never hosted much of a permanent population. Mo'omomi Beach has become the latest political hot potato on Molokai, with local residents combining to resist construction of a wind farm here.

Walking along the coastal track a mile west of Mo'omomi Bay brings you to prettier **Kawa'aloa Bay**, where the large sandy beach is slightly safer for swimming. The dunes here are an ecological treasure-trove, holding not only the fossils of extinct flightless birds, but also rare living species of plants. Casual strolling is not encouraged, but the Nature Conservancy of Hawaii in Kualapu'u (see p.319) organizes monthly **guided hikes**.

Kala'e

The tiny residential area of **KALA'E** is two miles northeast of Kualapu'u, 1500ft above sea level as Kala'e Highway climbs toward the top of the *pali* above Kalaupapa. Its rich wet farmland – the best on Molokai – was acquired in the 1850s by a German migrant, **Rudolph Meyer**, when he married the local high chiefess, Kalama.

During the 1870s Meyer ventured briefly into the sugar business. The roadside **R.W. Meyer Sugar Mill** operated only from 1878 until 1889 before Meyer returned to cattle ranching and went on to found the Molokai Ranch. Hawaii's smallest sugar mill then lay rotting for almost a century, but is now restored to

full working condition. Outside the main shed stands the original mule-powered cane crusher, while inside you can see the furnace, boiler, and the elaborate steam engine. So far, it's all quite underwhelming, but the modern hall behind holds the **Molokai Museum and Cultural Center** (Mon–Sat 10am–2pm; $6), which shows temporary exhibitions of Hawaii-related photographs.

Pālā'au State Park

A couple of miles beyond the sugar mill, and less than a mile past the mule stables and Kalaupapa trailhead (see p.324), Kala'e Highway ends its climb across Molokai in the forested parking lot of **Pālā'au State Park**.

A very short paved trail from the far end of the lot brings you to a railed **overlook** that faces east along the coast. Kalaupapa Peninsula spreads out far below, with the village of Kalaupapa clear on the near side, and the slight upswell of the central Kauhakō Crater behind it. The pinnacle of Mokapu island juts from the ocean beyond, but the original settlement of Kalawao (see p.327) is obscured by the slight curve of the *pali*. Captioned photographs explain the topography and history. A footpath continues left from the lookout, offering a pleasant half-hour hike but no better views. Plans have been announced to build further trails, leading east to the start of the path down to Kalaupapa (see p.324), in the near future.

Left of the parking lot, a broad and well-worn trail, which at first leads downward through the woods, takes five minutes to reach the top of the Pu'u Loa knoll, known for its **Phallic Rock**. This reshaped and much-fondled stone outcrop was in ancient times a fertility shrine known as Ka Ule O Nānāhoa – "the penis of Nānāhoa" – and used to stand fully exposed to the plains below, rather than deep in the forest. Women who brought offerings here and then spent the night were said to return home pregnant; the furrowed tip still holds cigarettes, dollar bills, flowers, and other gifts. Ancient petroglyphs are concealed beneath an overhanging rock nearby, while an extremely old *heiau* on a rocky point two miles to the west is surrounded by phallic emblems.

The Kalaupapa Peninsula

They were strangers to each other, collected by common calamity, disfigured, mortally sick, banished without sin from home and friends. Few would understand the principle on which they were thus forfeited in all that life holds dear; many must have conceived their ostracism to be grounded in malevolent caprice; all came with sorrow at heart, many with despair and rage. In the chronicle of man there is perhaps no more melancholy landing than this of the leper immigrants among the ruined houses and dead harvests of Molokai.

Robert Louis Stevenson

The **KALAUPAPA PENINSULA** is a dramatic volcanic afterthought, tacked on to Molokai's forbidding north coast and almost completely cut off by towering 2000ft cliffs. It was created long after the cliffs already stood in place, when lava from a minor eruption lapped against the vast bulk of the island to form a flat and exposed spit of land.

This remote outpost became world famous in the nineteenth century as the grim place of exile for Hawaiian sufferers from **leprosy**, and the site of the ministry of the saintly **Father Damien** (see box, pp.326–327). Although there is no further risk of the disease spreading, the peninsula is still reserved for former leprosy patients, and run as the Kalaupapa National Historic Park. It's also a somewhat

anomalous county in its own right, although it has no official county government, and all Hawaii's other counties consist of one or more entire islands. As no one under the age of 16 is allowed on the peninsula, this is the only **child-free** county in the US.

Kalaupapa is an inspiring place to visit, but you can only do so with a reserved ticket for an official **park tour**, operated (though sadly no longer personally led) by the residents as Damien Tours. Other than **flying** down to the peninsula, the only means of access is the long but safe **trail** that zigzags down the *pali*, which you can either **hike** or descend by **mule**.

If you don't have the time to visit the peninsula itself, it's possible to get a distant overview from the overlook in **Pālā'au State Park** (see p.323), at the top of Kala'e Highway.

The trail to Kalaupapa

The trailhead for the precipitous descent to Kalaupapa, the three-mile **Kukuiohapu'u Trail**, is located to the right of Kala'e Highway, almost three miles north of Kualapu'u and just beyond the headquarters of the **Molokai Mule Ride**. Molokai's most popular tourist attraction – famous for its slogan "Wouldn't You Rather Be Riding a Mule on Molokai?" – is a wonderfully escapist experience, though in essence it's simply an expensive, if enjoyable, means of transportation. Once at Kalaupapa, the riders dismount and join the same motorized tours (see opposite) as all other visitors.

Each day except Sunday, mule riders rendezvous by 8am to set off at 8.30am, and return at around 3.30pm. All riders must be aged 16 or over; the fee of $175 per person includes the ground tour and a picnic lunch, while round-trip airport transfers are $25 extra. For reservations, call ☎808/567-6088, 808/336-0802, or 1-800/567-7550, or email via ⓦwww.muleride.com, as far in advance as possible.

If you prefer to **hike**, there's nothing to stop you walking the full length of the trail and then climbing back up again, but you can only enter the peninsula itself if you meet up with a pre-arranged tour. Most hikers set off around 8.30am to coincide with the 10.15am Damien Tours tour.

Hiking down to the bottom of the cliffs takes around an hour and a quarter, while the mules take more like an hour and a half. For the first few hundred yards from the highway, the trail winds through bucolic meadows and guava orchards; then, suddenly, it comes to the edge of the cliff, above a sheer 1644ft drop. The section that follows is the narrowest of the lot, with the yawning abyss in full view to your left. Soon, however, you enter the shade of the forest and continue dropping steeply down 26 numbered switchbacks. The majestic *pali* stretches away to the horizon in both directions, with rainbows floating beneath the clouds and the plain of Kalaupapa laid flat at your feet.

Eventually the trail levels out to run the full length of **'Awahua Beach**, which you will have repeatedly glimpsed to the west of the peninsula on your way down. In winter, this broad expanse of slightly grimy sand can be stripped completely bare overnight. As on all the beaches at Kalaupapa, swimming is strictly forbidden.

Flying to Kalaupapa

Daily **flights** to Kalaupapa's tiny airstrip from Molokai's main airport at Ho'olehua are operated by Pacific Wings (☎808/567-6814 or 1-888/575-4546, ⓦwww.pacific wings.com). This seven-mile, nine-minute hop claims to be the shortest scheduled air service in the world, and carries the added bonus of a close-up view of the world's tallest sea cliffs, along Molokai's otherwise inaccessible northern coastline. Pacific

Hansen's disease

The disease familiar from the Bible as **leprosy** is known to scientists as **"Hansen's disease,"** in honor of the Norwegian Gerhard Hansen, who first identified the leprosy bacillus in February 1873. Despite popular misconceptions, Hansen's disease is not particularly contagious, and only around one person in twenty is even susceptible.

Any need for the isolation of patients, as practiced at Kalaupapa, was rendered obsolete by the development of **sulfone drugs** in the 1940s. These arrest the development of the disease in sufferers and eliminate the possibility of contagion. Nonetheless, although the disease has been all but eradicated both in Hawaii and the US as a whole, there are still two million sufferers worldwide, and some 600,000 new cases diagnosed each year.

In the last seventy years, Hawaiian state law regarding the official name of the disease has alternated three times between the terms "Hansen's disease" and "leprosy." While "Hansen's disease" is the current official choice, many of the patients at Kalaupapa continue to prefer "leprosy." Some are even content to be referred to as "lepers," despite what may seem to outsiders to be the negative connotations of the word.

Wings also offers direct flights to Kalaupapa from both Honolulu and Kahului. **Fares** for all these flights vary enormously, however, and can be exorbitantly high, at $200 or even $500 for the round trip. All passengers landing at Kalaupapa must have tour reservations.

The Molokai Mule Ride (T 808/567-6088 or 1-800/567-7550, W www.muleride .com) arranges day-trips to Kalaupapa, including round-trip flight, mule ride, and ground tour, from any hotel in Waikīkī, or from either airport on Maui. They'll even sell you a day-trip whereby you fly to and from Kalaupapa without taking the mule ride. Precise rates depend on airline prices and schedules.

Touring Kalaupapa

All **tours** of Kalaupapa Peninsula are organized by Damien Tours ($50; T 808/567-6088 or 1-800/567-7750). Every day except Sunday, their rickety minibuses or four-wheel-drive vehicles pick up tourists either from the airstrip or at the east end of 'Awahua Beach, just outside the settlement of **KALAUPAPA**, where the trail from Kala'e ends. Visitors are not allowed to wander unaccompanied, or to take photographs of residents. Even if you're on the mule ride, bring plenty of water; it can be a long hot day.

Exactly what is included on your tour depends on the whim of your guide. Sadly, the guides are no longer former patients, who used to provide an often very moving link with the history of the colony. Instead, they tend to be "top-siders," from the rest of Molokai, who are not always as knowledgeable or indeed sympathetic as you might expect. You may not see any residents at all, as many choose to stay behind closed doors rather than face scrutiny.

As a rule, you can expect to spend the first hour in Kalaupapa village, probably with stops at both *Fuesaina's* bar for drinks and ices, and at the **Kalaupapa National Historic Park Museum and Bookstore** (Mon–Sat 10.30am–12.30pm). The latter is a fancy name for a small house that holds ornaments and artifacts made by the residents, plus utensils that they adapted for their own use, and a fine selection of books.

Among other likely stops are a memorial to Father Damien; the gravesite of his successor Mother Marianne Cope; the church, where an outbuilding displays

Father Damien and the story of Kalaupapa

Within a century of its first contact with the outside world, the population of Hawaii dropped from around one million to just over fifty thousand. Among the main reasons was the susceptibility of native Hawaiians to imported **diseases**, and especially **leprosy**. Hawaii's first case of leprosy was diagnosed in 1835, on Kauai. Believed to have spread with the arrival of plantation laborers from China, it became known as *ma'i Pake*, or the "Chinese disease." By 1865, when one in fifty Hawaiians had contracted leprosy, King Kamehameha V decided to pursue a policy of rigorous **isolation**.

All persons deemed to be suffering from the disease – which effectively meant anyone with a visible skin blemish – had to surrender themselves for shipment to the Kalaupapa Peninsula, to live in permanent **exile**. Apart from one voluntary *kokua* (helper), they were separated forever from their homes and families. Bounty hunters scoured the islands in search of victims, and some sufferers, such as Kauai's legendary Koolau (see p.385), turned outlaw to escape their fate.

Although nowhere in Hawaii is more isolated than the Kalaupapa Peninsula, numerous shrines, *heiaus*, and gravesites attest to extensive ancient occupation. There was a substantial settlement here in the 1860s, but the villagers swiftly relocated "top-side" once sufferers began to arrive at nearby Kalawao Bay.

In its **early years**, the colony at Kalaupapa was a godforsaken place. Intended to be self-sufficient, it rapidly dissolved into anarchy. The first boatload of people were left to divide all the land among themselves; as additional exiles followed, it had to be re-divided again and again, occasioning bitter disputes each time. The strong dominated the weak, to be supplanted in turn as each succumbed to the disease. For fear of contagion, ships often refused to pull in closer to shore than Mokapu island, and many new arrivals were forced to swim for their lives through the rough surf.

The people of Kalaupapa were not regarded as patients; receiving no treatment, they were abandoned to die. There was little sympathy from the white-dominated government, which held the view that the natives had brought disease upon themselves by wanton promiscuity.

Matters only changed when the Belgian Catholic priest **Father Damien Joseph de Veuster** – who had worked for nine years on the Big Island – was posted to Kalaupapa in 1873. Only twelve of the 822 residents at that time were Catholic, but Father Damien dedicated himself to improving conditions for all. He was to spend the remaining sixteen years of his life on Molokai, in a sustained outpouring of sheer physical effort that doomed him to an early grave.

historical photos; and the small **boat landing** where all local supplies arrive. Just one barge per year now delivers cargo to Kalaupapa, including a hundred cases of Spam and 2700 cases of beer.

Kauhakō Crater

Kalaupapa is on the peninsula's sheltered, drier, western side. As you cross to the east, the vegetation grows rapidly thicker and greener, and groves of fruit trees appear. To the left of the one dirt road, the mound of **Kauhakō Crater** – the volcanic vent that created the peninsula – rises gently to a height of 400ft. White crosses stand on its rim, while the brackish lake inside is more than 800ft deep, reaching far below sea level. In the early years of the colony, residents are said to have sheltered overnight in caves down in the crater.

Off to the right of the road, the *pali* soars up into the clouds. After heavy rain, all the clefts in the cliff face become waterfalls; one, which runs red at first from the mud, takes twenty minutes to work its way down, filling six successive pools en route.

Damien's daily routine consisted of nursing, bathing, and dressing the sores of the sick, and carrying their corpses for burial with his bare hands. Although determined to build a new church at Kalawao, he regarded that task as less important and only allowed himself to work on its construction after dark. He also built three hospitals and over three hundred houses to replace the previous crude windbreaks, and constructed a pipeline to bring fresh water from high in Waikolu Valley.

One Sunday morning in 1885, Damien began his sermon "**We lepers…**" rather than the usual "my brethren". Out of more than a thousand helpers to have worked at Kalaupapa, he remains the only one ever to contract leprosy. His 82-year-old mother died the day after news of his illness reached Belgium; Damien himself died in Kalaupapa in April 1889, at the age of 49.

Damien has been eulogized ever since his death, by figures as disparate as the future King Edward VII of Britain and Mahatma Gandhi. One famous note of criticism, however, was sounded by Reverend Charles Hyde, a Protestant minister in Honolulu, who wrote of him as "a coarse, dirty man, headstrong and bigoted… Not a pure man in his relations with women." Robert Louis Stevenson, who visited Kalaupapa a month after Damien's death, sprang to his defense in an "Open Letter" that was reproduced all over the world.

Although Damien made it very clear that he wished to remain buried at Kalaupapa, his body was exhumed and taken to Belgium in 1936; his right hand was, however, returned to Molokai in 1995, and he was officially declared a **saint** in 2008. A poll conducted in Belgium in 2005 declared him to be the Greatest Belgian of all time.

Meanwhile, his work at Kalaupapa was carried on by such followers as Brother Joseph Dutton and Mother Marianne Cope. Over the years, the entire population shifted across the peninsula to the village of Kalaupapa itself, and Kalawao was abandoned altogether in 1932. The first effective treatment for leprosy appeared in the 1940s, and the formal separation of patients at Kalaupapa finally ended in 1969.

In all, more than eight thousand patients made their homes on the peninsula, with a peak population varying between the mid-700s and something over a thousand. As of 2010, fifteen of those patients were still alive, with the youngest being aged 69. They share Kalaupapa with around forty health workers and another forty park employees. No doctors live there; they simply visit for the day from Honolulu. As the saga gently draws to a close, the peninsula is turning into a historical monument; when the last patient dies, it will become wholly owned by the park service.

Kalawao

As you enter the original settlement of the "Lazaretto" (leper colony), **KALAWAO**, you pass the unobtrusive "birthing stone" where the chiefs of Molokai were traditionally born. The tasseled Australian casuarina tree alongside was planted by Father Damien in front of the third hospital he built in Kalawao.

Nothing now remains of the hospital. Indeed the only building left standing in Kalawao, which was inhabited from 1866 to 1932, is **St Philomena's Church**, where the road meets the sea. Shipped from Honolulu in 1872, this was greatly expanded by Damien and is widely known as "Damien's Church." The rectangular holes in the floorboards were cut by Damien himself, when he realized that the sickest patients were not attending Mass because they were afraid of despoiling the church by spitting. Before his body was taken to Belgium, Damien was buried in the gardens to the right; his grave remains decorated with *leis* and now contains his right hand once more.

▲ View of the north coast from Kalawao

Despite the horrific tales of misery and squalor, Kalawao is extraordinarily beautiful. From the lawns beyond the church, and especially from **Judd Park** at the end of the road, the **coastal views** are superb. Mists swirl beneath the gigantic *pali* to the east, occasionally parting to offer glimpses of the remote valleys that pierce it, while stark, rocky islands poke from the churning ocean. Daredevil ancient Hawaiians would swim out to **'Okala Island**, the closest to the shore, and leap from its 400ft summit clutching braided palm-leaf "parachutes."

Western Molokai

Western Molokai consists of what remains of the older of the island's two volcanoes, Mauna Loa. Similar in profile to its Big Island namesake, but much lower, the "long mountain" lies within the rainshadow of the larger East Molokai volcano. Because almost all the moisture carried by the prevailing winds has already fallen as rain before they reach this far, this end of the island is much drier, and there's been little erosion to dissect it into valleys.

Nonetheless, western Molokai held a considerable population in ancient times. As well as having the mysterious woodlands that witnessed the emergence of the hula and the fearsome poisonwood gods (see opposite), the upper slopes of its mountain were among Hawaii's best sources of the ultra-hard basalt used for making adzes – a precious commodity in a world without metal. Hence the region's name: **Kaluako'i**, "the adze pit."

In 1898, the entire west end of Molokai was sold for $251,000 to what became the **Molokai Ranch**. The ranch has been a dominant presence ever since, albeit by default since it ceased all operations in 2008. Having previously shifted from cattle ranching and pineapple farming toward real estate and tourism, and unveiled plans during the 1970s for the population of Kaluako'i to reach ten thousand, it has now abandoned the region to virtual dereliction. All that remains active is a smattering of smaller condo properties, a handful of private homes, no restaurants, and only the most basic of local stores.

Western Molokai has some magnificent beaches, such as the phenomenal **Pāpōhaku Beach**, but the surf is way too fierce to allow swimming. Instead, those few visitors who come this way tend to be here for the seclusion.

Maunaloa

Together with Kēʻē on Kauai (see p.379), **MAUNALOA** is one of two Hawaiian sites that claim to be the birthplace of hula. This tiny place also plays a prominent role in the legends of ancient Molokai. Only a few stone ruins remain of the pre-contact settlement, but a thriving community existed here until a couple of decades ago, when Maunaloa was among the most picturesque plantation villages in the state.

Perched high on the red-dirt flanks of western Molokai, enjoying views all the way to Diamond Head and Waikīkī on Oahu, modern Maunaloa took shape after Libby leased the nearby land to grow pineapples in the 1920s. At that time, it consisted of a cluster of simple timber cottages, shielded from the winds by stately rows of tall trees. Soon after passing into the hands of the Dole corporation in the 1970s, the pineapple fields were abandoned, the land reverted to the Molokai Ranch, and Maunaloa became a sleepy enclave of ranch hands, resort employees, and alternative artists.

In 1995, however, Molokai Ranch bulldozed most of the residential district of Maunaloa and replaced it with tracts of low-income housing further up the hillside. They subsequently added a small upscale inn, opened a bizarre "luxury

The poisonwood gods

Maunaloa was renowned throughout ancient Hawaii as the home of the dreaded **Kālaipāhoa**, or "**poisonwood gods**." According to legend, sometime in the sixteenth or seventeenth centuries a Molokai man called **Kāneiākama** lost everything he possessed playing ʻulumaika, which involved bowling stone disks down a hillside. As he was about to concede defeat, a god appeared to him and encouraged him to stake his life on the next throw. Upon winning, Kāneiākama sacrificed a pig to the mysterious god, who reappeared and gave his name as **Kāneikaulanaʻula**. Kāneiākama then watched as a grove of tall **trees** suddenly appeared in the hills above Maunaloa, and each different kind of tree was entered by a different deity.

When the then-chief of Molokai decreed that some of these magical trees should be chopped down and carved into **images** of the gods, the woodcutters died as soon as they were touched by flying chips or sap. Kāneiākama revealed sacrifices and ceremonies that made it safe to create the images; they passed into the control of the rulers of Molokai, while Kāneiākama became their kahuna, or priest.

Access to the images was ruthlessly restricted, and fear of them kept Molokai safe from attack. Eventually, however, Molokai was conquered, and the Kālaipāhoa passed first to Kahekili of Maui and then to Kamehameha the Great. Kamehameha kept the images by him during his final years at Kailua on the Big Island, and only he could resist their power.

Meanwhile the people of Molokai, and Maunaloa in particular, had begun to use the surviving trees for their own purposes. They used splinters or shavings of wood to poison each other's food, and even created magical bundles known as akua kumuhaka, that flew like flaming rockets through the night sky to seek out their enemies. Feared as an evil place of poʻokoʻi (**sorcery**), Molokai became known as the ʻaina hoʻounauna, "the land where spirits were sent on malicious errands."

Knowledge of the whereabouts of the Kālaipāhoa images died with Kamehameha, although at least one is thought to survive in Honolulu's Bishop Museum.

campsite" which not surprisingly never took off in the face of the $300-per-night charge for a tent, and instigated a program of outdoor activities such as rodeo and archery.

All have now closed down, and Maunaloa itself is all but silent. Its one center of activity is the Big Wind Kite Factory (Mon–Sat 8.30am–5pm, Sun 10am–2pm), whose convivial owner makes and sells colorful kites and is usually happy to demonstrate the finer points of kite-flying. The adjoining Plantation Gallery (same hours) stocks an excellent range of imported crafts from Bali, Nepal, and elsewhere.

Hale O Lono Harbor

Molokai's remote **southwestern shoreline** has long been inaccessible to visitors. However, the **Hale O Lono Harbor** reverted a few years ago to state ownership, after being leased to the Molokai Ranch for 35 years. Anyone who wants to can now drive down here, along a red-dirt road (very passable except after heavy rain) that starts in Maunaloa. En route, keener eyes might spot a phallic rock in a gully to the left that marks ancient burial caves.

Hale O Lono Harbor, which was constructed to ship sand from Pāpōhaku Beach to Oahu (see p.63), consists of a few concrete jetties with minimal facilities. In September and October each year it serves as the starting point of the prestigious men's and women's **outrigger canoe races** from Molokai to Oahu. Walking a couple of hundred yards east from the parking lot brings you to a small, sheltered beach.

Kaluako'i

Until construction began on the **Kaluako'i Resort** during the 1970s, just one person lived on the coast of western Molokai. That owes more to the fact that it belonged to the Molokai Ranch than to there being anything wrong with it. However, the lack of water has prevented the resort from growing to anything like the size originally envisaged. To this day, only one of its planned four hotels has ever been built, and even that, the *Kaluako'i Hotel*, has been closed since 2001.

As the hotel was home to the only stores or restaurants in the area, its closure has made staying in any of the nearby condo developments a much less appealing prospect, although it's still unquestionably worth making the trip here to enjoy splendid **Pāpōhaku Beach**.

Accommodation

The only **accommodation** in Kaluako'i is located on the headland where Kaluako'i Road reaches the ocean, dominated by the defunct *Kaluako'i Hotel*. For now, the hotel remains in a strange state of limbo; you can still wander in, and strangely enough its small gifts-and-grocery store remains open, but it's generally an eerie spot. Its swimming pool was cracked and empty when this book went to press, despite a court order obliging the Molokai Ranch to refill it. In addition to the properties listed below, other privately owned properties can be rented through the agencies listed on p.312.

Ke Nani Kai 50 Kepuhi Place ☎808/679-2016 or 1-800/490-9042, ⓦ www.kenanikai.com. Spacious and comfortable one- and two-bedroom condos, few of which have sea views, in a small, well-kept complex with its own pool and spa. ❺

Kepuhi Beach Condo Kaluako'i Rd ☎808/552-2222, 1-800/MOLOKAI, ⓦ www.1-800-molokai.com. A couple of upscale condos beside the defunct Kaluako'i golf course, very close to Pāpōhaku Beach, with good-value nightly or weekly rental rates. ❹

Paniolo Hale Lio Place; reserve through Swenson Real Estate ☎808/553-3648, ⓦ www.molokai-vacation-rental.com. An estate of studio apartments plus one- and two-bedroom condos, just north of the *Kaluako'i Hotel*. Some of the larger ones are complete houses and in very good condition. ❹

Kepuhi Beach and Kawākiu Iki Bay

Although the *Kaluako'i Resort* was positioned to enable guests to enjoy the long white sands of **Kepuhi Beach**, located directly in front of the *Kaluako'i Hotel*, it's only safe to swim here on calm summer days. Like most of the beaches of western Molokai, however, it looks fabulous and is ideal for sunset strolls.

A mile **north** of the resort, and reached by a very rough road – far too rough to drive – that starts by crossing the golf course beyond *Paniolo Hale*, pretty, crescent-shaped **Kawākiu Iki Bay** was a favorite fishing ground in ancient times. Mass protests in the 1970s persuaded the Molokai Ranch to grant free public access, and there's even a free but completely unequipped campground, but it's almost always deserted.

Pāpōhaku Beach

Immediately **south** of the hotel, it's possible to follow a track to the summit of the crumbling cinder cone of **Pu'u O Kaiaka** for views of the entire coastline and, with luck, across to Oahu. Beyond it lies the sublime, 2.5-mile-long **Pāpōhaku Beach**, one of Hawaii's broadest and most impressive white-sand beaches. It's so huge that for many years it was quarried for sand, much of which was used to build Waikīkī Beach.

Almost all the land to either side of Kaluako'i Road, which parallels Pāpōhaku a hundred yards back from the sea, was parceled off and sold for residential development many years ago. However, homes have only been built on a small proportion of the lots, and even those are seldom occupied, so you may have the full length of the beach to yourself. The relentless pounding of the surf is spectacular, but makes swimming extremely dangerous.

Three successive turnoffs connect Kaluako'i Road with the beach. The northernmost leads to **Pāpōhaku Beach Park**, a well-equipped county park that has picnic tables on its lawns and barbecue pits amid the trees. **Camping** is, however, currently not permitted. The southernmost turnoff, Papapa Place, appears as Kaluako'i Road starts to climb at the south end of the beach; it comes out near the gated tunnel through which sand destined for Waikīkī was carted off to the docks on the south coast.

Molokai Ka Hula Piko

On the third Saturday of May, between 8am and 4pm, Pāpōhaku Beach Park hosts **Molokai Ka Hula Piko**, a day-long celebration of Molokai's role as the birthplace of the hula (Ⓦwww.molokaievents.com). That's a slightly contentious boast – Kē'ē on Kauai also claims to be the home of Hawaii's oldest art form – but Ka Hula Piko is universally acknowledged to be one of the most authentic traditional festivals in the islands. As well as performances by dancers, musicians, and singers from all over Hawaii, it features local crafts and food stalls. Admission is free.

On Molokai, the story runs that the goddess **Laka** was taught to dance the hula by her sister **Kapo** amid the verdant *'ōhi'a lehua* groves of **Kā'ana**, near Maunaloa. After traveling through the Hawaiian islands teaching hula, Laka returned to Molokai to die, and lies buried beneath the hill of **Pu'unānā**.

Ka Hula Piko commences each year with a dawn ceremony at a ruined *heiau* at Kā'ana, to which the public is not admitted. However, the festival's organizers have in the past offered guided tours of related sites during the preceding week. At other times, the only way to see Kā'ana and Pu'unānā would be on a guided hike; contact the Molokai Visitors Association to see if anyone is currently leading them. The fact that the area is now almost entirely denuded of trees has made it possible to identify countless cultural sites.

For all-inclusive transport and accommodation packages to Ka Hula Piko, contact the Molokai Visitors Association (see p.313).

Dixie Maru Beach

Kaluako'i Road ends beyond Pāpōhaku Beach, but by turning right on to Pūhakuloa Road you can drive a couple of miles farther down the coast. A couple of beach access roads along the way lead to an exposed and rocky shoreline, but the final turnaround comes at the small sandy cove named **Dixie Maru Beach**, after a long-vanished shipwreck. Sparsely vegetated and relatively unattractive, the cove is enclosed enough to create a small lagoon of sheltered turquoise water, where the **swimming** is usually great.

Kaunalā Beach

From Dixie Maru Beach, it's possible to follow the coastal footpath for another mile south to reach **Kaunalā Beach**, where the ocean is muddier and much rougher. Beyond that, the remaining segment of the western coast belongs to the Molokai Ranch, though as usual in Hawaii anyone is free to walk along the shoreline below the high-water line.

Kauai

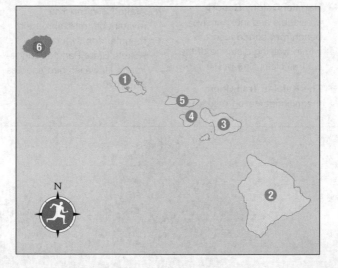

CHAPTER 6　**Highlights**

＊ **Helicopter trips** There's no place quite like Kauai for a flight-seeing extravaganza of hidden canyons, remote rainforests, velvety waterfalls and uninhabited valleys. See p.340

＊ **Lumaha'i Beach** The sublime (if dangerous) tropical beach where Mitzi Gaynor washed that man right out of her hair in the movie *South Pacific*. See p.377

＊ **Hanalei Colony Resort** Irresistible and inexpensive beachfront condo resort, within walking distance of the Nā Pali cliffs. See p.378

＊ **The Kalalau Trail** Utterly magnificent eleven-mile trail along Kauai's northern Nā Pali coastline; just hike the first stretch if time is limited. See p.382

＊ **Po'ipū Beach** Snorkel, boogie-board, sunbathe, or surf on Kauai's most popular family beach. See p.390

＊ **Waimea Canyon** An extraordinary gorge for such a tiny island, where rainbows complement the daily panoply of colors. See p.401

＊ **Alaka'i Swamp** The mysterious, mist-shrouded, mountaintop swamp, in Kōke'e State Park, abounds in rare Hawaiian bird species. See p.403

▲ Hanalei Colony Resort

6

Kauai

Although no point on the tiny island of **KAUAI** (rhymes with "Hawaii") is even a dozen miles from the sea, the sheer variety of its landscapes is quite incredible. This is the oldest of the major Hawaiian islands, and the forces of erosion have had over six million years to sculpt it into fantastic shapes. The resultant spectacular **scenery** – celebrated in movies from *South Pacific* to *Avatar* – is Kauai's strongest selling-point. In addition to such beauty spots as the plunging **Nā Pali cliffs** on the North Shore and mighty **Waimea Canyon**, every humble roadside town abounds in flowers, orchids, and greenery. The "Garden Island" is also fringed with stunning **beaches** of white and golden sand, in contrast to its rich red soil. On some beaches, on the north and west coasts in particular, it's seldom safe even to approach the ocean; others, especially around the southern resort of **Po'ipū**, are ideal for family bathing.

Kauai ranks fourth not only in size among the Hawaiian islands, but also in population and number of annual visitors. With only a little over sixty thousand inhabitants scattered around the shoreline, it holds no large towns. The administrative center, **Līhu'e**, is functional but unenthralling, while the main accommodation bases – **Po'ipū**, the coastal strip around **Kapa'a**, and **Princeville** – possess little identity of their own. If you're looking for the high life, stick to Waikīkī or Maui; Kauai is more suited to a quiet family holiday or romantic retreat. It's also a place to be active, on both sea and land. In addition to some of the world's most exhilarating **hiking** trails, it offers great **snorkeling** and **surfing**. Taking a boat trip along the North Shore is a can't-miss experience, and if you only go on one **helicopter** flight in your life, this is the place to do it.

A brief history of Kauai

Before the arrival of the Europeans, Kauai was always an independent kingdom; it was the only Hawaiian island never to be conquered by another. Even Kamehameha the Great opted to accept tribute from Kauai, after twice staging unsuccessful invasions.

Just as it was the first Hawaiian island "discovered" by Captain Cook, Kauai may well have been **colonized** before the rest, by a different group of Polynesian settlers. Its first settlers arrived from the Marquesas islands in southern-central Polynesia, perhaps as early as 200 AD. These may be the people later known as the *menehune*, though no tiny skeletons substantiate the legend that they were hairy dwarfs.

Thanks in part to the stormy ocean channel that separates it from Oahu, Kauai remained a land apart. Together with Niihau, it was a "leeward island," usually concealed from view of the other major, windward, islands. Its sailors were famous as raiders unafraid to sail out of sight of land. Known as Kauai *pule o'o* – "Kauai of strong prayers" – it also had a reputation as the home of devout prophets and seers.

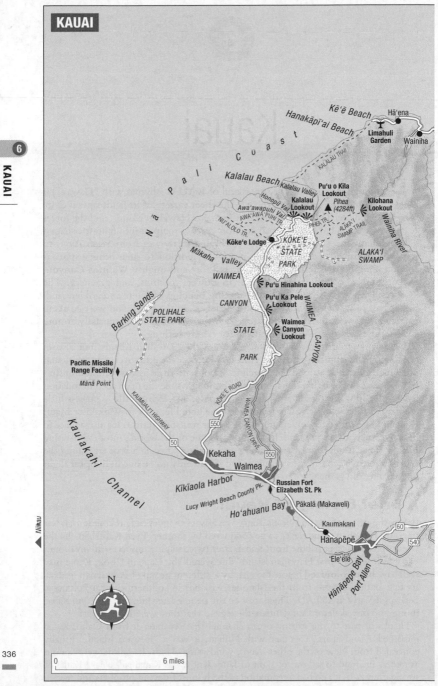

KAUAI

0   6 miles

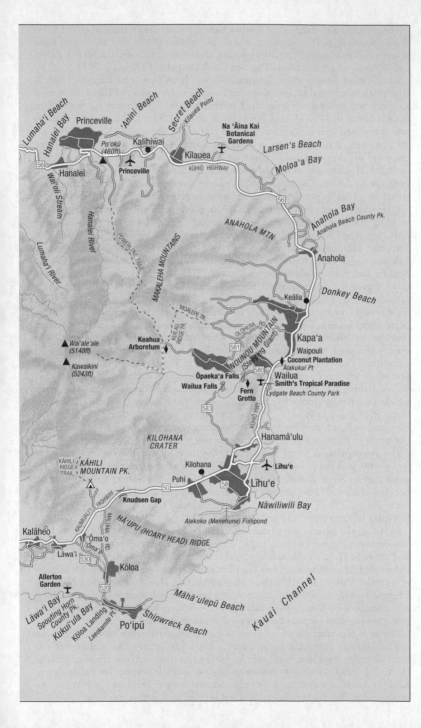

The greatest chiefs lived in the **Wailua Valley**, maintaining a chain of sacred *heiaus* that stretched up to the summit of Wai'ale'ale, where a phallic altar to the god Kane is said still to be standing. Other major population centers included the Nā Pali valleys and Waimea, which was where **Captain Cook** arrived in 1778 (see p.397.)

Kauai's most famous ruler, **Kaumuali'i**, was born two years later, in 1780. A slight man who traced his genealogy back over seven centuries to Tahiti, he learned to speak and write fluent English. Kamehameha the Great made his first bid to invade Kauai in 1796. A huge fleet set off at night from Oahu, but the attempt was abandoned after a storm sank several canoes. By the time of his next attempt, six years later, Kaumuali'i was in charge of Kauai. This time Kamehameha's force consisted of seven thousand Hawaiians and as many as fifty Europeans; his fleet included 21 schooners as well as traditional canoes and was equipped with eight cannons. As the force assembled on the eastern shore of Oahu, however, they were struck by a terrible pestilence, and the invasion plans were once more shelved.

After receiving envoys from Kamehameha, Kaumuali'i agreed to go to Honolulu in 1810. Kamehameha declined his face-saving offer to surrender Kauai in name only, replying "Return and rule over it. But if our young chief" – his eventual successor, Liholiho – "makes you a visit, be pleased to receive him."

Reports of a secret treaty between Kaumuali'i and the **Russian** envoy George Schäffer (see p.396) under which a joint Kauaian–Russian fleet would invade the other Hawaiian islands, alarmed Kamehameha. Shortly after his death, in 1821, Liholiho sailed to Kauai, supposedly for an unofficial visit. Having toured the island for six weeks, he invited Kaumuali'i to dine on his yacht, anchored off Waimea, on September 16, 1821. The boat set sail, and Kaumuali'i was abducted to Oahu. Within four days of landing he was married to Kamehameha's widow, Ka'ahumanu, who shortly afterwards married Kaumuali'i's son, Keali'iahonui, as well.

Kaumuali'i never returned to Kauai; he died in Honolulu in 1824. Kauai's final flourish of resistance against the Hawaiian monarchy came later that year. Another son of Kaumuali'i, **Prince George**, launched an armed **insurrection**. The rebels attacked the Russian fort at Waimea on August 8, 1824, but were swiftly cornered by forces from Oahu in Hanapēpē Valley, and all but wiped out. The victorious army remained on Kauai, indiscriminately confiscating land and property from local chiefs, and much of Kauai was parceled out among the descendants of Kamehameha.

The **corruption** of these newcomers, the inequities of the sandalwood trade (see p.419), and the founding of Hawaii's first sugar plantation at Kōloa in 1835, combined to erode Kauai's traditional way of life. Thereafter, Kauaian history becomes the usual Hawaiian tale of a diminishing and disinherited native population, the growth of American-owned agricultural concerns, and the influx of low-paid laborers from Asia and elsewhere.

By 1872, the island's population had slumped to just 5200. Agricultural land was increasingly given over to sugar, although there were experiments with silk and coffee in Hanalei, silk at Kōloa, and cattle ranching along the West Shore. As indentured Chinese workers left the plantations, they converted the taro terraces of Hanalei Valley into the largest **rice** paddies in Hawaii. Subsequently, many Chinese moved on to Honolulu, and taro production has since made something of a comeback on Kauai, while more recently farmers have attempted to diversify into growing such crops as corn, tropical fruits, and **coffee**.

The first Hawaiian island to grow sugar commercially also turned out to be the last. Kauai's final sugar harvest was in 2009, just as the other mainstay of the local economy, **tourism**, was badly hit by the recession. Anyone traveling around the island today can't fail to notice quite how many businesses have shut down. And yet Kauai's greatest asset – its phenomenal beauty – remains, and it's hard to imagine that the visitor industry will not bounce back before too long.

Kauai overview

Mount Wai'ale'ale, the extinct volcano responsible for creating Kauai, was the biggest of all the Hawaiian shield volcanoes. Lava streamed from it in all directions, so the island is roughly circular, measuring up to 33 miles north to south and 25 miles west to east. Little of the volcano's original outline, however, remains discernible. On all sides, but especially to the north and west, it is now furrowed with deep, lush valleys, while its summit has worn down to a mere 5000ft above sea level. The wettest place on earth, the summit is perched atop steepled cliffs and permanently shrouded in mist. Even on a helicopter tour (see p.340), you're unlikely to glimpse the highest peak.

Kauai's largest expanse of flat land lies in its southeast corner, where **Līhu'e** is home to its airport. While the county seat holds a small selection of hotels and an attractive little beach, most visitors head for more scenic areas almost as soon as they touch down. Six miles up the coast, north of the Wailua River, the beach strip from **Wailua** to **Kapa'a** abounds in relatively inexpensive hotels and a wide range of restaurants. The old wooden boardwalks of Kapa'a make for a diverting pause on the round-island drive, while fine hiking trails weave through the valleys inland.

Beyond Kapa'a, the highway steers clear of a succession of pretty and barely used beaches as it cuts through to the North Shore. **Princeville** here is a luxurious but soulless resort, guarding the headland above beautiful **Hanalei Bay**. At this point the green cliffs of the **Nā Pali** coast heave into view, towering above quirky Hanalei. From here on the **coast road** is breathtaking, passing gorgeous golden beaches pounded by endless surf. After ten miles, the ever-taller cliffs bar all further progress. The uninhabited Nā Pali valleys beyond can only be reached on foot, on the **Kalalau Trail**.

Po'ipū, at Kauai's southernmost tip, is the island's most popular resort, boasting several upscale hotels and condos. Its beaches remain the best for year-round family vacations, with great surfing and diving spots just offshore. **Waimea**, to the west, should in theory be a fascinating historic town, but lacks the commercial infrastructure to persuade visitors to linger.

A few miles west, **Polihale State Park** preserves Hawaii's longest beach, a dangerous but compelling fifteen-mile strand that ends at the western limit of the Nā Pali coast. High above, in the narrow gap between the mile-wide **Waimea Canyon** and the start of the Nā Pali valleys, **Kōke'e State Park** combines phenomenal roadside views with tremendous hiking trails. One of the most extraordinary leads through the land-locked **Alaka'i Swamp**, the last refuge of countless unique Hawaiian plant and bird species.

Getting to Kauai

Kauai's only commercial **airport**, just outside Līhu'e, is served by a handful of nonstop flights from **Los Angeles**, **San Francisco**, **Seattle**, and **Phoenix**. Hawaiian, Island Air, and Go! all offer nonstop flights to **Honolulu**, and Kahului on **Maui**, with connections to the other Hawaiian islands.

Kauai favorites: beaches	
'Anini Beach, p.368	Lumaha'i Beach, p.377
Kalalau Valley, p.384	Po'ipū Beach, p.390
Kalihiwai Beach, p.368	Polihale, p.399
Kē'ē Beach, p.379	Secret Beach, p.367

Getting around Kauai

As Kauai's resort areas tend to be spread out, and scenic spots like Waimea Canyon and the Nā Pali cliffs are a long way from the nearest places to stay, most visitors end up **driving** more than they expect. All the major car-rental chains are represented at Līhu'e airport.

As a rule, driving is a pleasure. There's just one main road, known as **Kaumuali'i Highway** south of Līhu'e, and **Kūhiō Highway** to the north, and only thirteen stoplights. However, all the way between Po'ipū and Princeville there's usually a fair amount of traffic; try to avoid the morning and evening "rush hours" between Līhu'e and Kapa'a. On both the narrow single-lane road along the North Shore – where you can be forced to a standstill as you wait for a chicken or a goose to cross the road – and the tortuous Waimea Canyon Drive, average speeds drop below 20mph.

By bus

The Kauai Bus operates a **bus service** to all parts of the island, with a flat fare of $2 (students and seniors $1; ℡ 808/241-6410 or Ⓦ www.kauai.gov). Large backpacks and suitcases are forbidden. Of the two main routes, one runs between Kukui Grove in **Līhu'e** and **Hanalei**, via Wailua, Kapa'a, Kīlauea, and Princeville (Mon–Fri 12 services daily, Sat 6 services; journey time 1hr 23min). The other connects **Līhu'e** and **Kekaha** via Hanapēpē and Waimea (Mon–Fri 13 services daily, Sat 6 services; journey time 1hr 15min). There are also five daily services from **Līhu'e** airport to Kōloa and Po'ipū, on weekdays only (journey time 40min).

Tours and taxis

Companies offering guided **minibus tours** include Roberts Hawaii (℡ 808/539-9400 or 1-866/898-2519, Ⓦ www.robertshawaii.com) and Polynesian Adventure Tours (℡ 808/246-0122 or 1-800/622-3011, Ⓦ www.polyad.com). Typical prices start at $50 for a half-day tour, $70 for a full day.

Hawaii Movie Tours (℡ 808/822-1192 or 1-800/628-8432, Ⓦ www.hawaiimovie tour.com) organizes a specialized all-day tour for $90 that concentrates on scenic

Helicopter flight-seeing

Kauai is the best Hawaiian island to see from the air. It's small enough, and its mountains are low enough, for a single **flight** to cover the whole island – and many of its most spectacular spots are impossible to reach any other way. Typical tours follow a clockwise route from Līhu'e, around to Waimea Canyon and along the north coast, then back via awesome Wai'ale'ale, and last 45 minutes to an hour. Official **rates** are generally around $150 for a 45-minute tour and $200 for an hour-long excursion, but many operators offer **discounts** for advance or online bookings, and you can also find bargains with the general activities operators listed on p.343.

Island Helicopters is unique in offering a highly recommended ($324) tour that includes a **landing** at remote Manawaiopuna Falls, seen in *Jurassic Park*. For details on Niihau Helicopters, which only runs excursions to the island of Niihau, see p.401.

	Number	Ⓦ www.	Departs
Blue Hawaiian	℡ 1-800/745-2583	bluehawaiian.com	Līhu'e
Inter-Island	℡ 1-800/656-5009	interislandhelicopters.com	Port Allen
Island	℡ 1-800/829-5999	islandhelicopters.com	Līhu'e
Jack Harter	℡ 1-888/245-2001	helicopters-kauai.com	Līhu'e
Safari	℡ 1-800/326-3356	safarihelicopters.com	Līhu'e
Sunshine	℡ 1-866/501-7738	helicopters-hawaii.com	Līhu'e and Princeville

Kauai spots that have featured in major Hollywood films (see p.437); they also offer a four-wheel-drive tour that reaches more inaccessible locations for $115. Aloha Kauai Tours (☏808/245-8809 or 1-800/452-1113, ⓦwww.alohakauaitours.com) offers four-hour tours of the backroads of Grove Farm Plantation in four-wheel-drive vans, starting from Kilohana at 8am and 1pm daily, for $70, as well as four-hour, $80 expeditions that involve a three-mile hike near the base of Mount Wai'ale'ale.

Guided hikes, usually on Saturdays, Sundays, and at the full moon, are organized by the local chapter of the Sierra Club (ⓦwww.hi.sierraclub.org).

Kauai **cab** operators include Kauai Taxi Company (☏808/246-9554, ⓦwww .kauaitaxico.com). Expect to pay perhaps $15 from the airport to Kapa'a, $25–30 to Pō'ipu, and $40 or more to the North Shore.

Where to stay

Kauai is small enough that you can base yourself pretty much anywhere and still explore the whole island. Away from Po'ipū and Princeville, room rates are generally lower than elsewhere in Hawaii. If finding **budget** accommodation is a priority, then the inexpensive inns and B&Bs from Līhu'e to Kapa'a are your best bet (see p.353). If you want a **beach-based** holiday in a family resort, opt for a hotel or condo in Po'ipū or Kapa'a. To rent a **tropical hideaway**, get in touch with the agencies in Princeville (see p.371).

Kauai offers great **camping**, especially along the North Shore and on the Nā Pali coast. Full details are available from the state and county parks offices in Līhu'e, as detailed on p.347. Other locations where you can pick up permits are detailed on the county website, ⓦwww.kauai.gov.

When to go

The best times to come to Kauai are late spring and fall, when room rates are often slightly lower and crowds are smaller. But since Kauai rarely feels either overcrowded or overpriced, it doesn't make that much of a difference.

Kauai favorites: campgrounds

'Anini Beach County Park, p.368   Kalalau Valley, p.384
Hā'ena Beach County Park, p.378   Kōke'e State Park, p.405
Hanalei Pavilion Beach County Park, p.375   Polihale State Park, p.399
For details on Nā Pali permits, see p.380.

Seasonal **weather** variations are relatively minimal. Along the south coast, Kauai's warmest region, daily maximum **temperatures** range up from the low seventies Fahrenheit (around 22°C) in winter (Jan–March), to almost 80°F (27°C) in summer (Aug–Sept). Po'ipu, the most popular base for beach holidays, is marginally warmer than Līhu'e and Kapa'a, and warmer again than Princeville, but the difference is negligible.

Rainfall statistics look far more dramatic on paper than they do on the ground. Mount Wai'ale'ale, as you'll often be reminded, is the wettest place in the world – its record of 683 inches of rain in a single year is not the most ever measured, but its annual average of 451 inches beats the 428 inches of second-ranked Cherrapunji in India. Figures for the coast, just a few miles away, are very different. Waimea receives less than twenty inches per year, Po'ipū less than forty, and Kapa'a less than fifty. Princeville nears a hundred inches, but even on the north shore you'd have to be unlucky to have your plans seriously affected. In all areas, significantly more rain falls in winter than in summer, but even then most of it falls at night. If your main priority is to spend time on the beach, then choose Po'ipū above Princeville, and summer above winter, but if you plan to tour the island as a whole, then you can usually reckon that on any one day you'll be able to escape any rain by driving far enough.

The state of the **ocean** changes much more than the weather. Between December and April, winter thunderstorms can render water activities unsafe on all but the most sheltered beaches. Nā Pali coast tours are obliged to follow different itineraries in winter, and are often canceled altogether for days at a time (see p.381). However, many visitors choose to come at precisely that time, in the hope of seeing whales.

Watersports and other activities

For energetic vacationers, Kauai offers an exhausting range of both water- and land-based activities. Operators stand ready to instruct beginners or pamper experts in watersports such as diving, kayaking, and windsurfing, while stunning landscapes make the island a wonderful playground for hikers, golfers, and horseback riders.

Kauai favorites: eating

These restaurants are listed in ascending order of price, not (necessarily) quality.
Hamura's Saimin, Līhu'e, p.352
Java Kai, Hanalei, p.376
Duane's Ono Char Burger, Anahola, p.363
Kalāheo Café & Coffee Co, Kalāheo, p.394
Mermaids Café, Kapa'a, p.365
Hanapēpē Café & Espresso, Hanapēpē, p.395
Hanamā'ulu Restaurant, Hanamā'ulu, p.352
Casa di Amici, Po'ipū, p.392
Roy's Po'ipū Bar & Grill, Po'ipū, p.393
The Beach House, Po'ipū, p.392

In addition to the specialized outfits listed below, several companies offer tours and activities of all kinds, often at discounted rates, and also rent out every piece of equipment you might need. At their best, they can be great sources of help and advice. Recommended businesses include Tom Barefoot's Cashback Tours (☎1-800/779-6305, ⓦwww.tombarefoot.com), Cheap Tours Hawaii (☎808/246-0009, ⓦwww.cheaptourshawaii.com), and Activity Warehouse (☎1-800/343-2087, ⓦwww.travelhawaii.com).

Outfitters Kauai offers an especially wide-ranging program of adventurous activities on the island (☎1-888/742-9887 or 808/742-9667, ⓦwww.outfitterskauai.com). In addition to bike and kayak rentals and guided tours, they organize expeditions on and near the Huleʻia River, close to Līhuʻe, that include hikes to jungle waterfalls; rope-swinging and jumping into rivers and waterholes; and a 50ft-high "**Zipline**" leap, in which you cross a mountain stream suspended from a pulley. Prices range from around $88 for half a day up to $150 for a full day.

Cycling

Kauai Cycle and Tours, 1379 Kūhiō Hwy, Kapaʻa (☎808/821-2115, ⓦwww.bikehawaii.com/kauaicycle), rents out **bicycles** for $20–35 per day and up to $150 per week, and offers guided tours from $65. Coconut Coasters, 4-1586 Kūhiō Hwy, Kapaʻa, rents out bikes by the hour, for use on the very easy, new coastal path nearby (☎808/822-7368, ⓦwww.coconutcoasters.com).

For most of the way around Kauai, conditions are generally flat, but only a real glutton for punishment would attempt to cycle up to Kōkeʻe State Park. It is, however, possible to be driven up to the Kalalau Lookout and then be given a bike on which to freewheel all the way back down again. Outfitters Kauai charge about $100 for the privilege.

Horseback riding

Several stables offer guided **horseback excursions** on Kauai. The best of the bunch for ordinary riders are the Silver Falls Ranch in Kīlauea (☎808/828-6718, ⓦwww.silverfallsranch.com), which offers rides every day of the week, and charges $95 for ninety minutes, $115 for two hours, and $135 for three hours, and CJM Country Stables near Poʻipū (☎808/742-6096, ⓦwww.cjmstables.com), as described on p.391.

Princeville Ranch Stables offers large-scale group rides on the North Shore (☎808/826-6777, ⓦwww.princeville ranch.com), detailed on p.369. Two smaller companies, based in Kapaʻa on the East Shore, make good choices for more proficient riders. Keapana Horsemanship offers private rides tailored to your requirements at $90 per rider, per hour (☎808/823-9303), while Esprit de Corps (☎808/822-4688, ⓦwww.kauaihorses.com), charges from $130 for a three-hour ride, up to $390 for eight hours.

Kayaking

Kauai is unique in Hawaii in offering **river kayaking** on several inland waterways. Guided trips are available along the Huleʻia Stream near Līhuʻe (Outfitters Kauai; see above), the Wailua River on the East Shore (Wailua Kayak Adventures ☎808/822-5795, ⓦwww.kauaiwailuakayak.com; from $43), and the Hanalei River on the North Shore (Kayak Kauai ☎808/826-9844, ⓦwww.kayakkauai.com; $60). These and other operators, including Pedal & Paddle in Hanalei's Ching Young Village on the North Shore (☎808/826-9069, ⓦwww.pedalnpaddle.com), also rent out kayaks for self-guided expeditions from as little as $20 for a couple of hours.

In general it's much safer for inexperienced kayakers to explore the rivers than to set off into the ocean. Only absolute experts should attempt to tackle the Nā Pali coast on their own; if you really want to see it, it's best to take a guided tour with Kayak Kauai (above; April–Sept only; $205).

Scuba diving

Although Kauai can't claim to be the very best of the Hawaiian islands for divers – the high North Shore seas preclude diving for most of the year, while the coast elsewhere tends to be short of spectacular coral – its waters still hold some truly superb **dive sites**. For novices, the best of the lot lie close to Po'ipū and are usually accessible year-round. **Sheraton Caverns**, just offshore from the *Sheraton* hotel, is a network of three massive lava tubes that shelters a large population of sea turtles and lobsters. At the slightly harder **General Store** site, colorful fish swarm through the wreckage of the steamship *Pele*, which foundered in 1895. In summer, popular North Shore snorkel sites such as **Tunnels Reef** and **Kē'ē Lagoon** also attract plenty of shore divers. The tiny islet of **Lehua**, off Niihau, is similar to Maui's Molokini (see p.223), but infinitely less crowded and polluted; however, it takes a long sea trip to reach it and considerable expertise to dive once you're there.

Dive operators based on the South Shore include Fathom Five (☎808/742-6691 or 1-800/972-3078, ⓦwww.fathomfive.com) and Mana Divers (☎808/335-0881 or 1-877/348-3669, ⓦwww.manadivers.com). Bubbles Below (☎808/332-7333 or 1-866/524-6268, ⓦwww.bubblesbelowkauai.com), Dive Kauai (☎808/822-0452 or 1-800/828-3483, ⓦwww.divekauai.com), and Seasport Divers (☎808/742-9303 or 1-800/685-5889, ⓦwww.seasportdivers.com) offer dives on both the South and East shores, while Hanalei is home to North Shore Divers (☎808/828-1223 or 1-877/688-3483, ⓦwww.northshoredivers.com). Expect to pay $120–150 for a two-tank boat dive.

Snorkeling

Snorkeling is more of a year-round activity on Kauai than diving, as even along the North Shore several mini-lagoons are sufficiently sheltered by offshore coral reefs to remain calm through most of the winter. Prime North Shore sites include **Kē'ē Beach** and **Tunnels Beach**, while the best spot along the East Shore is **Lydgate State Park**, just south of the Wailua River. Probably the safest and most convenient sites of all, however, are those abutting the resorts of Po'ipū, such as **Po'ipū Beach** and **Lāwa'i Beach**.

Outlets renting snorkel equipment include the ubiquitous Snorkel Bob's (ⓦwww .snorkelbob.com), here based at 4-734 Kūhiō Hwy in Kapa'a (☎808/823-9433) and 3236 Po'ipū Road in Kōloa (☎808/742-2206). Note also that most Nā Pali boat trips (see p.381) double as snorkel cruises, and equipment is provided.

Surfing and windsurfing

For surfers, Kauai is similar to Oahu, in that southern beaches such as Kalāpakī Beach and Po'ipū Beach are ideal places for beginners to learn the ropes, while the North Shore provides some great challenges for experts. **Hanalei Bay** in particular is immensely popular with serious surfers, with **Tunnels Beach** a close second. The best site on the East Shore is **Lydgate State Park** near Wailua.

Surfing lessons are offered by Titus Kinimaka's Hawaiian School of Surfing, in Hanalei (☎808/652-1116, ⓦwww.hawaiianschoolofsurfing.com), and, in Po'ipū, Kauai Surf School (☎808/651-6032, ⓦwww.kauaisurfschool.com) and Margo Oberg's Surfing School (☎808/332-6100, ⓦwww.surfonkauai.com). A two-hour group surfing lesson costs about $75 per person, a private lesson $100–150.

Kauai lū'aus

The *lū'aus* listed below charge $70–100 per adult and $30–50 per child; you should be able to get tickets for under $60 from activities operators all over the island.

Garden Lū'au Smith's Tropical Paradise, Wailua ☎808/821-6895, ⓦwww.smiths kauai.com. Summer Mon–Fri 5pm; winter Mon, Wed, & Fri 5pm (see p.356).

Grand Hyatt Kauai Lū'au *Grand Hyatt Kauai*, Po'ipū ☎808/240-6456. Thurs & Sun 5.30pm.

Lū'au Kalamaku Kilohana Plantation, Līhu'e ☎1-877/622-1780, ⓦwww.luaukalamaku .com. Tues & Thurs 5pm.

Surf to Sunset Lū'au *Sheraton Po'ipū*, Po'ipū ☎808/742-8200, ⓦwww.luaukilohana .com. Mon & Fri 5.30pm.

6

As for windsurfing, with the exception of sheltered **'Anini Beach** – where Windsurf Kauai offers instruction (☎808/828-6838, ⓦwww.windsurf-kauai .com), most of the North Shore is too dangerous for **windsurfers**. They head, instead, for the South Shore near Po'ipū. **Po'ipū Beach** is a good place to learn; the beaches of the **Māhā'ulepū** area are more favored by the already proficient.

Nightlife and entertainment

Barring the occasional big-name concert at the War Memorial in central Līhu'e, and promotional appearances by local stars at the Kukui Grove mall, virtually all Kauai's **nightlife** takes place in its hotels and restaurants. Among venues that can usually be depended upon for **live music**, especially at weekends, are the *Kauai Beach Resort* just outside Līhu'e; *Keoki's Paradise* in Po'ipū; and the *Hanalei Gourmet*, *Bouchons*, and *Tahiti Nui* in Hanalei. The North Shore, in particular, is where the funkier local musicians tend to hang out. Kauai Community Radio, broadcasting from Hanalei on 90.9 and 91.9FM (ⓦwww.kkcr.org), is a good source of up-to-date music and entertainment listings.

Līhu'e

Kauai's capital, **LĪHU'E**, will likely be the first and the last place you see on the island, and chances are you'll pass through it several times during your stay as well. Stretching back from the sea in the island's southeast corner, it's home to Kauai's main **airport** and **harbor**, and the midpoint of the highway that circles the island.

However, Līhu'e is not an attractive or exciting town, and few tourists spend more time here than they have to. With a population of just five thousand, its main effect on visitors tends to be to reveal just how rural Kauai really is. Several roads run through open fields without a sign of life, while downtown Līhu'e consists of a handful of tired-looking plantation-town streets lined with simple one- and two-story buildings.

That said, visitors shouldn't overlook Līhu'e completely. Its inland section offers Kauai's widest selection of **shops** and its best **museum**, while the area around

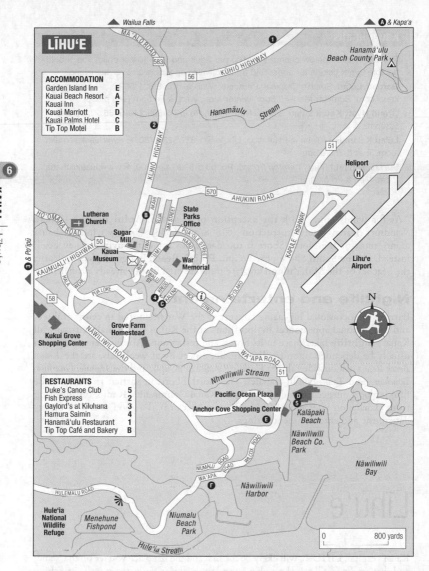

LĪHU'E

ACCOMMODATION
Garden Island Inn	E
Kauai Beach Resort	A
Kauai Inn	F
Kauai Marriott	D
Kauai Palms Hotel	C
Tip Top Motel	B

RESTAURANTS
Duke's Canoe Club	5
Fish Express	2
Gaylord's al Kilohana	3
Hamura Saimin	4
Hanamā'ulu Restaurant	1
Tip Top Café and Bakery	B

Nāwiliwili Bay holds some good hotels and restaurants, a fine sheltered white-sand beach, and a stretch of unspoiled riverfront that's a sanctuary for native water birds.

Līhu'e cannot boast a long history. It dates from the middle of the nineteenth century, when it was a village serving the Grove Farm sugar plantation. The area's sugar-growing days finally came to an end in 2000, and Grove Farm, which now belongs to AOL co-founder Steve Case, has diversified into real estate.

Until well into the twentieth century, Kauai's chief ports were Port Allen in the southwest, and Hanalei Bay in the north. Not until about 1930, when **Nāwiliwili Harbor** and the new airport were completed, did Līhu'e become the island's major port.

Arrival and information

Līhu'e's **airport** is only two miles east of downtown, near the ocean on Ahukini Road. All the major car-rental companies (see p.23) have offices across from the terminal. A **taxi** into Līhu'e costs around $10, while the fare from the airport to Wailua or Kapa'a is more like $20, and to Po'ipū $35 or so. Local cab companies include Akiko's Taxi (☎808/822-7588). For details on the Kauai Bus service north from Līhu'e to Hanalei, and west from Līhu'e to Kekaha and Kōloa, see p.340.

For official tourism information, stop in at the **Kauai Visitors Bureau** in central Līhu'e, on the first floor at Watamull Plaza, 4334 Rice St (Mon–Fri 8am–4.30pm; ☎808/245-3971 or 1-800/262-1400, ⓦwww.kauaidiscovery.com). The island's main **post office**, at 4441 Rice St (Mon–Fri 8am–4.30pm, Sat 9am–1pm), is opposite the Kauai Museum, immediately south of the Bank of Hawaii.

Accommodation

Although the opulent *Marriott* compares favorably with any luxury resort in Hawaii, Līhu'e itself is fundamentally a budget destination, where a handful of inexpensive **accommodation** options make reasonable bases from which to tour the entire island. The nearest place to **camp** is in Hanamā'ulu (see p.352).

Garden Island Inn 3445 Wilcox Rd, Kalāpakī Bay ☎808/245-7227 or 1-800/648-0154, ⓦwww.gardenislandinn.com. Nicely refurbished, good-value 21-room motel, dripping with purple bougainvillea, and set slightly back from the road that curves around Kalāpakī Beach. All the simple but appealing rooms have fridges and microwaves; those on the first floor have no views; on the second they have a/c and *lānais*; and on the third they're suites sleeping three to four guests. There's also a two-bed, two-story condo on the bluff behind. There are restaurants right across the street, and snorkel sets and boogie-boards are available for free; the one drawback is that the traffic can be busy. Rooms ❸, suites ❹, condo ❺

Kauai Beach Resort 4331 Kauai Beach Drive ☎808/245-1955 or 1-866/971-2782, ⓦwww.aquaresorts.com. Upscale oceanfront condo-hotel, three miles north of Līhu'e, and very convenient for

the airport. Its 350 comfortable, spacious rooms and suites have bright, contemporary island decor, and are set in four low-rise wings around an enticing three-segment swimming pool, complete with fern grotto. The beach alongside is pretty but poor for swimming, so there's an artificial beach on site. Rates are very reasonable, but beware hefty charges for extras like parking and wi-fi. Garden view ❹, ocean view ❺

Kauai Inn 2430 Hulemalu Rd, Niumalu ☎808/245-9000 or 1-800/808-2330, ⓦwww.kauai-inn.com. Simple, spotless motel-like inn, a mile beyond Kalāpakī Beach, which offers 48 good-value rooms arrayed around a small (and very shallow) pool. While not a destination in its own right, it's a handy central base. ❹

Kauai Marriott 3610 Rice St ☎808/245-5050 or 1-800/220-2925, ⓦwww.marriott.com/lihhi. Lavish resort alongside lovely Kalāpakī Beach, where most

---

Camping and hiking permits

If you haven't already made bookings online, Līhu'e is the place to gather any **camping** and **hiking permits** you may need during your stay on Kauai. The **state parks office**, which provides excellent, double-sided hiking and recreation maps of the island for $5, and the **Division of Forestry**, which controls camping in parts of Waimea Canyon, share adjoining offices on the third floor of the state building at 3060 Eiwa St (Mon–Fri 8am–3.30pm; ☎808/274-3444, ⓦwww.hawaiistateparks.org); the **county camping office** is not far away, in the Līhu'e Civic Center at 4444 Rice St (Mon–Fri 8am–4.15pm; ☎808/241-6660, ⓦwww.kauai.gov). Permit requirements for Nā Pali coast expeditions are outlined on p.380.

of the 345 tower-block rooms overlook Hawaii's largest swimming pool and its five whirlpool spas. The property boasts two golf courses, six restaurants, eight tennis courts, and eight miles of footpaths. Garden view **⑥**, ocean view **⑧**

🏃 **Kauai Palms Hotel** 2931 Kalena St ☏808/246-0908, ⓦwww.kauaipalmshotel .com. Pleasant, albeit very simple, plantation-style motel/inn in a quiet spot in downtown Līhu'e, with views out over the fields. Only the

larger of its 22 rooms, capable of sleeping three, have a/c, but the smaller ones are still tasteful and good value. **③**

Tip Top Motel 3173 Akāhi St ☏808/245-2333, Ⓔtiptop@aloha.net. Unprepossessing but well-equipped motel, hidden away on a backstreet. Each room has TV and a/c, and a shower but no bathtub, and costs just $65 per night. There's an inexpensive bakery-cum-diner plus a sushi restaurant onsite (see p.352). **②**

The town

A low-key assortment of stores, offices, and homes, scattered among rusting reminders of the plantation days and newer shopping malls, **Līhu'e** is divided into three distinct areas. The old **downtown**, along **Rice Street**, remains the administrative center of the island; in the middle of the day it's busy with local office workers, but barely a soul is left when evening comes. Driving a mile or so southeast beyond Rice Street brings you to **Nāwiliwili Bay**, where hotels and restaurants look out onto **Kalāpakī Beach**. The road that circles the island, running past the sugar mill at the northwest end of Rice Street, holds the bulk of Līhu'e's modern development. West of Līhu'e it bears the name **Kaumuali'i Highway**. About a mile out of town it passes the large **Kukui Grove Shopping Center**; after another mile it comes to the country-house mall **Kilohana**; from there it leads to Po'ipū and Waimea. Northeast of Līhu'e, the road is officially called **Kūhiō Highway**; for the first of the two miles that separate Līhu'e from the distinct community of **Hanamā'ulu**, it's lined with fast-food outlets and small malls.

Kauai Museum

The **Kauai Museum**, downtown Līhu'e's only significant attraction, occupies two buildings next to the state offices at 4428 Rice St (Mon–Sat 10am–5pm; adults $10, seniors $8, ages 13–17 $6, ages 6–12 $2; ☏808/245-6931, ⓦwww.kauaimuseum .org). If you've come to the island for sun, sea, and scenery, it may not hold your interest for long, but it does a creditable job of tracing Kauaian history from the mythical *menehune* onwards.

Visitors enter the museum through the older **Wilcox Building**, which holds the core of the collection – the private memorabilia of the missionary Wilcox family. Downstairs, there's a large assortment of traditional artifacts such as oval platters, *lei* standards, and calabashes made from *koa* wood. One colossal and highly polished calabash was used as a *poi* bowl by Kamehameha III; several have been skillfully repaired with butterfly-shaped patches, a process that was held to increase their value. Exhibits upstairs cover the growth of the sugar plantations and the great era of immigration. Photographs focus especially on the island's Japanese population, recording sumo tournaments, Bon dances, and Buddhist ceremonies.

The modern **Rice Building**, alongside the Wilcox Building, has a more comprehensive collection. It too has its fair share of calabashes, decorated gourd bowls, and bottles, but it also displays some more unusual ancient relics such as stone receptacles used in the *pule ana'ana* ("praying-to-death") rite, and a fearsome "thrusting spear." A relief model of the island shows where the Hawaiians had their original settlements, as well as the trails that connected them. Among the trails that no longer exist are those that lead down to the Nā Pali valleys from the heights of Kōke'e, and paths

from the summit of Mount Wai'ale'ale not only to Wailua, but also to Waimea and Hanapēpē. A diorama of Waimea at the time of Cook's first landfall depicts a settlement of a few thatched huts. Contemporary maps of Cook's voyages show tell-tale blank spaces for areas as yet unknown.

The whole history of Kauai is told in immense detail, tracing island genealogy as far back as Kamawae Lualani, said to have been *ali'i nui* or paramount chief in 310 AD. Illustrative exhibits include a letter from King Kaumuali'i, signing himself King Tamoree, and a soft sea-otter pelt brought by the Russians during their brief sojourn in Kauai (see p.396). Other displays cover mission and plantation life, and there's also a rain gauge that stood for many years atop Mount Wai'ale'ale, the wettest place on earth. It is capable of holding nine hundred inches of rain, but the most it ever received in a year was 682.94.

You can visit the museum's **gift store**, packed with books, maps, and wooden craft items, without paying for admission.

Nāwiliwili Bay

As Līhu'e has been a port for even less time than it has been a town, the oceanfront area around **Nāwiliwili Bay**, reached by heading east down Rice Street, is functional and without much character. So long as you stay on or near the golden sands of **Kalāpakī Beach**, however, that probably won't bother you. Despite the ugly developments that surround it, this sheltered quarter-mile stretch in front of the *Kauai Marriott* is actually a pretty good beach. Its smooth, shelving slope makes it ideal for family swimming, and it's also a good place to learn to **surf**, though beginners should avoid venturing out too far towards the open sea.

At the western edge of the beach, across the Nāwiliwili Stream – which, when it hasn't petered out altogether, is usually shallow enough to wade across – stands the **Anchor Cove Shopping Center**, home to a handful of restaurants, stores, and tour companies. The seafront at this point is no more than a wall, popular with anglers, but the lawns of **Nāwiliwili Beach County Park** are dotted with coconut palms. Immediately beyond the park, still within sight of the beach, stand the first structures of **Nāwiliwili Harbor**, which stretches away west at the mouth of the Hulē'ia Stream. The harbor was constructed in the 1920s to afford greater protection to large vessels than Port Allen could offer; it's also closer to Oahu than Port Allen. A long breakwater was pushed out into the bay from below Carter Point on the far side of the stream, and a combination of dredging the sea bed and using the silt as infill to create new flatland permanently changed the local topography. The harbor is now deep enough to accommodate mighty cruise-liners, which make an incongruous spectacle moored so closely to the low-key park facilities.

Menehune Fishpond and Hulē'ia National Wildlife Refuge

West of Nāwiliwili Harbor, Hulemalu Road climbs a hillside beyond the village of Niumalu to reach a viewpoint overlooking a pond. Officially this is the Alekoko ("Rippling Blood") Fishpond, but its nickname, the **Menehune Fishpond**, offers a better indication of its age. Created when the ancient Hawaiians sealed off a right-angle bend in Hulē'ia Stream with a half-mile-long low wall of rounded stones, the artificial lake was originally used for rearing mullet.

In popular mythology, the **menehune** were the earliest inhabitants of the islands, said to be hairy dwarfs given to erecting large monuments in the space of a single moonlit night. Such tales are especially prevalent on Kauai, which suggests that the island may have been populated by a different group of migrants than its neighbors.

Scholars now believe that the word *menehune* may be related to a Tahitian word for "commoner," and may refer to a social caste seen as inferior by later colonizers.

The Hawaiians were more sophisticated fish-farmers than any other Polynesian people, and the Menehune Fishpond is rivaled only by those on Molokai (see p.316) as the best-preserved such pond in the islands. It's now under private ownership, so unless you explore the stream by boat (guided kayak trips are offered by Outfitters Kauai, among others; see p.343), the overlook is as close as you can get to the actual pond. Most of the stone wall is overgrown with mangroves, so it's not a hugely impressive sight, but the overlook makes an appealing stop on a driving tour. The river spreads out below you, with just one little shack to interrupt the greenery along its banks. On the far side, the jagged **Hā'upu** (or "Hoary Head") **Ridge** is silhouetted against the skyline, its slopes thick with vegetation.

Standing at the fishpond viewpoint, you'll probably hear the cries of the water birds wheeling above the **Hulē'ia National Wildlife Refuge** just upstream. Like its equivalent at Hanalei in the north of the island (see p.373), this area still bears traces of terraces once used to grow first taro and later rice. It's now a sanctuary for endangered Hawaiian wetland birds, which can only be seen close-up in a **kayak**.

Grove Farm Homestead

Life on the nineteenth-century plantation to which Līhu'e owes its existence is recalled at the restored **Grove Farm Homestead**, hidden away on Nāwiliwili Road southwest of downtown (tours Mon, Wed & Thurs 10am & 1pm; reserve well in advance; adults \$10, under-12s \$5; ⓣ808/245-3202, ⓦwww.grovefarm.net). Although it's just a few hundred yards from Rice Street, you can only cross the deep channel of Nāwiliwili Stream down by the harbor or up at the main road, so it's too far to walk from town.

The plantation was opened in 1864 by George Wilcox, who was, in classic Hawaiian fashion, the entrepreneurial son of Hanalei-based missionaries. An ascetic bachelor, he lived in a cottage on the grounds; the larger *koa*-paneled mansion that's the center-piece of the two-hour guided tours belonged to his brother and his descendants. The tours also take in the plainly furnished home of the Japanese family who looked after the Wilcoxes, and George's personal orchard of fruit trees.

Kilohana Plantation

Kaumuali'i Highway commences its westward journey around the island from the top of Rice Street. Around a mile along, the **Kukui Grove Shopping Center**, Kauai's largest and best-equipped shopping mall, holds a Borders bookstore, plus assorted department stores and supermarkets. A mile past that, the stately house at **Kilohana Plantation** was built in 1935 by another scion of Līhu'e's founding family, Gaylord Wilcox. Most of the ground floor and veranda of the imposing mansion, which stands at the end of a sweeping driveway, is occupied by an excellent restaurant (*Gaylord's*; see p.352), while its two stories also hold upmarket crafts shops and galleries. Some of these can be rather quaint, but Kilohana is nevertheless one of Kauai's better options if you're looking for gifts to take home (shops open Mon–Sat 9.30am–9.30pm, Sun 9.30am–5pm).

Kilohana is named after the mountain peak that towers over the cane fields behind it. You can get a close-up view of the plantation itself on a forty-minute train tour, on the narrow-gauge **Kauai Plantation Railway** (departs daily 10am, 11am, noon, 1pm, 2pm, plus 5.30pm Tues & Fri only; \$18, ages 3–12 \$14; ⓣ808/245-7245, ⓦwww.kauaiplantationrailway.com). Every trip includes a stop at enclosures of farm animals like pigs and horses; paying \$75 also gives you a short guided forest hike and a picnic lunch.

The grounds also include a store by the **Kōloa Rum Company** (☎808/246-8900, ⓦwww.koloarum.com), which offers brief rum tastings, and are home to the **Lūʻau Kalamaku**, run by *Gaylord's* (Tues & Thurs 5pm; $99, ages 12–18 $69, ages 3–11 $49; ☎1-877/622-1780, ⓦwww.luaukalamaku.com). The *lūʻau* features an enjoyable theatrical spectacular telling the story of the earliest Polynesian voyagers, though as is so often the case, the catering is on too big a scale for the food to be worth recommending.

Wailua Falls

Just over a mile northeast of Rice Street, once the strip development along Kūhiō Highway has thinned out beyond the airport turnoff, Maʻalo Road leads away leftwards up to **Wailua Falls**. This picturesque 80ft drop interrupts the south fork of the Wailua River, a couple of miles upstream from the Fern Grotto (see p.356).

A parking lot, offering a side-on view both of the falls and of the streambed below, comes after a slow climb of three sinuous miles through the cane fields. Depending on recent rainfall, you're likely to see from one to three cascades, one of which emerges from a small tunnel a little way down the cliff face. You may

▲ Wailua Falls

have heard that it's possible to climb the guardrail and hike down to the base of the falls, but don't try it: several would-be hikers have fallen to their deaths.

Hanamā'ulu

The small community of **HANAMĀ'ULU** is located a short way beyond the road to Wailua Falls. Apart from the attractive *Restaurant and Tea House* (see below), it's mainly noteworthy as the site of the **Hanamā'ulu Beach County Park**, almost a mile out of town at the wooded mouth of the Hanamā'ulu Stream. Spreading along a broad and sheltered bay, this narrow strip of sand is an attractive place to spend a peaceful afternoon. However, the water is usually too cloudy for swimming. There's also a fully equipped campground, but locals tend to party at Hanamā'ulu well into the night, and visiting families usually prefer to camp elsewhere.

Eating and drinking

Downtown Līhu'e has a reasonable choice of **places to eat** during the day, but the highway malls offer standard fast-food chains and no more. Any quest for views or atmosphere – let alone fine dining – will take you away from the center, either down to the oceanfront, where there's also a handful of **bars**, or as far as Kilohana or Hanamā'ulu on the main road.

Duke's Canoe Club *Kauai Marriott*, 3610 Rice St ☏808/246-9599, ⓦwww.dukes.kauaimarriott .com. Cheerful, informal bar-restaurant right on Kalāpakī Beach, arranged around its own waterfall and carp pond, and enjoying gorgeous views. A burger or stir-fry lunch in the *Barefoot Bar* downstairs costs around $10, while dinner, served upstairs 5–10pm, might feature fish of the day prepared as you like for $20–30 or prime rib for $32. Dinner is accompanied by Hawaiian music on Thurs, Sat & Sun. Daily 11am–11pm.

Fish Express 3343 Kūhiō Hwy ☏808/245-9918. Very high-quality takeout fish dishes for around $10, available hot, cold, or in the example of the delicious *ahi poke* (tuna), raw. Mon–Sat 10am–6pm, Sun 10am–4pm.

Gaylord's at Kilohana 3-2087 Kaumuali'i Hwy ☏808/245-9593, ⓦwww.gaylordskauai.com. Delicious food served in the very British-influenced courtyard of a former plantation home, with views of extensive gardens and the mountains of the interior. Lunch consists mainly of sandwiches and salads, such as a Chicken Caesar ($15); Sunday sees a brunch buffet for $25; and pasta, steak, or fish dinner entrees cost $20–40. Mon–Sat 11am–3pm & 5.30–9pm, Sun 9am–2.30pm & 5.30–9pm.

Hamura Saimin 2956 Kress St ☏808/245-3271. This family-run diner and takeout spot is a much-loved Kauai institution, serving tasty and good-value Japanese-style fast

food at communal U-shaped counters. Just grab a seat if you spot one free. The specialty is heaped bowls of *saimin* (noodle soup), costing $5–6, or $6.75 with shrimp tempura. As a side order, try a satay skewer of barbecue chicken or beef for $1.50. Mon–Thurs 10am–11pm, Fri & Sat 10am–midnight, Sun 10am–9pm.

Hanamā'ulu Restaurant and Tea House 3-4253 Kūhiō Hwy ☏808/245-2511. A pleasant approximation of a Far Eastern teahouse, complete with fishponds and some nice private tearooms in the gardens, a mile from central Līhu'e. Surprisingly, they serve both Chinese and Japanese cuisine; both are good. As well as $10 Japanese lunch and dinner specials, they serve an Oriental seafood platter with fish marinated in ginger, tempura, and crab claws for $19, and three set dinner menus for $18–22. Sushi is offered in the evening only. Tues–Fri 10am–1pm & 4.30–8.30pm, Sat & Sun 4.30–8.30pm.

Tip Top Café and Bakery *Tip Top Motel*, 3173 Akāhi St ☏808/245-2333. Family-run diner in a quiet area of central Līhu'e, known for its simple and very filling food. The best bet is a breakfast of fruity pancakes or *malasadas* (Portuguese donuts) for $7–8, but they also offer plate lunches, stews, and basic meat dishes, as well as breads and pastries to take out, and sushi in the separate *Sushi Katsu* section. Café Tues–Sun 6.30am–2pm, sushi Tues–Sun 11am–2pm & 5.30–9.30pm.

The East Shore

Ever since Kauai was first settled, its population has been most heavily concentrated along the valley of the **Wailua River** and the nearby coastline. This region, starting roughly five miles north of Līhu'e, is now home to around twenty thousand people, but they're so spread out that you'd barely know they were there. Much more conspicuous are the guests in the oceanfront hotels and condos, here for the sun and fun rather than the relatively poor beaches along what's collectively known as the **Coconut Coast**.

Technically, Kūhiō Highway, the main artery, passes through several separate communities as it heads north beyond the river itself. The distinctions between the overlapping towns of **Wailua**, **Waipouli**, and **Kapa'a**, however, are far less significant or even noticeable than the contrast between the malls and high-rises along the highway and the residential districts a couple of miles inland. Tucked away behind long, low **Nounou Ridge** (the "Sleeping Giant"), which runs parallel to the coast, neat individual cottages are set amid gardens that erupt with spectacular blooms, and ramshackle farms still squeeze as much produce as possible from their few acres.

Beyond Kapa'a, there's far less development, and only rarely is access to the seashore at all easy. However, en route to Princeville you can stop at several little-known beaches.

Accommodation along the East Shore

In terms of number of beds, the East Shore, or Coconut Coast, ranks second to Po'ipū as Kauai's main vacation center, while competition at the mid-range level means room rates can drop amazingly low. Although the beaches here rank a distant third to both the south and north coasts, if you enjoy hanging out in lovely seaside resorts, this area has a lot going for it. As bases for exploring Kauai, the homely **B&Bs** a mile or two from the coast are ideal.

Note that downtown Kapa'a also holds the island's only **hostel**, the *Kauai International Hostel* at 4532 Lehua St (☎808/823-6142, ⓦwww.kauaihostel.net; ❶), but as the subject of consistently bad reports from travelers it cannot in good conscience be recommended.

B&Bs

Inn Paradise 6381 Makana Rd, Kapa'a
☎808/822-2542, ⓦwww.innparadisekauai.com. Great-value garden cottage, deep in the hills above Wailua, with three fully equipped en-suite B&B units. All share use of a roomy *lānai* and hot tub. ❸
Lani-Keha 848 Kamalu Rd, Kapa'a ☎808/822-1605, ⓦwww.lanikeha.com. Three comfortable en-suite B&B rooms in a large country house tucked in behind the Sleeping Giant; all have access to the main kitchen, living room, and a large *lānai*. Two-night minimum stay, no credit cards. ❸
Rosewood B&B 872 Kamalu Rd, Kapa'a
☎808/822-5216, ⓦwww.rosewoodkauai.com.

As well as a bunkhouse that holds three simple budget rooms sharing a single bathroom, the gorgeous gardens of this columned plantation-style house also hold two fully equipped cottages, and the owners serve as agents for several other East Shore B&B rooms, condos, and apartments. Bunkhouse ❷, rooms ❸, cottages and condos ❹–❾

Hotels and condos

Aston Aloha Beach Hotel 3-5920 Kūhiō Hwy, Wailua ☎808/823-6000 or 1-877/997-6667, ⓦwww.abrkauai.com. Much-remodeled hotel, with an exceptionally welcoming feel, looking

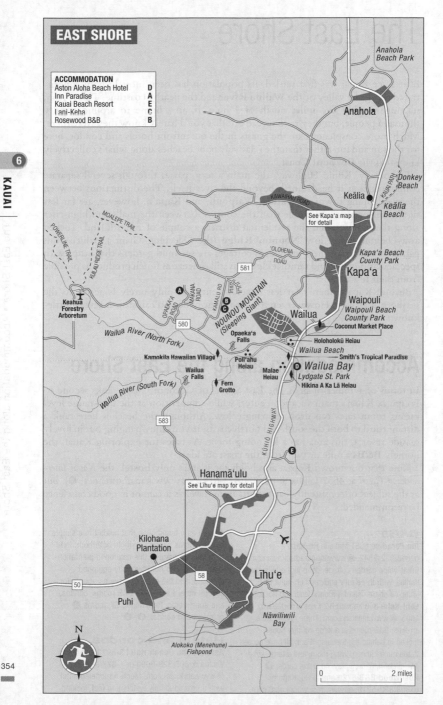

EAST SHORE

ACCOMMODATION

Aston Aloha Beach Hotel	D
Inn Paradise	A
Kauai Beach Resort	E
Lani-Keha	C
Rosewood B&B	B

Anahola Beach Park

Anahola

KUAI PATH

Donkey Beach

Keālia

KAWAIHAU ROAD

Keālia Beach

See Kapa'a map for detail

MOALEPE TRAIL

'OLOHENA ROAD

Kapa'a Beach County Park

POWERLINE TRAIL

KUILAU RIDGE TRAIL

581

Kapa'a

Keahua Forestry Arboretum

A

MAKANA ROAD

KAMALU RD

B

C

Waipouli

Waipouli Beach County Park

Coconut Market Place

OPAEKA'A ROAD

580

NOUNOU MOUNTAIN (Sleeping Giant)

Wailua

Wailua River (North Fork)

Opaeka'a Falls

Holoholokū Heiau

Kamokila Hawaiian Village

Poli'ahu Heiau

Wailua Beach

Smith's Tropical Paradise

Wailua Falls

Malae Heiau

D

Wailua Bay

Wailua River (South Fork)

Fern Grotto

Lydgate St. Park

Hikina A Ka Lā Heiau

583

KŪHIŌ HIGHWAY

E

Hanamā'ulu

See Līhu'e map for detail

Kilohana Plantation

50

58

Līhu'e

Puhi

Nāwiliwili Bay

N

Alokoko (Menehune) Fishpond

0   2 miles

over the ocean from above Lydgate State Park, immediately south of Wailua River. Thanks to its busy live entertainment schedule, and pro-kids policy, it's the liveliest of the Coconut Coast resorts. The location is especially good for families, close to the safe swimming and great playground at Lydgate Beach. Besides standard hotel rooms, they also have thirteen separate, more luxurious cottages, closer to the ocean. Rooms ❸, cottages ❹

Aston Islander on the Beach 440 Aleka Place, Kapaʻa ☎808/822-7417 or 1-877/997-6667, ⓦwww.astonhotels.com. Appealing, spacious beachfront "condotel" at the southern end of the Coconut Market Place with seven separate wings of individually owned rooms – all have *lānais*, safes, and showers rather than baths, and rates rise the closer you get to the sea – plus a small pool and spa. ❹

Aston Kauai Beach at Makaʻiwa 650 Aleka Loop, Kapaʻa ☎808/822-3455 or 1-877/997-6667, ⓦwww.astonhotels.com. The northernmost Coconut Market Place resort comprises several large beach-front wings holding 311 Hawaiian-themed rooms with private *lānais*; recent renovations have left them looking brighter. Guests enjoy use of the pool, spa, and free tennis courts; the beach here

is not good for swimming, but the coastal footpath passes right by. ❹

Hotel Coral Reef 1516 Kūhiō Hwy, Kapaʻa ☎808/822-4481 or 1-800/843-4659, ⓦwww .hotelcoralreefresort.com. Inexpensive suites in small, friendly, and recently renovated seafront hotel a short walk north of central Kapaʻa. All rooms have a/c, phones, and safes. ❹

Kauai Coast Resort at the Beachboy 520 Aleka Loop, Wailua ☎808/822-3441 or 1-866/678-3289, ⓦwww.kauaicoastresort.com. This renovated condo resort looks forbidding from the outside, with high lava-rock walls fronting the main road to the Coconut Market Place. Inside, it's far pleasanter. Three wings of comfortable guest rooms enclose spacious lawns and a pool; the fourth – open – side is the beach. All rooms have private *lānais* and two double beds. Garden view ❺, ocean view ❻

Lae Nani 410 Papaloa Rd, Wailua ☎808/822-4938 or 1-877/523-6264, ⓦwww.outrigger.com. Spacious low-rise complex of luxurious one- and two-bedroom condos, all capable of sleeping at least four guests, on a headland at the northern end of Wailua Bay, just south of the Coconut Market Place. The adjacent beach is ideal for inshore swimming, and there's also a pool, plus a ruined *heiau*, in the grounds. ❻

Wailua River

Kūhiō Highway crosses the **WAILUA RIVER** five miles out from central Līhuʻe, marking the start of Kauai's East Shore. For the ancient Hawaiians, the area to either side of the twin bridges here was *Wailua Nui Hoano*, or Great Sacred Wailua. Fertile, beautiful, and sheltered from the sea, it served as home to Kauai's greatest chiefs. A trail known as the **King's Highway**, lined with *heiaus* and other religious sites, ran beside the river all the way from the ocean to the rain-drenched summit of Mount Waiʻaleʻale.

In those days the Wailua flowed in two separate channels. It still has a South Fork and a North Fork, but they now fuse together for the last couple of miles. The resultant broad, flat stream is often called the only navigable river in Hawaii, although sandbars at its mouth usually stop vessels from entering it from the open sea. Exploring it in a **kayak** is a great way to spend a day; rental outlets are detailed on p.343.

The south bank of the river is set aside for agriculture, and almost entirely free of buildings or roads; it's impossible to head any farther inland than the Smith's Tropical Paradise theme park (see p.356), though tour boats leave regularly for the short cruise up to the **Fern Grotto**, which involves a brief walk along the south bank. Otherwise, few vantage points offer so much as a glimpse of its rolling fields and woodlands.

It was on the Wailua's north shore that Kauai's most famous ruler, Kaumualiʻi, had his own personal coconut grove and *heiau*. Several such historic sites are now preserved in **Wailua River State Park**, together with plenty of attractive scenery.

The Fern Grotto

Promoted as a romantic, fern-bedecked jungle cavern, the **Fern Grotto**, a short way up the Wailua River, used to be renowned as the island's premier beauty spot. Damage from successive hurricanes means it's now a shadow of its former self, but if you like old-fashioned *tiki*-tourism, you might enjoy the kitsch **river tours** that, unless you make your own way in a kayak, are the only way to visit.

Canopied barges, run by Smith's Motor Boats (daily 9.30am, 10am, 11.30am, 1.30pm, 2pm & 3.30pm; $20, under-13s $10; ☏808/821-6895, ⓦwww.smiths kauai.com), set off for the grotto from a marina on the south bank of the Wailua. Tours take an hour and twenty minutes.

As the barge heads upriver, a commentary on the few undramatic sights along the way is interspersed with local legends. For most of the route, you see little beyond the thick trees on both banks. After a couple of miles, the river divides. The Fern Grotto is just up its left (south) fork; to avoid the tour groups, most kayakers head off to the right.

Having disembarked at the grotto landing, you walk a short paved trail, lined with bananas and torch ginger plants, up to the cave, a large natural amphitheater that was hollowed out by a waterfall. These days it's only minimally festooned with the dense *a'e* ferns that once screened off its interior, but the acoustics remain unchanged, so tour parties are still serenaded with the *Hawaiian Wedding Song* by the guitar-toting crews of their barges.

There's plenty more ersatz Polynesian posturing at **Smith's Tropical Paradise**, alongside the marina. In the daytime, you can explore its thirty acres of colorful gardens in relative peace (daily 8.30am–4pm; $6). On several evenings each week, it reopens for a **Garden Lū'au** (summer Mon–Fri, winter Mon, Wed, & Fri; gates open 5pm, *lū'au* 8pm; ☏808/821-6895, ⓦwww.smithskauai; adults $78, ages 7–13 $30, ages 3–5 $19).

The King's Highway

Few of the **ancient sites** that once lined the Wailua River now amount to more than vague ruins. None has any formal opening hours or guided tours; you have to find them yourself and settle for reading whatever explanatory signs may have been erected.

Slightly back from the lava rocks of Lydgate State Park (see p.359), alongside the *Aloha Beach Hotel* on the southern bank of the Wailua at the river mouth, stands the **Hikina A Ka Lā** ("Rising of the Sun") **Heiau**. Only traces survive of the hundred-yard-long, 10ft-thick wall that once faced the rising sun here. Part of the area behind it was devoted to a "place of refuge" (see p.151), the Hauola O Hōnaunau, while the waters in front were popular, then as now, with expert surfers. On the other, *mauka*, side of the highway, just before the marina turnoff, a large mound covered with grass and trees in the middle of a cane field marks the site of **Malae Heiau**. Roughly a hundred yards square, this was the island's biggest temple.

As soon as you cross the Wailua, you're in the area where Kaumuali'i lived in his coconut grove. Kuamo'o Road, or Hwy-580A, follows the route of the old **King's Highway** trail inland from here. The first of the riverside parking lots on the left is the kayak and canoe launching ramp for **Wailua River State Park**, which encompasses the river itself and a thin strip along most of both banks. The second parking lot is at the foot of the low Ka Lae O Ka Manu ("Crest of the Bird" or cock's comb) ridge, where **Holoholokū Heiau** once stood. So tiny that it could only be entered on all fours, this was a *luakini*, used for human sacrifices. A few stone walls remain, but the hill itself is overgrown.

A little way further north around the base of the hill are the **Birthing Stones**, where all the great chiefs of Kauai were born. The mother was supposed to brace her back against one stone and her legs against the other as she gave birth, though they seem a bit too far apart for that to be very likely. An even slab at the edge of the small walled enclosure nearby was used to cover the corpses of dogs sacrificed on such occasions, while the infant's umbilical cord was inserted in the crack in the boulder behind.

From here on, the road steadily climbs along Kuamo'o ("Lizard") Ridge. After about a mile, a parking lot on the left commands a sweeping prospect of the broad flatlands beside a gentle curve in the Wailua. This spot on the bluff was the site of the palace of chief Ho'ono. The broad low walls of **Poli'ahu Heiau**, constructed of smooth stones from the riverbed, still stand, though with the thatched temple structures long gone they now enclose just grass and rubble. Coconut palms sway at either end, unusually high above the sea.

The birth of a new *ali'i* at the Birthing Stones was traditionally greeted by a hammer striking the **Bell Stone**, further upstream. To find it, head down the rutted dirt road off to the left just beyond the *heiau*, then follow a rough walkway down the hill. No one can now say for sure which among the pile of stones here is the correct one, so you'll just have to hit a few and make your own mind up.

Ōpaeka'a Falls and beyond

The next parking lot, this time on the right, is the overlook for **'Ōpaeka'a Falls**. Set amid thick green undergrowth, this wide, low waterfall splashes into a pool stained red with eroded earth, where native shrimp could once be seen churning in the water (*'Ōpaeka'a* means "rolling shrimp"). You can't walk any closer to the falls than this – a number of hikers have died trying in recent years – but you get a slightly better view from the highway bridge a few yards further up.

Carefully cross the road at this point for a fine panorama of Wailua Valley. Immediately below, you can see the huts of **Kamokila Hawaiian Village**, a re-creation of a traditional riverside settlement. Demolished by Hurricane Iniki in 1992, it was restored to serve as an African village in the 1995 Dustin Hoffman thriller *Outbreak*, and offers low-key tours that focus on daily life in ancient Kauai (daily 9am–5pm; $5; ☏808/823-0559, ⓦwww.villagekauai.com).

The King's Highway runs for several progressively wilder miles beyond 'Ōpaeka'a Falls. You're only likely to venture this way if you plan to do some backwoods **hiking**, along the excellent trails detailed on pp.361–362.

Wailua to Kapa'a

Although the East Shore's nicest beach, Lydgate State Park, is, like the Fern Grotto, on the south shore of the Wailua River, the strip development along the coast only gets going once you cross the river and enter **WAILUA** proper. At this point, a thin fringe of trees and sand is all that divides the highway from the sea, while an extensive grove of palms on the *mauka* side partially obscures the derelict **Coco Palms Resort**. Kauai's most famous hotel – the one through which Elvis and his new bride floated in *Blue Hawaii* – has remained closed ever since 1992's Hurricane Iniki, and there's no sign it will ever reopen.

Within less than a mile, as the gap between road and ocean starts to widen, the extensive **Coconut Market Place** complex appears *makai* of the highway. This centers on a mall of rather ordinary souvenir stores, fast-food outlets, bars, and restaurants, arranged around an open-air courtyard. Behind that lie half a dozen

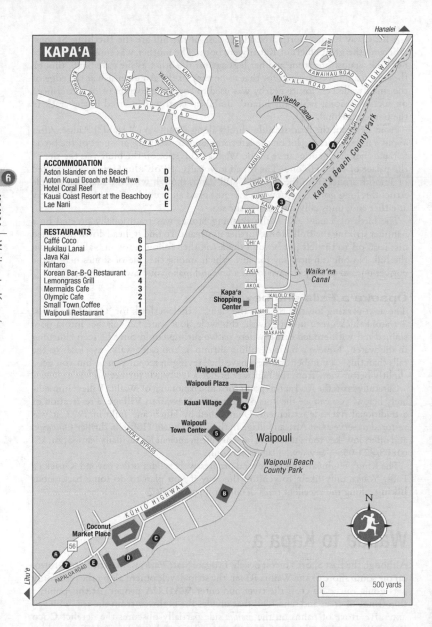

KAPA'A

Mo'ikeha Canal

Kapa'a Beach County Park

ACCOMMODATION

Aston Islander on the Beach	D
Aston Kauai Beach at Maka'iwa	B
Hotel Coral Reef	A
Kauai Coast Resort at the Beachboy	C
Lae Nani	E

RESTAURANTS

Caffé Coco	6
Hukilau Lanai	C
Java Kai	3
Kintaro	7
Korean Bar-B-Q Restaurant	7
Lemongrass Grill	4
Mermaids Cafe	3
Olympic Cafe	2
Small Town Coffee	1
Waipouli Restaurant	5

Waika'ea Canal

Kapa'a Shopping Center

Waipouli Complex

Waipouli Plaza

Kauai Village

Waipouli Town Center

Waipouli

Waipouli Beach County Park

Coconut Market Place

56

PAPALOA ROAD

KŪHIŌ HIGHWAY

KAPA'A BYPASS

N

Lihu'e ▲

0		500 yards

large hotels, while out of sight to the south are several condo buildings, not strictly speaking part of the complex.

Northbound traffic along the highway from here on in can get very congested; at busy times, it's well worth taking the alternative **bypass** system that follows the former sugar-cane roads inland, and rejoins Hwy-56 via Olohena Road in Kapa'a. Other than a few worthwhile restaurants (see p.364 for reviews), and the shops in the

Kauai Village shopping center, halfway between Wailua and Kapa'a in **WAIPOULI**, you miss nothing if you skip the main highway altogether.

KAPA'A itself is about the only recognizable town between Līhu'e and Hanalei. The old-fashioned boardwalks at the main intersection (not important enough to boast a stop light, but a welcome interruption in the monotonous strip) hold small shops, cafés, and restaurants. Equipment rental outlets offer kayaks, surfboards, and the like at reasonable rates, while a handful of quirky clothes and gift stores catch the eye.

The beaches

Although an almost unbroken ribbon of sand runs along the shore all the way from the mouth of the Wailua up to Kapa'a, it rarely deserves to be called a beach. The nearby mountains lend the area some scenic beauty, but the coastline is flat and dull, devoid of the sheltered coves and steepled cliffs that characterize the water-front further north. Strong waves and stronger currents rightly deter most bathers, so the swimming pools in the major hotels are kept busy.

Lydgate State Park

By far the most popular and attractive of the public beaches is the first one you come to heading north from Līhu'e. Hidden from the road, **Lydgate State Park** lies behind the *Aloha Beach Hotel* (see p.353) on the southern side of the mouth of the Wailua River. The murky, swirling waters where the river flows into the sea are of great interest to surfers, but for family swimming the two linked artificial pools in the park, lined with smooth lava boulders, are preferable. Regularly replenished by the sea, they are usually bursting with fish eager to be fed by snorkelers. There's a picnic spot alongside the pools, in the shade of a stand of ironwoods. The park is also the site of the **Kamalani Playground**, an intricate tangle of free-form wooden structures for children to climb on. In addition, Lydgate State Park holds an ancient *heiau*, described on p.356.

Wailua Beach

From the north bank of the river, the narrow crescent of **Wailua Beach** runs for something over half a mile, until its sand peters out at the rocky headland of Alakukui Point. Fringed with palms, the beach is an attractive place to stroll – especially at sunrise – if you're staying in the vicinity. However, it offers no amenities and, apart from the sheltered patch in front of the *Lae Nani* condos, the surf is generally high.

Waipouli Beach County Park

Waipouli Beach County Park, which starts just past the exposed Coconut Market Place strip, is rather less accessible than Wailua Beach, being backed for much of its length by small residential properties. In any case, only fitful patches of sand cover the rock at the ocean's edge, and if you do go into the water, the drop-off is alarmingly steep. You can admire the Pacific from the safe distance of a paved footpath lined with ironwoods, although you'll have to return to the main road to cross the small Moikeha Canal.

Kapa'a Beach County Park

A short way north of Waipouli Beach County Park comes **Kapa'a Beach County Park**. Almost as soon as it gets going, the beach here is interrupted by the Waika'ea Canal, built during plantation days to drain the inland marshes. The combination of silt deposited by the canal, and the more recent blasting of the shallow reef just offshore has badly eroded the shoreline. Little sand remains, and swimming from the rocks is unappetizing.

The Kauai Path

An excellent, paved **oceanfront trail**, officially called Ke Ala Hele Makalae but more generally known as simply the **Kauai Path**, follows the shoreline north from Kapaʻa Beach to Keālia Beach and beyond. Unveiled in 2009, for the shared use of cyclists and walkers, it has quickly become hugely popular with locals. It currently continues a short way beyond **Donkey Beach** (see p.363), but is planned to extend as far as the beautiful sands at Anahola, four miles north of Kapaʻa, as well as running all the way south through Wailua to Lydgate State Park. For the latest details, see ⓦ www.kauaipath.org.

Keālia Beach

Just beyond Kapaʻa, an unexpected stretch of low sand dunes at **Keālia Beach** are now the only dunes left along the East Shore. The tremendous surf that crashes almost onto the highway makes this the area's most exciting-looking beach. You'll probably see crowds of surfers and boogie-boarders getting pummeled half to death, especially at its northern end, but like all such "shorebreak" beaches – where there's no coral reef to protect you from the force of the open ocean – this is no place for inexperienced bathers.

East Shore hikes

If you have only a few days to spend **hiking** on Kauai, then the East Shore cannot compete with the splendors of the Kalalau Trail (see p.382) or the treks in Kōkeʻe Park (see p.403). However, some very enjoyable trails do lead through the hills above Wailua and Kapaʻa. The most compelling attraction here is the awe-inspiring crater wall of **Mount Waiʻaleʻale**, which looms before you as you head inland. It's no longer possible to walk to the top, as the ancients did, but despite the claims of the helicopter companies that it can be seen only from the air, keen hikers can trek to the wilderness at its base.

Nounou Mountain – "The Sleeping Giant"

The long, sharp crest of **Nounou Mountain**, known more often as the **Sleeping Giant**, parallels the shoreline between Wailua and Kapaʻa, roughly two miles back from the sea. Three separate trails lead up to the top of the ridge, where they join for a final assault on the summit. Whichever route you take, allow at least two hours for the round-trip hike.

The least demanding trail, from the **east**, starts near the end of Haleilio Road, a mile up from its junction with Kūhiō Highway. After an initial gentle zigzagging ascent through tropical vegetation, it gets a little hard to follow – head right, not left, at the fork half a mile along. Switchbacking across the northern end of the ridge, you get to see the high mountains inland as well as views back towards the ocean. Something over a mile along, the western trail links up from the right, and both continue left a short way to the picnic area.

Coming from the **west**, pick up the trail at the end of Lokelani Road, near the northern end of Kamalu Road, which connects Hwy-580 with Olohena Road. This is a shorter but steeper hike, more or less straight up the forested hillside. The highlight is a superb avenue of poker-straight Norfolk pines, recognizable by the raised ridges at regular intervals around their trunks.

Finally, it's also possible to climb the Sleeping Giant from the **south**, along a trail that starts a few hundred yards west of the ʻŌpaekaʻa Falls parking lot (see p.357). The two-mile trail is mostly in thick woodland as it meanders up the hillside, but

a picnic table in a clearing along the way offers some fine inland **views**. The trail meets the western route in the stand of pines mentioned above, with plenty of climbing still to go.

Whichever way you climb, you'll know you've reached the top when you arrive at the **Ali'i Vista Hale**, a sheltered picnic table set in a little clearing. So long as it isn't raining, you'll be able to see the entire coastline, from Līhu'e to Anahola, or look inland towards the residential areas of Wailua and Kapa'a.

If you're feeling intrepid, and conditions are not too slippery, it's possible to continue beyond the picnic area along a very dangerous, hair-raisingly makeshift trail. Were you down on the highway, you'd know this as the **Giant's Nose**; up here it's a sheer razorback ridge, with long drops to either side. Scrambling up the rocks at the end brings you out at a level and even better viewpoint. The soil underfoot is a rich red loam, which explains why such mountains erode so quickly; most of the slopes below are dense with small trees, but slashes of bare earth show where mudslides have taken place. Away to the west is the main ridge of Mount Wai'ale'ale, almost permanently wreathed in mist and cloud, while to the south lies the twisting, wooded gorge of the Wailua River. Anahola Mountain runs across the northern horizon, looking much like a sleeping giant itself.

Mount Wai'ale'ale Base Trail

For most visitors to the East Shore, the mountains of the interior remain a cloud-shrouded mystery. Behind the semi-permanent veil of mist, however, lies a landscape of extraordinary beauty. The very heart of the island is **Mount Wai'ale'ale**, whose annual rainfall of around 440 inches makes it the wettest spot on earth. Its highest point is less than a dozen miles west of Kapa'a, which receives a tenth as much rain. The name *Wai'ale'ale* means "overflowing water"; as you approach it from the ocean, it appears as a curved wall of velvet-green rock, furrowed by countless waterfalls. Most of its rain falls on the high ground of the Alaka'i Swamp, just behind the summit, then flows in every direction to create Kauai's major rivers. (Details of the amazing trail through the Alaka'i Swamp from Kōke'e State Park appear on p.408.) The escarpments of Wai'ale'ale are far too steep to climb, but hiking to the foot of the mountain is rewarding and far from strenuous.

To get here, drive along Hwy-580 beyond 'Ōpaeka'a Falls. The road ends roughly five miles further on at the **Keahua Forestry Arboretum**, where native trees are grown in controlled conditions. The arboretum also serves as the trailhead for the Kuilau Ridge Trail (see p.362) and the southern end of the Powerline Trail (see p.369), and was used for some location shooting for *Avatar*.

From here on, how far you can continue, first by car and then on foot, depends on the weather. Driving involves fording streams that cross the unpaved continuation of the road; if the water is at all high, don't try it. Otherwise, check your odometer, and set off across the stream at the arboretum. After 1.6 miles, a pull-out on the left offers the first clear views of Wai'ale'ale. Turn right at the T-junction after 2.2 miles, then left at the fork after 2.7 miles. Ignore the road to the left after 3.5 miles, but fork left a short way beyond that. The road ends at a yellow gate just under four miles from the arboretum, but you're free to walk on.

You're now heading directly towards Wai'ale'ale. After just over half a mile, the dirt road reaches a small dam, which is as far as it's safe to hike. This is the North Fork of the Wailua River, which has just plummeted down the face of the mountain. Upstream, its waters foam and tumble between the boulders, against the unforgettable backdrop of the high, green walls of Wai'ale'ale. If you're lucky, the cloud cover may clear long enough to offer a glimpse of the ridge at the top. The white specks of helicopters show up clearly against the green, and their

engines are just about audible above the river. It might look possible to continue even closer towards the mountain, but all the rudimentary footpaths on the far side of the dam peter out in a morass of mud, roots, ferns, and water.

It's simply not possible to climb to the summit of Wai'ale'ale from here; the trail of the ancient Hawaiians followed the ridge that leads up the flank to your right.

The Kuilau Ridge and Moalepe trails

Two further, less demanding trails traverse the upland forests above Kapa'a, leading through a rural landscape scattered with pink and purple blossoms and alive with birdsong. Each is a four-mile round-trip, but since they meet in the middle, you can combine the two if you arrange to be picked up at the opposite end from which you started.

A short way back down towards Wailua from the Keahou Forestry Arboretum (see above), a dirt road signed as the **Kuilau Ridge Trail** leads north from Hwy-580. As the name suggests, it climbs up the gradual slope of Kuilau Ridge, with views of Wai'ale'ale away to the left, and the Kamali'i Ridge of the Makaleha Mountains ahead. For much of the way it runs through dense tropical foliage, with flashes of color provided by bright-red, raspberry-like thimbleberries, *'ōhi'a lehua* blossoms down in the gullies, and a rich panoply of orchids. Not far beyond the picnic area that marks its halfway point, the trail rises sufficiently to let you see all the way to Līhu'e.

After just over two miles – perhaps 45 minutes of hiking – the trail seems to double back sharply on itself from a small clearing. In fact, as a very inconspicuous sign informs you, this is officially the end. Straight ahead of you is the highest, straightest segment of the Makaleha Mountains. A tiny footpath continues for a couple of hundred yards along the crest of Kuilau Ridge. You can push your way through the thorny undergrowth to get a few more views, including down to Kapa'a to your right, but it gradually gets more and more impenetrable. There is, in any case, no outlet to the hills.

You can also reach this point by following the **Moalepe Trail**, which leads from the top of the straight section of Olohena Road, six miles up from Kūhiō Highway. Park where the road turns to dirt, with one of its two tracks curving off north. It might look possible to drive the first few hundred yards of the trail, but it soon gets very rugged, by which time it's too narrow to turn around. Coming from this direction, too, you'll find the mountains confront you like a solid wall. You climb steadily, but the main ridge remains always on your right, and you never get near the summit. After half an hour the road becomes steep and rutted, but you're unlikely to lose your way; at the one confusing point, take the steeper option, towards the hills. At times, the ridge you're on has sheer drops to either side, but the vegetation is thick enough to meet up overhead, so you can't really see out. The clearing described above comes after around an hour's hiking, just beyond a final arduous climb.

Northeast Kauai

Once north of Kapa'a, the main highway stops running along the shoreline; it barely returns to sea level until Hanalei on the North Shore, twenty miles on. That leaves **Northeast Kauai** largely undisturbed by visitors. It is, in any case, sparsely inhabited, in part because it bears the full brunt of the trade winds and winter high seas. However, there are some spots where making your way down to the shore is rewarded by fine and often deserted beaches, though few are safe for swimming.

Donkey Beach

You can't see **Donkey Beach** from the highway, but the first beach north of Keālia can be reached via a simple half-mile downhill trail, as well as via the Kauai Path from Kapa'a, as described on p.360.

If you're driving, look out for a parking lot just over half a mile north of mile marker 11. Though there's no sign for the beach, an obvious paved trail sets off down towards the ocean, screened to either side by high hedges so you can't see the development that's taking place. When you hit the broad coastal path, turn right, and you'll soon reach the sandy crescent beach itself, curving north of Paliku Point.

The final slope down is carpeted with white-flowered *naupaka*, a creeping cross between an ivy and a lily, and there's no shade on the sands. The surf created by the steep drop-off attracts skilled surfers, but makes Donkey Beach unsafe for swimming. This area was traditionally sugar-growing country; the beach was named after the donkeys that hauled the cane here, and were left to graze nearby for much of the year. Later it became a popular spot for nude sunbathing, and then a gay hangout, but now that foot access is so easy its isolated days are over, and it's mainly used by dogwalkers and sightseeing tourists.

The coastal path continues a short way north of Donkey Beach, to a smaller cove that offers fine snorkeling, and will eventually extend as far as Anahola.

Anahola

Beyond Kapa'a, it's not possible to turn right from Kūhiō Highway until just after the mile marker 13, where a side road heads straight down to the sea then doglegs north. **Anahola Beach County Park** lies almost immediately below. The park is the southernmost stretch of the spellbinding curve of sand that rims Anahola Bay, sheltered by Kahala Point and therefore safe for family swimming (except in winter). Surfing is forbidden at this end, but boogie-boarders and surfers are free to enjoy the rest of the bay. There's no picnic pavilion or snack bar, but restrooms and showers are located among the palms.

Away from the beach, Anahola holds little to entice tourists, though the **Anahola Baptist Church**, set against a green mountain backdrop *mauka* of the highway, is worth a photograph. Nearby, just after the road crosses Ka'alua Stream, a tiny cluster of stores includes *Duane's Ono Char Burger* (Mon–Sat 10am–6pm, Sun 11am–6pm; ☎808/822-9181), where you can eat substantial, high-quality beef burgers under a spreading monkey-pod tree. A basic burger costs under $5, one with avocado is $7,and further variations include "Local Girls" and "Local Boys" burgers – the distinction is in the cheese. Be sure to try a marionberry milkshake while you're here.

The only **accommodation** around is a sophisticated, gay-owned, Japanese-style B&B, ⚵ *Mahina Kai* at 4933 'Aliomanu Rd, Anahola (☎808/822-9451 or 1-800/337-1134, ⓦwww.mahinakai.com; three-night minimum stay; ❺–❽). A couple of miles down a quiet side road that leads off the highway at mile marker 14, this lovely property perches above long, narrow 'Aliomanu Beach. Originally marketed as being exclusively gay, it nowadays welcomes all visitors. Its well-kept gardens boast a ruined *heiau*. In addition to two tasteful suites and a smaller guest room, there are also two separate cottages, plus a pool and hot tub.

Moloa'a Bay and Larsen's Beach

Ko'olau Road, a minor but passable road that cuts off a large bend in the highway from the fruit stand half a mile south of mile marker 17 until shortly before mile marker 20, provides access to a couple of little-known beaches. Neither is signed off the road, so both take a bit of finding.

First comes the beach at **Moloaʻa Bay**, accessible via Moloaʻa Road, a right turn a mile along that leads into a small oceanfront neighborhood of houses perched on high stilts. The deeply indented, treelined bay here is aligned so directly towards the trade winds that for most of the year it might as well not be sheltered at all. It's a pretty and very sandy spot, though, and in quiet periods the swimming and snorkeling can be excellent.

Larsen's Beach, further along, is most quickly reached from the north end of Koʻolau Road. Slightly over a mile down from there, a dirt road leads *makai* for a mile, leaving you with a five-minute walk at the end; access has been made deliberately difficult. The perfect sands of Larsen's Beach run for over a mile, interrupted in the middle by Pākala Point. Once again swimming is not recommended, this time because it's so shallow and rocky this side of the reef. The **snorkeling** can be good when the water's calm, provided you stay well away from the strong currents around the stream channel. At low tide, local families wade out to the edge of the reef to gather the edible red seaweed known as *limu kohu*.

Na ʻĀina Kai Botanical Gardens

Begun in the early 1980s as a labor of love by the former wife of *Peanuts* creator Charles Schulz, and open to the public since 2000, the **Na ʻĀina Kai Botanical Gardens** stand half a mile down Wailapa Road, which heads oceanward from the Kūhiō Highway halfway between mile markers 21 and 22 (Mon 8am–2pm, Tues–Thurs 8am–5pm, Fri 8am–1pm; tours $30–75; ☎808/828-0525, ⓦwww.naainakai .com). The plural is appropriate: the 240-acre site holds thirteen separately themed gardens, including a desert garden, a palm garden, a Japanese garden, a hardwood plantation, and a bog. It's all very exquisite, though you may feel it's less of a thrill to see these beautiful plants in such a manicured setting, scattered with slightly twee bronze sculptures.

Eating and drinking along the East Shore

Restaurants jostle for the attention of hotel guests all along the Wailua to Kapaʻa coastal highway, while the hotels themselves also generally hold dining rooms and **bars**. However, with one or two exceptions, the glossier-looking steak-and-seafood places tend to be less interesting than the cheaper ethnic alternatives. If you like to stroll around comparing menus before you eat out, only downtown Kapaʻa fits the bill.

Caffè Coco 4-369 Kūhiō Hwy, Wailua ☎808/822-7990, ⓦwww.restauranteur.com /cattecoco. Attractively ramshackle café, with a laidback hippy feel, set well back from the highway in central Wailua. Almost all the tables are outdoors in a graveled garden that's sometimes busy with mosquitoes. Wholesome, though not entirely vegetarian, lunches cost under $10; most dinner specials, such as grilled or roasted Italian-style meat dishes, and *ahi* prepared in various styles, are under $20. Tues–Fri 11am–2pm & 5–9pm, Sat & Sun 5–9pm.

Hukilau Lanai *Kauai Coast Resort at the Beachboy*, 520 Aleka Loop, Wailua ☎808/822-0600, ⓦwww .hukilaukauai.com. Much the nicest resort restaurant

on the East Shore, close to the Coconut Market Place but sadly not in sight of the ocean. There's a more adventurous tinge to appetizers such as *ahi poke* nachos ($7–13) than there is to the conventional steak or fish entrees ($18–28). Live entertainment nightly. Daily except Mon 5–9pm.

Java Kai 4-1384 Kuhio Hwy, Kapaʻa ☎808/823-6887, ⓦwww.javakai.com. Lively, friendly coffee bar in the heart of downtown Kapaʻa, serving good coffee drinks from the crack of dawn, and fine if expensive smoothies too. Mon–Sat 6am–5pm, Sun 7am–1pm.

Kintaro 4-3561 Kūhiō Hwy, Wailua ☎808/822-3341. Very large, very popular Japanese restaurant. Full sushi bar, plus teppanyaki meals and more unusual specialties such as grilled eel ($20) and *yose nabe*, a

sort of Japanese bouillabaisse with clams and crab (also $20). Mon–Sat 5.30–9.30pm.

Korean Bar-B-Q Restaurant 4-3561 Kūhiō Hwy, Wailua ⓣ808/823-6744. Modest, friendly, and very good-value barbecue joint. The meat dishes are all tasty, with combos at $8–15; vegetarian options include spicy *kimchee* vegetables. Takeout available. Mon & Wed–Sun 10am–9pm, Tues 4.30–9pm.

Lemongrass Grill 4-885 Kūhiō Hwy, Kapa'a ⓣ808/821-2888, ⓦwww.restauranteur.com/lemongrass. Smart, lively, attractive restaurant, serving a predominantly Japanese and seafood menu. Besides the outdoor tables, there's plenty more indoor dining space upstairs. Graze on delicious appetizers like the *togorashi* scallops for a lighter meal, or choose a more substantial entree such as broiled lamb loin, barbecued ribs, or grilled fresh catch ($15–28). Vegetarian options available. Daily 5.30–10pm.

Mermaids Cafe 1384 Kūhiō Hwy, Kapa'a ⓣ808/821-2026. Small, partly vegetarian café in central Kapa'a, alongside *Java Kai*, serving wholesome egg-and-fruit breakfasts and bargain Asian-flavored lunches and dinners such as chicken satay, tofu or *ahi* wraps, black bean burritos and the like for around $10, washed down with lemonade or hibiscus tea. Daily 11am–9pm.

Olympic Café 4-1354 Kūhiō Hwy, Kapa'a ⓣ808/822-5825. Large, open-sided, upstairs café, perched above central Kapa'a, that's a popular breakfast rendezvous for locals and visitors alike. Lunchtime sees sandwiches, burgers, and burritos at similarly inexpensive prices, while fish and meat dinner entrees range up to $25. Sun–Thurs 6am–9pm, Fri & Sat 6am–10pm.

Small Town Coffee 4-1495 Kūhiō Hwy, Kapa'a ⓣ808/821-1604. Ramshackle, friendly café, in an old house on the inland side of the highway just north of central Kapa'a, which keeps alternative-minded locals happy with espresso-fuelled breakfasts, and reopens for tango nights on Tues. Mon & Wed–Sun 5.30am–1pm, Tues 5.30am–1pm & 6.30–8.30pm.

Waipouli Restaurant Waipouli Town Center, 4-831 Kūhiō Hwy, Waipouli ⓣ808/822-9311. Simple plate-lunch restaurant, just south of Kauai Village. The menu includes roast pork, chicken, and other meats (it takes a huge combo to cost as much as $10), but the specialty is filling bowls of *saimin* noodles ($5–9). Mon & Sun 7am–2pm, Tues–Sat 7am–2pm & 5–8.30pm.

The North Shore

Kauai's **North Shore** may be the most astonishingly beautiful place you will ever see. If photographs of stunning Pacific landscapes – sheer green cliffs rippling with subtle variations of shade and light, and pristine valleys bursting with tropical vegetation – are what enticed you to come to Hawaii, this is where to find the real thing. On all the Hawaiian islands, the north and northeastern shores, being the most exposed to the ocean winds and rain, offer spectacular eroded scenery. As the oldest island, Kauai's coastline has had that much longer to be sculpted into fabulous formations, surpassing anything else in the state.

The **Nā Pali coast**, at the western end of the North Shore, is the most dramatic stretch. Though inaccessible by car, it can be seen from offshore boats, up close along a superb hiking trail, from high above in Kōke'e Park (see p.403), or from sightseeing flights.

Thanks to high rainfall (and local resistance), Kauai's northern coast is far less developed than its east and south shores, though **Princeville** has grown to become a somewhat faceless clifftop resort, albeit redeemed by sublime views. Beyond Princeville you reach sea level by crossing a succession of single-lane bridges, which serve to slow down not merely the traffic but the whole pace of life. **Hanalei Bay** is a ravishing mountain-framed crescent, home to the funky town of **Hanalei**, while the ten verdant miles to the end of the road are lined by beach after gorgeous beach.

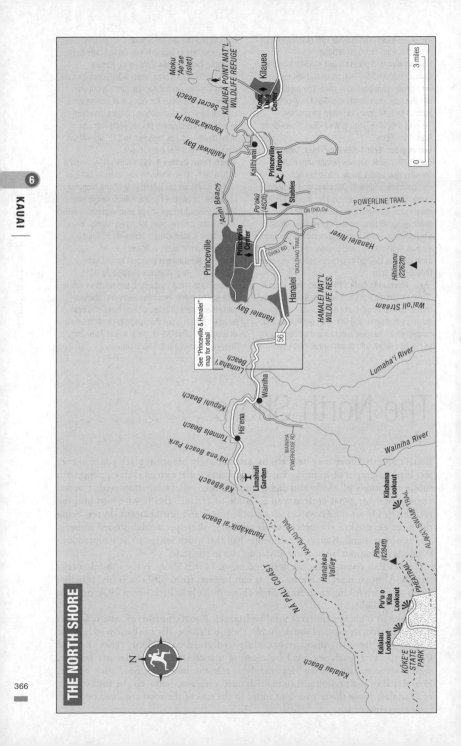

THE NORTH SHORE

Moku 'Ae'ae (islet)

KILAUEA POINT NAT'L WILDLIFE REFUGE

Kilauea

Kong Lung Center

Secret Beach

Kapuka'amoi Pt.

Kalihiwai Bay

Kalihiwai

Princeville Airport

Stables

Pō'okū (460ft)

PŌ'OKŪ RD

POWERLINE TRAIL

'Anini Beach

Princeville

Princeville Center

'ŌHIKI RD

'OKOLEHAO TRAIL

Hanalei River

Hanalei

Hihimanu (2262ft)

56

Hanalei Bay

HANALEI NAT'L WILDLIFE RES.

Waiʻoli Stream

See "Princeville & Hanalei" map for detail

Lumaha'i Beach

Lumaha'i River

Wainiha

Kepuhi Beach

Tunnels Beach

Hā'ena

WAINIHA POWERHOUSE RD

Wainiha River

Hā'ena Beach Park

Kē'ē Beach

Limahuli Garden

Hanakāpī'ai Beach

KALALAU TRAIL

NĀ PALI COAST

Kilohana Lookout

ALAKA'I SWAMP TRAIL

Hanakoa Valley

Pīhea (4284ft)

PĪHEA TRAIL

Pu'u o Kila Lookout

Kalalau Lookout

KŌKE'E STATE PARK

Kalalau Beach

N

0   3 miles

Kīlauea

The North Shore is commonly reckoned to start at Kauai's northernmost point, **KĪLAUEA**, which is more of a name on a map than a community in any real sense. Nine miles out of Anahola, a right turn from the highway leads past the small Kong Lung mall and two miles on to **Kīlauea Point**. This lonely promontory shares its name, "much spewing," with the volcano on the Big Island, but here the reference is to crashing waves, not erupting lava. When it was built, in 1913, the 52ft **lighthouse** at its tip boasted the largest clamshell lens in the world. The red-capped white shaft still stands proud, but it's no longer in use, having been supplanted by a 14ft tower just beyond.

The lighthouse is the focus of the **Kīlauea Point National Wildlife Refuge** (daily 10am–4pm; $5, National Parks passes accepted; ⓦwww.fws.gov/kilauea point), which protects such soaring Pacific sea birds as albatrosses, wedge-tailed shearwaters, red-footed boobies, frigate birds, and red- and white-tailed tropic birds. The refuge itself extends four miles east to Mokolea Point, while Mokuʻaeʻae Island just offshore is set aside for nesting. Detailed displays in the visitor center near the lighthouse explain the natural history, with a relief model of the whole island chain. Visitors can then walk out to the end of the promontory, where free binoculars offer close-up views of all those birds. During the winter, this exposed spot becomes a prime venue for **whale-watching**.

Practicalities

Kīlauea abounds in freshly grown tropical fruit, with the orchards of the Guava Kai farm rising *mauka* of the highway. If you fancy something more than fruit, the **Kong Lung Center**, half a mile off the highway, is your best bet. Tucked into the center's garden courtyard is the *Kīlauea Bakery & Pau Hana Pizza* (daily 6.30am–9pm; ☎808/828-2020), a friendly café-cum-bakery. It serves fresh breads and pastries to early risers, and then pizza (spiced up with smoked *ono* or tiger prawns) by the slice. Its closest neighbor, the *Lighthouse Bistro* (daily 11am–2pm & 5.30–9.30pm; ☎808/828-0480, ⓦwww.restauranteur.com/lighthouse), is a bit more formal, offering Italian-influenced food with an island twist, in a nice breezy setting. Lunchtime sandwiches and wraps cost $10–12, while evening entrees like mango cherry chicken are $24–30.

Kalihiwai

As you drive along the highway, it's easy to pass through **KALIHIWAI**, a couple of miles west of Kīlauea, without noticing anything more than a high bridge spanning a valley. Glancing to either side at this curve is a bit of a risk, but reveals glimpses of a pretty bay to the north, and tumbling Kalihiwai Falls to the south.

Until a *tsunami* whisked away another bridge, lower down, it was possible to loop off the highway, look at the beach, and climb back up on the far side. **Kalihiwai Road** still exists, but with the bridge gone it now consists of two separate segments, either side of the river. Its eastern end is no longer marked; look out for the *makai* turning just short of milepost 24.

Secret Beach

Long, golden **Secret Beach** – officially, Kauapea Beach – is one of Kauai's finest-looking strands of sand. It's "secret" partly because it's not visible from any road – in

fact you barely see it before you step onto it – and partly because, despite the opposition of local landowners, it has a reputation for attracting campers and nudists.

To reach it, turn onto the eastern half of Kalihiwai Road, as described above. Very soon, the road curves sharply to the left; turn right immediately beyond the bend to follow a well-surfaced dirt road, at first through a deep cutting. From a parking lot a few hundred yards down, a footpath skirts the edge of the hilltop, with fine homes to one side and a barbed-wire fence to the other, then drops down a steep and potentially very slippery gully to the beach. You'll hear the crashing surf well before you see the sea.

The path emerges at an inlet set slightly back from the ocean. From rocky Kapuka'amoi Point, immediately to your left, the beach runs east for just over half a mile towards Kīlauea Point, with the lighthouse at its tip. Depending on the season, it's either a magnificent expanse of coarse-grained yellow sand or, as winter progresses, a narrow, shelving ribbon battered by immense surf.

Only in its most placid midsummer moods is Secret Beach a safe place to take a swim, but a long stroll is always irresistible. Spinner dolphins can often be seen just offshore, while at the far end a waterfall cascades down the cliffs. You'll probably pass a handful of meditating nudists and would-be yogis scattered among the palms and fallen coconuts (bear in mind that Kauai's police can and do arrest nude sunbathers here).

Kalihiwai Beach

As you round the final sweeping curve of the eastern half of Kalihiwai Road, a mile or so down from the highway, **Kalihiwai Beach** spreads beneath you. Marking the point where the road is cut in two, this exquisite little crescent manages to hang on to its sand year-round. Residential properties line the *mauka* side of the road, but you can park in the shade of the high ironwoods rooted in the sand itself.

Surfers congregate below the cliffs to the east, while boogie-boarders and body-surfers ride into the heart of the beach, where the waves break across a broad sandbar. Rinse off the salt at the mouth of the Kalihiwai River, the put-in point for kayakers heading upstream (see below). There's hardly any sand on the far side of the river, at the end of the other half of the severed road.

'Anini Beach

Superb beaches come thick and fast as you continue along the North Shore. Turn right on the other branch of Kalihiwai Road, as the highway climbs west of the bridge, and fork left after a couple of hundred yards to find yourself back down at sea level skirting a gorgeous long strip of yellow sand known as **'Anini Beach**. No signs give the faintest inkling that the beach is here, but the road winds on for a full three miles, before reaching a dead end below Princeville.

All the way along, the beach is paralleled out to sea by one of the longest reefs in the state. Coral reefs take millions of years to form, so it's not surprising that Hawaii's largest are in the oldest region of its oldest island. This one shields an expanse of shallow, clear turquoise water that offers some of the North Shore's safest swimming. Snorkelers and scuba-divers explore the reef; if it's calm enough, you can peek at the huge drop-off beyond its outer edge. Other than during winter surf, the only area to avoid is around the outlet of the 'Anini Stream at the western end, which is plagued by treacherous currents that sweep out through a gap in the reef. The inshore area is a good place to learn to **windsurf**, but surfing and boogie-boarding are largely precluded by the jagged coral where the waves break.

Once a fishing ground of the kings of Kauai, 'Anini is still one of Kauai's most exclusive residential areas. That explains the **polo field** beside the road; ponies graze nearby all week, and you might see a game of a Sunday afternoon. The almond trees on the beach side, however, shelter a lovely **campground**, fully equipped with showers, rest rooms, and picnic pavilions. Reserve through the county parks office in Līhu'e (see p.347).

Po'okū

Roughly halfway between Princeville Airport and the Princeville resort itself, small, paved Po'okū Road runs off from the highway and into the hills. This area, officially known as **Po'okū**, was once the site of an important *heiau*, but now there's barely a building to be seen. Princeville Ranch Stables (Mon–Sat only; ⊤808/826-6777, ⓦwww.princevilleranch.com) operates **horseback** riding tours from its headquarters just up from the turnoff. Choices include picnic trips to the top of Kalihiwai Falls (3hr at $125, 4hr at $135), two- or three-hour "private rides" ($140 and $185), and a ninety-minute "Paniolo Cattle Drive Ride" ($135).

The Powerline Trail

Po'okū also marks the northern end of the thirteen-mile **Powerline Trail**, a broad dirt track that starts two miles down Po'okū Road. This was built for the local electricity company, whose cables stretch from pylon to pylon through the little-known interior of Kauai, but hikers are free to walk along it. Even if you just go a couple of miles rather than all the way to Keahou Arboretum (see p.361), it offers an easy and painless way to see high waterfalls and glorious flowers, without having to make any steep ascents. Starting with sweeping views of Hanalei Valley, it runs for most of its route along the crest of a ridge that parallels the Hanalei River.

Princeville

PRINCEVILLE, the main base for tourists on the North Shore, is a "planned resort community" rather than a town, consisting of neat rows of quasi-suburban vacation homes mixed in with a few larger condo complexes, two golf courses and a couple of luxury hotels. The general sense of placid domesticity is somehow heightened by the fact that the whole place is overlooked by the magnificent mountain wilderness that fills the western horizon.

Princeville stands on a well-watered plateau that abuts Hanalei Bay to the west and the open ocean to the north. In contrast to the farming lands of Hanalei Valley below, it served in ancient times as a residential area for the elite.

Soon after Europeans arrived on Kauai, the Russian-backed German adventurer **George Schäffer** (see p.396) renamed this district "Schäffertal" and constructed the short-lived **Fort Alexander** on the Pu'u Pōā headland now occupied by the *St Regis Princeville Resort*. The general outline of the fort is still discernible on the lawn near the main hotel entrance, and a small pavilion holds explanatory displays.

From the 1830s onwards, Princeville served variously as a cattle ranch, a sugar plantation, and a sheep farm; it took its name from the young Hawaiian Prince Albert, who visited with his parents King Kamehameha IV and Queen Emma in 1860. Finally, in 1969, the entire area was bought by an American consortium, and construction commenced on the **resort**. Its centerpiece, the *Princeville Resort*, opened in 1985 and

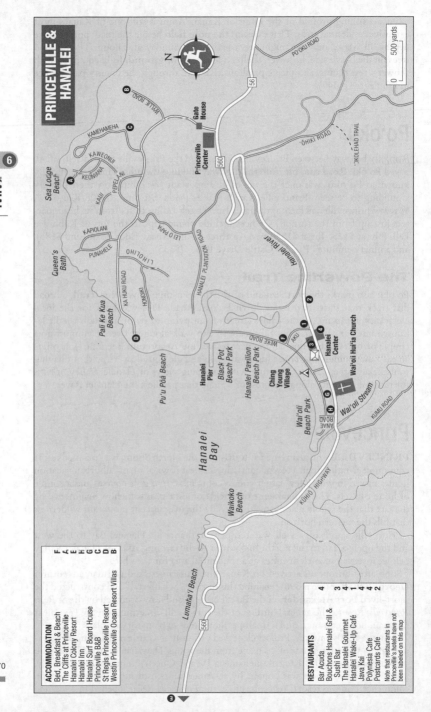

PRINCEVILLE & HANALEI

N

0   500 yards

ACCOMMODATION
Bed, Breakfast & Beach   F
The Cliffs at Princeville   A
Hanalei Colony Resort   E
Hanalei Inn   H
Hanalei Surf Board House   G
Princeville B&B   C
St Regis Princeville Resort   D
Westin Princeville Ocean Resort Villas B

RESTAURANTS
Bar Acuda   4
Bouchons Hanalei Grill &
Sushi Bar   3
The Hanalei Gourmet   4
Hanalei Wake-Up Café   1
Java Kai   4
Polynesia Cafe   4
Postcards Cafe   2

Note that restaurants in
Princeville's hotels have not
been labeled on this map

has changed hands repeatedly ever since, while continuing to rank among the world's top tropical hideaways. While Princeville these days can't be faulted as a relaxing base from which to explore North Kauai, there's nothing in particular to see, and the pretty little **beaches** tucked beneath the cliffs are no better than countless others along this stretch of coast. No airlines currently serve Princeville's small **airport**, a couple of miles east of the resort on the highway, though Sunshine Helicopters offers flight-seeing tours on demand (T 1-866/501-7738, W www.helicopters-hawaii.com).

Accommodation

Princeville is far from being an inexpensive place to **stay**, and neither is it very lively. Besides a pair of luxury resorts, there's little here apart from condo complexes, in most of which the apartments and villas are rented either directly by their owners, or through agencies such as Hanalei North Shore Properties (T 808/826-9622 or 1-800/488-3336, W www.rentalsonkauai.com), and Remax Kauai T 808/826-9675 or 1-877/838-8149, W www.remaxkauai.com). Note that the *Hanalei Bay Resort*, alongside the *St Regis* and sharing the same irresistible beach, is no longer a hotel, but a timeshare/condo property where individual units are available for rent.

The Cliffs at Princeville 3811 Edward Rd T 808/826-6219 or 1-800/367-8024, W www . cliffsatprinceville.com. Comfortable individual houses in Princeville's biggest condo complex, with a clifftop setting next to the golf course. Each unit has one bedroom, two bathrooms, a kitchen, and a *lānai*, and there are tennis courts and a pool. Try also the agents listed above. **6**

Princeville B&B 3875 Kamehameha Drive T 808/826-6733 or 1-800/826-6733, W www .pixi.com/~kauai. Luxury B&B accommodation in a plush private home that features two guest rooms and two upscale suites, with a garden *lānai* and views across the golf course to Kīlauea Lighthouse. Three-night minimum stay. Rooms **4**, suites **6/8**

St Regis Princeville Resort 5520 Ka Huku Rd T 808/826-9644, W www.stregis princeville.com. Set atop the bluffs, open to the full sweep of the Nā Pali cliffs across Hanalei Bay, the opulent resort hotel that is Princeville's *raison d'être* enjoys one of the world's most scenic

panoramas, and facilities more luxurious than you could ever need. The lobby is on the ninth floor; the hotel drops down the hillside in three tiers, with the infinity pool and lovely Pu'u Pōā Beach (see p.372) accessible from the lowest level. Some guest rooms are angled towards the inland mountains rather than the bay; few have *lānais*, and in the rest you can't even open the windows. Recently remodeled to create a less formal, more Hawaiian feel, it now also features the Haleala Spa. Garden view **8**, ocean view **9**

Westin Princeville Ocean Resort Villas 3939 Wyllie Rd T 808/827-8700, W www .westinprinceville.com. This luxurious new resort, which opened in 2008, does not literally consist of individual villas, but of 350 large rooms and suites spread through seven low-slung buildings. Most are condos, some are let as hotel rooms; all are set around nicely landscaped clifftop gardens, with good views but no readily accessible beach. Several pools make this a good family choice. **6**

The resort and its beaches

Not far west of milepost 27, just beyond the marked approach road to Princeville proper, the **Princeville Center** mall stands beside Kūhiō Highway, shielded by orange *lehua* trees. Apart from a supermarket, and a handful of snack bars and restaurants – plus the last gas station along the North Shore – its main business is real estate.

Princeville's quietest and most secluded **beaches** face north from the foot of the headland. That exposed position ensures that in winter the surf is too high for swimming and can obliterate the beaches altogether. At other times, however, stay within the reef and you can swim and snorkel safely. The three main alternatives are similar, each five to ten minutes' walk away along cliffside footpaths and stairways that can be slippery after rain.

Working from east to west, the first is **Sea Lodge Beach**, which despite its rich thick sand and fine summer snorkeling is often deserted. One route down starts at

the western edge of the ugly *SeaLodge* condo complex, but access is easier if you continue along the driveway at the end of Keoniana Road, then drop through some of Princeville's few surviving *hala* trees. Next comes the **Queen's Bath**, where there's little sand, but you can bathe in natural lava pools; it's reached by a meandering path off Kapiolani Road. **Pali Ke Kua Beach**, also known (especially by surfers) as **Hideaways**, lies down a steep staircase at the end of a path from the tennis courts of the *Pali Ke Kua* condos, not far from the *Princeville Resort*. Two distinct patches of sand nestle in the rocks, and the snorkeling here is great in summer, when you stand a good chance of spotting turtles, dolphins, and even monk seals.

Larger, sandier **Pu'u Pōā Beach**, below the *Princeville Resort*, is around the corner within Hanalei Bay. Set at the edge of a marsh that still holds vestiges of an ancient fishpond, it commands lovely views of the rising Nā Pali ridges. The inshore swimming and snorkeling is good; further out the waves get much higher. This is a perfect spot to watch surfers swirling and plummeting at the mouth of the bay. Access – as ever – is open to all, though the only facilities, back from the sea, are reserved for hotel guests. Walk a short way south to reach the Hanalei River, which should be shallow enough for you to wade across to Black Pot Beach County Park (see p.375). Hanalei itself is not far beyond.

Eating and drinking

While Princeville's hotel **restaurants** and **bars** gladly welcome non-guests, the only place where you can browse menus looking for a bite to eat is in the Princeville Center, beside the highway, which holds run-of-the-mill options like *CJ's Steak & Seafood*.

Kauai Grill St Regis Princeville Resort, 5520 Ka Huku Rd ☎ 808/826-9644, ⓦ www.stregisprinceville .com. Beautiful Pacific-Rim restaurant, at its best when softly spotlit by the gorgeous sunsets over Bali Hai. Overseen by Michelin-starred chef Jean-Georges Vongerichten – though he's based in New York – it serves a mélange of Asian and French cuisines, with plenty of raw or lightly seared fish, and desserts like *lilikoi* soufflé. The hearts-of-palm salad is a standout. Prices are sky high, with the $62 five-course set menu as the best deal. Tues–Sat 6–10pm.

Nanea *Westin Princeville Ocean Resort Villas*, 3939 Wyllie Rd ☎ 808/827-8736, ⓦ www .westinprinceville.com. This smart hotel dining-room, overlooking the *Westin*'s pool and gardens, is better value for a $10 burger or sandwich lunch than in the evening, when reasonable but not exceptional "Hawaiian Fusion" entrees like *opah* wrapped in pastry typically cost around $30. Mon–Sat 11am–2.30pm & 5.30–9pm, Sun 9am–1.30pm & 5.30–9pm.

Hanalei

With its perfect semicircular curve, fronted by tumbling white surf, fringed with coconut palms and yellow sand, and backed by jagged green peaks, **Hanalei Bay** is a strong candidate for the most beautiful bay in Hawaii. An easy thirty-mile drive from Līhu'e, it's not exactly inaccessible, but other than the *St Regis Princeville Resort*, peeking down from the east, it has been spared major development.

The local will to resist change is greatly aided by the fact that the Hanalei River, which meanders into the eastern side of the bay, can only be crossed via a flimsy single-lane bridge. What's more, this is just the first of seven similar bridges before the end of the road, which jointly ensure that the North Shore remains unspoiled. Even its largest community, **Hanalei** itself, is a relatively tiny affair, surviving partly on traditional agriculture and partly on tourism.

Until the Hanalei was bridged in 1912, all travelers, plus horses and baggage, were hauled across the river on a raft, guided by ropes suspended between a

mango tree on one side and a plum tree on the other. The flood plain to the west still constitutes one of Hawaii's largest **wetland** areas. Ancient Hawaiians waded knee-deep in gooey *lo'i* (see p.425) to grow taro to make into *poi*. Later attempts to cultivate sugar or coffee were unsuccessful, but for almost a century most of the valley was given over to the paddy fields of Chinese and Japanese immigrants. Now, however, it has reverted to taro production, and the landscape and its fauna are returning to their original state.

When driving on the North Shore, if an oncoming vehicle is crossing a narrow bridge towards you, etiquette dictates you allow three or four cars behind it to cross as well.

Accommodation

To the casual visitor, Hanalei seems to hold very little **accommodation**; the nearest sizeable lodging options are back in Princeville, or the *Hanalei Colony Resort* further down the coast (see p.378). However, there's a handful of **B&Bs**, while several Hanalei homes can be **rented** by the week through agencies such as those listed on p.371.

Bed, Breakfast & Beach 5095 Pilikoa Rd ☏ 808/826-6111, ⓦ www.bestvacationinparadise .com. Well-furnished private home, just back from the center of the beach near the foot of Aku Rd, where each of the three separate B&B rooms has its own en-suite bath. The same owner also lets out *Tutu's Country Cottage*, a detached two-bedroom cottage, by the week only. No credit cards. ❹–❺
Hanalei Inn 5-5468 Kūhiō Hwy ☏ 808/826-9333 or 1-877/445-2824, ⓦ www.hanaleiinn.com.

Small-scale inn a block from the bayfront, offering four very simple studio apartments, each of which has a kitchen and private bathroom. ❹
Hanalei Surf Board House 5459 Weke Rd ☏ 808/826-9825, ⓦ www.hanaleisurfboardhouse .com. English-owned B&B, just back from the beach, that offers two very comfortable en-suite studio units; one is bursting with Elvis memorabilia, the other has a "cowgirl" theme, and there's a three-night minimum stay. No credit cards. ❺

Hanalei National Wildlife Refuge

Immediately west of Princeville, just before Kūhiō Highway drops towards the river, an overlook offers the best view you can get of the full expanse of Hanalei Valley. The flat valley floor stretches west to the bay and south into the hills, crisscrossed by channels that create a green and brown patchwork of fields. As it curves its way around Hīhīmanu ("Beautiful") Mountain, the Hanalei River nestles between gentle grass slopes.

Most of what you can see belongs to the **Hanalei National Wildlife Refuge**. As Hawaii's natural wetlands have dwindled to cover just five percent of their former area, the population of **water birds** has declined in step. By helping farmers to reintroduce taro, the refuge provides an ideal habitat for them. The birds feed in the young taro patches, find shelter in the plants as they grow, and eventually breed on the mud flats and islands that appear during the annual cycle of planting, irrigation, and harvesting. Among the indigenous species here are the *'alae 'ula*, the Hawaiian gallinule or mud hen, with its yellow-tipped red beak, seen March through August; the *'alae ke'o ke'o*, or Hawaiian coot, seen March through September; the *koloa maoli*, Hawaiian duck, seen December through May; and the *ae'o*, or Hawaiian black-necked stilt, with its long red legs, which nests between March and July. The river itself holds introduced and native fish, such as the *o'opu* or native goby, and shrimp.

You'll get a close-up look at the valley as you cross the bridge down below. Turn left as soon as you're over and you can drive for a couple of miles along Ohiki Road, but venturing into the refuge is forbidden. The easiest way to explore is to rent a **kayak** (see p.343) and paddle your way upstream. It's a lovely ride, though if you start from the ocean you're in for a long haul before you reach the taro farms.

▲ Hanalei National Wildlife Refuge

It is also possible to **hike** up into the hills, for further stupendous views of the valley, by taking the **'Okolehau Trail**, which starts at a footbridge near the Chinese cemetery on the right of Ohiki Road, 0.6 miles from the bridge. The first section of this literally breathtaking climb follows a red-dirt road immediately to the left of the cemetery that's way too rutted to be passable in any vehicle. Two thirds of a mile up, at a massive utility-company pole, you double back sharply to the left onto a much narrower and even steeper foot trail. The path rapidly mounts a slick ridge that overlooks not only the valley and Hanalei Bay, but also more verdant valleys in the opposite direction towards distant Anahola. The trail ultimately dead-ends two miles up from the road, though you can turn back well before then and still be satisfied you've seen some of Kauai's finest scenery, in a round-trip hike of around ninety strenuous minutes.

Hanalei town

The town of **HANALEI** stretches for several hundred yards along the highway, around half a mile on from the bridge and a couple of hundred yards in from the beach. Little more than a village – you can almost be out the far end before you realize you've even arrived – it's home to an ever-changing mixture of laidback old-timers, spaced-out New Age newcomers, puffed-up surf bums, and hyper-active yuppies, who sadly, year on year, make it feel less like Kauai and more like a colony of California.

The main center of activity lies where two low-slung, somewhat ramshackle shopping malls face each other across the street. On the *mauka* side, the assorted buildings of the **Hanalei Center** include a converted school, and hold several restaurants and snack bars as well as a handful of upmarket clothing and gift stores. The Yellowfish Trading Co, tucked away in the back (℡808/826-1227), is highly recommended as a source of hard-to-find Hawaiiana, including some great 1950s souvenirs. The **Ching Young Village** opposite is a bit larger than it first looks, as it stretches a little way back from the road. In addition to a couple of outdoor-adventure and equipment-rental companies, it offers some grocery stores, and some cheaper eating options.

Hanalei was the location of Kauai's second Christian **mission** (the first was in Waimea), established in 1834 by Rev William Alexander. The mission buildings, gathered in a large meadow at the western end of town, are now Hanalei's only historic sites. The most photogenic is the clapboard **Wai'oli Hui'ia Church**, with its stained-glass windows and neat belfry. Painted bright green to blend in with the hills, and shaded by tall palms, it's a quintessential little Hawaiian church. It's a lot newer than its neighbors, however, having been built in 1912. Set back to the right is its predecessor, the original **Wai'oli Church**, which was erected in 1841. This long, low building, surrounded by a broad *lānai* and topped with a high slanted roof, now serves as the Wai'oli Social Hall.

Behind the two churches is the **Wai'oli Mission House** (tours Tues, Thurs & Sat 9am–3pm; donations welcome; T808/245-3202). Although it began life as the New England-style home of the Alexanders, it's better known now for having housed **Abner and Lucy Wilcox**, who ran the mission from 1846 until 1869. Members of the Wilcox dynasty became some of Kauai's leading landowners; you'll see the family name all over the island. Tours showcase the house outfitted with nineteenth-century artifacts, and provide a real sense of long-ago life in Hanalei. Out back you'll find the restored kitchen garden and family taro patch.

Hanalei Bay and its beaches

Hanalei means a *lei-* or crescent-shaped bay, and **Hanalei Bay** is lined for its entire sweeping two-mile curve with a wide shelf of yellow sand. Though it constitutes one of Kauai's very best **beaches**, each of its named segments has different characteristics, and not all are safe for swimming. **Weke Road**, which runs along the edge of the bay in Hanalei, is exclusively residential.

The underwater map of the bay is a lot more complex than what you see on the surface. The headlands to either side are ringed by coral reefs, but the channel through the middle is barely protected from the force of the ocean. While the resultant high surf places Hanalei among Kauai's favorite **surfing** destinations, it makes it a less than ideal **harbor**.

In May 1824, the royal yacht of King Liholiho, the son and heir of Kamehameha the Great, foundered in the bay. No lives were lost, but the *Pride of Hawaii* swiftly broke up. Kauaians saw a certain justice in the fact that the yacht had been used three years before to kidnap their own ruler, Kaumuali'i (see p.338), and that the loss occurred at the exact moment that Kaumuali'i died in exile. Marine archeologists who located the wreckage in the 1990s have retrieved a treasure-trove of artifacts.

For the next century, Hanalei was a significant port, shipping the valley's rice crop out and cattle and other supplies in. These days the bay is used only by pleasure craft.

The beach from which its jetty juts out takes its official name, **Black Pot Beach County Park**, from a large communal cooking pot that long served locals. Strong currents render it unsafe for swimming in winter, but it's busy the rest of the year. **Hanalei Pavilion Beach County Park**, a short distance west, is similar. When the surf isn't too ferocious, the lack of inshore rocks makes it a suitable spot to develop your surfing or boogie-boarding skills; otherwise, settle for enjoying a picnic in the open-fronted pavilion. With permission from the county parks office in Līhu'e (see p.347), you can **camp** here on Fridays, Saturdays, and holidays only.

The next beach along, **Wai'oli Beach County Park**, is marked by the fine stand of ironwood trees responsible for its nickname, "Pinetrees." Currents that swirl over the offshore sandbar, partly caused by Wai'oli Stream as it flows into the bay just to the west, lend it the more prosaic name of "Toilet Bowls." This is the most popular launching point for the champion surfers and paddleboarders who head out to the colossal waves in the mouth of the bay.

On the far side of Wai'oli Stream, right beside the highway towards the western end of the bay – further than you'd choose to walk from central Hanalei – **Waikoko Beach** is the safest beach for year-round family swimming. Thanks to a broad stretch of reef, the waters just offshore remain placid even in winter. The sea floor is sandy underfoot, and snorkelers can approach the coral with relative ease.

Eating and drinking

Most of Hanalei's enjoyable **restaurants** aim for a family or alternative feel rather than a romantic atmosphere. None has sea views, but the mountains and gardens compensate for that. Several breakfast places open at or before dawn, so early-bird hikers, surfers, and boaters can stock up, and there are plenty of **fast-food** takeouts around too.

While several Hanalei restaurants put on **live music** in the evenings, perhaps the most enjoyable place to hang out and listen to gentle Hawaiian sounds over an evening **drink** is *Tahiti Nui* (☎808/826-6277, ⓦwww.thenui.com), at Aku Road in the center of town, where there's something happening pretty much every night.

Bar Acuda Hanalei Center ☎808/826-7081, ⓦwww.restaurantbaracuda.com. This high-class, dinner-only restaurant, geared towards Spanish-style tapas, creates a bit of a conundrum. Its setting and decor, partly indoors and partly on a mountain-view terrace, across from the Ching Young Village in central Hanalei, are unarguably attractive. And the food is very good, ranging from $10 dishes like house-cured chorizo sausage, by way of seared scallops for $13 or braised short rib for $14, up to whole baked fish or grilled steak for almost $30. However, it attracts a braying Californian crowd that's totally at odds with Hanalei's usual laidback ambience. Daily except Mon 6–9pm.

Bouchons Hanalei Grill & Sushi Bar Ching Young Village ☎808/826-9701, ⓦwww.bouchons hanalei.com. As the unwieldy name suggests, this bustling second-floor dining room is something of a mixed bag, consisting of what were previously two separate restaurants sharing the same space. The lunchtime menu is a simple affair, with $9–14 burgers, sandwiches, and ribs; in the evening, alongside conventional entrees like pineapple chicken or steak, there's also top-notch Japanese food, as well as live music (Wed, Thurs, Sat & Sun), which includes jazz, reggae, Hawaiian, and blues, and usually keeps going long after the food service has ended. Sushi is sold by the piece ($4–10) and in a full range of pricey combos, and is available flash-fried. Daily except Mon 11.30am–10pm.

The Hanalei Gourmet Hanalei Center ☎808/826-2524, ⓦwww.hanaleigourmet.com. Mountain breezes blow through Hanalei's former schoolhouse to cool the open deck at the front. There you can enjoy tasty deli sandwiches ($10–12), salads, fish dips, or boiled shrimp, as well as $22–29 dinner specials, such as pan-fried crab cakes or mac-nut fried chicken, until 9.30pm. The same menu

is available from the takeout counter alongside, at the same prices. The bar is a busy center of local life, with live music every night except Mon & Thurs: jazz, Hawaiian (especially for the Sunday jam, 6–9pm), R&B, reggae, and rock'n'roll. Daily 8am–10.30pm.

Hanalei Wake-Up Café 148 Aku Rd ☎808/826-5551. Next to *Tahiti Nui* as you come into Hanalei from the east. Big breakfasts, such as omelets and "custard French toast," at low prices, are served from the crack of dawn. Daily 7–11am.

🏃 **Java Kai** Hanalei Center ☎808/826-6717. Small, friendly espresso bar across from the Ching Young Village. Hanalei's best bet for an early pick-me-up breakfast, with a nice *lānai* for specialty coffees and creamy waffles. Hours vary slightly seasonally, but typically it's open daily 6.30am–6.30pm.

Polynesia Cafe Ching Young Village ☎808/826-1999. Large deli/café where the eat-in seating is in a sort of open-sided bandstand a few yards away. They claim to serve "gourmet food on paper plates"; in fact the $16 daily dinner special, such as mahimahi green curry, is well below gourmet standards, and given the lack of service is a little overpriced, but the regular menu holds some real bargains, including a $10 Hawaiian Variety Plate of *kalua* pork, *ahi poke*, and *lomi lomi* salmon, and similarly cheap sandwiches and Chinese and Mexican offerings. Daily 8am–9pm.

Postcards Café Kūhiō Hwy ☎808/826-1191, ⓦwww.postcardscafe.com. Seafood and vegetarian restaurant in a former museum, *mauka* of the highway as it comes into Hanalei. Appetizers include home-grown taro fritters or lettuce wraps, both $10. Vegetarian entrees – some featuring tofu, others simply a mixture of sautéed or roasted vegetables – cost around $19, while fresh fish specials, cooked in assorted styles, are more like $20–30. Daily 6–9pm.

To the end of the road

Continuing west along the coast beyond Hanalei Bay, Hwy-56 becomes Hwy-560, and acquires the feel of a rural lane. For the half-dozen miles until the sheer Nā Pali cliffs definitively bar any further progress, it's lined by a succession of fabulous beaches. Some, like famous **Lumaha'i Beach**, are photogenic but treacherous; others are perfectly suited for surfing, snorkeling, diving, or swimming. Small private homes nestle in the undergrowth to either side, but there are no towns or villages, and only at **Hā'ena** has there been any commercial development.

Lumaha'i Beach

At the western edge of Hanalei Bay, just where a sharp hairpin bend in the highway finally takes you out of sight of Princeville, a makeshift roadside parking lot well before milepost 5 serves as both overlook and trailhead for **Lumaha'i Beach**. With its broad yellow sands, crashing white surf and green mountain backdrop, Lumaha'i has starred in such movies as *South Pacific*, but always seems to have enough space to accommodate another pair of wistful tourists. Romantic daydreams are a much safer way to spend time here than venturing into the water: currents are consistently ferocious, and there's no reef to stop unwary bathers from being swept far out to sea.

From beside the "Danger" sign at the head of the overlook, an easy trail drops down to the east end of the beach. Most of Lumaha'i's sand migrates here in winter; at other times the stark outcrops of black lava emerge more fully from the sea, making it clearer why this area is sometimes regarded as a separate beach in its own right, named Kahalahala.

In summer the sand piles in opulent drifts at the far end, two miles west near the mouth of the Lumaha'i River, occasionally blocking it altogether. That can make swimming in the river a possibility – it's one of the least spoiled in all Hawaii, bursting with native fish. For most of the year, however, it's extremely dangerous, with flash floods raging down from the mountains and the sea bed shelving away very steeply immediately offshore. Access to the beach's western end is straightforward, with a sea-level parking lot amid the ironwoods alongside the river.

Wainiha and Kepuhi

At a sweeping turn in the road shortly before milepost 7, Hwy-560 crosses two branches of the **Wainiha River** in quick succession, over a two-part wooden bridge. Sinuous Wainiha Valley winds several miles inland from this point, though unless you take a helicopter ride, you can only see its full extent by walking the full length of the mind-boggling Alaka'i Swamp Trail (see p.408). Now all but uninhabited, the valley once held a sizeable agricultural community. Historians wrestling over the existence of the *menehune*, supposedly the first settlers of Hawaii (see p.415), note that during the first census of Kauai, early in the nineteenth century, 65 people in Wainiha actually characterized themselves as *menehune*.

What the Hawaiians referred to as the "unfriendly waters" of Wainiha were harnessed in 1906, when a hydroelectric generating station was constructed a couple of miles upstream. It's still in use, with pylons carrying electricity around eastern Kauai (along the Powerline Trail; see p.369) to the south coast.

Neither **Wainiha Beach**, immediately west of the bridges, nor **Kepuhi Beach** just beyond that, is recommended for swimming. Silt churned up by the river keeps the sea almost permanently cloudy at Wainiha, precluding the growth of a protective reef, so the currents can drag swimmers way out into the ocean. There is a reef at Kepuhi, much frequented by local fishermen, but it is punctuated by so many gaps that it's equally unsafe.

Palm-fringed Kepuhi Beach nonetheless makes a superb setting for the North Shore's westernmost **hotel**, a delightful tropical retreat just two miles from the start of the Nā Pali coast. The highly recommended oceanfront ⚜ *Hanalei Colony Resort* (☎808/826-6235 or 1-800/628-3004, ⓦ www.hcr.com; ❻) consists of a cluster of two-story buildings following the curve of an exposed headland, affording magnificent beach and ocean views, and arrayed around a central lawn. Each of the units has two bedrooms and at least one bathroom, plus a kitchen, living room, and *lānai*, though no phones or TV; there's also a pool and hot tub, as well as a day-spa that offers massage therapies and yoga classes.

Housed in a seafront building that shares its parking lot with the *Hanalei Colony Resort*, and enjoying great views, the *Mediterranean Gourmet* **restaurant** (Mon–Sat 11am–9pm; ☎808/826-9875) serves mostly good meat and fish entrees, costing upwards of $20 for dinner (steer clear of the so-called "Euro-meat" though). Virtually every dish seems to come with copious quantities of the owner's delicious home-made hummus. A separate room beside the doorway holds a small espresso café, the *Nā Pali Art Gallery & Coffee Shop* (daily 7am–7pm; ☎808/826-1844).

Shortly before the *Hanalei Colony Resort*, three tenths of a mile past mile marker 7, *Hale Ho'o Maha*, 7083 Alamihi Rd (☎808/826-7083 or 1-800/851-0291, ⓦ www .aloha.net/~hoomaha; ❺), is a four-bedroom **B&B** a short walk from Tunnels Beach, where guests share use of a kitchen, living room, and whirlpool spa.

A short distance beyond the *Hanalei Colony Resort*, the *YMCA of Kauai Camp Naue* (☎808/246-9090, ⓦ www.ymcaofkauai.org; ❶) is a real bargain for budget travelers, though you can't reserve ahead. **Dorm beds** in either of its two simple oceanfront bunkhouses (bring your own linen), or setting up a tent on the grounds, costs $15.

Tunnels Beach and Hā'ena Beach County Park

From the first headland beyond Kepuhi Beach, just beyond milepost 8 and barely visible from the highway, a huge reef curves like a fishhook out to sea. In the calmer summer months, the lagoon it encloses is a safe anchorage for light sailing boats, as well as a great family snorkeling spot. Together with its fringe of golden sand, this popular area is known as **Tunnels Beach**, though divers and surfers dispute whether the name comes from its underwater lava tubes or its curling winter waves.

Tunnels can be accessed via a dirt road at the headland or by walking back to its western end from roadside **Hā'ena Beach County Park**. Manoa Stream ensures that the latter beach lacks a reef of its own, so it's no place to swim; but palms aplenty, broad lawns, and crisp white sands make it ideal for picnicking or lazing. It also offers a well-maintained country **campground** (closed Mon; for permits see p.347). While convenient to the Kalalau Trail, it's slightly too public for most campers to feel comfortable about leaving their gear unattended during the day.

Limahuli Garden and Preserve

Not far beyond Hā'ena Beach, halfway between mileposts 9 and 10, **Limahuli Garden** (Tues–Sat 9.30am–4pm) is part of the private National Tropical Botanical Garden, which has another branch on the South Shore (see p.392). The grounds can be seen either on self-guided tours (adults $15, under-13s free), or, by reservation, on two-and-a-half-hour guided tours (Tues–Sat 10am; $30, ages 10–12 $15; no under-10s; ☎808/826-1053, ⓦ www.ntbg.org).

The garden is set in a narrow, steep-sided valley reminiscent of Maui's 'Iao Valley (see p.251); the fifteen acres nearest the highway can be explored via a half-mile

walking trail, while a thousand more inaccessible acres further back are a natural preserve. Centuries-old terraces along the Limahuli Stream have been restored to cultivate taro in the ancient style, in small pond-like enclosures known as *lo'i*. Colorful native trees nearby include plumeria, with its white *lei*-making flowers; the *pāpala kepau*, whose sticky sap was used to trap birds; and several varieties of *'ōhi'a lehua*. From higher up the slopes, as the path skirts the cool mountain forest, you get superb views of the ocean, and there's a strong possibility of seeing whales in winter.

Hā'ena State Park and Kē'ē Beach

The western boundary of Hā'ena Beach County Park abuts the eastern edge of **Hā'ena State Park**, where the aim is to protect natural and archeological features from development rather than to display them to tourists. For most of its length, private residences stand between the road and the ocean, and only experienced surfers bother to make their way along the rocky seashore.

Few visitors see more of the park than glorious **Kē'ē Beach**, right where the highway ends alongside milepost 10. Swimming and snorkeling from its steep shelf of yellow sand is almost irresistible, but despite the usual crowds it's only safe when the sea is at its calmest. Lifeguards can advise. At such times, the waters inshore of the reef are ideal for fish-watching; at other times the surf that surges over the reef rushes out with even stronger force through gaps in it, especially at the western (left) end. Kē'ē Beach is a lovely spot for a sunset stroll; the further east you walk, away from the road, the further west it's possible to see along the majestic coastline.

The tale of Hi'iaka and Lohi'au

Several sites around Kē'ē Beach are renowned as the setting for the best-known legend of ancient Hawaii. However, no two sources agree exactly on what took place between its three central figures – **Pele** the volcano goddess, her sister **Hi'iaka**, and the Kauaian chief **Lohi'au**.

One version begins with Pele lying asleep in her home at **Kīlauea Crater** on the island of Hawaii, and finding her dreams filled with sweet, mysterious music. In search of its source, her spirit left her body and set off from island to island, until she finally came to this remote spot. The principal performer in the hula celebration that was taking place was the young chief Lohi'au, to whom Pele was uncontrollably drawn. After three days of blissful (though unconsummated) love, their idyll was shattered when Pele's slumbering body back at Kīlauea was awoken by her sister, Hi'iaka.

Pele despatched Hi'iaka to fetch Lohi'au. Her perilous voyage to **Kauai** involved countless obstacles on all the other islands, which Hi'iaka only survived thanks to the magical aid of her companion *wahine 'ōma'o*, or "green woman." Arriving on Kauai she found that Lohi'au had **hanged** himself in grief and lay buried nearby. She captured his free-floating spirit and managed to force it back into the corpse through a slit in the big toe, whereupon he rushed off to purify himself by surfing from Kē'ē Beach.

As they returned to Kīlauea, however, Hi'iaka and Lohi'au fell in love with each other. Lohi'au was repelled when he finally saw Pele's true bodily form (she was an elderly witch), and the jealous goddess retaliated by engulfing him in **lava**. This time it took two of Pele's brothers to restore him to life. They carried him back to Kauai, where he was reunited with Hi'iaka at Kapa'a.

According to local lore, the rudimentary walls of Lohi'au's **house** now poke from the undergrowth immediately opposite the foot of the Kalalau Trail, while the **hula platform** above the beach was the site of his first meeting with Pele, and his **grave** is just above Waikapala'e wet cave. It's also said that other houses nearby belonged to friends and relatives of Lohi'au who figured in the drama, and **rock formations** on the nearby cliffs are all that remain of *mo'o* (giant lizards) and other creatures killed by Hi'iaka.

Parking at Kēʻē Beach, which is also the start of the Kalalau Trail (see p.382), is very limited. During busy periods, you may well have to park back at Hāʻena Beach, and walk the mile from there.

Ke Ahu A Laka

A small trail heads west from Kēʻē Beach, along the black seafront rocks, and leads within a hundred yards to the ancient site of **Ke Ahu A Laka**. While the island of Molokai has stronger claims to being "the birthplace of **hula**" (see p.329), this was once the most celebrated *hālau hula* in all Hawaii, the highest academy where students were taught the intricacies of the form.

Although there are no directional or explanatory signs, finding the low-lying ruins is easy enough. No one knows whether the various structures were built simultaneously as parts of a single complex or are simply a group of unrelated buildings. Archeologists identify the site's lower level as the Ka Ulu A Pāʻoa *heiau*, which may have served some specific function for hula practitioners. Performances took place on the large flat terrace higher up, a few hundred yards back against the base of the *pali*. An altar, probably within a thatched enclosure, was dedicated to Laka, the patroness of hula. Local *hālau hula* come to the site in pilgrimage, but there are no public performances.

When a member of the *aliʻi* graduated from the *hālau hula*, or on other great occasions, the Hawaiians would celebrate by flinging flaming firebrands at night from the towering cliffs above Kēʻē. Burning branches of *hau*, *pāpala* and other light-wooded trees, dried and then soaked in *kukui* oil, were sent spinning out into the darkness, to be caught and held aloft by the trade winds as they curled up the cliff faces. Spectators would gather below in offshore canoes as the sky rained fire about them.

The Nā Pali coast

Beyond Kēʻē Beach, and beyond the reach of any vehicle, lie the green, inviolate valleys of the **Nā Pali coast**. Separated one from the next by knife-edge ridges of rock that thrust down to the ocean from heights of up to 4000ft, these are among the last great Hawaiian wildernesses, playing host to a magnificent daily spectacle

Nā Pali permits

To hike any further than Hanakāpīʻai, even for the day, to **camp** at either of the Kalalau Trail campgrounds, or to land by **boat** at Kalalau or Miloliʻi, in summer only, you must have a **permit**. With so many accidents and drownings along the way – and the possibility of a repetition of Hurricane Iniki, when 100ft waves necessitated the evacuation of all campers – a record of who may be missing is vital.

Hikers along the Kalalau Trail can camp for a total of five nights. As camping is no longer allowed at Hanakāpīʻai, and you're forbidden to spend two consecutive nights at Hanakoa, that means you can hike to Kalalau Valley with an optional overnight stop at Hanakoa in both directions. Up to sixty campers are allowed each day between mid-May and mid-September; for the rest of the year, that number drops to just thirty. Permits cost $20 per person per day, and are issued for groups of up to five named individuals; you have to specify exactly who is camping where each night. Reserve **online** via ⓦwww .hawaiistateparks.org/camping, or in person at the **state parks office** at 3060 Eiwa St in Līhuʻe (☏808/274-3444; weather information ☏808/245-6001). Spaces can be reserved up to a year ahead, but during the summer twenty permits for each night are only released 28 days in advance.

Nā Pali tours

Taking an **ocean-going tour** enables visitors to see the cliffs, valleys, beaches, and waterfalls of the Nā Pali coastline, looking even more dramatic than they do from the fly-on-the-wall perspective of the Kalalau Trail.

It's much better to take a Nā Pali boat tour that starts from the **North Shore** (from **Hanalei** or **'Anini Beach**) than one from the **West Shore** (from either **Kīkīaola Harbor**, 1.6 miles west of Waimea, or **Port Allen**). Tours from either side of the island end up at much the same places – most half-day trips include a view of Kalalau Valley and a snorkeling stop at the reef just off Nu'alolo Kai – but starting from the North Shore enables you to see Lumaha'i and Kē'ē beaches, as well as the full length of the Kalalau Trail. Boats that depart from the West Shore, on the other hand, cruise for much of the way alongside featureless sand dunes, though at least the western ports are more convenient to reach from the Po'ipū resorts.

Tour operators use either inflatable **Zodiac rafts** – highly maneuverable in calm waters, when they can dart into sea caves along the coast, but bumpy and slow in rougher conditions – or **catamarans**, which offer a smoother and faster ride but fewer close-up views and less of an adrenalin rush. Between December and April, when cruises can only cover shorter distances, the main compensation is the likelihood of seeing **whales**. Passengers scour the horizon for water spouts or a glint of tail flukes, and the catamarans venture a couple of miles out to sea in the hope of sightings. From that distance, the entire Nā Pali coast appears as a single rounded monolith.

Be warned that although tour operators give the impression that their trips depart to a regular schedule every day of the year, in fact, especially in winter (October to April), and especially from the North Shore, weather conditions can prevent them from sailing for days at a time.

Of the operators that sail **from the North Shore**, and typically charge around $140 for a six-hour snorkeling trip, the pick of the bunch is *Nā Pali Sea Breeze* (☎808/828-1285, ⓦwww.napaliseabreezetours.com), a powered catamaran that departs from **'Anini Beach**. Three catamarans sail from **Hanalei**: the highly maneuverable *Nā Pali Catamaran* (☎1-866/255-6853 or 808/826-6853, ⓦwww.napalicatamaran.com), the more expensive *Captain Sundown*, which hoists sails for part of its route (☎808/826-5585, ⓦwww.captainsundown.com), and Nā Pali Coast Hanalei Tours (☎808/826-6114, ⓦwww.napalitours.com), which runs to no fixed schedule.

Operators **from the West Shore** include Captain Andy (☎1-800/535-0830 or 808/335-6833, ⓦwww.napali.com) and Kauai Sea Tours (☎1-800/733-7997 or 808/826-7254, ⓦwww.kauaiseatours.com), both of which offer both catamaran and raft trips; Catamaran Kahanu (☎1-888/213-7111 or 808/645-6176, ⓦwww.catamaran kahanu.com) and Liko Kauai Cruises (☎1-888/732-5456 or 808/338-0333, ⓦwww .liko-kauai.com), which use catamarans; and Nā Pali Explorer (☎1-877/335-9909 or 808/338-9999, ⓦwww.napali-explorer.com), which uses hard-hulled rafts. Expect to pay $100–125 per adult for a four-hour snorkel trip and $130–170 for a longer tour (5hr 30min) that includes a beach picnic.

In addition to their regular Nā Pali tours, two more West Shore operators, both based at Port Allen – Blue Dolphin (☎1-877/511-1311 or 808/335-5553, ⓦwww.kauaiboats .com) and Holoholo (☎808/335-0815 or 1-800/848-6130, ⓦwww.holoholocharters .com) – offer extended tours that combine a Nā Pali trip with a cruise to the "Forbidden Island" of **Niihau**; see p.400.

It's also possible to join a guided **kayak** expedition from Hanalei. Kayak Kauai (☎808/826-9844, ⓦwww.kayakkauai.com) charges $205 for an escorted tour, available between April and September; only the most experienced of ocean kayakers should set off unaccompanied.

All Kauai's **helicopter** companies fly over the Nā Pali coast, but only Sunshine Helicopters offers flights from the North Shore; see p.340 for details.

of ever-changing colors. Intruders enter this world only on sufferance, clinging to the contours on perilous hiking trails or buffeted in small boats out at sea.

Nā Pali – "the cliffs" – comes from the same root as the name of the country, Nepal: the Himalayan word *pali* entered the Polynesian language long before recorded history, and is here applied to a landscape of truly Himalayan proportions. Although for the ancient Hawaiians, Kēʻē was proverbially the remotest spot on the islands, Nā Pali valleys such as Kalalau and Nuʻalolo Kai once held substantial populations of taro farmers. After the last Hawaiians left Kalalau in 1919, the region remained uninhabited until a sudden influx of hippies in the late 1960s. Official attempts to get rid of them led to the creation of the **Nā Pali Coast State Park**, and all access is now tightly controlled.

The Kalalau Trail

The eleven-mile **Kalalau Trail** passes through first **Hanakāpīʻai** and then **Hanakoa** valleys en route to **Kalalau Valley**, where it's defeated by a mighty buttress of stone. Honopū, Awaʻawapuhi, Nuʻalolo Kai and Miloliʻi valleys, further west, are only accessible by sea, though they can be surveyed from Kōkeʻe State Park far above (see p.403). Along the trail, there are **beaches** at Hanakāpīʻai (in summer) and Kalalau (all year) and **campgrounds** at Hanakoa (one-night stays only) and Kalalau. Arduous at all times, the trail also gets progressively more dangerous; indeed, the final five-mile stretch from Hanakoa to Kalalau, which involves scrambling along a precipitous, shadeless wall of crumbling red rock, is forced occasionally to close for repairs; check with the state parks office.

Any Kalalau Trail hike requires careful **preparation**. Most obviously, the 22-mile trek to Kalalau and back is too far to attempt in a single day. Hanakoa Valley itself being a grueling twelve-mile return trip (and one that requires a permit), the most realistic target for a **day-hike** is Hanakāpīʻai Beach, with a possible side-trip to the falls at the head of the valley. Allow a minimum of 4hr 30min for the trek from Kēʻē Beach to Hanakāpīʻai Falls and back. Neither food nor water is available at Kēʻe, let alone anywhere along the trail. However far you go, the path is rugged and uneven throughout, varying from slippery clay to shifting sand, so solid footwear is essential. And choose your hiking clothes carefully – thanks to the notorious red dirt, you may never be able to wear them again.

The trail rises and falls constantly, with several vertigo-inducing moments; it crosses, and can be blocked by, mountain streams; and emergency help is only available if fellow hikers manage to summon a helicopter. Bear in mind, too, that the sea undercuts the trail in many places; dropped or dislodged objects can hit passengers in boats below. Leaving a car overnight at the trailhead is not recommended; Hāʻena Beach County Park is safer.

The trail to Hanakāpīʻai

The Kalalau Trail climbs sharply away from its **trailhead** opposite milepost 10 at Kēʻē Beach, a few yards back from the ocean. Although much of its first half-mile was cobbled during the 1930s, the initial ascent is among the most demanding sections of the whole trail. It's also one of the most beautiful: conditions are much wetter here than further along, and the vegetation is correspondingly thicker. You soon find yourself clambering across the gnarled roots of the splay-footed *hala* (pandanus) tree, and sloshing through mini-waterfalls as they gush over the path.

Shortly after the trail rounds the first promontory, still during the first climb and still in sight of Kēʻē Beach, you may be able to make out the ruined walls of the Ka Ulu A Pāʻoa *heiau* on a small grassy oceanfront plateau below (see p.380). **Views** of the successive headlands that lie ahead, and of the islands of Niihau and Lehua further towards the horizon, start to open up half a mile along.

Ancient Hawaiians supposedly took just twenty minutes to reach Hanakāpī'ai Beach, but few modern hikers manage to cover the two-mile distance within an hour, and twice that is common. The obvious place to catch your breath en route is at the halfway point, where the trail tops out at 400ft before starting to drop back down again. A couple of small streams remain to be crossed, and the trail swings well away from the shoreline into a sheltered mini-valley, before Hanakāpī'ai spreads out at your feet. As you make the final descent, but still far above the valley, a warning sign marks the height to which you should climb if a tidal wave threatens.

Hanakāpī'ai Valley and Falls

Hanakāpī'ai Valley is the only spot between Kē'ē Beach and Kalalau Valley where the trail returns to sea level. Crossing Hanakāpī'ai Stream to reach the valley proper is normally straightforward; even if the stepping stones are submerged, there should be a strategically placed rope or branch to help you wade across. If the stream rises any higher than your thighs, turn back – it's not safe here, and it'll be worse still further along.

In summer Hanakāpī'ai boasts a broad white-sand **beach** which, though crowded with sunbathers, is notorious for **drownings**. Official statistics record 88 deaths here, chronicled on a grim notice-board, and anyone unfamiliar with Hawaiian waters should stay well clear of the ocean. Most victims are simply swept away as they wade at the shoreline. The dangerous currents are due to the lack of a reef, and that's what allows the sand to be swept away in winter, leaving a bare gray wall of small boulders.

Hanakāpī'ai no longer has a campground, but the portable restrooms are still there, a little way uphill beyond both beach and stream. If you detour away from the main trail to explore the valley, an energetic hour's hike, which requires several stream crossings and a lot of climbing up little rock faces and over fallen trees, brings you to the natural amphitheater of **Hanakāpī'ai Falls**. In addition to long-abandoned taro terraces, you'll pass the remains of a nineteenth-century coffee mill; coffee trees still grow wild throughout the valley.

Hanakāpī'ai to Hanakoa

For the nine miles between Hanakāpī'ai and Kalalau, the coastline is indented by successive "**hanging valleys**," cut by streams that end in cliff-top waterfalls. The trail out of Hanakāpī'ai switchbacks steeply up the *pali*, rising 840ft in little more than a mile. A false step here could be your last, and the concentration and effort of the climb allow little chance for enjoying the views. At the highest point a giant boulder *makai* of the trail – known to some as **Space Rock** – provides some welcome shade. Creep around behind it to confront the sheer drop down to the ocean, as well as a prospect that stretches from Kē'ē in the east to Kalalau in the west.

The nature reserve of **Ho'olulu Valley** comes next, swiftly followed by **Waiahuakua Valley**; the trail winds deep into both of them, forcing its way through the rampant undergrowth. Rounding each headland tends to involve a struggle against the swirling wind, but each brings a new view. Pristine green slopes soar skywards, their every fold covered with the intense blues, purples, and yellows of tiny flowers, and white tropic birds glide across the cavernous spaces in between.

Roughly an hour out of Hanakāpī'ai, immediately beyond a hair-raising section of trail, you reach the first overlook into Hanakoa Valley, with multi-tiered waterfalls tumbling far inland. This is also the first point where you're confronted by the full fluted majesty of the Nā Pali "cathedral," and the rounded Honopū headland in the distance.

Hanakoa Valley and Falls

Soon after entering **Hanakoa Valley**, you pass a cluster of **campgrounds** in a clearing on your right. This may seem a long way up from the sea, but it's as close as you'll get in the valley. Shortly afterwards, you cross **Hanakoa Stream** twice in very quick succession. Once again, don't attempt to get through if the water is high, but with several boulders scattered around the streambed you shouldn't have any problem. There are usually plenty of people around, bathing in the stream and picnicking beneath the trees. More campgrounds lie on the far side, set amid the stone walls of former taro terraces a little way up the hillside. The only drawback is the large population of **mosquitoes**.

Another side trail leads off inland from the terraces, this time to the 2000ft **Hanakoa Falls**, which you may have glimpsed as you came into the valley. Look out for ribbons tied to the trees, and be aware that if you don't re-cross the western channel of the stream within 100 yards of setting off, you've gone in the wrong direction. For steepness and mud this trail is even worse than the one to Hanakāpī'ai Falls, but only a third of a mile of spongy rotting trees have to be negotiated before you come to the sheer-walled waterfall, where you can cool off in the pool. However tempted you may be, don't drink the water; there are people, and goats, up top.

Hanakoa to Kalalau

The last five miles of the Kalalau Trail, from **Hanakoa to Kalalau**, include its most exposed stretches, though restoration work has rendered them less dangerous than they used to be. Each Nā Pali valley receives less rainfall than its neighbors to the east, so they grow progressively less indented and more precipitous. To the casual eye the vegetation still seems dense, but plants find it harder to grow. They therefore recover more slowly from the onslaught of wild goats, and the denuded slopes become prone to landslides. By this stage the trail cuts repeatedly across raw patches of red sandy gravel, where every footfall sends a shower of small stones tumbling down to the sea. With the path set at a slight angle to the hillside, open to the sun, and only in as good a condition as the last rains left it, such sections can be most unnerving.

However, the rewards at the end make it all worthwhile. Having skirted several small valleys, the trail emerges to access a full panorama of Kalalau Valley. Unfortunately, the final descent, while spectacular, is the worst of all. From the saddle that connects the pinnacle of **Pu'ukula**, or "Red Hill," with the main bulk of the island, the trail skitters down the crumbling hillside before pulling itself together to cross one last stretch of grassland down to Kalalau Stream.

Kalalau Valley

Kalalau Valley, the largest of the Nā Pali valleys at almost a mile wide and two miles deep, was the last to lose its native population. Its broad, gently sloping floor, cradled between mighty walls, nurtured many generations of Hawaiians before the arrival of the Europeans, and enough were left in the nineteenth century for missionaries to build a school and church here. Until 1919, when the last Hawaiians left, they were still living in thatched *hales*, cultivating taro and fishing with *hukilau* nets. They traded by canoe with their coastal neighbors, but were largely self-sufficient. For the next fifty years the valley was devoted to cattle ranching, but state authorities felt that cattle were damaging the valley's ecology and, when squatters began to move in as well, they set aside this whole section of coastline as a state park.

Before reaching the valley floor, hikers have first to wade the **Kalalau Stream**, where a rope serves as a handrail. The stream comes shortly after the 10-mile marker; take the right fork on the far side, and the final mile of the trail takes you down to, and along, the low bluffs above Kalalau's lovely white-sand **beach**. The only beach along the trail to retain its sand year-round, this nonetheless varies

Koolau the Leper

The "flower-throttled gorge" of Kalalau Valley was the setting of Jack London's famous short story *Koolau the Leper*, a flamboyant retelling of a true-life incident. The real **Koolau**, a *paniolo* from Waimea, was diagnosed as a leper in 1889 and condemned to permanent **exile**, far from family and friends, on the island of Molokai (see p.323). He fled instead with his wife and young child to the mountain fastness of **Kalalau**, to join a band of fellow sufferers. Sheriff Louis Stolz came in search of Koolau in June 1893, only to be shot dead, whereupon a large posse was sent to round up the fugitives. All except Koolau and his family were captured; Koolau, however, retreated to a cave only accessible via a knife-edge ridge, and picked off two of his pursuers as they inched their way after him. No one was ever to claim the $1000 reward for his arrest; his wife Pi'ilani emerged from Kalalau in 1896, to tell the world that both Koolau and their son had died.

greatly with the seasons. In winter it's a narrow shelf little more than 100 yards long, while in summer enough sand piles up for you to round the tumbled boulders and continue west for half a mile. Swimming during the winter or spring high surf is obviously dangerous, but even the calm summer seas are ripped through by powerful currents, and casual dips are never advisable.

Individual **campgrounds** line the trail above the beach, though some are prone to closure following landslides, and in any case the prime spot is considered to be around Ho'ole'a Falls at the far western end. When the sea caves here dry out in summer, campers pitch their tents inside, despite the risk of falling rocks. The falls are the valley's best source of fresh water, though it should still be purified before use.

Though camping is only permitted near the beach, the spur trail that forks left immediately after the stream crossing provides an easy and enjoyable two-mile walk back into the valley. Alternating between short climbs up to valley views, and jungle hikes through wild fruit groves (with guavas and mangoes for the picking), this ends after several hundred feet at a bathing hole known simply as **Big Pool**. Vegetation has reclaimed most signs of habitation in the valley, but you might glimpse the ruins of a *heiau* near the trail junction, or the stone walls of the mission church further inland.

Beyond Kalalau

The cliffs west of Kalalau are too fragile to hold a trail, so the magnificent valleys beyond can only be seen on the boat tours listed on p.381. The first of them, **Honopū**, is just half a mile from Kalalau; strong swimmers sometimes swim there, though heavy currents make the return leg all but impossible. Two beaches beautify the waterfront, but the valley itself stands atop a 150ft bluff.

Stunning **Awa'awapuhi**, a few hundred yards along, slithers out of sight behind the cliffs like the *puhi* (eel) after which it is named. It, too, is a hanging valley, so from water level there's little to see; only the Awa'awapuhi Trail in Kōke'e Park (described on p.409) offers complete views.

Next come **Nu'alolo 'Āina** and **Nu'alolo Kai**, respectively the inland and ocean-front portions of Nu'alolo Valley. Separated by a 75ft cliff, they were in ancient times connected by a perilous manmade ladder. Together they constitute one of the richest archeological sites in Hawaii, continuously occupied since the twelfth century. The overhanging cliff sheltered a row of stone-built house terraces, which have yielded layer upon layer of fishhooks, gourds, and the like. The valley floor above, though narrow and shaded, was extensively irrigated for taro. Most Nā Pali tour boats aim to spend an hour or two anchored at the coral reef that embraces Nu'alolo Kai, enabling passengers to snorkel among its plentiful fish; some also allow brief excursions ashore. Private individuals – kayakers for example – are not permitted to land.

Miloli'i, a mile on, is the last of the Nā Pali valleys, just four miles from the rolling dunes of Polihale State Park on the West Shore (see p.399). It, too, is protected by a reef, and was once home to a seafront fishing community. Boat landings on its pretty beach are permitted, but few operators do so; with a permit (see p.380), you can camp here for up to three nights.

The South and West shores

Thanks to its guaranteed sun and safe, sandy beaches, the **South Shore** is Kauai's main tourist center. Its only resort, **Po'ipū**, holds the island's largest concentration of upmarket hotels, condos, golf courses, and gourmet restaurants, but has never been a town in any real sense. It's very much a family destination, fine if watersports are your main priority, but holds next to nothing of interest otherwise. The plantation villages of **Kōloa**, nearby, and **Hanapēpē** ten miles on, boast some appealing, early twentieth-century storefronts but have definitely seen better days, while **Lāwa'i** and **Kalāheo** are just blink-and-you-miss-them highway intersections.

Waimea, the only sizeable town on the **West Shore**, was the site of Captain Cook's first Hawaiian landing. Although it offers one of Kauai's most characterful hotels (see p.398), it too suffers from an undistinguished present.

Few visitors would see the highway towns were they not en route to the wonderful state parks of **Waimea Canyon** and **Kōke'e**, described from p.399 onwards. As it is, however, all the settlements earn extra income catering to passing day-trippers, and there are a few interesting stores and galleries where you can while away the odd half-hour.

Kōloa

Immediately west of the **Knudsen Gap** – the narrow pass six miles west of Līhu'e where Hwy-50 squeezes between Hā'upu Ridge and the interior massif – Maluhia Road heads south from the highway. Its first straight stretch passes through an avenue known as the **Tree Tunnel**, where mighty eucalyptus trees meet and inter-mingle overhead. Three miles down, where the road ends, vehicles can shuffle either left or right to continue on to Po'ipū.

The small group of stores at this busy intersection constitutes **KŌLOA**, a nineteenth-century plantation town that was also the site of Kauai's first mission school. Its first teacher, in 1855, was Rev Daniel Dole; pupils included his son Sanford, the only president of the short-lived Republic of Hawaii (see p.422). Kōloa's raised wooden boardwalks hold assorted clothes and souvenir stores, as well as the open-sided, free-admission **Kōloa History Center**, just west of the Waikomo Stream, where wall displays recount snippets of local lore.

Practicalities

There's no **accommodation** in Kōloa, but the town's best-known **restaurant** is *Pizzetta* (daily 11am–9.30pm; ☎808/742-8881, ⓦ www.pizzettarestaurant.com), set

Kōloa and the sugar plantations

Though Kōloa has never been more than a small village, it played a crucial role in the development of modern Hawaii as the birthplace of the islands' first **sugar plantation**. From its origins in New Guinea, the sweet grass we know as sugar cane was carried throughout the Pacific by Polynesian voyagers. Ancient Hawaiians cultivated forty separate varieties of *ko*, which they chewed as medicine, an aphrodisiac, baby food, emergency rations, and simply for pleasure.

As **wild sugar** grew rampant in Kōloa, whose name meant "long cane," it made an ideal testing ground for commercial sugar production. In 1835, **Ladd & Co** secured permission from Kamehameha III to farm almost a thousand acres east of the Waihohonu Stream – the first such lease ever granted to outsiders – and sent 26-year-old William Hooper to establish a plantation. Hoping not only to make a profit but also to transform the Hawaiian way of life, he set 25 *kanakas* (native Hawaiians) to clear the grass.

Until that time ordinary Hawaiians were regarded as owing unlimited labor to the ruling *ali'i*, a form of serfdom that had been grotesquely abused in the sandalwood trade (see p.419). For Hooper, the plantation was an "entering wedge... to upset the whole miserable system of 'chief labor.'" To his **workers**, uprooted from seaside villages and brought to the new plantation settlement, however, this new system must have seemed little different from the old. They dragged the plows themselves, drilled the soil by hand using *'o'o* digging sticks, and crushed the raw cane using heavy *koa*-wood logs. By paying them in coupons that could only be redeemed at the company store, Hooper introduced them to consumerism. Each month, as the *kanakas* tired of the previous consignment of cheap goods and textiles from Honolulu, there'd be a frantic search for new items to import.

By 1838, the plantation employed one hundred laborers. An ever-increasing proportion of the sugar boilers were women, paid just six cents per day, less than half the men's wage. Hooper saw the Hawaiians as intelligent shirkers – "They display so little interest for their employment that it makes my heart ache" – who worked only when they were being watched and even learned to forge counterfeit coupons and avoid working altogether. As a result, he began to recruit **Chinese laborers** from a group who had been grinding wild cane at Waimea. These were housed in separate quarters at Kōloa, as were the white overseers, and patterns of race and class division emerged that became standard for all subsequent plantations. Soon after Hooper left in 1839, Ladd & Co managed to go **bankrupt**, despite being offered exclusive rights to all sugar production in Hawaii for a century. However, the plantation at Kōloa prospered, with the construction of a dam and a more sophisticated mill. The great **boom** came during the US Civil War, when the farms of the South stopped feeding the sweet tooth of the North. A leap in the price of Hawaiian sugar stimulated the opening of dozens of plantations, starting on the Big Island in 1863, and then on Oahu and Maui in 1864. When prices dropped at the end of the war, sugar dominated the Hawaiian economy; the US annexation of the islands was largely the result of campaigns by sugar producers to guarantee access to the American market.

Sugar production in Kōloa finally came to an end in 2000; the former sugar fields are progressively being replanted with coffee.

in a former *poi* factory along the boardwalk, with an open-air *lānai* out back. Huge, tasty lunchtime panini cost $9, a calzone is $13, pasta specials are $11–14, and full-size pizzas are $20–25. They also serve fine smoothies, and you can spend an interesting evening working your way through a long list of cocktails.

Both the food and the atmosphere in the garden courtyard of the nearby *Tom Kats Grille* (daily 7am–10pm; ☎808/742-8887) are similar. In addition to lunchtime burgers and sandwiches, they feature evening specials such as steak ($25) and seafood linguini ($20).

Po'ipū

PO'IPŪ, the southernmost point on Kauai, is also its principal vacation resort. Though *po'ipū* means "completely overcast," its **white-sand beaches** receive more sunshine than anywhere else on the island and are filled with tourists year-round. For surfing, windsurfing, scuba diving, snorkeling, or general family fun – and golf – it's a great place. However, beaches are about all there is here; there's no town to wander through and virtually nothing else to see or do. Even in daylight, most of the beaches are not visible from the confusing network of roads, so on first impression you might not even realize they were there. After dark, it's virtually impossible to find your way around, especially on foot.

Po'ipū is just about the only place on Kauai where the economy has not stalled completely in the recent recession – and that's probably because work was already too advanced on the huge **Kukui'ula** development just west of town. As it is, the large new Kukui'ula Village shopping mall opened in 2009, while thousands of new homes on the hillside are expected to be steadily unveiled over the next few years.

Accommodation

Hotels in Po'ipū tend to charge significantly more than their equivalents in, for example, Kapa'a, and unless you spend all your time on the beach you may not feel you're getting enough for your money. **B&B** rates are also unusually pricey, being aimed firmly towards the luxury end of the market.

Agencies that rent out individual **condos** in the virtually indistinguishable blocks along the shoreline include Parrish Collection Kauai (☎808/742-2000 or 1-800/325-5701, ⓦwww.parrishkauai.com) and Suite Paradise (☎808/742-7400 or 1-800/367-8020, ⓦwww.suite-paradise.com). Typical rates for a one-bedroom unit start as low as $100 per night in spring or fall, and for two-bedroom apartments at perhaps $140.

Garden Isle Cottages 2658 Pu'uholo Rd ☎808/639-9233 or 1-800/742-6711, ⓦwww .oceancottages.com. A small cluster of comfortable studio and one-bedroom apartments, in private cliff-top garden cottages overlooking Kōloa Landing. Kitted out with island-style paintings and furniture, and very peaceful by Po'ipū standards. Credit cards not accepted. ❺

Grand Hyatt Kauai Resort & Spa 1571 Po'ipū Rd ☎808/742-1234 or 1-800/492-8804, ⓦwww.kauai-hyatt.com. Six-hundred-room giant, sprawling along the seafront at the east end of Po'ipū, that's arguably the nicest tropical resort in Hawaii (especially for families). Top-of-the-range bedrooms and great sea views, plus amazing landscaping; the terraced gardens are filled with waterfalls and live swans, and you can swim from pool to pool, aided by waterslides, then drop down into a luscious network of artificial saltwater lagoons, squeezed in just back from the (unremarkable) beach. The *Tidepools* restaurant is reviewed on p.393. ❽

Kiahuna Plantation 2253 Po'ipū Rd; bookable through Outrigger ☎808/742-6411 or 1-800/542-4862, ⓦwww.outrigger.com, or Castle Resorts ☎808/742-2200 or 1-800/367-5004, ⓦwww.castleresorts.com. Huge oceanfront property, part managed by Outrigger and part by Castle Resorts (which tends to offer better rates online), who have separate offices at opposite ends. Each of the forty or so two-story "plantation-style" buildings is divided into condos with their own kitchens, living rooms, and *lānais*; all sleep at least four people, and rates rise considerably the closer you get to the sea. Manicured lawns lead down to a fine swimming and snorkeling beach. Castle ❺, Outrigger ❻

Ko'a Kea 2251 Po'ipū Rd ☎808/828-8888 or 1-877/806-2288, ⓦwww.koakea.com. It looks brand new, but this lovely, highly luxurious property occupies such a prime position beside Po'ipū's best beach because it's built on the exact "footprint" of the resort's first-ever hotel. Rooms in its low-rise buildings aren't particularly large, but they're kitted out with enormous ultra-comfortable beds, flat-screen TVs, espresso makers, and "rain" showers; there's a nice central pool and hot tub; and the high-class *Red Salt* restaurant adjoins the lobby. ❽

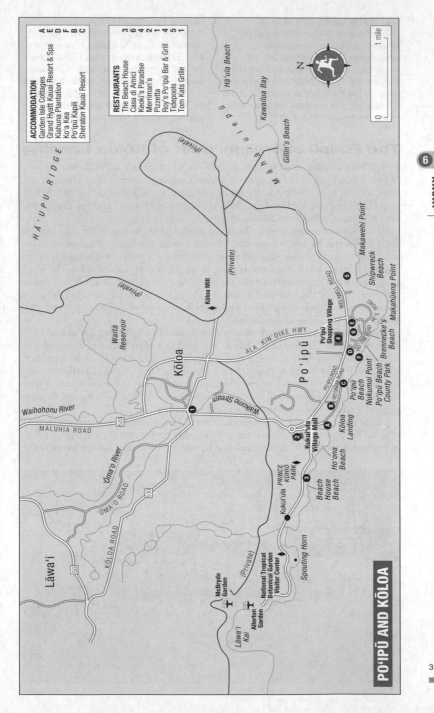

PO'IPŪ AND KŌLOA

ACCOMMODATION
Garden Isle Cottages	A
Grand Hyatt Kauai Resort & Spa	E
Kiahuna Plantation	D
Ko'a Kea	F
Po'ipū Kapili	B
Sheraton Kauai Resort	C

RESTAURANTS
The Beach House	3
Casa di Amici	6
Keok'i's Paradise	4
Merriman's	2
Pizzetta	1
Roy's Po'ipū Bar & Grill	7
Tidepools	5
Tom Kats Grille	1

0   1 mile

N

Hā'ula Beach

Māhā'ulepū

Kawailoa Bay

(Private)

Gillin's Beach

HĀ'UPU RIDGE

Makawehi Point

(Private)

Shipwreck
Beach

Kōloa Mill

Makahūena Point

Waitā
Reservoir

Po'ipū
Shopping Village

WELIWELI ROAD

Kōloa

ALA KIN'OIKE HWY

Po'ipū

Brennecke's
Beach   Makahūena Point

PO'IPŪ ROAD

HO'ONE ROAD

PE'E ROAD
HO'OWILI ROAD

Po'ipū Beach
County Park

Waihohonu River

Waikomo Stream

MALUHIA ROAD

Nukumoi Point

Po'ipū Beach

Kōloa
Landing

'Ōma'o River

Kukui'ula
Village Mall

Ho'ona
Beach

KŌLOA ROAD

PRINCE
KŪHIŌ
PARK

Beach
House Beach

Lāwa'i

McBryde Garden

National Tropical
Botanical Garden
Visitor Center

Allerton
Garden

Kukui'ula

(Private)

Lāwa'i
Kai

Spouting Horn

Poʻipū Kapili 2221 Kapili Rd
☎808/742-6449 or 1-800/443-7714,
ⓦ www.poipukapili.com. Very comfortable, spacious, and well-equipped one- and
two-bedroom condo apartments, each with kitchen
and *lānai*, and enjoying great sunset views in an
attractive, peaceful oceanfront location just east of
Kōloa Landing. Free use of pool and floodlit tennis
courts; five-day minimum stay. ⑥

Sheraton Kauai Resort 2440 Hoʻonani Rd
☎808/742-1661 or 1-866/716-8109, ⓦ www
.sheraton-kauai.com. As reflected in the room rates,
this luxury oceanfront resort ranks second best to
the *Hyatt Regency*. Rooms in the Ocean and Beach
wings enjoy spectacular views, but the Garden wing
is a bit disappointing. The pool is a little small, and
the restaurants are unexceptional, but with such a
good beach you may feel it doesn't matter. ⑥

The Poʻipū shoreline: east of Kōloa Landing

Poʻipū has two distinct sections of oceanfront, to either side of Waikomo Stream.
When Kōloa Plantation first opened, **Kōloa Landing**, on the eastern bank of the
river mouth, was briefly Kauai's major port, and as such Hawaii's third whaling
port after Lahaina and Honolulu. Only a basic boat ramp now survives, though the
area is popular with divers and snorkelers.

East of Kōloa Landing, a rocky headland marks the beginning of the long narrow
shelf of **Poʻipū Beach**, interrupted by two smaller headlands. The sea areas are
separated by parallel reefs; the inshore segment makes a perfect swimming spot for
young children, while windsurfers glide along the waters beyond when the wind
picks up, and an expert **surfing** site known as First Break lies half a mile out to sea.
Different parts of the beach are known by the names of the adjacent hotels; apart
from Sheraton Beach at the end of Hoʻonani Road, most of Poʻipū Beach can only
be reached by walking along the sand.

Nukumoi Point, the craggy easternmost point of Poʻipū Beach, is one of only
three *tombolos* in Hawaii, all on Kauai. A *tombolo* is a cross between an island and
a headland, joined to the mainland by a slender sandbar that all but disappears at
high tide. **Poʻipū Beach County Park**, beyond, has the only public facilities along
the Poʻipū coast, with a children's playground and a lifeguard station, and is thus
the beach of choice for local families. Swimming in the lee of Nukumoi Point is
generally safe, while snorkeling at its base is excellent.

A little way further along, boogie-boarders and body-surfers – surfers are banned
– jostle for position among the fierce waves that break over the offshore sandbar
at **Brennecke's Beach**. Brennecke's was named after a doctor whose house stood

▲ Poʻipū Beach

here until it was wrenched from its foundations by 1982's Hurricane Iwa. That hurricane took most of the sand from the beach too, and Iniki removed a lot more ten years later.

East of Brennecke's, the beaches are interrupted by conical **Poʻipū Crater**, a vestige of Kauai's final burst of volcanic activity. It's now ringed by small condos, with high bluffs along the seafront. On the far side, the *Hyatt Regency* dominates the crescent of **Shipwreck Beach**. Most of the sand scooped up by the hurricanes landed here, where it buried not only the eponymous shipwreck, but also a field of ancient petroglyphs. Even with all that sand, it's not much fun getting into the water across the shoreline rocks, so Shipwreck is largely the preserve of boogie-boarders and windsurfers.

Māhāʻulepū

Makawehi Point, at the eastern end of Shipwreck Beach, marks the start of the **Makawehi Dunes**, crisp-topped mounds of lithified sandstone filled with the bones of extinct flightless birds. Poʻipū Road ends alongside the golf course east of the *Hyatt*, but it's possible to keep going along the dirt road beyond. A couple of miles along, shortly after a closed gate forces you to turn right, you'll come to a gatehouse that is never manned, but marks the point where access is barred between sunset and sunrise daily. In daylight hours, you can proceed into the region known as **Māhāʻulepū**, which has three unspoiled, secluded beaches along its two-mile ocean frontage.

The road reaches the sea in the middle of **Gillin's Beach**, typical of the Māhāʻulepū beaches in being too exposed for safe swimming. Windsurfers prepared to carry their equipment this far take advantage of the strong waves, and naturalists set off into the dunes in search of rare native plants. Hikers head east, first to **Kawailoa Bay**, and then, across a stretch of lava indented with spectacular caves, to **Haʻula Beach** half a mile further along. CJM Stables runs **horseback trips** in the Māhāʻulepū area ($98–125; reservation required; ☎808/742-6096, ⓦwww.cjmstables.com).

The Poʻipū shoreline: west to Spouting Horn

Few beaches **west of Waikomo Stream** can compete with the luxuriant expanses to the east. Only for the first mile or so is there much sign of sand, and that tends to get stripped to almost nothing by each high tide. At **Hoʻona Beach**, the first possibility, the merest pocket of sand is tucked in among the rocks, and is appropriately nicknamed "Baby Beach."

Even less sand clings to the shoreline of Hoʻai Bay, just beyond. Across from the sea, the lawns of **Prince Kūhiō Park** commemorate the birthplace of Prince Jonah Kūhiō Kalanianaʻole (1871–1922), Hawaii's delegate to Congress from 1902 until 1922. Behind the bronze bust of the prince, the black-lava platform once held the Hoʻai *heiau*, which looks considerably sturdier than many of the new condos nearby.

Just past the next small headland is **Beach House Beach**, named after the nearby restaurant. This narrow roadside strip makes for a good, quick snorkel stop, and there are some expert-only surf breaks further out.

Coach tours galore continue beyond the bobbing yachts of tiny Kukuiʻula Harbor to **Spouting Horn County Park**, a natural freak a mile or so on at the end of the road. From the viewing area at the edge of the parking lot, you look down on to a flat ledge of black lava, just above sea level. As each wave breaks against it, clouds of spume and spray jet into the air through the "spouting horn," a hole in the lava. Obviously enough, the highest fountains coincide with the biggest waves, while rainbows hang in the spray when the eruptions come in quick succession. The rhythmic suction of air in and out of the hole creates a loud "breathing" sound, once attributed by Hawaiians to a giant *moʻo* or lizard.

If disappointment with what is often a less than enthralling spectacle tempts you to scramble down onto the rocks below, don't. The view isn't any better, and there's a risk of severe injury.

Allerton and McBryde gardens

Across the street from Spouting Horn, a restored plantation home serves as the visitor center for the **National Tropical Botanical Garden** (Mon–Sat 8.30am–5pm; ☎808/742-2623, ⓦwww.ntbg.org). Although it sells crafts and plant-related products, its main function is as the starting point for tours of **Allerton and McBryde gardens**, which fill over two hundred acres of the otherwise inaccessible **Lāwaʻi Valley**, a little further west. Originally created by the sole heir of a Chicago banking family, these beautiful gardens are now maintained as sanctuaries and research centers devoted to rare plant species, but Allerton in particular also makes a delightful spectacle for casual tourists. Bring insect repellent and drinking water.

Allerton Garden occupies the seaward half of the valley, stretching several hundred yards from the former Allerton home, which is not open to visitors, up to exquisite little **Lāwaʻi Kai** beach. Walking tours of the garden, which offer the only means of access, start with a tram ride down, and set off at 9am, 10am, 1pm, and 2pm, daily except Sunday (adults $45, ages 10–12 $20, under-10s not permitted). All tours last at least two and a half hours, and it's essential to make reservations as far in advance as possible.

Robert Allerton laid the garden out as a succession of "rooms," each with its own character; he was especially fascinated by leaves and foliage rather than flowers, and saw himself as creating "paintings." Even so, and despite the abundance of classical statuary, formal fountains, and gazebos, the overall impression is of a glorious profusion of tropical color. The plants are drawn from all over the world. Flaming torch gingers, lobster-claw heliconia, and birds of paradise erupt on all sides, and nature feels barely tamed. Appropriately enough, it was amid the roots of one especially enormous banyan tree that the dinosaur's egg was discovered in *Jurassic Park*.

McBryde Garden, by contrast – but like the NTBG's other Kauai property, at Limahuli (see p.378) – focuses exclusively on Hawaiian species. In fact, it holds the world's most extensive collection of Hawaiian plants. Trams down leave hourly on the half-hour, from 9.30am until 2.30pm daily; no reservations are necessary. Once at the bottom, you can take a self-guided walking tour before catching the tram back up (adults $20, ages 6–12 $10, under-6s free).

Eating and drinking

Poʻipū has a fine selection of gourmet **restaurants**, though only the *Beach House* is on the waterfront, and there's a distinct shortage of budget options. Most of the larger hotels have their own dining rooms, which serve reasonably good food, as well as **bars**, but only the *Hyatt* is especially worth visiting for a meal.

The Beach House 5022 Lāwaʻi Rd ☎808/742-1424, ⓦwww.the-beach-house.com. An irresistible oceanfront setting ensures this fashionable Pacific Rim restaurant is crammed to the brim early each evening; as the sunset gets under way, diners abandon their meals to take endless photos on the adjoining lawns. The food is almost as spectacular as the sunsets, making this Kauai's premier venue for romantic couples, and the prices are at premium levels. Appetizers such as *ahi* bruschetta or lettuce-wrapped Thai beef cost $12–18; entrees like the mint coriander rack of lamb or the rich seafood "Kauai Paella" are typically $28–38. Daily: April to mid-Sept 6–10pm; mid-Sept to March 5.30–10pm.

Casa di Amici 2360 Nalo Rd ☎808/742-1555, ⓦwww.casadiamici.com. Breezy, open-sided restaurant, tucked away in an obscure side street a hundred yards from the ocean, and serving high-class food at less than exorbitant prices. The bulk of the menu is Italian, with plenty

of pastas and delicious risottos, plus veal and chicken served in marsala, piccatta and gorgonzola sauces, all available in light ($20) and regular ($25) sizes. There are also a handful of adventurous Pacific Rim options, such as "Japanese mahogany glazed salmon and grilled black tiger prawns sprinkled with bonito *furikake* and served with black *frijoles chonitos* and jalapeño-tequila *aioli*" ($25), arguably the single best dish sold on Kauai. Everything is beautifully presented; the local-flavored side dishes, such as spinach creamed with coconut and corn with orange cilantro, are superb; and the staff are extremely friendly. Save room for Bananas Foster, at $12 for two. Daily 6–10pm.

Keoki's Paradise Po'ipū Shopping Village ☎808/742-7535, ⓦwww.restauranteur.com /keokis. Mall cocktail lounge that's been given an appealing Polynesian makeover, with a thatched bar, a waterfall, and a meandering lagoon; ersatz it may be, but it still turns dining here into an atmospheric experience. The food isn't bad, despite the mix'n'match approach to world cuisines, and there's live music Thurs–Sat. Lunchtime sandwiches and local plates are mostly under $10. For dinner, appetizers such as crab cakes ($11) and Thai shrimp sticks ($10) are followed by entrees generally priced under $20, though fresh fish specials cost a little more. Daily 11am–11pm.

Merriman's Kukui'ula Village Mall ☎808/742-8385, ⓦwww.merrimanshawaii.com. In a spacious building in Po'ipū's newest, rather bland, mall, Kauai's first outlet for chef Peter Merriman's "Hawaiian Regional Cuisine" is split between the all-day café downstairs,

where you order inside and they bring simple but tasty $10–14 salads, sandwiches, and plate lunches out to the breezy outdoor *lana'i*, and the dinner-only restaurant above it, which serves a pricier menu of more carefully crafted entrees from $24 (pork T-bone) up to $65 (lobster). Daily 11am–10pm.

Roy's Po'ipū Bar & Grill Po'ipū Shopping Village, 2360 Kiahuna Plantation Drive ☎808/742-5000, ⓦwww.roysrestaurant.com. Busy "Euro-Asian" joint, whose kitchens are visible at the back, and whose tables spread through this upscale mall. Appetizers range from pasta, satay, and snails ($10–15), to potstickers, crab cakes, and a Granny Smith apple salad. Entrees are $23–40, with standards like honey-mustard short ribs and hibachi salmon complemented by daily specials like Maui onion-crusted *opah*. Desserts include a legendary dark-chocolate soufflé at $9.50, and there's a great wine list. Everything tastes as good as it sounds; reservations are essential. Daily 5.30–9.30pm.

Tidepools *Grand Hyatt Kauai Resort*, 1571 Po'ipū Rd ☎808/742-6260, ⓦwww.kauai.hyatt.com. Very romantic dinner-only restaurant, consisting of semi-private open-air thatched huts arrayed around the resort's waterfalls and lagoon; the lights can be so low that you can hardly see your food. The relatively short menu features interesting appetizers like the $12 *poke, poke, poke*, a trio of raw *ahi*, octopus, and shrimp, while the entrees, at $22–48, include contemporary Hawaiian classics like seared *opah* alongside garlic-rubbed prime rib. Reservations are advisable. Daily 5.30–10pm.

Kāhili Mountain Park

Less than a mile beyond the Knudsen Gap on Hwy-50, a dirt road climbs for a mile inland to reach **Kāhili Mountain Park**. This idyllic private enclave holds some inexpensive rental **cabins**, but they're only available to guests with a connection to its owners, the Seventh-day Adventist Church (☎808/742-9921, ⓦwww.kahili park.org; ②–③).

The park is of more significance to visitors as the starting point of the **Kāhili Ridge Trail**, the finest hike on the southern side of Kauai, and one that makes an easy half-day outing for visitors based in Po'ipū. To find the **trailhead**, look for a water tower to the right of the dirt road, shortly beyond the final, highest cabin. Park nearby and follow a dirt track to a small clearing a hundred yards past the tower, then continue ahead through an obvious "tunnel" of overhanging low flowering shrubs.

As it climbs a slender spur towards the main mountain ridge, the trail swiftly degenerates to no more than a muddy rut. It's barely 2ft wide in places, and bursts of steep climbing are interspersed with precarious ridge-walking. Colorful flowers and orchids grow to either side, while the vegetation occasionally thins out to offer views down past Hā'upu Ridge to Līhu'e.

How far you get will depend on your head for heights and the rain conditions. It's not possible, however, to climb all the way to the 3089ft **summit** of Kāhili, which is itself just a pimple on the island's central spine, running north to Kawaikini. The trail ends instead at a radio mast less than two miles up from the park. Coming down is harder than going up, especially if the path is wet and slippery.

Kalāheo

Two miles on from Lāwaʻi, a minor junction where the three-mile rural Kōloa Road meets Hwy-50 ten miles west of Līhuʻe, the larger town of **KALĀHEO** consists of a cluster of shops, restaurants, and gas stations kept busy by its predominantly Portuguese community. Heading off the highway into the network of small roads to the south makes for some picturesque country driving, but you can't get as far as the sea. Much of this former sugar land is now given over to cultivating coffee instead, and extensive groves cover the sunny, south-facing slopes.

At **NUMILA**, just over two miles southwest of Kalāheo down Halewili Road, the **Kauai Coffee Company Visitor Center** explains the intricacies of coffee production and sells simple gifts (daily 9am–5pm; free; ☎808/335-0813, ⓦwww .kauaicoffee.com). Staff members offer free samples of local-grown java, while a coffee bar sells espressos, hot dogs, sodas, and pastries.

Practicalities

Surprisingly enough, Kalāheo boasts an old-fashioned **motel**, the *Kalāheo Inn*, a few yards south of the main road, but tucked out of sight at 4444 Papalina Rd (☎808/332-6023 or 1-888/332-6023, ⓦwww.kalaheoinn.com; ❸). It's a real bargain, with each of its fifteen very presentable suites offering its own kitchen, beach equipment available for free loan, and the self-explanatory *Kalāheo Steak & Ribs* **restaurant** alongside (daily 6–10pm; ☎808/332-9780). There's also inexpensive but good-quality **B&B** accommodation just up from Kalāheo at *Classic Vacation Cottages*, 2687 Onu Place (☎808/332-9201, ⓦwww.classiccottages.com; ❷–❸). They offer two houses, four garden cottages, and three studio apartments; all have private bathrooms and some form of kitchen.

If you're looking to pick up a snack as you pass through on the main highway – and especially useful if you're en route to or from Waimea Canyon – the ⚲ *Kalāheo Café & Coffee Co*, 2-2560 Kaumualiʻi (Mon & Tues 6.30am–2.30pm, Wed–Sat 6.30am–2.30pm & 5.30–9.30pm, Sun 6.30am–2pm; ☎808/332-5858), offers coffees from Kauai and beyond, plus cooked breakfasts, burgers, and salads later on, and dinner entrees like crispy eggplant parmesan or fresh catch.

Hanapēpē Valley

Shortly after Kalāheo, the fields to the right of the highway drop away, and a roadside pull-out overlooks a colorful and deeply worn gorge beneath a high mountain ridge. Many visitors imagine they're getting their first sight of Waimea Canyon, but this is in fact the similar but smaller **Hanapēpē Valley**. Watered by the broad Hanapēpē River, this fertile valley was once a major taro-growing center. As at Hanalei (see p.373), the land was turned over to rice by Chinese and Japanese immigrants at the end of the nineteenth century, but has since reverted to taro. The overlook was the scene of a bloody battle in 1824, when forces led by Governor Hoapili of Maui defeated insurgent Kauaians under Prince George, the son of the recently deceased chief Kaumualiʻi (see p.338).

'Ele'ele and Port Allen

As it starts to drop towards sea level, the highway reaches **'ELE'ELE**, making a sweeping rightward curve in front of the small 'Ele'ele Shopping Village complex. Following a minor road down behind the mall swiftly brings you to a dead end at **PORT ALLEN**, a small commercial harbor that's the base for several Nā Pali tour-boat companies (see p.381). Until the 1920s, when it was supplanted by Nāwiliwili Harbor, Port Allen was Kauai's main port.

The only reason you might pause in 'Ele'ele itself is for a bite to **eat** in the Shopping Village. Right on the highway, *Grinds* (daily 6am–9pm; ☎808/335-6027) is a diner that serves coffees and pastries to fishermen, boat trippers, and other early risers, full cooked breakfasts for around $8, and later, sandwiches, plate lunches, and pizzas for $8–10.

Hanapēpē

HANAPĒPĒ, at the foot of the hill beyond 'Ele'ele, is one of Kauai's quaintest little villages. Driving straight through on the highway you'd barely notice this former plantation town was there; to see anything, take the half-mile detour down its old main street, just inland. Captioned photos explain what each of the gently fading wooden stores used to be; several are now art galleries and specialty stores. Kauai Fine Arts (☎808/335-3778, ⓦwww.brunias.com) has some interesting old maps and aloha shirts, while Vintage Aloha (☎808/332-7405) sells funky postcards, prints and gifts, and the café (see below) is a welcoming place to stop. The whole town stays open late on Friday evenings, which is much the liveliest time to visit.

The **Hanapēpē River**, responsible for creating the valley, is not quite visible from the main street. For more views, either walk across the swinging rope bridge roughly opposite the café, which provides access to a footpath on the far side, or drive for a mile or two up Awawa Road just past the bridge at the west end of town.

Hanapēpē is also the only place where Hawaiian **"rock salt"** or *pa'a kai* is still manufactured by the traditional method of evaporation – a far from picturesque process, unfortunately. Turn *makai* of the highway just past town and you'll pass the "pans," expanses of red mud where sea water is collected and then allowed to dry away. Souvenir shops on Kauai sell what they call Hawaiian salt, but it's unlikely to be the genuine article.

The road continues as far as **Salt Pond Park**, a little further on at the flat, windswept southwestern corner of the island. Windsurfers come here in droves, and the sheltered inshore bathing is good for children, but Iniki scoured away what little beauty the crescent beach possessed.

Practicalities

Though Hanapēpē is devoid of accommodation, it does have a small selection of **restaurants**. On the old main street, the ⚔ *Hanapēpē Café & Bakery*, a former service station and drug store at 3830 Hanapēpē Rd (Mon–Thurs 11am–3pm, Fri 6–9pm; ☎808/335-5011), is a friendly, largely **vegetarian** establishment with a blue-tiled, horseshoe-shaped espresso bar. As well as smoothies and coffees it serves fine $8–10 sandwiches, like a roasted vegetable focaccia, as well as salads, frittatas, and specials like a $12 bouillabaisse. On Friday evenings it reopens for dinner, accompanied by slack-key guitar music; the menu changes every week, but the $20–28 entrees usually include international-themed dishes such as the baked eggplant Imam Biyaldi ($20).

Kaumakani

Kaumuali'i Highway turns northwest after Hanapēpē, heading towards Waimea through the extensive landholdings of the **Gay and Robinson family**. Though best known for owning the entire island of Niihau (see p.400), the family also owned Kauai's last **sugar plantation**, which ceased production in 2009. This corner of the island is a patchwork-quilt of fields, which have largely been turned over to growing seed corn, and open ranch land, used to pasture over three thousand head of cattle.

The plantation centers on the tiny community of **KAUMAKANI**, just over two miles out of Hanapēpē, where a picturesque Methodist church stands *mauka* of the highway. Across the road, an imposing avenue of trees leads down between twin rows of plantation houses.

Waimea

Six miles beyond Hanapēpē, the circle-island highway drops once more to sea level, crossing Waimea River to enter the town of **WAIMEA**. Sadly, despite being the spot where ancient Hawaiians first came into contact with European sailors, and despite its location at the portals of the magnificent Waimea Canyon, modern Waimea is a somewhat run down, even seedy place. It amounts to little more than a short street, off the far end of which leads the lesser of the two poorly marked roads up to the canyon.

When Captain Cook arrived in 1778, Waimea Valley was a major population center, with taro farmers exploiting the rich soil inland, and fishermen plundering both river and ocean. *Waimea* literally means "reddish water," but the red earth scoured by the river from the mountains is deposited along the shoreline as a fine gray silt, leaving the beaches looking dirty and unappealing. A statue of Captain Cook stands on Waimea's small central green – it's an exact replica of one in Cook's home port of Whitby, England – but the navigator's memory is not greatly honored. The beach where he landed, west of the river mouth, is pointedly named **Lucy Wright Beach Park**, after the first native Hawaiian teacher at the local school. A lava boulder commemorates the exact spot, but the National Park Service plaque that it bore has been vandalized, removed, and not replaced.

Head upriver on either Menehune Road or Ala Wai Road, and shortly after they join, a mile or so along, you may spot traces of the **Menehune Ditch** at the foot of the bluff on the left. Whether or not this ancient irrigation channel was built by the legendary *menehune* (see p.415), the care with which its stones were shaped makes it unique in Hawaii. However, little of it has survived.

Russian Fort Elizabeth State Historical Park

On the headland on the eastern side of Waimea River, the ruins of **Russian Fort Elizabeth** bear witness to a strange episode. When a Russian American Company ship was wrecked off Waimea in 1815, the Kauaian chief Kaumuali'i seized both the vessel and its cargo of Alaskan furs. The company sent a German surgeon, **George Schäffer**, disguised as a botanist, to persuade Kamehameha the Great to talk Kaumuali'i into returning its property. That circuitous plan failed, so Schäffer decided to negotiate directly with Kaumuali'i instead. Soon Kaumuali'i had secretly agreed that Schäffer would supply arms and ships for Kauai to invade Oahu, Maui, Molokai and Lanai, in return for Russian control over half of Oahu and other concessions. To strengthen Kauai's defences, Schäffer started construction of a star-shaped fortress at Waimea in 1816. However, American merchantmen got wind of his plans, were

The coming of Captain Cook

Captain James Cook sailed north from the Society Islands in December 1777, hoping to fulfill the aim of his third Pacific voyage – the discovery of the **Northwest Passage** back to the Atlantic. Instead he came upon an uncharted group of islands, north of the equator, in such a strategic location that he immediately recognized this as the crowning moment of his career.

Cook's two ships, the *Resolution* and the *Discovery*, had sailed from London in July 1776. On January 18, 1778, having passed far to the west of Hawaii and Maui, lookouts sighted first Oahu, and then **Kauai**. The following day, off the southeast corner of Kauai, two canoes came alongside, each carrying three or four men: "We were agreeably surprised to find them of the same Nation as the people of Otaheite [Tahiti] and the other islands we had lately visited," Cook wrote in his journal.

The ships sailed along the south coast looking for a place to land. With those canoes that dared to approach, they exchanged nails and small pieces of iron for "roasting pigs and some very fine Potatoes." When they finally found a safe anchorage, Cook allowed the natives of the nearest village, "Wymoa," to come aboard:

"I never saw Indians so much astonished at the entering a ship before, their eyes were continually flying from object to object... However the first man that came on board did not with all his surprise, forget his own interest, the first moveable thing that came in his way was the lead and line, which he without asking any questions took to put into his Canoe and when we stopped him said 'I am only going to put it into my boat.'"

On the next day, January 20, Third Lieutenant Williamson was sent ashore in a small boat. Before he could set foot on dry land, he found himself besieged by curious Hawaiians. With the "greatest reluctance," he shot and **killed** "a tall handsome man about 40 years of age [who] seemed to be a chief." Williamson didn't even mention the incident to Cook until some weeks later, but wrote that "These barbarians must be [initially] quelled by force, as they afterwards readily believe that whatever kindness is then shown them proceeds from love, whereas otherwise they attribute it to weakness, or cowardice."

Cook himself landed near the mouth of the **Waimea River** later that day. "Several hundreds ... were assembled on a sandy beach before the Village... they all fell flat on their faces, and remained in that humble posture till I made signs to them to rise. They then brought a great many small pigs and gave us without regarding whether they got anything in return." Together with a small party of sailors, Cook walked up the valley, which was planted with taro, sugar, plantains, and paper mulberry trees. He was led to a nearby *heiau* and told it had recently been used for human sacrifice.

Above all else, the Hawaiians were eager to trade for **iron**. That they already owned tiny quantities of the metal suggests previous, unrecorded contact with Spanish explorers. Cook's men, however, speculated that the iron might have arrived attached to driftwood. Local women found it easy to obtain scraps of metal from the sailors, and **venereal diseases** along with it, which despite all Cook's hand-wringing were established throughout the islands within a year.

The English ships had spent just three days at Waimea when rough seas forced them to move on – first to Niihau, and then northwards. Cook's rendition of the name of Kauai as **Atoui** was not such a bad mistake, for it came from a mishearing of "and Kauai"; as the most leeward of the islands, Kauai tends to come at the end of the list. He named the archipelago the **Sandwich Islands**, in honor of the Earl of Sandwich (the same one for whom the sandwich had been named in 1762).

For an account of Cook's return to Hawaii in 1779, and his death at Kealekekua Bay, see p.148. Waimea was thereafter a principal port of call for Western ships, with the first fur-traders arriving in 1786. Captain John Kendrick of the *Lady Washington*, who picked up firewood here in 1791, sailed straight back again when he realized that his load included precious **sandalwood**. In doing so, he sparked the first boom in the Hawaiian economy, and fatally undermined the old political order (see p.419).

told by other Russians that Schäffer was not acting on orders, and hatched their own plot to get rid of him. They managed to convince the whole population of Kauai, including Schäffer, that Russia and the United States were at war. In May 1817, Schäffer fled, as he thought, for his life.

Nonetheless, the fort was completed and used by the Hawaiian government until 1864. Though it has now been minimally reconstructed, it would take a lot of imagination to derive any interest from this tumbledown relic, overgrown with dandelions.

Practicalities

Western Kauai's only **accommodation** possibility is one of the most appealing on the island. ⚑ *Aston Waimea Plantation Cottages*, just west of Waimea at 9400 Kaumualiʻi Hwy (☏808/338-1625 or 1-866/774-2924, ⓦwww.waimea-plantation .com; ❻–❾), are the former homes of Waimea Sugar Mill Company employees, gathered in a coconut grove and fully renovated. Ordinary plantation workers may not have lived this close to the sea, or have had such luxurious bathrooms, but the atmosphere feels authentic, and the wooden floors, linen draperies, and breezy *lānais* make the cottages a delight. The sea isn't safe for swimming, but there's a pool and spa, and the garden hammocks have good views of Niihau.

Adjoining the plantation headquarters, just off the highway amid the coconut palms, the *Grove Café* is both a **restaurant**, serving hearty local food such as short ribs ($8) or shrimp scampi ($14), and the self-proclaimed "world's westernmost **brewpub**," selling such locally produced beers as the wittily named Waiʻaleʻale Ale (daily 11am–9pm; ☏808/338-2300). It's a pleasant spot, with plenty of shaded seating out on the terrace.

Waimea proper also holds a handful of inexpensive restaurants, including the central *Wranglers Steakhouse* (Mon–Thurs 11am–8.30pm, Fri 11am–9pm, Sat 5–9pm; ☏808/338-1218), and the good *Shrimp Station* (daily 11am–5pm; ☏808/338-1242, ⓦwww.shrimpstation.com), just before the canyon turnoff.

West of Waimea

Virtually all the tourists who make it as far west as Waimea are en route to Waimea Canyon and Kōkeʻe State Park, described on p.399 onwards. If you ignore both the roads that head off up the canyon, however, it's possible to continue further **west from Waimea** as far as one of the longest, largest beaches in all Hawaii.

Kekaha

Just over a mile beyond *Waimea Plantation Cottages*, the highway passes the approach road to the small-boat harbor at **Kīkīaola**, the point of departure for some Nā Pali boat tours (see p.381). A mile or so on, it briefly runs along the shoreline at **KEKAHA**. The beach here starts to consist of sand, rather than the muddy dirt of Waimea, but very little of it is left. Only expert surfers enter the water; the waves are usually too powerful for swimming.

Away from the sea, Kekaha boasts a few minor **churches** and a gigantic, rusting sugar mill. A little mall at the foot of Kōkeʻe Road, the second and more important canyon approach road (see p.402), holds a couple of snack places.

Pacific Missile Range Facility

The long straight section of Kaumualiʻi Highway immediately past Kekaha, much loved by motorcycle freaks, ends ten miles out of Waimea, where a sharp left turn leads to the US Navy's **Pacific Missile Range Facility**.

Originally part of a network of naval early warning systems developed after the attack on Pearl Harbor, the base is now a linchpin of US defense strategy. The world's only research site that can test space craft, aircraft, surface warships and submarines, it benefits from having over forty thousand square miles of open ocean to the northwest that are entirely unused by commercial aircraft. Lying, supposedly, within range of North Korea's nuclear capability, the facility has played a crucial role in developing and testing the so-called "Son of Star Wars" missile shield. As well as increasingly successful intercepts of incoming dummy missiles by the Navy's SM-3 missiles, it's also the headquarters for work on the Army's equivalent program, known as Theater High Altitude Area Defense (THAAD).

Polihale State Park

So long as you don't mind driving on unsurfaced roads, you can skirt around the test facility and continue up the coast. Keep going straight past the entrance, and the main road veers sharply inland, where a sign soon directs you left onto a straight dirt road. Bumpy and dusty it may be, but it's perfectly manageable. Slowly the hills to the right climb upwards and turn into cliffs, until progress is barred after just over five miles by the start of the Nā Pali coast.

This spot, **Polihale State Park**, protects a segment of a fifteen-mile-long **beach** that stretches to Kekaha. The main parking lot is half a mile short of the boulders that mark the first Nā Pali headland; trudge to the end and you'll be able to make out another three or so headlands beyond that. While the endless sands and crashing surf make a compelling spectacle, drownings in the mighty waves are all too common; even beachcombers have been swept away. Facilities remain minimal to say the least, but with an $18-per-night permit (available either **online** via ⓦ www.hawaii stateparks.org/camping, or from the state parks office; see p.347) you're welcome to **camp**. Walking back south along the coast from Polihale, you soon come to the undulating dunes known as the **Barking Sands**. Rising up to 100ft high at the Nohili Point headland, they owe their name to an ability to produce strange sounds, variously described as growling or hooting as well as barking. Each grain of sand is said to be hollow, so they reverberate when rubbed together. Suggested methods of making the sands perform include grinding handfuls together, sliding down the dunes, and dragging a companion as fast as possible across them.

Waimea Canyon and Kōke'e State Park

Two of Hawaii's greatest scenic attractions – the gorge of **Waimea Canyon** and **Kōke'e State Park** (with its views of the Nā Pali coast to one side and the Alaka'i Swamp to the other) – can only be reached from the west coast of Kauai. Waimea Canyon is always seen from above, from the viewpoints along the eighteen-mile **Waimea Canyon Drive**, which climbs its western flank,

Very few outsiders see anything more of the island of **Niihau** than a misty silhouette on the horizon, eighteen miles off the west coast of Kauai. The "Forbidden Island" remains the private property of the Scottish **Gay and Robinson family**, who bought it during the nineteenth century. Paradoxically, by turning the whole island into a cattle ranch, they also effectively froze it in time, and Niihau is widely seen as a sanctuary of traditional Hawaiian culture. Under the Robinsons' quasi-feudal patronage, the islanders are reasonably free to come and go, but unauthorized visitors are arrested and expelled.

The smallest of the seven inhabited Hawaiian islands, Niihau measures eighteen miles long by six miles wide. It receives just twelve inches of rain a year, so almost all its 73 square miles are desert, and there are no permanent forests. While the bulk of the island consists of low, arid dunes, its northeast coast – the part most easily seen from Kauai – is lined by sheer sea-cliffs. These formed the west rim of the volcano that created Niihau (the rest is long since submerged); the highest point is **Pānī'au**, at 1281ft. Off the north coast is the islet of **Lehua**, an eroded crescent-shaped tuff cone like Molokini off Maui (and equally good for divers). The southern plains hold two lakes, the 182-acre **Halulu** and the 860-acre **Halali'i**, Hawaii's largest lake.

Little is known of Niihau's ancient history, but it's thought that ten thousand Hawaiians lived here, fishing and growing yams and sugar cane – enough people for two rival chiefs to fight a war before the island could be united.

Captain Cook called at Niihau in 1778, and it was the recipient of his first gifts: goats, pigs, pumpkin and melon seeds, and onions. On Kauai, he had been relatively successful in preventing his crew from spreading venereal diseases to the Hawaiians. Here, however, they proved uncontrollable, and the infections had spread throughout the entire island chain by the time he returned a year later.

The population of Niihau had slumped by 1864, when **Elizabeth Sinclair** arrived with her extended family. She had previously farmed for twenty years in Scotland, and another twenty in New Zealand. A widow with five children (two of whom had married men called **Gay** and **Robinson**), she was en route to a new life in California when she decided to live in Hawaii instead. Negotiating with King Kamehameha IV for a $10,000 tract of farming land, she was offered a stretch of the Oahu coastline that took in all of Waikīkī and most of what's now downtown Honolulu. Instead, she opted for the island of Niihau; family tradition has it that the Sinclair party arrived to inspect the island shortly after one of its very rare rain showers, and were deceived by the greenness.

The people of Niihau were appalled at the idea of their homeland being sold. They petitioned the king to be allowed to buy it themselves, and many emigrated when the sale went through. One family had already purchased their own lands, but the Sinclairs soon bought them out, stacking $1000 in dollar coins, one by one, until they could resist no longer. Barely a hundred islanders were left when **Niihau Ranch** was set up.

Well before she died in 1892 at the age of 93, Mrs Sinclair had realized Niihau was of only marginal use for agriculture and started to buy land on western Kauai. Her descendants have continued to do so ever since, and Gay and Robinson (as the family business is known) now holds almost as many acres on Kauai as on Niihau.

enters Kōke'e State Park beyond the canyon proper, and ends at the vertiginous cliffs above Kalalau Valley.

Although you can rent a cabin or camp overnight in Kōke'e, the great majority of visitors see both canyon and park on a single day-trip. While you can enjoy superb and widely differing views without having to **hike**, trails – such as the Cliff Trail, or the Canyon Trail – lead off to further unforgettable spots, by way of dry gullies, lush vegetation, and pretty waterfalls.

The Robinson family imposed a strict way of life on the island, obliging every inhabitant to attend church services and banning the ownership of dogs. The policy of isolation from the outside world, however, only developed after Hawaii was annexed by the US in 1898, when the Robinsons became convinced it was their mission to preserve Niihau from the changes taking place elsewhere in the islands.

Around 130 people now live on Niihau, almost all of them in its one village, **Pu'uwai** ("heart"), a tangle of red-dirt roads on the west coast. The island has no airport, cars, or even running water. In the last few years, raising sheep and cattle on the Niihau Ranch has proved increasingly unprofitable, so there are no real jobs beyond maintaining the ranch infrastructure at a minimal level. Instead, almost all island families are on welfare, supplementing their income perhaps by fishing, raising mullet, making charcoal, and collecting honey. Niihau is also renowned for necklaces made from the tiny shells that wash up on its beaches. Most households run small electric generators, and have radios but not TVs; they're not allowed to smoke or drink.

What makes Niihau truly unique, however, is that it's the only place where everyone still speaks **Hawaiian** as a first language. As the island never fell prey to the missionary attempts to standardize and simplify the language (see p.455), the version spoken on Niihau is believed to be the purest, and most authentically pronounced, that survives.

The people of Niihau were alone among Hawaiians in voting against statehood in 1959, and the state government has repeatedly tried to buy back the island. Particularly controversial is the fact that the Robinsons refuse to recognize the state law that guarantees free access to all Hawaiian beaches. The Hawaiian media has a tradition of running exposés that "reveal" the true state of affairs on Niihau – one TV documentary, for example, alleged that its inhabitants were kept in conditions not far removed from slavery – and its public image in the rest of the state is not good.

The only legal way to set foot on Niihau is as a passenger in the **helicopter** that serves as an air ambulance for island medical emergencies. To defray costs, this runs three-hour trips from western Kauai to Niihau whenever five passengers are prepared to pay Niihau Helicopters $385 each for the privilege (☎1-877/441-3500 or 808/335-3500, ⌾www.niihau.us/heli.html). It briefly overflies Pu'uwai, and lands at either the northernmost or southernmost beaches on the island, Kamakalepo Point or Keanahaki.

You can also get a close-up view of the island on a **snorkeling cruise** from Port Allen. Both Holoholo Charters (☎808/335-0815 or 1-800/848-6130, ⌾www.holoholo charters.com; $164) and Blue Dolphin (Tues & Fri only; scuba available; ☎1-877/511-1311 or 808/335-5553, ⌾www.kauaiboats.com; $175), run seven-hour trips that combine a Nā Pali cruise with crossing the Kaulakahi Channel to Niihau. There they sail just offshore and stop either in the lee of South Point, where the lack of runoff and scant visitation creates some of the very best snorkeling conditions in all of Hawaii, or at Lehua.

Waimea Canyon

It was supposedly Mark Twain who first called **Waimea Canyon** the "Grand Canyon of the Pacific." In fact, Twain never visited the island, but the comparison is not unreasonable. At something over 3000ft, it may not be quite as deep as its Arizona rival, but the colors – all shades of green against the red earth – and the way it is squeezed into such a tiny island, are absolutely breathtaking.

Like all the Hawaiian islands, Kauai was once a vast volcano, of whose original contours little trace remains. Torrential rains have eroded Waimea Canyon into its present form, but that process began when a massive geological fault cracked the island down the middle. Eventually, the canyon will wear its way back to meet Kalalau Valley, and split the island in two; for the moment, the two are separated by the eerie basin of the Alaka'i Swamp.

Waimea Canyon Drive

The most dramatic route up to Waimea Canyon, **Waimea Canyon Drive** (Hwy-550), turns right off the highway as you leave Waimea, just after a sign indicating that you should *not* turn right. The other route, **Kōke'e Road** (Hwy-55), sets off from Kekaha, roughly three miles on. Because of its greater width and shallower gradient, all tour buses go that way, so it's likely to be a much slower drive.

Not that you should race up Waimea Canyon Drive. Speeding around its curves is far too dangerous, and even if you don't stop, it takes almost an hour to drive the eighteen miles to the top. Following Waimea Canyon Drive from the start enables you to watch the canyon grow alongside you, turning from a gentle tree-covered valley to an ever-deeper gash.

By the time Kōke'e Road comes in from the left, after eight miles, the canyon is a mile wide. It's worth stopping at each of the roadside lookouts from here on. The first – **Waimea Canyon Lookout**, 10.5 miles up from Waimea – is also the lowest, of course, but 3400 feet straight down still seems a very long way. Located at the junction of several distinct fissures, it tends to be very misty in the morning. The bare red earth slips away beneath your feet into the vagueness, while the weathered cliffs immediately below resemble the pinnacles of the Nā Pali coast. In the late afternoon the view is utterly different, glowing orange and red in the setting sun.

Next comes the **Pu'u Ka Pele Lookout**, shortly before milepost 13. From opposite the start of Polihale Ridge Road – which runs a short distance towards the cliffs above Polihale – this surveys a side chasm as it drops down towards the main canyon. On the far wall, you may be able to make out Waipo'o Falls (see opposite).

Less than a mile further on, perched above crumbling jagged slopes, the large **Pu'u Hinahina Lookout** looks straight down the head of another gorge. Far below, Waiahulu Stream plunges towards the main valley, echoing with the distant bleating of goats. A thousand shades of two main colors fill the canyon walls, mixed in different proportions as the shadows lengthen: by the evening, one side radiates warm russet highlights, the other luxuriates in dark green, and gray mists spill over both edges. The Canyon Trail (see below) runs along the promontory almost directly in front of you, slightly below and off to the left.

For the first half of each day, the **Niihau Lookout**, to the right of the same parking lot, offers views out to the cloud-shrouded island of Niihau, floating on the Pacific. Its profile is three-dimensional, with flat leaves of land jutting from below a central plateau; to its right is tiny, pyramid-shaped **Lehua**.

Waimea Canyon hikes

The best way to take a **day-hike** in Waimea Canyon is to combine the Cliff, Canyon, and Black Pipe trails, which lead off **Halemanu Valley Road**. This dirt road heads right shortly after milepost 14 on Waimea Canyon Drive, but is seldom fit to drive in an ordinary vehicle; park at a pull-out near the intersection, and set off on foot.

All the above trails start on the same path, which cuts away to the right after half a mile once the road has dipped to cross Halemanu Stream and then risen again. Ignore the turnoff for the Canyon and Black Pipe trails not far along, and keep going towards the end of the **Cliff Trail**, a walk of barely five minutes.

The narrow footpath soon emerges from the woods to run along a railed bluff, with the green, sharp planes of the canyon to your right and wooded hills to your left; from here you can look all the way down the canyon. Though the trail appears to continue, first on to a ridge immediately below you, and then across to a worn red-earth track above the steep drop ahead, there's no direct connection, and the promontory in front of the railing is not recommended.

However, you can reach the trail visible in the distance – the **Canyon Trail** – by retracing your steps as far as the intersection mentioned above and turning right. As this path dips into the gullies between the exposed headlands, the terrain constantly changes, from dry brush in semi-desert to lush green. The Canyon Trail proper starts a third of a mile along, with a sharp descent through thick woodlands. It then comes out on the rounded red ridge you've already seen from the Cliff Trail, which gently curves away towards an abysmal drop. Pick your way along that, and the path soon doubles back on itself towards two small waterfalls, reached by clambering through thick vegetation and across boulders. The pool at the upper end of the **Waipo'o Falls**, where the stream springs out of the rock, is ideal for cooling off after the hike; lower down, you can let the main flow tumble over you. Don't try to go any lower, however; the huge main falls soon bar your way.

From this point you can head back to join the **Black Pipe Trail**, which loops through the forest to rejoin Halemanu Valley Road after some steep but spectacular climbing. That makes a total hike of two to three hours. Alternatively, the Canyon Trail heads onwards around the lip of the canyon to meet up with Kumuwela Ridge, from which you can complete a larger loop, via two other trails, back to your starting point. At least two day-hikes in Kōke'e park are more rewarding, however (see p.406), so that option only makes sense if you have several days to spare.

Kōke'e State Park

The boundaries that separate Waimea Canyon State Park from Kōke'e State Park – and, for that matter, from the Pu'u Ka Pele and Nā Pali-Kona forest reserves – are imperceptible, and in places not even defined. Broadly speaking, **Kōke'e State Park** starts beyond the Pu'u Hinahina Lookout, as the highway veers away from the canyon rim. To the south and east, the park abuts the high valleys that lead into Waimea Canyon; to the north and west, it drops to the sheer cliffs of the Nā Pali coast. Waimea Canyon Drive follows the crest of Kaunuohua Ridge as it climbs and narrows through the woods until it finally peters out.

Although much of Kōke'e consists of alpine forest, its most remarkable feature is the all-but-impenetrable **Alaka'i Swamp**. In this natural volcanic bowl, cupped between the mountaintops, the heaviest rainfall on earth collects to form a strange, primordial quagmire. More of a very wet rainforest than a conventional swamp, it remains home to a unique range of flora and fauna. The few humans who manage to penetrate the mists are assailed on all sides by the shrills, whistles, and buzzes of a jungle without any mammals (save the odd tiny mouse) or snakes. The word "Alaka'i" means "leader" or "to lead" in Hawaiian; the name reflects the fact that anyone venturing into the swamp alone before the modern trail was built was very likely to get lost.

The park headquarters: Kanaloahuluhulu

Kōke'e State Park has its headquarters in a grassy clearing, left of the road just after milepost 15. Ancient Hawaiians who paused here on the trek to Kalalau called this meadow **Kanaloahuluhulu**, claiming it had been cleared by the god Kanaloa to get rid of an evil spirit who had been attacking travelers.

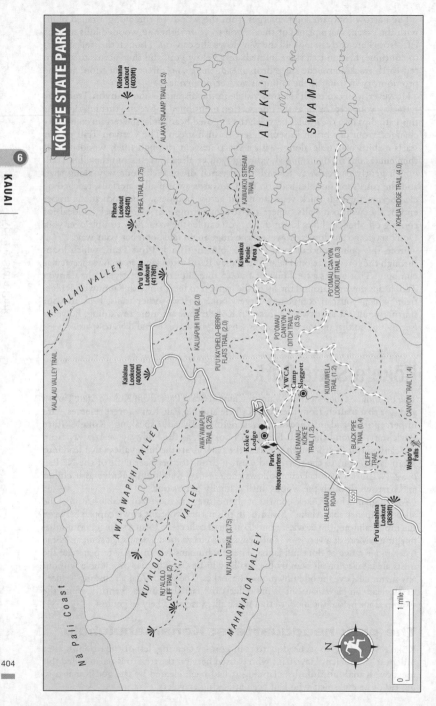

KŌKE'E STATE PARK

Kilohana Lookout (4030ft)

ALAKA'I SWAMP TRAIL (3.5)

PIHEA TRAIL (3.75)

Pihea Lookout (4284ft)

KAWAIKOI STREAM TRAIL (1.75)

A L A K A ' I   S W A M P

KOHUA RIDGE TRAIL (4.0)

Pu'u O Kila Lookout (4176ft)

Kawaikoi Picnic Area

PO'OMAU CANYON LOOKOUT TRAIL (0.3)

KALALAU VALLEY

KALIUAPUHI TRAIL (2.0)

Kalalau Lookout (4000ft)

KALALAU VALLEY TRAIL

PU'U KA'OHELO-BERRY FLATS TRAIL (2.0)

PO'OMAU CANYON DITCH TRAIL (3.5)

YWCA Camp Sloggett

KUMUWELA TRAIL (1.2)

A W A ' A W A P U H I   V A L L E Y

AWA'AWAPUHI TRAIL (3.25)

Kōke'e Lodge

Park Headquarters

HALEMANU–KŌKE'E TRAIL (1.2)

BLACK PIPE TRAIL (0.4)

CANYON TRAIL (1.4)

CLIFF TRAIL

Waipo'o Falls

N U ' A L O L O   V A L L E Y

NU'ALOLO CLEFT TRAIL (2)

NU'ALOLO TRAIL (3.75)

HALEMANU ROAD

550

Pu'u Hinahina Lookout (3636ft)

M A H A N A L O A   V A L L E Y

N ā   P a l i   C o a s t

1 mile

N

0

A wooden cabin here serves as the **Kōke'e Natural History Museum** (daily 10am–4pm; $1 donation; ☎808/335-6061, ⓦwww.kokee.org), where staff sell books and maps and provide up-to-the-minute hiking tips. All the major trails are shown on a relief model of the island; wall displays cover meteorology and, especially, Hurricane Iniki, and there are several cases of stuffed birds.

The larger **Kōke'e Lodge** nearby holds a souvenir store, public restrooms, and a reasonable and inexpensive cafeteria open daily for breakfast (served 9–11am) and lunch (10am–2.30pm). Takeout sandwiches are available from 9.30am onwards, while lunch specials include local dishes such as the $6.25 Portuguese bean soup.

Footpaths lead up behind the lodge to the ⨝ *Kōke'e Lodge Housekeeping Cabins* (☎808/335-6061, ⓦwww.thelodgeatkokee.net; ❸). Each of these **rental cabins** sleeps from three to seven persons, and is available for a maximum of five days (Fri & Sat can only be rented together). They have bed linen, hot water, fridges, and wood stoves – bring your own food for evening meals and buy firewood from the store, as it gets cold up here at night.

You can also **camp** just north of the meadow, so long as you have a permit, available either **online** via ⓦwww.hawaiistateparks.org/camping, or from the state parks office in Līhu'e, which can also provide details of other campgrounds tucked away on the dirt roads to either side of Waimea Canyon Drive. *YWCA Camp Sloggett* (☎808/245-5959, ⓦwww.campingkauai.com; ❶), across the highway from the Kanaloahuluhulu meadow, offers **hostel** accommodation in its bunkhouse for $25 per bed (bring your own linen). There's also a ten-person lodge, rented out to one group of five or more visitors at a time, again for $25 each; a rental cottage that holds up to four, for $85 per night; and a campground that charges tent campers $10.

The highway lookouts

Waimea Canyon Drive continues three miles beyond *Kōke'e Lodge* before squeezing to a halt above Kalalau Valley. There's little to see in this final stretch – you pass a couple of trailheads (see p.409) and glimpse the white "golf ball" belonging to Kauai's missile defense system – before the **Kalalau Lookout** at milepost 18.

As you leave your car to walk towards the viewing area, it looks as though nothing lies beyond the railings. If the mist has rolled in, as it often does later in the day, there may indeed be nothing to see. With luck, on the other hand, you'll be confronted by the vast, sublime panorama of **Kalalau Valley**, seen here from the head of its slightly shorter west branch, and framed by scattered *lehua* trees and arching ferns. To either side of the broad valley floor, rich with trees, sheer green walls soar 4000ft high, pleated into deep clefts through which plunge slender white waterfalls. Occasional red slashes in the hillsides show where landslides have sheared the razorback ridges. Reaching up from immediately below you, and hard to distinguish from the background, are several separate stand-alone pinnacles.

Tear your gaze away to trace the brief ridge that curves east from where you're standing towards the end of the road. This is the last tiny remnant of the caldera rim of the volcano that built Kauai.

Depending on the state of the road beyond the Kalalau Lookout, which frequently closes for repair, you can either walk or drive another half-mile to reach the **Pu'u O Kila Lookout**, which commands another stunning prospect, looking directly down the main body of Kalalau Valley. Only one wall is revealed in all its majesty, but the bonus here is that you can look inland as well, across the wilderness of the Alaka'i Swamp to the summit of Mount Wai'ale'ale.

Clouds appear from nowhere; you won't see them approach across the ocean, as this is the spot where they are born, when Pacific winds are forced to climb four thousand feet. One second the entire valley basin can be brimming with mist; the next second the swirling clouds may unveil a staggering prospect of the Nā Pali coastline.

Kōke'e hikes

Kōke'e boasts several excellent **hiking trails**, easy to follow and equipped with small, yellow-on-brown wayside signs marking each quarter-mile. Some trails marked on older maps, however, no longer exist; call at Kōke'e Museum (see p.405) for information before you set off. Whichever route you choose, get going **early**, before the clouds set in. Note also that **hunting** (for feral goats and pigs) is allowed on weekends and holidays, so casual hikers should wear bright clothing.

Stick to the named trails, but don't feel obliged to follow just one trail from start to finish; most of the best hikes involve **combinations** of different trails. If you have just one day, an ideal route is to follow the **Pihea Trail** down from Pu'u O Kila Lookout as far as its intersection with the **Alaka'i Swamp Trail**, walk the last two miles of that to Kilohana, and then retrace your steps. The round-trip takes six hours, allowing for an hour's stop at the end. You can walk the other half of both trails – less exciting but, at two hours, much quicker – by taking the Alaka'i Swamp Trail from its trailhead to the same intersection, then following the Pihea Trail down as far as the **Kawaikoi Stream Trail**, and looping back to the Alaka'i trailhead along that.

For the best views of the Nā Pali cliffs, another good combination – which again takes six hours, and is not recommended for anyone with vertigo – is to hike down the **Awa'awapuhi Trail**, follow the **Nu'alolo Cliff Trail** along the ridge, and return to the road via the **Nu'alolo Trail**.

The Pihea Trail

Waimea Canyon Drive was originally intended to run on beyond the Pu'u O Kila Lookout, and to connect somehow with the North Shore. Mountain mud swallowed several earth-moving vehicles before that project was abandoned, but its planned route remains obvious. This broad, undulating groove, cutting straight ahead from the lookout through the red clay of the ridge, now forms the start of the **Pihea Trail**. A short out-and-back stroll will give you views of both Kalalau Valley and the Alaka'i Swamp, while a more demanding trek leads down into the swamp itself.

The first mile of the Pihea Trail follows the high crest of Kalalau Valley. At the far end, the **Pihea Lookout** is (at 4284ft) the highest peak of all. If you can see it below the clouds from Pu'u O Kila, it makes for a great hour's hike. For over half the way, the trail is wide and even; then you have to pick your way over tree roots and scramble up hills. Though safe and manageable, it narrows at times to a few feet, with precipitous drops on either side, while visibility regularly drops to nothing as clouds siphon across the ridge.

Just before the final climb up to the Pihea Lookout – which is almost vertical, and usually extremely muddy – the Pihea Trail proper makes a sharp right turn to descend into the swamp. After a hundred yards of slithering down the clay slope, a plank boardwalk makes an appearance. It soon becomes a smooth, gradual staircase down the hillside, which reaches the obvious **four-way intersection** of boardwalks with the Alaka'i Swamp Trail 1.75 miles from the parking lot.

Turning left at this point enables you to combine the best of both trails; how the trail continues if you choose to do so is described on p.408. If you continue down the Pihea Trail, however, the boardwalk ends within a minute or two and the path drops ever more steeply. In dry weather, this is a green and lovely walk. The ground is so spongy underfoot, with its thick carpeting of moss, and the trees and shrubs to either side are so small and stunted, that it can feel almost surreal, as though you've blundered into Lilliput.

The trail zigzags down the thickly vegetated *pali* to reach babbling Kawaikoi Stream, then heads right, following the bank through pleasant woodlands, and crossing small side-streams. Shortly after a picnic shelter at mile marker 3, you ford the wide main stream via rocks in the river bed, then join the **Kawaikoi Stream Trail** on the far side.

The birds of Kōkeʻe

Kōkeʻe State Park is one of the last great sanctuaries for native Hawaiian **birds**, safe here from their two main predators. When the **mongoose** was imported into Hawaii (see p.434), it lived off the eggs of defenseless ground-nesting birds. Kauai, however, was the only island spared the mongoose invasion, so many native species of bird survived; recent reported sightings of mongooses on Kauai might augur the worst. **Mosquitoes** first came to Hawaii when a whaling ship taking on fresh water on Maui discharged its stagnant casks into a stream; the insects have been infecting native birds with avian malaria ever since. In theory, they can't live more than 3500ft above sea level, so the Alakaʻi Swamp has remained protected, though Hawaiian mosquitoes seem to be evolving to cope with higher altitudes.

Those birds that established themselves in Hawaii before the arrival of the Polynesians did so by chance. Thus a single blown-astray finch evolved into over fifty species of honey-creeper, each adapted to some specific habitat or diet. In Kōkeʻe these included the bright scarlet **ʻiʻiwi**, with its black wings, orange legs, and salmon-colored sickle-shaped bill, perfect for sipping nectar; the **ʻapapane**, which also has a red body and black wings but a short, slightly curved black bill; the tiny greenish-yellow **ʻanianiau**; and the predominantly black **mamo**. In addition there was the **pueo**, or Hawaiian owl, which flies by day, not night, and the rust-colored **ʻelepaio** flycatcher. Meanwhile, majestic **tropic birds** soar above the Nā Pali coast and Waimea Canyon. The white-tailed variety, the *koaʻe kea*, cruises the wind-currents high above the valleys, then plummets into the ocean in pursuit of fish and squid.

Ancient Hawaiians never lived in Kōkeʻe, but climbed this high to collect feathers. The *mamo* would be trapped on a sticky branch, its long yellow tail plucked for use in ceremonial cloaks and *leis*, and then released; the *ʻiʻiwi* was stripped bare and kept for food. The Hawaiians also came looking for the tall, straight *koa* trees, thrusting from the steepest valleys, that made the best canoes. They were guided by the *ʻelepaio*; if it settled for too long on a *koa*, the tree was riddled with insects and thus unsuitable for use.

All the native birds found on Kauai at the time of Captain Cook survived until 1964, when the last *akialoa* died. After that, the rarest was another honey-creeper, the **ʻōʻō ʻāʻā**, whose yellow "garter" feathers were prized by the Hawaiians. Before Hurricane Iwa hit Kōkeʻe in 1982, there were thought to be fewer than ten birds left, living deep in the Alakaʻi Swamp. Only one was ever subsequently spotted, tending its treetop nest and calling for a mate that never answered.

By far the most conspicuous bird in Kōkeʻe today is the **moa**, or **Red Jungle Fowl**. Descended from the chickens brought by the Polynesians, these raucous creatures strut around outside the museum and restaurant at Kanaloahuluhulu, or scurry down the trails. For all their haughty demeanor, they're not exactly intelligent; they peck away indiscriminately, and will no doubt try to eat your license plate or rearview mirror.

For more about Hawaiian birds, see p.432.

Away to the left, this makes a mile-long loop around some luscious mountain streams; turning right brings you (in about fifteen minutes) to a plank footbridge, two miles from Alakaʻi junction, that marks the end of the trail.

The **Kawaikoi Picnic Area** here is a broad meadow with two more shelters and a restroom. If you turn right on to the dirt road at the far end, a fifteen-minute climb brings you to the Alakaʻi Picnic Area and the trailhead of the **Alakaʻi Swamp Trail**. If you've parked up at Puʻu O Kila, you could walk to the Pihea/Alakaʻi intersection, then back up the Pihea Trail, and be back at your car within about five hours. By road, following the dirt road to the park headquarters and then climbing Waimea Canyon Drive, it's much farther.

Another four miles or so of dirt road lie beyond the Kawaikoi Picnic Area, but you'd need a four-wheel-drive vehicle, and a lot of time, to take advantage of the remote trails that lead along and down the far side of Waimea Canyon.

The Alaka'i Swamp Trail

The **Alaka'i Swamp Trail** was long renowned as not only the most arduous hike on Kauai, but also the dirtiest, a protracted wade through thigh-deep mud. These days, though, a boardwalk covers almost its entire 3.5-mile length, and it's nowhere near as fearsome as legend suggests.

Nonetheless, hikers still have to wage a constant battle of wits against the cloying black swamp, as thrusting tree roots and subsiding mud holes ensure that the boardwalk is never totally dependable. Apart from the magnificent **view** at the far end, the main reward for hikers is the swamp's rare and resplendent **vegetation**. Giant ferns dangle above the trail, and orchids gleam from the undergrowth, while the trees – especially in June – erupt into brilliant flowering displays.

As outlined on p.406, the second and more interesting half of the trail can be combined with walking the Pihea Trail from the Pu'u O Kila Lookout. If you want to hike the whole thing, however, start by driving as close as possible to the trailhead along the dirt road (marked *YWCA Camp Sloggett*) that leads right from Waimea Canyon Drive just beyond the Kōke'e State Park headquarters. Keep going beyond the YWCA camp, and park at the sign, 1.7 miles from the highway, that warns only four-wheel-drive vehicles can proceed.

Now walk about a mile further along the road, first sharply down to cross the Kauaikanana Stream and then back up again, until you come to a sign announcing the Nā Pali-Kona Forest Reserve, and another pointing to the trails nearby. This spot is the **Alaka'i Picnic Area**; ahead of you spreads your first large-scale overview of the swamp itself, while on the horizon to the left is the ridge that holds the highway and the Kalalau lookouts.

Before continuing, take the short spur trail to your right. After a few yards it stops at the end of a high promontory pointing straight towards **Po'omau Canyon**, one of the narrow gorges that feed into the top end of Waimea Canyon. A sheltered picnic table at the edge of the abyss commands superb views of the chasm below.

The Alaka'i Swamp **trailhead** is a five-minute walk down the rutted ridge-top track that leads left off the road. The narrow path starts by dropping abruptly, shored up against the precipices to either side; it then climbs and widens again to become a pleasant, grassy path. Half a mile along, the **boardwalk** – two parallel planks overlaid with rusty wire mesh – begins. Despite the mud, the trail is high and exposed, and for a while the trees thin out altogether. Another half-mile on, you meet the Pihea Trail at the **four-way intersection** (see p.406).

Continuing on the Alaka'i Swamp Trail from here, the boardwalk turns into a playful, willful companion. For most of the time one plank meets the next, but at some point, as they grow tauntingly further apart, you're bound to slip into the mud. For the first half-mile, the trail drops toward a gentle tributary of the Kawaikoi Stream, most of the descent on a wooden stairway. As you cross the stream, by stepping stones, you're still a full hour short of the end. Soon afterwards, the boardwalk stops as the trail climbs a high and relatively dry ridge through the forest, with thick green moss to either side. While the last significant climb is now behind you, the highest part of the swamp turns out to be the wettest, little more than one large pool of gloopy mud. Only the red blossoms of tiny, stunted *'ohi'a lehua* plants relieve the monotony. The boardwalk then returns to guide you across first a bog, then a rainforest, and finally a bleak, marshy plain.

The trail eventually comes to a dead end at a small wooden platform high on a hillside, engulfed for much of the time in swirling mists. Waiting for the clouds to clear, in the wettest place in the world, can feel like a loser's game, but the wind forever rustling the trees around you is a guarantee that they will. You'll then see that you've walked the length of the Nā Pali coast. This viewpoint – named **Kilohana** – stands atop the towering western wall of Wainiha Valley; far below, Wainiha Stream flows towards the ocean. Down the coast beyond the mouth of the valley curves the crescent of Hanalei Bay, while away to the right, inland, the high *pali* opposite stretches as far as the eye can see.

A constant succession of clouds race in to stream up the slopes, feeding the dense rainforest that somehow clings to their sides. In the intervals when you seem entirely cut off, you can reflect that in January 1871, Queen Emma (see p.84) reached this lonely eminence with a retinue of over a hundred companions. They camped out along the way, with the Queen singing songs to keep their spirits up, but were disappointed at the last. According to the commemorative chant, "*ē huli hoʻiʻo ka lani, ua kū ka ʻohu i nā pali*" – "the queen turned to go back, for the fog rested on the mountain."

A ground-level description of Wainiha Valley appears on p.377.

The Awaʻawapuhi Trail

From the left of Waimea Canyon Drive, halfway between the Kōkeʻe headquarters and Kalalau Lookout, the **Awaʻawapuhi Trail** drops steeply through three miles of forest to the **Awaʻawapuhi Valley**, tucked between the Nā Pali cliffs. Walking to the end takes little more than an hour, though climbing back up again is a different matter. The only views come right at the end, but they're stupendous enough to make this one of Kauai's finest hikes. Before you set off, be aware that the Awaʻawapuhi trailhead is notorious for vehicle break-ins, so leave nothing valuable in your car.

As the trail begins its inexorable descent, it's easy underfoot. At first the forest is largely *ʻohiʻa*, but as the path drops into hotter, drier territory, *koa* starts to predominate. Though most of the route remains in shade, after 1.5 miles the tree cover begins to thin out, and you get your first glimpses of the high parallel ridges to either side. At the 2.75-mile marker, a magnificent *hala pepe* tree has individual palm-like fronds growing from its branches. Shortly after that, keep going past the junction with the Nuʻalolo Cliff Trail (see below).

The end of the trail comes at mile marker 3, when suddenly, 2400ft above sea level, it runs out of ridge. The railing ahead marks the overlook at the head of the Awaʻawapuhi Valley. Far below, the Awaʻawapuhi River twists its way between two equally sinuous red ridges. Ancient Hawaiians said the valley was shaped by an eel slithering into the sea; its final thrashings mean that its ocean outlet is not visible. You can, however, see a huge expanse of ocean, and hear the distant roar of the surf. Most visitors venture a few steps beyond the railing, in search of the perfect photo; some fall and die.

Back to your left, another viewpoint looks out across Nuʻalolo Valley to the bare red top of the higher Nuʻalolo Ridge. Unlike in the Awaʻawapuhi Valley, which is in perpetual shade, trees can be seen on the valley floor. If the sight of the exposed ridge makes you reluctant to attempt the Nuʻalolo Trail, you won't be comforted to know that where you're standing looks just as bad from over there.

The Nuʻalolo Cliff Trail

In order to combine the Awaʻawapuhi and Nuʻalolo trails you have to edge your way along the gulf between the two, by means of the two-mile **Nuʻalolo Cliff Trail**. This is the one Kōkeʻe trail that you really *must* avoid if you have problems with vertigo.

From the intersection described above, the Nuʻalolo Cliff Trail dips down into a small patch of rainforest. There it crosses a gentle stream, slowly gathering pace as it approaches the plummet ahead, then traverses some attractive meadows, one of which holds a picnic shelter. Near the 1.75-mile marker, it rounds a fearsome bend above a colossal drop. The ground is loose red gravel, the trail a narrow slanting groove scuffed against the hillside. Dislodged pebbles tumble thousands of feet into the abyss, and the wayside rock, clutched for support, crumbles to dust in your hand.

Just after that you join the Nuʻalolo Trail, here 3.25 miles from its starting point, with the Lolo Vista Point (see below) another three-quarters of a mile away to your right.

The Nuʻalolo Trail

Like the parallel but slightly shorter Awaʻawapuhi Trail, the **Nuʻalolo Trail** is a footpath down a long ridge that culminates with sweeping Nā Pali views. If you're making the loop trip with the Awaʻawapuhi Trail, as outlined on p.406, it's best to walk the Nuʻalolo Trail from bottom to top, as it's a marginally easier climb. The description that follows, however, starts from the road and works down.

From its trailhead just below *Kōkeʻe Lodge*, the Nuʻalolo Trail starts with a surprise, switchbacking up and over Kaunuohua Ridge. Thereafter it drops progressively downhill, at times winding gently through the thick grass of the pretty upland meadows. After two miles, it begins to descend ever more steeply through a channel in places worn deep into the mud. While seldom dangerous, the last half-mile is precipitous in the extreme, straight down the slippery crest of the ridge. The fifteen-minute totter beyond the junction with the Nuʻalolo Cliff Trail (see above), along the exposed ridge towards **Lolo Vista Point**, is regarded as a separate trail, and one best left to the brave.

Contexts

Contexts

History

If a big wave comes in, large fishes will come from the dark Ocean which you never saw before, and when they see the small fishes they will eat them up. The ships of the white men have come, and smart people have arrived from the great countries which you have never seen before, they know our people are few in number and living in a small country; they will eat us up, such has always been the case with large countries, the small ones have been gobbled up.

David Malo, to the future King Kamehameha IV, 1837

The human history of Hawaii divides into three very distinct chapters. First came the era when the islands developed their own unique culture, as Polynesian settlers adapted their traditional way of life to this remote and pristine archipelago. Then came the islands' encounter with the rest of the world, and a hundred years of increasingly doomed resistance to the inevitable takeover by stronger foreign powers. The third stage began when Hawaii was incorporated into the United States, in 1898. Ever since then, the islands have been at the mercy of economic and political events in the rest of the world.

The age of migrations

The fiery origins of the Hawaiian islands have decisively shaped their destiny. These are the remotest islands on earth; as they have never been attached to a larger continent, humans have only ever been able to get here by crossing at least two thousand miles of treacherous ocean. Furthermore, being composed entirely of lava, they are devoid of metals and workable clays, the raw materials used to build civilizations elsewhere.

Until less than two thousand years ago, the islands remained unknown specks in the vast Pacific, populated by the mutated descendants of what few organisms had been carried here by wind or wave (see p.432). Carbon dating of fishhooks and artifacts found at sites such as Bellows Beach on Oahu and Ka Lae (South Point) on the Big Island suggests that Hawaii's earliest human settlers arrived during the second or third centuries AD. Except perhaps for their first chance landfall, they came equipped to colonize, carrying goats, dogs, pigs, coconut palms, bananas, and sugar cane, among other essentials.

These first inhabitants were **Polynesians**, and probably arrived from the Marquesas Islands, northeast of Tahiti. Their ancestors had originally spread from the shores of Asia to inhabit Indonesia and the Solomon Islands around thirty thousand years ago. Such migrations, across coastal waters shallower than they are today, involved for the most part hopping from island to island without having to cross open ocean. Twenty-five thousand years later they acquired the techniques to venture further afield. For more on how such migrations were carried out, see p.429.

Just over three thousand years ago, when the "Little Climatic Optimum" made wind and sea conditions milder, the voyagers reached Fiji. They then spread via Tahiti

The ancient Hawaiians

For more on the daily life, traditions, and culture of the **ancient Hawaiians**, see p.425; for more about their **voyaging techniques**, see p.429.

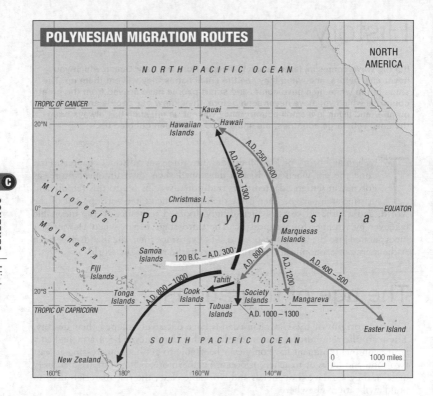

POLYNESIAN MIGRATION ROUTES

to populate the entire "Polynesian Triangle," extending from Easter Island in the east to Hawaii in the north and finally down to New Zealand in the south.

Thanks to DNA testing, it is now known for certain that the Polynesians entered the Pacific from Southeast Asia. Thor Heyerdahl's argument for an American origin, as also promulgated by the Mormon Church in Oahu's Polynesian Cultural Center, has been finally disproved. On the other hand, Polynesians do seem to have reached the Americas. Evidence of Polynesian-style religious structures, dating to 600 AD, has been found on the Channel Islands, off the coast of California. Some voyagers must have returned to Polynesia via South America, too, as that's the only way the sweet potato could have reached the islands.

Traditional historical accounts of the settling of Hawaii describe the arrival of successive waves of migrants at widely spaced intervals. Marquesas Islanders are said to have continued to arrive until the eighth century, after which there was a gap before they were followed by Tahitians between the eleventh and fourteenth centuries. It's said that the warrior-priest **Pa'ao** was forced to flee Tahiti for some transgression, chanced upon the peaceful islands of Hawaii, and returned to Tahiti to report that these wonderful new lands were ripe for the picking. Certainly, as described on p.428, the elaborate, restrictive *kapu* system, along with the cult of human sacrifice, seems to have reached Hawaii around the twelfth century, and it seems clear that a new hierarchical order was imposed by force, with each island being violently invaded and conquered in turn. The very name **"Hawaii"** is known previously to have been an alternative, "poetic" name for the largest of the leeward Tahitian islands, Raiatea, the site of the voyaging temple of Taputapuatea.

This may not have been the first time the Marquesans were overrun. In legend, the earliest Hawaiians frequently figure as the **menehune**, often described these days as hairy elves or leprechauns who worked at night and hid by day. It seems likely that the word is, in fact, a corruption of the Tahitian *manhune*, which means "lacking in lineage," and was applied to the original Polynesian people of Tahiti. These could well have been displaced by warriors from Raiatea, first from their homeland to the Marquesas, then forced to escape from there to Hawaii, before the Tahitians finally followed them to Hawaii itself. Rather than literally being dwarfs, they were probably treated as social inferiors by their conquerors, and became the lowest caste in Hawaiian society.

It's not known for certain whether large-scale migration from Tahiti actually took place, or whether a small warrior elite simply arrived and took over. It's still possible to meet Hawaiians, who proudly trace their ancestry back to the Marquesans rather than the Tahitians. Whether or not Tahitians did reach Hawaii in significant numbers, by the time the Europeans appeared, no two-way voyaging between Hawaii and the South Pacific had taken place for perhaps as long as five hundred years.

The coming of the foreigners

No Western ship is known for certain to have chanced upon Hawaii before that of **Captain Cook**, in January 1778; the first European to sail across the Pacific, the Portuguese Ferdinand Magellan, did so without seeing a single island. When Cook first encountered Hawaii, he failed to spot both Maui and the Big Island before stumbling upon the western shores of Kauai. He was en route to the north Pacific, in search of the Northwest Passage (which at the time did not exist, though it has recently been created thanks to climate change). When he returned to Hawaii a year later, his two ships, the *Discovery* and the *Resolution*, skirted Maui and then, to the fury of their crews, cruised the coast of the Big Island for almost seven weeks, before anchoring in Kealakekua Bay. There Cook met with the island's chief, Kalaniopu'u, and was greeted in ceremonies at the Hikiau *heiau*; there, too, within a few weeks, he was killed. See p.148 for an account of the events leading to his death, and the legends that grew up around it.

Cook named the **"Sandwich Islands"** after Lord Sandwich. News of their existence reached the rest of the world after his death by way of the **Russians**, as his ships later halted for provisions on the Siberian coast. Hawaii swiftly became a

Did Cook come first?

Although Captain Cook is always credited with "discovering" Hawaii, considerable evidence points to pre-Cook contact between Hawaiians and outsiders. **Spanish** vessels disappeared in the northern Pacific from the 1520s onwards, while during the two centuries, starting in 1565, that the "Manila Galleons" made annual voyages across the Pacific between Mexico and the Philippines, at least nine such ships were lost. Cook observed that the first Hawaiians he encountered were familiar with iron, and even suggested that some bore European features.

Hawaiian legends speak of several plausible encounters. Thanks to the many detailed genealogies of Hawaiian families, it's possible to work out roughly when they took place. The earliest known was in the middle of the thirteenth century, when a vessel remembered as *Mamala* arrived at Wailuku on Maui. The crew of five, men and women, were pale, and became the ancestors of a light-skinned family. As no Europeans were in the Pacific at that time, it's possible they had drifted astray from **Japan**.

On the Big Island, during the reign of Keali'iokaloa, the son of Umi, a ship called *Konaliloha* was wrecked on the reef in or near Kealakekua Bay. The only survivors were a brother and sister who swam ashore, where they remained and had children. That can be dated to November 1527, when two small Spanish ships, the *Santiago* and the *Espiritu Santo*, went missing in the north Pacific. Distorted versions of the same story are told on Maui and Kauai, and it's also said that more Spanish mariners were shipwrecked on the north coast of Lanai later in the sixteenth century. Lanai's museum holds objects thought to have been carved from the ballast of such a wreck.

Written evidence from Western sources includes the log of the Dutch ship *Lefda* in 1599, which spoke of eight seamen deserting to an unknown island at this latitude. Most compelling of all, in 1555, the Spanish navigator Juan Gaetano named and charted what he called the Islas de Mesa, or "The Table Islands." This group subsequently appeared on Spanish naval maps, at the correct latitude but roughly ten degrees too far east. Longitude at the time was estimated by dead reckoning, so such mistakes were easily made, especially in the face of unfamiliar ocean currents. British sailors captured such a map in 1742, showing "La Mesa," "Los Monges," and "La Desgraciada," and Cook's crew debated whether these were the same islands that they had found.

Spanish influence might explain the similarity of the red and yellow feather headdresses of Hawaiian warriors to the helmets of Spanish soldiers, and account for the phenomenal speed with which syphilis spread through the islands after it was supposedly introduced by the Cook expedition. A skeleton of a young woman has been unearthed on Oahu who appears to have died of syphilis in the mid-seventeenth century; other contemporary burials contain small scraps of sailcloth. Finally, there are also much earlier legends of inter-island wars for the possession of a mighty Excalibur-style iron sword, which may have been washed ashore accidentally from medieval Japan.

port of call for all traders crossing the ocean, and especially for ships carrying furs from the Pacific Northwest to China.

Kamehameha the Great

For a few brief years the Hawaiians remained masters of their own destiny. The major beneficiary of the change in circumstances was the astute young Big Island warrior **Kamehameha**.

Although he remains the greatest Hawaiian hero, to some extent Kamehameha played into the hands of the newcomers who flocked to the islands from all over the world. Most governmental representatives were under orders not to trade **guns** with the Hawaiians, but Russian fur traders, in particular, had no such scruples,

and surprise Hawaiian attacks on merchant vessels also enabled Kamehameha to build up his own arsenal of foreign weapons. His subsequent conquest of the entire archipelago, and his creation of a single Hawaiian kingdom, greatly simplified the maneuvers that enabled outsiders to achieve first economic, and eventually political, domination over the islands.

The future Kamehameha the Great was born in northern Kohala on the Big Island, in 1758. Both his mother, Kekuiapoiwa, and father, Keōuau, were of royal blood, though it's not clear whether they were niece and nephew of the then ruler of the Big Island, Alapa'i, or of **Kahekili**, the ruler of Maui. It has even been suggested that Kahekili himself was Kamehameha's true father. The infant Kamehameha was raised in seclusion in Waipi'o Valley.

By the time Kamehameha grew to adulthood, Kalaniopu'u had become high chief of the Big Island. As a valuable warrior for the king, Kamehameha was present on the waterfront at the death of Captain Cook. When Kalaniopu'u died in 1782, he designated his son Kīwala'o to be his heir, but civil war broke out almost immediately. By defeating Kīwala'o in battle, Kamehameha took control of the Kona, Kohala, and Hāmākua regions; however, Kīwala'o's brother **Keōua** survived to establish his own power base in Ka'ū.

For more than a decade a three-way struggle for domination raged back and forth between Kamehameha, Keōua, and Kahekili, who at this point ruled both Maui and Oahu. It briefly looked as though Kahekili might unite all the islands, but his hopes of capturing the Big Island were dashed by the **Battle of the Red-Mouthed Gun** off Waipi'o Valley in 1791, when for the first time Hawaiian fleets were equipped with cannons, operated by foreign gunners. The long campaign against Keōua (many of whose warriors were wiped out by an eruption of Kīlauea; see p.206) finally came to an end that same year. At the dedication of the great *heiau* at Pu'ukoholā, the last of the *luakinis*, Keōua himself was the chief sacrifice.

Kamehameha had previously conquered **Maui** through a bloody victory at 'Īao Valley in 1790, only to lose it again when he was forced to turn his attention back to Keōua. As sole ruler of the Big Island, he went on to reconquer first Maui and Lanai, then to capture **Molokai** in 1794, and to take **Oahu** after one last battle at Nu'uanu Valley, in 1795. Finally, after two unsuccessful attempts to invade **Kauai**, he settled for accepting tribute from its ruler, Kaumuali'i. So eager was Kamehameha to obtain military assistance from the Europeans at this time that he briefly ceded the Big Island to Great Britain, though this was never made formal (hence the British "Union Jack" that's still incorporated into the Hawaiian flag). Kamehameha even considered the possibility of launching expeditions against the islands of the South Pacific.

By now, many Europeans had settled permanently on the islands. Kamehameha's most important foreign advisers were John Young and Isaac Davis (see p.234), who, in return for royal patronage, led his armies into battle, personally gunning down enemy warriors in droves. In addition, European artisans such as blacksmiths, carpenters, and stonemasons introduced practical skills of all kinds to the islands.

For some time Kamehameha had his capital in the fledgling port of Lahaina on Maui. By the time he died in 1819, however, he had returned to live in a palace at Kailua on the Kona coast of the Big Island.

The end of the old order

Kamehameha's successor, his son Liholiho – also known as **Kamehameha II** – was a weak figure who was dominated by the regent **Queen Ka'ahumanu** (see p.288). As a woman, she was excluded from the *luakini heiaus* that were the real center of political power, so she set out to bring down the priesthood. Liholiho was plied with drink and cajoled into dining with women at a public banquet; that simple act brought

about the end of the *kapu* system (see p.428) and precipitated a civil war in which the upholders of the ancient religion were defeated in a battle near Hōnaunau on the Big Island. Altars and idols at *heiaus* throughout Hawaii were overthrown and destroyed.

That threw Hawaii into moral anarchy at the very moment when the first Puritan **missionaries** arrived. The creation of the Sandwich Islands Mission stemmed from a visit to New England by **Henry ʻOpukahaʻia**. A *kahuna* priest from Hikiau *heiau* on the Big Island, he converted to Christianity, but died in his early twenties while a student at the Foreign Mission School in Cornwall, Connecticut. As he breathed his last, he lamented his failure to return to Hawaii to convert his brethren.

The heartfelt prayer and hard cash of New England worthies, deeply moved by the young man's tragic end, enabled the mission's first two ministers, **Rev Hiram Bingham** and **Rev Asa Thurston**, to sail from Boston in the brig *Thaddeus* on October 23, 1819. According to their instructions, they were sent for "no private end, for no earthly object," but "wholly for the good of others and for the glory of God our Savior. You are to aim at nothing short of covering those islands with fruitful fields and pleasant dwellings, and schools and churches."

After a five-month, eighteen-thousand-mile journey, they reached Kailua Bay on April 4, 1820. Among the Hawaiians, there was considerable debate as to whether the missionaries should be allowed to land at all; Kaʻahumanu didn't exactly jump at the chance to replace the old priests with a new bunch of interfering moralizers. In the end, the counsel of the aging John Young played a decisive role, but only Thurston was allowed to remain in Kailua. Bingham was obliged to settle in Honolulu, where he denounced his flock as the "stupid and polluted worshippers of demons."

The missionaries' wholehearted capitalism, and their harsh strictures on the easygoing Hawaiian lifestyle, might have been calculated to compound the chaos. They set about obliging Hawaiian women to cover unseemly flesh in billowing *muʻumuʻu* "Mother Hubbard" dresses, condemning the hula as lascivious and obscene, and discouraging surfing as a waste of time, liable to promote gambling and lewdness.

Meanwhile, Liholiho, who never quite took to the new faith, had been seized with an urge to visit England. He died of measles in London in 1824, without ever meeting King George IV (who referred to him as a "damned cannibal"). When the news reached Hawaii, he was succeeded by his brother Kauikeaouli, who reigned as **Kamehameha III**, although Queen Kaʻahumanu remained very much in control. She had become an enthusiastic promoter of Christianity after being nursed through a grave illness by Bingham's wife, Sybil.

In general, the missionaries concentrated their attentions on the ruling class, the *aliʻi*, believing that they would then bring the commoners into the fold. They also devised Hawaii's first alphabet and founded countless schools; one on Kauai famously started out using surfboards for desks. On Maui in particular, the support of the ardently Christian Governor Hoapili facilitated a hugely successful program of education, to the extent that Hawaii achieved the highest literacy rate on earth.

At first, great tensions manifested themselves between the missionaries and the new breed of foreign entrepreneurs. These were to disappear as their offspring intermarried, acquired land, and formed the backbone of the emerging middle class.

The foreigners take control

For ordinary Hawaiians, the sudden advent of capitalism was devastating. Any notion of Hawaiian self-sufficiency was abandoned in favor of selling the islands' resources for cash returns. The most extreme example of this was the earliest: the **sandalwood** trade.

Even greater than the economic impact of the foreigners was the physical impact of the **diseases** they brought with them. Epidemic after epidemic swept the islands, reducing the native Hawaiian population from something between 300,000 and 500,000 when Cook arrived to little over fifty thousand a century later. As agricultural laborers were imported from the rest of the world, the Hawaiians came to be outnumbered in their own islands.

Sandalwood logs were first picked up from Hawaii in 1791, when the crew of the *Lady Washington* spotted them in a consignment of fuel collected at Waimea on Kauai. Traders had been searching for years for a commodity to sell to the Chinese in return for tea to meet English demand. Once it was realized that the Chinese would pay enormous prices for the fragrant wood (the scent of a bowl of sandalwood chips lasts for up to fifty years), the race was on.

Kamehameha had a monopoly on the trade until his death, but thereafter individual chiefs out for their own profit forced all the commoners under their sway to abandon taro farming and fishing and become wage slaves. The wood was sold in units known as *piculs*, which weighed just over 133 pounds. "*Picul* pits," the exact size and shape of a ship's hold, were dug in the hills and filled with logs. Men, women, and children then carried the wood down to the sea on their naked backs. As the trees became rarer, the burden of the laborers, forced to search ever higher in the mountains, grew worse; it's said that they deliberately uprooted saplings to drive the tree to extinction to insure that their children would not have to do the same cruel work.

Each *picul* of sandalwood sold for one cent in Hawaii and 34 cents in China; most of the profits went to New England merchants. By the end of the 1820s, the forests were almost entirely denuded, the traditional Hawaiian agricultural system had collapsed, and many chiefs found themselves greatly in debt to foreign merchants, with no obvious way to pay.

Whaling

The first **whaling ships** arrived in Hawaii in 1820, the same year as the missionaries. Their impact was equally dramatic. With the ports of Japan closed to outsiders, Hawaii swiftly became the center of the industry. Not that any whales were actually hunted in Hawaii; visitors often assume that it was the humpback whales seen in Hawaiian waters today that attracted the whaling fleets, but humpbacks were not hunted during the nineteenth century. When caught with the technology of the time, they sank uselessly to the ocean floor. Instead, the whalers chased other species in the waters around Japan in winter and in the Arctic in summer, and called at Hawaii each spring and fall to unload oil and baleen to be shipped home in other vessels, to stock up, and to change crew.

Any Pacific port would have seemed a godsend to the whalers, who were away from New England for three years at a time and paid so badly that most were either fugitives or plain mad. Hawaii was such a paradise that up to half each crew would desert, to be replaced by Hawaiian *sailamokus*, born seafarers eager to see the world.

From the very first, Westerners recognized **Honolulu** as possessing the finest deep-water harbor in the Pacific (in reference to the current city, not Pearl Harbor, which did not become usable until it was dredged much later). Hawaiians had never required such anchorages, and Honolulu in ancient times had been a tiny village. It swiftly became the whalemen's favorite port, a status it retained until the capital, and the missionary presence that went with it, moved to Honolulu from **Lahaina** on Maui in 1845. The whalers swapped the other way, and both ports became notorious for such diseases as syphilis, influenza, measles, typhoid, and smallpox.

Provisioning the whaling ships became the main focus of the Hawaiian economy. The uplands of Maui were irrigated to grow temperate crops such as white potatoes, while cattle ranches were established on both Maui and the Big Island. The Hispanic cowboys imported to work there, known as **paniolos** (a corruption of *españoles*), were among the first of the many overseas ethnic groups to make their homes in Hawaii.

The Great Mahele

By 1844, foreign-born fortune-seekers dominated the Hawaiian government. Fourteen of King Kamehameha III's closest advisers were white, including his three most important ministers. Various foreign powers jostled for position; it's easy now to forget that it was not inevitable that the islands would become American. After all, it was not until the 1840s that New Zealand was snapped up by the English, and Tahiti by the French, and both those European powers retained ambitions in Hawaii. In 1843, a British commander captured Honolulu, claiming all Hawaii for Queen Victoria, and it took six months for word to arrive from London that it had all been a mistake. (At the restoration celebration in Honolulu, on July 31, 1843, King Kamehameha III delivered the short speech that remains the official motto of Hawaii – "*ua mau ke ea o ka 'āina i ka pono*," "the life of the land is perpetuated in righteousness".) In 1849, a French admiral did much the same thing, but this time everyone simply waited until he got bored and sailed away again.

The most important obstacle to the advance of the foreigners was that they could not legally own **land**. In the old Hawaii there was no private land; all was held in trust by the chief, who apportioned it to individuals at his continued pleasure only. The king was requested to "clarify" the situation. A land commission was set up, under the direction of a missionary, and its deliberations resulted in the **Great Mahele** ("Division of Lands") in 1848. In theory the land was parceled out to native Hawaiians only, with sixty percent going to the Crown and the government, thirty-nine percent to just over two hundred chiefs, and less than one percent to eleven thousand commoners. However, claiming and keeping the land involved complex legal procedures and required expenditures that few Hawaiians were able to meet. In any case, within two years the *haoles* (non-Hawaiians) were also permitted to buy and sell land. The often-heard jibe that the missionaries "came to Hawaii to do good – and they done good" stems from the speed with which they amassed vast acreages. Their children became Hawaii's wealthiest and most powerful class.

Many Hawaiians were denied access to the lands they had traditionally worked, arrested for vagrancy, and used as forced labor on the construction of roads and ports for the new landowners. Meanwhile, a simultaneous **water grab** took place, with new white-owned plantations diverting water for their thirsty foreign crops from the Hawaiian farmers downstream.

The sugar industry and the US Civil War

At the height of the whaling boom, many newly rich entrepreneurs began to put their money into **sugar**. Hawaii's first sugar plantation started in 1835 in Kōloa on Kauai (see p.387), and it swiftly became clear that this was an industry where large-scale operators were the most efficient and profitable. By 1847 the field had narrowed to five main players, four of whom had started out by provisioning whaling ships. These **Big Five** were Hackfield & Co (later to become Amfac), C. Brewer & Co, Theo Davies Co, Castle & Cooke (later Dole), and Alexander & Baldwin. Thereafter, they worked in close cooperation with each other, united by common interests and, often, family ties.

When **Civil War** hit the United States, and the markets of the North cast about for an alternative source of sugar to the Confederate South, Hawaii was poised to take advantage. The consequent boom in the Hawaiian sugar industry, and the ever-increasing integration of Hawaii into the American economic mainstream, was the most important factor in the eventual loss of Hawaiian sovereignty.

The Civil War also coincided with the **decline of whaling**. Several ships were bought and deliberately sunk to blockade Confederate ports, while the discovery of petroleum diminished the demand for whale oil. The final disaster came in 1871, when 31 vessels lingered in the Arctic too long at the end of the season, became frozen in, and had to be abandoned.

By the 1870s, cane fields were spreading across all the islands. The ethnic mixture of modern Hawaii is largely the product of the search for laborers prepared to submit to the draconian conditions on the plantations. Once the Hawaiians had demonstrated their unwillingness to knuckle under, agents of the Hawaiian Sugar Planters Association scoured the world in search of peasants eager to find new lives.

As members of each ethnic group in turn got their start on the plantations, and then left to find more congenial employment or establish their own businesses, a new source of labor had to be found. It soon became clear that few single men chose to stay on the plantations when their contracts expired – many left for California to join the Gold Rush – so the planters began to try to lure families to Hawaii, which meant providing better housing than the original basic dormitories.

First came the **Chinese**, recruited with a $10 inducement in Hong Kong, shipped over for free, and then signed to five-year contracts at $6 or less per month. The **Portuguese** followed, brought from Madeira and the Azores from 1878 onwards by planters who thought they might adjust more readily to the dominant *haole*-Hawaiian culture. **Koreans** arrived during the brief period between 1902, when they were first allowed to leave their country, and 1905, when it was invaded by the **Japanese**, who themselves came in great numbers until 1907, when the so-called Gentleman's Agreement banned further immigration. **Filipinos**, whose country had been annexed by the US in 1898, began to arrive in their stead, to find similar climate, soil, and crops to their homeland.

Smaller-scale plantations were also established to grow other crops, such as **pineapples** (discovered in Paraguay early in the sixteenth century), which spread to cover much of Oahu, Maui, and Lanai, and **coffee**, which was brought to Hawaii by Chief Boki in 1825 and grew most successfully on the Kona slopes of the Big Island (see p.145).

The end of the Kingdom of Hawaii

Hawaii is ours. As I look back upon the first steps in this miserable business, and as I contemplate the means used to complete the outrage, I am ashamed of the whole affair.

US President Grover Cleveland, 1893

After sugar prices dropped at the end of the Civil War, the machinations of the sugar industry to get favorable prices on the mainland moved Hawaii inexorably toward **annexation** by the US. In 1876 the Treaty of Reciprocity abolished all trade barriers and tariffs between the US and the Kingdom of Hawaii; within fifteen years, sugar exports to the US had increased tenfold.

By now, the Kamehameha dynasty had come to an end, and the heir to the Hawaiian throne was chosen by the national legislature. The first such king, William Lunalilo, died in 1874, after barely a year in office. In the ensuing elections, **Queen Emma**, the Anglophile widow of Kamehameha IV (see p.84), lost to **King David Kalākaua**. The "Merrie Monarch" is affectionately remembered today for his role

The Hawaiian monarchy	
Kamehameha I	1791–1819
Kamehameha II (Liholiho)	1819–1824
Kamehameha III (Kauikeaouli)	1825–1854
Kamehameha IV (Alexander Liholiho)	1854–1863
Kamehameha V (Lot Kamehameha)	1863–1872
William C. Lunalilo	1873–1874
David Kalākaua	1874–1891
Lili'uokalani	1891–1893

in reviving traditional Hawaiian pursuits such as hula and surfing, but he was widely seen as being pro-American, and a riot protesting his election in 1874 virtually destroyed Honolulu's Old Court House. King Kalākaua was to a significant extent the tool of the plantation owners. In 1887 an all-white (and armed) group of "concerned businessmen" forced through the "Bayonet Constitution," in which he surrendered power to an assembly elected by property owners (of any nationality) rather than citizens. The US government was swiftly granted exclusive rights to what became Pearl Harbor.

Kalākaua died in San Francisco in 1891. In his absence, his sister **Lili'uokalani** had served as regent, and she now became queen. When she proclaimed her desire for a new constitution, the same group of businessmen, who had now convened themselves into an "**Annexation Club**," called in the US warship *Boston*, then in Honolulu, and declared a **provisional government**.

President Grover Cleveland (a Democrat) responded that "Hawaii was taken possession of by the United States forces without the consent or wish of the government of the islands…[It] was wholly without justification…not merely a wrong but a disgrace." With phenomenal cheek, the provisional government rejected his demand for the restoration of the monarchy, saying the US should not "interfere in the internal affairs of their sovereign nation." They found defenders in the Republican US Congress and declared themselves a **republic** on July 4, 1894, with **Sanford Dole** as their first President.

Following an abortive coup attempt in 1895, Queen Lili'uokalani was charged with **treason**. She was placed under house arrest, first in 'Iolani Palace and later at her Honolulu home of Washington Place. Though she lived until 1917, all hopes of a restoration of Hawaiian independence were dashed in 1897, when a Republican president, McKinley, came to office claiming "Annexation is not a change. It is a consummation." The strategic value of Pearl Harbor was emphasized by the Spanish–American War in the Philippines, and on August 12, 1898, Hawaii was formally **annexed** as a territory of the United States.

A territory and a state

At the moment of annexation there was no question of Hawaii becoming a state; the whites were outnumbered ten to one and had no desire to afford the rest of the islanders the protection of US labor laws, let alone to give them the vote. (Sanford Dole said that natives couldn't expect to vote "simply because they were grown up.") Furthermore, as the proportion of Hawaiians of Japanese descent (*nisei*) increased (to 25 percent by 1936), Congress feared the prospect of a state whose inhabitants might consider their primary allegiance to be to Japan.

Consequently, Hawaii remained for the first half of the twentieth century the virtual fiefdom of the Big Five, who, through their control of agriculture (they owned 96 percent of the sugar crop), dominated transport, banks, utilities, insurance, and government.

The endemic racism of Hawaii's ruling elite was notoriously exposed during the 1930s by the so-called **Massie Case**. After Thalia Massie, the (white) wife of a naval officer, alleged that she'd been gang-raped in 1931, a group of five young men, of assorted ancestry, were arrested on flimsy evidence. When a jury failed to reach a guilty verdict, Thalia's mother and husband abducted and murdered one of the supposed suspects. Several elements in the case – including threats by a senior US naval official at Pearl Harbor to promote a coup if the verdict was not to his liking; the astonishing anti-Hawaiian racism of the US media; and the release of the murderers after an hour's detention – all unexpectedly conspired to create a new solidarity among ordinary Hawaiian residents. For the first time, Hawaii's many immigrant groups found common cause with each other and with the native Hawaiians, and a new identity started to emerge that was to reshape the islands.

That change truly took effect during World War II. The Japanese offensive on Pearl Harbor (see p.88) meant that Hawaii was the only part of the United States to be attacked in the war, and demonstrated just how crucial the islands were to the rest of America. Military bases and training camps were established throughout Hawaii, many of which remain operational. In addition, Hawaiian troops played an active role in the war. Veterans of the much-decorated 442nd Regimental Combat Team – composed of Japanese Hawaiians who, for obvious reasons, were sent to fight in Europe – became a leading force in Hawaiian politics.

The main trend in Hawaiian history since the war has been the slow decline of agriculture and the rise of **tourism**. Strikes organized along ethnic lines in the sugar plantations had consistently failed in the past, but from 1937 on, labor leaders began to organize workers of all races and all crafts, in solidarity with mainland unions. In 1946, the plantation workers won their first victory. Thanks to the campaigns that followed, the long-term Republican domination of state politics ended, and Hawaii's agricultural workers became the highest paid in the world. Arguably, this led to the eventual disappearance of all their jobs in the face of Third World competition. Only one sugar plantation now survives in the whole of Hawaii, on Maui.

Hawaii finally became the fiftieth of the United States in 1959, after a plebiscite showed a seventeen-to-one majority in favor, with the only significant opposition coming from the few remaining native Hawaiians. **Statehood** coincided with the first jet flight to Hawaii, which halved the previous nine-hour flight time from California. These two factors triggered a boom in **tourism** – many visitors had had their first sight of Hawaii as GIs in the war – and also in migration from the mainland to Hawaii.

Official figures showing the growth of the Hawaiian economy since statehood conceal a decline in living standards for many Hawaiians, with rises in consumer prices far outstripping rises in wages. Real-estate prices in particular have rocketed, so that many islanders are obliged to work at two jobs, others end up sleeping on the beaches, and young Hawaiians emigrate in droves with no prospect of being able to afford to return.

The sovereignty movement

During the late 1980s, broad-based support mushroomed for the concept of **Hawaiian sovereignty**, meaning some form of restoration of the rights of native Hawaiians. Pride in the Polynesian past was rekindled by such means as the

voyages of the *Hōkūle'a* canoe (see p.429) and the successful campaign to claim back the island of **Kaho'olawe**, which had been used since the war as a Navy bombing range (see p.260).

In retrospect, the movement can be seen to have culminated in 1993, when massive demonstrations outside 'Iolani Palace commemorated the centenary of the coup against Queen Lili'uokalani. Later that year, President Clinton signed an official **Apology to Native Hawaiians**, in which the US government formally acknowledged the illegality of the US overthrow of the Hawaiian monarchy. At that point, everyone in Hawaii seemed to expect that some form of sovereignty lay just over the horizon.

Since then debate as to the shape sovereignty might take has revealed deep divisions in the state. There has been a considerable backlash among elements of Hawaii's non-native (and, in particular, Caucasian) population. High-profile court cases have seen successful challenges to various state programs designed to benefit native Hawaiians.

There now seems less prospect than ever of the solution advocated by many Hawaiian activists – the re-emergence of Hawaii as an independent nation. After the federal indifference of the Bush years, however, the election of a Hawaiian-born president has helped to re-kindle the possibility of some degree of recognition of Hawaiian sovereignty. As this book went to press, the so-called **Akaka Bill**, sponsored by veteran Hawaii senator Daniel Akaka, was trundling through Congress. While its ultimate provisions remain a matter for speculation, it's rooted in the granting to native Hawaiians of nation-within-a-nation status, as with Native American groups on the mainland. The major bone of contention is what that will mean for restitution or otherwise of **land** claimed by native Hawaiians – it also precludes for the moment any right to operate casinos in Hawaii.

Although Hawaiians are hugely proud that **Barack Obama** was born and raised on Oahu – for details, see p.83 – his career has been entirely played out on the mainland, and has had little impact on the islands' political scene. Much the biggest news of recent years has been instead the latest economic downturn, and especially its effect on **tourism**. Visitor numbers have been dropping, and investment drying up, and once again Hawaii finds itself at the mercy of international forces over which it has minimal control.

Ancient culture and society

No written record exists of the centuries between the arrival of the Polynesians and the first contact with Europeans. Sacred chants, passed down through the generations, show a history packed with feuds and forays between the islands, and the rise and fall of dynasties, but the specific dates are conspicuous by their absence. However, oral traditions do provide a detailed picture of the day-to-day life of ordinary Hawaiians.

Developing a civilization on such isolated islands, without metals and workable clays, presented the settlers with many challenges. Nevertheless, by the late eighteenth century, the Hawaiian islands were home to around a million people. Two hundred years later, the population has climbed back to a similar level. Now, however, virtually no pure-blooded Hawaiians remain, and the islands are no longer even close to being self-sufficient. The population distribution has changed, too; early explorers often described being greeted by vast numbers of canoes in areas that are now all but uninhabited. The Big Island's population would have been far larger than the 176,000 it is today, and Oahu's population smaller, but no precise figures are known.

Daily life

In a sense, ancient Hawaii had no economy, not even barter. Although then, as now, most people lived close to the coast, each island was organized into wedge-shaped land divisions called **ahupua'a**, which stretched from the ocean to the mountains. *Ahupua'a* literally means a place where hogs were stored or gathered, and the boundaries between one and the next were marked by an altar bearing a carved image of a pig's head. The abundant fruits of the earth and sea were simply shared among the inhabitants within each *ahupua'a*.

While there's some truth in the idea of pre-contact Hawaii as a leisured paradise, it took a lot of work to make it that way. Coconut palms were planted along the seashore to provide food, clothing, and shade for coastal villages, and bananas and other food plants distributed inland. Crops such as sugar cane were cultivated with the aid of complex systems of terraces and irrigation channels. Taro, whose leaves were eaten as "greens" and whose roots were mashed to produce the staple *poi*, was grown in *lo'i*, which (like rice paddies) are kept constantly submerged, in the lush windward valleys such as Hanalei on Kauai, Waimea on Oahu, Hālawa on Molokai, and Waipi'o on the Big Island.

Most **fishing** took place in shallow inshore waters. Fishhooks made from human bone were considered especially effective; the most prized hooks were made from the bones of chiefs who had no body hair, so those unfortunate individuals were renowned for their low life expectancy. Nets were never cast from boats, but shallow bays were dragged by communal groups of wading men drawing in *hukilau* nets. (Elvis did it in *Blue Hawaii*, and you occasionally see people doing it today.) There was also a certain amount of freshwater fishing in the mountain streams, especially for shrimp, catfish, and goby. Fish were caught by placing basket-like nets at a narrow point, then dislodging stones upstream.

In addition, the art of **aquaculture** – fish farming – was more highly developed in Hawaii than anywhere in Polynesia. It reached its most refined form in the extensive networks of fishponds that ringed much of Hawaii's shoreline; the best surviving examples are along the southeast coast of Molokai (see p.316) and near

Līhu'e on Kauai. Such fishponds were usually constructed to demonstrate the power of a particular chief and increase his wealth; the fish would be reserved for his personal consumption.

Few people lived in the higher forested slopes, but these served as the source of vital raw materials such as *koa* wood for canoes and weapons. The ancients even ventured to the summit of Mauna Kea on the Big Island; as the only point in the Pacific to be glaciated during the last Ice Age, it has the hardest basalt on the islands. Stone from the **adze quarry**, 12,400 feet up, was used for all basic tools.

Ordinary commoners – the **maka'āinana** – lived in simple windowless huts known as *hales*. Most of these were thatched with *pili* grass, though in the driest areas ordinary people didn't bother with roofs. Buildings of all kinds were usually raised on platforms of stone; rounded boulders were taken from riverbeds and hauled long distances for that purpose, and were also used to make roads. Matting would have covered the floor, while the pounded tree bark called *kapa* (known as *tapa* elsewhere in the Pacific, and decorated with patterns) served as clothing and bedding. Lacking pottery, households made abundant use of gourds, wooden dishes, and woven baskets; chiefs would sometimes decorate bowls and calabashes with the teeth of their slain enemies, as a deliberate desecration of their remains.

The most popular pastime was **surfing**. Petroglyphs depicting surfers have been found, and there were even surfing *heiaus*. Ordinary people surfed on five- to seven-foot boards known as *alaia*, and also had *paipus*, the equivalent of the modern boogie-board; only the *ali'i* used the thick sixteen-foot *olo* boards, made of dark oiled *wiliwili* or *koa* wood. On land the *ali'i* raced narrow sleds on purpose-built, grass-covered *hōlua* slides, and staged boxing tournaments.

The ali'i

The ruling class, the **ali'i**, stood at the apex of Hawaiian society. In theory, heredity counted for everything, and great chiefs demonstrated their fitness to rule by the length of their genealogies. In fact the *ali'i* were educated as equals, and chiefs won the very highest rank largely through physical prowess and force of personality. To hang on to power, the king had to be seen as devoutly religious and to treat his people fairly.

For most of Hawaiian history, each island was divided into a varying number of chiefdoms, with huge potential for intrigue, faction, and warfare. Canoes being the basic means of transportation, it was also feasible for chiefs to launch inter-island campaigns. Kauai managed to remain consistently independent, thanks to the wide, dangerous channel separating it from the windward islands, but as the centuries went by large scale expeditions between Oahu, Maui, and the Big Island became ever more frequent. Lanai and Molokai usually fell under the sway of Maui.

Complex genealogies of the great *ali'i* still survive, but little is recorded other than their names. Among the most important was **'Umi-a-Liloa**, who some time between the twelfth and sixteenth centuries became the first ruler to unite the Big Island, from his base amid the taro fields of Waipi'o Valley. 'Umi is said to have inherited the throne by defeating his brother in a *hōlua* sledding contest. Listed as representing the sixtieth generation after the sky god Wākea, he was responsible for Hawaii's first legal code – the *kanawai*, which concerned itself with the equal sharing of water from Waipi'o's irrigation ditches – and was among the first to make human sacrifice an instrument of state policy. Other significant individuals include the sixteenth-century **Pi'ilani**, who was the first chief to control all

Maui and built the first paved road around any island, and the ferocious tattooed **Kahekili**, also from Maui, who almost conquered the entire archipelago shortly before Kamehameha the Great finally did so.

Perhaps the most enigmatic figure was **Lono**, who may have been ʻUmi's grandson. Legends suggest that he lost his throne after quarreling with, or even murdering, his wife and left the Big Island in a half-crazed fit of self-loathing. Some say that he regained his sanity, returned to unite the island, and was subsequently deified as Lonoikamakahiki, patron of the annual *makahiki* festival. Others claim that the Hawaiians predicted his return for centuries and believed these prophecies to be fulfilled by the arrival of Captain Cook (see p.148).

Religion

It's all but impossible now to grasp the subtleties of ancient Hawaiian **religion**. So much depends on how the chants and texts are translated; if the word *akua* is interpreted as meaning "god," for example, historians can draw analogies with Greek or Hindu legends by speaking of a pantheon of battling, squabbling "gods" and "goddesses" with magic powers. Some scholars, however, prefer to translate *akua* as "spirit consciousness" – which might correspond to the soul of an ancestor, or even the motivational force present in a modern wristwatch – and argue that the antics of such figures are peripheral to a more fundamental set of attitudes regarding the relationship of humans to the natural world.

The **Kumulipo**, the chant that contains Hawaii's principal creation myth, has been preserved in full, passed down from generation to generation. It tells how, after the emergence of the earth "from the source in the slime…[in] the depths of the darkness," more complicated life forms developed, from coral to pigs, until finally men, women, and "gods" appeared. Not only was there no Creator god, but the gods were much of a kind with humans. It took a hundred generations for the divine ancestors of the people of Hawaii to be born: Wākea, the god of the sky, and Papa, an earth goddess.

It may well be misleading to imagine that all Hawaiians shared the same beliefs; different groups sought differing ways to augment their *mana*, or spiritual power. Quite possibly only the elite *aliʻi* paid much attention to the bloodthirsty warrior god **Kū**, while the primary allegiance of ordinary families and, by extension, villages and regions, may have lain toward their personal *ʻaumākua* – a sort of clan symbol, which might be a totem animal such as a shark or an owl, or a more abstract force, such as that embodied by **Pele**, the volcano goddess.

Spiritual and temporal power did not necessarily lie in the same hands, let alone in the same places. Hawaiian "priests," known as **kahunas** – literally, "men who know the secrets" – were the masters of ceremonies at temples called **heiaus**. The design of a *heiau* was not always consistent, but as a rule it consisted of a number of separate structures standing on a rock platform (*paepae*). These might include the *hale mana* ("house of spiritual power"), the *hale pahu* ("house of the drum"), and the *anuʻu* ("oracle tower"), from the top of which the *kahunas* would converse with the gods. Assorted *kiʻi akua*, symbolic wooden images of different gods, would stand on all sides, and the whole enclosure was fenced or walled off. In addition to the two main types of *heiau* – the **luakinis**, which were dedicated to the war god Kū, and held *leles* or altars used for human sacrifice, and **māpeles**, peaceful temples to Lono – there were also *heiaus* to such entities as Laka, goddess of the hula. Devotees of Pele, on the other hand, did not give their protectress formal worship at a *heiau*.

Most *heiaus* were built for some specific occasion and did not remain in constant use. Among the best-preserved examples are the *luakinis* at Puʻukoholā on the Big Island, at Puʻu O Mahuka on Oahu, and at Kahanu Garden on Maui; the hula *heiau* above Kēʻē Beach on Kauai; and the healing *heiau* at Keaīwa, outside Honolulu.

Hawaiian religion in the form encountered by Cook was brought to the Big Island, and subsequently to the rest of the archipelago, by the Tahitian warrior-priest **Paʻao**, who led the last great migration to Hawaii. The war god Kū received his first human sacrifices on the Big Island, at *luakini* temples such as Wahaʻula Heiau near Kīlauea, which was destroyed by lava flows during the 1990s.

Paʻao is also credited with introducing and refining the complex system of **kapu**, which circumscribed the daily lives of all Hawaiians. *Kapu* is the Hawaiian version of the Polynesian *tabu*, often written in English as "taboo." Like all such systems, it served many purposes. Some of its restrictions were designed to exalt the power of the kings and priests, while others regulated domestic routine or attempted to conserve scarce natural resources.

Many had to do with **food**. Women were forbidden to prepare food or to eat with men; each husband was obliged to cook for himself and his wife in two separate ovens and to pound the *poi* in two distinct calabashes. The couple had to maintain separate houses, as well as a *hale noa*, where a husband and wife slept together. Women could not eat pork, bananas, or coconuts, or several kinds of fish. Certain fish could only be caught in specified seasons, and a *koa* tree could only be cut down provided two more were planted in its place.

No one could tread on the shadow of a chief; the highest chiefs were so surrounded by *kapus* that some only went out at night. Although bloodlines defined one's place in the *kapu* hierarchy, might dominated over right, so the ruling chiefs did not necessarily possess the highest spiritual status. One of Kamehameha's wives, Kapiʻolani, was so much his superior that he could only approach her naked, backwards, and on all fours.

The only crime in ancient Hawaii was to break a *kapu*, and the only punishment was death. It was possible for an entire *ahupuaʻa* to break a *kapu* and incur death, but the penalty was not always exacted. One way for guilty parties to avoid execution was by hotfooting it to a *puʻuhonua*, or "place of refuge." Each island is thought to have had several of these; the one in Hōnaunau on the Big Island remains among the best-preserved ancient sites in all Hawaii (see p.150). In addition, the monarch was considered to be a *puʻuhonua*.

The return of the voyagers

Although archeological and linguistic evidence had long made it clear that the Polynesians deliberately colonized the Pacific, how they did so remained a mystery until surprisingly recently. In 1973, a group of Hawaiians set out to rediscover the skills and techniques of their ancestors. Ben Finney, an anthropologist from Honolulu's Bishop Museum, Tommy Holmes, a racing canoe paddler, and the artist Herb Kane founded the **Polynesian Voyaging Society** to build replicas of the ancient ocean-going vessels and use them to reproduce the early voyages. They were determined to prove that it was possible to make sustained, long-distance return trips across the Pacific without modern instruments or charts, despite the trade winds that consistently blow from the northeast.

The great Polynesian **sailing canoes**, or *wa'a*, were developed to their ultimate level of sophistication in Hawaii itself. This followed the discovery of the native Hawaiian *koa*, a gigantic hardwood tree whose wood was the perfect material for canoe construction. Each canoe was scooped from a single *koa* trunk, six feet in diameter and at least fifty feet long, using stone adzes and knives made of bone, shell, or coral. Surfaces were sanded with the skin of manta rays, and the hulls waterproofed with gum from the breadfruit tree. When lashed together, two such vessels formed a double-hulled long-distance sailing canoe. Using the word "canoe" to describe a *wa'a* is somewhat misleading to modern ears; each was up to 150ft long and capable of carrying five or six hundred people. For comparison, they were three times the size of the largest Viking longboat and faster than nineteenth-century clipper ships, traveling an average of 120 nautical miles per day.

Voyaging canoes were equipped with sails made from plaited pandanus leaves (*lau hala*), while a *lei hulu*, made from bright feathers, was the attractive equivalent of a windsock. The crew would be unlikely to catch many fish on the long voyage between Tahiti and Hawaii, but they could cook on a hearth lined with stone and coral, and lived mainly on fermented breadfruit.

The Polynesian Voyaging Society's first vessel was the **Hōkūle'a**, named after the "Star of Gladness" that passes over Hawaii. Though constructed of plywood and fiberglass rather than *koa*, it was designed to replicate the performance of a traditional double-hulled canoe. Petroglyph images served as blueprints for the shape of the sails, and extensive sea trials were required before the crew felt confident in handling the unfamiliar craft.

Perhaps the biggest problem was finding a **navigator**. In ancient times, the children of master navigators were apprenticed from the age of five to learn the secrets of their trade. Eventually the student would have, as a nineteenth-century canoe captain explained, "his head all same as compass." Navigators prepared intricate "stick charts," using twigs and shells to depict ocean currents, swells, and islands. Memorized rather than carried on board, these were used to guide canoes across the Pacific. Once settled in Hawaii, however, the Polynesians had no need of such skills, and as the older generations died, the knowledge was lost. Only the barest details of the migrations could be gleaned from Hawaiian lore.

When the *Hōkūle'a* embarked on its maiden long-distance voyage in 1976, it was navigated by **Mau Piailug**, from the Central Caroline islands of Micronesia, who was able to chart his course owing to years of experience on the Pacific and the relative familiarity of the night sky. In personal terms, thanks in part to the presence of a team from *National Geographic*, the voyage was fraught with tensions; by reaching Tahiti in just thirty days, however, it triumphantly achieved its purpose.

In subsequent years, the *Hōkūle'a* sailed all over the Pacific. By using a north wind to sail east from Samoa to Tahiti, it refuted Heyerdahl's statement that it was

impossible for canoes from Asia to sail into the trade winds of the Pacific. Between 1985 and 1987 it went to New Zealand and back, a twelve-thousand-mile round-trip. Meanwhile, a young Hawaiian crew member of the *Hōkūle'a*, **Nainoa Thompson**, became fascinated with the lost art of navigation and set out to rediscover the specific techniques that the ancient Hawaiians themselves would have used.

The navigator's task consists of two main elements: way-finding and land-finding. **Way-finding** is the ability to plot and keep track of a long-distance course as accurately as possible. Although way-finding involves constantly monitoring the state of the ocean, the winds, and the currents (except for brief catnaps, the navigator has to remain awake for the entire voyage), it is rooted in close astronomical observation. In a fascinating partnership with modern science, Thompson gleaned a lifetime's worth

Western myths and misconceptions

Western scientists, unwilling to credit **Polynesian culture** with any degree of sophistication, struggled for two hundred years to account for the very existence of the Hawaiians. When Captain Cook reached the Hawaiian islands, he was amazed to find a civilization that shared a culture and language with the people of the South Pacific.

Europeans had only just developed the technology to make expeditions such as Cook's possible. The recent development of a pendulum-free clock that remained accurate at sea – which earned its inventor a prize of £20,000 – had finally enabled sailors to calculate their longitude. As a result, they found it hard to believe that the Polynesians were already able to plot and sail a precise course across a three-thousand-mile expanse of ocean. The Hawaiians in turn were unable to explain how their ancestors had achieved this feat; although their chants and legends were explicit about their Tahitian origin, they no longer undertook long-distance sea trips, so the specific **navigational skills** had been forgotten.

At first it was proposed that the Hawaiians came from an as-yet-undiscovered continent; when that proved not to exist, it was suggested that they had survived its submergence. Some argued that the islanders had simply been deposited by God. The consensus came to be that the Polynesians had drifted accidentally from island to island, with groups of storm-tossed unfortunates making lucky landfalls on unoccupied islands. One hypothesis, "demonstrated" by **Thor Heyerdahl** in his 1947 *Kon Tiki* expedition, was that the Polynesians came originally from South America, having been swept out to sea on balsa-wood rafts as they fished off the coast.

There are strong reasons to reject the theory of accidental drift. The islands of the Pacific are so tiny and so far apart that vast quantities of drifting rafts would be required to populate every one. Moreover, the fact that migratory groups clearly brought the plants and animals necessary for survival indicates that the colonization was planned, and almost certainly involved return trips to the home base. But the most crucial evidence, in the case of Hawaii, is that neither wind nor wave alone will carry a vessel across the Equator; travel between Hawaii and Tahiti is only possible on a craft that uses some form of power, be it oar or maneuverable sail. Modern authorities believe the most likely explanation for the discovery of Hawaii was as part of a deliberate program of exploration for new lands. The most likely strategy for that would have been for Polynesian seafarers to wait until a moment the wind was blowing in the opposite direction to usual, then to sail before it as far as possible until supplies began to run short and/or the wind reversed direction once again.

One linchpin of Heyerdahl's argument was the presence in Polynesia of the sweet potato, which is unquestionably of South American origin. His claims that Polynesian languages showed South American roots have, however, been disproved by modern analysis, which shows a linguistic spread from Asia, as well as by conclusive DNA evidence. At some point, quite possibly deliberately, Polynesians must have reached South America and succeeded in returning.

of experience of the motions of the night sky through spending long hours in the planetarium at Honolulu's Bishop Museum. The precise techniques he developed, which involved finding "matching pairs" of stars that set or rise at the same time, may not be identical to those used by the original Polynesians. They have, however, conclusively demonstrated that long voyages without navigational aids are possible.

The other essential component to navigation is **land-finding**, the art of detecting land when you know it must be close. From the deck of a sailing canoe on the open Pacific, the horizon is just four miles away; to avoid sailing right past your objective, you have to watch for the many signs that land is nearby. The most obvious of these is the behavior and color of cloud formations; the Big Island, for example, is usually "visible" from about a hundred miles away, thanks to the stationary clouds over its giant volcanoes. The nightly homeward flight of birds to their island nests is another indication, while much can also be read into the swells and currents of the sea itself.

The **Hawai'iloa**, a canoe made of wood at the Bishop Museum and launched in 1993, went another step toward reproducing past glories. Unfortunately, no *koa* tree large enough to build such a canoe was found; instead the Tlingit of Alaska donated two four-hundred-year-old Sitka spruces. Soon afterwards, the **Mauloa**, a 26ft-long, single-hulled *koa*-wood canoe, was constructed at the Pu'uhonua O Hōnaunau on the Big Island, under the supervision of Mau Piailug.

According to legend, during the heyday of Polynesian voyaging, regular gatherings of canoes from throughout the Pacific took place at the *Marae Taputapuatea* (temple of Lono) at **Raiatea**, not far from Tahiti in what are now called the Society Islands. The last such occasion, in 1350 AD, broke up after a Maori navigator was murdered. The Maori placed a *kapu* on the temple, and the era of ocean voyaging came to an end. After that date, no further expeditions sailed to or from Hawaii, although the last known long-distance voyage in Polynesia was as recent as 1812, from the Marquesas Islands.

In 1995, the canoes gathered again, for the first time in more than six centuries. Both the *Hōkūle'a* and *Hawai'iloa* sailed from Hawaii to Tahiti, taking a mere three weeks, and then continued on to Raiatea. Maori elders conducted ceremonies at the *marae* to lift the ancient *kapu*, and canoes from Tahiti, New Zealand, and the Cook Islands joined their Hawaiian counterparts in proclaiming a new era of pan-Polynesian solidarity. Five years later, the *Hōkūle'a* traveled safely to and from Rapa Nui, or Easter Island. By venturing to this remote spot in the southeast Pacific, it formally completed the final leg of the "Polynesian Triangle," demonstrating that the ancient Polynesians did indeed deliberately colonize the entire ocean.

The canoes have become perhaps the most potent symbol of a Polynesian Renaissance. Their every movement is eagerly followed by children throughout the Pacific, and a new generation of navigators is being trained to assume the mantle of Nainoa Thompson and Mau Piailug. The latest plan is for the *Hōkūle'a* to sail around the entire world, starting in 2012. For news and updates, access the Polynesian Voyaging Society's website, ⓦpvs.kcc.hawaii.edu.

The Hawaiian environment

Of all the places in the world, I should like to see a good flora of the Sandwich Islands.

Charles Darwin, 1850

Much of the landscape in Hawaii seems so unspoiled and free from pollution that many visitors remain unaware of how fragile the environmental balance really is. Native life forms have had less than two millennia to adapt to the arrival of humans, while the avalanche of species introduced in the last two centuries threatens to overwhelm the delicate ecosystems altogether.

Hawaii is a unique ecological laboratory. Not only are the islands isolated by a "moat" at least two thousand miles wide in every direction, but, having emerged from the sea as lifeless lumps of lava, they were never populated by the diversity of species that spread across the rest of the planet.

Those plants and animals that found a foothold evolved into specialized forms unknown elsewhere. Of the more than ten thousand species of insect catalogued in the islands, for example, 98 percent are unique to Hawaii, while at least five thousand further species are thought to remain unidentified. Recent discoveries include the tiny "happy-face spiders" of the rainforests, whose markings are now familiar from postcards sold all over the state.

Such species are particularly vulnerable to external threats; half of Hawaii's indigenous plants and three-quarters of its birds are already extinct, while the US Fish & Wildlife Service currently classifies 377 Hawaiian species as threatened or endangered. More than one hundred species of Hawaiian plants now have fewer than twenty remaining individuals in the wild.

The arrival of life

During the first seventy million years after the Hawaiian islands started to arise from the ocean, new plants and animals arrived only by sheer happenstance, via a few unlikely routes. Such were the obstacles that a new species only established itself once every 100,000 years. That makes seven hundred altogether, of which the great majority arrived from the west, from Asia and the Pacific.

Some drifted, clinging to flotsam washed up on the beaches; others were borne on the wind as seeds or spores; and the odd migratory bird found its way here, perhaps bringing insects or seeds. The larvae of shallow-water fish from Indonesia and the Philippines floated across thousands of miles of ocean to hatch in the Hawaiian coral reefs.

Of **birds**, only the strongest fliers made it here; the nēnē, Hawaii's state bird, is thought to have evolved from a Canadian goose injured during its annual migration and forced to remain on the islands. Its descendants adapted to walking on raw lava by losing the webbing from their feet. No land-based amphibians or reptiles reached Hawaii, let alone large land mammals. At some point a hoary bat and an intrepid monk seal must have got here, as these were the only two mammals whose arrival pre-dated that of humans.

Each species mutated from a single fertilized female to fill numerous ecological niches with extraordinary speed. Hundreds of variations might develop from a single fruit fly or land snail, and many species adapted themselves to conditions in specific areas of individual islands.

Although the Hawaiian environment was not entirely free of competition, many plants prospered without bothering to keep up their natural defenses. Thus there are nettles with no stings, and mints with no scent. Conversely, normally placid creatures turned savage; caterpillars content to munch leaves elsewhere catch and eat flies in Hawaii. These evolutionary changes have taken place so fast that five species of banana moth have evolved in the 1500 years since the Polynesians brought the banana to the islands.

As each new island emerged, it was populated by species from its neighbors as well as stragglers from further afield. This process can still be seen on the Big Island – the youngest and least densely populated island – where Hawaii's last remaining stand of pristine rainforest still attempts to spread onto the new land created by Kīlauea. Although lava flows destroy existing life, fresh lava is incredibly rich in nutrients. Water collects in cavities in the rock, and seeds or spores soon gather. The basic building block of the rainforest is the *hapu'u* tree fern. Patches of these grow and decay, and in the mulch the *'ohi'a lehua* gains a foothold as a gnarled shrub; in time it grows to become a gigantic tree, forcing its roots through the rock. After several hundred years, the lava crumbles to become soil that will support a full range of rainforest species. In addition, lava flows swirl around higher ground, or even random spots, to create isolated "pockets" of growth that quickly develop their own specialized ecosystems.

The Polynesian world

The first humans to arrive on the Hawaiian scene swiftly realized that the islands lacked the familiar comforts of their South Seas homelands. Many of what might now seem quintessentially Hawaiian species, such as **coconut** palms, **bananas**, **taro**, and **sugar cane**, were in fact brought from Tahiti by the Polynesians, who also introduced the islands' first significant mammals – **goats**, **dogs**, and **pigs**.

The settlers set about changing the islands' physical environment to suit their own needs. They constructed terraces and irrigation channels in the great wetland valleys, such as Hālawa on Molokai and Waipi'o on the Big Island, planted coconuts along the shoreline, and built fishponds out into the ocean (see p.316). While their animals wrought destruction on the native flora, the settlers also had a significant impact on the **bird** population. Around twenty species of flightless birds, for example, swiftly became extinct. Forest birds were snared so their feathers could be used to make cloaks, helmets, and *leis*; bright red feathers came from the *i'iwi* bird, while yellow became the most prized color of all, so yellow birds such as the *mamo* and *'ō'ō* grew progressively rare. The *nēnē* was hunted for food, and the *auku'u* heron, the curse of the fishponds, was driven from its native habitat.

On the whole, however, the Hawaiians lived in relative harmony with nature, with the *kapu* system helping to conserve resources. It was the arrival of foreigners, and the deluge of new species that they introduced, that really strained the ecological balance of Hawaii. Among the first victims were the Hawaiians themselves, decimated by the onslaught of foreign **diseases**.

Foreign invaders

The ships of early European explorers of the Pacific were explicitly intended to play the role of Noah's Arks. They carried food plants and domestic animals around the world in order to adapt newly discovered lands to the European

image, and present their benighted natives with the accoutrements deemed necessary for civilization. Hawaii's first **cattle**, for example, were presented to Kamehameha the Great by Captain George Vancouver of the *Discovery* in 1793. Allowed to run wild on the Big Island, they ate through grasslands and forests, as well as the crops of the Hawaiians. When they were eventually rounded up and domesticated, it formalized the change in land usage they had already effected. **Horses** had a similar initial impact, and wild goats remain a problem to this day.

Foreign **plants**, too, were imported, ranging from the scrubby mesquite trees of the lowlands (now known as *kiawe*) to the Mexican cacti that dot the mountainsides of Maui and the strawberry guava that runs riot along forest trails.

Along with such deliberate introductions came stowaways, such as rats and forest-choking weeds. An especially unwelcome arrival was the **mosquito**. Scientists have pinpointed the exact moment it turned up, in 1826, when the whaling vessel *Wellington* emptied its rancid water casks into a stream near Lahaina prior to filling up with fresh water; they've even decided from which Peruvian river the water, and the mosquito larvae it contained, was originally drawn.

Another spectacular disaster came when sugar plantation owners imported the **mongoose** to Hawaii, hoping it would keep down the rat population. Unfortunately, while rats are nocturnal, mongooses are not. The rodents continued to thrive while the mongooses slept, having gorged themselves on birds' eggs during the day. Only Kauai, where the mongoose never became established – myth has it that an infuriated docker threw the island's consignment into the sea after he was bitten – now retains significant populations of the many Hawaiian birds who, in the absence of predators, had decided it was safe to build their nests on the ground. Even here, there have been alarming recent reports of mongoose sightings.

Wild pigs have also had a ravaging effect. It is said that for every twenty humans in Hawaii, there lurks a feral pig. Though tourists are unlikely to spot one, their impact on the rainforests has been devastating. For the ancient Hawaiians, the pig god Kama'pua'a was the embodiment of lusty fertility, plowing deep furrows across the islands with his mighty tusks. His modern counterparts combine the strongest characteristics of the Polynesian pigs with those of later European imports. Rooting through the earth, eating tree ferns, eliminating native lobelias and greenswords, and spreading the seeds of foreign fruits, the pigs destroy the canopy that should prevent direct sunlight and heavy raindrops from hitting the forest floor. In addition, they create muddy wallows and stagnant pools where mosquitoes thrive – the resultant avian malaria is the major single cause of bird extinctions.

Eradicating wild pigs is a priority for conservationists. Although that goal gels with the desire of amateur hunters for sport, bitter "Pig Wars" pit hunters who want to leave enough wild pigs for hunting to continue against scientists who want to eliminate them altogether.

Unwanted alien species continue to arrive. Among those reported recently are the **coqui frog** from Puerto Rico, which has already achieved dense populations on four islands, and the Madagascar **giant day gecko**, a foot-long orange-spotted lizard now established on Oahu. Environmentalists fear that Hawaii's next likely arrival will be the **brown tree snake**. Originally found in the Solomon Islands, it has hitchhiked its way across the Pacific since World War II, sneaking into the holds of ships and planes, then emerging to colonize new worlds that have never seen a single snake. In Guam it has already established itself in concentrations of up to thirty thousand individuals per square mile, happy to eat virtually anything, and wiping out local birds.

Issues and prospects

Hawaii has a short and unimpressive history of legislating to conserve its environment. One positive development is that the whole state is now a **humpback whale** sanctuary, despite much opposition from local fishermen.

Conservationists are struggling to combat the disappearance of Hawaii's indigenous **wildlife**. High-profile successes have included the preservation of the extraordinary **silversword** plants of Haleakalā on Maui (see p.276) and the breeding of *nēnē* geese on both Maui and the Big Island. However, the rarest bird species survive only in isolated mountain-top sanctuaries like Kōke'e State Park on Kauai (see p.407), Molokai's Kamakou Preserve (see p.319), and Maui's Kīpahulu Valley (see p.290). So long as they stay at least 3500ft above sea level, the mosquitoes can't reach them; nonetheless, birds such as the *'ō'ō a'a* honey-creeper are becoming extinct at an alarming rate. Activists concerned about the destruction of Hawaiian plants by casually imported newcomers point out that all passengers leaving Hawaii for the US are subjected to stringent inspections, to prevent Hawaiian species from reaching the mainland, but there are no checks on arriving passengers.

Throughout Hawaii, a resurgence of interest in what are seen as native Hawaiian values has dovetailed with the influx of New Age *haoles* to create an active **environmental movement**. In particular, the cyclical depressions to which the Hawaiian economy is prone have made the islands vulnerable to grandiose schemes designed to attract outside funding.

Controversy recently erupted over the **Hawaii Superferry**, a high-speed catamaran that commenced sailings between Oahu and Maui in 2007. Following mass objections focusing on its environmental impact, the service never expanded to reach Kauai and the Big Island, and the legal consequences of its failure to carry out impact surveys eventually drove it into bankruptcy in 2009. However, while the Superferry might indeed have harmed marine mammals, and spread alien species between the islands, much of the opposition was rooted in political and commercial rivalries.

Other contentious issues have included the ongoing operations to harness the geothermal power of the Kīlauea volcano, an abortive plan to build a commercial spaceport nearby, and a scheme to get rid of surplus carbon dioxide by pumping it into the deep ocean off Honokōhau, all on the **Big Island**; the US Army's missile program on **Kauai** (see p.398); the proposed construction of wind farms on **Molokai** and **Lanai**; and the long-standing wrangle over the future of **Kaho'olawe**, described on p.260. For up-to-date information on all such issues, visit the **Environment Hawaii** website, at ⓦwww.environment-hawaii.org.

There has also been much discussion over what is to become of the islands' **irrigation channels**, developed long before European contact, and falling rapidly into disrepair. As the ancient Hawaiians knew all too well, maintenance is extremely labor-intensive; without swift action, however, the opportunity to revive small-scale agriculture may soon pass.

The greatest debates of all, however, have revolved around **tourism**. The power of the development lobby has for the last few decades been great enough to override environmental objections to the growth of resorts across all the islands. There are also concerns that the resorts are damaging their immediate environment; the combination of golf courses and coral reefs may be ideal for vacationers, but that won't last if fertilizer and silt washed down from the greens and fairways end up choking the reef to death. However, it now looks as though the era of resort building has drawn to a close, albeit due more to economic factors than environmental pressure.

Hawaii in the movies

Moviegoers may not always have known what they were seeing, but the spectacular scenery of Hawaii has featured prominently on the silver screen since the earliest days of the cinema. **Kauai**, for example, has not only appeared as a tourist paradise in its own right in movies such as *Blue Hawaii* (1961), *Throw Momma from the Train* (1987), and *Honeymoon in Vegas* (1992), but has also doubled as a Caribbean island in *Jurassic Park* (1993) and the latest *Pirates of the Caribbean* (2010), as South America in *Raiders of the Lost Ark* (1981), as Vietnam in *Tropic Thunder* (2008), as Africa in *Outbreak* (1995), and even as Neverland in *Hook* (1992) and the planet Pandora in *Avatar* (2009).

The very first footage shot in Hawaii was a travelogue, made by Thomas Edison's company in 1898; you can see it in Lahaina's Wo Hing Temple on Maui (see p.231). By 1913, Universal Studios had made a silent feature on Oahu, *The Shark God*, which established a tradition of Hawaii as an all-purpose exotic backdrop for tales of **terror**, mysterious rites, and unbridled passion. Later examples include Boris Karloff's 1957 *Voodoo Island*; Roger Corman's *She God of Shark Reef*, from the following year; the 1976 remake of *King Kong*; and *Aloha Donny and Marie*, featuring the Osmonds, in 1978.

A separate genre, the Hawaii-based **musical comedy**, was instigated by *Waikiki Wedding* in 1937, in which **Bing Crosby** crooned *Blue Hawaii* and *Sweet Leilani*. Hawaii provided a glamorous setting for star vehicles featuring Hollywood's biggest names. Thus Shirley Temple and Betty Grable donned grass skirts and *leis*, while those home-grown actors who managed to appear on camera, such as the singer Hilo Hattie (whose name lives on in her chain of aloha-wear stores) and legendary surfer Duke Kahanamoku, simply played bit parts to add a little local color.

With the invention of Technicolor, film-makers began fully to appreciate the potential of Hawaii. In *Pagan Love Song* (1950), Esther Williams performed one of her trademark aquatic ballets in Kauai's Hanalei Bay – supposedly Tahiti – while the smash-hit Rodgers and Hammerstein musical *South Pacific* (1958) turned Kauai into a South-Seas Eden. However, it was **Elvis Presley**, whose Cherokee ancestry made him at least semi-plausible as a Polynesian, who became most closely identified with Hawaii. As tour guide Chad Gates in his greatest box-office success, *Blue Hawaii* (1961) – promoted with the lame but accurate slogan "You'll Want to Visit Hawaii, After You See *Blue Hawaii*" – Elvis preened at countless Honolulu and Waikīkī locations before finally tying the knot with Joan Blackman in a gloriously kitsch wedding ceremony at Kauai's now-defunct *Coco Palms Resort*. He returned to Hawaii in 1962, for *Girls, Girls, Girls*, but as his adventures as a charter-boat skipper were allegedly taking place off Louisiana, not a single sequence shows a recognizable Hawaiian landmark. By contrast, during his *Paradise, Hawaiian Style* (1966), the camera seizes every opportunity to drift away from the flimsy plot line and linger lovingly on the North Shore cliffs of Kauai.

After World War II, Hawaii also became the ideal location to film stories of the War in the Pacific, whether the producers needed an accessible stand-in for some other, more remote, Pacific island, or wanted to depict actual events on Hawaii. The most famous re-enactment of the attack on Pearl Harbor, for example, came as the climax of **From Here to Eternity**, which won the Academy Award for Best Picture in 1953 (and tends to be best remembered for the scene in which Burt Lancaster and Deborah Kerr frolic in the surf at Oahu's Hālona Cove). **Frank Sinatra**, who received an Oscar for his portrayal of Private Maggio in that movie – having won the role with the behind-the-scenes maneuvering on which the horse's-head incident in *The Godfather* is allegedly based – directed his own war

epic on Kauai a dozen years later. The war-torn Pacific beach in *None But the Brave* was Pīlaʻa Beach, east of Kīlauea. During filming, Sinatra had to be rescued from drowning when he found himself in difficulties swimming off Wailua Beach. Big **John Wayne** made a number of war movies in Hawaii, including *The Sea Chase*, filmed on the Big Island in 1955, and Otto Preminger's *In Harm's Way* (1965), which featured another depiction of the Pearl Harbor attack. He had a rather happier time touring Kauai's coastline with Dorothy Lamour in the John Ford-directed comedy *Donovan's Reef* (1963).

Visitors seeking specific **movie locations** should head straight for **Kauai**. The landscape of **South Pacific**'s fictional Bali Haʻi was created by melding the peak of Makana, near Kēʻē Beach, with assorted Fijian scenes, but the movie's showstopping songs were filmed at genuine North Shore locations. These included a waterfall on Kīlauea River, for *Happy Talk*; Hanalei Bay, for *Some Enchanted Evening*; and Lumahaʻi Beach, under the name of Nurses' Beach, where Mitzi Gaynor sang *I'm Gonna Wash that Man Right Out of My Hair*. The opening sequence of **Raiders of the Lost Ark**, in which Harrison Ford escapes by seaplane from a posse of Amazonian headhunters – portrayed by Kauai locals with pudding-basin haircuts – was shot on the Hulēʻia Stream just outside Lihuʻe. The first attempt to film on the inaccessible Nā Pali coast came in 1976, when remote Honopū Beach stood in as Skull Island in that year's remake of **King Kong**. Helicopters were again deployed to ferry the crew of **Jurassic Park** into the island's interior, and a helicopter tour is the only way tourists can hope to see the waterfalls in and around Hanapēpē Valley where much of the action takes place. The movie's heroes, however, were disturbed by a sneezing dinosaur as they slept in the branches of a Moreton Bay fig at Allerton Garden on the South Shore, while the gates to the park itself were erected on a cane road above Wailua that leads toward Mount Waiʻaleʻale. Filming on *Jurassic Park* was brought to an abrupt end by Hurricane Iniki in September 1991 – which may explain why the sequel was shot elsewhere – and the movie includes a brief sequence of the hurricane's onslaught on Nawiliwili Harbor. Many Kauai landmarks are even recognizable in Disney's 2002 animation, *Lilo and Stitch*, while Keahua Arboretum stood in for Pandora in *Avatar*.

Finally, Hawaii may be even more familiar from **television**. Between 1968 and 1980, 262 episodes of **Hawaii Five-O** were filmed on Oahu. Jack Lord starred as Steve McGarrett and James MacArthur as Dano; their archenemy, Wo Fat, took his name from a real-life Honolulu restaurant. One in four visitors to Hawaii during the 1970s cited the program as a factor in their decision to come. Upon its demise, *Hawaii Five-0* was immediately replaced by Tom Selleck's **Magnum P.I.**, which ran in turn until 1988. Both *Fantasy Island* (1978–84) and *Gilligan's Island* (1964–67) were also filmed at least partially in Hawaii. Most recently, the hit series **Lost** was filmed almost entirely on Oahu. Location-spotting fans have pointed out that the crash site of Oceanic Flight 815 was Mokulēʻia Beach; the survivors' initial explorations took place in Kaʻaʻawa Valley, home to the Kualoa Ranch; many rainforest scenes were shot near the *Turtle Bay Resort*; and the Hawaii Convention Center doubled as Sydney Airport.

Hula and Hawaiian music

From the moment Europeans first reached the Hawaiian islands, in 1778, **Hawaiian music** has been constantly adapting and changing, as new waves of immigrants and visitors have introduced their own traditions and instruments. Appropriately enough, Hawaii provided perhaps the earliest **world music** craze of all, around a hundred years ago, when its distinctive slide-guitar sound and hula dances were taken up first across the US and subsequently all over the world. Even so, despite the islands' lengthy entanglement with tourism, their music has continued to follow its own highly individual path.

Roots

Although the ancient Hawaiians were devotees of the poetic chants they called **meles**, they had no specific word for "song." *Meles* were composed for various purposes, ranging from lengthy genealogies of the chiefs, put together over days of debate, through temple prayers, to lullabies and love songs. Unaccompanied chanting was known as *mele oli*; when the chant was accompanied by music and dance, the combined performance was known as **mele hula**. The invention of the hula was generally credited to the goddess Laka, who is said to have danced for the first time either in the *'ōhi'a lehua* groves near Maunaloa on Molokai (see p.329) or above Kē'ē Beach on Kauai (see p.379).

Music was created using instruments such as gourds, rattles, and small hand or knee drums made from coconuts. A larger kind of drum, the *pahu*, which was made by stretching shark skin over hollow logs, was said to have been introduced by Hawaii's final wave of settlers from Tahiti, around the thirteenth century; legend tells of the voyagers booming out this menacing new sound as they pulled towards shore.

As a rule the tonal range was minimal and the music monotonous, though occasionally bamboo pipes may also have been played. Complexity was introduced by the fact that the dance, the chant, and the music were all likely to follow distinct rhythmic patterns.

The telling of the story or legend was of primary importance; the music was subordinate to the chant, while the feet and lower body of the dancers served mainly to keep the rhythm, and their hand movements supplemented the meaning of the words. Dancers underwent training in a *halau hula* – part school, part temple – and performances were hedged around by sacred ritual and *kapu*.

Missionaries and immigrants, kings and queens

When the first Christian **missionaries** reached Hawaii in the 1820s, immediately after the collapse of the *kapu* system, they saw hula as a lascivious manifestation of the islands' general lack of morality. It's clearly true, for example, that the religious subtleties of the so-called "genital hula" dances, celebrating the genitals of leading members of the *ali'i*, were lost on visiting whalemen. Their own church music, however, served to introduce western instruments, concepts

of harmony, and vocal styles. Inspired by the *hīmeni* they learned from the first Hawaiian hymn book, local musicians were soon creating their own songs in the Western tradition.

The population of Hawaii changed rapidly, as a massive influx of settlers and sailors, whalemen and laborers was matched by a precipitous decline in its indigenous peoples. Specific immigrant groups exposed the islands to a wide range of musical influences; thus the Mexican cowboys (known as *paniolos*) who came to work the cattle ranches of the Big Island introduced **guitars**, while Portuguese sugar farmers arrived from the Azores with the *braguinha*, an early form of '**ukulele**.

Towards the close of the nineteenth century, and championed especially by the Hawaiian royal family, a new kind of Hawaiian music emerged. The coronation in 1883 of **King David Kalākaua** – the so-called "Merrie Monarch," who had his own 'ukulele group, and co-wrote Hawaii's national anthem, *Hawaii Ponoi* – was marked by the first public hula performance in two generations. Kalākaua also recruited bandleader **Henry Berger** from the Prussian army to establish the Royal Hawaiian Band, a brass band that performed arrangements of Hawaiian songs as well as marches and ragtime compositions. For good measure, Berger also taught **yodeling**, which helped to add an idiosyncratic twist to Hawaii's already developing tradition of **falsetto** singing, in which the *hai*, or break in the voice between falsetto and "normal" singing, is emphasized rather than hidden. As part of the process of adapting music and dance to suit foreign tastes, incidentally, the **grass skirt** was imported to Hawaii from the Gilbert Islands in the 1870s, as somehow looking more Polynesian.

King David was succeeded in 1891 by his sister, **Queen Lili'uokalani**, who remains perhaps the most celebrated of all Hawaiian composers. She was deposed by a US-inspired coup in 1894, and subsequently imprisoned in her own palace; small wonder she's remembered for such haunting songs as the oft-covered *Aloha Oe*.

Thanks in part to their strong association with the much-mourned royal family, and despite the fact that they're already a self-evident mixture of Polynesian forms with musical influences from all over the world, it's the songs from this era that are now thought of as typifying traditional Hawaiian music.

The 'ukulele – a Portuguese gift to the Pacific

The **'ukulele** – one of the most ubiquitous instruments in Hawaiian (and Polynesian) popular music – is essentially the *braguinha*, a small four-stringed instrument that originated on the **Portuguese** island of Madeira (and a variant of the more common *cavaquinho* of the Portuguese mainland).

In September 1878, a hundred and twenty Madeira islanders arrived in Honolulu as Hawaii's first Portuguese immigrants, ready to work on the sugar plantations. They were joined a year later by another four hundred settlers, including one **João Fernandes**, who had borrowed a *braguinha* from a fellow passenger and learned to play it during the voyage of almost five months. When the boat finally arrived in Honolulu the passengers celebrated their safe arrival with a dance, and Fernandes played the instrument, to the delight of both settlers and Hawaiians. He soon became a fixture at balls and parties and eventually formed a group, which played on occasion for the Hawaiian royalty.

A fellow passenger on that same boat, Manuel Nunes, opened a shop where he made and sold *braguinhas* – by now renamed 'ukuleles. He and other craftsmen began to use local *kou* and *koa* wood and before long the *braguinha* became a national instrument. The Hawaiian word *'ukulele* literally means "jumping flea," and is said to originate from the nickname of a small Englishman, Edward Purvis, who played the instrument with quick, jerky movements.

Slack-key and steel guitar

In conventional guitar tuning, strumming the open strings produces a discord. In the late nineteenth century, however, Hawaiians started to retune the strings to create a harmonious chord, and from there developed a whole range of open tunings – a new style that they called *kī hōʻalu* or **slack key**. A further innovation soon followed, with the development of the Hawaiian **steel guitar** (*kika kila*): a new guitar sound and a new guitar posture, with the instrument played on the lap or on a stand. Previously, the violin or flute would often figure as the lead instrument in Hawaiian music; now the steel guitar took over as lead, while slack-key strumming maintained the rhythm.

After the islands were annexed by the US in 1898, the **hapa haole** ("half white") style of song began to emerge, as Hawaiian musicians strove to please visiting Americans and win audiences on the mainland. Though *hapa haole* is often characterized as a form in which English or nonsense lyrics were set to traditional Hawaiian melodies, in truth the music too was heavily influenced by whatever was currently popular in the US. For that matter, at the peak of its popularity much of it was actually written on Tin Pan Alley, by songsmiths who had never visited the islands. Thus while the earliest *hapa haole* songs owed much to ragtime, they shifted towards jazz and blues by the 1920s, big-band sounds in the 1930s, and even rock'n'roll by the late 1950s. Often there was a comedy or novelty element,

---

Slack-key and steel guitar

Slack-key guitar, as its name suggests, involves slackening or loosening the strings in order to retune the guitar to achieve an open chord. Thus if you take the standard guitar tuning (from high to low – EBGDAE) and slacken the first string from E to D, the fifth from A to G and the sixth from E to D, you get a tuning of DBGDGD. Not only does this produce an open chord of G when strummed, but if you then place a finger (or steel bar) across the strings at the fifth and seventh frets, you get the other two chords needed for any three-chord song, like a blues.

This is one of the simplest tunings. During the prewar craze for the music, Hawaiian guitarists made an art out of different tunings, some of which were closely guarded secrets. They also developed two ways of playing with open tunings – slack key and steel guitar. **Slack key** involved picking the strings, with the thumb providing a constant bass while the other fingers play a melody (often a slightly altered version of the sung melody) on the upper strings.

The fact that Portuguese guitars often used steel rather than gut strings, and the creation of the National Steel guitar in the 1920s, to aid Hawaiian musicians in the days immediately before electric amplification, have obscured the reality that the "steel" in **steel guitar** is simply another word for "slide." And although many people think that slide guitar originated with blues musicians, it's a Hawaiian invention. **Joseph Kekuku**, an 11-year-old Oahu schoolboy, realized in 1885 that if he slid a solid object up or down the strings after plucking or strumming them, the chord would slide up and down in a glissando. He tried all kinds of objects before settling on the hand-tooled steel rod that gave the style its name; further experiments led him to play seated, with the guitar placed horizontally across his lap, and also to raise his strings so the steel would not touch the frets.

The first electric guitar – a Rickenbacher nicknamed the "frying pan" – was actually a Hawaiian lap steel guitar made in 1931. In the US this developed into the pedal steel guitar, with its mechanical devices to change tunings and volume. This became the characteristic sound of country music, though it is less favored by Hawaiian musicians.

in which the real or supposed sounds of the Hawaiian language were exaggerated for comic event, as with the *Hawaiian War Chant*.

At San Francisco's Panama-Pacific Exposition in 1915 – which celebrated the opening of the Panama Canal – the new Territory of Hawaii invested heavily in its pavilion. America fell in love with the sounds of Hawaii, and by 1916 more Hawaiian records were being sold in the US than any other type of music. Groups such as the **Kalama Quartet** introduced four-part falsetto harmony singing with two steel guitars playing counterpoint, while other recordings featured virtuoso Hawaiian steel-guitarists.

Another cultural collision occurred as these musicians discovered jazz. **Bennie Nawahi** was a key figure in this early fusion – a steel-guitar wizard who performed with equal dexterity on mandolin and 'ukulele. He started out as a busker, then worked a cruise ship with his brothers, developing an extraordinary showmanship, playing the steel guitar with his feet and the 'ukulele behind his head with one hand. With America in the grip of 'ukulele madness, Nawahi played the vaudeville circuit as "King of the Ukulele" with huge success in the 1920s, and launching a recording career that stretched nearly fifty years.

During his early busking days Nawahi also worked with steel-guitarist **Sol Hoopii**, who played a technically brilliant synthesis of American jazz and traditional Hawaiian music. Hoopii developed the tuning that led to the development of the pedal steel guitar and the Nashville country music sound. He too recorded extensively, from 1925 until the 1950s, and his advanced use of chords, harmony, and phrasing had a profound effect on a generation of island musicians

Inspired by such figures, musicians the world over explored the Hawaiian sound. From the 1930s, Hawaiian-style bands and steel-guitar players started to appear as far afield as Britain and Germany, Japan, India, and Indonesia. In London, for example, the Felix Mendelssohn Hawaiian Serenaders were a hugely popular radio and dancehall act, performing a mix of traditional Hawaiian, *hapa haole*, jazz, and popular songs.

Back in Hawaii, a magazine article was complaining as early as 1923 that "the truth of the matter is that the real Hawaiian hula has little in common with the coarse imitations served up to sight-seers, magazine readers, and the general public."

Tourism and the Sons of Hawaii

As **tourism** to Hawaii increased, "Hawaiian music" became an ever more important part of the experience. Visitors were lured to the islands by such means as the *Hawaii Calls* radio program, broadcast around the world from 1935 onwards from the *Moana Hotel* on Waikīkī Beach, and entertained once they arrived by grass-skirt revues with an emphasis on entertainment rather than education.

An even greater boom in tourism followed after Hawaii became the fiftieth US state in 1959, and the simultaneous arrival of quick jet travel. By the time Elvis Presley filmed *Blue Hawaii* in the islands in 1961, young Hawaiians were turning away from steel guitar towards rock'n'roll. And yet the seeds of a revival of the old-style music were already being sown.

The major figure in the resurgence was slack-key guitarist **Gabby Pahinui**. By the late 1950s, his virtuosity, honed through twenty years of playing in Waikīkī's clubs and revues, meant he was ready to step to the forefront and play slack key as a lead rather than simply a rhythm instrument. He joined with 'ukulele virtuoso **Eddie Kamae** to form the **Sons of Hawaii**, and together they championed the

Iz: May 20, 1959 – June 26, 1997

In 1997, the Hawaiian music scene lost the man who was in every sense its biggest star. **Israel Kamakawiwoʻole**, who started out singing in the Makaha Sons of Niʻihau and then went solo in 1990, died of respiratory difficulties in a Honolulu hospital.

During his twenty-year career, "Iz" came to epitomize the pride and the power of Hawaiian music. His extraordinary voice adapted equally well to rousing political anthems, delicate love songs, pop standards, and "Jawaiian" reggae rhythms, while his personality and his love for Hawaii always shone through both in concert and on record. Like his brother Skippy before him – also a founder member of the Makaha Sons – Iz eventually succumbed to the health problems caused by his immense size. At one point, his weight reached a colossal 757 pounds; he needed a fork-lift truck to get on stage, and could only breathe through tubes. His strength in adversity did much to insure that he was repeatedly voted Hawaii's most popular entertainer, and after his death he was granted a state funeral, with his body lying in state in the Capitol.

Iz's enduring legacy will be the music on the four solo albums released during his lifetime – *Ka Anoi* (1990), *Facing Future* (1993), *Ala E* (1995), and *'n Dis Life* (1996). His medley of *Somewhere over the Rainbow/What a Wonderful World* has become a staple of movie and TV soundtracks, while his haunting rendition of *Hawaiʻi 78* (on *Facing Future*) became the anthem of campaigners seeking to restore native Hawaiian sovereignty.

traditional music of Hawaii. Kamae traveled the remote backwaters of the islands in search of old songs and performers, seeking out Hawaii's heritage before it was lost for ever. So few people speak fluent Hawaiian that only elders and experts could tell him the true meaning and pronunciation of many lyrics. Hawaiian is an intensely poetic language, and traditional songs often work on several levels, perhaps celebrating some beautiful place while also hymning the beauty of a loved one, all overlaid with sexual innuendo.

A significant change came into Hawaiian music during the 1970s, when many of the bands that sprang up in the wake of the Sons of Hawaii began to write new songs about contemporary island issues as well as performing older Hawaiian-language material. This new generation was hugely inspired by a wave of pan-Polynesian feeling, triggered especially by the success of the *Hōkūleʻa* canoe; one side effect was that even the hula now considered most authentic has come to incorporate elements from elsewhere in Polynesia, especially Tahiti and Samoa. Among groups who came to prominence during this Hawaiian Renaissance were the **Sunday Manoa**, consisting of Peter Moon alongside brothers **Robert and Roland Cazimero**, and **Hui Ohana**, another trio comprising Ledward and Nedward Kaʻapana and Dennis Pavao. By now, the *hapa haole* label had become an embarrassment to younger musicians, and ceased to be applied to newly made music, although arguably Hawaiian music remained as susceptible as ever to outside influences, including the "soft rock" then sweeping California.

Meanwhile, Gabby Pahinui had left the Sons of Hawaii for a solo career that saw him team up with other slack-key legends like Atta Isaacs and Sonny Chillingworth, and with his four sons, Martin, Bla, Cyril, and Philip. Gabby's recordings with **Ry Cooder**, who sought him out after buying one of his records in Honolulu, crossed slack key over into the US mainstream for the first time. Worn out by a life of hard labor and hard liquor, however, Gabby died aged 59 in 1980.

Hawaiian music today

The typical sound of the Pahinui-inspired revival of Hawaiian groups has settled into a regular, unplugged format of guitars, 'ukulele, steel guitar, bass, and vocals, but no drums. Most play a mix of traditional music, country, rock covers, pop, pan-Pacific styles, and reggae – all in a typically inclusive Hawaiian way. The musicians don't tour outside of the islands too often, and most discs are local releases, so you really have to go there to hear Hawaiian music at its best.

Hula remains an integral part of performance; Gabby himself was an expert dancer, for example, and musicians will often appeal to the audience: "Does anyone know the hula to this one?" Two main forms of hula coexist. The first, *kahiko*, is closer to the old style, consisting of chanting to the beat of drums; the dancers wear knee-length skirts of flat *ti* leaves, and anklets and bracelets of ferns. *'Auana* is the modern style of hula, featuring bands of musicians playing Western-style instruments.

Among the finest currently active performers are **Hapa**, consisting of sweet-voiced singer-guitarists Barry Flanagan and Nathan Aweau, plus chanter Charles Ka'upu; the Maui-based *kumu hula* (hula teacher) **Keali'i Reichel**, equally acclaimed for a succession of fine albums and his charismatic performing style; slack-key maestros **Dennis Kamakahi** and **Ledward Ka'apana**; **Amy Gilliom**, whose crystal-clear voice brings out all the beauty of her classic Hawaiian-language material; 'ukulele whiz-kid **Jake Shimabukuro**; **Kaumakaiwa Kanaka'ole**, a chanter, dancer, and singer from the Big Island who's keeping up a great family tradition; and **Raiatea Helm**, a young female falsetto singer from Molokai. **Eddie Kamae** still performs as well, though most of his energies in recent years have gone into making compelling documentary movies about Hawaiian music and musicians.

Discography

Among the few US record companies to feature Hawaiian music are **Rounder**, the Boston-based American roots-music label (ⓦwww.rounder.com), and **Dancing Cat Records** based in Santa Cruz, California (ⓦwww.dancingcat .com), who have done sterling work to raise the profile of slack-key guitar music. Their series of Slack Key Master CDs has grown to include pretty much every player of note. Also in California, **Cord International** (ⓦwww .cordinternational.com) is steadily re-releasing classic Hawaiian recordings of yesteryear. For a comprehensive online selection of Hawaiian music, see ⓦwww.mele.com.

Hawaii live

The best way to experience Hawaiian music is to hear it on its home ground, though it can be hard to track down the finest practitioners amid the countless tourist revues. A handful of hotels and restaurants, especially in Honolulu and Waikīkī – as detailed on p.96 – feature authentic performers; the *Napili Kai Beach Resort* on Maui hosts wonderful weekly slack-key concerts (see p.225); and Hanalei on Kauai also stages regular concerts (see p.345).

There's also a rich year-round program of **festivals**, as detailed on p.30.

Compilations

Hana Hou! Do it Again! Hawaiian hula chants and songs (Pan, Netherlands). Traditional chants and contemporary dance songs performed in their basic form. Only one or two singers with minimal accompaniment of *ipu heke* (gourd drum), 'ukulele, or guitar.

Hawaiian Drum Dance Chants: Sounds of Power in Time (Smithsonian/Folkways, US). A record of the earliest known forms of Hawaiian music, some of it from old cylinder recordings. As close as you can get to the stuff Captain Cook would have heard.

Steeling Round the World (Harlequin, England). This utterly delightful, if bizarre, chronicle of how the world went mad for Hawaii features Hawaiian-esque performances recorded in the 1930s and 1940s by soloists and groups from as far afield as Sweden, Indonesia, Greece, Hungary, India, South Africa, and New Zealand, plus home-grown Hawaiian acts like the great Kanui and Lula, recorded in Paris in 1934.

Vintage Hawaiian Music: The Great Singers 1928–1934 (Rounder, US). A hugely seductive collection of slack-key classics compiled by Bob Brozman, featuring Mme Riviere's Hawaiians, the all-male Kalama's Quartet and Sol Hoopii Trio, and lots more besides. Plenty of falsetto vocals and steel guitar.

Vintage Hawaiian Music: Steel Guitar Masters 1928–1934 (Rounder, US). A companion volume highlighting the golden age of acoustic steel guitar. Tracks from Tau Moe, Sol Hoopii, King Benny Nawahi and Jim & Bob the Genial Hawaiians.

Vintage Hawaiian Treasures Vol 7 (Cord International, US). A reissue of the first commercial releases of slack key from the 1940s, including seminal Gabby Pahinui cuts. Other standout tracks include Tommy Blaisdell pieces that stomp along like barrelhouse blues.

Individual artists

Sol Hoopii

Sol Hoopii (1902–53) made his fame in the US after stowing away on a liner to San Francisco. Most famous for his classic acoustic recordings, he switched to electric guitar in 1934, then in 1938 became an evangelist and gave up his career in secular music.

Sol Hoopii – Vol 1: 1926–1929 and Vol 2: 1927–1934 (Rounder, US). Classic tracks from probably the most influential of all Hawaiian steel-guitarists. Both albums are recommended.

Tau Moe Family

Born in Samoa in 1908, steel-guitarist and singer Tau Moe embarked on an astonishing fifty-year world tour in the 1920s. His wife Rose joined Mme Riviere's Hawaiians (Tau and his three uncles) in 1927, for a tour of Asia that lasted from 1928 until 1934; they then toured India and the Middle East until the late 1940s when they moved to Europe, performing there through the 1950s and 1960s, and finally retired back to Lā'ie on Oahu in the late 1970s. In the mid-1980s, American steel-guitarist Bob Brozman received a letter from Moe ordering a couple of his records, and recognized Moe's name from his legendary 1929 recordings. Brozman called up and discovered to his amazement that it was the self-same man. After Brozman met Moe and Rose, he suggested that they re-record the songs from those old 78s.

Tau Moe Family with Bob Brozman: Remembering the Songs of Our Youth (Rounder, US). Although this disc dates from 1989, it reprises the songs, style, and instrumentation of the 1920s and 1930s, with Rose Moe, then in her eighties, handling the lead vocals, backed up by Tau and their two kids Lani and Dorien (in their sixties), vocals from the family, and the hugely talented Bob Brozman on steel-guitar parts learnt from Tau. It kicks off with the beautiful *Mai Kai No Kauai*, the 1929 version of which opens the Steel Guitar Masters compilation on p.444. An amazing CD.

Bennie Nawahi
Bennie Nawahi (1899–1985) was a key figure in the acoustic era of Hawaiian guitar. He lost his sight, inexplicably, while driving home from a performance in 1935.

Hot Hawaiian Guitar 1928–1949 (Shanachie/Yazoo, US). A lovely disc of Nawahi performing jazz-inflected Hawaiian numbers with fellow master Sol Hoopii.

Mahi Beamer
All-round musician Mahi Beamer comes from one of Hawaii's great musical dynasties, and has spent much of his fifty-year career playing piano and guitar, as well as dancing hula, but he's most renowned for his stunning falsetto voice.

The Remarkable Voice of Hawaii's Mahi Beamer in Authentic Island Songs (Hula Records/EMI Music). Seldom can an album have been more accurately named. Originally released in 1959, it showcases the extraordinary male falsetto of Mahi Beamer, performing songs exclusively in Hawaiian and mostly written by his grandmother. The hauntingly minimal backing includes traditional hula implements.

Lena Machado
As she grew up in Honolulu a century ago, Lena Machado's adoptive parents disapproved of her singing. She practiced in secret, was overheard by a producer as she sang high in a mango tree, cut her first record in 1927, and went on to enjoy a fifty-year career. Her 'ukulele playing, her jazzy song-writing, and above all her unique falsetto style still hold an elevated place in Hawaiian hearts.

Hawaiian Song Bird (Cord International). Most of this lovely CD dates from 1962, but it also includes a few earlier numbers, including Lena's 1927 debut and a version of her trademark *Keyhole Hula* backed by Sol Hoopii in 1935. Her falsetto is a constant joy, especially on her own sassy, jazz-tinged material like *E Kuu Baby Hot Cha Cha*.

Gabby Pahinui
Gabby Pahinui (1921–80) is without doubt the biggest influence on modern Hawaiian music. A slack-key guitar-player and singer, he released the first commercial recording ever of slack key, *Hi'ilawe*, in 1946, and in the 1960s was responsible for launching not only a revival of interest in slack key, but in Hawaiian culture in general.

Gabby Pahinui Hawaiian Band Volume 1 and Volume 2 (Edsel, UK). Breathtaking discs of slack-key guitar, steel guitar, and bass from a band of legends – Sonny Chillingworth, Atta Isaacs and the Pahinui Brothers, Cyril, Bla, Phillip, and Martin – as well as Gabby himself and a little fairy-dust from Ry Cooder. Along with the **Rabbit Island Music Festival** (Panini, Hawaii), recorded by the same band but without Cooder, these three albums of Hawaiian string-band music are unequalled.

The Sons of Hawaii

Conceived in the late 1950s by Gabby Pahinui and Eddie Kamae, who were subsequently joined for the band's classic line-up by bassist Joe Marshall and steel-guitarist extraordinaire David "Feet" Rogers, the **Sons of Hawaii** spearheaded a revolution in Hawaiian music. Although Pahinui left in the early 1970s, and the other original members have now all passed away, Kamae has continued to use the name on and off, and a roster of greats has passed through the ranks, including slack-key maestro Dennis Kamakahi.

The Folk Music of Hawaii (Panini Records, Hawaii). This classic was the fruit of a reunion of the Sons' original quartet in 1971, joined by Moe Keale on 'ukulele and vocals. Everything about it is just perfect, from Gabby's singing and playing to the long-lost songs rediscovered and burnished by Eddie Kamae, but if one element makes it truly transcendent, it's the staggeringly understated yet precise fills provided by "Feet" Rogers on steel guitar.

Hapa

As singer, songwriter, and slack-key guitarist, New Jersey transplant Barry Flanagan has so deeply immersed himself in Hawaiian musical traditions that his group **Hapa**, which has been through various line-ups, has since the mid-1990s provided the islands' definitive soundtrack.

Hapa (Coconut Grove, Hawaii). No album by a Hawaiian group has sold more copies than Hapa's eponymous 1995 debut, packed with infernally catchy melodies, Hawaiian lyricism, and beautiful singing and guitar work.

Israel Kamakawiwoʻole

As described on p.442, the solo career of Hawaii's much-loved megastar Iz was cut short by his tragically early death, but he raised the profile of Hawaiian music around the world.

Facing Future (Mountain Apple Company, Hawaii). Iz's 1993 masterpiece is an unqualified delight, showcasing the extraordinary power and resonance of his voice on *Hawaii 78*, his spritely 'ukulele work on island favourites like *Amaama* and *Henehene Kou Aka*, and his delicacy on *Somewhere over the Rainbow*.

Books

An extraordinary number of books have been written about Hawaii and all matters Hawaiian, though you're only likely to come across most of them in bookstores on the islands themselves. Titles marked with 🏃 are particularly recommended.

History

Gail Bartholomew *Maui Remembers.* Large-format paperback history of Maui, with lots of early photographs and entertaining stories.

🏃 **Emmett Cahill** *The Life and Times of John Young.* Lively biography of one of the most fascinating figures of the immediate post-contact era: the Welsh seaman who became Kamehameha's most trusted military adviser.

Gavan Daws *Shoal of Time.* Definitive if dry single-volume history of the Hawaiian islands, tracing their fate from European contact to statehood.

🏃 **Greg Dening** *The Death of William Gooch.* Elaborate anthropological and metaphysical speculations spun around the 1792 murder of three European sailors in Oahu's Waimea Valley.

Michael Dougherty *To Steal a Kingdom: Probing Hawaiian History.* An eccentric and entertaining look at Hawaiian history, which focuses on the famous names of the nineteenth century and pulls no punches.

🏃 **Michael Kioni Dudley and Keoni Kealoha Agard** *A Call for Hawaiian Sovereignty* (2 vols). Two short books, indispensable for anyone interested in Hawaiian sovereignty. The first attempts to reconstruct the world-view and philosophies of the ancient Hawaiians; the second is the clearest imaginable account of their dispossession.

Edward Joesting *Kauai, the Separate Kingdom.* Dramatic and very readable account of Kauai's early history and how the island resisted incorporation into the Hawaiian mainstream.

Noel J. Kent *Hawaii: Islands Under the Influence.* Rigorous Marxist account of Hawaiian history, concentrating on the islands' perennial "dependency" on distant economic forces.

Lili'uokalani *Hawaii's Story by Hawaii's Queen.* Autobiographical account by the last monarch of Hawaii of how her kingdom was taken away, written in 1897 when she still cherished hopes of a restoration.

Gananath Obeyesekere *The Apotheosis of Captain Cook.* An iconoclastic Sri Lankan anthropologist reassesses Captain Cook from an anti-imperialist – but, according to most authorities, historically inaccurate – perspective.

🏃 **Gordon W. Prange** *At Dawn We Slept* and *The Verdict of History.* Definitive, best-selling analysis of the attack on Pearl Harbor. Over two volumes, Prange exhaustively rebuts conspiracy theories.

A. Grenfell Price (ed) *The Explorations of Captain James Cook in the Pacific.* Selections from Cook's own journals, including entries about his first landfall on Kauai and his ill-fated return to the Big Island. The story of his death is taken up by his successor as captain.

Luis I. Reyes *Made in Paradise.* Lovingly prepared coffee-table history of how Hollywood has depicted Hawaii, with some great illustrations.

Marshall Sahlins *How Natives Think…about Captain Cook, for example.* An impassioned and closely argued

response to the Obeyesekere book reviewed above.

David A. Stannard *Honor Killing*. A riveting account of the Thalia Massie rape-and-murder case on Oahu in the 1930s (see p.423), which brilliantly dissects the racist attitudes towards "natives" that permeated both Hawaii and the US mainland.

Ronald Takaki *Pau Hana*. Moving history of life on the sugar plantations and the trials experienced by generations of immigrant laborers.

Rerioterai Tava and Moses K. Keale Sr *Niihau, The Traditions of an Hawaiian Island*. Comprehensive collection of fact and legend surrounding Hawaii's least-known island, so detailed that it names each of the island's five breadfruit trees.

Haunani Kay Trask *From a Native Daughter: Colonialism and Sovereignty in Hawaii*. A stimulating and impressive contribution to the sovereignty debate, from one of Hawaii's best-known activists.

Ancient Hawaii

Ross Cordy *Exalted Sits The Chief: The Ancient History of Hawai'i Island*. Cordy has assembled a great deal of valuable raw material about the early history of the Big Island, but the book's poor organization and dry style make it a disappointingly heavy read.

Stephen L. Desha *Kamehameha and His Warrior Kekūhaupi'o* (Kamehameha Schools Press). An invaluable narrative drawn from oral traditions of Kamehameha the Great, originally published in Hawaiian, as newspaper articles, during the 1860s and 1870s.

Abraham Fornander *Ancient History of the Hawaiian People* (Mutual Publishing). While a circuit judge on Maui in the 1870s, the Swedish-born Abraham Fornander assiduously gathered oral histories, to fill the gaps in Hawaii's unwritten history. The result can be heavy going, but wonderful tales are scattered throughout.

Samuel M. Kamakau *The People of Old* (3 vols). Anecdotal essays, originally written in Hawaiian in the 1860s. Packed with fascinating nuggets of information, they provide a compendium of Hawaiian oral traditions. Kamakau's longer *Ruling Chiefs of Hawaii* (Bishop Museum Press) details all that is known of the deeds of the kings.

Patrick Kirch *Feathered God and Fishhooks* and *Legacy of the Past*. The former is the best one-volume account of ancient Hawaii, though nonspecialists may find the minutiae of archeological digs hard going. The latter is an excellent guide to specific Hawaiian sites.

David Malo *Hawaiian Antiquities*. Nineteenth-century survey of culture and society, written by a native Hawaiian brought up at the court of Kamehameha the Great. As with Kamakau, Malo's conversion to Christianity colors his account, but this is the closest we have to a contemporary view of ancient Hawaii.

Valerio Valeri *Kingship and Sacrifice: Ritual and Society in Ancient Hawaii*. Detailed academic analysis of the role of human sacrifice in establishing the power of the king – an aspect of Hawaiian religion that many other commentators gloss over.

Koko Willis and Pali Jae Lee *Tales from The Night Rainbow*. A fascinating curiosity: an oral history of nineteenth-century Molokai, as told by the matriarchal Kaili'ohe Kame'ekua, said to have lived from 1816 to 1931. It's hard to sift a coherent narrative from her tales, but they offer glimpses of the world-view of a Hawaiian who witnessed astonishing changes.

Music and hula

Dorothy B. Barrère, Mary K. Pukui, and Marion Kelly *Hula: Historical Perspectives*. Essays on ancient Hawaii's most important art form, packed with early eyewitness accounts, and with a special emphasis on Kauai.

Ronna Bolante and Michael Keany *The Fifty Greatest Hawai'i Albums*. If you're a newcomer to Hawaiian music, this authoritative list, assembled by *Honolulu Magazine*, will point you to some wonderful discoveries.

Rick Carroll *Iz – Voice of the People*. A lavishly illustrated celebration of the great Israel Kamakawiwo'ole (see p.442).

Samuel H. Elbert and Noelani Mahoe *Nā Mele O Hawai'i Nei*. A definitive short introduction to Hawaiian songs and songwriting, describing how 101 of Hawaii's favorite songs came to be written, and exploring the themes in Hawaiian music.

Jerry Hopkins *Elvis in Hawaii*. An irresistibly obsessive blow-by-blow account of the King's love affair with Hawaii, from the Arizona Memorial concert of 1961 to *Aloha from Hawaii*.

James D. Houston with Eddie Kamae *Hawaiian Son: The Life and Music of Eddie Kamae* ('Ai Pōhaku Press). Still proselytizing for the islands and their music, the much-loved Eddie Kamae serves up the fascinating inside story of the Sons of Hawaii.

George S. Kanahele (ed) *Hawaiian Music and Musicians: An Illustrated History* (University of Hawaii Press). Put together by a team of experts, this fabulous five-hundred-page encyclopedia was published in 1979, and is now only available secondhand, for almost $200 – but for authoritative details on long-neglected performers and styles, it's the only source there is.

Travelers' tales

Isabella Bird *Six Months in the Sandwich Islands*. The enthralling adventures of an Englishwoman in the 1870s, including sojourns on all the major islands and a cold expedition up Mauna Loa on the Big Island.

A. Grove Day and Carl Stroven (eds) *A Hawaiian Reader* and *The Spell of Hawaii*. Lively paperback anthologies of writings on Hawaii, including pieces by Mark Twain, Jack London, Isabella Bird, and Robert Louis Stevenson.

William Ellis *A Narrative of an 1823 Tour Through Hawai'i*. On his exhausting tour around the Big Island, early missionary Ellis proved to be a surprisingly sympathetic observer of the traditional Hawaiian way of life he and his fellows were about to destroy.

James Macrae *With Lord Byron at the Sandwich Islands in 1825*. Short

pamphlet of extracts from the diary of a Scottish botanist, including descriptions of Honolulu as a small village and the first-known ascent of Mauna Kea.

Andy Martin *Walking on Water*. An English journalist attempts to immerse himself in the surfing culture of Oahu's North Shore.

Robert Louis Stevenson *Travels in Hawaii*. The Scottish novelist spent several months in Hawaii in the late nineteenth century; the highlight here is a moving account of his visit to Kalaupapa on Molokai, which includes his famous "Open Letter" in defense of Father Damien (see p.327).

Hunter S. Thompson *The Curse of Lono*. Inimitably overwrought account of a winter fishing vacation on the Big Island, involving such escapades as

abandoning a demented Doberman in Kailua's *King Kamehameha* hotel.

Mark Twain *Letters from Hawaii.* Colorful and entertaining accounts of nineteenth-century Hawaii, with rapturous descriptions of the volcanoes of Maui and the Big Island, written as a cub reporter. Twain reworked much of the best material for inclusion in *Roughing It.*

Navigation

Ben Finney *Hōkūleʻa: The Way to Tahiti.* Gripping story of the sailing canoe's first eventful voyage to Tahiti, by a founder of the Polynesian Voyaging Society.

Tommy Holmes *The Hawaiian Canoe.* Compendious, beautifully illustrated coffee-table presentation of traditions and techniques involved in building and navigating sailing canoes, from the ancient Polynesians to the present day.

Will Kyselka *An Ocean in Mind.* Detailed account of the rediscovery of traditional Polynesian navigational techniques and the voyages of the *Hōkūleʻa.*

Natural sciences

Peter S. Adler *Beyond Paradise.* Personal essays about life in Hawaii, illuminating if occasionally self-indulgent, with an interesting account of the "Wounded Island" of Kahoʻolawe.

Peter Crawford *Nomads of the Wind.* Enjoyable, well-illustrated overview of the human and natural history of Polynesia.

Pamela Frierson *The Burning Island.* The most exciting and original volume written about the Big Island; a history and cultural anthropology of the region around Mauna Loa and Kīlauea, combined with a personal account of living with the volcanoes.

Garrett Hongo *Volcano.* The "Volcano" of the title is the Big Island village where Hongo was born; the book itself is a lyrical evocation of its physical and emotional landscape.

Gordon A. Macdonald and Agatin A. Abbott *Volcanoes in the Sea.* Thorough technical examination – sadly not illustrated in color – of how fire and water have shaped the unique landscapes of Hawaii.

Frank Stewart (ed) *A World Between.* Stimulating collection of essays by authors such as Peter Matthiessen and Maxine Hong Kingston, covering all aspects of Hawaiian natural history.

Food

Roy Yamaguchi and John Harrisson *Roy's Feasts From Hawaii.* Well-illustrated cookbook of delicious recipes, from the kitchens of a prime mover of "Euro-Asian cuisine."

Hawaii in fiction

David Lodge *Paradise News.* The enjoyable tale of a dry English academic succumbing despite himself to the charms of Hawaii.

Herman Melville *Typee.* Largely set in the Marquesas Islands, but with echoes of his time in Hawaii, Melville's wildly romanticized

version of the South Seas – originally published as nonfiction – makes a perfect escapist read.

W.S. Merwin *The Folding Cliffs*. A compelling, visually evocative blank-verse retelling – in over three hundred pages – of the story of Koolau the Leper (see p.385), by a leading contemporary poet.

James Michener *Hawaii*. Another romanticized romp, whose success was a major factor in the growth of Hawaiian tourism.

Paul Theroux *Hotel Honolulu*. This very entertaining slice of reportage brilliantly captures the flavor of life in Oahu, packed with tourists passing through as well as local characters; there's even a cameo appearance from Iz.

Richard Tregaskis *The Warrior King*. Fictionalized biography of Kamehameha the Great that serves as a readable introduction to a crucial period in Hawaiian history.

Kathleen Tyau *A Little Too Much Is Enough*. Atmospheric and amusing account of growing up as a Chinese-Hawaiian, with an appetizing emphasis on food.

Sylvia Watanabe *Talking to the Dead*. Short, haunting evocation of village life in West Maui, in the days before the resorts.

Language

Language

Hawaiian

The Hawaiian language is an offshoot of languages spoken elsewhere in Polynesia, with slight variations that arose during the centuries when Hawaii had no contact with the islands of the south Pacific. Among its most unusual features is the fact that there are no verbs "to be" or "to have," and that, although it lacks a word for "weather," it distinguishes between 130 types of rain and 160 types of wind.

Although barely two thousand people speak Hawaiian as their native tongue, it remains a living language, and has experienced a revival in recent years. While visitors to Hawaii are almost certain to hear Hawaiian-language songs, it's rarely spoken in public, and there should be no need to communicate in any language other than English. However, everyday conversations tend to be sprinkled with some of the more common Hawaiian words below, and you'll also spot them in many local place-names.

The Hawaiian alphabet

Hawaiian only became a written language when a committee of missionaries gave it an alphabet. The shortest in the world, it consists of just twelve letters – a, e, h, i, k, l, m, n, o, p, u, and w – plus two punctuation marks. When the missionaries were unable to agree on the precise sounds of the language, they simply voted on which letter to include – thus k beat t, and l beat r. As a result, the language has been oversimplified, and scholars argue that no one really knows how it used to sound.

Hawaiian may look hard to **pronounce**, but in fact with just 162 possible syllables – as compared to 23,638 in Thai – it's the least complicated on earth. The letters h, l, m, and n are pronounced exactly as in English; k and p are pronounced approximately as in English but with less aspiration; w is like the English v after an i or an e, and the English w after a u or an o. At the start of a word, or after an a, w may be pronounced like a v or a w.

The **glottal stop** (') has the effect of creating the audible pause heard in the English "oh-oh." Words without macrons (ˉ) to indicate stress are in theory pronounced by stressing alternate syllables working back from the penultimate syllable. Thanks to the frequent repetition of syllables, this is usually easier than it may sound. "Kamehameha," for example, breaks down into the repeated pattern Ka–meha–meha, pronounced Ka–mayha–mayha.

Pronunciation

a	*a* as in above	ā	*a* as in car
e	*e* as in bet	ō	*ay* as in day
i	*y* as in pity	ī	*ee* as in bee
o	*o* as in hole	ō	*o* as in hole (but slightly longer)
u	*u* as in full	ū	*oo* as in moon

Glossary of Hawaiian terms

'A'ā rough lava

Ahupua'a basic land division, a "slice of cake" from ocean to mountain

Aikāne friend, friendly

'Āina land, earth

Akua god, goddess, spirit, idol

Ali'i chief, chiefess, noble

Aloha love; hello; goodbye

'Aumākua personal god or spirit; totem animal

'Elepaio bird

Hala tree (pandanus, screw pine)

Halāu longhouse used for hula instruction; also a hula group

Hale house, building

Hana work

Haole (white) non-native Hawaiian, whether foreign or American resident

Hapa half, as in *hapa haole*, or half-foreign

Hāpu'u tree fern

Heiau ancient place of worship

Honua land, earth

Hui group, club

Hula dance/music form (*hula 'auana* is a modern form; *hula kahiko* is traditional)

Imu pit oven

Ka'a car

Kahuna priest(ess) or someone particularly skilled in any field; *kahuna nui* is chief priest

Kai sea

Kālua to bake in an *imu* (underground oven)

Kama'aina Hawaiian from another island; state resident

Kāne man

Kapa the "cloth" made from pounded bark, known elsewhere as *tapa*

Kapu forbidden, taboo, sacred

Kapu moe prostration

Kaukau food

Keiki child

Kiawe thorny tree, mesquite

Ki'i temple image or petroglyph

Kīpuka natural "island" of vegetation surrounded by lava flows

Koa dark hardwood tree

Kōkua help

Kona leeward (especially wind)

Kukui candlenut tree, whose oil was used for lamps

Lānai balcony, terrace, patio

Lau leaf

Lehua or **'Ōhi'a lehua** native red-blossomed shrub/tree

Lei garland of flowers, feathers, shells, or other material

Liliko'i passionfruit

Limu seaweed

Lomi lomi massage or raw salmon dish

Luakini temple of human sacrifice, used by ruling chiefs

Lū'au traditional Hawaiian feast

Mahalo thank you

Mahimahi white fish or dolphin fish (not the mammal)

Makai direction: away from the mountain, toward the sea

Malihini newcomer, visitor

Mana spiritual power

Mauka direction: away from the sea, toward the mountain

Mele ancient chant

Menehune in legend, the most ancient Hawaiian people, supposedly dwarfs

Mo'o lizard, dragon

Mu'umu'u long loose dress

Naupaka a shrub with small white flowers

Nei this here, as in *Hawaii nei*, "this [beloved] Hawaii"

Nēnē Hawaiian goose – the state bird

Nui big, important

O of; or

'Ohana family

'Ōhelo sacred red berry

'Ōhi'a lehua see *lehua*

'Ono delicious

'Ō'ō yellow-feathered bird

'Ōpae shrimp

'Opihi limpet

Pāhoehoe smooth lava

Pali sheer-sided cliff

Paniolo Hawaiian cowboy

Pau finished

Pili grass, used for thatch

Poi staple food made of taro root

Poke raw fish dish

Pua flower, garden

Pua'a pig

Pueo owl

Puka hole; door

Pūpū snack

Pu'u hill, lump

Saimin noodle soup

Taro Hawaiian food plant

Tūtū grandparent; general term of respect

Wa'a sailing canoe

Wahine woman

Wai water

Wikiwiki hurry, fast

Wiliwili native tree

Travel store

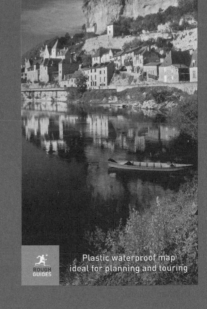

Travel

Andorra The Pyrenees, Pyrenees & Andorra Map, Spain
Antigua The Caribbean
Argentina Argentina, Argentina Map, Buenos Aires, South America on a Budget
Aruba The Caribbean
Australia Australia, Australia Map, East Coast Australia, Melbourne, Sydney, Tasmania
Austria Austria, Europe on a Budget, Vienna
Bahamas The Bahamas, The Caribbean
Barbados Barbados DIR, The Caribbean
Belgium Belgium & Luxembourg, Bruges DIR, Brussels, Brussels Map, Europe on a Budget
Belize Belize, Central America on a Budget, Guatemala & Belize Map
Benin West Africa
Bolivia Bolivia, South America on a Budget
Brazil Brazil, Rio, South America on a Budget
British Virgin Islands The Caribbean
Brunei Malaysia, Singapore & Brunei [1 title], Southeast Asia on a Budget
Bulgaria Bulgaria, Europe on a Budget
Burkina Faso West Africa
Cambodia Cambodia, Southeast Asia on a Budget, Vietnam, Laos & Cambodia Map [1 Map]
Cameroon West Africa
Canada Canada, Pacific Northwest, Toronto, Toronto Map, Vancouver
Cape Verde West Africa
Cayman Islands The Caribbean
Chile Chile, Chile Map, South America on a Budget
China Beijing, China,

Hong Kong & Macau, Hong Kong & Macau DIR, Shanghai
Colombia South America on a Budget
Costa Rica Central America on a Budget, Costa Rica, Costa Rica & Panama Map
Croatia Croatia, Croatia Map, Europe on a Budget
Cuba Cuba, Cuba Map, The Caribbean, Havana
Cyprus Cyprus, Cyprus Map
Czech Republic The Czech Republic, Czech & Slovak Republics, Europe on a Budget, Prague, Prague DIR, Prague Map
Denmark Copenhagen, Denmark, Europe on a Budget, Scandinavia
Dominica The Caribbean
Dominican Republic Dominican Republic, The Caribbean
Ecuador Ecuador, South America on a Budget
Egypt Egypt, Egypt Map
El Salvador Central America on a Budget
England Britain, Camping in Britain, Devon & Cornwall, Dorset, Hampshire and The Isle of Wight [1 title], England, Europe on a Budget, The Lake District, London, London DIR, London Map, London Mini Guide, Walks In London & Southeast England
Estonia The Baltic States, Europe on a Budget
Fiji Fiji
Finland Europe on a Budget, Finland, Scandinavia
France Brittany & Normandy, Corsica, Corsica Map, The Dordogne & the Lot, Europe on a Budget, France, France Map, Languedoc & Roussillon, The Loire, Paris, Paris DIR,

Paris Map, Paris Mini Guide, Provence & the Côte d'Azur, The Pyrenees, Pyrenees & Andorra Map
French Guiana South America on a Budget
Gambia The Gambia, West Africa
Germany Berlin, Berlin Map, Europe on a Budget, Germany, Germany Map
Ghana West Africa
Gibraltar Spain
Greece Athens Map, Crete, Crete Map, Europe on a Budget, Greece, Greece Map, Greek Islands, Ionian Islands
Guadeloupe The Caribbean
Guatemala Central America on a Budget, Guatemala, Guatemala & Belize Map
Guinea West Africa
Guinea-Bissau West Africa
Guyana South America on a Budget
Holland see The Netherlands
Honduras Central America on a Budget
Hungary Budapest, Europe on a Budget, Hungary
Iceland Iceland, Iceland Map
India Goa, India, India Map, Kerala, Rajasthan, Delhi & Agra [1 title], South India, South India Map
Indonesia Bali & Lombok, Southeast Asia on a Budget
Ireland Dublin DIR, Dublin Map, Europe on a Budget, Ireland, Ireland Map
Israel Jerusalem
Italy Europe on a Budget, Florence DIR, Florence & Siena Map, Florence & the best of Tuscany, Italy, The Italian Lakes, Naples & the Amalfi Coast, Rome, Rome DIR, Rome Map, Sardinia, Sicily, Sicily Map, Tuscany & Umbria, Tuscany Map,

Venice, Venice DIR, Venice Map
Jamaica Jamaica, The Caribbean
Japan Japan, Tokyo
Jordan Jordan
Kenya Kenya, Kenya Map
Korea Korea
Laos Laos, Southeast Asia on a Budget, Vietnam, Laos & Cambodia Map [1 Map]
Latvia The Baltic States, Europe on a Budget
Lithuania The Baltic States, Europe on a Budget
Luxembourg Belgium & Luxembourg, Europe on a Budget
Malaysia Malaysia Map, Malaysia, Singapore & Brunei [1 title], Southeast Asia on a Budget
Mali West Africa
Malta Malta & Gozo DIR
Martinique The Caribbean
Mauritania West Africa
Mexico Baja California, Baja California, Cancún & Cozumel DIR, Mexico, Mexico Map, Yucatán, Yucatán Peninsula Map
Monaco France, Provence & the Côte d'Azur
Montenegro Montenegro
Morocco Europe on a Budget, Marrakesh DIR, Marrakesh Map, Morocco, Morocco Map,
Nepal Nepal
Netherlands Amsterdam, Amsterdam DIR, Amsterdam Map, Europe on a Budget, The Netherlands
Netherlands Antilles The Caribbean
New Zealand New Zealand, New Zealand Map

DIR: Rough Guide **DIRECTIONS** for short breaks

Available from all good bookstores

For more information go to www.roughguides.com

Small print and

Index

A Rough Guide to Rough Guides

Published in 1982, the first Rough Guide – to Greece – was a student scheme that became a publishing phenomenon. Mark Ellingham, a recent graduate in English from Bristol University, had been travelling in Greece the previous summer and couldn't find the right guidebook. With a small group of friends he wrote his own guide, combining a highly contemporary, journalistic style with a thoroughly practical approach to travellers' needs.

The immediate success of the book spawned a series that rapidly covered dozens of destinations. And, in addition to impecunious backpackers, Rough Guides soon acquired a much broader and older readership that relished the guides' wit and inquisitiveness as much as their enthusiastic, critical approach and value-for-money ethos.

These days, Rough Guides include recommendations from shoestring to luxury and cover more than 200 destinations around the globe, including almost every country in the Americas and Europe, more than half of Africa and most of Asia and Australasia. Our ever-growing team of authors and photographers is spread all over the world, particularly in Europe, the US and Australia.

In the early 1990s, Rough Guides branched out of travel, with the publication of Rough Guides to World Music, Classical Music and the Internet. All three have become benchmark titles in their fields, spearheading the publication of a wide range of books under the Rough Guide name.

Including the travel series, Rough Guides now number more than 350 titles, covering: phrasebooks, waterproof maps, music guides from Opera to Heavy Metal, reference works as diverse as Conspiracy Theories and Shakespeare, and popular culture books from iPods to Poker. Rough Guides also produce a series of more than 120 World Music CDs in partnership with World Music Network.

Visit www.roughguides.com to see our latest publications.

Rough Guide credits

Text editor: Melissa Graham
Layout: Nikhil Agarwal
Cartography: Deshpal Dabas
Picture editor: Harriet Mills
Production: Rebecca Short
Proofreader: Diane Margolis
Cover design: Nicole Newman, Dan May
Photographer: Greg Ward
Editorial: **London** Andy Turner, Keith Drew,
Edward Aves, Alice Park, Lucy White, Jo Kirby,
James Smart, Natasha Foges, Róisín Cameron,
James Rice, Emma Beatson, Emma Gibbs,
Kathryn Lane, Monica Woods, Mani Ramaswamy,
Harry Wilson, Lucy Cowie, Alison Roberts,
Lara Kavanagh, Eleanor Aldridge, Ian Blenkinsop,
Joe Staines, Matthew Milton, Tracy Hopkins;
Delhi Madhavi Singh, Jalpreen Kaur Chhatwal
Design & Pictures: **London** Scott Stickland, Dan
May, Diana Jarvis, Mark Thomas, Nicole Newman,
Sarah Cummins, Emily Taylor; **Delhi** Umesh
Aggarwal, Ajay Verma, Jessica Subramanian,
Ankur Guha, Pradeep Thapliyal, Sachin Tanwar,
Anita Singh, Sachin Gupta

Production: Liz Cherry, Louise Daly, Erika Pepe
Cartography: **London** Ed Wright, Katie Lloyd-
Jones; **Delhi** Rajesh Chhibber, Ashutosh Bharti,
Rajesh Mishra, Animesh Pathak, Jasbir Sandhu,
Swati Handoo, Lokamata Sahu
Online: **London** Faye Hellon, Jeanette Angell,
Fergus Day, Justine Bright, Clare Bryson, Aine
Fearon, Adrian Low, Ezgi Celebi; **Delhi** Amit
Verma, Rahul Kumar, Narender Kumar, Ravi
Yadav, Debojit Borah, Rakesh Kumar, Ganesh
Sharma, Shisir Basumatari
Marketing & Publicity: **London** Liz Statham,
Jess Carter, Vivienne Watton, Anna Paynton,
Rachel Sprackett, Laura Vipond; **New York**
Katy Ball; **Delhi** Aman Arora
Digital Travel Publisher: Peter Buckley
Reference Director: Andrew Lockett
Operations Assistant: Becky Doyle
Operations Manager: Helen Atkinson
Publishing Director (Travel): Clare Currie
Commercial Manager: Gino Magnotta
Managing Director: John Duhigg

Publishing information

This sixth edition published January 2011 by
Rough Guides Ltd,
80 Strand, London WC2R 0RL
11, Community Centre, Panchsheel Park,
New Delhi 110017, India

Distributed by the Penguin Group

Penguin Books Ltd,
80 Strand, London WC2R 0RL

Penguin Group (USA)
375 Hudson Street, NY 10014, USA

Penguin Group (Australia)
250 Camberwell Road, Camberwell,
Victoria 3124, Australia

Penguin Group (NZ)
67 Apollo Drive, Mairangi Bay, Auckland 1310,
New Zealand

Rough Guides is represented in Canada by
Tourmaline Editions Inc. 662 King Street West,
Suite 304, Toronto, Ontario M5V 1M7

Cover concept by Peter Dyer.

Typeset in Bembo and Helvetica to an original
design by Henry Iles.

Printed in Singapore
© Greg Ward, 2011
Maps © Rough Guides
No part of this book may be reproduced in any
form without permission from the publisher except
for the quotation of brief passages in reviews.
480pp includes index
A catalogue record for this book is available from
the British Library
ISBN: 978-1-84836-529-2
The publishers and authors have done their best
to ensure the accuracy and currency of all the
information in **The Rough Guide to Hawaii**,
however, they can accept no responsibility for
any loss, injury, or inconvenience sustained by
any traveller as a result of information or advice
contained in the guide.

1 3 5 7 9 8 6 4 2

FSC
www.fsc.org
MIX
Paper from
responsible sources
FSC™ C018179

Help us update

We've gone to a lot of effort to ensure that the
sixth edition of **The Rough Guide to Hawaii** is
accurate and up-to-date. However, things change
– places get "discovered", opening hours are
notoriously fickle, restaurants and rooms raise
prices or lower standards. If you feel we've got it
wrong or left something out, we'd like to know,
and if you can remember the address, the price,
the hours, the phone number, so much the better.

Please send your comments with the subject
line "**Rough Guide Hawaii Update**" to ✉mail
@uk.roughguides.com. We'll credit all contributions
and send a copy of the next edition (or any other
Rough Guide if you prefer) for the very best emails.
   Find more travel information, connect with
fellow travellers and book your trip on ⑩www
.roughguides.com

SMALL PRINT

ROUGH
GUIDES

Acknowledgements

Very much love and thanks above all to my wife Sam Cook, and thanks once again to the many people who helped to make travelling through the Hawaiian islands such a great joy: Candy Aluli, Teddi Andersen, Barbara Anderson, Bronwen Batey, Julie Bicoy, Keli'i Brown, Maggie Brown, Nedielyn Bueno, Linda Bukoski, Nancy Daniels, Diane Farnsworth, Jessica Ferracane, Erin Franklin, Emele Freiberg, Sandy Frewer, Edie Hafdahl, Waynette Kwon, Dara Lum, Brooke Miller, Megan Mooney, Roxanne Murayama, Rebecca Pang, Mirjam Peternek, Tracy Potter, Monica Salter, Becky Smith, Liz and Sage Spalding, and Sandi Yara.

Thanks also to all the great team at Rough Guides, and especially to Melissa Graham for her diligent and creative editing.

Photo credits

All photos by Greg Ward © Rough Guides, except the following:

Introduction

Kekaha Kai State Park © Robert Harding World Imagery/Getty

Plumeria flowers © Tor Johnson/Photo Resource Hawaii

Nā Pali Coast State Park, Kauai © Jeffrey A. Cable/Getty Getty

Man harvesting taro plants, Kauai © Joseph Sohm/Visions of America, LLC/Alamy

Waikīkī, Oahu © Chad Ehlers/Photolibrary.com

Hula dancer © Pictures Colour Library/Alamy

Windsurfing at Ho'okipa Beach, Maui © Russ Bishop/Photolibrary.com

Things not to miss

01 Haleakalā cinder cone crater, Maui © Danita Delimont Stock/AWL Images Ltd

04 Garden of the Gods, Lanai © Walter Bibikow/Getty

06 'Akaka Falls, Big Island © Glowimages/Getty

07 Common nectar-feeding Hawaiian honeycreeper © Jack Jeffrey/ PhotoResourceHawaii.com

08 Shrine on Mauna Kea, Big Island © Marc Lepage/istockphoto

09 Oahu's Circle-Island Drive © James Randklev/Corbis

11 Surfer, North Shore, Oahu © Chris Dyball/Innerlight/Getty

12 Riding mules, Kalaupapa peninsula, Molokai © Panoramic Images/Getty

13 Merrie Monarch Festival © Val Kim/PhotoResourceHawaii.com

14 Whale's tail © Jan Sonnenmair/Getty

15 Helicopter flies over Nā Pali coast, Kauai © Michael T. Sedam/Corbis

16 Lava flow from Kīlauea Crater, Big Island © Roger Ressmeyer/Corbis

18 Hiking the Kalalau Trail, Kauai © David Samuel Robbins/Corbis

19 Wai'ānapanapa State Park black-sand beach © Nigel Hicks/DK Images

Blue Hawaii

Surfing at Pipeline, North Shore, Oahu © Sean Davey/Getty

Polihua Beach, Lanai © Joe Solem/PhotoResourceHawaii.com

Punalu'u black-sand beach, Big Island © Ethel Davies/Robert Harding/Corbis

Humpback whale breaching © Doug Perrine/Naturepl.com

Duke Kahanamoku © Hulton Archive/Getty

Shinpei Horiguchi surfs the Banzai Pipeline, North Shore, Oahu © Kelly Cestari/epa/Corbis

Hiking in Hawaii

Kalalau Trail © Hutch Axilrod/Getty

Awa'awapuhi Trail © David Boynton/PhotoResourceHawaii.com

Sliding Sands Trail, Maui © Tor Johnson/PhotoResourceHawaii.com

Pēpē'ōpae Trail, Molokai © Richard A. Cooke/Corbis

Hālawa Falls, Molokai © Jon Ogata/PhotoResourceHawaii.com

Kīlauea Iki © Wayne Levin/PhotoResourceHawaii.com

Lava flowing from Kīlauea Volcano © Michele Falzone/AWL Images Ltd

Black and whites

p.253 Maui Ocean Center © Nigel Hicks/DK Images

p.303 Hulopo'e Beach, Lanai © Nigel Hicks/DK Images

p.351 Wailua Falls, Kauai © Christopher and Sally Gable/DK Images

Index

Map entries are in color.

I

INDEX

INDEX

Map symbols

maps are listed in the full index using colored text

▬H1▬	Freeway	⊛	Crater
═50═	Highway	⚠	Campsite
═══	Road	✹	Shipwreck
▬▬▬	Pedestrianised road	━	Boat
━◦━◦	Track	⌂	Park headquarter
-----	Trail	◉	Hotel/restaurant
━╍━	Railway	✈	Airport
───	River	Ⓗ	Helipad
⟵	One-way street	▣	Parking
▲	Peak	▤	Gas station
𝕏	Waterfall	ⓘ	Tourist office
⩊	Marshland	⊠	Post office
⚘	Viewpoint	⛩	Chinese temple
🌳	Tree	⌂	Buddhist temple
🌱	Public garden	⚱	Church (regional maps)
✦	General point of interest	✚	Church (town maps)
∴	Ancient site	▬	Building
♟	Museum	▢	Market
❦	Winery	▦	Park/national park
⌣	Bridge	▨	Lava flow
⚑	Lighthouse		

So now we've told you about the things not to miss, the best places to stay, the top restaurants, the liveliest bars and the most spectacular sights, it only seems fair to tell you about the best travel insurance around

WorldNomads.com
keep travelling safely

Recommended by Rough Guides

Hawaii

written and researched by

Greg Ward

**ROUGH
GUIDES**

www.roughguides.com

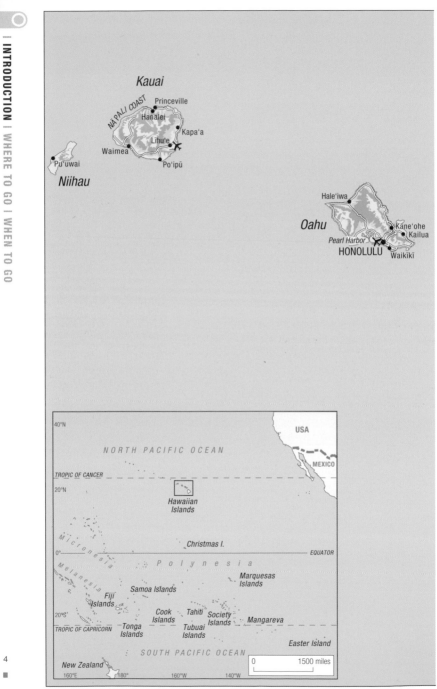

Contents

Hiking in Hawaii
color section
following p.176

Blue Hawaii
color section
following p.304

◄◄ Kalawao, Kalaupapa Peninsula, Molokai ◄ Kekaha Kai State Park, The Big Island